HISTORY OF THE WATERLOO CAMPAIGN

NAPOLEONIC LIBRARY

CHATEAU AND FARM OF HOUGOMONT

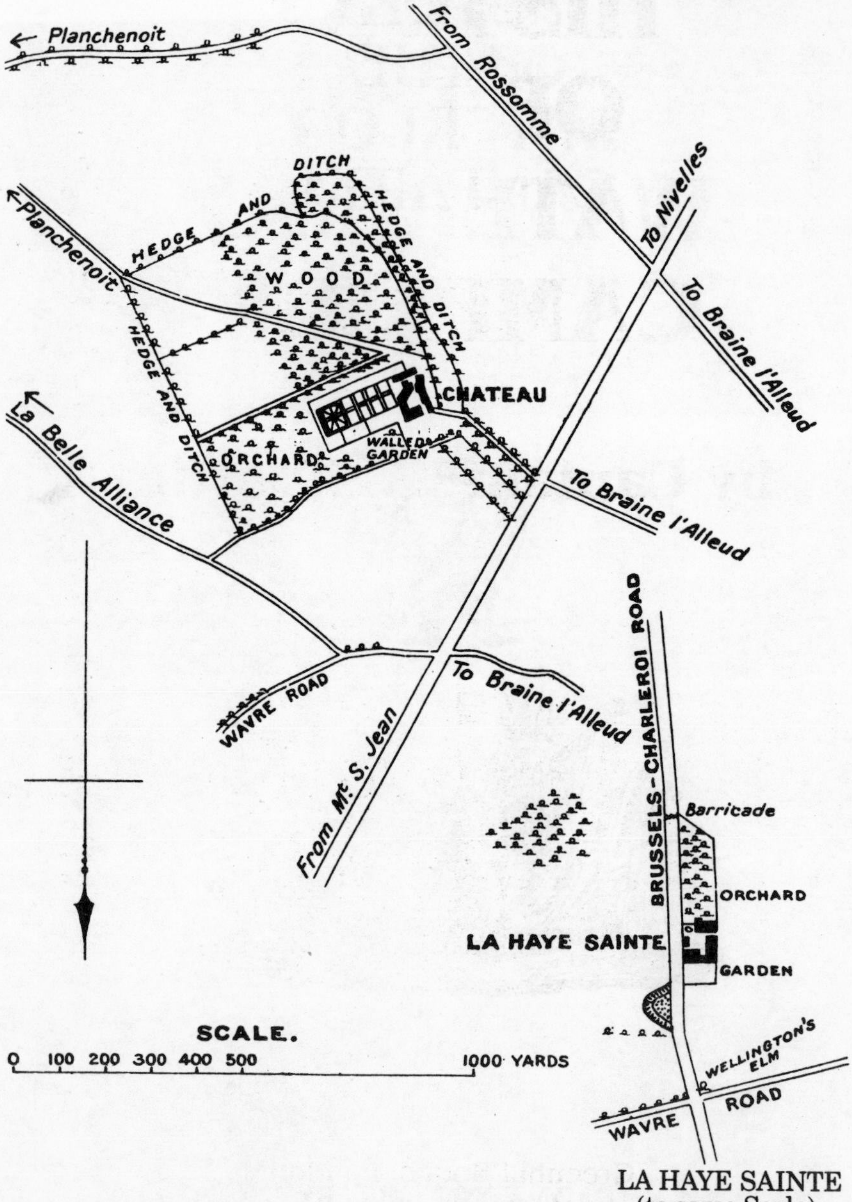

LA HAYE SAINTE
(to same Scale).

HISTORY OF THE WATERLOO CAMPAIGN

by Captain W. Siborne

Greenhill Books, London
Stackpole Books, Pennsylvania

This edition of *History of the Waterloo Campaign*
published 1990 on the 175th Anniversary
of the Battle of Waterloo
Reprinted 1995 on the 180th Anniversary of the Battle of Waterloo
by Greenhill Books, Lionel Leventhal Limited, Park House
1 Russell Gardens, London NW11 9NN
and
Stackpole Books
5067 Ritter Road, Mechanicsburg, PA 17055, USA

British Library Cataloguing in Publication Data
Siborne, W. (William)
History of the Waterloo Campaign
1. Napoleonic Wars. Battle of Waterloo
I. History of the war in France and Belgium in 1815   II. Title
940.27

ISBN 1-85367-069-3

Library of Congress Cataloging-in-Publication Data available

Publishing History
History of the Waterloo Campaign was first published under
the title *History of the War in France and Belgium in 1815*
in 1848 (T. and W. Boone) and the text is reproduced now
exactly as the original edition, complete and unabridged,
with additional illustrations and maps.

Printed and bound in Great Britain
by Biddles Limited, Guildford and King's Lynn

TO THE

QUEEN'S MOST EXCELLENT MAJESTY.

MADAM,

IN graciously deigning to accept the dedication of these pages, Your Majesty has afforded the greatest possible encouragement to my humble endeavours to record, with simplicity, impartiality, and truth, the incidents of an eventful war, resulting in a long enduring peace; a war which shed a new and brighter lustre on the valour and discipline of the British Army, and once more called forth the consummate sagacity and far-extending prescience of that illustrious Chief, whom Your Majesty, with wise appreciation and a just pride, retains at its head.

Earnestly hoping that the result of those endeavours may prove not altogether undeserving of Your Majesty's approbation,

I have the honour to be,
With profound respect,

MADAM,

Your Majesty's most humble
And most devoted servant,

WILLIAM SIBORNE,
Captain Unattached.

PREFACE

TO THE THIRD EDITION.

In offering to the Public this Third Edition, I feel called upon to state, by way of explanation, in what respect it differs from the two former editions. During the interval which has elapsed, I have not failed to avail myself of every opportunity to correct and improve any points which further investigation rendered desirable; and I have been much gratified in finding that the general plan and arrangement of the work, together with the elucidation of the military operations, and the views of their tendency and effect, have been generally borne out and approved; and that, consequently, in these repects little alteration has been required.

The exceptions, which consist principally in details, and amount in number to only four or five, have been rectified in this edition. They are chiefly the result of discussions which have appeared in the pages of the "United Service Magazine," and relate to a portion of the proceedings of Sir Colin Halkett's and Sir Denis Pack's brigades at Quatre-Bras and Waterloo.

Through the kindness of His Excellency the Prussian Ambassador, Chevalier Bunsen, and of the Prussian Generals von Canitz and von Krauseneck, and of Major Gerwien of the Prussian head-quarters staff, I have obtained additional interesting details connected with the Prussian operations; more especially as regards the opening of the campaign.

A Dutch work published, apparently under authority, by Major Van Löben Sels, Aide-de-camp to his Royal Highness Prince Frederick of the Netherlands, and entitled "Bydragen

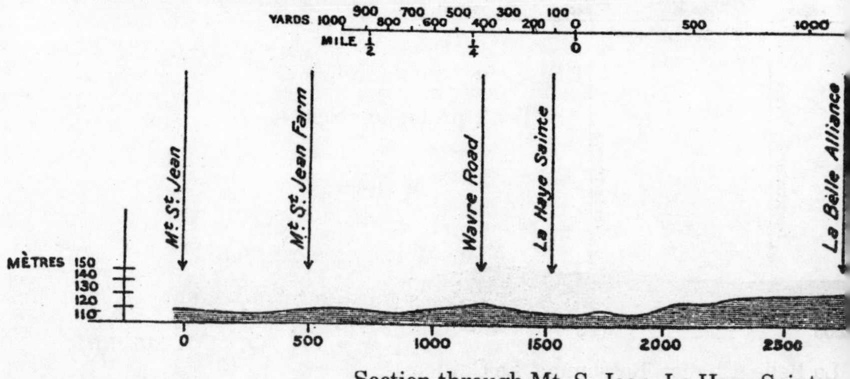

Section through Mt. S. Jean, La Haye Sainte,

tot de Krÿgsgeschiedenis van Napoleon Bonaparte," of which I was not previously in possession, has enabled me to give additional particulars respecting the movements and dispositions of the most advanced portion of the Dutch-Belgian troops, on the first advance of the enemy; and also to explain particular circumstances and qualify some observations respecting those troops which appeared in former editions.

The Editor of an article in "The Quarterly Review, No. CLI.," entitled "Marmont, Siborne, and Alison," having, in his comments upon this work, denied the accuracy of one or two important facts therein stated, I have, in notes at pages 57 and 152, entered into more minute details, which explain the grounds that warrant me in adhering to the original statements.

The observations made in the Preface of a volume of "Murray's Home and Colonial Library," entitled "The Story of Waterloo," and the palpable embodyment of the present work into the pages of the latter, have been such as could scarcely fail to attract attention, and I have accordingly appended to this edition, in a separate form, some remarks upon that publication. Public opinion (if I may judge by the unanimous consent of the press) having so distinctly pronounced its acknowledgment of the value of my work, as one of history, I could not disregard the conduct of a writer, who, in the first place endeavours to depreciate that value, and then unblushingly makes the most ample and unlicensed use of it for his own purposes.

W. SIBORNE.

18th June, 1848.

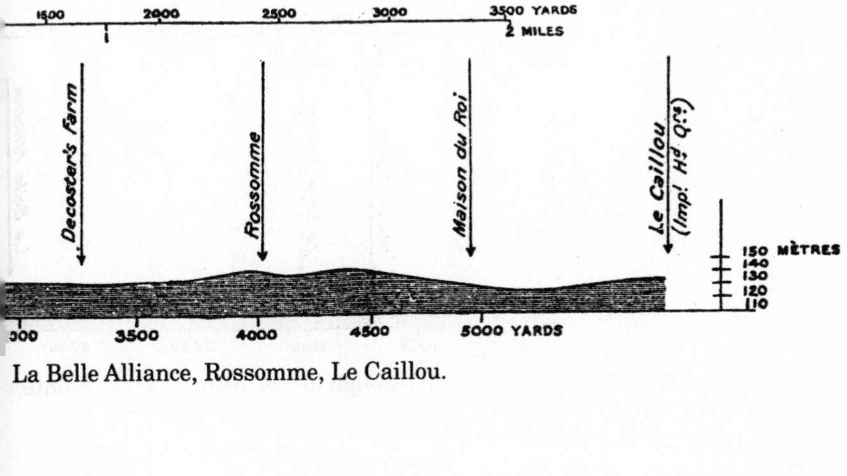

La Belle Alliance, Rossomme, Le Caillou.

PREFACE

TO THE SECOND EDITION.

THE circumstance of the first edition having been sold off within a very few days, combined with the highly favourable notices taken of the work by professional as well as other critics, and, I may be permitted to add, the very flattering encomiums which have been pronounced upon it by so many who, from their position, are the most competent to form an opinion on its merits, cannot fail to afford proofs, the most satisfactory to the Public, and, at the same time, the most gratifying to the Author, that, in the production of these volumes, upon a subject of such stirring national interest, neither the expectations of the former have been altogether disappointed, nor the labours of the latter bestowed in vain.

The present edition contains corrections on one or two points of trivial importance, to which my attention has been directed, and I shall be happy to receive further information from surviving eye-witnesses who may discover any instances in which the facts related appear either inaccurately or insufficiently explained.

W. SIBORNE.

August 23rd, 1844.

PREFACE.

Some years ago, when constructing a Model of the Field of Waterloo, at a particular period of the battle, I found it necessary to make great exertions to procure that detailed information for which I had sought in vain in the already numerous *published* accounts of the military transactions of 1815. Anxious to ensure the rigorous accuracy of my work, I ventured to apply for information to nearly all the surviving eye-witnesses of the incidents which my model was intended to represent. In every quarter, and among officers of all ranks, from the general to the subaltern, my applications were responded to in a most liberal and generous spirit; and the result did indeed surprise me, so greatly at variance was this historical evidence with the general notions which had previously prevailed on the subject. Thus was suggested the *present* work. I was induced by the success of this experiment to embrace a wider field, and to extend my enquiries over the entire battle, and, ultimately, throughout the campaign itself, from its commencement to its close.

Having become the depository of such valuable materials, I felt it a duty to the honourable profession of which I am an humble member, to submit to it, and to the world, a true and faithful account of this memorable epoch in the history of Britain's military greatness.

Though not so presumptuous as to imagine that I have fully supplied so absolute a desideratum, yet I consider myself fortunate in being the instrument of withdrawing so far the veil from Truth. One of my Waterloo correspondents has humorously remarked, that "if ever truth lies at the bottom of a well, she does so immediately after a great battle, and it takes an amazingly long time before she can be lugged out." The time of her emerging appears to have at length arrived, but, while I feel that I have brought to light much that was involved in obscurity, I cannot but be sensible that I may have fallen into errors. Should such be the case, I shall be most ready, hereafter, to make any corrections that may appear requisite, on my being favoured, by *eye-witnesses,* with further well authenticated information.

I take this opportunity of returning my sincere thanks to the numerous officers of the British Army, who have so kindly committed to my keeping their recollections of the events which I have attempted to describe. Similar thanks are likewise due to the officers of the King's German legion and Hanoverian subsidiary corps; as also to the General Officers who respectively furnished me with such information as related to the troops of Brunswick and Nassau.

I beg also to express my obligations to the Prussian Minister of War, and the officers of the Prussian general staff in Berlin, for the readiness and liberality with which they have supplied me with such details concerning the dispositions and movements of the troops of their sovereign, as were essential to me in prosecuting the task I had undertaken.

Having briefly explained the circumstances that led to the construction of the work which I thus venture to place before the Public, I have now only to express a hope that my labours may be crowned with usefulness. Should such a result occur, I shall then have obtained the only fame I seek.

W. SIBORNE.

March, 1844.

REMARKS

UPON

"THE STORY OF WATERLOO,"

BY THE REV. G. R. GLEIG:

FORMING A VOLUME OF THE "HOME AND COLONIAL LIBRARY."

The great demand for cheap literature by the middle and lower classes of society, is a healthy sign of the times, a manifest token of the vast increase of education, and the consequent thirst for knowledge, which, by the joint exertions of the Government, of public bodies, and of private individuals, have started into existence within, comparatively, a very brief period. To meet this demand, those useful literary caterers for the public taste, authors and publishers, have been industrious and painstaking. Several well-conducted serial publications have been, and continue to be, issued from the press, containing new editions, or re-prints, of various standard works, on subjects of general information or unfailing interest. Among the more prominent of these are the "Home and Colonial Library," "Chambers's Journal," &c. With a view to procure the best materials for these publications, works of a high character, but the copyrights of which have expired, are re-edited, and liberal purchases are made of copyrights still extant. In this manner, vested rights are respected, and the interests of both authors and publishers satisfactorily adjusted. Such is the general rule, which, however, like numerous other general rules, appears to be subject to exceptions; and it is in consequence of such an exception, involving the spoliation of literary property, that the publishers of the "History of the War in France and Belgium in 1815" have been seriously injured.

In last June, a volume of the "Home and Colonial Library" was published, entitled, "The Story of Waterloo," by the Rev. G. R. Gleig. Into this volume nearly the entire of the present work has been embodied, the arrangement of the military operations, in all their details, copied in the same consecutive order, to deduce which cost me so much labour and research in the collection of evidence from eye-witnesses: paragraph after paragraph has been transferred to his pages, not containing the *same words*, but presenting the same facts and incidents in another dress—in short, to use a literary expression, "*re-written*;" and parallel passages innumerable appear throughout the book. "The Story" commences with a view of the state of Europe previously to the opening of the campaign, but without conveying any more necessary information on this point than what I have thought proper to furnish, in a different style, in my own introduction of the general subject: it also contains two or three chapters descriptive of the "state of feeling" at Brussels before, during, and after the battle, for all of which ample materials are afforded in the numerous publications of that time, such as Mudford's and Booth's accounts, "Paul's Letters to his Kinsfolk," &c. With these and some other exceptions of minor import, the "Story" appears to be "*got up*," as booksellers say, from the History of the Campaign of 1815 which I have constructed, not with materials furnished by previous publications, but with the diligently collated, and well authenticated, evidence of eye-witnesses of all ranks. In the Preface, after a few complimentary remarks, a broad insinuation is made by Mr. Gleig, that, in my History, I have represented battles as won by "feats of individual heroism." I quote the following paragraph.

"I have not applied to many of the minor actors in the "great game for information respecting its details. Captain "Siborne, in his valuable work, has saved all who may be "curious in those matters, a great deal of trouble; and if I "shall seem somewhat to have overlooked the advantages "which he offers to me, I trust that he will not on that account consider that I think lightly of what he has done. "His History will always stand upon its own merits; I am "glad to acknowledge my many obligations to it; and his "plans I have found, while studying my subject, to be invaluable. But I confess that my recollections of war lead me "somewhat to undervalue—perhaps in a measure to distrust "—the stories told in perfect good faith by parties who happen "to be the heroes of them. Modern battles are not won by "feats of individual heroism; indeed, many gallant deeds "achieved embarrass more than they facilitate the accom- "plishment of the General's plans. I have, therefore, endea- "voured as much as possible to avoid entering into minute "narrations of these things, except where simple facts were to "be stated; and I hope that this course will prove satisfac- "tory to my readers."

Now if my work be of that character which Mr. Gleig here assigns to it, and if he alone have described the means and motives of action which constitute the highest branch of the art of war, better known by the term "strategy," we have assuredly confounded the *titles* of our respective works, for, in that case, *his* should be the "History of the War in France and Belgium in 1815," and *mine*, "The Story of Waterloo." But I make no such admission, and I indignantly repudiate the insinuation which he has thus publicly put forth; and I do so, not only from a firm conviction of its utter groundlessness, but from the fact that the main object which I had in view, when undertaking the work, was particularly to elucidate the strategy of the campaign. as will be seen by the following extract from the Prospectus previously issued by my Publishers.

"Numerous as are the accounts already published of this "great conflict, the information which they convey is generally "of too vague and indistinct a nature to satisfy either the mili- "tary man who seeks for professional instruction, or the "general reader who desires to comprehend more clearly, in "all its details, that gorgeous machinery, if it may be so "termed, which was put in motion. regulated, and controlled, "by the greatest masters of their art, who, in modern times, "have been summoned forth to wield the mighty engines of "destruction wherewith nation wars against nation. How "just is the observation of Jomini, one of the most ta- "lented military writers of the day—'Jamais bataille ne fut "plus confusément décrite que celle de Waterloo.' On con- "sulting these accounts the public glean little beyond the "fact that at Waterloo the Allied army stood its ground "the whole day, in defiance of the reiterated attacks by the "French, until the Duke of Wellington led it forward to crown "its exertions with the most splendid victory. They afford "us but a faint idea of those strategical movements and com- "binations upon which the grand design of the campaign "was based by the one party, and with which it was assailed "by the other; and we seek in vain for the development of "those tactical dispositions by which the skill of the com-

"manders and the valour of the combatants were fairly "tested. From the want of due consecutive arrangements in "the details, and the tendency too frequently manifested to "compensate for this deficiency by mere anecdotic narration, "the motives by which, in the great game of war, the illus-"trious players are actuated, are left out of view, while cir-"cumstances which especially call forth the skill of subordi-"nate officers in command, as also the courage, the discipline, "and the prowess, of particular brigades, regiments, or even "minor divisions of the contending masses, are either imper-"fectly elucidated, or, as is often the case, *unhesitatingly set* "*aside to make way for the exploits of a few individuals whose* "*deeds, however heroic they may be deemed, constitute but* "*isolated fractional parts of that great sum of moral energy* "*and physical force combined, requisite to give full effect to* "*the application of the mental powers of the chieftains under* "*whose guidance the armies are respectively placed* These "remarks have reference, more or less, not only to the "generality of the accounts of the Battle of Waterloo, with "which the public have hitherto been furnished, but also "to those of Quatre-Bras, Ligny, and Wavre; the first of "which, brilliant as was the reflection which it cast upon the "glory of the victors, became eclipsed solely by the more "dazzling splendour of the greater, because more important, "triumph of Waterloo. To endeavour to remedy these de-"ficiencies, through the medium of the evidence of eye-"witnesses most willingly and liberally supplied, as well as "carefully collated, examined, and, at the same time, proved, "wherever practicable, by corroborative testimony—every "component piece of information being made to dovetail, as "it were, into its adjacent and corresponding parts—is the "chief object of the present publication."

The above extract, whilst it affords a most explicit declaration of the great object which I had in view in publishing my "History of the War in France and Belgium in 1815," indicates with sufficient clearness, by the lines which are printed in *Italics*, my views of the value to be attached, in military historical composition, to "feats of individual heroism." I have not the presumption to imagine that I have completely acted up to the spirit, and literally fulfilled the promise, of this portion of the Prospectus of my publication; but I have the resolution to affirm that such has been the object of my humble and strenuous endeavours. My critics have been most numerous, and it is with pride and satisfaction that I refer to their opinions, so freely and extensively pronounced through both the professional and the public press; and, until the promulgation of Mr. Gleig's remarks in his Preface to the "Story of Waterloo," I have never, in a single instance, been represented as deficient in those qualifications which are so essentially requisite in the author of a military History. Even the writer of the article in the Quarterly Review for June 1845, to which Mr. Gleig deems it necessary to adhere in one or two points of some importance,* does not hesitate to view the work "as a history, and not as a collection of anecdotes." In constructing a complete history of the campaign, the introduction of "feats of individual heroism" in connexion with the military operations is unavoidable; and Mr. Gleig has found it very convenient to copy nearly all those feats which I have described, as well as numerous incidents detailed in my work, into his "Story," merely taking care not to employ precisely the same words, for this would be rather too glaring an act of literary piracy. I could never have anticipated that this would be made a pretext for detracting from the character of my "History," whatever may be its demerits in other respects. With due deference, I would venture to hint that it would have been more candid on the part of that Gentle-

* In a casual conversation which I had with Mr. Gleig, respecting the above article in the "Quarterly," I mentioned that —— (naming the writer) had fallen into a great error in stating that the Duke of Wellington could, from the field of Quatre-Bras, distinctly see that of Ligny. I adverted to the line of argument I intended to adopt for the purpose of refuting the error; and, on my instancing the intervening heights of Marbais, Mr. Gleig remarked, "Ah! you have him there!" At that time he was preparing his "Story of Waterloo" for the press, but I was wholly ignorant of the fact, and he did not think proper to disclose it to me. When his book was published, I became curious to see what he had written upon this particular point, and I was not a little amused to find that in his desire to follow in the wake of the writer in the "Quarterly," and, at the same time, to overcome the difficulty which I had pointed out, he had represented* that "the fields of action were near enough the one to the other to permit his" (the Duke's) "seeing, from each height as he ascended it, the smoke of the battle of Ligny rise in thick volumes over the intervening woods." This is the first time we have heard of the Duke having ascended *each* height on his own field, to see what Blücher was about at Ligny. However, in the third sentence beyond the one above quoted, Mr. Gleig forgets the woods which, as if with a magic wand, he has caused to spring up between the two fields of action, and, borrowing that extraordinary telescope which the writer in the "Quarterly" puts into the Duke's hands, and which at once levels both woods and heights, and clears away smoke, mist, and even darkness,† he actually enables the Duke to *see* "the failure of that cavalry-charge which led to Blücher's misfortune, and immediately preceded the general retreat of his army,"—which charge, be it recollected, took place at a distance of seven miles, and after darkness had set in!

* "Story of Waterloo," page 106.

† See my remarks in the note at page 154 of the present edition.

man, to have openly stated that he had been engaged by Mr. Murray to edit such a cheap account of the battle as would be suitable for a volume of his "Home and Colonial Library:" and, at all events, he ought so far to have respected the existing copyright of an author as to have acknowledged the authority for his several facts and incidents, however inconvenient it might have proved to have had that author's name figuring as such authority on almost every page of his book.*

If, with the courtesy usually observable in such matters, Mr. Gleig had previously communicated with me, or Mr. Murray with my Publishers, either of those gentlemen would have ascertained that it was the intention of the latter to put forth a cheaper edition of my work as soon as arrangements could be made for that purpose. The withholding of any such communication looks very like "stealing a march" upon both author and publishers, and tends to the inference that a work which was sold for two guineas a copy, and the popularity of which was so strikingly evinced by the fact that its first edition was exhausted within a few weeks of its publication, presented a temptation not easily resisted by individuals who would not scruple to "get up" the identical subject, embodying all the contents of that work, with perhaps a new head and tail, as well as a new title, and at a low price—in short, with a book at six shillings to drive one at two guineas out of the market.

I shall perhaps be reminded that Waterloo is a subject on which so much has been written, that sufficiently numerous materials were at hand to render any particular recourse to mine inexpedient: but I challenge Mr. Gleig to name any work, or set of works, published previously to mine, in which he could have found precisely the same facts, the same occurrences, the same incidents, the same details, arranged in the same consecutive order, and so perfectly connected, so closely dovetailed into one another as to present a minutely tactical elucidation of the great battle, as are contained in my "History." Could Mr. Gleig have furnished the public with his "Story" in the shape in which we find it, without having made the most unscrupulous use of my work? Let

* In one instance only, throughout his whole "Story," does Mr. Gleig allude to me; and then he does so † solely for the purpose of endeavouring to convict me of error, as regards a comparatively trivial incident, mentioned by me in a note,‡ namely, the death of Corporal Shaw of the Life Guards. My reply to this imputation of inaccuracy will be found in the "United Service Magazine" for August 1847, and my original statement remains unaltered.

† "Story of Waterloo," page 191.

‡ See page 260 of the present edition.

him set apart all that he has taken from the latter, and what will then remain? The shadow in place of the substance.

An enumeration of parallel passages in the two works would extend to an inordinate length the few remarks I have felt myself called upon to make in justice to my Publishers. I shall therefore content myself with requesting such persons as may be curious in these matters to compare the two accounts of any prominent or leading feature of the great battle. Let them select, for instance, the attack and defence of Hougomont, from the commencement to the close, and they will find in Mr. Gleig's book all the occurrences and incidents related by him, not in the *same words*, for that would have been actionable, but in the same consecutive order in which they are arranged in my work. Only one little exception occurs, and that consists in his making the fire break out at Hougomont much earlier, to which he is apparently induced by a desire, while adverting to the conduct of Serjeant Graham of the Coldstream Guards, to introduce at the same place an incident which I have related respecting him; but, when subsequently following up my narrative, as if forgetful of having thus anticipated the circumstance, he makes the fire break out at a much *later* period!* These remarks apply equally to the description of the grand attack made by d'Erlon's corps and Kellermann's cuirassiers against the British centre and left wing, and of its repulse; also to the attack and defence of La Haye Sainte, the French grand cavalry-attack of the British right wing and centre; and to the several dispositions and movements connected with the final attack by the French imperial guard. In a similar, if not a still more glaring manner, has Mr. Gleig copied the arrangement of dispositions and movements of the various troops engaged at the battle of Quatre-Bras, with all the occurrences and incidents in the same consecutive order in which they appear in my "History." These arrangements of the details of the military operations, the result of a mass of most valuable evidence, I should observe, are original, and not to be found in *any* previous work on the subject. In so unscrupulously adopting them Mr. Gleig was bound at least to quote, as he proceeded in his "Story," the authority whence he had derived his information.

A comparison of the two works will fully attest the correctness of my remarks. As regards parallel passages, however, I shall select two at random—the following, for instance, from our respective accounts of the contest at Hougomont;

* "Story of Waterloo," page 204.

premising that mine is deduced from the positive evidence of eye-witnesses, and Mr. Gleig's (with some variation, which however slight, leads to error and confusion) from the result of that evidence as given in my own work, and which he could not have obtained from any other source.

Mr. Gleig, page 176.

"Scarcely was this feat of nobleness* performed, when the enemy, having collected in denser masses, made a new rush against the gate. They failed in bursting it open; but presently upon the top of the wall appeared a French grenadier, who had led the way for the purpose of removing the defences from the interior, and whose bold bearing shewed that he would not be deterred by a trifle. It happened that Serjeant Graham

Captain Siborne, page 240.†

"During this advance of the French skirmishers against the extreme right of the Allied front line, the troops which formed their support attempted again to force open the rear gate of Hougomont. The individuals before mentioned as having closed the gate, were at the time occupied in rendering it more secure by placing against it some pieces of ash timber that lay in the yard. The French, failing in their endeavours to

* The following extracts contain Mr. Gleig's description of this "feat," and the parallel passage in my "History"—the latter written down from the account given to me personally by Serjeant Graham.

Mr. Gleig, page 175.

"At this moment Serj. Graham, who stood upon the banquette, and bore himself with unrivalled bravery, begged permission of Colonel Macdonnell to retire for a moment. Col. Macdonnell, who knew the nature of the man, merely said, 'By all means, Graham, but I wonder you should ask leave now.' 'I would not, Sir,' was the answer; 'only my brother is wounded, and he is in that outbuilding there, which has just caught fire. Give me leave to carry him out; I will be back in a moment.' The leave was granted, of course, with eagerness, and Graham, laying down his musket, ran off, lifted his brother in his arms, and placed him in a ditch. He was back at his post before his absence could well have been noticed, &c."

Captain Siborne, Note, *page* 238-9.†

"This individual deserves honourable mention, having greatly distinguished himself during the memorable defence of Hougomont. At a later period of the day, when in the ranks along the garden-wall facing the wood, and when the struggle was most severe in that quarter, he asked Lieut. Colonel Macdonnell's permission to fall out. The Colonel, knowing the character of the man, expressed his surprise at the request made at such a moment. Graham explained that his brother lay wounded in one of the buildings then on fire, that he wished to remove him to a place of safety, and that he would then lose no time in rejoining the ranks. The request was granted: Graham succeeded in snatching his brother from the horrible fate which menaced him; laid him in a ditch in rear of the inclosures, and, true to his word, was again at his post, &c."

† Present edition.

had given his musket to Captain Wyndham, and was in the act of piling some heavy substance against the gate. 'Do you see that fellow, Graham,' cried the Captain. 'Yes, Sir,' was the laconic answer; whereupon a log of wood which he carried was dropped, and resuming his weapon, he took aim at the grenadier, and shot him dead. None dared to follow where this brave man died, and the enemy forthwith abandoned their attempt on the gate and turned elsewhere.

"Away they now rushed along the inner edge of the orchard, there they found a gap communicating from the wood with the interior of the latter inclosure, and they sprang through it in great numbers, confident that they should have the edifice in reverse. But Lord Saltoun with his gallant band was here. He did not stop to skirmish—he formed his men in line, and with a shout rushed upon the head of the column. A brief but desperate struggle ensued, in which the guards abated nothing of their accustomed daring, and backwards by sheer force the intruders were borne, leaving many behind who there struck their last blow and fired their last shot. Nevertheless the weight of numbers was overpowering. From other quarters of the wood crowds of men broke in, and Lord Saltoun fought push in the gate, a brave grenadier volunteered to climb over and open it from the inside. Captain Wyndham, on perceiving the latter at the top of the gate, instantly desired Serjeant Graham, whose musket he was holding whilst the latter was bringing forward another piece of timber, to drop the wood, take his firelock, and shoot the intruder. The order was instantly obeyed; and the intrepid assailant, who, for any useful result, ought to have been accompanied by a score of his comrades, fell beneath Graham's deadly aim. It was at this moment that the French skirmishers who had advanced against the main position, were falling back upon their support, and the whole of these troops were driven off by the advance of the four companies of the Coldstream guards, detached from the main position, as previously described.

"In the mean time, the French infantry in the wood, finding their advance against the garden so suddenly checked, endeavoured to turn it by its left. With this view they were debouching through a large gap in the fence, forming an outlet from the wood into the orchard, when Lieut. Colonel Lord Saltoun, seizing the favourable opportunity, made a most gallant charge upon the head of the column with the light companies of as became the descendant of his race, disputing every tree, but was compelled to give ground till in a hollow-way, rearward of the inclosure, he found some cover. There he stoutly maintained himself: and it is said that he would have been succoured by the light troops of Alten's division, had not the Prince of Orange interposed in a very characteristic manner to prevent it. 'Don't stir,' was his exclamation; 'depend upon it that the Duke has seen that move, and will take steps to counteract it.'* And his Royal Highness was right. Just as he spoke two companies of the 3rd guards were seen to descend the brow of the hill, and to advance along the same hedge by which the enemy were approaching, exactly in front of them. Saltoun saw and felt the advance of his friends. His retreat had drawn the enemy into such a position that they were terribly galled by a flank-fire from the garden wall, and now he sprang up, and shouted to his men to follow. They were over the inner side of the ditch in a moment, and the relieving companies

the 1st brigade of guards, and succeeded in driving the enemy back into the wood.

"Shortly afterwards a large body of the enemy's light troops began to advance stealthily along the eastern hedge of the Hougomont inclosures, communicating at the same time with the infantry in the wood on their left. This was immediately followed by a direct front attack upon the orchard, which compelled Lord Saltoun gradually to withdraw his greatly reduced force from tree to tree, until he reached the hollow-way in rear of that inclosure.

"The light troops in front of Alten's division, having perceived the French creeping along the hedge so as to turn the left flank of Hougomont, were on the point of forming to oppose them, but on the latter being pointed out to the Prince of Orange, who had just come to the front to make his observations, he coolly remarked:—'No, don't stir—the Duke is sure to see that movement, and will take some step to counteract it.' He had scarcely spoken, when two companies of the 3rd regiment

* So guarded is Mr. Gleig against employing my language that he extends this rule even to the varying of the precise words uttered by individuals as related to me by those who actually heard them. To the above example I will merely add the following. An officer of the Inniskilling dragoons, who was upon the left flank of that regiment as it advanced, with the remainder of Ponsonby's brigade, to charge d'Erlon's columns of attack between one and two o'clock, having related to me the exclamation made by the late Duke of Richmond at that moment, I have given it in the words which he heard his Grace utter; namely, "Now's your time!" Mr. Gleig, in copying this incident, has thought proper to alter the Duke's actual expression to "At 'em, my lads; at 'em, now's your time."

pushing forward at the same time, the French were driven back at a pace much more rapid than that which had carried them forward in their tide of success. Lord Saltoun's loss was severe; indeed, more men fell during this brief struggle in the orchard than in the defence of the buildings, though protracted for several hours; but his triumph was complete. He cleared the orchard, re-occupied its front hedge, and effectually secured the important post from risk on that side; and as his comrades were equally successful, chasing the enemy into the hollow ground from which they had debouched, he felt, as soon as they had joined themselves to his party within the fence, that for the present all was safe. And he was right."

of British guards, detached from the Allied line, were seen advancing along the same hedge, in an opposite direction, to meet them. Lord Saltoun being thus reinforced upon his left, and the French skirmishers in his front having become exposed to a sharp flanking fire from the guards lining the eastern garden-wall, he resumed the offensive, cleared the orchard of the enemy, and re-occupied its front hedge; while the detachment on the left drove the French along the outer hedge, and down into the hollow whence they had debouched, and then joined the troops in the great orchard. The front hedge of the orchard, the front wall of the garden, with the lane and avenue on the right, constituted at this time the outer line of the defence of Hougomont."

On hastily perusing these passages, a person might merely be struck by their parallelism, and by the evidence which they afford of the one having been put together from the other. This, however, is only an injury which affects my Publishers. The evil lies in the deception so frequently imposed upon the public by persons engaged in "re-writing," and giving out as original productions, passages in wholesale from other works, without acknowledgment of their source, or regard to an author's copyright. Thus, for instance, Mr. Gleig, desirous of embodying *in other words* all the incidents related by me in the extracts selected, falls into great inaccuracy and confusion. He says of the French,—"Away they now rushed along the inner hedge of the orchard. There they found a gap communicating from the wood with the interior of the latter inclosure, and they sprang through it in great numbers, confident that they now should have the edifice in reverse. But Lord Saltoun with his gallant band was here. He did not stop to skirmish—he formed his men in line, and with a shout, rushed upon the head of the column." Now, these troops did *not* rush "along the inner hedge of the orchard." They had nothing to do with the "gap communicating from the wood with the interior of the orchard." Had they "rushed along the inner hedge of the orchard," as Mr. Gleig says they did, towards the "gap communicating from the wood," they would have come up *in rear* of Lord Saltoun, who, at that time, occupied the orchard! The orchard and the gap were on the *east* side of Hougomont. The troops alluded to retired by the lane on the *west* side of the château (as described by me in the paragraph immediately preceding the first one quoted,* and which Mr. Gleig has also copied, as usual, together with other matters, in a preceding paragraph of his own). They were engaged with the four companies of the Coldstream guards, under Lieut. Colonel Woodford, and *not* with the light companies of the 1st brigade of guards, under Lieut. Colonel Lord Saltoun. It is therefore evident that Mr. Gleig, either through ignorance of the localities, or, which is much more apparent, from his eagerness to put an original narrative into a new dress, and disregarding due attention to the proper adjustment of its several parts, has failed to convey the very clear explanation which I have given on this point in the passages above quoted. Mr. Gleig, proceeding with his plagiarism, but wishing to avoid making use of my expression that "shortly afterwards a large body of the enemy's light troops began to advance stealthily along the eastern hedge of the Hougomont inclosures, communicating at the same time with the infantry in the wood on their left," and, further, that "this was immediately followed by a direct front attack of the orchard, which compelled Lord Saltoun gradually to withdraw," &c. affirms that "from other quarters of the wood crowds of men broke in," which is quite contrary to the fact; for this "gap," which was at the south-west angle of the orchard, and at which Lord Saltoun's struggle with the defenders of the wood took place, was the only outlet from the latter into the orchard. The front attack upon the orchard at this moment was *not* made by "crowds of men from other quarters of the wood," but by the enemy's light troops above mentioned. In copying the incident which I have furnished in connection with an exclamation made by the Prince of Orange to the light troops of Alten's division, namely, "Don't stir, depend upon it the Duke has seen that move, and will take steps to counteract it," Mr. Gleig makes no previous mention of the movement to which the word "*that*" in this exclamation particularly refers, but, in endeavouring to vary his language from mine, leaves it to be vaguely inferred

* See page 239—240 of the present edition.

from a *subsequent* sentence. Judging from the concluding portion of Mr. Gleig's plagiarism above quoted, the reader might be led to imagine that Lord Saltoun had communicated to him what were his views and feelings at the moment indicated; but this, I know, has not been the case, and Mr. Gleig's assertions in this respect rest entirely upon his own assumption.

It will be seen by the quoted passage from Mr. Gleig, that to avoid using my language in describing the incident which I have given respecting Serjeant Graham, he converts it into a dialogue between the latter and Captain Wyndham, without a tittle of evidence; and this constitutes an essential point of difference between us, for I never relate in my work any conversation or exclamation without having direct evidence respecting it.

Mr. Gleig never allows Lord Saltoun to attack the enemy without raising a "shout," and yet he has no evidence in support of such statements. In one instance, a very remarkable one—that of the attack by the British guards upon the imperial guards of France—I certainly mention that his Lordship called out "Now's the time, my boys!" but I had previously ascertained that such was the fact; not, however, from the reminiscences with which his Lordship favoured me, but from the distinct evidence of officers of the guards who heard his exclamation.

I will now select two parallel passages from our respective accounts of the contest at La Haye Sainte, not so much for the purpose of showing any precise parallelism between them, as for that of affording an instance of error into which Mr. Gleig is occasionally led by studiously varying his language from mine.

Mr. Gleig, page 211.	*Captain Siborne, page* 280.*
"Major Baring, however, having been joined by two companies of green Germans, planted them, together with a detachment from his own battalion, in the garden:† with	"Meanwhile, Major Baring having applied for a reinforcement, two companies were detached to his post from the 1st light battalion of the King's German legion. To

* Present edition.

† In the preceding portion of the paragraph above quoted, Mr. Gleig, again misled by the "Quarterly," fairly outdoes the Reviewer on this point, by boldly asserting that "all on the English right and rear of the pile was solid masonry, through which, by some grievous oversight or other, no aperture had been broken; and the consequence was, that let the battle go as it might, there were no means of reinforcing the garrison except from the Charleroi road." Having resided in the farm of La Haye Sainte during a period of six months, and made myself thoroughly

the rest he occupied the house, barn, stables, and other outbuildings, and, abandoning the orchard, as too extensive for his force, prepared to make a stout resistance, and hoped to make it an effectual one.

"On came the French cavalry, sweeping like a stormy sea up the face of the hill. They soon passed Baring by, driving in the skirmishers which connected him with the main position, and presently Donzelot's infantry moved towards him. They presented a very formidable appearance, marching with a quick yet steady pace along the great road, and covering themselves as usual with clouds of skirmishers. It was not long ere the firing began. The Germans plied their rifles vigorously from loophole and window, and over the copings of the wall, behind which they had erected with benches and these and a part of his own battalion, he intrusted the defence of the garden; and, abandoning altogether the orchard, he placed the remainder of his force in the buildings, distributing their defence among the three officers who had so courageously maintained them during the previous attack. The French columns advanced against this post with the most undaunted resolution, and the most conspicuous gallantry. The well-aimed bullets of the German rifles, though they told quickly and fearfully amidst their masses, arrested not their progress for a moment. They rushed close up to the walls, and seizing the rifles as they protruded through the loopholes, endeavoured to wrest them from the hands of the defenders. They also made a most furious assault against the gates and doors, in the

acquainted with even its most minute features, and also constructed a model of it upon a large scale, as it appeared on the morning of the battle, I am enabled to assure Mr. Gleig that there was no necessity for breaking an "aperture," as more than one aperture already existed. At the back of the house, facing the garden, were a door and four windows, instead of "solid masonry;" and there was a passage from that door through the house to the front door; and it was through this passage that Major Baring received his several reinforcements, and that his gallant comrades retreated. But if, as Mr. Gleig states, "there were no means of reinforcing the garrison except from the Charleroi road," which was raked by the enemy's artillery, he ought to have explained how Major Baring managed to receive the several reinforcements detached to him in the course of the day, and why that officer should, as stated in the passage above quoted, have "planted' his "green Germans in the garden;" where, in consequence of the "solid masonry," they became, as soon as the enemy advanced, cut off from all communication with him. Subsequently, however, in copying the incidents contained in my description of the capture of La Haye Sainte, and of the retreat of the Germans *through the house*, Mr. Gleig gets rid of the "solid masonry," and admits that "there was a narrow passage leading through the house to the garden in the rear"!! (See page 222.)

other articles of furniture a somewhat insecure banquette, and the French replied to them with volleys of musketry. But the latter soon closed upon the pile, and made determined efforts to force an entrance from the orchard, and over the wall wherever it seemed to be accessible. The main attack was of course from the Charleroi road. The assailants found there a large doorway imperfectly barricaded, and leading into one of the barns. They forced it open, and rushed in with loud cries of "Vive l'Empereur!"—but not a man penetrated beyond the threshold. A score of rifles were pointed, and a score of bullets, delivered at the distance of a few feet by steady marksmen, caused a heap of dead to block up in a moment further ingress to the living."

defence of which many lives were sacrificed. The greatest struggle was at the western opening to the large barn, the door of which was wanting. The French, determined to make good an entrance, encountered the brave Germans, equally resolute to prevent them. The foremost Frenchmen, dashing boldly on to force their way, were struck down by the deliberate fire from the rifles the instant they reached the threshold, and seventeen of their dead bodies already formed a rampart for those who continued to press forward to carry on the struggle."

In this passage, by Mr. Gleig, it would appear that, wishing to avoid falling into my expression—"the greatest struggle was at the western opening to the large barn, the door of which was wanting,"—he affirms, without knowing, or at least satisfying himself, which was really the "*western opening*," that "the main attack was of course from the Charleroi road," and that "the assailants found there a large doorway, imperfectly barricaded, and leading into one of the barns"—further that, "they forced it open and rushed in." Now it so happened that the great struggle was *not* on the Charleroi road, or eastern side, but on the *opposite* side of the farm, at the opening into the barn, the door of which had unfortunately been used for firewood. It was *here* where the French penetrated, and it was from *this* side that they ultimately gained possession of the farm. They never effected an entrance from the "*Charleroi road.*"

I could adduce innumerable parallel passages, all couched in language so guardedly worded as possibly to constitute a dexterous evasion of the law of copyright—a law so vague and indefinite, and so entirely dependent on the peculiar views which a judge may entertain respecting it, that, except in cases of actual *verbatim* copies, authors of works of a high class and of a necessarily expensive nature, are placed completely at the mercy of certain publishers, who engage persons to write upon the subjects of such works, and embody all the information which these contain, in a different and a cheaper form.

A greater proof of plagiarism on the part of any writer could scarcely be adduced than the circumstance of his transcribing not merely the substance of an author's statements, but also his errors: for since the publication of the second edition of my History, I have ascertained, partly through discussion in the "United Service Magazine", and partly through additional correspondence with surviving eye-witnesses, that it contained four or five errors. It is curious that these *identical errors,* which have been rectified in the present edition, should have been faithfully copied by Mr. Gleig into his "Story"—I say *copied,* because it is impossible, in the face of them, to draw any other conclusion.

The first of these copied errors occurs in Mr. Gleig's narrative, at page 79, in which he makes the advance of Halkett's brigade at Quatre-Bras and the French attack upon the 69th regiment *precede* the charge by the 92nd Highlanders. This is in accordance with the arrangement in the former edition of my work, but, on reference to the present one, it will be seen that I have reconstructed my description of that part of the action so as to completely invert the order of those movements.

The second error copied by Mr. Gleig occurs at page 170-171 of his book, where he assigns the opening of the cannonade at Waterloo to Captain Cleeves's battery of the King's German legion. I have since ascertained that Captain Sandham's battery opened the fire of the Allied artillery.

The third copied error is to be found in his description of the attack and defeat of a dense column of the French imperial guard by Maitland's brigade of British guards—a description, which, though as usual, not taken exactly *verbatim* from mine, certainly contains the same matter and follows the same order—wherein he makes the whole of Maitland's brigade run back to the ridge after having attacked the first column of the French guards. This agrees with my former statement, but I now find, on the best authority, that on this point I committed *one* mistake; for it was not the *whole*, but only *one wing* of the brigade, that fell back in the manner represented.

The fourth error copied by Mr. Gleig occurs at page 238 of his book, where he represents Halkett's brigade as being "fiercely engaged with Donzelot's troops" during the attack by the first column of the Imperial guard; but it will be seen that I have also corrected this error in the present edition, having satisfied myself that the *whole* of Halkett's brigade was at that time engaged with the Imperial guard, and not with Donzelot's troops.

Will Mr. Gleig give a similar correction of these errors in the next edition of his "Story"?

I have already stated that as regards the battle of Waterloo, Mr. Gleig has transferred to his pages, in another dress, and in the same consecutive order, nearly all the facts, occurrences, and incidents, comprised in my representation of the several acts of that sanguinary drama. These are, the attack and defence of Hougomont; the attack by d'Erlon's corps and Kellermann's cavalry upon the British centre and left wing, and its repulse; the attack and defence of La Haye Sainte; the cavalry-attack upon the British right wing and centre; and the dispositions and movements connected with the final attack by the French imperial guard.* The only exception to Mr. Gleig's general rule in this respect occurs immediately

* In describing the advance of the first column of the imperial guard to this attack, Mr. Gleig allows his fancy strangely to mislead him. Thus, at page 236, he says, "Down the slope went the leading column of the guard, the detached masses of d'Erlon's corps operating an effective diversion in their favour. Now they were in the hollow—now they began to ascend the lower wave of ground which intervenes between the positions of the two armies—now they crown this height, and while their own guns ceased firing for a space, those on the external slope of the English position open with terrible effect. Now the shot plunged and smashed among the companies as they went over that ridge! Now one after another their files seemed to be wrenched asunder by the weight of the salvoes that greeted them. But they never paused for a moment. The survivors closed up into the spaces which the dead and wounded had left, and in due time the entire mass was again under cover of a valley; then the French batteries renewed their fire, and so fierce and incessant was it that the uninitiated bystander might have been apt to imagine that a desire to take vengeance on the slayers of their countrymen had animated these vigorous cannoneers. But this did not last long. By and bye the leading sections began to breast the English hill," &c. &c. Now along the track of the advance of this column, there was *no* intermediate "ridge", *no* "lower wave of ground which intervenes between the positions of the two armies." From the moment the column commenced its advance, until it reached the brow of the Allied position, it continued within view of the British artillery. Hence no such scene as that represented could have taken place. This is merely the indulgence of fancy at the sacrifice of truth!

after his description of the last mentioned contest, when he narrates the manner in which the second column of attack of the imperial guard was repulsed by the British. As in this part of his "Story" Mr. Gleig introduces facts at variance with those which I have given, and which are founded upon the most extensive and the clearest evidence, I feel it necessary to undeceive those persons who may imagine the former to be founded on my work, by pointing out a few of the most decided errors which are therein put forth. It is *not* true that when "Colonel Colborne (now Lord Seaton), who that day commanded the 52nd, changed the front of his regiment so as to bring its line directly upon the flank of the French column, he paused only till his brigadier should have time to lead up the 71st, so as to head it." He made *no pause whatever*. Any pause at that moment would have been utterly inconsistent with the spirit in which this daring but judicious movement had been conceived. The 71st did *not* "head" the French column. The three regiments of Adam's brigade did *not* "pour a fire simultaneously into the mass." A body of cuirassiers did *not* "charge the 52nd," neither did "a squadron of the 23rd light dragoons gallop past it," at this moment. Maitland's and Adam's brigades did *not* "envelope the devoted column and sweep it from the field." It was Colborne's brilliant charge which "swept it from the field." It is *not* a true description that when "the whole line advanced, scenes commenced of fiery attack and resolute defence—of charging horsemen and infantry stern, such as there is no power, either in pen or pencil, adequately to describe." As far as the line itself was concerned, all fighting had ceased. Its advance was one of triumph, not of attack. Adam's, Vivian's, and Vandeleur's brigades, were the only troops still engaged. The first, continuing its victorious advance, reached the height on which were posted the rallied remnant of the first attacking column of the imperial guard; charged the latter, who fled; and pursued them as far as Rossomme: the second, (Vivian's), completely routed the French cavalry-reserves near La Belle Alliance, and continued in pursuit; while the third, (Vandeleur's), dispersed or made prisoners large bodies of infantry more to the right, and also went on in pursuit. In these transactions the only encounter which presented a severe struggle was that which took place between a squadron of the 10th hussars and a square of the imperial guard; but no contest occurred between even these advanced brigades and their opponents, such as Mr. Gleig's language above quoted would imply;

and, as regards the line itself, *none whatever* took place. The two squares of the imperial guard which remained in support of the attacking columns of that force, did *not* stand "at the bottom of the descent," but on the high ground of La Belle Alliance. It was *not* Adam that moved "towards the further face of one of these masses with the apparent design of falling upon it." The 52nd regiment did *not* "change its front for a moment," and gain possession of the battery which "opened upon the flank of Adam's brigade."

These are some of the errors into which Mr. Gleig has fallen in the only part of his account of the battle wherein he has not copied the facts, occurrences, and incidents, and the order in which they are related, as they appear in my work. If I am asked whether I affirm them to be errors simply because in this single portion of the "Story" the facts alluded to are not taken, as in the other parts of it, from my "History," my answer is that I affirm them to be such because they are at direct variance with the most distinct and undeniable evidence which I have in my possession from actors in the scene described. Has Mr. Gleig any evidence of a similar character to prove that they are *not* errors? If any person will take the trouble to compare the two accounts of this portion of the battle, namely, its closing scene, he will find that these errors mostly consist in a mis-timed and distorted relation of somewhat *similar* facts originated in my own description!

I am not disposed to dwell longer on this unpleasant subject. I feel satisfied that I am fully justified in offering these remarks in vindication of my own reputation, and of the rights of my Publishers. It can scarcely be presumed that an author, conscious of having, by dint of indefatigable industry, minute research, and deep study, produced an *original* work, will submit without a murmur to so unscrupulous a spoliation of his general plan, and arrangement of his views, his facts and incidents, as that which has been made of my "History of the War in France and Belgium in 1815," by one from whom, considering his connection with the same honourable profession to which I myself belong, a more generous and friendly treatment might have been expected.

W. SIBORNE.

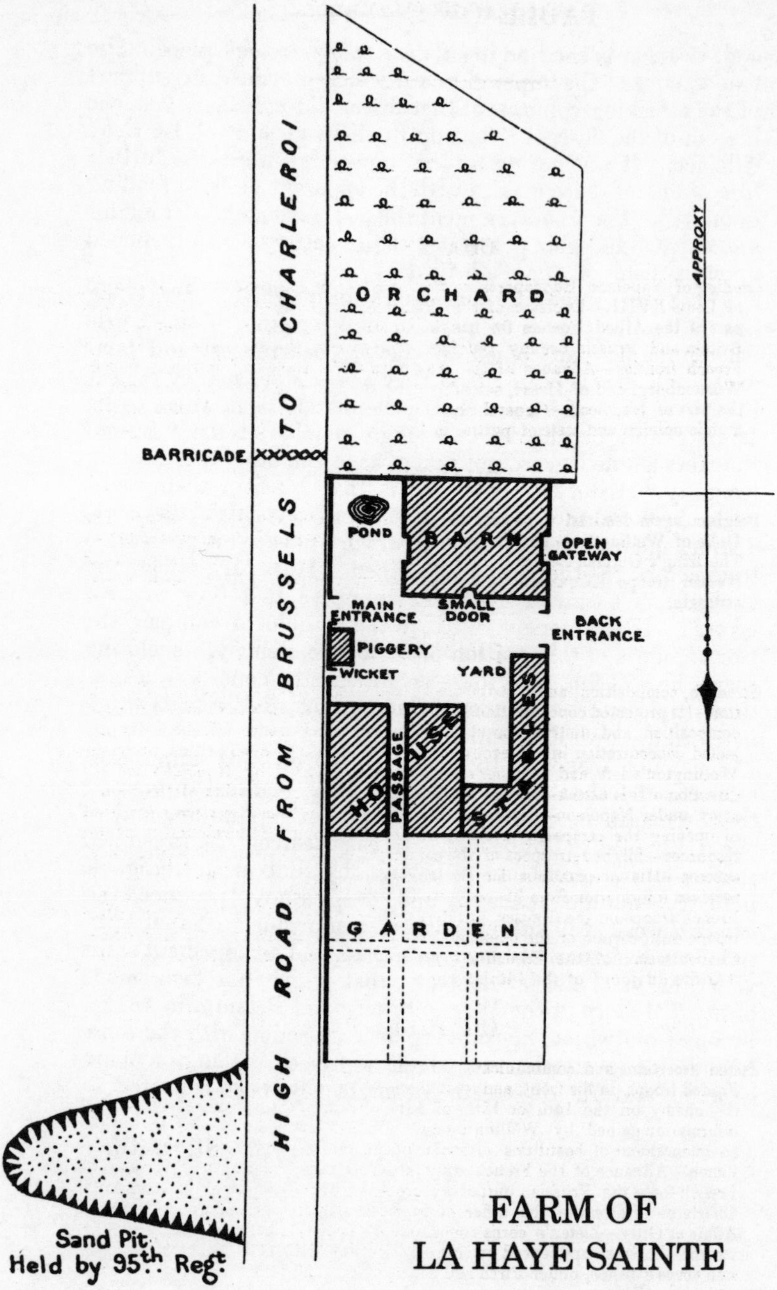

FARM OF
LA HAYE SAINTE

TABLE OF CONTENTS.

CHAPTER I.

CHAPTER II.

CHAPTER III.

CHAPTER IV.

CHAPTER V.

CHAPTER VI.

CHAPTER VII.

CHAPTER VIII.

CHAPTER IX.

CHAPTER X.

CHAPTER XI.

CHAPTER XII.

CHAPTER XIII.

CHAPTER XIV.

CHAPTER XV.

CHAPTER XVI.

CHAPTER XVII.

CHAPTER XVIII.

CHAPTER XIX.

CHAPTER XX.

APPENDIX.

THE ENGRAVINGS

are reproduced from
THE BATTLE OF WATERLOO,
WITH THOSE OF LIGNY AND QUATRE-BRAS
by George Jones, Esq. R.A.
Published by John Booth and T. Egerton,
London, 1817

1. "The Duke of Wellington having shown the Duke of Brunswick a letter, changed his horse, and they then set off together."

2. Battle of Ligny
"It was here a contest began, the most obstinate recorded in history."

3. Battle of Ligny
"Marshall Blücher, stunned by the violent fall, lay entangled under his horse."

4. Battle of Quatre-Bras
"Sir Thomas Picton ordering the charge of Sir James Kempt's Brigade."

5. Battle of Quatre-Bras
"The 28th remained steady."

6. Battle of Quatre-Bras
Lieut.-Col. Macara of the 42d Regiment.

7. Battle of Quatre-Bras. The 71st Highlanders.
"The piper suddenly struck up the Pibroch and followed into the thickest of the fight."

8. Marquis of Anglesey charging on 17th June.

9. The Duke of Wellington and Staff at the commencement of the Battle.

10. Hougomont

"The Artillery Officers had the range so accurately that every shot and shell fell into the very centre of their masses."

11. “The Duke led on a Brigade consisting of the 52d and 95th Regts.”

12. La Sainte Haye
"Close by a large building occupied alternately by Friend and Foe."

13. Waterloo, 2pm - Left of the British Line
Charge of the Royals, Greys, and Inniskillings. The body of Gen. Picton is borne from the field.

14. Ponsonby's Brigade
"At this critical minute, the Marquis of Anglesey galloped up."

15. Ponsonby's Brigade charging
"The Greys preserved a beautiful line at speed."

16. The fall of Major General Sir Wm. Ponsonby, KCB.

17. “French Cuirassiers advanced to the mouth of our cannon.” About 3 o’clock.”

18. The Hon. Lieut.-Col. Ponsonby, 12th Dragoons.

19. Lieut-General Sir Thomas Picton fell in the thickest of the fight.

20. "The Greys and 92d cheered and huzza'd 'Scotland for ever!'"

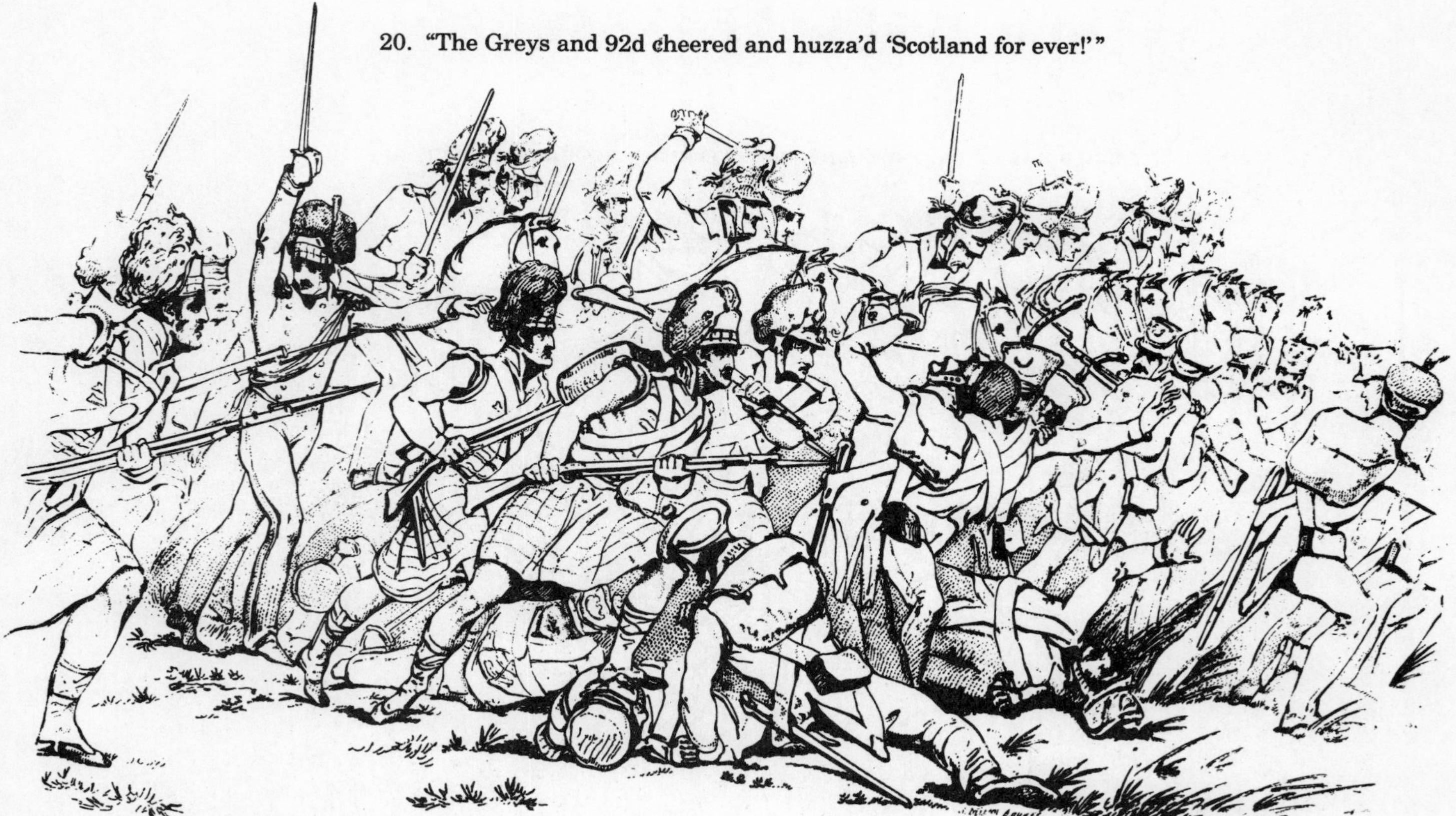

21. Corporal Shaw of the Life Guards dealing destruction to all around him.

22. Sergeant Taylor, 18th Hussars, and French Cuirassiers.

23. General Lord Hill and 13th
"Drive them back, 13th!"

24. Waterloo, 8pm - Right of the British Line
The Duke of Wellington ordering the general advance.

25. Waterloo 8pm - Centre of the British Line
The Marquis of Anglesey, on the general advance, directing the Brigades of Cavalry on the right of La Haye Sainte.

26. “Now every man must advance!”

27. "It was at La Belle Alliance, pierced thro' and thro', that Marshals Blücher and Wellington accidentally met."

28. The Retreat at Genappe
"The Duke fell yesterday, and thou shalt also bite the dust."

HISTORY

OF THE

WAR IN FRANCE AND BELGIUM

IN 1815.

CHAPTER I.

The history of Europe records but few events so universally and so intimately involving the policy and interests of her component states, as the escape of Napoleon Buonaparte from the island of Elba, on the 26th of February, 1815—his landing in France, and his again ascending, unopposed, that throne, from which Louis XVIII. had fled with precipitation, upon learning the triumphal approach towards the capital, of his successful and formidable rival. With the rapidity of lightning the intelligence spread itself over the whole Continent, and with all the suddenness and violence of an electric shock, did it burst amidst the delegates from the different states, who were then assembled in Congress at Vienna. This important assembly, so unexpectedly interrupted, had been called together to deliberate upon measures of international security and prosperity; and to solve those intricate questions of policy necessarily arising out of the various combinations, which, in the course of a general war, carried on with unmitigated violence, and but little intermission, for nearly a quarter of a century, had so fatally unhinged and dismembered the previously existing social order and polity of Europe. With one accord, a fresh appeal to the sword was decided upon; the military resources of every nation were again called into requisition. From state to state the cry "To arms!" was responded to with cheerfulness and alacrity, and immense armies were put in motion towards the French frontier, all animated with the sole object and fixed determination of annihilating, for ever, the common foe whom they had already conquered, but whom, as it would then appear, they had but ineffectually humbled. The openly declared project of the Allied Sovereigns to employ all their means, and combine all their efforts, towards the accomplishment of the complete overthrow of the resuscitated power of Napoleon, with whom they had determined, thenceforth, to enter into neither truce nor treaty,* was singularly favoured by the circumstance of their armies being still retained upon a war establishment. The forces of the several Powers were continued on that scale, in consequence of the difficulties experienced in the Congress in dealing with and settling many perplexing questions of international policy, and moderating the warmth of the discussions that took place upon them. It was considered expedient to keep up powerful reserves, available both for home service, and for any contingencies that might arise out of combinations and revolts among those minor states, whose aversion to the new political arrangements was more than suspected. Thus it had been found necessary to detach bodies of troops from the main bulk of the forces, in consequence of the state of the Poles placed under the protection of Russia, and of the Saxons inhabiting that portion of their country which had been ceded to Prussia; as also, in consequence of the powerful diversion, as regarded Austria, caused by the sudden irruption of Murat, king of Naples, into the north of Italy. Notwithstanding these necessary deductions, however, it was found practicable to assemble, by the end of May, an efficient force of not less than 500,000 men, upon different points contiguous to the French frontier, with all the supplies necessary for the prosecution of a vigorous campaign.†

The most important portion of this extensive line of frontier was undoubtedly that which fronted the Netherlands; for although it had been planned by the Allies that no advance was to be made by the troops in Belgium, until the remainder of their forces had reached a line of connecting points along the French frontier, when all their armies were to march, in combined movement, upon the capital, still it was reasonably to be expected, that Napoleon would not wait for the com-

* See the Declaration, on the 13th of March, of the Allied Powers, on the return of Napoleon Buonaparte to France—Appendix I.

† See the Treaty of Alliance, of the 25th of March, 1815, concluded between Austria, Russia, Prussia, and Great Britain—Appendix II.

pletion of this plan, but rather that he would endeavour, by a decisive effort, if not to frustrate its accomplishment, at least to diminish its efficacy. It required no great exercise of military sagacity or political foresight to predict, that after having adopted a maturely considered disposition of force, on the most important points along his general line of defence, and placed his frontier fortresses upon a respectable footing, Napoleon would open the tremendous game, upon which his crown, his political existence, and the fate of France were now fairly staked, by a bold, sudden, and resolute advance into Belgium—straining every nerve to vanquish, in detail, the allied forces in that densely populated country, of which a vast portion was already prepared to declare in his favour. His authority once established in Brussels, through the means of some great and signal triumph, the accession to his moral influence over the entire mass of the French nation would be immense; and then, flying to the succour of his nearest corps menaced from the banks of the Rhine by the approach of hostile forces, (upon which his possession of Belgium would operate as a powerful check by the facilities thus afforded for a combined attack in front and flank,) a series of brilliant successes, supported by fresh levies from the interior, might enable him even to dictate terms to the Allies, who had indignantly rejected all his overtures.

Hence the importance of narrowly watching the Belgian frontier, and of making due preparations for meeting any attack in that quarter, was too obvious not to form a principal feature in the general plan of the Allies. Its defence was assigned to an army under the Duke of Wellington, comprising contingent forces from Great Britain, from Hanover, the Netherlands, Brunswick, and Nassau; and to a Prussian army, under Field Marshal Prince Blücher von Wahlstadt.

At the moment of the landing of Napoleon on the French shore, the only force in the Netherlands consisted, in addition to the native troops, of a weak Anglo-Hanoverian corps, under the command of His Royal Highness the Prince of Orange; but the zeal, energy, and activity displayed by the government of Great Britain, in engrafting upon this nucleus a powerful army, amounting, at the commencement of hostilities, to about 100,000 combatants, notwithstanding the impediments and delays occasioned by the absence of a considerable portion of its troops in America, were truly surprising. At the same time, the extraordinary supply of subsidies furnished by the British Parliament, without which not one of the armies of the Allied Sovereigns could have commenced operations, and by means of which England thus became the great lever whereby the whole of Europe was set in motion towards the attainment of the one common object, was admirably illustrative of the bold, decided, and straightforward policy of the most determined, the most indefatigable, and the most consistent enemy of Napoleon.

Within the same period, the Prussian forces, originally limited to a corps of 30,000 men, under General Count Kleist von Nollendorf, occupying the Prussian territories bounded by the Rhine, the Meuse, and the Moselle, were augmented to an effective army of 116,000 combatants, with all the rapidity and energy which a keen sense of the wrongs and miseries their country had endured, under the ruthless sway of their inveterate foe, and a salutary dread of a repetition of such infliction, could not fail to inspire.*

Great Britain and Prussia thus occupied the post of honour, and formed the vanguard of the mighty masses which Europe was pouring forth to seal the doom of the Napoleon dynasty.

A Russian army, under Field Marshal Count Barclay de Tolly, amounting to 167,000 men, was rapidly traversing the whole of Germany, in three main columns, of which the right, commanded by General Dochterow, advanced by Kalisch, Torgau, Leipzig, Erfurt, Hanau, Frankfort, and Hochheim, towards Mayence; the centre, commanded by General Baron Sacken, advanced by Breslau, Dresden, Zwickau, Baireuth, Nuremberg, Aschaffenburg, Dieburg, and Gross-Gerau, towards Oppenheim; while the left column, commanded by General Count Langeron, took its direction along the line of Prague, Aube, Adelsheim, Neckar, and Heidelberg, towards Manheim. The heads of the columns reached the Middle Rhine, when hostilities were on the point of breaking out upon the Belgian frontier. The intimation to these troops, of another campaign in France, and of a probable re-occupation of Paris, had imparted new life and vigour to the spirit of inveterate hatred and insatiable revenge, which they had so thoroughly imbibed against the French, and which had so invariably marked their career since the memorable burning of Moscow.†

An Austrian army of about 50,000 men, commanded by Field Marshal Prince Schwartzenburg, and the army of reserve, under the Archduke Ferdinand, amounting to 40,000 men, were gradually occupying the most important points

* See the Proclamation of the King of Prussia to his army—Appendix III.

† See Address of the Emperor Alexander, to a numerous body of Russian troops which he reviewed on the 5th of April, 1815—Appendix IV.

along the right bank of the Rhine, between Basle and Manheim. In addition to this force, about 120,000 men were then assembling on the plains of Lombardy, upon the termination of the decisive campaign against Murat, which secured the deposition of the latter, and the restoration of King Ferdinand to the throne of Naples. Vigorous and energetic measures such as these on the part of Austria, clearly indicated that her government, discarding alike the circumstance of a family alliance with Napoleon, and the views which had once induced it to enter into a league with him, and with the southern German states, as a security against its formidable northern neighbours, still adhered with inflexible resolution to its subsequently adopted policy of entering into, and fostering, a general European compact, having for its object the complete annihilation of the despotic sway of the ambitious soldier-sovereign of the French.

The assembling also, on the Upper Rhine, of a Bavarian army, commanded by Prince Wrede, of the contingents of Baden and Wurtemberg, under the hereditary Prince of Wurtemberg, and of the troops of Hesse, amounting altogether to about 80,000 men, offered a sufficient guarantee for the line of policy espoused by the confederated states of the Rhine.

Formidable as was the attitude assumed by the Allies towards France, and imposing as was their array of armies assembling upon her frontier, they nevertheless found their great antagonist prepared, on learning that they had determined on an irrevocable appeal to the sword, to throw away the scabbard. He assumed a bold and resolute posture of defence—armed at all points, and prepared at all hazards, either to ward off the blows of his adversaries, or to become himself the assailant. The indefatigable exertions of Napoleon in restoring the empire to its former strength and grandeur, were really astonishing; and never, perhaps, in the whole course of the extraordinary career of that extraordinary man, did the powerful energies of his comprehensive mind shine forth with greater brilliancy and effect, than in his truly wonderful and incredibly rapid development of the national resources of France, on this momentous occasion. The truth of this assertion will be best confirmed by briefly enumerating some of the most important objects accomplished within the limited interval of three months—from his landing at Cannes, to his taking the field against the Allies. Among them were—the complete overthrow of all obstacles in the way of his re-ascending the throne; the reconciliation, to a very considerable extent, of the several factions whose discordant views and interests had distracted the whole nation; the suppression of the insurrectionary movements in La Vendée, and the establishment of his authority over every part of the empire; the projection of various public measures, laws, and ordinances; the remodelling of the civil and military administrations; the restoration of the army to its previous organization under the imperial regime; the placing of the numerous fortresses of the kingdom in an efficient state; the erection of fortified works around Paris, Lyons, and other important points; the re-organization of the national guard *d'élite*, to the extent of 112,000 men, divided into 200 battalions, and destined principally for garrisoning the fortresses; the adoption of the most active operations in all the arsenals, and the employment of vast numbers of additional workmen in the manufacture of arms and ammunition. Before all these we ought to place the raising, clothing, arming, drilling, and organizing of 410,000 men, (including the national guard d'élite,) which, in addition to the 149,000 men of which the royal army consisted on the 1st of March, formed, on the 1st of June, an effective force of 559,000 men, available for the national defence.

Of this number, the effective force of the troops of the line amounted to 217,000 men, and the regimental depôts to 146,000 men: the remainder, consisting of 200 battalions of the national guard d'élite, of 20 regiments of marines, of 10 battalions of marine artillery, of coast guards, veterans, and organized pensioners, and amounting to 196,000 men, constituted the "*armée extraordinaire*," to be employed in the defence of the fortresses and of the coast.

Napoleon having calculated that an effective force of 800,000 men would be requisite to enable him to oppose the Allies with full confidence of success, had given orders for the formation, at the regimental depôts, of the 3rd, 4th, and 5th battalions of every regiment of infantry, and of the 4th and 5th squadrons of every regiment of cavalry; also for the additional formation of 30 battalions of artillery-train, of 20 regiments of the young guard, of 10 battalions of waggon-train, and of 20 regiments of marines. These and other measures he anticipated, would furnish the force desired, but not until the 1st of October. The movements of the Allies, however, and his projected plan of active operations, precluded the possibility of his waiting for their full accomplishment. To augment the means of local defence, instructions were also issued for the reorganization of the national guard throughout the empire, by which it was divided into 3130 battalions, and was to form, *when complete*, no less a force than 2,250,000 men !

Out of the disposable force of the troops of the line, and partly also out of the national guard d'élite, were formed 7 *corps d'armée*, 4 corps of reserve-cavalry, 4 corps of observation, and an army of the West, or of La Vendée.

The army of the North, generally designated the grand army, was to be considered as acting under the immediate orders of the Emperor. It consisted of 5 corps d'armée, (the 1st, 2nd, 3rd, 4th, and 6th,) all the reserve-cavalry, and the imperial guard. Its total force amounted to nearly 120,000 men; and its distribution, in the early part of June was as follows:—

The 1st corps d'armée, commanded by Count D'Erlon, had its head-quarters at Lille; the 2nd, under the orders of Count Reille, was cantoned in the environs of Valenciennes; the 3rd, under Count Vandamme, was assembled in the environs of Mezieres; the 4th, under Count Gérard, in the environs of the Metz; and the 6th corps, commanded by Count Lobau, was stationed at Laon. The four corps of reserve-cavalry, under the chief command of Marshal Grouchy, were in cantonments between the Aisne and the Sambre. The imperial guard was in Paris.

The 5th corps d'armée, commanded by Count Rapp, formed the basis of an army of the Rhine, and consisted of about 36,000 men. Its head-quarters were at Strasburg, and it occupied the principal points along that part of the frontier between Landau and Hagenau; communicating with the 4th corps d'armée on its left, as also with the 1st corps of observation on its right.

The 7th corps d'armée, commanded by the Duke of Albufera, formed the basis of the army of the Alps. It did not at that time amount to more than 15,000 men, but arrangements were made for its augmentation, by the end of June, to 40,000 men. It held the passes along the Italian frontier—was strongly posted at Grenoble, and at Chambery—communicating on its left with the 1st corps of observation, and covering the approach to Lyons, where very extensive works were carried on with the utmost vigour and activity.

The 1st corps of observation, called the army of the Jura, commanded by Lieutenant General Lecourbe, guarded the passes along the Swiss frontier; had its head-quarters at Altkirch, and occupied the line between Huningen and Béfort—communicating on its right with the army of the Alps, and on its left with the army of the Rhine. It did not, at that time, consist of a larger force than 4500 men, which, however, was to be augmented to 18,000 on the arrival of additional battalions from the national guard d'élite, then in course of active organization.

The 2nd corps of observation, called the army of the Var, commanded by Marshal Brune, had its head-quarters at Marseilles; occupied Toulon and Antibes, and watched the frontier of the Maritime Alps. Its force, which then amounted to 5300 men, was to be joined by sixteen battalions of the national guard d'élite, and, in this way, increased to 17,000 men.

The 3rd corps of observation, called the army of the Eastern Pyrenees, commanded by Lieutenant General Count Decaen, had its head-quarters at Perpignan. It did not then consist of more than 3000 men, but was to be augmented by thirty-two battalions of the national guard d'élite, to 23,000 men.

The 4th corps of observation, called the army of the Western Pyrenees, or of the Gironde, was commanded by Lieutenant General Clauzel; had its head-quarters in Bourdeaux; consisted of the same force as that of the 3rd corps; and was to be augmented in a similar manner.

The army of La Vendée, commanded by General Lamarque, was occupied in restoring tranquillity to that part of the empire. It consisted of about 17,000 men, including detachments supplied temporarily from the 3rd and 4th corps of observation.

Arrangements had also been made for reinforcing, at the end of June, the two armies of the Rhine and of the Alps, with 50,000 men from the troops of the line organized in the regimental depôts, and with 100,000 men from the national guard d'élite; and with a view to afford a second line and support to the grand army, commanded by Napoleon in person, the latter was to be augmented by 100,000 men of the national guard, and by 60,000 men of regular troops taken from the depôts, where the additional battalions and squadrons of regiments were in course of daily organization.

The general aspect of France at that moment was singularly warlike. It was that of a whole nation buckling on its armour: over the entire country armed bodies were to be seen in motion towards their several points of destination: every where the new levies for the line, and the newly enrolled national guards were in an unremitting course of drill and organization: the greatest activity was maintained, day and night, in all the arsenals, and in all the manufactories of clothing and articles of equipment: crowds of workmen were constantly employed in the repair of the numerous fortresses, and in the erection of entrenched works. Every where appeared a continued transport of artillery, waggons, arms, ammunition and all the material of war; whilst upon every road forming an approach to any of the main points of assembly in the vicinity of the frontiers, might be seen those well-formed veteran bands, Napoleon's followers through many a bloody field, moving forth with all the order, and with all the elasticity of spirit, inspired by the full confidence of a renewed career of victory —rejoicing in the display of those standards which so proudly recalled the most glorious fields that France had ever won, and testifying by their acclamations their enthusiastic devotion to the cause of their Emperor, which was ever cherished by them as identified with that of their country.

The sentiments which so generally animated the troops of the line, must not, however, be understood as having been equally imbibed by the remaining portion of the army, or indeed by the major part of the nation. There was one predominant cause, which, though its influence acted as an additional stimulus to the army, was, to a very considerable extent, the sole incentive to exertion with the civil portion of the community. It was the general prevalence of that unconquerable aversion and undisguised contempt entertained by the French for the mass of their foreign invaders, whose former humiliation and subjection, the result of an almost uninterrupted course of victory and triumph, to which the history of France presented no parallel, had served to flatter and to gratify the national vanity. It was this feeling, combined with a dread of that retributive justice which would inevitably follow in the train of a successful invasion, that operated so powerfully upon the mass of the nation, with whom the cry of "Vive l'Empereur!" merged into that of "Vive la France!" To the above cause may also be traced the temporary reconciliation of the different factions which it was one of the main objects of Napoleon's celebrated "*Champ de Mai*,"* to establish. This convocation of the popular representatives, which had in a measure been forced upon the Emperor by the political vantage-ground the people had gained during even the short constitutional reign of Louis XVIII., and of which they had begun to feel the benefit, did not in any degree fulfil the expectations of its projector. The stern republicans were dissatisfied with the retention of a chamber of peers, which, in the late reign, they had regarded as an English importation; and the royalists were no less

* See Appendix V.

disgusted with the materials out of which such a chamber had been constructed; while both parties felt it to be a mere semblance of a constitutional body, destined to be composed of the willing slaves of the despot, his ready instruments for counteracting and paralyzing the effects of any violent ebullition of the popular will. When it is considered that an overwhelming majority of the members of the new chamber of deputies were men of avowed republican principles, and that in their very first sittings, they evinced by the tone of their debates, and by the tenor of their measures, a determination to uphold the authority vested in them by the people, and to make even the military power of the Emperor subservient to their views of popular government; when, also, it is considered that the two predominant parties in the state, the republicans and the royalists, relied upon, and awaited but, the issue of events, for the ultimate success and realization of their respective principles, it need not excite surprise that Napoleon, on quitting the capital to take the field, should have appeared to feel that he left behind him a power even more dangerous to the stability of his authority, and more destructive of his ambitious projects, than that which he was going personally to confront. He naturally calculated largely upon the enthusiasm of his troops and their devotion to his cause; but he must have entertained serious doubts as to whether this spirit was shared by the great majority of the nation; and must have foreseen that it would only be by means of a successful result of the approaching contest, that he could possibly avert the dangers to which his sovereignty was exposed, as much by the machinations of political opponents at home, as by the combinations of hostile forces abroad. He was now made painfully sensible of the vast change which the result of all his former wars, the restoration of the legitimate monarch, and the newly chartered liberty of the subject, had gradually wrought in the political feelings and sentiments of the nation. In short, he found that he had to contend with a new, a mighty, and an uncontrollable power—the great moral power of public opinion—compared with which, the military power, centred in a single individual, however brilliant the latter in genius and in conception, however fertile in expedients, and however daring and successful in enterprise and in execution, can acquire no permanent stability, when not based upon, and emanating from, the broad and comprehensive moral energies of the nation; and even a succession of dazzling triumphs, when gained through the instrumentality of an arbitrary drain upon the national resources, and in opposition to the real interests and welfare of the state, tends but to hasten the downfall of the military dictator, whose career may be aptly likened to a Grecian column erected upon a loose foundation, displaying around its lofty capital an exuberance of meretricious ornament, which, by its disproportionate weight, destroys the equilibrium of the ill-supported shaft, and involves the entire structure in one confused and irretrievable ruin. Its fall may startle the world with its shock; the fragments may strew the earth in a wreck as gigantic as were its proportions when it drew the gaze of admiring or trembling nations; but they are but the more striking proofs of the destruction that has overtaken it;—it is a ruin still.

CHAPTER II.

Belgium, the frequent battle-ground of Europe, whose every stream and every town is associated with the memory of bygone deeds of arms, was destined, in 1815, to witness another and a mighty struggle—a struggle in which were arrayed, on the one side, the two foremost of the confederated armies advancing towards the French frontiers; and, on the other, the renowned "*grande armée*" of imperial France, resuscitated at the magic call of its original founder—the great Napoleon himself. During the months of April and May, troops of all arms continued to enter upon, and spread themselves over, the Belgian soil.

Here might be seen the British soldier, flushed with recent triumphs in the Peninsula over the same foe with whom he was now prepared once more to renew the combat; and here the Prussian, eager for the deadly strife, and impatiently rushing onward to encounter that enemy whose ravages and excesses in his fatherland still rankled in his memory. The Englishman was not fired by the desire of retribution, for it had pleased Divine Providence to spare Great Britain from the scourge of domestic war, and to preserve her soil unstained by the foot-print of a foreign enemy. The Prussian soldier looked forward with a sullen pleasure to the prospect of revenge: vengeance seemed to him a sacred duty, imposed upon him by all the ties of kindred, and by all those patriotic feelings, which, in the hour of Prussia's need, had roused her entire people from the abject state to which they had been so fatally subdued; which, when the whole country lay prostrate at the conqueror's feet, so wonderfully, so powerfully, and so successfully prompted her sons to throw off the yoke. History will mark this deliverance as the brilliant point in Prussia's brightest era, affording as it does, a clear and beautiful parallel to that in which an equally forcible appeal to the energies of the nation was made with similar success by that illustrious statesman and general, Frederick the Great, when opposed single-handed to the immense armies and powerful resources of surrounding states. France was about to expiate by her own sufferings the wrongs she had wrought upon his country and his kind, and the Prussian panted for an opportunity of satiating his revenge.

The Briton, if he had no such spur as that which urged the Prussian soldier forward, did not want a sufficiently exciting stimulus; he cherished, in an eminent degree, that high feeling and proud bearing which a due sense of the obligations imposed on him by his country, and of her anxious expectations of his prowess, could not fail to inspire; determined resolutely and cheerfully to discharge the former, and, if possible, to more than realize the latter.

These feelings and dispositions of the soldiery in the two most advanced of the allied armies were concentrated with remarkable intensity in the characters of their respective chiefs. With peculiar propriety may it be said of the illustrious Wellington, that he personified, as he ever has done, the pure ideal of the British soldier—the true character of his own followers. Resolute, yet cool, cautious, and calculating in his proceedings; possessing a natural courage unshaken even under the most appalling dangers and difficulties; placing great yet not vain reliance upon physical and moral strength, as opposed to the force of numbers;—it was not surprising that he should have inspired with unbounded confidence, soldiers who could not but see in his character and conduct the reflection and stamp of their own qualities, the worth of which he so well knew, and which he had so often proved during the arduous struggle that had been brought to so brilliant and so glorious a conclusion. But besides these traits in his character, which so completely identified him with a British army, there were others which peculiarly distinguished him as one of the greatest captains that his own or any other nation ever produced, and which might well inspire confidence as to the result of the approaching contest, even opposed as he was to the hero of a hundred fights, with whom he was now, for the first time to measure swords. The eagle-glance with which he detected the object of every hostile movement, and the promptitude with which he decided upon, and carried into effect, the measures necessary to counteract the enemy's efforts; the lightning-like rapidity with which he conducted his attacks, founded as they frequently were upon the instantaneously discovered errors of his opponents; the noble and unexampled presence of mind with which he surveyed the battle-field, and with which he gave his orders and instructions; unaffected by merely temporary success, unembarrassed by sudden difficulties, and undismayed by unexpected danger; the many proofs which his operations in the Peninsula had afforded of his accurate knowledge, just conception, and skilful discrimination, of the true principles of the science of strategy—all tended to point him out as the individual best fitted by his abilities, his experience, and his character, to head the military array assembled to decide the all-important question whether the star of Napoleon was to regain the ascendant, or to set in darkness; whether his iron despotism was again to erect its mighty head, or to be now struck down and crushed —finally and effectually crushed.

The character of the commander of the Prussian army in this memorable campaign, the veteran Marshal Prince Blücher von Wahlstadt, was, in like manner, peculiarly adapted for concentrating within itself all those feelings and emotions already adverted to as animating this portion of the enemies of France—possessing, to a degree bordering on rashness, a high spirited daring in enterprise; distinguished, on critical occasions in the field, when the unrestrained feelings and nature of the *ci-devant* bold hussar started forth in aid of the veteran commander, by a personal display of chivalrous and impetuous bravery; ever vigilant for an opportunity of harassing his enemy; and fixedly relentless in the pursuit, so long as he retained the mastery; qualities, which, in his own country, had acquired for him the soubriquet of "*Marschall Vorwärts*"—he was eminently fitted to be both the representative and the leader of the Prussians.*

Here, too, in close alliance and amity with the British sol-

* The fiery impetuosity of his character was finely tempered by the sage counsels of his chief of the staff, the veteran Lieutenant General Count von Gneisenau, in whose talents, foresight, and judgment, he invariably placed implicit confidence. Blücher always took great pleasure in publicly expressing his obligations to his old and faithful companion in arms; a circumstance, which, while it redounded so highly to the merits of his friend, at the same time brought forth, in prominent relief, the perfect openness of his own character, and the extreme modesty of his nature. Numerous instances might be cited of the manifestation of this generous and kindly feeling: the two following are humorous, and at the same time highly characteristic. When at Oxford, in 1814, along with the Emperor of Russia, the King of Prussia, the Prince Regent, the Duke of Wellington, and Prince Metternich, he received an intimation that the heads of the university intended to confer upon him, as well as upon those illustrious personages, the dignity of a Doctor. Blücher, who had never once dreamed of the possibility of his becoming one of the learned, could not refrain from laughter, and jocularly remarked, "Well, if I am to be a doctor, they cannot do less than make Gneisenau an apothecary; for we both work together—and it is he who has to make up the pills which I am in the habit of administering." In 1818, he happened to be in the midst of a very large party in Berlin, where, in the course of the evening, much merriment and jesting arose from the proposal and solution of enigmas. Blücher at once absorbed the attention of the guests, by remarking, "Come, I will do what none of you can—I will kiss my own head!" and while all were expressing their surprise, and wondering how this was to be accomplished, the old man added, with an air of the utmost singleness and assurance, "This is the way," when, rising, he advanced towards Gneisenau, whom he kissed and embraced most heartily.

dier, were seen the German-legionary, the Hanoverian, and the Brunswicker, who had so nobly shared with him, under the same chief, all the toils and all the glories of the war in the Peninsula; and who were now prepared to defend the threatened liberties of their respective countries, the very existence of which, as independent states, hung upon the issue of the impending struggle. Although the British were but little acquainted with their other allies, the Dutch, the Belgians, and the Nassau troops in the service of the King of the Netherlands, still the fact that it was upon their own soil the brunt of the coming contest was to fall, and in all probability to decide the question whether it should become a portion of imperial France, or continue an independent state, coupled with the knowledge which the British troops possessed of the character of the prince at their head, who had gained his laurels under their own eyes, and who had thus ingratiated himself in their favour, encouraged great hopes of their hearty exertions in the common cause.

It was naturally to be expected that Napoleon, from the moment he re-ascended the throne of his former glory, would devote the utmost energies of his all-directing mind to the full development of whatever military means France, notwithstanding her recent reverses, yet retained; but the rapidity and the order with which so regular and so well organized a force as that which was now concentrating on the French side of the Sambre, had been collected and put in motion, were truly wonderful. The speedy and almost sudden re-appearance of the old army in all its grandeur, with its corps and divisions headed by men, who, by a series of daring and successful exploits, had proved their just titles to command, and endeared themselves to the old campaigners, was such that it seemed as if the French had realized the fable of the dragon's teeth, which it might be said they had sown as they crossed their frontiers in the previous year, when retreating upon the capital before the victorious Allies. Never did any army contain within itself so much of that necessary essence in the composition of a military force,—unbounded enthusiasm, combined with the purest devotion to its leader. The oft-told tale of the veteran of so many a hard-fought field, indulging in the hope of aiding by his exertions, at any sacrifice, in again carrying the eagles to the scenes of their former triumphs, excited the ardour of many a youthful aspirant to share with him the glory of wiping out the stain which had dimmed the lustre of his country's fame, and darkened a most eventful page in her annals.

Such being the nature of the elements ready to rush into collision, it was easy to foresee that the shock which that collision would produce, would be both violent and terrible; but no one could have anticipated that within the short space of four days from the commencement of hostilities, the die would be irrevocably cast, annihilating for ever the imperial sway of Napoleon, and securing to Europe one of the longest periods of peace recorded in her history.

CHAPTER III.

By the middle of June, the Anglo-allied army which had been gradually assembling in Belgium, under the command of the Duke of Wellington, amounted to about 106,000 men, and was composed in the following manner:—

INFANTRY.

British	23,543
King's German Legion	3,301
Hanoverian	22,788
Brunswick	5,376
Nassau (1st regiment)	2,880
Dutch and Belgian	24,174
	82,062

CAVALRY.

British	5,913
King's German Legion	2,560
Hanoverian	1,682
Brunswick	922
Dutch and Belgian	3,405
	14,482

ARTILLERY.

British	5,030	102 guns
King's German Legion	526	18 ,,
Hanoverian	465	12 ,,
Brunswick	510	16 ,,
Dutch and Belgian	1,635	56 ,,
	8,166	204 guns.

ENGINEERS, SAPPERS AND MINERS, WAGGON-TRAIN, AND STAFF CORPS.

British	1,240

TOTAL.

Infantry	82,062
Cavalry	14,482
Artillery	8,166
Engineers, waggon-train, &c.	1,240
	* 105,950 men and 204 guns.

* For detailed returns see Appendix VI. They are founded on the following data: those of the British infantry and cavalry, as also of the British engineers, sappers and miners, waggon-train, and staff corps, are taken from the twelfth volume of the Despatches of the Duke of Wellington, compiled by Colonel Gurwood, C.B., p. 486; those of the British artillery from documents furnished

The infantry was divided into two corps and a reserve.

The 1st corps, commanded by General His Royal Highness the Prince of Orange,* was composed of the 1st division, under Major General Cooke;† of the 3rd division under Lieutenant General Sir Charles Alten; of the 2nd Dutch-Belgian division, under Lieutenant General de Perponcher; and of the 3rd Dutch-Belgian division, under Lieutenant General Baron Chassé.

The left of this corps rested upon Genappe, Quatre-Bras, and Frasne, on the high road leading from Brussels to Charleroi on the Sambre, and communicated with the right of the first corps d'armée of the Prussian army, the head-quarters of which corps were at Charleroi. De Perponcher's Dutch-Belgian division formed the extreme left, having its head-quarters at Nivelles, on the high road from Brussels to Binche. On its right was Chassé's Dutch-Belgian division, more in advance, in the direction of Mons and Binche, and quartered principally in Roeulx, and in the villages between the latter place and Binche. The next division on the right was Alten's, having its head-quarters at Soignies, on the high road from Brussels to Mons, and occupying villages between this town, Roeulx, Braine-le-comte, and Enghien. The right division, Cooke's, had its head-quarters at Enghien.

The 2nd corps, commanded by Lieutenant General Lord Hill,§ consisted of the 2nd division, under Lieutenant General Sir Henry Clinton;|| of the 4th division, under Lieutenant General the Hon. Sir Charles Colville;¶ of the first Dutch-Belgian division, under Lieutenant General Stedmann; and of a brigade raised for service in the Dutch colonies, called the Indian brigade, under Lieutenant General Baron Anthing.

by the Ordnance Department; those of the King's German Legion and Hanoverian troops from returns compiled by Major Benne, K.H., under the direction of the Hanoverian military authorities: those of the Brunswick troops from information furnished by Lieutenant General von Herzberg of that service: those of the Nassau troops from returns supplied by General von Kruse, who commanded them; and those of the Dutch-Belgian troops from returns obtained from the Dutch Government.

* His Majesty the present King of Holland; General in the British service; G.C.B.

† Lieutenant General Sir George Cooke, K.C.B. died in February, 1837.

‡ Count Alten, Major General in the British service, G.C.B.; G.C.H., died in April, 1840.

§ General Lord Viscount Hill; G.C.B.; G.C.H.; K.C., died on the 10th of December, 1842.

|| Lieutenant General Sir Henry Clinton, G.C.B.; G.C.H., died on the 11th of December, 1830.

¶ General the Honorable Sir Charles Colville, G.C.B.; G.C.H., died on the 27th of March, 1843.

The 2nd division, which formed the left of this corps, communicated with Alten's right; its head-quarters were at Ath, on the Dender, and upon the high road leading from Brussels to Tournai, and one brigade, (the 3rd,) occupied Lens, situated about midway between Ath and Mons.

The 4th division was the next on the right, having its head-quarters at Audenarde on the Scheldt, and occupying also Renaix. One brigade of this division, (the 6th Hanoverian,) garrisoned the fortress of Nieuport on the coast. The 1st Dutch-Belgian division was cantoned in villages bordering upon the high-road connecting Grammont with Ghent; and the so-called Indian brigade occupied villages between this line and Alost.

The reserve consisted of the 5th division, under Lieutenant General Sir Thomas Picton;* of the 6th division, under Lieutenant General the Hon. Sir Lowry Cole;† of the Brunswick division under the Duke of Brunswick;‡ of the Hanoverian corps under Lieutenant General von der Decken;§ and of the contingent of the Duke of Nassau, which comprised the 1st regiment of Nassau infantry, containing three battalions, and forming a brigade under the command of General von Kruse.‖

The 5th and 6th divisions, and the Brunswick division, were quartered principally in and around Brussels, excepting the 7th brigade, which together with von der Decken's corps, the 13th veteran battalion, the 1st foreign battalion, and the 2nd garrison battalion, garrisoned Antwerp, Ostend, Nieuport, Ypres, Tournai, and Mons; and von Kruse's Nassau brigade was cantoned between Brussels and Louvain.

Of the fortresses already mentioned, those which had not been destroyed by the French when they gained possession of the country in 1794, namely, Antwerp, Ostend, and Nieuport, were strengthened, and each rendered capable of holding out a siege. By taking every possible advantage offered by the remains of the old fortifications, and by the

* Lieutenant General Sir Thomas Picton, K. C. B., was killed at the battle of Waterloo.

† General the Honorable Sir Galbraith Lowry Cole, G.C.B., died on the 5th of October, 1842.

‡ His Serene Highness, Frederick William, Duke of Brunswick Œels, Lieutenant General in the British army, was killed at the Battle of Quatre-Bras.

§ Lieutenant General Count von der Decken, G.C.H., died on the 22nd of May, 1840.

‖ The 2nd regiment of Nassau infantry had been, since 1814, in the immediate service and pay of the King of the Netherlands; it now constituted, with the regiment of Orange-Nassau, the 2nd brigade of de Perponcher's Dutch-Belgian division, and was commanded by Colonel Prince Bernhard of Saxe-Weimar.

continued employment of 20,000 labourers, through requisitions on the country, in addition to the military working parties, and by the accession of artillery and stores from England and Holland, the towns of Ypres, Tournai, Mons, Ath, and the citadel of Ghent were placed in a state of defence, and a redoubt was constructed at Audenarde to protect the sluice-gates, which afforded the means of inundating that part of the country.*

The cavalry of the Anglo-allied army, commanded by Lieutenant General the Earl of Uxbridge,† consisted of seven brigades, comprising the British and the King's German Legion; of a Hanoverian brigade; of five squadrons of Brunswick cavalry; and of three brigades of Dutch-Belgian cavalry.

The British and King's German Legion cavalry, with the Hanoverian brigade, were stationed at Grammont and Ninove, and in villages bordering upon the Dender. The Brunswick cavalry was dispersed in the vicinity of Brussels. The 1st brigade of Dutch-Belgian cavalry was cantoned in the neighbourhood of Roeulx; the 2nd brigade, in villages between Roeulx and Mons; and the 3rd brigade, partly on the south side of Mons, in the direction of Maubeuge and Beaumont, and partly between Binche and Mons.

The wide dissemination of the Duke of Wellington's forces which the advanced line of cantonments presented—a line forming a considerable portion of a circle, of which Brussels was the centre, and the Tournai, Mons, and Charleroi, roads were the marked radii—tended greatly to facilitate the means of subsisting the troops, and to render that subsistence less burthensome to the country; while, at the same time, it offered to the Duke, in conjunction with the interior points of concentration, and with the efficient reserve stationed around the capital, full security for his being prepared to meet any emergency that might arise. The main points of interior concentration were (commencing from the right) Audenarde, Grammont, Ath, Enghien, Soignies, Nivelles, and Quatre-Bras. From whatever point, therefore, offensive operations might be directed against that portion of the Belgian frontier, occupied by the army under Wellington—whether from Lisle, by Courtrai, or by Tournai, between the Lys and the Scheldt; from Condé, Valenciennes, or Maubeuge, by Mons, between the Sambre and the Scheldt; or from Maubeuge, Beaumont, or Philippeville, by Charleroi, between the Sambre and the

* Orders for the defence of the towns of Antwerp, Ostend, Nieuport, Ypres, Tournai, Ath, Mons, and Ghent, will be found in the Appendix VII.

† The present Marquess of Anglesey; Field Marshal; K.G.; G.C.B.; G.C.H.; Master General of the Ordnance.

Meuse—the Duke, by advancing to the threatened point with his reserve, and placing the remainder of his troops in movement, had it in his power to concentrate at least two-thirds of his intended disposable force for the field, upon the line of the enemy's operations, within twenty-two hours after the receipt of intelligence of the actual direction and apparent object of those operations.*

* That the Duke was prepared, as far back as the 30th of April, to meet any attack that might be made upon him, may be seen by the following

'SECRET MEMORANDUM

'*For H. R. H. the Prince of Orange, the Earl of Uxbridge, Lord Hill, and the Quarter Master General.*

'Bruxelles, April 30th, 1815.

'I. Having received reports that the Imperial Guard had moved from Paris upon Beauvais, and a report having been for some days prevalent in the country that Buonaparte was about to visit the northern frontier, I deem it expedient to concentrate the cantonments of the troops, with a view to their early junction in case the country should be attacked, for which concentration the Quarter Master General now sends orders.

'II. In this case the enemy's line of attack will be either between the Lys and the Scheldt, or between the Sambre and the Scheldt, or by both lines.

'III. In the first case, I should wish the troops of the 4th division to take up the bridge of the Scheldt, near Avelghem, and with the regiment of cavalry at Courtrai, to fall back upon Audenarde, which post they are to occupy, and to inundate the country in the neighbourhood.

'IV. The garrison of Ghent are to inundate the country in the neighbourhood likewise, and that point is to be held at all events.

'V. The cavalry in observation between Menin and Furnes are to fall back upon Ostend; those between Menin and Tournai, upon Tournai, and thence to join their regiments.

'VI. The 1st, 2nd, and 3rd divisions of infantry are to be collected at the head-quarters of the divisions, and the cavalry at the head-quarters of their several brigades, and the whole to be in readiness to march at a moment's notice.

'VII. The troops of the Netherlands to be collected at Soignies and Nivelle.

'VIII. In case the attack should be made between the Sambre and the Scheldt, I propose to collect the British and the Hanoverians at and in the neighbourhood of Enghien, and the army of the Low Countries at and in the neighbourhood of Soignies and Braine-le-Comte.

'IX. In this case, the 2nd and 3rd divisions will collect at their respective head-quarters, and gradually fall back towards Enghien with the cavalry of Colonel Arentschildt's and the Hanoverian brigade.

'X. The garrisons of Mons and Tournai will stand fast; but that of Ath will be withdrawn, with the 2nd division, if the works should not have been sufficiently advanced to render the place tenable against a *coup de main*.

'XI. General Sir W. Ponsonby's, Sir J. Vandeleur's, and Sir H. Vivian's brigades of cavalry will march upon Hal.

'XII. The troops of the Low Countries will collect upon Soignies and Braine-le-Comte.

'XIII. The troops of the 4th division and the 2nd hussars, after taking up the bridge at Avelghem, will fall back upon Audenarde, and there wait for further orders.

'XIV. In case of the attack being directed by both lines supposed, the troops of the 4th division and 2nd hussars, and the garrison of Ghent, will act as directed in Nos. III. and IV. of this memorandum; and the 2nd and 3rd

The Prussian army, under the command of Prince Blücher von Wahlstadt, amounted to nearly 117,000 men, and was thus composed :—

Infantry	99,715
Cavalry	11,879
Artillery, waggon train, and engineers	5,303
	116,897 men & 312 guns.*

It was divided into four corps d'armée.

The 1st corps, commanded by Lieutenant General Zieten,† consisted of the 1st brigade, under General Steinmetz; of the 2nd brigade, under General Pirch II.;‡ of the 3rd brigade, under General Jagow; of the 4th brigade, under General Count Henkel; of a cavalry-reserve, under Lieutenant General Röder; and of an artillery-reserve, under Colonel Lehmann.

The right of this corps d'armée, the head-quarters of which were at Charleroi, communicated with the left of the 1st corps of the Duke of Wellington's army. Its right brigade, the 1st, was cantoned in and around Fontaine l'evêque, which lies midway between Charleroi and Binche; the second brigade, in Marchienne-au-Pont, on the Sambre; the 3rd brigade, in Fleurus; the 4th brigade, in Moustier-sur-Sambre; the reserve-cavalry in Sombref, and the reserve-artillery in Gembloux. The line of advanced posts of this corps extended from Bonne Esperance (two miles south-west of Binche) along the frontier of Lobbes, Thuin, and Gerpinnes, as far as Sossoye.

The 2nd corps d'armée, commanded by General Pirch I., consisted of the 5th brigade, under General Tippelskirchen; of the 6th brigade, under General Krafft; of the 7th brigade, under General Brause; of the 8th brigade, under Colonel Langen; of a cavalry-reserve, under General Jürgass; and of an artillery-reserve, under Colonel Röhl.

The head-quarters of this corps were at Namur, situated

divisions, and the cavalry, and the troops of the Low Countries, as directed in Nos. VIII., IX., X., XI., and XII.

'WELLINGTON.'

—*Despatches of the Duke of Wellington, compiled by Colonel Gurwood.*—Vol. xii. p. 337.

* For detailed returns, see Appendix VIII.

† In order to avoid the constant repetition of the prefix "von" to the names of the German officers, I have omitted it altogether in the present edition; an omission, however, which I feel persuaded those officers will not consider as involving any breach of courtesy or respect.

‡ Prussian general officers bearing the same family name, are usually distinguished by the addition of the Roman numerals. General von Pirch I. is named above.

at the confluence of the Sambre and the Meuse, where also its 1st brigade (the 5th) was stationed; the 6th brigade was cantoned in and around Thorembey-les-Beguignes; the 7th brigade in Heron; the 8th brigade in Huy; the reserve-cavalry in Hannut; and the reserve-artillery along the high road to Louvain. The line of advanced posts of this corps extended from Sossoye as far as Dinant on the Meuse, about midway between Namur and Givet.

The 3rd corps d'armèe, commanded by Lieutenant General Thielemann, consisted of the 9th brigade, under General Borke; of the 10th brigade, under Colonel Kämpfen; of the 11th brigade, under Colonel Luck; of the 12th brigade, under Colonel Stülpnagel; of a cavalry-reserve, under General Hobe; and of an artillery-reserve, under Colonel Mohnhaupt.

The head-quarters of this corps were at Ciney: the 9th brigade was stationed at Asserre; the 10th brigade at Ciney; the 11th brigade at Dinant; the 12th brigade at Huy, on the Meuse; the reserve-cavalry between Ciney and Dinant; and the reserve-artillery at Ciney. The line of advanced posts of this corps extended from Dinant as far as Fabeline and Rochefort.

The 4th corps d'armée, commanded by General Count Bülow von Dennewitz, consisted of the 13th brigade, under Lieutenant General Hacke; of the 14th brigade, under General Ryssel; of the 15th brigade, under General Losthin; of the 16th brigade, under Colonel Hiller; of a cavalry-reserve under General his Royal Highness Prince William of Prussia; and of an artillery-reserve, under Lieutenant Colonel Bardeleben.

The head-quarters of this corps were at Liege, where was also stationed the 13th infantry-brigade; the 14th brigade was cantoned in and around Waremme; the 15th brigade at Hologne; the 16th brigade at Liers; the 1st brigade of reserve-cavalry at Tongern; the 2nd brigade at Dalhem, and the 3rd brigade at Lootz; the reserve-artillery was cantoned in and about Gloms and Dalhem.

Prince Blücher's head-quarters were at Namur.

The points of concentration for the respective corps were therefore Fleurus, Namur, Ciney, and Liege. The four corps were so disposed that each could be collected at its own head-quarters within twelve hours; and it was fully practicable to form a junction of the whole army at any one of these points within twenty-four hours from the time of such collection. At Namur, the most central point, it would of course be accomplished in much less time. Blücher had decided, in the event of an advance by the French across the line of the Sambre, by Charleroi, upon concentrating his army in a position in front of Sombref, a point upon the high road between Namur and Nivelles, about fourteen miles from the former place, and only seven miles and a half from Quatre-Bras, the point of intersection of this road with the one leading directly from Charleroi to Brussels, and at which Wellington had agreed, in that case, to concentrate as large a force as time would admit, in order to check any advance in this direction, or to join Blücher's right flank, according to circumstances. Should the enemy advance along the left bank of the Meuse towards Namur, this place would become the point of junction of the 1st, 2nd, and 4th corps of the Prussian army, whilst the 3rd, collecting at Ciney, would, after presenting a stout resistance at Dinant, operate as effectively as circumstances would admit, against the right of the line of attack; and should he advance by the right bank of the Meuse towards Ciney, the army would concentrate at this point, with the exception of the 4th corps, which would assemble at Liege as a reserve, for the better security of the left flank and of the communications with the Rhine.

Such were the dispositions of the allied commanders, who contemplated no change in their arrangements until the moment should arrive of the commencment of hostile demonstrations of a decided character, for which they were perfectly prepared, and for which a vigilant look-out was maintained along the general line of the advanced posts.

From the foregoing, however, it would appear that the concentration of Wellington's army on its own left, and that of Blücher's army on its own right, required longer time than that in which they could have been respectively accomplished on other points; and further that the distribution of the former was better calculated to meet the enemy's advance by Mons, and that of the latter to meet it by Namur, than to oppose a line of attack by Charleroi. This peculiar feature in the dispositions of the two commanders did not escape the vigilance of Napoleon, who, as will be seen in the sequel, made it subservient to his hopes of beating their armies in detail.

The French troops destined to constitute the grand army with which Napoleon had decided upon taking the field against the allied forces in Belgium, comprised the 1st, 2nd, 3rd, 4th, and 6th, corps d'armée; 4 corps of cavalry; and the imperial guard: amounting altogether to 116,124 men:—

Infantry	83,753
Cavalry	20,959
Artillery, waggon-train, and engineers	11,412
	*116,124 men and 350 guns.

The 1st corps d'armée, commanded by Lieutenant General Count d'Erlon, consisted of the 1st infantry-division under Lieut. General Alix; of the 2nd infantry-division, under Lieut. General Baron Donzelot; of the 3rd infantry-division, under Lieut. General Baron Marcognet; of the 4th infantry-division, under Lieut. General Count Durette; and of the 1st light cavalry-division, under Lieut. General Jaquinot; with 5 batteries of foot, and one of horse, artillery.

In the beginning of June this corps was stationed in and around Lille.

The 2nd corps d'armée commanded by Lieut. General Count Reille, consisted of the 5th infantry-division, under Lieut. General Baron Bachelu; of the 6th infantry-division, under Lieut. General Prince Jerome Napoleon; of the 7th infantry-division, under Lieut. General Count Girard; of the 9th infantry-division, under Lieut. General Count Foy; and of the 2nd light cavalry-division, under Lieut. General Baron Piré; with 5 batteries of foot, and 1 of horse, artillery.

This corps was stationed in and around Valenciennes.

The 3rd corps d'armée, commanded by Lieut. General Count Vandamme, consisted of the 8th infantry-division, under Lieut. General Baron Le Fol; of the 10th infantry-division, under Lieut. General Baron Habert; of the 11th infantry-division, under Lieut. General Berthezene; and of the 3rd light cavalry-division, under Lieut. General Baron Domon; with 4 batteries of foot, and 1 of horse, artillery.

This corps was assembled in and around Mezières.

The 4th corps d'armée, commanded by Lieut. General Count Gérard, consisted of the 12th infantry-division, under Lieut. General Baron Pecheux; of the 13th infantry-division,

* For detailed returns see Appendix IX. The above-mentioned force is computed from the detailed returns published in the "Journal des sciences militaires" for 1840, as the "Situation de l'Armée du Nord au mois de Juin 1815," and which give the entire strength as consisting of 5,510 officers and 116,124 men—making a grand total of 121,634. There is reason, however, to believe, that this force was somewhat greater. In the Appendix to the "Geschichte des Feldzugs von 1815," by Damitz, it is stated that, according to the information obtained by the Allies immediately before the commencement of hostilities, the total amount was 130,000 men.—See Appendix X. According to a memorandum written by the Duke of Wellington at Brussels on the 16th May, 1815, the amount was then estimated at 126,000 men.—See Despatches of the Duke of Wellington, vol. xii. p. 394.

under Lieut. General Baron Vichery; of the 14th infantry-division, under Lieut. General de Bourmont; and of the 6th light cavalry-division, under Lieut. General Maurin; with 4 batteries of foot, and 1 of horse, artillery.

This corps occupied Metz, Longwy, and Thionville, and formed the basis of the army of the Moselle; but it was now decided that it should approach the Sambre, and unite itself with the grand army.

The 6th corps d'armée, commanded by Lieut. General Count Lobau, consisted of the 19th infantry-division, under Lieut. General Baron Simmer; of the 20th infantry-division, under Lieut. General Baron Jeannin; of the 21st infantry-division, under Lieut. General Baron Teste; with 4 batteries of foot, and 1 of horse, artillery.

This corps was assembled in and around Laon.

The four corps forming the reserve-cavalry were placed under the command of Marshal Count Grouchy. The 1st, commanded by Lieut. General Count Pajol, consisted of the 4th cavalry-division (hussars), under Lieut. General Baron Soult; and of the 5th division (lancers and chasseurs), under Lieut. General Baron Subervie; with 2 batteries of horse artillery. The 2nd corps, commanded by Lieut. General Count Excelmans, consisted of the 9th division (dragoons), under Lieut. General Strolz; and of the 10th division (dragoons), under Lieut. General Baron Chastel; with 2 batteries of horse artillery. The 3rd corps, commanded by Lieut. General Count de Valmy (Kellermann), consisted of the 11th division (dragoons and cuirassiers), under Lieut. General Baron L'Heritier; and of the 12th division (carabiniers and cuirassiers), under Lieut. General Roussel d'Hurbal; with 2 batteries of horse artillery. The 4th corps, commanded by Lieut. General Count Milhaud, consisted of the 13th division (cuirassiers), under Lieut. General Wathier, and of the 14th division (cuirassiers), under Lieut. General Baron Delort; with 2 batteries of horse artillery.

The principal portion of the reserve-cavalry lay in cantonments between the Aisne and the frontier.

The infantry of the imperial guard consisted of the 1st and 2nd regiments of grenadiers, under Lieut. General Count Friant; of the 3rd and 4th regiments of grenadiers, under Lieut. General Count Roguet; of the 1st and 2nd regiments of chasseurs, under Lieut. General Count Morand; of the 3rd and 4th regiments of chasseurs, under Lieut. General Count Michel; of the 1st and 3rd regiments of tirailleurs, under Lieut. General Count Duhesme; and of the 1st and

3rd voltigeurs, under Lieut. General Count Barrois. The cavalry of the guard consisted of two regiments of heavy cavalry (grenadiers à cheval and dragoons), under Lieut. General Count Guyot; and of 3 regiments of light cavalry (chasseurs à cheval and lancers), under Lieut. General Lefèbvre-Desnouettes. Attached to the guard were 6 batteries of foot, and 4 batteries of horse, artillery, with 3 batteries of reserve-artillery; comprising altogether 96 pieces of cannon, under the command of Lieut. General Desvaux de St. Maurice. These troops were principally in Paris.

The French Emperor having, upon the grounds explained in a former chapter, determined to take the field against the allied armies in Belgium, the commencement of active operations could no longer be deferred. When we reflect upon the disparity of force with which he was going to contend against two such generals as Wellington and Blücher, we are bound to acknowledge that it was an undertaking daring and perilous in the extreme, even for an individual of the dauntless and adventurous character of Napoleon. A delay of only a few weeks would have secured for him, by means of the vast organization which was in constant and rapid progress, a sufficient accession of disposable troops to have enabled him to effect a powerful diversion upon either Wellington's right, or Blücher's left, flank, and thus to impart an infinitely greater degree of weight and stability to his main operations; but then, on the other hand, this delay would also have brought the powerful armies of the confederated sovereigns across the whole line of his eastern frontier, and have led to the consummation of that combined movement upon the capital, the execution of which it was his great aim to frustrate. But it was not the first time that Napoleon had advanced against such fearful superiority of numerical strength. In the previous year, when nearly surrounded by the victorious forces of Prussia, Austria, and Russia, when apparently overwhelmed by a succession of disasters, and when his army was daily diminishing by the desertion of newly-raised conscripts, and presenting the mere wreck of its former self, he was at the very *acme* of his mental energy, and in the full possession of his determinate and all-subduing will. His great genius seemed to acquire additional vigour and elasticity, with the increasing desperation of his position; and darting with electric suddenness and rapidity, now upon one adversary and then upon another, maintaining with the renowned leaders of his detached forces, a combination of movements developing the highest order of strategy, he succeeded by his brilliant triumphs at Champaubert, Montmirail, and Monterau, not only in stemming the torrent of invasion, but in causing the resumption of the diplomatic preliminaries of a peace. This peace, however, these very triumphs induced him, as if by a fatality, to reject with scorn and indignation, although the terms were honourable in the highest degree under his then existing circumstances. Hence, with such a retrospect, Napoleon might well indulge in hope and confidence as to the result of the approaching campaign, notwithstanding the want of sufficient time for a greater development of his resources. A finer or a more gallant army, or one more complete and efficient in every respect, than that which he was going to lead in person, never took the field. He had selected for the line of his main operations the direct road to Brussels, by Charleroi, that being the road, as before remarked, on which Wellington's left, and Blücher's right respectively rested, and which he designed to maintain by first overcoming the Prussian army, which was the most advanced on that line, and then attacking the Anglo-allied troops before they could be collected in sufficient strength to prevent his further progress; his grand object being to impede the junction of the two armies; to vanquish them in detail; to establish himself in Brussels; to arouse the dense population of Belgium, of which a vast proportion secretly adhered to his cause; to re-annex the country to the French empire; to excite the desertion of the Belgian soldiery from the service of Holland; to prevent a check by these means to the operations of the invading armies crossing the Rhine; perhaps also to enter into negotiations; and, at all events, to gain, what was to him of vital importance, *time* for the advance and co-operation of further reinforcements from France.

The necessary orders were now despatched for the concentration of the grand army; and in order to mask its movements as much as possible, the whole line of the Belgian frontier was studded with numerous detachments of the national guards furnished by the garrisons of the fortresses, more especially along that part of the frontier which passes in advance of Valenciennes, Condé, Lille, and even as far as Dunkirk; all the debouchés of which line were strongly occupied, the outposts tripled, and there was every apparent indication that either the principal attack, or at least a formidable diversion, was in course of preparation in that quarter.

These measures had the effect of strengthening the anticipations which Wellington had previously formed of offensive movements from the side of Lille and Valenciennes, and consequently of placing him still more upon his guard against any hasty and incautious junction of his forces with those of Blücher, until fully satisfied as to the true direction and object of Napoleon's main operation.*

On the 12th of June, Lieut. Colonel Wissell,† whose regiment, the 1st hussars of the King's German Legion, formed an extensive line of outposts in front of Tournai, reported to Major General Sir Hussey Vivian‡, to whose brigade the regiment belonged, that he had ascertained, from information on which he could rely, that the French army had assembled on the frontier, and was prepared to attack. Vivian desired him to report upon the subject to Lord Hill, to whose corps his regiment was attached while employed on this particular service. The next morning Vivian repaired in person to the outposts, and found that a French cavalry-picquet which had previously been posted opposite to Tournai, had a short time before marched to join the main army, and had been relieved by *douaniers*. These, upon being spoken to by Vivian did not hesitate to say that their army was concentrating, and that if the Allies did not advance, their troops would attack. On returning to his quarters, Vivian communicated what he had seen and heard both to Lord Hill and the Earl of Uxbridge, by whom the circumstances were made known to the Duke of Wellington. His Grace, however, for the reasons before stated, did not think the proper moment had arrived for making any alteration in the disposition of his forces.

Gérard's corps quitted Metz on the 6th of June, with orders to reach Philippeville by the 14th. The imperial guard began its march from Paris on the 8th, and reached Avesnes on the 13th, as did also Lobau's corps from Laon. D'Erlon's corps from Lille, Reille's corps from Valenciennes, and Vandamme's corps from Mezières, likewise arrived at Maubeuge and Avesnes on the 13th. The four corps of reserve-cavalry concentrated upon the Upper Sambre.

The junction of the several corps on the same day, and

* This circumstance has been entirely overlooked by certain historians who have blamed the Duke for not having effected a more rapid concentration of his troops at Quatre-Bras on the 16th, by means of which he might have been enabled to detach an efficient force to the immediate support of Blücher's right flank at Ligny.

† Lieut. Colonel Wissell, K.C.H., died on the 30th of May, 1842.

‡ Lieut. General Lord Vivian, G.C.B.; G.C.H., died on the 20th of August, 1842.

almost at the same hour, (with the exception of the 4th, which joined the next day,) displayed the usual skill of Napoleon in the combination of movements. Their leaders congratulated themselves upon these auspicious preparations, and upon finding the "grand army" once more assembled in "all the pomp and circumstance of glorious war:" the appearance of the troops, though fatigued, was all that could be desired; and their enthusiasm was at the highest on hearing that the Emperor himself, who had quitted Paris at three o'clock on the morning of the 12th, and passed the night at Laon, had actually arrived amongst them.

Upon the following day the French army bivouacked on three different points. The left, consisting of d'Erlon's and Reille's corps, and amounting to about 44,000 men, was posted on the right bank of the Sambre at Solre-sur-Sambre. The centre, consisting of Vandamme's and Lobau's corps, of the imperial guard, and of the cavalry-reserves, amounting altogether to about 60,000 men, was at Beaumont, which was made the head-quarters. The right, composed of Gérard's corps, and of a division of heavy cavalry, amounting altogether to about 16,000 men, was in front of Philippeville. The bivouacs were established in rear of some slight eminences, with a view to conceal their fires from the observation of the enemy.*

The army, while thus assembled, on the eve of opening the campaign, received through the medium of an "*ordre du jour*" the following spirit-stirring appeal from its chief:—

"Napoleon, by the Grace of God and the Constitutions of the Empire, Emperor of the French, etc., to the Grand Army.

"At the Imperial Head-quarters,
Avesnes, June 14th, 1815.

"Soldiers! this day is the anniversary of Marengo and of Friedland, which twice decided the destiny of Europe. Then, as after Austerlitz, as after Wagram, we were too generous! We believed in the protestations and in the oaths of princes, whom we left on their thrones. Now, however, leagued together, they aim at the independence, and the most sacred rights of France. They have commenced the most unjust of aggressions. Let us, then, march to meet them. Are they and we no longer the same men?

"Soldiers! at Jena, against these same Prussians, now so arrogant, you were one to three, and at Montmirail one to six!

* For a detailed explanation of the position occupied by the French army on the 14th of June, see the "Ordre du Jour" of the 13th of June—Appendix XI.

"Let those among you who have been captives to the English, describe the nature of their prison-ships, and the frightful miseries they endured.

"The Saxons, the Belgians, the Hanoverians, the soldiers of the confederation of the Rhine, lament that they are compelled to use their arms in the cause of the princes, the enemies of justice and of the rights of all nations. They know that this coalition is insatiable! After having devoured twelve millions of Poles, twelve millions of Italians, one million of Saxons, and six millions of Belgians, it now wishes to devour the states of the second rank in Germany.

"Madmen! one moment of prosperity has bewildered them. The oppression and the humiliation of the French people are beyond their power. If they enter France they will there find their grave.

"Soldiers! we have forced marches to make, battles to fight, dangers to encounter; but, with firmness, victory will be ours. The rights, the honour, and the happiness of the country will be recovered!

"To every Frenchman who has a heart, the moment is now arrived to conquer or to die!

"NAPOLEON."

"THE MARSHAL DUKE OF DALMATIA,
Major General."

CHAPTER IV.

Napoleon, by his precautionary measures of strengthening his advanced posts, and of displaying along the whole line of the Belgian frontier an equal degree of vigilance and activity, had effectually concealed from his adversaries the combined movements of his several corps d'armée, and their concentration on the right bank of the Sambre. During the night of the 13th, however, the light reflected upon the sky by the fires of the French bivouacs, did not escape the vigilant observation of Zieten's outposts, whence it was communicated to the rear that these fires appeared to be in the direction of Walcourt and of Beaumont, and also in the vicinity of Solre-sur-Sambre; further, that all reports received through spies and deserters, concurred in representing that Napoleon was expected to join the French army on that evening; that the imperial guard and the 2nd corps had arrived at Avesnes and Maubeuge; also that, at one o'clock in the afternoon of that day, four French battalions had crossed the river at Solre-sur-Sambre, and occupied Merbes-le-Chateau; that late in the night the enemy had pushed forward a strong detachment as far as Sart-la-Bussière; and lastly, that an attack by the French would certainly take place on the 14th or 15th.

On the 14th of June, the Dutch-Belgian General van Merlen, who was stationed at St. Symphorien, near Mons, and who commanded the outposts between the latter place and Binche, which formed the extreme right of the Prussians, ascertained that the French troops had moved from Maubeuge and its vicinity by Beaumont towards Philippeville, that there was no longer any hostile force in his front, except a picquet at Bettignies, and some national guards in other villages. He forwarded this important information to the Prussian General Steinmetz, on his left, with whom he was in constant communication, and by whom it was despatched to General Zieten at Charleroi. The Prussian General Pirch II., who was posted on the left of Steinmetz, also sent word to Zieten that he had received information through his outposts that the French army had concentrated in the vicinity of Beaumont and Merbes-le-Chateau; that their army consisted of 150,000 men, and was commanded by General Vandamme, Jerome Buonaparte, and some other distinguished officers; that since the previous day all crossing of the frontier had been forbidden by the French under pain of death; and that a patrol of the enemy had been observed that day near Biercée, not far from Thuin. During the day frequent accounts were brought to the troops of Zieten's corps, generally corroborative of the above, by the country-people who were bringing away, and seeking some place of safety for, their cattle. Intelligence was also obtained of the arrival of Napoleon, and of his brother, Prince Jerome. Zieten immediately transmitted the substance of this information to Prince Blücher and to the Duke of Wellington; and it was perfectly consistent with that which the latter had received from Major General Dörnberg,* who had been posted in observation at Mons, and from General van Merlen (through the Prince of Orange) who, as already mentioned, commanded the outposts between that place and Binche. Nothing, however, was as yet positively known concerning the real point of concentration, the probable strength of the enemy, or his intended offensive movements, and the allied commanders therefore refrained from making any alteration in their dispositions, and calmly awaited the arrival of reports of a more definite character concerning the enemy's designs.

Zieten's troops were kept under arms during the night, and were collected by battalions at their respective points of assembly.

Later in the day Zieten ascertained, through his outposts, that strong French columns, composed of all arms, were assembling in his front, and that every thing portended an attack on the following morning.

Zieten's communication of this intelligence reached Blücher between nine and ten o'clock on the night of the 14th. Simultaneous orders were consequently despatched by eleven o'clock for the march of Pirch's corps from Namur upon Sombref, and of Thielemann's corps from Ciney to Namur. An order had already, in the course of the day, been forwarded to Bülow at Liege, desiring him to make such a disposition of his corps d'armée as should admit of its concentration at Hannut in one march; and at midnight a further order was despatched, requiring him to concentrate his troops in cantonments about Hannut. Zieten was directed to await the advance of the enemy in his position upon the Sambre, and, in the event of his being attacked by superior numbers, and compelled to retire, to effect his retreat as slowly as circumstances would permit, in the direction of Fleurus, so

* Now Sir William de Dörnberg, K.C.B.; G.C.H.; Lieut. General in the Hanoverian service.

as to afford sufficient time for the concentration of the other three corps in rear of the latter point.

The vigilance which was thus exercised along both the Anglo-allied and Prussian line of outposts, obtained for Wellington and Blücher the fullest extent of information which they could reasonably have calculated on receiving respecting the dispositions of the enemy immediately previous to an attack. They had been put in possession of the fact that considerable masses of French troops had moved by their right, and assembled in front of Charleroi. Still, this baring of the frontier beyond Tournai, Mons, and Binche, of the troops which had previously occupied that line, and their concentration in front of Charleroi, might be designed to mask the real line of operation, to draw the Anglo-allied troops towards Charleroi, upon which a feigned attack would be made, while the real attack was intended to be by Mons. Hence no alteration was made by the Duke in the disposition of his forces; but the Prussian Field Marshal immediately ordered the concentration of his own troops at a point where they would be at hand in case Charleroi should be the real line of attack, and whence they could far more readily move to the support of Wellington, should that attack be made by the Mons road.*

Zieten's position, and his line of advanced posts, have already been described.† His right brigade (the 1st), having its head-quarters at Fontaine-l'Evêque, held the ground between Binche and the Sambre; his centre brigade (the 2nd) lay along the Sambre, occupying Marchienne-au-Pont, Dampremy, La Roux, Charleroi, Châtelet, and Gilly; a portion of his 3rd brigade occupied Farciennes and Tamines, on the Sambre, while the remainder was posted in reserve between Fleurus and the Sambre; and his left brigade (the 4th) was extended along this river nearly as far as Namur. The reserve-cavalry of the 1st corps had been brought more in advance, and was now cantoned in the vicinity of the Piéton, having Gosselies for its point of concentration.

In this position, Zieten, without making the slightest alteration, remained fully prepared for the expected attack on the morrow.§

* The facts which I have already detailed in connexion with the eve of the opening of the campaign, will, I presume, afford a sufficient refutation of the charge so frequently brought against the allied commanders, that the French attack took them by surprise.

† See page 22, chap iii.

§ A further proof of the perfect readiness in which Zieten had for a long time previously held his corps to meet the enemy's first attack, is presented by the instructions contained in his orders of the 2nd of May. See Appendix XII.

While Napoleon was occupied in prescribing his intended order of attack, he received a despatch from Count Gérard announcing that Lieut. General de Bourmont, and Colonels Clouet and Villoutreys, attached to the 4th corps, had deserted to the enemy—a circumstance which induced the Emperor to make some alteration in his dispositions.*

The morning of the 15th had scarcely broken, when the French army commenced its march towards the Sambre, in three columns, from the three bivouacs already mentioned as having been taken up during the previous night. The left column advanced from Solre-sur-Sambre, by Thuin, upon Marchienne-au-Pont; the centre from Beaumont, by Ham-sur-Heure, upon Charleroi; and the right column from Philippeville, by Gerpinnes, upon Châtelet.†

As early as half-past three o'clock in the morning, the head of the left column came in contact with the Prussian troops in front of Lobbes, firing upon, and driving in, the picquets of the 2nd batt. of the 1st regiment of Westphalian landwehr, commanded by Capt. Gillhausen. This officer who was well aware that the French troops that had assembled, the night before, in great force in his front, intended to attack him in the morning, had posted his battalion so as to afford it every advantage to be derived from the hilly and intersected ground it occupied. The French, however, inclined more to their right, and joined other troops advancing along the road to Thuin, which lay on his left. Shortly after, they drove back an advanced cavalry-picquet, and, at half-past four, commenced a fire from four guns upon the outpost of Maladrie, about a mile in front of Thuin.

This cannonade, which announced the opening of the campaign by the French, was heard by the Prussian troops forming the left wing of Steinmetz's brigade; but the atmosphere, which was extremely thick and heavy, was most unfavourable for the conveyance of sound; so much so, that the greater portion of the right wing of the brigade remained for a considerable time in ignorance of the enemy's advance.

* When General de Bourmont was presented to Blücher, the latter could not refrain from evincing his contempt for the faithless soldier; and to those who endeavoured to appease him, and to impress him more favourably towards the general by directing his attention to the white cockade which he wore in a conspicuous fashion, the Prince bluntly remarked—"Einerlei, was das Volk für einen Zettel ansteckt! Hundsfott bleibt Hundsfott!"—an expression of which the following may be considered but a mild translation: "It matters not what a man sticks in his hat for a mark—a mean-spirited scoundrel always remains the same!"

† For the order of movement of the French army on the 15th of June, see Appendix XIII.

The firing, however, was distinctly heard at Charleroi; and Zieten, who, by the reports which he forwarded on the 14th to Wellington and Blücher, had fully prepared these commanders to expect an attack, lost no time in communicating to them the important fact, that hostilities had actually commenced. Shortly before five o'clock, he despatched courier-jägers to their respective head-quarters, Brussels and Namur, with letters containing the information that since half-past 4 o'clock, he had heard several cannon-shots fired in his front, and at the time he was writing, the fire of musketry also, but that he had not yet received any report from his outposts. To Blücher he at the same time intimated that he should direct the whole corps to fall back into position, and, should it become absolutely necessary, to concentrate at Fleurus. His report to the Duke of Wellington arrived in Brussels at 9 o'clock in the morning; that to Prince Blücher reached Namur between 8 and 9 o'clock. The former, while it placed the British commander on the *qui vive*, did not induce him to adopt any particular measure—he awaited further and more definite information; but the latter satisfied the Prussian Field-Marshal that he had taken a wise precaution in having already ordered the concentration of his several corps in the position of Sombref.*

* In the present edition I have given a somewhat more minute description of the circumstances which occurred on the morning of the 15th, and of the measures adopted by General Zieten, because I think it but due to the memory of this gallant and distinguished officer to defend him from the imputation made against him by the Rev. George Gleig, the author of a volume of the "Home and Colonial Library," entitled "The Story of Waterloo," of negligence in not having made any communication to the Duke of Wellington of the attack by the French army. I have already shown that Zieten forwarded reports to his Grace on the 13th and 14th (either directly or through General Müffling), of the actual state of affairs in his front, and that these were found to be perfectly consistent with those which had been received from other quarters. Such was their tendency that in a letter, still extant, written by General Müffling on the morning of the 15th, to General Count Gneisenau, the chief of the Prussian staff, it appears that at the Duke's head-quarters it had been considered very probable that the enemy would have attacked even on the 14th. He had thus fully prepared the Duke for that which there was abundant reason to expect would very shortly take place. He knew also that his brigadier, General Steinmetz, would, in accordance with previous orders, communicate to the Dutch General van Merlen the fact of the attack by the French, and the consequent retreat of his brigade. Hence he concluded that after having, on the morning of the 15th, informed the British commander of the actual commencement of hostilities, the instructions he had received to forward to the Duke of Wellington timely information of hostile demonstrations in his front, had been fulfilled, and that his Grace would thenceforth receive reports of occurrences in front from the commander of the Anglo-allied corps on his (Zieten's) immediate right, as also any information respecting military dispositions adopted in consequence of the French advance, from the Prussian head-quarters at Namur. He may also have concluded, if he bestowed upon the matter any further consideration, that the above mentioned commander—the

The Prussian troops at Maladrie checked, for a time, the advance of the French upon Thuin, and maintained their ground for more than an hour, with the greatest bravery

Prince of Orange—would immediately despatch officers in observation of occurrences on the right of the Prussian army. I am quite ready to admit, judging *after* events, that if between eleven and twelve o'clock in the forenoon, Zieten had forwarded a despatch to the Duke stating that the French had obtained possession of Charleroi, and that it had become evident that their advance was a real attack, and not a mere diversion, some valuable time would have been gained. The Duke might, in this way, have received by four o'clock the information which did not reach him until nearly ten o'clock at night—a difference of six hours; not of twelve hours, as supposed by Mr. Gleig. But the fact is, that Zieten, who had rigidly adhered to his instructions up to the moment of the French attack, did not consider himself called upon to continue his reports to the British head-quarters after that moment had arrived. It is scarcely reasonable to expect that he should have weighed in his own mind the question whether the British commander-in-chief would, or would not, act upon the report which he had made to him of the commencement of hostilities, as from this moment he, in all probability, considered himself bound to devote his undivided attention to his own immediate operations, and to address all reports respecting them to the Prussian head-quarters at Namur.

I very much regret that any English writer should have cast so severe a censure of negligence upon our gallant Prussian allies for not having communicated to the British head-quarters earlier intelligence of the events upon the Sambre on the morning of the 15th of June. Such a writer should be prepared to encounter the retorts of the military critics of Prussia, who might perhaps tell him that if "negligence" existed in any quarter, he must seek it nearer home; and ask him why General van Merlen, who was posted at St. Symphorien, within two miles and a half from Mons, whence there was a direct road to Brussels by Braine-le-Comte and Hal, exceeding the one from Charleroi by three or four miles only, did not despatch an orderly to the Duke with the information communicated to him by Major Arnauld, at eight o'clock, that the French had attacked Zieten's troops, driven in his outposts, and forced his 1st brigade, which adjoined the left of his (van Merlen's) own outposts, to retreat. They might also ask how it was that neither van Merlen nor the Prince of Orange, the commander of the 1st Anglo-allied corps, and who was with the former early that morning, and who remained with the advanced posts until between nine and ten o'clock, did not proceed to make any personal reconnaissance, or detach any staff officers on that duty, with a view to obtain intelligence of events on the left flank. Had this been effected, the troops at Frasne, Quatre-Bras, Genappe, Hautain-le-val, and Nivelles, might, shortly after the capture of Charleroi, have been prepared for the enemy's advance, instead of having been left to learn it, late in the day, through the medium of a wounded Prussian soldier, and a Belgian officer of the maréchaussées, the fact being that the firm countenance and gallant stand presented at Quatre-Bras during the evening of the 15th, was mainly attributable to the decision and intelligence evinced by Prince Bernhard of Saxe-Weimar, previously to the receipt of any orders from the head-quarters of the 1st corps. If a degree of vigilance commensurate with the occasion had been exercised, the Duke of Wellington might have been informed, by two o'clock, that the enemy had driven in the Prussian advanced posts at Lobbes and Thuin, and appeared disposed to attack Charleroi; and he might also have been informed, by four o'clock, of the crossing of the Sambre and the capture of Charleroi by the French. Nothing of this kind, however, occurred, and it appears, according to Mr. Gleig's own statement, that when the Prince of Orange reached Brussels and imparted the first intelligence to the Duke, his Royal Highness knew so very little about the matter, that "he described the enemy as having occupied and subsequently abandoned Binche"! Hence it is obvious that the question of "negligence" is

They were overpowered, and driven back upon Thuin. This place was occupied by the 3rd battalion of the 2nd Westphalian landwehr, under Major Mönsterberg, who, after an obstinate and gallant resistance, during which the battalion suffered an immense loss, was forced to retire, about 7 o'clock, upon Montigny, where he found Lieut. Colonel Woisky, with 2 squadrons of the 1st West Prussian dragoons. The French succeeded in taking this village, and the retreat was then continued in good order, under the protection of Woisky's dragoons, towards Marchienne-au-Pont; but before reaching this place, the latter were attacked, and completely overthrown by the French cavalry; and the infantry getting into disorder at the same moment were partly cut down, and many were taken prisoners. Indeed so severe was the loss which the 3rd battalion of the 2nd Westphalian landwehr suffered in this retreat, that the mere handful of men which remained could not possibly be looked upon as constituting a battalion in the proper meaning of the term. It was reduced to a mere skeleton. Lieut. Colonel Woisky was wounded on this occasion, but continued, nevertheless, at the head of his dragoons.

Captain Gillhausen, who, as before stated, commanded the Prussian battalion posted at Lobbes, as soon as he had satisfied himself that Thuin was taken, saw the necessity of effecting his own retreat, which he did, after the lapse of half an hour, drawing in his picquets, and occupying the bridge over the Sambre with one company. He then fell back, and occupied the wood of Sar de Lobbes, where he received an order, as soon as the post of Hoarbes was also taken by the enemy, to continue his retreat, taking a direction between Fontaine l'Evêque and Anderlues. The post at Abbaye d'Alnes, occupied by the 3rd battalion of the 1st Westphalian landwehr, under the temporary command of Captain Grollmann, also fell into the hands of the French, between eight and nine o'clock.

As soon as the commander of the 1st Prussian brigade—

one of a very delicate nature, and it is one which, in my humble opinion, it would have been well if Mr. Gleig had never raised.

Mr. Gleig states, in furtherance of his imputation against General Zieten, that "neither was there any reason, in the local situations of the head-quarters of the two Marshals, why the one should have been kept in ignorance of what was communicated to the other. Brussels is not further removed from Charleroi than Hannut. Both may be about thirty English miles distant from that town; and the road to the former was, in 1815, at least as passable as the road to the latter." This line of argument is founded upon an entirely false assumption, and it is scarcely credible that Mr. Gleig, as a military writer, should have been ignorant of the fact that Blücher's head-quarters were *not* then at Hannut, but at Namur, which is little more than half the distance!

General Steinmetz—was made acquainted with the attack upon his most advanced posts along the Sambre, he despatched an officer of his staff—Major Arnauld—to the Dutch-Belgian General van Merlen at St. Symphorien, situated on the road between Binche and Mons, to make him fully acquainted with what had taken place, and with the fact that his brigade was falling back into position. On his way, Major Arnauld directed Major Engelhardt, who commanded the outposts on the right, to lose not a moment in withdrawing the chain of picquets; and on arriving at Binche, he spread the alarm that the French had attacked, and that the left of the brigade was warmly engaged, which rendered it necessary that the right should retire with the utmost expedition. Until this officer's arrival, the Prussian troops in this quarter were wholly ignorant of the attack, the state of the atmosphere, to which allusion has already been made, having prevented their hearing the slightest sound of any firing. They had a much greater extent of ground to pass over in retreat than the rest of the brigade, and yet, by the above unfortunate circumstance, they were the last to retire.

Zieten, having ascertained, about eight o'clock, that the whole French army appeared to be in motion, and that the direction of the advance of its columns seemed to indicate the probability of Charleroi and its vicinity being the main object of the attack, sent out the necessary orders to his brigades. The 1st was to retire by Courcelles to the position in rear of Gosselies; the 2nd was to defend the three bridges over the Sambre, at Marchienne-au-Pont, Charleroi, and Châtelet, for a time sufficient to enable the 1st brigade to effect its retreat towards Gosselies, and thus to prevent its being cut off by the enemy, after which it was to retire behind Gilly; the 3rd and 4th brigades, as also the reserve-cavalry and artillery, were to concentrate as rapidly as possible, and to take up a position in rear of Fleurus.

The three points by which the 1st brigade was to fall back, were Mont St. Aldegonde, for the troops on the right, Anderlues for those in the centre, and Fontaine l'Evêque for the left. In order that they might reach these three points about the same time, Zieten ordered that those in front of Fontaine l'Evêque should yield their ground as slowly as the enemy's attack would admit. Having reached the line of these three points, about ten o'clock, the brigade commenced its further retreat towards Courcelles, having its proper left protected by a separate column consisting of the 1st regiment of Westphalian landwehr and two companies of Silesian rifles, led by Colonel Hoffmann, in the direction of Roux and Jumet, towards Gosselies.

At Marchienne-au-Pont stood the 2nd battalion of the 6th Prussian regiment, belonging to the 2nd brigade of Zieten's corps. The bridge was barricaded, and with the aid of two guns, resolutely maintained against several attacks; after which these troops commenced their retreat upon Gilly, by Dampremy. In the latter place were 3 companies of the 1st battalion of the 2nd regiment of Westphalian landwehr, with 4 guns. These also retired about the same time towards Gilly, the guns protecting the retreat by their fire from the churchyard; after which they moved off as rapidly as possible towards Gilly, while the battalion marched upon Fleurus; but the 4th company, which defended the bridge of La Roux until Charleroi was taken, was too late to rejoin the latter, and therefore attached itself to the 1st brigade, which was retreating by its right flank.

Lieut. General Count Pajol's corps of light cavalry formed the advanced guard of the centre column of the French army: it was to have been supported by Vandamme's corps of infantry, but by some mistake, this general had not received his orders, and at six o'clock in the morning had not quitted his bivouac. Napoleon, perceiving the error, led forward the imperial guards in immediate support of Pajol. As the latter advanced, the Prussian outposts, though hard pressed, retired, skirmishing in good order. At Couillet, on the Sambre, about a mile and a half below Charleroi, the French cavalry fell upon a company of the 3rd battalion of the 28th Prussian regiment, surrounded it, and forced it to surrender. Immediately afterwards, the French gained possession of Marcinelles, a village quite close to Charleroi, and connected with this town by a dike 300 paces in length, terminating at a bridge, the head of which was palisaded. Along this dike the French cavalry ventured to advance, but was suddenly driven back by the Prussian skirmishers, who lined the hedges and ditches intersecting the opposite slope of the embankment; a part of the village was retaken, and an attempt made to destroy the bridge. The French, however, having renewed the attack with increased force, succeeded in finally carrying both the dike and the bridge, and by this means effected their entrance into Charleroi. Major Rohr, who commanded this post, now felt himself under the necessity of effecting his retreat with the 1st battalion of the 6th Prussian regiment, towards the preconcerted position in rear of Gilly, which he did in good order, though hotly pursued by detachments of Pajol's dragoons.

By eleven o'clock, the French were in full possession of Charleroi, as also of both banks of the Sambre above the town, and Reille's corps was effecting its passage over the river at Marchienne-au-Pont.

The right column of the French army, commanded by Count Gérard, having a longer distance to traverse, had not yet reached its destined point, Châtelet on the Sambre.

The 4th brigade of Zieten's corps, as also the advanced portion of the 3rd, continued their retreat towards Fleurus; General Jagow, who commanded the latter, having left the two Silesian rifle-companies and the fusilier-battalion* of the 7th Prussian regiment at Farciennes and Tamines, for the purpose of watching the points of passage across the Sambre, and of protecting the left flank of the position at Gilly. But, from the moment the French made themselves masters of Charleroi, and of the left bank of the Sambre above that town, the situation of the 1st brigade under General Steinmetz became extremely critical. Zieten immediately ordered General Jagow, whose brigade was in reserve, to detach Colonel Rüchel with the 29th regiment of infantry to Gosselies, for the purpose of facilitating General Steinmetz's retreat. The Colonel found that General Röder (commanding the reserve-cavalry of the corps) had posted there the 6th regiment of Prussian Uhlans (lancers) under Lieut. Colonel Lützow, to whom he confided the defence of Gosselies, which he occupied with the 2nd battalion of the 29th regiment, while he placed himself in reserve with the other two battalions.

As soon as the French had assembled in sufficient force at Charleroi, Napoleon ordered Count Pajol to detach General Clary's brigade towards Gosselies, and to advance with the remainder of the 1st corps of reserve-cavalry towards Gilly. General Clary, with the 1st French hussars, reached Jumet, on the left of the Brussels road, and only but little more than a mile from Gosselies, before the 1st Prussian brigade had crossed the Piéton. He now advanced to attack Gosselies, but was met by Lieut. Colonel Lützow and his dragoons, who defeated and repulsed him, and thus secured for General Steinmetz time to pass the Piéton; and as soon as the latter

* The Prussian regiments of infantry generally consisted of three battalions, of which the third was the fusilier-battalion.

had turned the defile of Gosselies, Colonel Rüchel with the 29th regiment moved off to rejoin the 3rd brigade.

The check thus experienced by General Clary led to his being supported by Lieut. General Lefebvre-Desnouettes, with the light cavalry of the guard and the two batteries attached to this force; and a regiment from Lieut. General Duhesme's division of the young guard was advanced midway between Charleroi and Gosselies as a reserve to Lefebvre-Desnouettes. The advanced guard of Reille's corps, which had crossed the Sambre at Marchienne-au-Pont, was also moving directly upon Gosselies, with the design both of cutting off the retreat of Zieten's troops along the Brussels road, and of separating the Prussians from the Anglo-allied army. D'Erlon's corps, which was considerably in the rear, received orders to follow and support Reille.

General Steinmetz, upon approaching Gosselies, and perceiving the strength of the enemy and the consequent danger of being completely cut off, with the utmost promptitude and decision directed the 2nd battalion of the 1st Westphalian landwehr to march against the enemy's left flank, with a view to divert his attention and to check his advance, while, protected by the 6th lancers and the 1st Silesian hussars, he continued his retreat towards Heppignies. This plan was attended with complete success; and Steinmetz reached Heppignies with scarcely any loss, followed by General Girard at the head of the 7th division of the 2nd French corps d'armée, with the remainder of which Reille continued his advance along the Brussels road. Heppignies was already occupied by the 2ud and 3rd battalions of the 12th Prussian regiment, and with this increase of strength Steinmetz drew up in order of battle, and upon Girard's attempting to force the place, after having previously occupied Ransart, he advanced against him, and drove him back in the direction of Gosselies. A brisk cannonade ensued, which was maintained on the part of the Prussians, only so long as it was deemed necessary for covering their retreat upon Fleurus.

In conformity with Zieten's orders, General Pirch II., when forced to abandon Charleroi, retired to Gilly, where, having concentrated the 2nd brigade, about two o'clock, he took up a favourable position along a ridge in rear of a rivulet; his right resting upon the abbey of Soleilmont, his left extending towards Châtelineau, which flank was also protected by a detachment occupying the bridge of Châtelet, Gérard's corps not having as yet arrived at that point. He posted the fusilier-battalion of the 6th regiment in a small wood which lay in advance on the exterior slope of the ridge; 4 guns on the right, upon an eminence commanding the valley in front; 2 guns between this point and the Fleurus road, as also 2 guns on the right of the road, to impede as much as possible the advance of any columns towards Gilly. The sharpshooters of the fusilier-battalion of the 6th regiment, by lining some adjacent hedges afforded protection to the artillery. The 2nd battalion of the 28th regiment was stationed beyond the Fleurus road, near the abbey of Soleilmont, in such a manner as to be concealed from the enemy. The 1st battalion of this regiment stood across the road leading to Lambusart; and its fusilier-battalion was posted more to the left, towards Châtelet. The 2nd battalion of the 2nd Westphalian landwehr was posted in support of the battery in rear of Gilly. The 1st battalion of this regiment, previously mentioned as on the march from Dampremy to Fleurus, passed through Lodelinsart and Soleilmont, and rejoined the brigade in rear of Gilly, before the affair had terminated. The 1st and 2nd battalions of the 6th regiment formed the reserve. The 1st West Prussian dragoons were posted on the declivity of the ridge towards Châtelet: they furnished the advanced posts, and patrolled the valley of the Sambre, maintaining the communication with the detachment at Farciennes, belonging to the 3rd brigade.

General Pirch, foreseeing that in the event of the enemy succeeding in turning his right, a rapid advance along the Fleurus road would be the means of greatly molesting, if not of seriously endangering, his retreat upon Lambusart, took the precaution of having this road blocked up by an *abatis* in the wood through which it led.

Vandamme did not reach Charleroi until three o'clock in the afternoon, when he received orders to pursue the Prussians, in conjunction with Grouchy, along the Fleurus road. It was, however, a considerable time before any advance was made. In the first place, the whole of Vandamme's corps had to cross the Sambre by a single bridge; secondly, both generals were deceived by exaggerated reports concerning the strength of the Prussians in rear of the Fleurus woods; and Grouchy who had gone forward to reconnoitre, returned to the Emperor with a request for further instructions. Upon this, Napoleon undertook a reconnaissance in person, accompanied by the four squadrons *de service;* and having formed an opinion that the amount of force in question did not exceed 18, or 20,000 men, he gave his orders for the attack of General Pirch's brigade.

The French generals having directed their preparatory dispositions from the windmill near the farm of Grand-drieu, opened the engagement about six o'clock in the evening, with a fire from two batteries. Three columns of infantry advanced in echelon from the right, the first directing its course towards the little wood occupied by the fusilier-battalion of the 6th Prussian regiment; the second passing to the right of Gilly; and the third winding round the left of this village. The attack was supported by two brigades of General Excelmans' cavalry-corps, namely, those of Generals Bourthe and Bonnemain; of which one was directed towards Châtelet, thus menacing the Prussian left flank, and the other advanced along the Fleurus road.

The battery attached to the 2nd Prussian brigade was in the act of replying with great spirit to the superior fire from the French artillery, and the light troops were already engaged, when General Pirch received Zieten's orders to avoid an action against superior numbers, and to retire by Lambusart upon Fleurus. Perceiving the formidable advance and overwhelming force of the enemy, he did not hesitate a moment in carrying those orders into effect, and made his dispositions accordingly; but the retreat had scarcely commenced when his battalions were vigorously assailed by the French cavalry. Napoleon, in the hope of profiting by this retrograde movement, sent against the retreating columns the four squadrons *de service* of the guard, under General Letort, a distinguished cavalry officer attached to his staff. The Prussian infantry withstood the repeated attacks of the French cavalry with undaunted bravery, and, aided by the gallant exertions of Lieut. Colonel Woisky, who boldly met the enemy with the 1st West Prussian dragoons, and checked his progress, the greater part of it succeeded in gaining the wood of Fleurus. The fusilier-battalion of the 28th regiment (of which it will be recollected, one company had previously been captured on the right bank of the Sambre) was the only column broken on this occasion. It had been ordered to retire into the wood by Rondchamp, but before it could complete the movement, it was overtaken by the enemy's cavalry, by which it was furiously assailed, and suffered a loss of two-thirds of its numbers. The fusilier-battalion of the 6th regiment was more fortunate. When about five hundrd paces from the wood, it was attacked by the enemy's cavalry on the plain, but forming square, and reserving its fire until the French horsemen had approached within twenty or thirty paces, it gallantly repelled several charges. As the vigour with which these attacks were made began to slacken, the battalion cleared its way with the bayonet through the cavalry that continued hovering round it. One of its companies immediately extended itself along the edge of the wood, and kept the French cavalry at bay. The latter suffered severely on this occasion, and General Letort who led the attacks was mortally wounded.

The Brandenburg dragoons had been detached by Zieten in support of Pirch's brigade, and opportunely reaching the field of action, made several charges against the French cavalry, which they repulsed and compelled to relinquish its pursuit.

Pirch's brigade now took up a position in front of Lambusart, which was occupied by some battalions of the 3rd brigade, and General Röder joined it with his remaining three regiments of cavalry and a battery of horse artillery. At this moment the French cavalry, which was formed up in position, opened a fire from three batteries of horse artillery, and thus brought on a cannonade, with which, however, the affair terminated.

The 1st Prussian brigade having safely executed its retreat from Heppignies, towards Fleurus, reached St. Amand about eleven o'clock at night. The detachments left by the 3rd brigade at Farciennes and Tamines, had been previously called in, and effected their retreat without any molestation, as did also, subsequently, the 2nd brigade from Lambusart, by Boulet, towards Fleurus, protected by the reserve-cavalry.

Zieten's corps, at three o'clock in the morning had possessed a line of advanced posts, from Dinant on the Meuse, crossing the Sambre at Thuin, and extending as far as Bonne Esperance, in advance of Binche; thus stretching along a space of from forty to fifty miles in length: its main force occupied the Sambre from Thuin as far as its confluence with the Meuse, an extent of, at least, thirty-six miles, exclusive of the numerous windings throughout the whole course of the river between those two points. The men had, since daybreak, been constantly under arms, in motion, and almost as constantly engaged, pursued, and assailed upon all points by an overwhelming superiority of force, headed by the élite of the French cavalry; and it was not until about eleven o'clock at night that the corps effected its concentration in position between Ligny and St. Amand, at a distance varying from fourteen to twenty miles in rear of its original extended line of outposts; after having successfully and gloriously fulfilled the arduous task imposed upon it of gaining sufficient time for the concentration, on the following day, of all the Prussian corps, by stemming, as well as its scattered force would admit, the imposing advance of the whole French army.

The loss of the 1st Prussian corps d'armée on the 15th of June amounted to 1200 men. The fusilier-battalions of the 28th regiment and of the 2nd Westphalian landwehr, reduced to mere skeletons, were united, and formed into one battalion.

Before ten o'clock on the morning of the 15th a further order was despatched from the Prussian head-quarters to the 3rd corps d'armée, to the effect that after resting during the night at Namur, it was to continue its march upon the morning of the 16th towards Sombref. At half-past eleven o'clock in the forenoon a despatch was forwarded to Bülow, announcing the advance of the French, and requesting that the corps after having rested at Hannut, should commence its march upon Gembloux by daybreak of the 16th at the latest. By three o'clock in the afternoon of the 15th, the 2nd corps d'armée had taken up the position assigned to it between Onoz and Mazy in the immediate vicinity of Sombref, with the exception, however, of the 7th brigade, which, having been stationed in the most remote of the quarters occupied by the corps, did not reach Namur until midnight. Here the latter found an order for its continuance in Namur until the arrival of the 3rd corps d'armée; but as this had already taken place, the brigade, after a few hours' rest, resumed its march, and joined its corps at Sombref about ten o'clock in the morning of the 16th June. Thielemann passed the night at Namur, which he occupied with the 10th brigade; the 9th brigade bivouacked on the right, and the 11th on the left, of Belgrade, a village at a short distance from the town, on the road to Sombref; the 12th brigade in rear of the 9th; the reserve-cavalry at Flavinne, between that road and the Sambre; and the reserve-artillery on the left of the road.

It has already been explained that on the 14th Blücher sent off a despatch to Bülow desiring him to make such a disposition of his corps as should enable his troops to reach Hannut in one march; and that at midnight of the 14th, a second despatch was forwarded, requiring him to concentrate the 4th corps at Hannut. The first of these despatches reached Bülow, at Liege, at five o'clock on the morning of the 15th; when he issued the necessary orders with an instruction that they should be acted upon as soon as the troops had dined, and forwarded a report of this arrangement to head-quarters.

These orders to his troops had been despatched some hours, and the consequent movements were for the most part in operation, when, towards noon, the second despatch arrived. Bülow, considering the effect which the change required by this new order would have upon the troops, inasmuch as their reception was prepared in quarters to which, in this case, they would no longer proceed, and they would have nothing provided for them in the destined bivouac near Hannut, also as a great proportion of them could not receive the orders for the change in the direction of their march until evening, decided upon deferring the new movement until daybreak of the 16th. The despatch, moreover, did not require him to establish his head-quarters at Hannut, but merely suggested that the latter appeared the most suitable for the purpose. The General was, besides, perfectly unconscious of the commencement of hostilities, which, indeed, he had expected would be preceded by a declaration of war; and he had also good grounds for an opinion which he had formed that it was in contemplation to assemble the whole army at Hannut. He made a report to head-quarters of his reasons for deferring the execution of the order, with the intimation that he would be at Hannut by mid-day of the 16th. Captain Below, on Bülow's staff, who carried this despatch, arrived at nine o'clock in the evening of the 15th at Namur, where he discovered that the head-quarters of the army had been transferred to Sombref. At half-past eleven o'clock in the forenoon of the 15th, another despatch was forwarded to Bülow from Namur, announcing the advance of the French, and requesting that the 4th corps, after having rested at Hannut, should commence its march upon Gembloux, by daybreak of the 16th at latest. The orderly who carried it was directed to proceed to Hannut, the presumed head-quarters of Bülow's corps on that day. On reaching that place, the orderly found the previous despatch lying in readiness for the general, and, mounting a fresh horse, he then went on with both despatches to Liege, where he arrived at sunrise. The orders which they contained had now, however, become impracticable, in consequence of Bülow's not having immediately carried into effect the *first* order to collect at Hannut; and thus by one of those mischances, which, in war, occasionally mar the best planned operations, the opportune arrival of the 4th Prussian corps at the battle of Ligny, which would, in all probability, have changed the aspect of affairs, was rendered a matter of impossibility.*

* Had this order been accompanied by the slightest intimation that it was given in consequence of information received respecting the concentration of the French army, the hero of Dennewitz, whose zeal, intelligence, and activity had

Late in the evening, and after Prince Blücher had established his head-quarters at Sombref, Captain Below arrived with the before-mentioned report from Count Bülow ; on receiving which his Highness was made sensible that he could no longer calculate with certainty upon being joined by the 4th corps on the following day.

It was seven o'clock in the evening of the 15th, when Marshal Ney, who had just arrived, joined the Emperor near Charleroi, at the point where the road to Fleurus branches off from the one to Brussels.* Having expressed the pleasure he felt at seeing him, Napoleon gave him the command of the 1st and 2nd corps d'armée ; explaining at the same time that Reille was advancing with three divisions upon Gosselies ; that d'Erlon would pass the night at Marchienne-au-Pont ; that he would find under his orders Piré's light cavalry-division ; as also the two regiments of chasseurs and lancers of the guard, of which, however, he was not to make use except as a reserve. "To-morrow," added the Emperor, "you will be joined by the reserve-corps of heavy cavalry under Kellermann. Go and drive back the enemy."

It has already been shown in the preceding chapter, that the extreme left of the Duke of Wellington's army, composed of de Perponcher's 2nd Dutch-Belgian division, rested upon the Charleroi road to Brussels. The 2nd brigade of

shone forth on so many important occasions, would not have hesitated an instant in fulfilling its instructions to the letter ; but he looked upon it as a mere matter of precaution, and being utterly ignorant of the outbreak of hostilities, he deemed it needless to issue the second order while the troops were acting on the first one. He considered that if a change in their order of march was made, instead of halting in the quarters already prepared for them, they would be compelled to bivouac at Hannut, which place they could not reach before night, and then only in an exhausted condition. He thought it better therefore to order their march to be resumed at day-break of the 16th, and directed upon Hannut. From the moment, however, that he received the third pressing order, for his speedy march upon Sombref, and was made sensible of his error, his exertions to repair the latter by accelerating in every possible way the advance of his corps, were most conspicuous ; but there was no longer any chance of reaching Sombref in sufficient time to support the remainder of the army on the field of battle. He had also entertained an idea that a general concentration of the army would be effected at Hannut, and that as his corps was the nearest to that point, its movements need not partake of the character of a forced march. An error of this kind, however, though committed in ignorance of the commencement of hostilities, can only be palliated, not justified, by such considerations.

* It was not until the 11th of June, on the eve of Napoleon's departure from Paris, that Ney received an order to join the army. He reached Beaumont late in the night of the 14th, but was unable the next morning to follow the Emperor (who had started at two o'clock) in consequence of his not having any horses at his disposal, his own not having arrived. However, on hearing that Marshal Mortier was detained in the town by illness, he bought two horses from him, as did also his first aid-de-camp, Colonel Heymès, who had accompanied him from Paris, whereupon they both proceeded towards the army.

this division, under Colonel Gödecke, was thus located:—1st battalion of the 2nd regiment of Nassau, at Hautain-le-val; the 2nd battalion, at Frasne and Villers-Peruin; the 3rd battalion, at Bézy, Sart-à-Mavelines, and Quatre-Bras; both battalions of the regiment of Orange-Nassau, at Genappe. There was also at Frasne a Dutch battery of horse artillery, under Captain Byleveld.

Early on the morning of the 15th, these troops were lying quietly in their cantonments, perfectly unconscious of the advance of the French army, when they heard a brisk cannonade at a distance in the direction of Charleroi; but not having received the slightest intimation of the enemy's approach, they concluded that the firing proceeded from the Prussian artillery practice, which they had frequently heard before, and to which they had therefore become accustomed. Gradually towards noon, however, the cannonade became more distinctly audible; and, in the afternoon, the arrival of a wounded Prussian soldier completely set at rest all doubt as to the advance of the French. An orderly was immediately despatched with the intelligence to the regimental head-quarters, whence it was also communicated to General de Perponcher's head-quarters at Nivelles. In the meantime, Major Normann, who commanded the 2nd battalion of the 2nd regiment of Nassau, drew up the latter with the battery in position in rear of Frasne, and upon the road to Quatre-Bras, after having posted a picquet of observation in advance of the village.

Perponcher lost not a moment in ordering both brigades of his division to hasten towards their respective points of assembly; the 1st brigade, under General Bylandt to Nivelles, and the 2nd, under Colonel Gödecke to Quatre-Bras.

Before this order, however, could possibly reach these troops, Prince Bernhard of Saxe-Weimar, who commanded the regiment of Orange-Nassau, at Genappe, having been informed by the officer of the Dutch-Belgian *maréchaussées*, who had been compelled to quit his post at Charleroi, that the French were advancing from that place, took upon himself to move forward with the above regiment from Genappe to Quatre-Bras, and despatched a report of such movement to the head-quarters of the brigade at Hautain-le-val, as also, subsequently, to General de Perponcher at Nivelles, by Captain Gagern, of the Dutch-Belgian staff, who happened to be just then at Genappe, for the purpose of collecting information.

About six o'clock in the evening, parties of lancers belonging to Piré's light cavalry-division of Reille's corps appeared in front of Frasne, and soon drove in Major Normann's picquet. This officer placed a company on the south or French side of Frasne, for the purpose of preventing as long as possible the entrance of the French into the village. Byleveld's battery took post on the north side of the village, and the remaining companies of the 2nd battalion of the 2nd regiment of Nassau drew up in its support. Two guns were upon the road, and three on each side of it. After some time, the lancers, having been reinforced, compelled the company before mentioned, to retire through the village and fall back upon the main body, which then opened a vigorous fire, by which this front attack by the French cavalry was defeated. The latter then made a disposition to turn the left flank of these troops; on perceiving which Major Normann and Captain Byleveld, resolved upon falling back to within a short distance in front of Quatre-Bras. The retreat was conducted in excellent order, the battery continuing to fire along the high road.

Quatre-Bras was the *rendezvous* of the 2nd brigade; and the 3rd battalion of the 2nd regiment of Nassau, which was cantoned in its immediate vicinity, had already, without waiting for the receipt of superior orders, assembled at that point. Prince Bernhard, on arriving there with the regiment of Orange-Nassau, and learning the particulars of the engagement at Frasne, assumed the command as senior officer, and being fully impressed with the importance of securing the point of junction of the high road from Charleroi to Brussels, with that from Namur to Nivelles, came to the resolution of making a firm stand at Quatre-Bras. This decision accorded entirely with the spirit of the orders which had in the mean time been despatched from Braine-le-Comte, the Dutch-Belgian head-quarters, on the receipt of intelligence of the French having crossed the Sambre. General de Perponcher, who commanded the division, had also approved of the Prince's determination, and Colonel Gödecke who was at Hautain-le-val, and who had hitherto commanded the 2nd brigade, now tendered his command to his Serene Highness, who immediately accepted it. The Prince pushed forward the 3rd battalion of the 2nd regiment of Nassau, in column, upon the high road towards Frasne, detached two companies of the 1st battalion, and the volunteer jägers, to the defence of the wood of Bossu, and the remaining companies on the high road towards Hautain-le-val; and posted the remainder of the brigade at Quatre-Bras, along the Namur road. Of

Byleveld's horse-battery, four guns were posted in advance in the direction of Frasne, two on the road to Namur, and two in rear of the main body.*

By the determined show of resistance which his Serene Highness displayed, as well as by the vigorous cannonade which he maintained, Piré's advanced guard, the left flank of which became endangered by the Dutch occupying the wood of Bossu, was forced to retire in its turn, which it did unmolested, and brought back intelligence that Quatre-Bras was occupied by ten battalions with artillery, and that Wellington's troops were moving to concentrate at this important point.

At ten o'clock at night Ney's forces were thus disposed:— Piré's light cavalry-division and Bachelu's infantry-division occupied Frasne, a village situated upon the Brussels road, about two miles and a half on the French side of Quatre-Bras;† the two regiments of chasseurs and lancers of the guard were in reserve in rear of Frasne; Reille was with two divisions, and the artillery attached to them, at Gosselies: these divisions ensured the communication until the arrival of d'Erlon's corps, which was to remain that night at Marchienne-au-Pont. The remaining division of Reille's corps (Girard's) was at Heppignies, and thus served to maintain the communication with the main column under Napoleon. The troops were greatly fatigued by having been kept constantly on the march since three o'clock in the morning; the strength of the different regiments, the names of their colonels, and even of the generals, were unknown to the Marshal, as also the number of men that had been able to keep up with the heads of the columns at the end of this long march. These circumstances, combined with the information brought in from Quatre-Bras, induced Ney to decline risking a night attack upon that point; and he contented himself with taking up a position in advance of Frasne. Having issued such orders as he deemed essential,

* In the report which the Prince forwarded to Lieut. General de Perponcher respecting these dispositions, he represented the inadequacy of the force at his command for any lengthened resistance at the point of Quatre-Bras, and remarked at the same time upon the great deficiency in the supply of ammunition to some of his troops; the 2nd battalion of Orange-Nassau, (provided with French muskets) having only 10 rounds of ball-cartridge a man, and the volunteer jägers having rifles of four different kinds of calibre, and only 10 rounds in each pouch.

† The village of Frasne is a little to the left of the high road. There is also a hamlet of the same name on the other side of that road, and a mile and a quarter nearer to Quatre-Bras: it is situated upon what are usually termed the heights of Frasne.

and enjoined the most vigilant look-out, he returned to Charleroi, where he arrived about midnight; partook of supper with Napoleon (who had just arrived from the right wing of the army), and conferred with the Emperor upon the state of affairs until two o'clock in the morning.

The first intimation which the Duke of Wellington received on the 15th, of hostilities having commenced, was conveyed in the report already alluded to, as having been forwarded by General Zieten, shortly before five o'clock in the morning, and as having reached Brussels at nine o'clock. It was not, however, of a nature to enable the Duke to form an opinion as to any real attack being contemplated by the enemy in that quarter. It simply announced that the Prussian outposts in front of Charleroi were engaged. It might be the commencement of a real attack in this direction, but it might also be a diversion in favour of an attack in some other direction, such as Mons. In fact, until further information was received, it could only be considered in the light of an affair of outposts.

Not long after three o'clock in the afternoon, the Prince of Orange arrived in Brussels, and informed the Duke that the Prussian outposts had been attacked and forced to fall back. His Royal Highness had ridden to the front at five o'clock in the morning, from Braine-le-Comte, and had a personal interview at St. Symphorien, with General van Merlen, whose troops were on the immediate right of the Prussians, who had retired. After having given to this General verbal orders respecting his brigade, the Prince left the outposts between nine and ten o'clock, and repaired to Brussels to communicate to the Duke all the information he had obtained respecting the enemy's attack upon the Prussian advanced posts. This, however, was not sufficiently conclusive to induce his Grace to resolve upon any immediate step; but, in about an hour afterwards, that is, about half-past four, General von Müffling, the Prussian officer attached to the British head-quarters, waited upon the Duke with a communication which had been despatched from Namur by Prince Blücher at noon, conveying the intelligence that the French had attacked the Prussian posts at Thuin and Lobbes on the Sambre, and that they appeared to be advancing in the direction of Charleroi. The Duke was fully prepared for this intelligence, though uncertain how soon it might arrive. The reports which had been made to him from the outposts, especially from those of the 1st hussars of the King's German legion, stationed in the vicinity of Mons and

Tournai, gave sufficient indication that the enemy was concentrating his forces. But, as observed in the preceding chapter, his Grace was determined to make no movement until the real line of attack should become manifest;* and hence it was, that if the attack had been made even at a later period, his dispositions would have remained precisely the same.†

The Duke at once gave orders for the whole of his troops to assemble at the head-quarters of their respective divisions and to hold themselves in immediate readiness to march. At the same time an express was despatched to Major General Dörnberg, requiring information concerning any movement that might have been made on the part of the enemy in the direction of Mons.

The following were the movements ordered by the Duke.‡ Upon the left of the army, which was nearest to the presumed point of attack—Perponcher's and Chassé's Dutch-Belgian divisions were to be assembled that night at Nivelles, on which point Alten's British division (the 3rd) was to march as soon as collected at Braine-le-Comte; but this movement was not to be made until the enemy's attack upon the right of the Prussian army and the left of the Allied army had become a matter of certainty. Cook's British division (the 1st) was to be collected that night at Enghien, and to be in readiness to move at a moment's notice.

Along the central portion of the army—Clinton's British division (the 2nd) was to be assembled that night at Ath, and to be in readiness also to move at a moment's notice. Colville's British division (the 4th) was to be collected that night at Grammont, with the exception of the troops beyond the Scheldt, which were to be moved to Audenarde.

* When, in the evening, Lord Fitzroy Somerset, whilst in conversation with the Duke respecting the advance of the French, observed, with an air of confidence, "No doubt we shall be able to manage those fellows," his Grace said "There is little doubt of it, provided I do not make a false movement." A writer in the "Quarterly Review," No. lxx, has truly remarked that "the Duke of Wellington has never hesitated to avow his opinion, that, of all the chiefs of armies in the world, *the one* in whose presence it was most hazardous to make a false movement was Napoleon Buonaparte."

† I had hoped that the statements so erroneously made by some writers, imputing to the Duke that he was taken by surprise, were not countenanced at the present day, since such statements, when submitted to an impartial military investigation of all the concurrent circumstances, must be found totally groundless; but I regret to perceive that in a work recently published, and enjoying a considerable degree of celebrity, great pains are taken to prove that the Duke really did allow himself to be surprised, and to show that the allied commanders were "*out-generaled*" by Napoleon, because their armies were not respectively concentrated at *Waterloo* and *Wavre*, *before* the opening of the campaign!

‡ Appendix, No. XIV.

Upon the right of the army—Stedmann's Dutch-Belgian division, and Anthing's Dutch-Belgian (Indian) brigade were, after occupying Audenarde with 500 men, to be assembled at Sotteghem, so as to be ready to march in the morning.

The cavalry were to be collected that night at Ninhove, with the exception of the 2nd hussars of the King's German Legion, who were to remain on the look-out between the Scheldt and the Lys; and of Dörnberg's brigade, with the Cumberland hussars, which were to march that night upon Vilvorde, and to bivouac on the high road near to that town.

The reserve was thus disposed—Picton's British division (the 5th), the 81st British regiment, and Best's Hanoverian brigade (of Cole's division), were to be in readiness to march from Brussels at a moment's notice. Vincke's Hanoverian brigade (of Picton's division) was to be collected that night at Hal, and to be in readiness at day-light on the following morning to move towards Brussels, and to halt on the road between Alost and Assche for further orders. The Duke of Brunswick's corps was to be collected that night on the high road between Brussels and Vilvorde. Kruse's Nassau brigade was to be collected at day-light on the following morning upon the Louvain road, and to be in readiness to move at a moment's notice. The reserve-artillery was to be in readiness to move at day-light.

It was ten o'clock at night when the first intelligence of the attack made by the French in the direction of Frasne, was received at the Prince of Orange's head quarters, at Braine-le-Comte. It was carried by Captain Gagern, who, as previously mentioned, (see page 49) had been despatched by Prince Bernhard of Saxe-Weimar, with his Serene Highness's report of the affair, to General Perponcher at Nivelles, and who was subsequently sent on by the General, with this information to the above head-quarters. Lieutenant Webster, aide-de-camp to the Prince of Orange, started soon afterwards for Brussels, with a report from the Dutch-Belgian Quarter-Master-General, de Constant Rebecque, stating what had taken place, and detailing the measures which he had thought proper to adopt. These measures did not entirely coincide with the instructions above given, as issued by the Duke, because they were consequent upon the affair at Frasne, with which his Grace at that time was unacquainted; but they were perfectly consistent with the spirit of those instructions, inasmuch as they were not adopted "until the enemy's attack upon the right of the Prussian army, and the left of the Allied army had become a matter of certainty." The enemy's advance along the Charleroi road had already heen successfully checked at Quatre-Bras, and the necessity of immediately collecting at this important point, the troops ordered by the Duke "to be assembled that night at Nivelles" was too obvious to be mistaken.

A little before ten o'clock on the same evening, a further communication reached the Duke from Prince Blücher, announcing the crossing of the Sambre by the French army, headed by Napoleon in person; and the required intelligence from other quarters having arrived almost at the same moment, and confirmed him in the opinion "that the enemy's movement upon Charleroi was the real attack," he issued, at ten o'clock, P.M. the following orders for the march of his troops to their left:*—Alten's division to continue its movement from Braine-le-Comte upon Nivelles. Cooke's division to move from Enghien upon Braine-le-Comte. Clinton's and Colville's divisions to move from Ath, Grammont, and Audenarde, upon Enghien. The cavalry to continue its movement from Ninhove upon Enghien.

The disposition of the French left column, under Ney, during the night of the 15th, has already been shown. The centre column of the French army was thus located—Vandamme's corps bivouacked in the wood of Fleurus; Pajol's corps of light cavalry at Lambusart; the 3rd light cavalry-division, under Domon, on the left, at the outlet of the wood, and the heavy cavalry-corps of Excelmans between the light cavalry and Vandamme; the guards bivouacked between Charleroi and Gilly; and Lobau's corps, together with Milhaud's heavy cavalry-corps, lay in rear of Charleroi. The right column, consisting of Gérard's corps, bivouacked in front of the bridge of Châtelet, which point it had reached during the evening.

The result of the proceedings on the 15th was highly favourable to Napoleon. He had completely effected the passage of the Sambre; he was operating with the main portion of his forces directly upon the preconcerted point of concentration of Blücher's army, and was already in the immediate front of the chosen position, before that concentration could be accomplished; he was also operating with another portion upon the high road to Brussels, and had come in contact with the left of Wellington's troops; he had also placed himself so far in advance upon this line, that even a partial junction of the forces of the allied commanders was already rendered a hazardous operation, without a previous

* Appendix, No. XV.

retrograde movement; and he thus had it in his power to bring the principal weight of his arms against the one, whilst, with the remainder of his force, he held the other at bay. This formed the grand object of his operations on the morrow. But however excellent, or even perfect, this plan of operation may appear in theory, still there were other circumstances, which, if taken into consideration, would scarcely seem to warrant a well-grounded anticipation of a successful issue. Napoleon's troops had been constantly under arms, marching, and fighting, since two o'clock in the morning, the hour at which they broke up from their position at Solre-sur-Sambre, Beaumont, and Philippeville, within the French frontier: they required time for rest and refreshment; they lay widely scattered between their advanced posts and the Sambre; Ney's forces were in detached bodies from Frasne as far as Marchienne-au-Pont, the halting-place of d'Erlon's corps; and although Vandamme's corps was in the wood of Fleurus, Lobau's corps and the guards were halted at Charleroi, and Gérard's corps at Châtelet. Hence, instead of an imposing advance, with the first glimmering of the dawn of the 16th, the whole morning would necessarily be employed by the French in effecting a closer junction of their forces, and in making their preparatory dispositions for attack; an interval of time invaluable to the Allies, by the greater facility which it afforded them for the concentration of a sufficient force to hold their enemy in check, and to frustrate his design of defeating them in detail.

In taking a calm retrospect of the dispositions made by Napoleon on the night of the 15th of June, we become strongly impressed with a conviction, that to the laxity of those dispositions, to the absence which they indicated of that energetic perseverance and restless activity which characterized the most critical of his operations in former wars, may, in a very great degree, be attributed the failure of the campaign on the part of the French. The great advantages derived by Napoleon from the result of his operations during the 15th, have been already set forth; but of what avail were those advantages to him, if he neglected the requisite measures for effectually retaining them within his grasp; or if, having secured them, he hesitated in following them up with the promptitude and energy which their complete development demanded of him? His position, if judged by that of his most advanced forces, was all that could be desired; but, by fatally neglecting to concentrate the remainder of his troops in the immediate support of that advance, the important advantages which such a position held forth were completely neutralized. Doubtless the troops required rest; but, if one portion required it more than another, it was that which now lay most in advance: they had performed the longest march, and had withstood, in addition, the whole brunt of the action; so that there was no reason whatever why the remainder of the French army should not have been so far advanced as to afford direct support to the important position taken up by the leading divisions: that which had been so successfully effected by the heads of the columns, might have been attained with infinitely greater ease and security by the masses which followed. And even supposing that serious impediments stood in the way of the full accomplishment of this concentration, such as the usual delays occasioned by the lengthening out of the columns of march, to what did they amount in comparison with so many brilliant instances of what had been overcome by the noble and heroic efforts of a French army headed by Napoleon? Had it even required some sacrifice, which at the most could only have consisted in the temporary diminution of strength, by the loss of stragglers on the march, what was this when placed in the balance with the fulfilment of the grand design of Napoleon's invasion of Belgium—preventing the junction of the allied armies, and overthrowing them in detail? The commencement of this design, in which the essential requisite was rapidity of movement, had been eminently successful: a vantage-ground had been gained which offered the most encouraging prospect of success: of Blücher's four corps, only one, Zieten's, had assembled in the chosen position of Ligny on the night of the 15th; Pirch's, which had arrived from Namur, was in bivouac between Onoz and Mazy, about six miles from Ligny; Thielemann's corps, which had quitted its cantonments around Ciney at half-past seven o'clock in the morning, passed the night at Namur, about fifteen miles from Ligny; Bülow's corps, supposed by Blücher to be then at Hannut, was still at Liege, about sixty miles distant from Ligny. Between this position of Ligny and that occupied by the leading divisions of Napoleon's main army, namely the villages of Lambusart, Wagnée, and the wood of Fleurus, there was an interval of not more than from two to three miles! Hence every thing was favourable to the French Emperor's plan, which only required to be carried on with the same vigour and activity that had marked its commencement; the fate of Napoleon, of France, and of Europe, hung upon its issue; not an hour, not a moment should have been suffered to pass unheeded; and had the

French right been concentrated during the night in this position, as also the left under Ney, between Gosselies and Frasne, and had an impetuous attack, with overwhelming force, been made not later than five o'clock on the following morning, upon both Zieten's and Pirch's corps, not at that time united, it is very possible that these troops would have been beaten in detail, that Thielemann's corps, advancing from Namur, would either have shared the same fate, or have moved off in the direction of Hannut or Liege to effect a junction with Bülow, whilst Ney would either have been enabled to secure the important point of Quatre-Bras before the arrival of any considerable portion of the Anglo-allied troops, or would have held his own force advantageously disposed for a junction with that of Napoleon, on the latter moving to the left, by the Namur road, for the purpose of bringing the great mass of his army against Wellington. Instead of this, what happened? Of the French right, its main force remained the whole night at Charleroi and Châtelet, on the Sambre, whilst between the advance of Ney's forces at Frasne and his rear at Marchienne-au-Pont, there was an interval of about twelve miles. Napoleon did not advance towards Fleurus until between eleven and twelve o'clock on the 16th, by which time Zieten's, Pirch's, and Thielemann's corps were all concentrated and in position, and he did not commence the battle of Ligny until nearly three o'clock in the afternoon; while Ney, on his side, in consequence of his operations having been rendered subordinate to those of the Emperor, delayed to advance with any degree of vigour until between two and three o'clock, about which time Wellington's reserve reached Quatre-Bras, from Brussels, and joined the forces then engaged in front of that point!*

* Upon the above passages the following remark has been made in an article in the "Quarterly Review," No. CLI.:—

"He (Captain Siborne) criticises the conduct of the Emperor Napoleon for not following up with sufficient activity, on the 16th, the movement which he had made with so much success on the 15th; but a little reflection upon the information which he has obtained on the movements of the French army must have convinced him that the troops which had been on their extreme left in French Flanders, and which formed the rear of the column, of which the head was engaged on the Sambre on the 15th, could not be closed up till a late hour on the 16th. It is easy to speculate on possible consequences of supposed circumstances. Those who indulge in such speculations would do well to consider that rapidity is purchased by exhaustion."

As this is the only instance adduced by the reviewer of an incorrect military opinion on my part, I am desirous of offering a few observations upon it. No commander of an army could be justified in exacting from his troops a rapidity of movement to such an extent as to render them powerless through exhaustion at a moment when their active services in the field are urgently required. This would, in fact, be a suicidal act. On the other hand, however, a commander would be perfectly justified in making a forced march, even at the sacrifice of leaving on the road all the feeble and sickly portion of his troops, in an enterprise depending, as upon this occasion, on celerity of movement for success. I have not argued that the march of the French troops on the 15th should have been one of greater extent than that which was made by the heads of the columns, but simply that these columns should have been well closed up by nightfall, so that they might have been ready for an advance to attack *early* on the morning of the 16th. The reviewer is mistaken in supposing that "the troops which had been on their extreme left in French Flanders, and which formed the rear of the column of which the head was engaged on the Sambre on the 15th, could not be closed up till a late hour on the 16th." The French army was fully collected together on the 14th, and bivouacked at Philippeville, Beaumont, and Solre-sur-Sambre; and was perfectly fresh for the opening of the campaign. The centre column advanced from its bivouac, which was a league in front of Beaumont, and gained possession, by eleven o'clock, of Charleroi, distant about 17 miles. In the evening it occupied the wood of Fleurus, having its advance at Lambusart, distant about 7 miles from Charleroi. The left column, from Solre-sur-Sambre, by Lobbes and Thuin, reached Marchienne-au-Pont, where it effected its passage across the Sambre, also by eleven o'clock, having marched about 17 miles. At night its advanced guard was at Frasne, about 10 miles from Marchienne. Reille's corps was at Gosselies, about half that distance, and d'Erlon's corps was halted at Marchienne. The right column, from its bivouac in advance of Philippeville, reached Châtelet, a distance of about 19 miles, in the evening, and bivouacked during the night in front of the bridge at that point. The heads of the left and centre columns, which had been fighting as well as marching during the day, betrayed no exhaustion when halted for the night; and I repeat that the columns themselves ought to have been closed up before dark, and that supposing a few thousand men had been left upon the road as stragglers, this admitted of no consideration in comparison with the accomplishment of the great object in view. It will surely be admitted that the French were capable of enduring as much fatigue on the 15th as the Anglo-allied troops underwent on the following day. The Duke of Wellington's reserve marched at daybreak from Brussels towards Quatre-Bras, which it reached before three o'clock in the afternoon—a distance of about 23 miles. The 3rd division marched from Soignies to Quatre-Bras, where it arrived between five and six o'clock—a distance of about 22 miles. Shortly afterwards the 1st division reached Quatre-Bras from Enghien, a distance of about 25 miles. Thus it will be seen that there was very little difference between the extent of march of the heads of the French columns on the 15th, and that of the march of the Anglo-allied troops on the 16th. A most important difference, however, occurred in one respect. The latter, as they arrived in succession on the field of Quatre-Bras, became engaged with the enemy, (who, in comparison, was perfectly fresh), and fought a desperate battle until nightfall; and I feel satisfied that the reviewer will agree with me in opinion that their conduct on that glorious occasion was not such as to evince any symptom of "*exhaustion*." The cavalry made a still longer march, namely, one of more than 40 miles. Only a portion of it reached Quatre-Bras in time to witness the termination of the battle; but it was all collected together, and fully prepared for action by daybreak of the 17th.

These considerations, I am persuaded, afford sufficient grounds whereon to justify the course of reasoning which I have adopted, and to render inapplicable to such reasoning, the censure implied by the reviewer's remark.

CHAPTER V.

With the early dawn of the 16th of June, the whole of the Duke of Wellington's forces were in movement towards Nivelles and Quatre-Bras. Previously to starting from Brussels for the latter point, his Grace despatched an order for the movement of the cavalry and of Clinton's British division upon Braine-le-Comte, as also of the troops under Prince Frederick of the Netherlands, consisting of Stedmann's Dutch Belgian division, and of Anthing's Dutch-Belgian (Indian) brigade, from Sotteghem to Enghien, after leaving 500 men, as before directed, in Audenarde. Picton's division quitted Brussels by the Charleroi road about two o'clock in the morning; and the Duke of Brunswick's corps somewhat later. Kruse's Nassau brigade received orders to follow along the same road, but having been dispersed in extended cantonments between Brussels and Louvain, it required some considerable time to collect together, and did not therefore reach Quatre-Bras sufficiently early to take part in the action.

The disposition made by Colonel the Prince Bernhard of Saxe Weimar at this point, on the night of the 15th, with the 2nd brigade of Perponcher's Dutch-Belgian division, has already been described. Soon after ten o'clock on that evening, Major Count Limburg Stirum, Dutch aide-de-camp to the Prince of Orange, left Braine-le-Comte for Nivelles, with a verbal order from the Dutch-Belgian Quarter-Master-General, enjoining General Perponcher to hold his ground to the last extremity, to support his 2nd brigade by the 1st, and even to ask for aid from the 3rd Anglo-allied division, and from the Dutch-Belgian cavalry-division; and, at all events, to send an officer to acquaint the commanders of these divisions with the state of affairs. This message appears to have reached Nivelles about midnight. Previously to this, that is, between nine and ten o'clock in the evening, Captain Crassier's company of the 27th battalion of chasseurs moved out from Nivelles towards Quatre-Bras *en reconnaissance.* About two o'clock in the morning, Perponcher himself followed with the remainder of the chasseurs, which body reached Quatre-Bras at four o'clock. General Bylandt, who commanded the 1st brigade, ordered the remaining battalions of the latter, and his artillery, to commence their march from Nivelles at five o'clock. The 7th Dutch line-battalion was directed to remain at Nivelles until relieved by Alten's division.

At three o'clock in the morning, Perponcher arrived at Quatre-Bras, and after having reconnoitred the position, immediately commenced operations for recovering the ground lost on the previous evening. Just at this time, a detachment of about 50 Prussian hussars of the 2nd Silesian regiment, under Lieutenant Zehelin, who, on the previous day, had been driven back from near Gosselies, and had retreated towards Hautain-le-val, gallantly advanced to the front, attacked the enemy's out-posts, forced them to retire, and then formed a chain of vedettes. As soon as the Dutch-Belgian troops had advanced to within a short distance of these Prussian hussars, the latter moved off by their left towards Sombref.*

Prince Bernhard of Saxe Weimar's brigade penetrated deeper into the wood of Bossu, and secured the entrances into it from the French side. Perponcher directed the 2nd battalion of the 2nd regiment of Nassau to take post on an eminence in advance towards Frasne, and stationed the 3rd battalion of this regiment more to the left. The latter, however, was soon relieved by the 27th chasseurs, which battalion, on reaching Quatre-Bras, at four o'clock in the morning, had detached two companies to the left. These moved steadily forward in extended order towards the wood of Delhutte,† outside of which the enemy showed his light troops. They succeeded in forcing back the French into a hollow-way bordering the wood, where the latter maintained themselves for some little time, and then retired into the wood itself. Taking advantage of the cover afforded by the edge of the wood, the French now poured a deadly fire upon their assailants, who retreated to some favourable ground a little in advance of their battalion.

The Prince of Orange arrived at Quatre-Bras about six o'clock, and immediately reconnoitred the position of the enemy, and that occupied by his own troops. Having expressed his perfect satisfaction with all the arrangements and dispositions which had been made, both on the previous evening and on that morning, he ordered the troops then present to take up a position more in advance, for the purpose

* Captain Gagern, on his way to Quatre-Bras, at daybreak, fell in with this Prussian detachment, and invited Lieutenant Zehelin to join temporarily the Dutch-Belgian troops.

† Although called "Delhutte," this is in fact the northern portion of the wood of Villers-Peruin.

of imposing upon the enemy; enjoining at the same time, all unnecessary firing, it being desirable under then existing circumstances, to avoid bringing on prematurely an attack by the enemy.

Ney, having quitted Charleroi at a very early hour in the morning, returned to Gosselies, where he communicated with Reille, whom he ordered to assemble the force then with him, consisting of two infantry-divisions and their artillery, and to advance upon Frasne; to which point the Marshal repaired in person. Here he collected all the information which the generals and other officers had been able to obtain respecting the enemy; and being naturally anxious to make himself acquainted with the details of the force placed so suddenly under his orders, he desired Colonel Heymès, his first aide-de-camp, to repair to every regiment, and note down their strength and the names of the commanding officers; after the performance of which duty, Colonel Heymès laid before the Marshal a return of the troops in the field.

The uncertainty in which Ney was placed as to the amount of force concentrated by the Allies during the night in rear of Quatre-Bras, and the conviction which he had reason to entertain that the Prussians were in strong force at no very great distance on his right, and that therefore any check experienced by the main column under Napoleon, would endanger his right flank and even his line of communication, rendered him cautious in attacking a point so considerably in advance of the Emperor's left, without ample means at hand to enable him, in case of disaster, to maintain that line, or, in the event of success, to effectually establish himself at Quatre-Bras, and derive every possible advantage from its possession, by checking, if not defeating in detail, any body of troops that might be approaching it as a point of concentration from either Nivelles or Brussels. Hence he became extremely anxious for the arrival of d'Erlon's corps and the promised 3rd corps of heavy cavalry under Kellermann; the more so, as although Lefebvre-Desnouette's light cavalry of the guard was nearer at hand, he had been desired by Napoleon not to make use of it. Officers of the chasseurs and lancers of the guard (in consequence of the deficiency of staff-officers) were sent to the rear in the direction of Marchienne-au-Pont, with orders to hasten the march of the 1st corps upon Frasne; while Ney himself was busily occupied in reconnoitring the enemy's position and movements.

Whilst so employed, a despatch reached him from the

Emperor,* acquainting him that he had just ordered Kellermann's dragoons to march to Gosselies, where they would be at his disposal; stating, at the same time, his intention to withdraw Lefebvre-Desnouette's light cavalry of the guard from the force under his command; and expressing a wish to be informed of the exact disposition of the 1st and 2nd corps, and of the cavalry-divisions attached to them, as also of the probable strength of the enemy, and of the particulars which had been obtained concerning him.

The 5th battalion of Dutch militia, which arrived at Quatre-Bras about seven o'clock, was ordered, some time afterwards, to occupy the farm of Gemioncourt. The other battalions of Bylandt's brigade, as they arrived in succession, formed a reserve, extending itself from the point of intersection of the two high roads along the Nivelles road, and in rear of the wood of Bossu. About nine o'clock Captain Stievenaar's foot-battery attached to Bylandt's brigade also arrived at Quatre-Bras.

Aided by these reinforcements, the Prince of Orange made his dispositions for impeding as much as possible the expected French attack, and maintaining his ground in front of Quatre-Bras until the arrival of the allied troops, which he knew were rapidly approaching from Brussels and Nivelles. The arrival of the 1st brigade induced him to make a further advance, and extension to the right, of the 2nd brigade; retaining a firm hold of the wood of Bossu. He disposed of his artillery in the following manner: upon the high road, in advance of his centre and in front of Frasne, he placed two guns of Perponcher's divisional horse-artillery; three guns a little in left rear of these, and three guns towards the left, so as to keep the road to Namur in view. He also placed six guns of the divisional foot-artillery a little to the right of, and in line with, the advanced guns of the horse-battery, and the remaining two guns on the right wing of his first line. His Royal Highness had unfortunately no cavalry in the field; yet such was the firm countenance which he displayed in the arrangement of his nine battalions and 16 guns that the enemy, unaware of this circumstance, and probably misled by the appearance, at an early hour, of the chain of vedettes formed by the Prussian detachment of hussars, to which allusion has previously been made, and also conceiving that a considerable force had already assembled at Quatre-Bras, made no vigorous attempt, until the afternoon, to dislodge him from his position.

* Appendix XVI.

Between ten and eleven o'clock the Duke of Wellington arrived in person at Quatre-Bras, where he joined the Prince of Orange, of whose dispositions he fully approved. He reconnoitred the ground; observed only a few of the enemy in front, who occasionally fired a shot; saw that there was a little popping musketry, but that nothing more serious was at that time threatened in this quarter. Conceiving that the enemy was not in any great force at Frasne, while at the same time, accounts reached him that Prince Blücher, in his position at Ligny, was menaced by the advance of considerable masses; the Duke, accompanied by his staff and a small escort of cavalry, shortly afterwards rode off to hold a conference with the Prussian commander, whom he found at the windmill of Bussy, between Ligny and Bry; whence he had an opportunity of observing the French preparatory dispositions for attack. These having led the Duke to conclude that Napoleon was bringing the main force of his army to bear against Blücher, he at once proposed to assist the Prince by first advancing straight upon Frasne and Gosselies, as soon as he should have concentrated sufficient force, and then operating upon the enemy's left and rear, which would afford a powerful diversion in favour of the Prussians, from the circumstance that their right wing was the weakest and most exposed, and considering the object of Napoleon's movement, the one most likely to be attacked. Upon a calculation being made, however, of the time which would elapse ere the Duke would be able to collect the requisite force for undertaking this operation, and of the possibility of Blücher being defeated before it could be carried into effect, it was considered preferable that Wellington should, if practicable, move to the support of the Prussian right by the Namur road. But a direct support of this kind was necessarily contingent on circumstances, and subject to the Duke's discretion. The latter having expressed his confident expectation of being enabled to afford the desired support, as also of his succeeding in concentrating, very shortly, a sufficient force to assume the offensive, rode back to Quatre-Bras.

It was nearly eleven o'clock when General Flahaut, an aide-de-camp of the Emperor, after passing through Gosselies, arrived at Frasne, with the following letter from the latter to the Marshal:

"Au Maréchal Ney.

"Mon Cousin—Je vous envoie mon aide-de-camp, le Général Flahaut, qui vous porte la présente lettre. Le major-général a dû vous donner der ordres;

mais vous recevrez les miens plus tôt, parceque mes officiers vont plus vite que les siens. Vous recevrez l'ordre du mouvement du jour, mais je veux vous en écrire en détail, parceque c'est de la plus haute importance. Je porte le Maréchal Grouchy avec les 3e et 4e corps d'infanterie sur Sombref. Je porte ma garde à Fleurus, et j'y serai de ma personne avant midi. J'y attaquerai l'ennemi si je le rencontre, et j'éclairerai la route jusqu'à Gembloux. Là d'après ce qui ce passera, je prendrai mon parti peut-être à trois heures après midi, peut-être ce soir. Mon intention est que, immédiatement après que j'aurai pris mon parti, vous soyez prêt à marcher sur Bruxelles, je vous appuierai avec la garde qui sera à Fleurus ou à Sombref, et je désirerais arriver à Bruxelles demain matin. Vous vous mettriez en marche ce soir même si je prends mon parti d'assez bonne heure pour que vous puissiez en être informé de jour et faire ce soir trois ou quatre lieues et être demain à sept heures du matin à Bruxelles. Vous pouvez donc disposer vos troupes de la manière suivante:—Première division à deux lieues en avant des Quatre-Chemins s'il n'y a pas d'inconvénient. Six divisions d'infanterie autour des Quatre-Chemins, et une division à Marbais, afin que je puisse l'attirer à moi à Sombref, si j'en avais besoin. Elle ne retarderait d'ailleurs pas votre marche. Le corps du Comte de Valmy, qui a 3,000 cuirassiers d'élite, à l'intersection du chemin des Romains et de celui de Bruxelles, afin que je puisse l'attirer à moi, si j'en avais besoin; aussitot que mon parti sera pris, vous lui enverrez l'ordre de venir vous rejoindre. Je désirerais avoir avec moi la division de la garde que commande le Général Lefebvre-Desnouettes, et je vous envoie les deux divisions du corps du Comte de Valmy pour la remplacer. Mais dans mon projet actuel, je préfère placer le Comte de Valmy de manière à le rappeler si j'en avais besoin, et ne point faire de fausses marches au Général Lefebvre-Desnouettes, puisqu'il est probable que je me déciderai ce soir à marcher sur Bruxelles avec la garde. Cependant, couvrez la division Lefebvre par les deux divisions de cavalrie d'Erlon et de Reille, afin de ménager la garde, et que, s'il y avait quelque échauffourée avec les Anglais, il est préférable que ce soit sur la ligne que sur la garde. J'ai adopté comme principe général pendant cette campagne, de diviser mon armée en deux ailes et une réserve. Votre aile sera composée des quatre divisions du 2e corps, de deux divisions de cavalerie légère, et de deux divisions du corps de Valmy. Cela ne doit pas être loin de 45 à 50 mille hommes.

Le Maréchal Grouchy aura à peu près la même force, et commandera l'aile droite. La garde formera la réserve, et je me porterai sur l'une ou l'autre aile, selon les circonstances. Le major-général donne les ordres les plus précis pour qu'il n'y ait aucune difficulté sur l'obéissance à vos ordres lorsque vous serez détaché, les commandants de corps devant prendre mes ordres directement quand je me trouve présent. Selon les circonstances, j'affaiblirai l'une ou l'autre aile en augmentant ma réserve. Vous sentez assez l'importance attachée à la prise de Bruxelles. Cela pourra d'ailleurs donner lieu à des accidents, car un mouvement aussi prompt et aussi brusque isolera l'armée Anglaise de Mons, Ostende, etc. Je désire que vos dispositions soient bien faites pour qu'au premier ordre, vos huit divisions puissent marcher rapidement, et sans obstacle sur Bruxelles.

N.

"Charleroi, le 16 Juin, 1815."

This letter, which was intended to convey to Ney a general notion of Napoleon's intentions, prescribed to him, at the same time, as a principle, that he was to consider his movements subordinate to those of the Emperor. The latter intimated his purpose of attacking the enemy at Fleurus, should he find him there, and of pushing on as far as Gembloux, where he would decide upon his plan of further operation, "perhaps at three o'clock in the afternoon, perhaps in the evening;" immediately *after* which Ney was to be ready to march upon Brussels, supported by Napoleon with the guards, it being the Emperor's desire to reach that capital in the morning. The idea of advancing upon Gembloux, and of capturing Brussels by a *coup de main*, which could only be effected by a vigorous repulse and signal defeat of the corps of Zieten, and by a successful turning and partial dispersion of those of Pirch and Thielemann, as also by the rapid march of a closely collected force under Ney, proves that Napoleon had either been insufficiently informed as to the general dispositions of his opponents, or had greatly miscalculated the degree of energy and promptitude required in his movements for the execution of such a design.

Very shortly afterwards, Ney received the official order of movement* to which Napoleon adverted in his letter as having been sent by Soult. It instructed him to put the 2nd and 1st corps d'armée, as also the 3rd corps of cavalry which had been placed at his disposal, in movement upon Quatre-Bras; to take up a position at that point; thence to push forward reconnaissances as far as possible on the roads to Brussels and Nivelles, "d'où probablement l'ennemi s'est retiré;" to establish, should he meet with no impediment, a division with some cavalry at Genappe; and to detach another division towards Marbais, in order to cover the interval between Sombref and Quatre-Bras. He was also to desire the general officers commanding the two corps d'armée to assemble their troops, collect the stragglers, and order up all the waggons belonging to the artillery and to the hospitals that might still be in the rear.

In pursuance of these instructions, Ney despatched orders of movement to Counts Reille and d'Erlon. The former was desired† to put the 2nd corps immediately on the march, for the purpose of taking up the following position:—the 5th division in rear of Genappe, upon the heights which command that town, the left appuied upon the high road; one or two battalions covering all the débouchés in advance on the Brussels road; the 9th division, following the movement of the 5th, to take up a position in second line on the heights to the right and left of the village of Bauterlet; the 6th and 7th divisions at Quatre-Bras. It was at the same time intimated to Reille that the three first divisions of d'Erlon's corps were to take post at Frasne; the right division to establish itself at Marbais along with Piré's division of light cavalry; that

* Appendix XVII. † Appendix XVIII.

the former was to cover his (Reille's) march towards Brussels, and both his flanks; that two divisions of Kellermann's corps were to take post at Frasne and Liberchies; and that the regiments of the guard under Generals Lefebvre-Desnouettes and Colbert were to remain in their actual position at Frasne.

This order had scarcely been sent off to Reille when Ney received from the latter a despatch, dated Gosselies, 16th June, a quarter past ten, a.m.* announcing his having just received from Girard (whose division was still at Heppignies,) a verbal report by one of his officers, to the effect that the enemy continued to occupy Fleurus with light cavalry; that hostile masses were observed advancing along the Namur road, the heads of their columns reaching as far as St. Amand; that these troops were gradually forming, and gaining ground; that as far as could be judged at that distance, the columns appeared to consist of six battalions each; and that movements of additional troops were perceived in their rear. Reille added that General Flahaut, in passing through Gosselies, had made him acquainted with the purport of the orders he was conveying to the Marshal, whereupon he had communicated with Count d'Erlon, in order that the latter might follow the movement which he (Reille) had intended to commence as soon as the divisions were under arms, but that in consequence of this report from Girard he would wait for the Marshal's further instructions, holding the troops ready to march.

About the same time, orders reached Ney from Napoleon,† desiring him to unite the corps under Reille and d'Erlon, and the cavalry-corps under Kellermann, which latter, it was stated, was on the point of commencing its march towards him; remarking also, that with these troops he ought to be able to destroy whatever forces the enemy might bring forward; that Grouchy was going to advance upon Sombref; and that the Emperor was setting off for Fleurus, to which place the Marshal was to address his reports.

In consequence of these instructions, Ney became anxious for the speedy concentration of his troops, and again sent orders to Reille and d'Erlon to move up their divisions. The information which he had obtained concerning the enemy in his front, and Girard's report of the assembling of troops in front of Fleurus, induced him to be cautious in his proceedings, and not to attempt any impetuous onset until he could have all his force more in hand, instead of the greater

* Appendix XIX. † Appendix XX.

portion of it being, as it then was, lengthened out in columns of route along the Charleroi high road; and, in this respect, his views were in perfect accordance with the last despatch which he had received from the Emperor, enjoining him in the first instance, to unite the two corps of Reille and d'Erlon. Hence, in debouching from his position at Frasne, about one o'clock, his advance was by no means vigorous: it was limited to a gradual pressing forward of the light troops, and amounted to little more than a reconnaissance.

About two o'clock, Ney, calculating that d'Erlon's corps could not be far in his rear, and hoping that the sound of his cannonade would hasten its march, resolved to attack the enemy's forces which intercepted his advance upon Quatre-Bras. Piré's light cavalry, constituting a strong line of skirmishers with well-disposed supports, covered the advance of the infantry-divisions of Bachelu and Foy, whilst that of Jerome followed as a reserve.

The force with which Ney thus entered the field, consisted of 3 divisions of Reille's corps, of Piré's light cavalry, of 4 batteries of foot, and 1 of horse, artillery: altogether—

16,189 infantry
1,729 cavalry
38 guns.

The Prince of Orange's force consisted of de Perponcher's division (with the exception of the 7th Dutch line-battalion); of 1 battery of foot, and 1 of horse, artillery: altogether—

6,832 infantry
16 guns.

It was not long after two o'clock when the Duke of Wellington returned to Quatre-Bras from the Prussian army. He observed attentively, with his glass, the movements of the French, and told the Prince of Orange he would be attacked directly. In a few minutes, the French advanced, and the Dutch-Belgian troops gradually retired; but the Prince, aware of the great advantages which the position of Quatre-Bras would derive from the possession of the farm of Gemioncourt, adjoining the Charleroi road, as also of the wood of Bossu on the right, and of the inclosures of Piermont on the left, flank, endeavoured, with that view, to make a stand, as soon as his centre reached the first-named point. The 5th battalion of Dutch militia which occupied this post, successfully withstood several attacks, during which Ney drew up his forces along the ridge which, intersecting the high road in the immediate (French) rear of Gemioncourt, extends on one side towards the wood of Bossu, and on the other in the direction of Piermont.

The vast preponderance of force on the part of the French, was now quite manifest to the Prince of Orange, who found himself compelled to withdraw the main body of his troops into the wood of Bossu, still retaining, however, the post of Gemioncourt. He gave an order to Captain Stievenaar's foot-battery to fall back and take up a flanking position near the wood. Here this officer, who possessed the highest merit, lost not a moment in re-opening his fire, but scarcely had he done so when he was mortally wounded. At the same moment one gun was damaged so as to become useless. The enemy rapidly advanced in such superior force as to compel the battery to resume its retreat. Captain Byleveld's horse-battery retired by the opposite side of Gemioncourt. One of its limbers blew up, severely wounding an officer, and occasioning the gun attached to it to be relinquished. The French pressed forward with their light troops; and part of Piré's light cavalry, seizing a favourable opportunity, gallantly charged the 27th Dutch light infantry, threw it into confusion, and made many prisoners. At this time a portion of Bachelu's infantry-division on the right advanced towards the village of Piermont.

It was about half-past two, or perhaps a quarter before three o'clock, when the Prince of Orange, whose situation had become extremely critical, as he directed his anxious looks towards that point of the horizon which was bounded by the elevated ground about Quatre-Bras, had the inexpressible satisfaction of recognizing, by their deep red masses, the arrival of British troops upon the field.

These comprised the 5th infantry-division, commanded by Lieut. General Sir Thomas Picton,* and consisting of the 8th British brigade, under Major General Sir James Kempt,† the 9th British brigade, under Major General Sir Denis Pack,‡ and of the 4th Hanoverian brigade,§ under Colonel

* These troops had been halted at Waterloo, both for the purpose of resting, and of awaiting further orders, so that they might be moved upon either Nivelles or Quatre-Bras, (the roads to which points unite at Mont St. Jean,) according as the Duke might think proper to direct, on his becoming acquainted with the exact state of affairs. They were soon joined by the Brunswick troops, which, after a short rest, proceeded on to Genappe, where they again halted. As the Duke, who was proceeding as quickly as possible to Quatre-Bras, (where he arrived between ten and eleven o'clock,) passed Picton, he ordered the 5th division to resume its march upon that point. Proceeding through Genappe, it passed the Brunswickers, who soon followed along the same road.

† Now General the Right Honorable Sir James Kempt, G.C.B.; G.C.H.

‡ Major General Sir Denis Pack, K.C.B., died on the 24th of July, 1823.

§ The 5th Hanoverian brigade, under Colonel Vincke, properly belonged to

Best.* The head of the column, leaving Quatre-Bras on its right, turned down the Namur road, along which the division was speedily drawn up; the British brigades in front, and the Hanoverian brigade in second, line. Captain Rettberg's† battery of Hanoverian foot artillery took post on the right, and Major Rogers's‡ battery of British foot artillery on the left, of the division. The 1st battalion of the 95th British regiment, commanded by Colonel Sir Andrew Barnard,§ was despatched in haste towards the village of Piermont, of which it was to endeavour to gain possession.

The French, on perceiving the arrival of the British infantry, opened a furious cannonade from their batteries, with a view to disturb its formation, while Ney, anxious to secure the vantage-ground of a field which he plainly foresaw, was likely to become the scene of a severe contest, renewed his attack upon Gemioncourt, still bravely defended by the 5th Dutch militia. Hereupon, Perponcher, having received an order to advance this battalion along the high road, immediately placed himself at its head, as did also the Prince of Orange himself, who rode up to it at the same moment. The manner in which His Royal Highness personally led on his national militia on this occasion, was distinguished by the most resolute and conspicuous gallantry. The battalion was exposed to a most destructive fire from some guns which the Prince seemed determined to capture. Placing himself frequently at its head, and waving his hat, he presented in his own person so brilliant and heroic an example, that for a considerable time the battalion maintained its ground most bravely against the far superior number of the enemy. It was composed, however, of young and inexperienced soldiers, who had not attained sufficient confidence to fight in anything like deployed order; and, therefore, when, a few minutes afterwards, a swarm of cavalry rushed upon it, it soon lost its compactness, and broke into a confused and hasty retreat; whilst the French infantry succeeded in obtaining possession of the farm, in which they firmly established themselves.

The Duke of Wellington, who now assumed the command, was so much alive to the importance of maintaining Gemion-

the 5th division, but in consequence of some mistake in the disposition of the troops, Colonel Best's brigade held the place of the former in this division both at Quatre-Bras and at Waterloo.

* Major General Best, K.C.H., (Lieut. Colonel in the British service,) died on the 5th of December, 1836.

† Now Captain von Rettberg (Colonel in the Hanoverian artillery).

‡ Colonel Rogers, C.B., died on the 9th of August, 1839.

§ Now Lieut. General Sir Andrew Barnard, G C.B.; G.C.H.

court and its inclosures, that he gave directions for its immediate occupation by a British regiment, but the one destined for this service having by some accident been otherwise disposed of, some delay occurred, and the 28th British regiment, commanded by Colonel Sir Charles Philip Belson,* was then marched down towards that point, under the guidance of Lieut. Colonel Gomm,† on the staff of the 5th division. As the battalion approached the farm, the latter was discovered to be already occupied by the French, whereupon it was withdrawn to its division.

The 3rd Dutch-Belgian light cavalry-brigade, under General van Merlen, had shortly before this reached the field, and now advanced to the support of the Dutch infantry retiring from Gemioncourt, but they were met and defeated by Piré's cavalry, and pursued along the high road nearly to Quatre-Bras, where they arrived in great disorder, a portion of them coming in contact with the Duke of Wellington himself, and carrying his Grace along with them to the rear of Quatre-Bras. The latter, however, succeeded in arresting their further flight, and in bringing them again to the front. The French cavalry did not, on this occasion, follow up the pursuit, evidently hesitating to approach very near to the allied infantry, the latter appearing well-formed, and fully prepared to receive them. The Dutch-Belgian infantry retreated to the wood of Bossu, abandoning four guns to the enemy,‡ who closely pursued them, and now began to penetrate into the wood.

Meanwhile, Bachelu, on the French right, threw a considerable force into Piermont, in sufficient time to secure its possession before the 1st battalion 95th British regiment had approached the village, and was pushing forward another strong body towards a small wood that lay still more in advance, on the opposite side of the Namur high road, the possession of which along with that of Piermont would have effectually cut off the direct communication between Quatre-Bras and Ligny. Here, for the first time in this

* Major General Sir Charles Philip Belson, K.C.B., died in November, 1830.

† Now Lieut. General Sir William Gomm, K.C.B.

‡ The Dutch-Belgian artillery succeeded in recovering their guns, mainly through the gallantry of Captain Gey, commanding the half horse-battery attached to van Merlen's brigade, (but of which only two guns had been brought into the field), who dashed forward with his horse-artillerymen, and being followed by others, drove off the enemy's cavalry, already busily occupied in removing the guns.

campaign, the troops of the two nations became engaged. The skirmishers who successfully checked the further advance of the French, and secured the wood, were the 1st battalion of the British 95th rifles,* whom the old campaigners of the French army, at least those who had served in the Peninsula, had so frequently found the foremost in the fight, and of whose peculiarly effective discipline and admirable training they had had ample experience.

The possession of Gemioncourt proved of the utmost importance to Ney's position, which now assumed a definite character, and, in a purely tactical point of view, offered great advantages. The southern portion of the wood of Bossu was occupied by his extreme left, while his extreme right was in full possession of Piermont; and these points were connected by a narrow valley extending along his whole front, bounded on either side by a hedge-row, and intersecting the Charleroi road close to Gemioncourt. The outer fence was strongly occupied by his light troops, ready to cover the formation and advance of his columns of attack, for the support of which by artillery, the heights constituting his main position in rear of Gemioncourt, offered every facility.

Scarcely had Picton's division taken up its ground, when the Duke of Brunswick's corps arrived upon the field. It was not complete; its artillery (under Major Mahn) and the 1st and 3rd light battalions (commanded by Major Holstein and Major Ebeling,) having been stationed in distant cantonments, had not yet joined. The 2nd light battalion (under Major Brandenstein) was immediately detached to the wood near Piermont on the left of the position, and of which the possession had already been secured by the 1st battalion of the British 95th regiment: the two rifle companies of the advanced-guard-battalion (under Major Rauschenplatt) were moved into the wood of Bossu; on the right of which some detachments of cavalry were posted for the purpose of observing the enemy's dispositions in that quarter. The remainder of these troops, by a movement to their left, when close upon Quatre-Bras, deployed in rear of, and in a direction parallel to, the Namur road, thus forming a reserve to Picton's division. The absent portion of the corps reached the field in the course of the action, as will hereafter be explained.

* Now the rifle brigade.

The Duke of Wellington's force in the field at this moment was as follows:—

		Infantry.	Cavalry.	Guns.
British	8th infantry brigade . . .	2,471		
	9th do. do. . . .	2,173		
K. G. Legion .	Battery of foot artillery . .			6
Hanoverians .	4th infantry brigade . . .	2,582		
	Battery of foot artillery . .			6
Brunswickers .	Advanced-guard-battalion .	672		
	2 battalions of the light infantry brigade	1,344		
	Line infantry brigade . .	2,016		
	Regiment of Hussars . . .		690	
	Squadron of lancers . . .		232	
Dutch-Belgians	2nd infantry brigade* . .	6,832		
	3rd cavalry brigade . . .		1,082	
	Half Battery of horse artillery			2†
	Battery of foot artillery . .			8
	Do. horse do. . .			8
		18,090	2,004	30

The following is the amount of force which Marshal Ney had actually in the field:—

	Infantry.	Cavalry.	Guns.
5th infantry division . . .	5,003		
6th do. do.	6,591		
9th do. do.	4,595		
3 divisional foot batteries . .			24
1 reserve foot battery . . .			8
2nd cavalry division . . .		1,729	
1 battery of horse artillery .			6
	16,189	1,729	38

The cannonade which had opened against the 5th British division as it took up its ground, continued with unabated vigour. The French light troops were now observed advancing from the inclosures that skirted the foot of their position, and to meet them the light companies of the different regiments of Picton's division were immediately thrown forward. On the French extreme right all further progress was checked by the gallant manner in which the 1st battalion 95th British regiment, though opposed by a much superior

* Deducting the 7th Dutch line battalion—See page 60—61.

† See note, page 71.

force, retained possession of the Namur road, which they lined with their skirmishers, while the wood in rear was occupied by the battalion-reserve and the 2nd Brunswick light battalion. On the French left, however, the incessant rattle of musketry in the wood of Bossu plainly indicated by its gradual approach in the direction of Quatre-Bras, that the Dutch-Belgian infantry were yielding to the fierce onset of the enemy in that quarter.

The protection which the French would derive from the possession of the eastern portion of this wood for the advance of their masses over the space between it and the Charleroi road, instantly became apparent to the British commander; in fact, the previous pursuit of the Dutch-Belgian cavalry along this road proved the expediency of establishing some restraint to such facility for a hostile advance in that direction; and he therefore requested the Duke of Brunswick to take up a position with a part of his corps between Quatre-Bras and Gemioncourt, so as to have his left resting upon the road, and his right communicating with Perponcher's division, part of which was deployed along the skirt of the wood. The Duke of Brunswick immediately ordered forward the guard-battalion, (under Major Pröstler,) the 1st line-battalion, (under Major Metzner,) and the two light companies of the advanced-guard-battalion, which he posted in close columns upon, and contiguous to, the road, on the ground indicated, and threw out a line of skirmishers connecting these columns with the two jäger-companies in the wood. As an immediate support to the infantry, he stationed the Brunswick hussars (under Major Cramm) and lancers (under Major Pott) in a hollow in their rear; while as a reserve to the whole, the 2nd and 3rd line-battalions (under Major Strombeck and Major Norrmann) were posted *en crémaillère* contiguously to the houses of Quatre-Bras, which important point they were to defend to the last extremity.

Whilst this disposition on the Anglo-allied right was in progress, two heavy French columns were observed descending into a valley below Gemioncourt, where, under cover of the strong line of skirmishers which had been for some time engaged with those of Picton's division, they were divided into separate smaller columns of attack. The cannonade from the French heights, which now sensibly quickened, was telling fearfully amidst the 5th British division; and a fresh impulse having been given to the enemy's light troops by the near approach of their own attacking columns, the British skirmishers, overpowered by numbers only, were seen darting, alternately and at short distances, to the rear, through the line of smoke that had been raised midway between the contending armies. At this critical moment, when the rapid progress of the French in the wood of Bossu, and their imposing advance against his left wing, threatened to compromise his disposal of the Brunswick troops on the right of the Charleroi road, Wellington, by one of thôse electric inspirations of his master-mind, with which he had been wont in former campaigns to frustrate the best-devised plans of his opponents, resolved not to await the attack, but to meet it. He instantly ordered the advance of Kempt's and Pack's brigades, with the exception of the 92nd regiment, which (under the command of Lieut. Colonel Cameron*) was to continue at its post on the Namur road, close to Quatre-Bras.

During the advance of these two brigades, which was made with admirable steadiness and in the best order, the skirmishers fell back upon their respective battalions, all of which now presented a clear front to the enemy. From the heads of Ney's columns, as well as from the thick lines of skirmishers by which they were connected, a severe and destructive fire was opened and maintained against the British line, along which the gallant Picton, the far-famed leader of the no less renowned "fighting division" of the British army in the Peninsular campaigns, was seen galloping from one regiment to another, encouraging his men, and inciting them by his presence and example. The troops significantly responded to his call by those loud and animating shouts with which British soldiers are wont to denote their eagerness to close with their enemies. The interval between the adverse lines was rapidly diminishing: the fire from the French suddenly began to slacken; hesitation, quickly succeeded by disorder, became apparent in their ranks; and then it was, that, animating each other with redoubled cheers, the British regiments were seen to lower their bristling bayonets, and driving everything before them, to pursue their opponents down to the outer fence of the valley, whence the French line had advanced in the full confidence of triumph.

Kempt's brigade, in consequence of the greater proximity of its original position to that of the enemy, was the first to overthrow the French infantry. The 79th Highlanders, on the left of the line, (commanded by Lieut. Colonel Douglas†)

* Lieut. Colonel John Cameron was killed in this battle.

† Now Lieut. General Sir Neil Douglas, K.C.B., K.C.H.

made a gallant charge down the hill, dashed through the first fence, and pursued their opponents, who had advanced in two battalion columns, not only across the valley, but through the second fence; and, carried on by their ardour, even ventured to ascend the enemy's position. By this time, however, their ranks were much broken: they were speedily recalled, and as they retraced their steps across the valley, they derived considerable support from the adjoining battalion in the line, the 32nd regiment, (commanded by Lieut. Colonel Maitland,*) which was keeping up from the first hedge a vigorous fire against the French, who now lined the second fence. The remaining regiments of both brigades had all in like manner charged down as far as the nearest hedge, whence they inflicted a severe loss upon their enemies as these precipitately retired, with their ranks completely broken and disordered on passing through the inclosure. On the right of the line, the 42nd Highlanders (commanded by Lieut. Colonel Sir Robert Macara,†) and 44th regiment (commanded by Lieut. Colonel Hamerton,‡) had advanced to within a very short distance of Gemioncourt, in which, and behind the hedges lining the valley, the French were seeking shelter.

During the progress of this contest on the Anglo-allied left of the Charleroi road, the Brunswick troops were not permitted to remain in quiet possession of their advanced position on the right, which indeed was well calculated to attract Ney's attention. A battery was immediately drawn up on the opposite height westward of Gemioncourt, from which, as also from the incessant fire maintained by the enemy's skirmishers posted at no great distance from the front of the line, a very destructive fire was maintained against the Brunswick troops. The regiment of hussars particularly suffered, standing in line, and frequently receiving an entire discharge from the battery. The Brunswickers were, for the most part, young and inexperienced soldiers—in every sense of the word, *raw* troops: and the numerous casualties which befel their ranks in this exposed situation might have produced a fatal influence upon their discipline, but for the noble example of their Prince, whose admirable tact and calm demeanour were most conspicuous on this trying occasion. Quietly smoking his pipe in front of his line, he gave out his orders as if at a mere field-day; and was only restrained from taking offence

* Colonel James Maitland died on the 6th September, 1826.

† Lieut. Colonel Sir Robert Macara, K.C.B., was killed in this battle.

‡ Now Lieut. General Hamerton, C.B.

at the representations made to him by some of his staff of the imminent danger to which he was exposing himself, from a consciousness of the kindly motives by which they were dictated.

At length, the continued havoc created amongst his devoted followers by the fire from the French heights, excited the impatience of the Duke himself for at least the means of retaliation; and as his own artillery was still upon the march from its cantonments, he sent to the Duke of Wellington a request to be furnished with some pieces of cannon. This was immediately acceded to, and four guns were moved forward and posted on the right of the Brunswick infantry; but they had scarcely fired a few rounds when the enemy's cannonade was redoubled; two of the guns were quickly disabled, and several of the horses attached to the limbers were killed. At the same time, two columns of French infantry were seen advancing in succession along the edge of the wood of Bossu, preceded by a battalion in line, and supported by some cavalry, of which description of force there also appeared a considerable mass advancing along the Charleroi road. As the French infantry rapidly approached the right of the line of the Brunswick skirmishers, the latter were forced to retire, as were also the Dutch-Belgian infantry that lined the wood at this part of the field. The Duke of Brunswick, perceiving that the bend of the wood in rear of his regiment of hussars was likely to impede the freedom of its movements, immediately ordered the latter to proceed to the opposite side of the Charleroi road, and retire towards Quatre-Bras, there to remain in readiness to act according to circumstances. Then, placing himself at the head of his lancers, he gallantly charged the advancing infantry, which, however, received them with so much steadiness and good order, and opened upon them so destructive a fire, that the attack completely failed, and the regiment withdrew to Quatre-Bras. Finding the strength of the enemy's forces to be so overpowering, the Duke now ordered the infantry posted contiguously to the Charleroi road, also to retire upon the main position. The 1st line-battalion moved hastily along the road, while the guard-battalion, with which the Duke himself was at this time present, retired across the fields eastward of the isolated house upon the Charleroi road, towards the Allied line, posted upon the road to Namur. Major Pröstler, who commanded the guard-battalion, rendered himself conspicuous by his exertions to execute this movement in as orderly a manner as possible, but the eager and close pursuit by the French light troops, now emboldened by success, a shower of round shot upon the column, and the approach of the enemy's cavalry, spread such a panic among these young troops that they fled in confusion, some through Quatre-Bras, and others through the Anglo-allied line on the left of that point; and it was in the moment of attempting to rally his soldiers, not far from the little garden of the house before mentioned, that the Duke of Brunswick was struck from his horse by a shot which terminated the career of this gallant Prince.*

In the mean time the Brunswick hussars were ordered forward to cover the retreat of the infantry, and repel the advance of the French cavalry, which was now seen in rapid motion along the Charleroi road, as if incited and emboldened by the loud shouts of triumph sent forth by their light troops in front. The hussars, whose order while advancing, was quickly disturbed by a straggling fire from the French infantry, to which their right flank became exposed, failed in producing the slightest check upon the cavalry, and were soon seen wheeling about and in full flight, closely pursued by their opponents.

To the 42nd Highlanders and 44th British regiment, which were posted on a reverse slope, and in line, close upon the left of the above road, the advance of French cavalry was so sudden and unexpected, the more so as the Brunswickers had just moved on to the front, that as both these bodies whirled past them to the rear, in such close proximity to each other, they were, for the moment, considered to consist of one mass of Allied cavalry. Some of the old soldiers of both regiments were not so easily satisfied on this point, and immediately opened a partial fire obliquely upon the French lancers, which, however, Sir Denis Pack and their own officers endeavoured as much as possible to restrain; but no

* No officer of his staff was with him at the moment except Major Wachholtz, who immediately caused him to be removed across the road to the rear of the line by some men of the guard-battalion. Here, several officers searched in vain for a surgeon; not one could be found: while the deadly paleness of his countenance and his half-closed eyes betokened the worst. Once he looked up, recognised his attendants, and asked for Colonel Olfermann, the next in command. He then requested some water, which, however, could not be procured at the moment. As the proximity of the fight increased, fears were entertained of his falling into the hands of the enemy in the event of a retreat, and he was therefore carried still further to the rear, along the Charleroi road, as far as the group of houses called La Baraque. Here they found the staff-surgeon of the corps, Dr. Pockels, who, having examined the wound, declared the Prince to have breathed his last. The fatal shot appeared to have been a musket-ball which entered his right wrist and passed diagonally through his body. Thus fell in the battle-field—the bed of glory in which reposed so many of his illustrious house—Frederick William, Duke of Brunswick, in the forty-fourth year of his age.

sooner had the latter succeeded in causing a cessation of the fire, than the lancers, which were the rearmost of the cavalry, wheeled sharply round, and advanced in admirable order directly upon the rear of the two British regiments. The 42nd Highlanders having, from their position, been the first to recognise them as a part of the enemy's forces, rapidly formed square; but just as the two flank companies were running in to form the rear face, the lancers had reached the regiment, when a considerable portion of their leading division penetrated the square, carrying along with them, by the impetus of their charge, several men of those two companies, and creating a momentary confusion. The long-tried discipline and steadiness of the Highlanders, however, did not forsake them at this most critical juncture: these lancers, instead of effecting the destruction of the square, were themselves fairly hemmed into it, and either bayoneted or taken prisoners, whilst the endangered face, restored as if by magic, successfully repelled all further attempts on the part of the French to complete their expected triumph. Their commanding officer, Lieut. Colonel Sir Robert Macara, was killed on this occasion, a lance having pierced through his chin until it reached the brain; and within the brief space of a few minutes, the command of the regiment devolved upon three other officers in succession: Lieut. Colonel Dick,* who was severely wounded, Brevet Major Davidson, who was mortally wounded, and Brevet Major Campbell,† who commanded it during the remainder of the campaign.

If this cavalry-attack had fallen so unexpectedly upon the 42nd Highlanders, still less had it been anticipated by the 44th regiment. Lieut. Colonel Hamerton, perceiving that the lancers were rapidly advancing against his rear, and that any attempt to form square would be attended with imminent danger, instantly decided upon receiving them in line. The low thundering sound of their approach was heard by his men before a conviction they were French flashed across the minds of any but the *old* soldiers who had previously fired at them as they passed their flank. Hamerton's words of command were, "Rear rank, right about face!"—"Make ready!"—(a short pause to admit of the still nearer approach of the cavalry,)—"Present!"—"Fire!" The effect produced by this volley was astonishing. The men, aware of their perilous position, doubtless took a most deliberate aim at their opponents, who were thrown into great confusion.

* Major General Sir Robert Dick, K.C.B., K.C.H., was killed at the battle of Sobraon, on the 10th February, 1846.

† Colonel John Campbell, C.B., died on the 31st March, 1841.

Some few daring fellows made a dash at the centre of the battalion, hoping to capture the colours, in their apparently exposed situation; but the attempt, though gallantly made, was as gallantly defeated. The lancers now commenced a flight towards the French position by the flanks of the 44th. As they rushed past the left flank, the officer commanding the light company, who had very judiciously restrained his men from joining in the volley given to the rear, opened upon them a scattering fire; and no sooner did the lancers appear in the proper front of the regiment, when the front rank began in its turn to contribute to their overthrow and destruction,

Never, perhaps, did British infantry display its characteristic coolness and steadiness more eminently than on this trying occasion. To have stood in a thin two-deep line, awaiting, and prepared to receive, the onset of hostile cavalry, would have been looked upon at least as a most hazardous experiment; but, with its rear so suddenly menaced, and its flanks unsupported, to have instantly faced only one rank about, to have stood as if rooted to the ground, to have repulsed its assailants with so steady and well-directed a fire that numbers of them were destroyed—this was a feat of arms which the oldest or best-disciplined corps in the world might have in vain hoped to accomplish; yet most successfully and completely was this achieved by the gallant 2nd battalion of the 44th British regiment, under its brave commander, Lieut. Colonel Hamerton.

In this attack occurred one of these incidents which, in daring, equal any of the feats of ancient chivalry, which make the wildest fables of the deeds of the knights of old appear almost possible; which cause the bearing of an individual to stand out, as it were, in relief amidst the operations of the masses; and which, by their characteristic recklessness, almost invariably insure at least a partial success. A French lancer, gallantly charged at the colours, and severely wounded Ensign Christie,* who carried one of them, by a thrust of his lance, which, entering the left eye, penetrated to the lower jaw. The Frenchman then endeavoured to seize the standard, but the brave Christie, notwithstanding the agony of his wound, with a presence of mind almost unequalled, flung

* I have failed in my endeavours to trace the subsequent career of this officer. He was a lieutenant on half-pay of the 44th regiment, on the 24th of June, 1827; but in consequence of his having ceased to receive or apply for any further issue of half-pay during more than four years from that date, he was struck off the half-pay list, in conformity with the usual practice in like cases.

himself upon it—not to save himself, but to preserve the honour of his regiment. As the colour fluttered in its fall, the Frenchman tore off a portion of the silk with the point of his lance; but he was not permitted to bear the fragment beyond the ranks. Both shot and bayoneted by the nearest of the soldiers of the 44th, he was borne to the earth, paying with the sacrifice of his life for his display of unavailing bravery.*

In the mean time the leading portion of Piré's light cavalry, from which the lancers that attacked the 42nd and 44th British regiments had been detached, as already described, continued its advance along the high road towards Quatre-Bras, driving in the Brunswick hussars, who were now galloping confusedly upon the 92nd Highlanders then lining the ditch of the Namur high road contiguous to Quatre-Bras. Pursued by the chasseurs à cheval, and finding no opening for their passage, they made for the right flank of the regiment:† and, as they were flying past, the grenadier company was wheeled back upon the road so as to oppose a front at that point to the flank of the pursuing cavalry, upon which the Highlanders now poured a most destructive volley. The shock thus occasioned to the French cavalry was immediately perceptible; but though thrown into confusion, the main body soon re-formed, and retired with much steadiness and regularity. The front of the column, however, impelled by the furious ardour with which it had advanced, or, perhaps, imagining itself still followed and supported by the main body, dashed in amongst the houses of Quatre-Bras, and even advanced to some distance beyond them, cutting down several stragglers whom they found there, principally belonging to the routed Brunswick infantry, as also groups of wounded. Many of them rushed through the large opening into the farm yard of Quatre-Bras, which was situated immediately in rear of the right of the 92nd. A few daring fellows finding they had proceeded too far to be able to retire by the same direction in which they had advanced, wheeled round

* The part of the colour thus torn off by the French lancer, was in the possession of the late Major General O'Malley, C.B. then Lieut. Colonel of the 44th regiment, to the command of which he succeeded, on Lieut. Colonel Hamerton being wounded at a later period of the battle. The colours themselves are in the safe keeping of the latter officer, whose decision, firmness, and bravery, on this occasion, well entitle him to the guardianship of these sacred and glorious relics of his gallant corps.

† The Duke, on this occasion, was nearly overtaken by the French cavalry; and being obliged to gallop towards the 92nd Highlanders, he called out to the nearest men to lie down in the ditch, when he fairly leaped over them.

suddenly at the point where the high roads intersect each other, and galloped right through the grenadier-company of the Highlanders, shouting, and brandishing their swords, and receiving a fire from some of the rear rank of the regiment as they dashed along the road. None of them escaped: one, an officer of the chasseurs à cheval, had already reached the spot where the Duke of Wellington was at that moment stationed in rear of the Highlanders. Some of the men immediately turned round and fired: his horse was killed, and at the same moment a musket-ball passed through each foot of the gallant young officer.* Those of the French chasseurs who had entered the farm-yard, finding no other outlet, now began to gallop back, in small parties of two or three at a time, but few escaped the deadly fire of the Highlanders.

About this time Kellermann reached the field, with the 11th heavy cavalry-division under Lieut. General L'Heritier. This augmented Ney's forces to the following amount:

	Infantry.	Cavalry.	Guns.
Force already in the field . .	16,189	1,865	38
11th cavalry division		1,743	
1 battery of horse artillery . .			6
	16,189	3,608	44

The French infantry upon the extreme left had by this time possessed themselves of the greater portion of the wood of Bossu, from the Allied rear of which numerous groups of wounded and runaways were now seen to emerge; indeed, it soon became evident that no dependance could be placed on the continued occupation of the wood by the Dutch-Belgian forces, and that the whole brunt of the battle would have to be borne by the British, Hanoverian, and Brunswick forces. Upon the extreme French right, all attempts to turn the opposite flank of the Allies, were successfully checked by the steadiness and gallantry of the 95th British regiment, supported by the 2nd Brunswick light battalion.

* It may here be mentioned as one of the numerous instances of the extraordinary mutation of circumstances under which, among civilized nations, military men are frequently thrown together, that an officer of the 92nd Highlanders, present at this scene, (Lieutenant Winchester,* who was severely wounded at Waterloo,) was afterwards billeted along with this French officer (Monsieur Bourgoine) in the same house, for six months at Brussels, at the expiration of which period, he proceeded with him to Paris, where he received great kindness and attention from him and his family.

* Lieut. Colonel Winchester, K.H. died on the 23rd July, 1846.

Ney, although he had failed in his first general attack upon the Anglo-allied line, had fully ascertained that the raw troops of which the Dutch-Belgian and Brunswick cavalry in the field were composed, were totally incapable of competing with his own veteran warriors of that arm, and he therefore determined to take advantage of Kellermann's arrival for the execution of a vigorous cavalry attack. Retaining General Piquet's brigade in reserve, he combined, for this purpose, General Guyton's brigade, consisting of the 8th and 11th cuirassiers, with Piré's light-cavalry division; and also taking advantage of his greatly superior artillery-force, he caused the attack to be preceded and covered by a tremendous cannonade, occasioning great havoc in the ranks of the Anglo-allied infantry, the range for which the French gunners had by this time ascertained with fearful precision. It was not long before the British battalions most in advance were warned of the approach of hostile cavalry by the running in of their skirmishers; and scarcely had they formed their squares when the batteries respectively opposed to them having ceased their fire, a rushing sound was heard through the tall corn, which, gradually bending, disclosed to their view the heads of the attacking columns; and now began a conflict wherein the cool and daring intrepidity with which British infantry are accustomed to defy the assaults of cavalry, was exemplified in a manner that will ever reflect honour and glory upon the regiments to whose lot it fell, on this memorable field, to assert and maintain their country's prowess. A rolling fire from the muskets of the 42nd Highlanders and 44th British regiment, given at a moment when the enemy's horsemen were almost close upon their bayonets, though most destructive in its effects upon their own immediate opponents, checked not the ardour and impetuosity of the general attack. These two diminutive squares, now completely surrounded by the French cavalry, seemed destined to become a sacrifice to the fury with which a rapid succession of attacks was made upon them; no sooner was one squadron hurled back in confusion, than another rushed impetuously forward upon the same face of a square, to experience a similar fate; and sometimes different faces were charged simultaneously. A strong body of cuirassiers now passed the right flank of the two regiments, along the high road, with an evident intention of making another attempt upon Quatre-Bras.

Picton, who had been watching with intense anxiety the contest maintained by the 42nd and 44th British regiments in their exposed situation, and who had become convinced of the utter hopelessness of obtaining any efficient support from the Allied cavalry then in the field, could no longer restrain his impatience to fly to the rescue of the devoted squares; and, as a substitute for cavalry, he decided upon immediately assailing that of the enemy with his own oft-tried infantry. With this view, he united the Royals (under Lieut. Colonel Colin Campbell*) and the 28th regiment, both of which corps were at that moment standing in column at quarter distance. Led on by both Picton and Kempt, the united column, with loud shouts, boldly advanced into the midst of the enemy's cavalry; the whole extent of ground along its front appeared to swarm with lancers, chasseurs à cheval, and cuirassiers, a considerable portion of whom were now seen rapidly forming for an attack upon the column; but Picton constantly on the alert, and at the same time desirous of arriving at such a distance as would enable him to present an efficient flank fire in support of the 44th regiment, continued advancing until the last moment, when he suddenly formed it into square. The repeated and furious charges which ensued, were invariably repulsed by the Royals and the 28th, with the utmost steadiness and consummate bravery; and although the lancers individually dashed forward and frequently wounded the men in the ranks, yet all endeavours to effect an opening, of which the succeeding squadron of attack might take advantage, completely failed. The ground on which the square stood was such that the surrounding remarkably tall rye concealed it in a great measure, in the first attacks, from the view of the French cavalry until the latter came quite close upon it; but to remedy this inconvenience, and to preserve the impetus of their charge, the lancers had frequently recourse to sending forward a daring individual to plant a lance in the earth at a very short distance from the bayonets, and they then charged upon the lance-flag as a mark of direction.

The advance of the Royals and the 28th had been almost immediately followed, under the same form, by that of the 32nd regiment, which, having reached a convenient distance, halted, and formed square so as to support, at the same time, by a flank fire, the Royals and 28th, and the square of the 79th Highlanders, which latter regiment constituted a connecting link with the 95th British regiment upon the extreme left.

Upon the advance of the regiments belonging to Kempt's

* Lieut. Colonel Colin Campbell, C.B., died in March, 1833.

and Pack's British brigades, Best's Hanoverian brigade occupied the Namur road in their rear, along which the landwehr-battalions Lüneburg, Osterode, and Münden, (respectively commanded by Lieut. Colonel Ramdohr, Major Reden, and Major Schmid,) were deployed, while the landwehr-battalion Verden, (under Major Decken,) also in line, was posted somewhat in advance.

In this position, Picton's division sustained repeated assaults of the French cavalry, which attacked the squares simultaneously, and in every direction: as a portion rushed upon one square, other squadrons passed on to assail the next; some parties, taking advantage of sinuosities of the ground, awaited, like birds of prey, the favourable moment for pouncing upon their victims; no sooner was one attacking squadron driven back and dispersed by a stream of musketry from the face of a square, than a fresh party would rush from its cover upon the same ranks, in the vain hope that the means of breaking its onset had been expended; but a reserved fire never failed to bring down upon it a similar fate. Viewed from a little distance, the British squares could at times be scarcely discerned amidst the surrounding cavalry; and as the latter was frequently observed flying back from sudden discharges of musketry, a spectator might easily have imagined the squares to be so many immense bombs, with every explosion scattering death and confusion among the masses that rushed so daringly into their fatal vicinity.

The French cavalry, by its repeated failures to make any impression on the British infantry by the manner in which it had passed through and through the intervals between the squares, and in which the charging squadrons when dispersed had got intermingled, was now in great disorder—lancers, chasseurs, and cuirassiers, were mixed together and crossing one another in every direction, seeking out their respective corps. To retire and re-form had therefore become with them an absolutely necessary measure; but this afforded no respite to the devoted squares, against which the batteries upon the French heights now played with terrific effect.

During the French attack of the British squares on the eastern side of the Charleroi road, a considerable body of cuirassiers advanced along the latter, with the evident design of making another attack upon the Anglo-allied centre at Quatre-Bras. The Belgian cavalry, which was again ordered forward, endeavoured to check this movement, but with no better effect than that which attended its former attempt; in fact, it retired sooner, charged and pursued by the cuirassiers, against whom a rapid fire was now opened from the 92nd Highlanders, who still lined the ditch of the Namur road, close to Quatre-Bras, a fire so destructive in its effects that the steel-clad warriors were completely staggered, and the order of their advance so thoroughly shaken, that they were compelled to retire in confusion.

In addition to the furious cannonade to which they were subjected, the foremost of Picton's British battalions, more especially the 42nd and 44th regiments, were exposed to a rapid and destructive fire, which, as soon as the enemy's cavalry had been withdrawn, was opened upon them by the French troops advancing from the inclosures of Gemioncourt. To check this, skirmishers were thrown forward, but from the want of sufficient ammunition, they could reply but very feebly to the fire of their opponents, who, not suffering the same disadvantage, were picking them off as fast as they could load. Their line soon became fearfully thinned, and finally their ammunition was totally exhausted, to which circumstance the officer on whom the command of them had devolved (Lieutenant Riddock,* 44th regiment) called the attention of Sir Denis Pack, who ordered him to close his men to their centre and to join his own regiment. He had just executed the first part of the order, when the French cavalry having rallied and re-formed, renewed their attacks upon the British squares. Squadrons of cuirassiers and lancers, in their onward course, swept past Lieutenant Riddock and his party, while others intercepted his direct line of retreat. He instantly formed four deep, and with his front rank at the charge, he made good his way through the enemy's cavalry, as far as the south face of the square formed by the 44th regiment; which, however, was so hotly pressed at the moment as to be unable to receive him, whereupon he ordered his men to lie down close to their bayonets, until a favourable opportunity should offer for their admission within the square.

A repetition of the former scene on this part of the field now took place, and the attacks, which were conducted with similar impetuosity, were met by a resistance equally undaunted. As if to overawe the square formed by the Royals and 28th British regiments, the French cavalry now made a simultaneous attack upon three of its faces, and these consisted mainly of the latter corps. Picton, who was again in the square, upon perceiving the approach of this apparently

* Lieutenant Alexander Riddock, on half-pay of the 44th regiment, died in February 1845.

overwhelming force, suddenly and emphatically exclaimed, "28th! remember Egypt!" They answered him with a loud cheer, and reserving their fire until the cavalry had approached within a few yards of the square, their muskets were coolly and deliberately levelled at their assailants, who in the next moment were hurled back in wild disorder, horses and riders tumbling over one another, and creating indescribable confusion. Similar in their results were all the attacks, made upon the other British squares, which maintained their ground with the same unshaken steadiness and gallantry. These repeated charges by the French cavalry, though conducted by veteran soldiers, with admirable order and compactness, and though affording innumerable instances of individual gallantry and daring, were certainly not carried on in a manner calculated to ensure success over infantry distinguished by such high training and such undaunted bravery as the British proved themselves to possess on this memorable occasion. There was no indication of a systematic attack upon any particular point by a rapid succession of charging squadrons—no *forlorn-hope-like* rush upon the opposing bayonets by the survivors of a discharge of musketry levelled at a leading squadron, and that rush followed up with lightning-like rapidity by the next squadron, which, in spite of the intervening space encumbered with the bodies of men and horses overthrown in the first charge, would thus obtain the greatest chance of effecting by its own weight and compact order, a breach in the square at the point originally selected for the assault. No such system of attack was attempted; but, on the contrary, it almost invariably happened that the leading squadron no sooner received the fire from the point attacked, than it either opened out from the centre to the right and left, and retired, or, it diverged altogether to one flank, leaving the succeeding divisions, in both cases, to observe the same movement; and, in this manner, the whole of the attacking force exposed itself to a far more extended range of fire and consequent loss, than if it had pursued the more daring, and at the same time, more decisive, mode of attack just described.

Whilst a considerable portion of the French cavalry was thus fruitlessly assailing the British squares, a body of lancers, which had advanced considerably in the rear of those squares, made a sudden and unexpected charge upon the Hanoverian landwehr-battalion Verden, which was then, as previously explained, deployed a short distance in front of the Namur road: it was completely successful, and the greater part of the battalion was cut down by the lancers, who, emboldened by this triumph, were preparing to cross the Namur road, where a well-directed fire opened upon them by the landwehr-battalions Lüneburg and Osterode, lying concealed in the ditch by which it was lined, threw them into disorder, and forced them to a precipitate retreat.

The whole of the French cavalry was now withdrawn for the purpose of re-forming its broken and disordered ranks, leaving the Anglo-allied infantry to be again assailed by a vigorous cannonade from the heights above Gemioncourt. The only movement on the part of the Anglo-allied forces was the advance of the Brunswick guard-battalion and 2nd line-battalion in front of Quatre-Bras, by the right of the Charleroi road, as a precautionary measure against any flank attack that might be attempted from the wood of Bossu upon the advanced battalions of Picton's right.

It was long past five o'clock. The French infantry in the wood of Bossu was continually making progress towards the Namur road, across which increased numbers of the Dutch-Belgian troops, to whom the defence of the wood had been entrusted, were seen hastily retiring. In Piermont, the French light troops had been reinforced, and they were now evidently preparing for a more vigorous attack upon the extreme left of Wellington's forces; whilst certain movements in the vicinity of Gemioncourt gave intimation of an intended renewal of the attack upon Quatre-Bras. All prospect of the Anglo-allied cavalry encountering Ney's veteran dragoons with any chance of success had entirely vanished; whilst, on the other hand, the latter were on the point of being reinforced by the arrival of another cavalry-division. Pack's brigade had expended nearly the whole of its ammunition; its exposed position, and the continued cavalry-charges in its rear having precluded the transmission of the necessary supply. The Brunswickers had been greatly discouraged by the death of their gallant Prince; and the losses sustained by all the troops engaged had already been truly frightful. It was at this very moment, when Wellington's situation had become so extremely critical, that two infantry-brigades of the 3rd division, under Lieut. General Sir Charles Alten, most opportunely reached the field of action by the Nivelles road. They were the 5th British brigade, commanded by Major General Sir Colin Halkett,* and the 1st Hanoverian brigade, under Major General Count Kielmansegge;† and

* Now General Sir Colin Halkett, K.C.B.; G.C.H,

† Now General Count Kielmansegge, G.C.H.

were accompanied by Major Lloyd's* battery of British foot artillery, and by Captain Cleeves's† battery of Hanoverian foot artillery.‡

By the arrival of these troops Wellington's force was augmented as follows:—

		Infantry.	Cavalry.	Guns.
British	Force already in the field	18,090	2,004	30
	5th infantry brigade	2,254		
	Battery of foot artillery			6
King's German Legion	Do. do. do.			6
Hanoverians	1st infantry brigade	3,189		
Dutch-Belgians	7th Dutch line battalion§	731		
		24,234	2,004	42

About the same time, Ney's troops were reinforced by the remaining division of Kellermann's corps of heavy cavalry, so that his whole force was constituted as follows:—

	Infantry.	Cavalry.	Guns.
Force already in the field	16,189	3,472	44
12th cavalry-division		1,502	
1 battery of horse artillery			6
	16,189	4,974	50

Ney, on perceiving the arrival of this reinforcement to the Anglo-allied toops, despatched a peremptory order to d'Erlon to hasten to his support and join him without a moment's delay; and having well calculated the advantages he still retained, he resolved upon a bold and vigorous effort to secure the victory. The greater portion of the wood of Bossu was now in his possession; and this circumstance appeared to him to present the means of establishing himself at Quatre-Bras, and of thus enabling him effectually to turn Wellington's right flank, and cut off his line of retreat upon Brussels. With this view he had already greatly reinforced his infantry in the wood through which he had even ordered the advance of two

* Major Lloyd was mortally wounded at the battle of Waterloo.

† Lieut. Colonel Cleeves, K.H. of the Hanoverian artillery, died on the 8th of June, 1830.

‡ The remainder of this division, consisting of the 2nd brigade of the King's German legion, under Colonel Ompteda, had been detached by Alten when on the march from Soignies, and placed in observation on the Mons road, near the village of Arquennes; but it rejoined the division at Quatre-Bras during the night.

§ As soon as Alten's division arrived at Nivelles, the 7th Dutch line battalion quitted that town to join its division at Quatre-Bras.—See page 60-61.

batteries, in a direction parallel to, and within a very short distance of, its eastern boundary, so that they might be prepared to act upon the plain, as soon as circumstances rendered such a proceeding advisable or expedient. He now also threw forward additional light troops to strengthen his extreme right in the vicinity of Piermont; whilst his cavalry, so vastly superior, both in numbers and in efficiency, to that which the British Commander had brought into the field, constituted his main central force, and compensated in a great measure for the deficiency created in this point of his line by the drawing off of the infantry to the flanks.

The two French batteries above alluded to as having advanced along the interior of the wood of Bossu, suddenly opened a destructive fire from the edge of the latter upon the Brunswick troops posted on the right of the Charleroi road, just as Lloyd's battery arrived at Quatre-Bras. The Duke instantly ordered the advance of this battery into the open space between the Charleroi road and the wood, for the purpose of silencing the French guns; but before the British artillerymen could unlimber, several horses of the battery were killed, wheels were disabled, and, from the proximity of the enemy's guns, some of the gunners were literally cut in two by the round shot with which they were so closely assailed. Nevertheless, the battery succeeded, not only in silencing its opponents, but also in forcing back into the wood a French column of infantry, which, advancing directly towards the Brussels road, had endeavoured to turn its right flank: after which brilliant services, Lloyd, perceiving no adequate support, judged it prudent, in the then crippled state of his battery, to retire to his former post, abandoning two guns for which he had not a sufficient number of horses remaining, and which consequently could not be recovered until the termination of the action.

Halkett's brigade, shortly after passing Quatre-Bras, was ordered to bring up its left shoulders; and, entering the rye fields in front of the Namur road, it proceeded some little distance in advance, and halted. Kielmansegge's brigade continued its march along the Namur road, and received orders to strengthen the extreme left, as also to support, and, where necessary, to relieve the exhausted British battalions, which had so bravely withstood the fiercest onsets of a most daring and well-organised cavalry, and had so unflinchingly endured the incessant cannonade maintained against them by the well-served batteries on the French heights.

It was during the advance of the 3rd British division to

take up its ground—Halkett proceeding directly to the front, and Kielmansegge moving along the Namur road to the left—and under cover of the heavy cannonade which was maintained against the Allied line at this time, that again a column of French infantry advanced from out of the wood, towards the Brussels road, and entering the latter by the isolated house southward of Quatre-Bras, established itself in and about that building and its inclosures. Shortly afterwards another column advanced in support of the former one, which then emerged from its cover, and began to ascend that part of the Anglo-allied position occupied by the 92nd Highlanders. On perceiving this, Major General Barnes,* Adjutant General to the British forces, who had just ridden up to the right of the regiment, placed himself very conspicuously at the head of the Highlanders, waving his hat, and exclaiming, "92nd, follow me!" In an instant the latter sprang out of the ditch in which they had hitherto been posted, and with great gallantry and steadiness charged down the slope. The French infantry hastily fell back, until having gained the partial shelter afforded them by the isolated house and its inclosures, they opened a most destructive fire upon the Highlanders, who nevertheless slackened not their pace, but drove the French out of their cover. Their commanding officer, Colonel Cameron, here received his death wound, and having lost the power of managing his horse, the latter carried him at its utmost speed along the road until he reached Quatre-Bras, where his servant was standing with his led horse, when the animal, suddenly stopping, pitched the unfortunate officer on his head. The supporting column, however, securing the garden opposite to the house and on the right of the road, seemed resolved to make a stand against the further advance of the Highlanders; but the latter, by a judicious disposition of their force in three divisions—one towards each flank of the garden, and the other directly to the gate in front—and again uniting as soon as these points were secured, once more rushed upon their foes with the bayonet, displaying, under a terrific fire, the most undaunted bravery. As soon as the French turned their backs, the 92nd poured upon them a volley which proved most destructive, and continued their advance, pursuing the enemy along the edge of the wood, into which they finally retired upon perceiving a disposition on the part of the French cavalry to charge, and finding themselves exposed to a heavy cannonade which was rapidly thinning their ranks to a fearful

* Lieut. General Sir Edward Barnes, G.C.B., died on the 19th of March, 1838.

extent. Subsequently, in consequence of their very severe loss, they were withdrawn through the wood to Quatre-Bras.

Again the French skirmishers were creeping up the slope from the Gemioncourt inclosures, and Pack, who had united the remains of the 42nd and 44th regiments into one battalion, made the best show of resistance in his power to their teazing *tiraillade;* but being aware how very small a quantity of ammunition remained in his men's pouches, his anxiety on this point became extreme, the more so as he had good reasons for apprehending fresh attacks of cavalry. His advanced position in the immediate proximity of the formation of the enemy's columns of attack, naturally kept him on the look-out for effective British support; and on observing the head of Halkett's brigade, as the latter was advancing from Quatre-Bras, he instantly despatched an aide-de-camp to that general, with a message, that his own brigade had expended nearly the whole of its ammunition, and that if he did not offer him a support, he would be under the necessity of almost immediately abandoning his position. Halkett at once acceded to the proposal by sending forward the 69th British regiment, and desiring its commanding officer, Colonel Morice* to obey any orders he might receive from General Pack.

In pursuance of orders received from the Duke, Halkett moved the remainder of his brigade into the space between the wood of Bossu and the Charleroi road, fronting the French left wing. Here he found the Brunswick infantry retiring with precipitation: he immediately put himself in communication with their commanding officer, Colonel Olfermann, and by aid of the support which his brigade presented to their view, he succeeded in bringing them up under cover, in the ditch which, traversing the space between the wood and the high road, ran nearly parallel with the enemy's line. Leaving his brigade in the position he had taken up, in support of the Brunswickers and of Pack's brigade, and pending the arrival of further instructions from the Duke, Halkett galloped to the front, nearly beyond the farm of Gemioncourt, for the purpose of ascertaining, if possible, the disposition and intentions of the enemy. He was not kept long in suspense, Ney's arrangements for another general attack having been concluded; and, observing the cavalry destined to advance against the Allies on both sides of the Charleroi road in motion, he turned round his horse and hastened to dispose his brigade in such a manner as to render it fully prepared to

* Colonel Morice was killed at the battle of Waterloo.

brave the coming storm. On his way, he sent an intimation to Pack of his discovery, and orders to the 69th regiment to prepare forthwith to receive cavalry.

A sudden and heavy cannonade had already opened from the French heights—a sure prelude to the attack which was about to take place—and the 69th regiment was in the act of forming square, when the Prince of Orange rode up to it and asked what it was doing. Colonel Morice explained that he was forming square in pursuance of the instructions he had received; upon which His Royal Highness, remarking that he did not think there was any chance of the cavalry coming on, ordered him to re-form column, and to deploy into line. During this last movement a strong body of French cuirassiers, taking advantage of the surrounding high corn, and of the circumstance of the regiment lying in a hollow, approached unperceived quite close to the spot, and rushing suddenly and impetuously upon a flank, succeeded in completely rolling up the regiment, riding along and over the unfortunate men, of whom great numbers were cut down, and in the midst of the confusion thus created, captured and carried off one of the colours; in defence of which Major Lindsay,* Lieutenant Pigot,† and Volunteer Clarke,‡ highly distinguished themselves, and were desperately wounded. Some officers and men took shelter in the square formed by the 42nd and 44th regiments; the mounted officers gained the other side of the road, pursued by about twenty of the enemy, and escaped by riding through one of the Hanoverian battalions lining the Namur road.

The 30th regiment, which had also been deployed into line by the orders of the Prince of Orange, most fortunately discovered, in sufficient time, the approach of cavalry, (notwithstanding the extraordinary height of the rye, which greatly impeded all observation,) formed square with remarkable rapidity, and, reserving their fire until the very last moment, they completely dispersed and drove off a body of Piré's lancers, and a portion of Kellermann's cuirassiers, which troops had made a charge upon them, enveloping two faces of their square. Picton, who, from the opposite side of the high road, was an eye-witness of this scene, was so much

* Major Henry Lindsay, not having drawn his half-pay during four years, was struck off the establishment in 1831; but whether this omission on his part was caused by death, or otherwise, I know not.

† Now Captain Brooke Pigot, retired full pay, of the 69th Regiment.

‡ Lieutenant Christopher Clarke of the 42nd Highlanders died on the 23rd of September, 1831.

pleased with the perfect steadiness of the regiment, that, seizing a favourable opportunity of galloping up to it, he called for the commanding officer, and told Lieut. Colonel Hamilton* that he should report to the Duke the gallant conduct of his corps. Indeed the steadiness and gallantry of the 30th in this battle were so conspicuous as also to draw upon them the well merited commendations of the Prince of Orange, and Generals Alten, Halkett, and Kielmansegge. The 73rd regiment (under Colonel Harris†), and the Brunswickers, were equally on the alert, but the French cavalry, on finding them prepared, diverged towards the high road.

The 33rd regiment (under Lieut. Colonel Elphinstone,‡) had formed square upon its leading company (the grenadiers) at the moment the latter had reached some rising ground; in which position it became a conspicuous mark for the fire, at point blank distance, of a French battery which opened upon it with great spirit. It was deemed advisable to deploy it into line, in which formation the regiment advanced towards the two Brunswick battalions then fiercely engaged with the enemy's light troops near the skirt of the wood; but upon approaching the latter, a report was spread along the line that French cavalry was in its rear, whereupon the regiment rushed precipitately into the wood, within which it was speedily re-formed.

Whilst that portion of Kellermann's dragoons which had dispersed the 69th regiment, were sweeping gallantly onwards in their bold career along the high road towards Quatre-Bras, the greater body of this corps advanced into the open space on the right of that road. Here Picton's gallant little bands found themselves again involved in one general onset of cavalry, made with a violence and fury which seemed to betoken a desperate resolve to harass the devoted squares to the last extremity, and to carry every thing by main force. At the same time a dense cloud of skirmishers, bursting forth from the inclosures of Piermont, threatened to turn the extreme left of the Anglo-allied army; whilst the French infantry in the wood of Bossu, close upon the northern boundary of the latter, equally endangered its extreme right.

At this moment, Ney's prospects were bright enough to justify his hopes of success, and he hailed the captured colour, presented to him by the cuirassier Lami of the 8th

* Colonel Alexander Hamilton, C.B., died in June, 1838.
† Lieut. General Lord Harris, C.B., K.C.H., died on the 30th of May, 1845.
‡ Major General Elphinstone, C.B., died at Cabul in 1842.

regiment, as the harbinger of victory. In fact, on whatever point of his line Ney now directed his view, his operations were full of promise as to the result.

It was certainly a most anxious moment to the British chief: but frightfully crippled as were his resources by the failure and hasty retreat of the great bulk of the Dutch-Belgian infantry, by the evident inferiority and utter helplessness of his cavalry, and by the dreadfully severe losses already inflicted upon his British regiments, he calmly surveyed the field of slaughter, and deliberately calculated upon the extent to which the heroic valour and admirable spirit so unequivocally displayed by the British and German infantry would enable him to bear up against the storm that now spread its fury along his whole line, until his eagle-glance might detect some favourable opening, seize some critical moment, to deal the stroke that, by a combination as sudden as the launching of the thunderbolt of the storm itself, should avert its fury, or oppose to it a barrier that might exhaust its strength.

The arrival of Lloyd's British, and Cleeves's German, batteries, attached to Alten's division, had already made a most important addition to the Duke's artillery-force; the former took post in front of Quatre-Bras on the right, the latter on the left, of the Charleroi road. Almost immediately afterwards, Major Kuhlmann's* battery of horse artillery of the King's German legion, belonging to the 1st division, which it had preceded on the Nivelles road, reached the field, and moved rapidly to the point of intersection of the Brussels and Nivelles road, where it came into action, at the very moment the cuirassiers who had fallen upon Halkett's brigade were advancing in mass along the former road towards Quatre-Bras. Two guns under Lieutenant Speckmann† were posted so as to bear directly upon the French column, and completely to enfilade the road; and as the cuirassiers approached with the undaunted bearing that betokened the steadiness of veterans, and with the imposing display that usually distinguishes mailed cavalry, a remarkably well-directed fire was opened upon them: in an instant the whole mass appeared in irretrievable confusion; the road was literally strewed with corses of these steel-clad warriors and their gallant steeds; Kellermann himself was dismounted, and compelled like many of his followers to retire on foot.

* Lieut. Colonel Kuhlmann, K.H., of the Hanoverian artillery, died on the 19th of March, 1830.

† Captain Theodore Speckmann died on the 17th of September, 1834.

It was at this moment that Colonel Laurent, who had been despatched from the imperial head-quarters, reached Ney, with a pencilled note requiring the Marshal to detach the 1st corps towards St. Amand. Having fallen in with the head of the column of that corps, he had taken upon himself to alter the direction of its march; and, on coming up with Count d'Erlon, who had preceded his corps, and was then in front of Frasne, he showed him the note, and explained to him where he would find the head of his column. Shortly afterwards, General d'Elcambre, chief of the staff to the 1st corps, arrived to report the movement which was in course of execution.*

Ney now saw clearly that at the very moment he required the aid of d'Erlon's corps, not only to counterbalance the arrival of reinforcements which had joined Wellington, but to give an efficient support to the renewed general attack he had projected, that corps had been placed beyond his reach, and that he must, in all probability, continue to fight the battle without any addition to the force he had already in the field. Nevertheless, he did not allow the circumstance to suspend the execution of his operations; and, with the hope of yet securing the assistance of the 1st corps, he sent back General d'Elcambre, with a peremptory order for its return towards Quatre-Bras.

It was soon after this that Ney received another despatch from Napoleon, dated at two o'clock. From its general tenor it was evidently written previously to the departure of Colonel Laurent with the order for the flank movement of d'Erlon's corps, and therefore the bearer of it must have taken longer time than was necessary in conveying it to the Marshal. It announced that the Prussians were posted between Sombref and Bry, and that at half-past two Grouchy was to attack them with the 3rd and 4th corps d'armée, and expressed the Emperor's wish that Ney should also attack whatever enemy might be in his front, and, after having repulsed the latter, fall back in the direction of Ligny, to assist in enveloping the Prussians. At the same time it stated, that should Napoleon succeed in defeating the latter beforehand, he would then manœuvre in Ney's direction, to support in like manner the Marshal's operations. It concluded by requesting information both as to Ney's own dispositions and those of the enemy in his front.† This

* A further explanation of the movements of d'Erlon's corps will be given in the account of the battle of Ligny, in Chapter VI.

† The despatch (see Appendix XXI.) was addressed—" A. M. le Maréchal

despatch reached Ney at a moment when he was most seriously engaged, when the issue of the battle was extremely doubtful, and the probability of his being enabled to afford the support required by Napoleon most questionable.

Upon the extreme left of the Anglo-allied forces, the advance of the French light troops from Piermont and its vicinity was met in a most determined and gallant manner by the head of Kielmansegge's Hanoverian brigade, (which after having moved along the Nivelles road, exposed to the continued fire from the batteries on the French heights, had just reached that part of the field), in conjunction with the 1st battalion 95th British rifles, and the 2nd Brunswick light battalion. The most determined efforts were made by the enemy to turn the Anglo-allied flank. The French infantry had already gained the high road, and were boldly pressing forward, when the British rifles, the Brunswick light infantry, and the Hanoverian field-battalion Lüneburg (under Lieut. Colonel Klencke) dashed in amongst them. The contest was obstinate and severe; but the Allied light troops having been reinforced by the Hanoverian field-battalion Grubenhagen, (under Lieut. Colonel Wurmb,) gradually obtained the ascendancy, and, dislodging their opponents from one inclosure after another, continued steadily advancing, and gaining ground.

Along the whole front of the central portion of the Anglo-allied army, the French cavalry was expending its force in repeated but unavailing charges against the indomitable squares. The gallant, the brilliant, the heroic, manner in which the remnants of Kempt's and Pack's brigades held their ground, of which they surrendered not a single inch throughout the terrific struggle of that day, must ever stand pre-eminent in the records of the triumphs and prowess of British infantry. To relieve them as much as possible from the severe pressure they experienced, now that their ammunition was almost entirely exhausted, some of the Hanoverian battalions were judiciously thrown forward so as to afford

Prince de la Moskowa, à *Gosselies*, sur la route de Bruxelles;" and the route to be taken by the bearer was thus pencilled on the back:—"Wagnée—Bois de Lombuc." A duplicate of the despatch was forwarded, bearing the same address, and having the route marked—"Wagnée—Ransart." This circumstance proves that Napoleon was under the impression that Ney had *not* at that time (two o'clock) commenced his attack, but was still at Gosselies, and is of itself sufficient to correct the gross misstatements which appear in the "Mémoires Historiques de Napoléon," and in the "Campagne de 1815, par le Général Gourgaud," censuring the Marshal for having neglected to act in accordance with the Emperor's instructions, because he did not attack Quatre-Bras, and gain possession of that post, on the morning of the 16th.

them a close, immediate, and efficient, support, while others continued to line the Namur road; a disposition for which the arrival of Kielmansegge's brigade had presented the ready means, and which imposed an impregnable barrier to any further advance of the French cavalry, whose ranks were now thoroughly disordered, and their numbers greatly diminished, by their perseverance in a contest the hopelessness of which began to appear but too evident.

During that part of the battle just described, Ney received a further despatch from the Emperor by Colonel Forbin Janson. It was dated a quarter past three, and announced to the Marshal that Napoleon was at that moment seriously engaged. It desired Ney to manœuvre immediately so as to turn the right of the Prussians and fall upon their rear, and contained the remark that the latter would thus be taken *en flagrant délit* at the moment they might be endeavouring to join the English.* The impossibility of Ney's complying with these directions was already sufficiently apparent.

At this time Wellington received an addition to his forces by the arrival of the 1st and 3rd Brunswick light battalions, and the Brunswick brigade of artillery under Major Mahn, consisting of a battery of horse, and another of foot, artillery. The guns were immediately posted close upon the Namur road, at a short distance to the left of Quatre-Bras; and their fire, combined with that of the British and German batteries, soon produced a very perceptible effect upon the French artillery. The infantry reinforced the 1st and 3rd Brunswick line-battalions occupying the houses of Quatre-Bras.

The most important reinforcement, however, was the arrival, at nearly the same moment—about half-past six o'clock—of the 1st British division, under Major General Cooke, consisting of the 1st brigade of guards, commanded by Major General Maitland,† and the 2nd brigade of guards, commanded by Major General Sir John Byng.‡ Their line of march having been by the Nivelles road, they came very opportunely upon the most critical point of the Anglo-allied position, namely, its extreme right, just at the moment when the French light troops, having driven out the Dutch-Belgian infantry, showed themselves in force along the northern boundary of the wood of Bossu, and some of their skirmishers had almost gained the high road.

Wellington's force was still further augmented by the recently arrived troops as follows:—

* Appendix XXII. † Now General Sir Peregrine Maitland, K.C.B.
‡ Now General the Earl of Strafford, G.C.B.; G.C.H.

		Infantry.	Cavalry	Guns.
	Force already in the field .	24,234	2,004	42
British . .	1st infantry division . . .	4,061		
	Battery of foot artillery . .			6
K. G. Legion .	Do. horse do. . . .			6
Brunswick . .	1st and 3rd light battalions .	1,344		
	Battery of foot artillery . .			8
	Do. horse do. . .			8
		29,639	2,004	70

Ney's force actually present continued as before :—

Infantry.	Cavalry.	Guns.
16,189	4,974	50

The Prince of Orange, who had galloped along this road to meet the guards, immediately ordered the light companies under Lieut. Colonel Lord Saltoun,* to enter the wood. They rushed forward with a loud cheer, and commenced a brisk fire on their opponents, who were soon made sensible of the superior description of force now brought against them. The remainder of the brigade speedily followed, and the loud, sharp, animated rattle of musketry, which was progressing rapidly into the very heart of the wood, plainly indicated that even in this quarter, where the French had hitherto been the most successful, and whence they might not only have molested the Anglo-allied troops on the eastern boundary of the wood, but have most seriously endangered the right of the British position, they were now encountering a most vigorous and determined resistance.

Halkett's brigade, with the Brunswickers, resolutely maintained the ground on which they had been charged by the French cavalry. As the latter retired, the light companies of the brigade, with a portion of the Brunswickers on the right, and some Hanoverian riflemen on the left, advanced in pursuit. The French threw forward a line of tirailleurs to check them, and a brisk fire was maintained on both sides. The cannonade on this side of the field was also kept up with great spirit. At length the French cavalry advanced, forcing back Halkett's skirmishers upon their respective columns, on which they then charged. Their attack, however, was not made with much energy, and, upon their being uniformly

* Now Lieut. General Lord Saltoun, K.C.B.; G.C.H.

repulsed, the light troops resumed their former ground. Halkett pushed forward his battalions to the line of his skirmishers, and then moving towards his right, in the direction of the ravine, which descends from the wood, drove across the rivulet a body of French infantry, from which a portion of his brigade had suffered a severe fire. In this part of the affair one of Picton's battalions—the Royals—co-operated. The two Brunswick battalions continued boldly to advance even beyond this line, resting their right close upon the wood.

In the mean time, Byng's brigade had closely followed up Maitland's in support, having previously sent forward its light companies under Lieut. Colonel Macdonell* round by Quatre-Bras, skirting the eastern border of the wood. The spirited and determined nature of the advance of the British guards not admitting of that restraint which, considering the many intricate parts of the wood, was essential for the preservation of order, led to great confusion in their ranks by the time they reached the southern extremity, after having fairly driven out the French; and in this state they ventured to pursue the enemy on the open ground, but were quickly repulsed by his reserves; and the French artillery poured so destructive a fire into this portion of the wood, that Maitland deemed it advisable to withdraw the 2nd battalion (under Colonel Askew†) to the rivulet, where it was immediately joined from the rear by the other battalion of his brigade (the 3rd, under Colonel the Hon. William Stuart.‡)

The time which would have been occupied in restoring the order and regularity that had been so completely lost during the progress of these battalions through the wood, was considered too precious for that purpose at such a moment, and the brigade was ordered to form line to its left, outside the wood, the men falling in promiscuously as fast as they emerged from their cover, and extending the line into the plain between the wood and the Brussels road. Thus formed, the line advanced, through but for a short distance, when it opened and continued a brisk fire, under which the French infantry, in its immediate front, deployed with the utmost steadiness and gallantry. This advance had been followed by the Brunswick guard-battalion, which was now manœuvring to form on the left of Maitland's brigade. The

* Now Lieut. General Sir James Macdonell, K.C.B.; K.C.H.

† Now Lieut. General Sir Henry Askew, C.B.

‡ Lieut. General the Honorable William Stuart, C.B., died on the 15th of February, 1837.

French cavalry, which had been watching for an opportunity to charge the brigade, now made a dash at its left flank. When the irregular formation of the latter, which has been already explained, is considered, it is evident that any attempt to form square at that moment would have involved the British guards in inextricable confusion, and have rendered them an easy prey to the French horsemen. Rapid as was the advance of the latter, its object was frustrated in a manner which testifies the extraordinary discipline of the men of that brigade. Mere discipline it was not; it was an instinctive momentary impulse, which seemed to animate the whole corps with the sole conviction, that the only step to be taken, the only chance left for safety, consisted in a general and instantaneous movement to the ditch which bounded the wood on their right. This was accomplished with complete success, and the French cavalry, which had advanced in full confidence of an easy triumph, were hurled back in confusion by a volley from the ditch, which the brigade had lined with a rapidity, a dexterity, and a precision, quite wonderful; while at the same moment, the Brunswick battalion threw itself into square, and received the cavalry with a degree of coolness, steadiness, and gallantry, which won for it the warmest admiration and encomiums of the British who witnessed the manœuvre. The flanking fire which was thus brought to bear so suddenly on the French cavalry by the Brunswickers, and the destructive front fire so deliberately poured in amongst them by the British guards from the ditch, fairly drove them out of this part of the field.

More to the left, the French were retiring before Halkett in perfect order, covered by their skirmishers. As that General's brigade neared the farm-house of Gemioncourt, Major Chambers* of the 36th regiment, an experienced officer, incited by the desire of capturing a post which had been throughout the day a point d'appui to the French centre, led on two companies of his corps towards it. They made a gallant rush into the court-yard, but were met by a smart fire which forced them back. Major Chambers, however, rallied his men in the orchard, and having instructed them how to proceed in their attack, the place was instantly carried.

The further advance upon the Anglo-allied left had, in the mean time, kept equal pace with that on the right. Ney had been compelled to yield the strongholds by aid of which he had hoped to force the Duke's position: his infantry had

* Major T. W. Chambers was killed at the battle of Waterloo.

been driven out of Piermont and the inclosures in front of his right, as also out of the wood of Bossu on his left: Gemioncourt, also, in front of his centre, had been captured; while the plain between the two positions, over which his cavalry had executed innumerable charges—charges that were occasionally suspended merely that the scattered bands might rally afresh to renew the onslaught with redoubled vigour, and that his artillery might pour upon the devoted squares its destructive missiles, by which each was shattered to its very centre,—was now completely cleared from the presence of a single horseman.

It was long after sunset, and darkness was sensibly approaching, when Wellington, now that his flanks and centre were relieved, in the manner already described, from the severity of a pressure of such long duration, led forward his victorious troops to the foot of the French position. The loud shouts which proclaimed the triumphant advance of his forces on either flank were enthusiastically caught up and responded to by those who constituted the main central line, and who had so nobly and so resolutely withstood and defied the impetuous battle-shock by which they had been so repeatedly and so pertinaciously assailed.

Ney, convinced of the utter futility, if not imminent hazard, of protracting the contest, withdrew the whole of his forces, and concentrated them on the heights of Frasne, throwing out a strong line of picquets, to which Wellington opposed a corresponding line, having the southern extremity of the wood of Bossu on the right, the inclosures south of Piermont on the left, and Gemioncourt in the centre, for its main supports.

The French picquets manifested an extraordinary degree of vigilance; the slightest movement on the side of the Anglo-allied picquets instantly attracted attention, and was noticed by a concentrated fire from the watchful sentries of the enemy. No movement, however, of any consequence was made on either side during the night. The wearied combatants sought that rest of which they stood so much in need, and the silence in which the Anglo-allied bivouac soon became hushed, was only disturbed by the arrival of additional reinforcements, consisting principally of British cavalry.

Ney was joined by the 1st corps, after the termination of the action. At nine o'clock, d'Erlon presented himself to the Marshal for the purpose of reporting to him his proceedings, and of receiving his orders, after which the corps was bivouacked in the rear of Frasne; with the exception, however, of Durutte's division, (the 4th), and Jaquinot's light cavalry brigade, which d'Erlon had left on the field of Ligny, in front of the extreme right of the Prussian army; a measure which he had deemed advisable in order to prevent the enemy from debouching into the plain between Bry and the wood of Delhutte.

It is singular that Napoleon, who at Fleurus held so powerful a reserve as that consisting of the imperial guard and the 6th corps, and who was in perfect ignorance of the true state of affairs at Quatre-Bras, should have ventured to withdraw from Ney a force amounting to more than one half of that which he had originally placed at his disposal. It was decidedly a false step, from which no advantage resulted on his own field of battle, whilst there can be very little doubt that it lost him that of Quatre-Bras.

The losses sustained in this battle by the Anglo-allied army in killed, wounded, and missing, were as follows:—

British	2,275 *
Hanoverians	369 †
Brunswickers	819 ‡
	3,463 men.

To these must be added the loss of the Dutch-Belgian troops, amounting probably to about 1,000 killed and wounded,§ which makes the entire loss of the Anglo-allied army equal to about 4,463 men.

The French loss amounted to about 4,000 killed, wounded, and missing.

Such was the battle of Quatre-Bras: a battle in which the British, the Hanoverian, and the Brunswick, infantry, covered itself with imperishable glory; to estimate the full extent of which we must constantly bear in mind, that the whole brunt of the action fell upon that infantry; that throughout the greater part of the day it was totally unaided by any cavalry, that arm of the Allies in the field having, at the outset, proved itself incompetent to engage

* For a detailed return, including officers and non-commisioned officers—See Appendix XXIII.

† The above number is taken from the *London Gazette* of the 8th of July, 1815. No detailed regimental returns exist of the losses of either the King's German legion, or the Hanoverian subsidiary corps, on each day of the 16th, 17th, and 18th of June, *separately:* the returns which will be found in the Appendix embrace the casualties that occurred during those three days.

‡ For a detailed return, including officers—See Appendix XXIV.

§ A detailed return of the killed, wounded, and missing, of the Dutch-Belgian troops, during the 16th, 17th, and 18th of June, will be found in the Appendix.

with the French; and, lastly, that it was completely abandoned in the latter part of the action by the 2nd Dutch-Belgian infantry-division, amounting to no less than 7533 men.*

When the imagination dwells upon that which constitutes one of the most prominent features of the battle—the manner in which the gallant Picton, on finding there was no cavalry at hand wherewith to charge effectively that of the enemy, led on the British infantry, and dashed into the midst of the French masses, stoutly maintaining his ground in defiance of

* It is but an act of justice to the Dutch-Belgian troops that some explanation should be given of the peculiar circumstances under which they were called upon to take the field in defence of Belgium. They were almost entirely composed of young soldiers hastily collected together, after the peace of 1814, to form the army of the recently united kingdom of the Netherlands. The time for their training had been too short, and altogether, they might be considered in no other light than that of raw and inexperienced troops. It must also be observed, that in that brief period, a cordial unity of sentiment, and a thorough identity of interests between the levies raised in Holland, and those in the Belgian provinces, was scarcely to be expected; and it is well known that from old associations and reminiscences, a very considerable proportion of the population of Belgium was favourably inclined towards the French. Had it not been for the great popularity which the Prince of Orange had acquired with both sections of the nation, matters might have been infinitely worse. These troops frequently manifested an eager desire to merit the approbation of the Prince; and the conduct of their officers was, in general, both praiseworthy and encouraging. It has been shown that on the evening of the 15th, and morning of the 16th, they effected, considering their numbers, all that could reasonably be expected from troops similarly situated. When however, the French began to convert that which had hitherto been little more than a skirmish into a regular attack with compact bodies, and the Dutch-Belgians found themselves placed in that critical position invariably experienced by raw troops called upon to manœuvre, under a vigorous fire, in the presence of well-trained and highly disciplined opponents, they were unable, notwithstanding the increase which had, in the mean time, been made to their numbers, to hold their ground. When withdrawn into the wood of Bossu, they stoutly maintained for a time, its northern boundary; but here the boldness of their enemies, inspired by long experience acquired in this kind of warfare, soon overpowered their efforts. Not long afterwards, whilst they were in the heart of the wood, an impression gained ground among them that the enemy's fire was approaching the wood on both sides, and that as there were no troops in their vicinity to afford them assistance they would be surrounded. Bylandt's brigade suffered very much before it retired from the wood to rally in rear of the main position. Van Merlen's cavalry-brigade also suffered a heavy loss before it retired, upon the failure of its charge. Their artillery, more particularly Byleveld's horse-battery, had been engaged in a heavy cannonade, and after it had retired to re-fit, several of its guns that were still serviceable, took post on the flanks of the British and German batteries. That there existed in the Dutch-Belgian ranks several disaffected *mauvais sujets*—men who were either personally interested in the restoration of the Napoleon *regime*, or were the ready tools of others that cherished the hope of such an event, there can be no doubt. I have the evidence of officers of the 1st British division, that as they approached the wood, and inquired of the various groups of their infantry, the cause of their retiring so hastily, the answers which they received plainly indicated that a certain portion of them entertained sentiments by no means favourable to the cause of the Allies.

their oft-repeated assaults, invariably scattering back their charging squadrons in confusion, and this, too, in the face of a splendid cavalry, animated by the best spirit, and headed by a Kellermann, whose fame and merit were so universally acknowledged—with what exulting pride and heartfelt gratitude must not the British nation reflect on the heroic valour displayed by her sons in their noble fulfilment of the desires and expectations of her Cambrian chief!

The zealous and cordial support which the Hanoverians and the Brunswickers afforded to their British brethren in arms, the devotion with which they commingled with them in the thickest of the fight, are indelibly engraven in the grateful memory of every true German, and remain recorded as a lasting theme of admiration in the history of their fatherland.

The defeat sustained by the French was certainly not attributable, in the slightest degree, to any deficiency on their part, of either bravery or discipline. Their deportment was that of truly gallant soldiers, and their attacks were all conducted with a chivalric impetuosity, and an admirably sustained vigour, which could leave no doubt on the minds of their opponents as to the sincerity of their devotion to the cause of the Emperor.

In a strategical point of view, both parties gained certain important advantages, and lost others, which had been comprised within their respective plans of operation. Ney had succeeded in preventing the junction of the Anglo-allied army with the Prussians, and might have obtained still more important results, had he not been deprived of the services of d'Erlon's corps, the arrival of which he had been so fully led to expect. Wellington, though he had been compelled to relinquish all hope of being enabled to afford that aid to Blücher which, in the morning, he had proffered to him, yet, by maintaining his ground at Quatre-Bras sufficiently long to admit of the arrival of reinforcements which enabled him to obtain a brilliant victory, he completely succeeded in frustrating the grand object of Ney's movements, which had been to defeat the Anglo-allied troops thus advancing, in detail, and also to operate upon Blücher's right flank. The Duke's success gave ample and convincing evidence of the sagacity and foresight with which his plans had been devised and matured, as also of the soundness of those calculations by which he had for some time previously placed himself, with the confident security of a master of his art, in a posture of defence, fully prepared to meet every emergency, from whatever point, or however suddenly, the coming storm might arise. And now that he had gained the battle, and secured the important point of Quatre-Bras, upon which the remainder of his troops were advancing, and where the greater portion of them would arrive in the evening and during the night, he was perfectly ready and willing, should the Prussians prove victorious at Ligny, to renew the contest on the following morning, by attacking Ney with his collected force; and then, if successful, (of which little doubt could be entertained,) by a junction with Blücher's right, to operate upon Napoleon's left, so as to bring the great mass of the combined armies to bear directly upon the main body of the French; or, in case of a defeat of the Prussians, to make good his retreat along his principal line of operation, in such a manner, as to secure a position between Quatre-Bras and Brussels, favourable for a co-operation of Blücher's forces with his own, and for presenting a bold and determined stand against the further advance of the French Emperor.*

* Ney has been frequently reproached for not having established himself at Quatre-Bras early on the morning of the 16th, in pursuance of orders alleged to have been given by Napoleon to that effect; and certain writers, desirous both of exculpating the errors of the French Emperor, by attributing the failure at Quatre-Bras to Ney's want of energy, and of detracting from the merits of Wellington by representing that he was taken by surprise, have argued that had Ney, in obedience to orders, united his whole force and commenced his attack at an earlier hour, he would have frustrated the concentration of the Anglo-allied army. To such arguments, as far as Ney is concerned, the facts and circumstances which have been detailed, and the recorded instructions of Napoleon, offer a complete refutation: and as regards Wellington, it requires but a slight insight into his dispositions, to prove that they were most fully calculated to ensure sufficient time for the assembling of his forces on the French line of attack. It has already been explained that Genappe, Quatre-Bras, and Frasne, were the points upon the Charleroi road on which the left of the Anglo-allied army rested. Frasne was the advanced post of the troops occupying the two first-named points, and was distant about ten miles from the Sambre, and about thirty miles from the French frontier. The passages along this river in its front were occupied by Prussian troops, whose outposts were extended to about midway between the Sambre and the line of frontier from which the enemy would have to advance. Hence, however early in the morning the enemy might commence his march, he would have to drive in the Prussian outposts, to force the passages of the Sambre, and, in addition to all the delays, impediments, and mischances to which such an advance would be subjected, he would have to perform altogether a march of more than thirty miles from the nearest point of the French territory, before he could reach even the advanced post of Frasne, which was about three miles in front of Quatre-Bras. Under such circumstances, it was not at all probable that any overpowering force could arrive at Quatre-Bras in one day's march. Now let us compare the extent of such a march with that which would have been required of the nearest Anglo-allied troops ordered to collect at Quatre-Bras. Enghien, the head-quarters of the most remote division of the 1st corps, was about twenty-five miles distant from Quatre-Bras; the reserve, at Brussels, was about twenty-three miles distant. The whole of these troops, therefore, amounting to more than 30,000 men, could be collected at Quatre-Bras before any similar amount of force could be brought against that point by the enemy, provided a vigilant look-out was maintained, and

Orders were now forwarded for the movement of Clinton's division on the following morning, at daybreak, from Nivelles

the necessary measures were taken for procuring the earliest intelligence of the enemy's advance. The Duke of Wellington had given special instructions to the Prince of Orange to watch the enemy's movements in front of his advanced posts. These extended to the left as far as Binche, which was occupied by the extreme right of the advanced line of the Prussian army, and to which the Prince of Orange had repaired in person at an early hour. He had also directed Major General Sir William Dörnberg, to obtain the earliest information concerning any movements along that part of the French frontier facing Mons, at which point he was posted for this purpose; whilst Lieut. Colonel Wissell, with the 1st hussars of the King's German Legion, kept up a good look-out along the line of Tournai, Ypres, and Furnes. In fact, the Duke's arrangements as regarded the disposition of his forces, the selection of the interior points of concentration, and the necessary precautions enjoined along the line of outposts, were fully calculated to guard against any attempted surprise. It now remains to be shown how far the intentions of his Grace, as developed by these arrangements, were carried into effect by his subordinates in command. Solre-sur-Sambre, whence the French left main column of attack debouched at two o'clock on the morning of the 15th, and Lobbes, where the Prussian outposts first became engaged with the advanced guard of that column were equidistant about nine miles from Binche, whence the Prussians were withdrawn at eight o'clock, on the arrival of Major Arnauld, on his way to St. Symphorien, to communicate with General van Merlen the fact of the Prussian outposts having been attacked and forced to retire.* Van Merlen must, therefore, have received this intelligence before nine o'clock. Three hours would have sufficed for the transmission of orders from the Prince of Orange, who had proceeded in person to St. Symphorien and Binche, early in the morning, to the whole of the troops of the 1st corps of the Anglo-allied army to assemble at their respective head-quarters of brigades, and to prepare to march at a moment's notice. By means of a vigilant reconnaissance, the object of the enemy's advance and his attack upon Charleroi at ten o'clock, might have been known at Binche between eleven and twelve, and at St. Symphorien soon after twelve o'clock, and the entire 1st corps might have been put in movement upon Quatre-Bras by three o'clock; at which important point the troops would thus have been gradually collected, and the whole have been assembled before night. By a properly organized system of expresses along the high road from Binche to Brussels, the first intelligence of the French advance could certainly have been conveyed to head quarters by a little after twelve o'clock, and that of the French attack upon Charleroi, by four o'clock in the afternoon. The Duke would thus have been enabled to place all the troops of the 2nd corps, of the cavalry, and of the reserve, in readiness, in the middle of the day, to move at a moment's notice; and subsequently to have put them in movement that evening in support of the 1st corps at Quatre-Bras, where his whole army might have been assembled at a very early hour on the following morning. When, therefore, those who venture to censure Ney, for not having established himself at Quatre-Bras early in the morning of the 16th, assert that *if* that Marshal had thus acted, Wellington, by having allowed himself to be surprised, would have exposed his troops to the risk of being 'crushed in detail,' they ought at least to concede, that if the excellent arrangements made by the Duke had been duly and promptly acted upon by his subordinates, Ney could not have fulfilled the task they are pleased to assign to him, even supposing him to have received the order, and to have possessed the means, for its accomplishment, which, as I trust having clearly shown, was by no means the case. Unfortunately, the commander of the 1st Anglo-allied corps did not act up to the spirit of his instructions, but making *himself* the bearer of the intelligence of the French advance, proceeded to Brussels, where he arrived soon after three o'clock,

* See page 39.

to Quatre-Bras: and of Colville's division, at the same hour, from Enghien to Nivelles. The reserve-artillery was di-

in the afternoon. The only real surprise which the Duke experienced on this occasion, was in finding the Prince of Orange on the night of the 15th at the Duchess of Richmond's ball, when he delicately suggested to his Royal Highness the expediency of his returning to his corps. There was also a certain degree of remissness on the part of Major General Sir William Dörnberg, who, as before stated, was posted in observation at Mons. This point was about eleven miles from Binche, and seventeen from Solre-sur-Sambre, so that if a vigilant look-out had been maintained, and a system of rapid communication along the line of outposts established, that officer could not have remained long ignorant of the commencement of hostilities; but it was not until he received, late in the day, the dispatch from the Duke requiring information as to appearances in front of Mons, that he communicated at all with his Grace. It is right, however, to observe that as no movement was made by the French in his direct front, he had nothing to communicate to head-quarters on that point, and that as no intimation of an attack reached him from the outposts of the 1st corps, on his left, he may have concluded that nothing of consequence had taken place.

My object being to relate only that which actually occurred, I do not feel myself called upon to enter into the question of what would have taken place under other circumstances; and perhaps even the brief remarks I have here made may be already considered too digressive; but I cannot refrain from still further noticing the assertions made by the writers before alluded to, as to what would have resulted, had Ney attacked Quatre-Bras at an earlier hour of the 16th, with both the 1st and 2nd corps d'armée. Let us, for the sake of argument, suppose that by an extraordinary exertion on the part of the French army, these two corps under Ney had succeeded in gaining that post on the morning of the 16th—Do these gentlemen imagine that in this case the Anglo-allied troops would have continued to march upon Quatre-Bras, in detached bodies, from their respective cantonments, so as to afford Ney the opportunity of 'crushing'* them in detail? Can they not conceive the difference between troops marching upon a point for concentration, and troops marching towards a point occupied by an enemy? Can they not conceive the possibility of Nivelles and Genappe then becoming the points of general concentration? Can they not conceive that at these two points such concentration could be effected with more rapidity, and in greater force, than at Quatre-Bras? Can they not conceive the possibility of Wellington taking up a sufficiently strong position on the heights commanding the defile of Genappe, and preparing at the same time, to operate, with his collected force at Nivelles, upon the left flank of the enemy's advance? Can they not conceive the possibility of Ney, having Napoleon with the main army at such a distance as Fleurus, the whole Prussian army on his right, a very considerable portion of the Anglo-allied army on his left, and the remainder of the latter force in his front, being induced by the knowledge which he must have had of the energetic and decisive character of Wellington, to hesitate in advancing, under such circumstances, along the direct road to Brussels? Can they not conceive the possibility of Ney (who, they must admit, was a general possessing both great abilities and long experience,) not venturing to advance beyond Quatre-Bras, without leaving in his rear at least one-half of his force to secure his line of operation against any hostile attempt on the part of either the Prussians by the Namur road, or the Anglo-allies along that of Nivelles, as also to prevent any interruption of his communication with Napoleon,—a precaution which would subject him to the

* "It was well for the British corps that the French Marshal did not concentrate his whole army together, and commence his attack with his united force; for if so, they must inevitably have been crushed."—*Alison's History of Europe*, vol. x. page 929.

rected to move at daybreak, on the following morning, to Quatre-Bras, there to receive further orders; and the 10th infantry-brigade, under Major General Sir John Lambert,* was directed to march, at the same hour, from Assche to Genappe, there to remain until further orders.

The tremendous roar of artillery in the direction of Ligny gave a sufficient intimation to the Duke that a great battle had taken place in that quarter, but as it seemed to continue stationary, and only ceased as night set in, he was doubtful of the result, and remained in this state of suspense and uncertainty until the following morning; the officer who had been despatched in the night to Quatre-Bras from the Prussian head-quarters with the expected communication, having been surprised in the dark, and made a prisoner by the French.

risk of finding his further progress opposed by superior force in both front and flank, of suffering his own troops to be beaten in detail, and, consequently, of compromising the safety of the main French army? Can they not—but it is needless to pursue the subject further. If they cannot conceive these *possibilities*, they should pause before they presume to attempt to diminish, in the estimation of the world, the merits of Britain's illustrious chieftain, by boldly hazarding assertions so utterly incompatible with *probabilities*.

* Now General Sir John Lambert, G.C.B.

CHAPTER VI.

PRINCE Blücher having ascertained, on the morning of the 16th, that his communication with the left division of the Duke of Wellington's forces by Quatre-Bras, continued uninterrupted, resolved upon accepting battle in the position in rear of Fleurus, which had been previously fixed upon as the one most eligible, in the event of the enemy's adoption of that line of operations respecting which all doubt and uncertainty had now ceased. Its importance in a strategical point of view, apart from tactical considerations, was manifest. Wellington having, on his part, selected Quatre-Bras as the point whereon to concentrate his forces, the position in question, connected as it was with the latter by a paved road over an extent of not more than six or seven miles, offered great facility for co-operation and mutual support upon whichever point the great mass of the French army might be directed. Should it prove tenable, then, considered in conjunction with the advance of the Russians from the Rhine, the whole line of the Meuse below Namur, and the communications with Aix-la-Chapelle and the Prussian states, were effectually secured. If, on the other hand, either position should be forced by the enemy, then Mont St. Jean and Wavre, upon parallel lines of retreat towards Brussels and Louvain, would likewise offer the means of co-operation on the south side of the forest of Soignies; and supposing Blücher willing to risk for a time his communication with the right bank of the Meuse, concentric lines of retreat upon Brussels would bring the two armies in combined position in the immediate front of that capital. Supposing also that Napoleon's plan had been to advance by Mons, the concentration of the Prussian forces could not have been effected upon a more favourable point than that of Sombref, whence they could have advanced in support of their allies, leaving a sufficient portion of Zieten's corps to watch the approaches by Charleroi: and, finally, had the French Emperor directed his main attack by Namur, the retreat of Thielemann's corps would have secured time for effecting the concentration of the 1st, 2nd, and 3rd Prussian corps d'armée, if not also of the 4th, while the Duke of Wellington's forces might have assembled at Quatre-Bras, for the purpose of meeting any secondary attack from the Charleroi side, and of forming a junction with the Prussian army.

The position itself comprises the heights of Bry, Sombref, and Tongrines, contiguous to the high road connecting Namur with Nivelles, by Quatre-Bras, and to the point of junction of that road with the one from Charleroi, by Fleurus. These heights are bounded upon the south-west and western sides, or right of the position, by a ravine, through which winds a small rivulet along the villages of Wagnelé, St. Amand-la-Haye, and St. Amand, near the lower end of which last, it unites with the greater rivulet of the Ligny; and, along the whole of the south side, or front of the position, by a valley, through which flows the Ligny, and in which lie, partly bordering the stream itself, and partly covering the declivities, the villages of Ligny, Mont Potriaux, Tongrenelles, Boignée, Ballatre, and Vilrets. At the last-named point, another small rivulet falls into the Ligny on quitting a deep ravine, which commences northward of the village of Botey, and thus tends to the security of the extreme left of the position. The extreme right, however, resting upon the Namur road, in the direction of Quatre-Bras, was completely en l'air. The heights in rear of St. Amand, Ligny, and Sombref, are somewhat lower than those on the opposite or Fleurus side of the valley; and, from the nature of the ground, troops, particularly artillery, are more exposed on the former than on the latter, where the undulations afford better cover. The descent from either side into the villages of Wagnelé, St. Amand-la-Haye, and St. Amand, is gentle: between the latter point and Mont Potriaux the sides of the valley descend more rapidly: and below that village they become steep, particularly about Tongrines, Boignée, and Balatre; while the ground above commands alternately from side to side. Above Mont Potriaux, the bed of the valley is soft, and occasionally swampy: below that point it partakes still more of this character. The buildings in the villages are generally of stone, with thatched roofs, and comprise several farm-houses with court-yards, presenting great capabilities for defence. St. Amand and Boignée are the most salient points of the position, the central portion of which retires considerably, particularly near Mont Potriaux.

In the morning of the 16th, the 1st corps, (Zieten's) occupied that portion of the position which is circumscribed by the villages of Bry, St. Amand-la-Haye, St. Amand, and Ligny. The four brigades of this corps had been very much mixed up together when occupying these villages during the night, which will account in some measure for the promiscuous manner in which their several battalions appear to have been distributed during the battle. The main body of the corps was drawn up on the height between Bry and Ligny, and upon which stands the farm and wind-mill of Bussy, the highest point of the whole position. Seven battalions of the 2nd brigade (General Pirch II.) were formed immediately in rear of this farm; the 28th regiment and 2nd Westphalian landwehr in the first, and the 2nd and 3rd battalions of the 6th regiment in the second line; while the 3rd battalion of the latter regiment occupied the farm itself, which was put into a state of defence. Two battalions of the 4th brigade, (General Count Henkel,) namely, the 2nd battalions of the 19th regiment and of the 4th Westphalian landwehr, stood on the slope between the 2nd brigade and Ligny; while the remaining four battalions of the brigade—the 1st and 3rd of the 19th regiment, and the 1st and 3rd of the 4th Westphalian landwehr—were charged with the defence of Ligny. The village of Bry was occupied by the 3rd battalions of the 12th and 24th regiments, belonging to the 1st brigade (General Steinmetz); and the 2nd battalion of the 1st Westphalian landwehr was posted in rear of the village in support. The 1st and 3rd companies of the Silesian rifles, attached to this brigade, were distributed about the intersected ground between Bry and St. Amand-la-Haye. The remainder of the first brigade was posted on the height in the rear of St. Amand, its right resting on St. Amand-la-Haye; the 1st and 2nd battalions of the 12th regiment on the right, and the 1st and 2nd battalions of the 24th regiment on the left, forming a first, and the 1st and 3rd battalions of the 1st Westphalian landwehr forming a second, line. The defence of St. Amand was confided to three battalions of the 3rd brigade (General Jagow)—the 1st and 2nd of the 29th regiment, and the 2nd battalion of the 3rd Westphalian landwehr. The remaining six battalions of this brigade were posted in reserve northward of Ligny, and near the Bois du loup. The 2nd and 4th companies of the Silesian rifles were thrown into Ligny. The reserve-cavalry of Zieten's corps continued in advance, upon the Fleurus high road, watching the movements of the enemy.

It was eight o'clock when these dispositions were completed; and about eleven o'clock Pirch's corps, which more than an hour before had quitted its bivouac near Mazy, was formed up in reserve to Zieten. The 5th brigade (General Tippelskirchen) stood across the high road, near its intersection with the old Roman road, in the customary Prussian brigade-order of three lines of columns of battalions at deploying intervals, and had in its front the two batteries, Nos. 10 and 37. The 6th brigade (General Krafft) was posted in similar order in the rear of the farm of Bussy, and in left-rear of Bry. The 7th brigade (General Brause) stood more to the left: it had only the 14th regiment then present, for the 22nd regiment and the Elbe landwehr did not rejoin it until one o'clock in the afternoon. The 8th brigade (Colonel Langen) was ordered to remain upon the high road leading from Sombref to Fleurus, until the arrival of the 3rd corps (Thielemann's). One of its battalions—the 3rd of the 21st regiment—as also two squadrons of the Neumark dragoons attached to this corps, had been left in the line of outposts beyond the Meuse, towards Philippeville, and did not rejoin it until the 20th of June.

The reserve-cavalry of Pirch's corps, under General Jürgass, was stationed in rear of the high road, and on the west side of Sombref.

The twelve-pounder batteries, Nos. 4, and 8, and the horse-batteries, Nos. 5, and 18, remained in reserve, near Sombref.

Thielemann's corps which had quitted Namur about seven o'clock in the morning, had reached Sombref before twelve. It was immediately assigned its position in that part of the field which lies between Sombref and Balatre, and was posted in columns upon both high roads, here to remain available for either a movement to the right, or for the occupation of the position in left front of Sombref, along the heights in rear of the Ligny rivulet.

Such were the dispositions made by Blücher previously to Napoleon's advancing from Fleurus. The occupation of Ligny and St. Amand—the most salient part of the position—by Zieten's corps, and the posting of the reserve-cavalry of the latter in the intervening space between those villages and Fleurus, were justly calculated to secure for the Prussian commander ample time for further developing his line of battle in such a manner as the direction and mode of his opponent's attack might render most expedient.

In the morning of the 16th, the French troops which lay along the Sambre, and which belonged to that main portion of the army which was more immediately under the orders and guidance of Napoleon, quitted their bivouacs, and marched to join their leading columns, the position of which in front of Fleurus was described in the fourth Chapter. It was past ten o'clock when these troops debouched in two columns from the Fleurus wood—the one along the high road, the other more to the right—and drew up in two lines within a short distance of Fleurus. In the first line, Pajol's light, and Excelmans' heavy, cavalry, formed the right, and Vandamme's corps, the left, wing; while Gérard's corps which had not received the order to march until half past nine o'clock, arrived much later, and occupied the centre. Girard's division was detached some little distance on the extreme left. The imperial guard and Milhaud's corps of cuirassiers constituted the second line. More than an hour was passed in this position before the arrival of the Emperor, who then rode along the line of vedettes, and reconnoitred the enemy's dispositions.

It appeared to Napoleon that Blücher had taken up a position perpendicular to the Namur road, and had, in this way, completely exposed his right flank; whence he inferred that the Prince placed great reliance upon the arrival of auxiliary forces from the Duke of Wellington's army.*

A single glance at the Prussian position, as it has been described, will suffice to prove that the French Emperor was in error as regarded Blücher's assumed line of battle, and that so far from its having been perpendicular to, it was, in the general military acceptation of the term, parallel with, the Namur road. At the same time it is proper to remark, that he may have been misled by the massing of the Prussian troops between the salient point of the position, St. Amand, and the road in question, as well as by the direction of the line of the occupied villages of St. Amand, Ligny, and Sombref.† It must also be acknowledged that although the inference was incorrectly drawn, it accorded in substance with the real fact, that Blücher did rely upon the arrival of a

* He may also have inferred from the disposition which he imagined Blücher to have made that the latter designed retiring upon Quatre-Bras in the event of a defeat, and should this view be correct, it strengthens the probability of Napoleon's having been ignorant of the non-arrival of Bülow's corps, notwithstanding the insinuation made of the contrary in the historical memoirs collected at St. Helena, and in which it is admitted that he was unacquainted with the disposition even of Thielemann's corps, inasmuch as he imagined its arrival to have taken place during the battle, whereas it had entered the field by twelve o'clock in the morning, and was fully assembled at Sombref, though not distributed in position, at the time of his reconnaissance.

† The following remark by Gamitz, in his "Geschichte des Feldzugs von 1815," offers, if not a correct, at least a very reasonable view of this question:—"Napoleon was too practical a general to judge of the position of an opponent by the direction and extent of lines. It is much more probable that he made use of the expression, reported by persons who were present, 'Le vieux renard ne débusque pas.' This would at all events have exhibited on his part a better judgment of his adversary than does the opinion he has since asserted to have formed at the time upon the Prussian position."

portion of Wellington's forces by the Namur road from Quatre-Bras.

Napoleon having returned from his reconnaissance, immediately gave his orders for the advance of the army, and for the disposition of each individual corps in his intended line of battle. Impressed with the important advantage which, according to his assumed view of Blücher's position, might accrue from a vigorous and well-timed attack upon the right and rear of the Prussians, while vigorously assailing them himself in their front, he directed Soult to address to Ney the despatch, dated two o'clock,* to which reference was made in the preceding Chapter, acquainting the Marshal that in half an hour thence he proposed attacking Blücher, posted between Sombref and Bry, and desiring that he would, on his part, also attack whatever might be in his front, and that after having vigorously repulsed the enemy, he should move towards the Emperor's field of battle, and fall upon the right and rear of the Prussians; adding, at the same time, that should the Emperor be first successful, he would then move to the support of the army at Quatre-Bras.

The French light troops moved forward against Fleurus, of which place they gained possession between eleven and twelve o'clock, and then opened from their light artillery a cannonade upon the Prussian cavalry-posts taken up by the 6th uhlans. The latter immediately retired, and formed upon the left of the Brandenburg dragoons, which regiment had been placed in front of the Tombe de Ligny, along with the horse-battery No. 2, in support. The Brandenburg uhlans were also in support, but more to the rear, and on the left of the high road.

At this time, Napoleon was on the height of Fleurus, again reconnoitring the Prussian position; and it was also about the same period that Wellington joined Blücher in person near the mill of Bussy.†

As soon as Röder perceived the imposing array of the French columns in full advance, he ordered the immediate retreat of his cavalry, which he covered with the 6th uhlans and the Brandenburg dragoons, together with two pieces of horse-artillery. He sent the main body, which he had stationed in a hollow, in rear of the Tombe de Ligny, as also the remainder of the artillery, across the Ligny, with directions to take post between the village of that name and Sombref. He himself continued with the above two regiments, and the

* Appendix XXI. † See page 63.

two guns, near the Tombe de Ligny, until he received orders also to retire.

In the mean time the main body of the French army advanced in great regularity in columns of corps. The left column, consisting of the 3rd corps d'armée under Vandamme, to which was attached the infantry-division under Lieut. General Girard, belonging to Reille's corps, (then with Ney) being destined to advance against St. Amand, the most salient point of the Prussian position, and therefore having the shortest distance to pass over, was the first to take up its ground, preparatory to attack. Whilst thus engaged in making its preliminary dispositions for this purpose, it was cannonaded by the Prussian batteries posted on the heights in rear of the village. Girard's division took post on the left of Vandamme's corps, and Domon's light cavalry-division on the left of Girard.

The centre column, consisting of the 4th corps d'armée, under Gérard, advanced along the Fleurus high road, and took up, somewhat later, a position upon the heights fronting Ligny, and parallel to the general direction of that village; its left being near the Tombe de Ligny, and its right resting on an eminence southward of Mont Potriaux.

The right column, under Grouchy, comprising the cavalry-corps of Pajol and Excelmans, moved by its right, and took post, as did also the light cavalry-division under Lieut. General Maurin, belonging to the 4th corps d'armée, on the right of Gérard, and showing front towards the villages of Tongrines, Tongrenelle, Boignée, and Balatre. Grouchy disposed this cavalry so as to protect Gérard from any attempt which the Prussians might make to debouch in his rear from Mont Potriaux or Tongrenelle; as also to watch any hostile movements on their left, and to divert their attention from the centre. Pajol's corps, which was formed on the right, detached along the cross road which leads to Namur. The villages of Boignée and Balatre being situated on the French side of the valley, and occupied by Prussian infantry, Grouchy was supplied with two battalions from Gérard's corps. The 1st and 2nd squadrons of the 3rd Kurmark landwehr cavalry belonging to Thielemann's corps, which had been posted in advance, upon the Fleurus road, retired skirmishing until they reached the barrier at the bridge, whither they were pursued by the French cavalry. Here, however, the latter were checked and driven off by the 3rd battalion of the 4th Kurmark landwehr, belonging to Colonel Luck's brigade.

The imperial guard and Milhaud's cuirassiers were halted

in reserve, the former on the left, and the latter on the right, of Fleurus.

The numerical strength of the French Emperor's forces prepared to engage with the Prussian army amounted to:—

Infantry	43,412
Cavalry	12,614
Artillery	6,856
Total . .	62,882 men, with 204 guns.

If to this we add Lobau's corps, which was on the march from Charleroi, the total amount of available force was:—

Infantry	51,564
Cavalry	12,614
Artillery	7,788
Total . .	71,966 men, with 242 guns.*

The Prussian army in the field amounted to:—

Infantry	73,040
Cavalry	8,150
Artillery	3,437
	84,617
Deduct loss of 1st corps on 15th June	1,200
Total . .	83,417 with 224 guns.†

As soon as the direction of the enemy's movements for attack became sufficiently manifest, Blücher made such further disposition of his force as appeared to him requisite to meet that attack. He ordered the batteries of the first corps d'armée (Zieten's) to be suitably posted for impeding the enemy's advance. The three heavy batteries of the corps were immediately drawn up on the height between Ligny and St. Amand. They were supported by the battery of the first brigade, posted in rear of St. Amand. Somewhat later, when the direction of attack by Gérard's corps became more developed, the battery of the 3rd brigade was placed on the right of Ligny, near a quarry, and the battery of the 4th brigade on the left of the village, upon the declivity descending to the rivulet. The battery of the 2nd brigade, the foot battery No. 1, and the horse-battery No. 10, remained in reserve. Of the remaining horse-batteries of the corps, one continued with the cavalry under General Röder, (which was posted in a hollow, as before stated, between Ligny and Sombref), and

* For detailed return—See Appendix XXV. Loss on the 15th of June not known; but it was trifling.

† For detailed return—See Appendix XXVI.

the other was with the first Silesian hussars, which regiment had been detached in observation on the right flank of the army, and posted between the northern extremity of the village of Wagnelé and a large pond contiguous to the old Roman road.

By the time the action commenced in front of St. Amand and Ligny—half-past two o'clock—Blücher was satisfied that no necessity existed for any movement of his 3rd corps d'armée to the right; and he therefore ordered it to proceed from the position it had hitherto held in columns upon the two high roads near Sombref, and form the left wing of his line of battle; resting its right upon Sombref, and occupying the heights, at the foot and on the declivities of which are situated the villages of Mont Potriaux, Tongrines, Tongrenelle, Boignée, Balatre, Vilrets, and Botey The 9th brigade (General Borke) was formed in brigade-order in rear of Sombref and northward of the Namur high road, having detached one of its battalions (the 3rd of the eighth regiment) with the foot-battery No. 18, to Mont Potriaux, where the former posted itself on the north, and the latter took up a favourable position on the south, side of the church. The 11th brigade (Colonel Luck) with the 12-pounder battery No. 7, stood across the Fleurus high road, in front of the junction of the latter with the Namur road upon the height of le Point du Jour, having detached the 3rd battalion of the 4th Kurmark landwehr into the valley, where it occupied the houses in its immediate vicinity. Four battalions of the 10th brigade (Colonel Kämpfen) were drawn up on the height of Tongrines, resting their right on this village, and having in their front the foot-battery No. 35, and at a short distance from their left, the horse-battery No. 18. The remaining two battalions of the brigade were detached, the 3rd battalion of the 27th regiment, to occupy Tongrines and the castle of Tongrenelle, and the 3rd battalion of the 2nd Kurmark landwehr, to hold the villages of Boignée and Balatre. The 2nd battalion of the 3rd Kurmark landwehr, belonging to the brigade, as also 2 squadrons of the 6th Kurmark landwehr-cavalry, and 2 squadrons of the 9th hussars, attached to this corps, still continued in the line of outposts in the vicinity of Dinant, to observe Givet; and rejoined on the morning of the 17th of June. The 12th brigade (Colonel Stulpnagel) with the horse-battery No. 20, was formed in brigade order, in reserve, near the windmill, on the height of le Point du Jour. The reserve-cavalry of this corps, with the horse-battery No. 19, was posted on the extreme left of the position between Botey and

Vilrets, whence it detached the 3rd squadron of the 7th uhlans to Onoz, in observation.

This position and the order of battle which was thus developed, were well calculated to answer the object which Blücher had in view, namely, to hold his ground long enough to gain sufficient time for the arrival of at least a portion of Wellington's forces, expected to join the Prussian extreme right by the Namur road; as also, perhaps, for the arrival and co-operation of Bülow's corps, in rear of Thielemann, by the Gembloux road. In either of these cases, if not previously favoured by the circumstances of the general battle about to take place, such a marked accession to his strength would enable him to assume the offensive, whilst, in the first mentioned, Wellington would effectually prevent a junction between Napoleon's and Ney's forces.

The position had been long before selected, and the whole of the ground had even been surveyed, with a view to meet the contingency which had now actually occurred; but then it must be remembered, that in this design the co-operation of the 4th corps d'armée was fully contemplated, whereas the latter had now become a doubtful question: and hence it was that Blücher was led to place more reliance upon a direct support from Wellington, than would otherwise have been the case. To accept a battle, notwithstanding the absence of Bülow's corps, was undoubtedly the wisest course. The enemy's force in the field did not appear to exceed that of the Prussians; and therefore, considering the nature of the position, the contest would, in all probability, become protracted, perhaps until the arrival of Bülow, perhaps, also until the close of day, without any distinct advantage being gained by either party. In the former case, the required preponderance might instantly give a decidedly favourable turn to the scale; in the latter, the junction of the 4th corps during the night would enable Blücher on the following morning to attack his opponent with every prospect of success, and either to relieve Wellington, if necessary, from any pressure in his front, or so to combine his further operations with those of the British commander, should the latter have held his ground and concentrated his army, as to lead to the complete overthrow of both Napoleon's and Ney's forces. To have declined the contest, and retired so as to effect a junction with his 4th corps, he must still, if he wished to act in close concert with Wellington, have abandoned his direct communication with the Meuse and the Rhine, whence he drew all his supplies; a result which might as well be trusted to the chances of a battle. These considerations were also, in all probability, strongly seconded by a desire on the part of the Prussian commander, and one perfectly in keeping with his ardent character, to take every possible measure which was at all warranted by the actual posture of affairs, for vigorously opposing Napoleon's advance.

In a tactical point of view, the position was undoubtedly defective. Nearly the entire of the ground situated between the line of villages of Ligny, St. Amand, and Wagnelé, and the great Namur road, was exposed to the view of the enemy; and as there was every probability of a protracted village-fight along the front of the position, the supports and reserves required to maintain a contest of that nature, would necessarily be subjected to the full play of the batteries on the opposite heights. Upon the space above mentioned every movement could be detected from the French side, where, on the contrary, the undulations were such as to admit of the concealment of the disposition of considerable masses of troops. The defect in this respect was subsequently made strikingly manifest, by the fact that the gradual weakening of the Prussian centre for the purpose of reinforcing the right, was closely observed by Napoleon, who took advantage of the insight thus obtained into his opponent's designs, by collecting in rear of the heights of Ligny that force with which, when he saw that the Prussians had no reserve remaining, he so suddenly assailed and broke the centre of their line.

Napoleon's dispositions having been completed, the battle commenced, about half-past two o'clock, with an attack upon the village of St. Amand, by Lieut. General Lefol's division of Vandamme's corps. The attack, which was made in three columns, proved successful; the three battalions of the 29th Prussian regiment which defended it, were compelled, after a stout resistance, to yield to greatly superior numbers, and were driven out of the village. General Steinmetz, whose brigade was posted in rear of St. Amand, pushed forward all the sharpshooters of the 12th and 24th regiments to their support. These, however, being unable to make head against the enemy, who already made a disposition to debouch from the village, the 12th and 24th regiments were led forward to renew the contest. In the mean time, just as the French appeared at the outlet of the village, a shower of grape and canister was poured right down amongst them from the foot-battery No. 7. Immediately upon this, both battalions of the 12th regiment descended into the ravine, rushed upon the inclosures, and, driving the enemy's shattered infantry before them, regained possession of the village. The 24th regiment advancing by wings of battalions—the one in line and the other in column of reserve respectively—supported this attack upon the left, and established itself in the lower part of St. Amand.

In the course of this short prelude, the batteries ranged along the little eminences which rose on either side of the valley of the Ligny, opened a furious cannonade along the whole extent of the front lines of the contending armies. Ligny, as also St. Amand, (when repossessed by the Prussians,) both of which lay so directly under the French guns, seemed devoted to destruction. Their defenders, sheltered in a great degree by stone walls, hollow ways, and banked-up hedges, appeared perfectly motionless while the deluge of shot and shell poured fast and thick around them; but no sooner did those in Ligny discover a dusky mass emerging from the clouds of smoke which enveloped the heights above them, and wending its course downwards upon the lower portion of the village, than they rushed out of their concealment, and lining with their advanced skirmishers the outermost inclosures, prepared to meet the onset which would probably bring them into closer contact with their enemies, and lead to a struggle in which physical strength and innate courage, combined with individual skill and dexterity, might effect a result unattainable by a recourse to projectiles alone.' It was the 2nd battalion of the 19th Prussian regiment, which, issuing from its cover, where it had stood in column, rapidly deployed, and, by a well directed volley, shook the advancing mass, which it then threw into disorder by following up this advantage with a well-sustained fire. Twice was this attack repeated on the part of Gérard's troops, but with a similar result. A second column now advanced against the centre of the village, and shortly afterwards a third was launched against the upper part of it, near the old castle; but their attempts to penetrate within its precincts proved equally futile, and the four Prussian battalions of Henkel's brigade gallantly maintained the post of Ligny. As the French column withdrew, their batteries played with redoubled energy upon the village, and fresh columns prepared for another assault.

The troops of Vandamme's corps renewed the attack upon St. Amand with the utmost vigour, and forcing back the 12th and 24th Prussian regiments, which suffered most severely, penetrated into the village, where the fight became obstinate, and the fire most destructive. Steinmetz had only two more battalions of his brigade remaining at his disposal—the 1st and 3rd battalions of the 1st Westphalian landwehr—and these he pushed forward into the village, to restore confidence to the defenders, whose numbers were so fearfully reduced, and, if possible, to stem the progress of the assailants. They had scarcely got fairly into action, however, when their commanding officers were wounded, and both battalions gave way before the furious onset of the French, the 3rd battalion leaving numbers of its men killed, along the outlets of the village. The whole brigade, which, within a short period, had suffered a loss of 46 officers and 2,300 men, having rallied in rear of St. Amand, retired into position between Bry and Sombref, and the three battalions which had first occupied the village, marched to rejoin the 3rd brigade, whilst the loud shouts of "*vive l'Empereur!*" which immediately followed the cessation of the sharp rattle of the musketry, heard even amidst the incessant thunder of the artillery, proclaimed the triumph of the French infantry.

In the meantime, another assault was made upon Ligny, whose defenders had been reinforced by the two remaining battalions of Henkel's brigade. The French now changed their mode of attack. They advanced simultaneously, against the centre with the view of gaining the church-yard, and against the lower end of the village in order to turn the left flank of the defenders; and taking advantage of the unusually great height of the corn, their line of skirmishers, strengthened by whole battalions so as to give it a decided superiority over that of the Prussians, approached so cautiously and silently as to continue unperceived until they suddenly possessed themselves of the outermost hedges and gardens. A hand-to-hand contest ensued, and the Prussians, pressed in front by superior numbers, and taken in flank at the same time, were forced to yield. Presently, however, stimulated by the combined exertions of the commanding officers, Majors Count Gröben, Kuylenstierna, and Rex, they recovered themselves, rallied, and again faced their enemies.

The battle, on this part of the field, now presented an awfully grand and animating spectacle, and the hopes of both parties were raised to the highest state of excitement. Intermingled with the quick but irregular discharge of small arms throughout the whole extent of the village, came forth alternately the cheering "*En avant!*" and exulting "*Vive l'Empereur!*" as also the emphatic "*Vorwärts!*" and the wild "*Hourrah!*" whilst the batteries along the heights, continuing their terrific roar, plunged destruction into the masses seen descending on either side to join in the desperate struggle in the valley, out of which there now arose, from the old castle of Ligny, volumes of dark, thick smoke, succeeded by brilliant flames, imparting additional sublimity to the scene.

The Prussians gradually gained ground, and then pressing forward upon all points of the village, succeeded in clearing it of the French, who, in retreating, abandoned two guns which had been moved close down to the principal outlet on that side. General Jagow's brigade (the 3rd) had made a change of front to its left, and approached the village; the 3rd battalions of both the 7th and 29th regiments had been detached to the right, to protect the foot-batteries Nos. 3 and 8, and to remain in reserve; the four remaining battalions descended into the village as a reinforcement.

Beyond an occasional cannonading, the action on the eastern side of the field, between the corps of Grouchy and of Thielemann, was comparatively languid, being limited to a contest, varied in its results, for the possession of the village of Boignée, and, subsequently, of those houses of Tongrines which were situated along the bottom of the valley, as also to some skilful manœuvring on the part of Grouchy with his cavalry, with a view of menacing the Prussian left.

In the mean time, the French maintained possession of St. Amand, but Zieten's 12-pounder batteries, which were now moved forward, presented a formidable obstruction to their debouching from that village. Napoleon directed General Girard, on the extreme left, to take possession, with his division, of St. Amand-la-Haye, and this operation having been successfully accomplished, gave the French the advantage of outflanking from thence any attack upon St Amand itself. Blücher ordered General Pirch II. to retake this village; whereupon the latter advanced with his brigade from the height of Bry, and withdrew the 1st battalion of the 6th regiment from the windmill of Bussy, which was then occupied by the 2nd battalion of the 23rd regiment (8th brigade) and near to which the 1st Westphalian landwehr-cavalry remained during the whole of the action. At the same time, the Prussian chief, fully sensible of the very critical position in which he would be placed, were the French, following up the advantages they had already gained upon his right, to debouch from St. Amand and St. Amand-la-Haye, in sufficient force to overpower Zieten's corps, and thus cut off his communication with Wellington, he decided upon occupying the village of Wagnelé, whence repeated attacks might be directed against the enemy's left flank; and, with this view, he desired General Pirch I., who commanded the 2nd corps, to detach the 5th brigade (General Tippelskirchen's) to the latter village, and to place it under the orders of General Jürgass, who was also sent to that part of the field, with Lieut. Colonel Sohr's brigade of cavalry, (consisting of the 3rd Brandenburg, and 5th Pomeranian, hussars,) together with two squadrons of the 6th Neumark dragoons, and the horse-battery No. 6. Colonel Marwitz, of Thielemann's corps, was also ordered to join these troops with two regiments of his brigade, the 7th and 8th uhlans. The brigade of General Brause, (the 7th,) which had been rejoined by detached battalions, was pushed forward as far as the Roman road, to occupy the position vacated by the advance of General Tippelskirchen's brigade, to which it was to act as a support in case of necessity.

It was four o'clock when General Pirch II. who had formed his brigade for the attack of St. Amand-la-Haye, having his left flank protected by the 12th regiment, which had re-assembled in rear of St. Amand, moved his front line against the former village. As it advanced, however, its ranks were dreadfully shattered by the fire from the French artillery, nor were they less thinned by that of the musketry as they entered the village; and such was the determined resistance on the part of the French, that they were unable to penetrate beyond the centre of the village; and though reinforced by the 1st battalion of the 6th regiment, from the second line, they found it quite impracticable to drive the enemy out of a large building which was surrounded by a stone wall, and which formed the point of connection between the two villages. The Prussians having got into great disorder, and being closely pressed by the French, were compelled to abandon the village, in order to collect their scattered remnants, and to re-form. General Girard, whose division had, under his own immediate guidance, so gallantly maintained the village, fell mortally wounded on this occasion.

Blücher now decided on a renewed attack upon St. Amand-la-Haye, in order to occupy the front of Girard's division, while he should carry into effect his previously projected movement against the enemy's left flank; and, anxious to ensure the due execution of his instructions and to direct the attacks himself, he repaired in person to this part of the field. General Tippelskirchen's brigade, having advanced along the Roman road, was already formed in brigade order, in rear of Wagnelé, while Jürgass had posted his cavalry more to the left, and opposite to the interval between that village and St. Amand-la-Haye, whence he could with considerable advantage fall upon the enemy, should the latter venture to debouch in that direction.

These movements did not escape the watchful eye of Napoleon, who detached a division of the young guard and a battery of the same corps in support of his left wing, as also General Colbert's brigade of lancers from Count Pajol's corps, to reinforce the cavalry on the left, and to preserve the communication with Ney.

When all was ready for the attack, Blücher, who felt how much depended on its result, galloped up to the leading battalions, and thus earnestly and impassionately ordered the advance:—"Now, lads, behave well! don't suffer the '*grande nation*' again to rule over you! Forward! In God's name—forward!"* Instantly his devoted followers rent the air with their re-echoing shouts of "*Vorwärts!*" Nothing could surpass the undaunted resolution and intrepid mien which Pirch's battalions displayed as they advanced against, and entered, St. Amand-la-Haye, at a charging pace; they completely swept the enemy before them, while Major Quadt, who commanded the 28th regiment, supported by some detachments of the 2nd regiment (from Tippelskirchen's brigade) gained possession of the great building. The 1st battalion of the 6th regiment, after having forced its way right across the village, sallied forth from the opposite side, in pursuit of the enemy, with a degree of impetuosity which its officers had the utmost difficulty in restraining, while numbers of the men were on the point of plunging into the very midst of the French reserves. The cavalry on the right of the village seemed to have caught up the intrepid spirit and enthusiastic devotion of the infantry, and, as if impatient to join in the struggle, a squadron of the Brandenburg uhlans supported the attack of the village by a charge upon the enemy's cavalry; after which, the remainder of this regiment, with the 1st Kurmark landwehr-cavalry, advanced under General Treskow, into the plain on the left of the village, of which the whole contour now bristled with the bayonets of the 46th regiment, while the 28th regiment held the post of the great building, which it had so gallantly carried, and the 2nd Westphalian landwehr stood in second line, as a reserve.

So completely absorbed was the attention of the 12-pounder battery No. 6, which stood in a somewhat isolated position, by the contest in St. Amand-la-Haye, which it

* "Kinder, haltet Euch brav! lasst die Nation nicht wieder Herr über Euch werden! Vorwärts—vorwärts in Gottes Nahmen!"

covered by its fire, that it had not noticed the stealthy advance of a troop of the enemy's horsemen, wearing the uniform of the light artillery of the guard, and most unexpectedly found itself attacked in flank by these bold adventurers. This gave rise to a curious scene, for the Prussian gunners, in the first moment of surprise, could only defend themselves with their rammers and handspikes, but with these they plied the intruders with so much adroitness and resolution as to hurl their leaders to the ground, and force the remainder to betake themselves to a hasty flight.

Prince Blücher had, in the mean time, on perceiving Colbert's French lancers hovering upon, and stretching out beyond, his extreme right, ordered General Pirch to detach two more cavalry regiments—the Queen's dragoons and the 4th Kurmark landwehr-cavalry—as a reinforcement to the cavalry of Zieten's corps.

The nearly simultaneous attack upon Wagnelé by Tippelskirchen's brigade, previously mentioned as having taken post in rear of that village, was not attended with an equal degree of success. The 1st and 2nd battalions of the 25th regiment advanced in column through the centre of Wagnelé; but on debouching, the 2nd battalion, which led the advance, was suddenly assailed by a fire from the French skirmishers who lay concealed in the high corn. Although its order was thus considerably disturbed, it succeeded, nevertheless, in effecting its deployment. The 1st battalion also deployed, but, in doing so, its left wing covered the right of the second battalion; and while executing a second movement, intended to clear the front of the latter, the French battalions pressing forward, drove in the Prussian skirmishers upon the regiment, which consisted mostly of young soldiers; when, notwithstanding the conspicuously meritorious exertions of all their officers, they were overthrown and dispersed in such a manner that it became impracticable to lead them back into action in any other way than by separate detachments. The 3rd battalion of this regiment shared nearly the same fate; for, having plunged into the high corn, it received a volley which disordered its ranks, and killed its three senior officers; and although it maintained for some time a fire in return, it was eventually compelled to retire, as were also the 1st and 2nd battalions of the 5th Westphalian landwehr, under precisely similar circumstances. The brigade was re-formed, under the protection of the 2nd Prussian regiment, which now advanced from the reserve, boldly encountered the enemy, and, aided by the efficacious fire of the foot-battery No. 10, stemmed the further progress of the French, and thus gained time for the remaining battalions to re-form in rear of Wagnelé. Upon the advance, however, of a French column towards its left flank, it fell back as far as the entrance into the village.

The French now renewed their attacks upon St. Amand-la-Haye, and made their appearance simultaneously in front and in both flanks of that village. The fight again became desperate. Pirch's brigade had, however, exhausted both its ammunition and its strength, when Blücher pushed forward the 3rd battalion of the 23rd regiment (from the 8th brigade —Colonel Langen's), and soon afterwards the 3rd battalion of the 9th regiment, together with the whole of the 26th regiment (from the 6th brigade—General Krafft's), whereupon General Pirch withdrew his battalions, which had suffered so severely, to the rear of Bry. The foot-battery No. 3, belonging to Pirch's brigade, had at an earlier period moved to its left, and had taken up a position near the quarries on the right of Ligny, by the side of the foot-battery No. 8, of Jagow's brigade.

While the struggle in the villages in front of the right of the Prussian position continue to wear an indecisive and unsettled aspect, let us return for a moment to Ligny, which we left in possession of Count Henkel's 4th Prussian brigade, supported by the 3rd brigade under General Jagow.

The 1st and 2nd battalions of the 7th regiment (of Jagow's brigade) were ordered to traverse the village, and to advance in column against the enemy. Just as they debouched, they found in their immediate front, several French battalions, in close column, moving directly against the village. Both parties at once came to a halt; the Prussians without being able to deploy in the defile, and the French without attempting to do so, probably unwilling to lose the time which such a movement would require. A fire of musketry commenced which lasted half an hour, and caused much loss. Other battalions now hastened across the village, but all at once, a rumour flew rapidly among them, that the French were in possession of the church-yard, and in a moment several muskets were aimed in that direction, and either thoughtlessly or nervously discharged. Those battalions that were in front, at the outlet of the village, became alarmed by this unexpected firing in their rear. At the same time, a discharge of grape, from some guns suddenly brought forward by the French, in their immediate front, augmented their confusion, and forced them to a retreat. They were closely pursued by the enemy, whose skirmishers made a dash at the colour of the 2nd battalion of the 7th regiment, which they would have captured but for the noble and determined gallantry with which it was defended.

General Krafft, from whose brigade (the 6th) five battalions had already been detached, namely, four for the defence of St. Amand-la-Haye, and one in aid of that of Ligny, now received Blücher's order with his remaining four battalions, (the 1st and 2d of the 9th, and the 1st and 3d of the 1st Elbe landwehr,) to drive the enemy out of the latter village. The foot-battery No. 15, was posted between the left of Ligny and the Bois-du-loup, and the foot-battery No. 37, was directed towards St. Amand. The other batteries posted between Ligny and St. Amand received orders to retire accordingly as they expended their ammunition, for the purpose of refitting; and they were successively relieved by the foot-battery No. 1, the horse-battery No. 10, and the 12-pounder batteries Nos. 4 and 8. The horse-battery No. 14 was advanced across the stream between Ligny and Sombref, and took post on the other side of the valley, where it was much exposed to the enemy's fire, and lost 19 gunners and 53 horses.

General Krafft moved forward, in the first instance, only two battalions, and kept the others in reserve; but all of them soon became engaged; for the French, though driven back at first, received considerable reinforcements.

The fight throughout the whole village of Ligny was now at the hottest: the place was literally crammed with the combatants, and its streets and inclosures were choked up with the wounded, the dying, and the dead: every house that had escaped being set on fire, was the scene of a desperate struggle: the troops fought no longer in combined order, but in numerous and irregular groups, separated by houses either in flames, or held as little forts, sometimes by the one, and sometimes by the other party; and in various instances, when their ammunition failed, or when they found themselves suddenly assailed from different sides, the bayonet, and even the butt, supplied them with the ready means for prosecuting the dreadful carnage with unmitigated fury. The entire village was concealed in smoke; but the incessant rattle of the musketry, the crashing of burning timbers, the smashing of doors and gateways, the yells and imprecations of the combatants, which were heard through that misty veil, gave ample indication to the troops posted in reserve upon the heights, of the fierce and savage nature of the struggle beneath. In the mean time, the relieving batteries on the Prussian side, which had arrived quite fresh from the rear, came into full play, as did also a reinforcement, on the French side, from the artillery of the imperial guard. The earth now trembled under the tremendous cannonade; and as the flames, issuing from the numerous burning houses, intermingled with dense volumes of smoke, shot directly upwards through the light-grey mass which rendered the village indistinguishable, and seemed continually to thicken, the scene resembled for a time some violent convulsion of nature, rather than a human conflict—as if the valley had been rent asunder, and Ligny had become the focus of a burning crater.

Long did this fierce and deadly strife continue without any material advance being made on either side. At length the French gained possession of a large house, as also of the church-yard, into which they brought forward two pieces of cannon. General Jagow vainly endeavoured with the 7th regiment to retake this house. The 1st battalion of the 3rd Westphalian landwehr displayed the most inflexible perseverance in its endeavours to drive the French out again from the church-yard: it made three unsuccessful attempts to cross an intervening ditch, and subsequently tried to gain a hollow-way, which lay in the flank of that post, but falling upon the French reinforcements that were advancing towards it, they were compelled to abandon the enterprise.

Fresh victims were still required to satiate the "king of terrors," who might be said to hold a gala-day in this "valley of death." Blücher had ordered Colonel Langen's brigade (the 8th) to follow in succession that of General Krafft. The position vacated by the former, in front of Sombref, was taken up by Colonel Stülpnagel's brigade (the 12th) of Thielemann's corps, and the chain of skirmishers of the latter brigade extended along the rivulet as far as Ligny. As soon as Colonel Langen had reached the immediate vicinity of Ligny, he posted the 1st and 2nd battalions of the 21st regiment upon an eminence near the village, and the foot-battery No. 12, covered by two squadrons of the 5th Kurmark landwehr-cavalry, upon the left of the road leading to Ligny. The 21st regiment made no less than six different attacks, partly in conjunction with the other troops that fought in Ligny, and partly isolated, without succeeding in disturbing the position of the enemy in that portion of the village which lies on the right bank of the Ligny. Colonel Langen, observing the increased fury and obstinacy of the fight in Ligny, detached thither also the 1st battalion of the 23rd regiment, and the second of the 3rd Elbe landwehr: he then took up a position, with the remainder of his brigade, near the mill of Bussy, into which he threw the 2nd battalion of the 23rd regiment. The 1st battalion of this corps, having formed two columns, rushed into the village, and, after crossing the stream, received a sharp fire from the windows of the houses on the opposite side. The left column of the battalion stormed a farm-house, of which, after it had burst in the gates with hatchets, it gained possession, and thus protected the advance of the right column. At this moment, Napoleon's final and decisive attack commenced on this point; but previously to entering upon an account of it, it will be necessary to resume the narrative of the contest along the remainder of the line of battle.

On the right, Tippelskirchen's brigade (the 5th) was ordered to renew the attack upon St. Amand-la-Haye, and, as an auxiliary movement, a bold push was to be made upon the group of houses in rear of that village, and of Wagnelé, called the Hameau de St. Amand. Both of the 3rd battalions of the 2nd and 25th regiments, under Major Witzleben, advanced against the latter point, while the 1st and 2nd battalions of the 2nd regiment, the 3rd battalion of the 5th Westphalian landwehr, and a battalion of the 25th regiment made a direct attack upon St. Amand-la-Haye. Both movements were supported by the foot-batteries Nos. 10 and 37, and Colonel Thümen was detached, with the Silesian uhlans, and the 11th hussars, to cover the right of the brigade: the 1st and 2nd squadrons of the 5th Kurmark landwehr-cavalry were posted in reserve. The 3rd battalion of the 2nd regiment opened the attack upon the Hameau de St. Amand, and being well protected on their right by the 11th hussars, carried it by storm. The French appeared determined to regain this point, which from its position, was, in fact, the key to the defence of the three villages of St. Amand, St. Amand-la-Haye, and Wagnelé, and the struggle for its possession was most obstinate and sanguinary. All the battalions of Tippelskirchen's brigade became successively engaged. Four times was St. Amand-la-Haye lost and retaken by the 2nd regiment, which suffered severely. General Jürgass ordered forward the horse-battery No. 6, on the right of which the foot-battery No. 10 then took post. The Silesian uhlans and the 11th hussars suffered considerably from their exposure to the enemy's artillery. Colonel Thümen was killed at their head, by a cannon-shot, and was succeeded by Lieut. Colonel Schmiedeberg, who ordered both these regiments to make a change of front to the right; when the Prussian lancers dashed forward to meet the advance of a French regiment, which they completely defeated, and having followed up the attack with a vigorous pursuit, fell all at once among the enemy's reserves; but they immediately recovered themselves, and rallied with great celerity, order, and precision.

About this time, the light cavalry-brigade of Colonel Marwitz, already mentioned as having been ordered from the left, reached the right flank, and was formed up in two lines: also the four battalions that had been detached from General Krafft's brigade, arrived upon the right of St. Amand-la-Haye, and came into action. The battle on both sides on this part of the field continued to rage with unabated violence, and with such indefatigable ardour did the Prussians continue the struggle, that when the fire of their infantry-skirmishers was observed to slacken, from the men having expended their ammunition, the soldiers of the 11th hussars rushed into the midst of them, and supplied them with such cartridges as they had of their own; an act of devotion to which many of them fell a sacrifice. General Jürgass ordered forward the brigade (7th) of General Brause in support of that of General Tippelskirchen which had suffered a very severe loss. When General Brause had, at an earlier period, taken post at the Trois Burettes, upon Tippelskirchen advancing from that point to Wagnelé, (as previously explained,) he stationed both the 3rd battalions of the 14th and 22nd regiments upon an eminence on the left of the high road, for the purpose of keeping up the communication with Tippelskirchen; and he pushed on the other two battalions of the 14th regiment towards Bry, that they might be nearer at hand, if required, for the contest in the villages of Wagnelé and St. Amand-la-Haye, while the two squadrons of the Elbe landwehr-cavalry, attached to his brigade, kept a look-out upon both sides of the road. These two battalions, thus posted, caught the eye of Blücher as he looked round for the nearest available force, and he immediately ordered them to advance, and join in the contest; and General Brause, on being made acquainted with this disposition, led forward the 3rd battalions of the 14th and 22nd regiments, and the 1st battalion of the 2nd Elbe landwehr, while the four remaining battalions of his brigade, making a change of front to their left, formed up, in reserve, in rear of the Namur road. On approaching the more immediate scene of the action, General Brause came upon the 3rd battalion of the 9th regiment, which had expended all its ammunition: he procured for it a fresh supply, and ordered it to return into the village, along with the 2nd battalion of the 14th regiment; while the first battalion of this regiment threw itself into St. Amand-la-Haye, and relieved the 2nd regiment, which now retired, as did also the remainder of Tippelskirchen's brigade to the rear of Wagnelé, where it re-formed.

Here, in these villages on the right, as well as at Ligny, the fight never slackened for a moment: fresh masses, from both sides, poured in among the burning houses as often as the fearfully diminished numbers and dreadfully exhausted state of the combatants rendered relief imperatively necessary; partial successes on different points were constantly met by corresponding reverses on others; and so equally were the courage, the energies, and the devotion of both parties balanced, that the struggle between them appeared, from its unabated vigour, likely to continue until the utter exhaustion of the one should yield the triumph to the greater command of reserves possessed by the other. The anxiety at that time on the part of Blücher for the arrival of either a portion of Wellington's forces, or Bülow's corps, was extreme; and frequently, as he cheered forward his men in their advance to take part in the contest, did he address them with the exhortation, "Forward, lads! we must do something before the English join us!" In fact, his only reserve remaining was the 9th brigade (General Borcke's), the withdrawal of which would greatly expose his centre; and Napoleon, who had already entertained a suspicion that such was the case, resolved upon terminating the sanguinary combat in the valley, by boldly advancing a portion of his own intact reserves, consisting of the guard and Lobau's corps (which had just arrived and was posted on the right of Fleurus) against the Prussian centre.

For the execution of his project the French Emperor destined the imperial guard, with Milhaud's corps of cuirassiers in support. He wished to conceal this movement as much as possible from the enemy, and caused it to be made to the right, along the rear of the corps of Gérard, a portion of whose batteries was ordered to be withdrawn, for the purpose of affording greater protection to the guard, by diverting the enemy's fire to other points, and of deceiving him as to the real object of the movement, if observed previously to the actual execution of the Emperor's design.

This far-famed band of veteran warriors, and Milhaud's splendid corps of mailed cuirassiers, were in full march towards the lower extremity of Ligny, where they were to cross the stream, when, all at once, they were halted by an order direct from the Emperor, who had decided upon suspending the movement, until he should ascertain the result of an incident that had occurred upon his extreme left, and which had placed him for the time in considerable doubt and anxiety respecting its real nature. He had received a message from Vandamme, informing him that a strong column, composed of infantry, cavalry, and artillery, was advancing towards Fleurus; that it had at first been looked upon as the corps detached from Ney's forces, until it was discovered that it moved by a different road from that along which those troops had been expected, and in a direction towards the French left rear, instead of the Prussian extreme right; that Girard's division had been consequently induced to fall back, and take up a position to cover Fleurus; and that the effect produced upon his own corps by the sudden appearance of this column was such, that if His Majesty did not immediately move his reserve to arrest its progress, his troops would be compelled to evacuate St. Amand and commence a retreat. This intelligence could not fail to create alarm in the mind of the French Emperor, who concluded that the corps in question had been detached against his rear, as a diversion in favour of Blücher, from the army of Wellington, who had probably obtained some signal triumph over Ney. Another officer arrived from Vandamme, reiterating the account previously given. Napoleon instantly gave the order for the halt of the imperial guard; and despatched one of his aides-de-camp to reconnoitre the strength and disposition of the column, and to discover the object of its movement.

The commencement of the march of the imperial guard and Milhaud's cuirassier-corps towards Ligny, had been conducted with so much skill, and the manœuvring of these troops at one point in their line of march to shelter themselves from the fire of the Prussian batteries, to which they had become suddenly exposed, bore so much the appearance of a retrograde movement, accompanied as it was by the withdrawal of a portion of the guns of Gérard corps, that the Prussians were completely deceived by it. Intelligence was hastily conveyed to Blücher that the enemy was retreating; whereupon he ordered the march of all the remaining disposable battalions of Colonel Langen's brigade (the 8th) upon St. Amand, to enable him to take advantage of the circumstance by pressing upon the enemy's left.

In the mean time, Colonel Marwitz had been menaced by the advance of a considerable line of cavalry and a battery, which latter annoyed him but little. This cavalry did not, however, seem much disposed to risk a close encounter: once it put forward a detachment, which was overthrown by two squadrons of the 7th and 8th uhlans, and then a regiment of French chasseurs à cheval fell upon the skirmishers of the 2nd regiment of infantry, but was driven back by two squadrons of the 5th Kurmark landwehr-cavalry. Colonel Marwitz had been ordered by General Jürgass to send out patroles in different directions from the right flank, for the purpose of seeking out the communication with the Duke of Wellington's forces. These brought in prisoners, from whom it was ascertained that a whole French corps, the 1st, under Count d'Erlon, was in that vicinity. Subsequently French cavalry was perceived between Mellet and Villers-Perruin; whereupon Colonel Marwitz, who had been reinforced by two squadrons of the Pomeranian hussars, ordered a change of front of his brigade in this direction, then deployed his eight squadrons in two lines, with considerable intervals, and withdrew them, alternately, towards the high road; followed, though not vigorously, by three French regiments of cavalry and a battery, comprising Jaquinot's light cavalry-brigade, attached to d'Erlon's corps.* As he approached the chaussée, the 2nd and 3rd battalions of the 2nd Elbe landwehr, as also the 3rd battalion of the 22nd regiment advanced to his support.

Until about six o'clock the action along that part of the line which extended from Sombref to Balatre, had not been carried on with any degree of energy, and the occupation of the opposing forces was generally limited to mutual observation. Now, however, the French infantry, (of which only a small portion was attached to Grouchy's cavalry) penetrated as far as the precincts of the village of Tongrines; but Colonel Kämpfen's brigade, (the 10th,) having been successively reinforced by all the battalions of Colonel Luck's brigade (the 11th) excepting one which was left in reserve, the French were easily repulsed, and the Prussians maintained full possession of all this portion of their original position.

It was about seven o'clock when the aide-de camp* returned from his reconnaissance, and reported to Napoleon that the column in the distance which had caused so much uneasiness proved to be d'Erlon's corps; that Girard's division, upon being undeceived, had resumed its position in the line of battle; and that Vandamme's corps had main-

* See page 102-103.

† There is reason to believe that it was General Labedoyère. It was certainly not General Dejean, as stated in the "Mémoires de Napoleon," livre IX.

tained its ground. This movement of d'Erlon's corps admits of being satisfactorily explained. Napoleon, having received information that d'Erlon had been left in reserve in front of Gosselies, and inferring, perhaps, from this circumstance that Ney was sufficiently strong to be able to hold his ground at Quatre-Bras, without further aid than what he had at hand, resolved upon employing this corps against the Prussian right flank; but in the mean time, d'Erlon had, in pursuance of instructions from Ney, continued his march towards Quatre-Bras; and having himself proceeded in advance, had reached Frasne, at which place Colonel Laurent found him, and communicated to him the Emperor's order for the march of his corps upon St. Amand; adding that on coming up with the head of his column, he had taken upon himself to change its direction of march into that of St. Amand. D'Erlon hastened to comply with Napoleon's wishes, and despatched General d'Elcambre, his chief of the staff, to make known the movement to Marshal Ney. His route from Frasne towards St. Amand the point prescribed by the order, lay through Villers-Perruin, and the movement was altogether one of a retrograde nature. Hence the direction of the column, as seen in the distance, was well calculated to alarm the troops of the French extreme left; as also to excite surprise in the mind of Napoleon, who having formed no expectation of the arrival of any French troops in the field by any other direction than that from Gosselies upon St. Amand, or perhaps from Quatre-Bras upon Bry, also participated in the opinion that the column in question, under its attendant circumstances and general disposition, could be no other than that of an enemy. As d'Erlon debouched from Villers-Perruin, and advanced upon the prescribed point, St. Amand, he threw out his cavalry (Jaquinot's) to his left, for the protection of this flank; and it was before this cavalry that the Prussian brigade, under Colonel Marwitz, retired in the manner already explained, a movement which fully restored confidence to Girard's division. All at once this column was observed to halt, to indicate an indecision in its intentions, and finally to withdraw from the field. D'Erlon had in fact just received from Ney a peremptory order to join him without delay, with which he resolved to comply, probably concluding that he was bound to do so from the circumstance of his having been in the first instance placed under the Marshal's immediate command; having ascertained also from the Emperor's aide-de-camp that he was not the bearer of any instructions whatever from Napoleon as to his future movements, and that the appearance of his corps upon that part of the field of battle had been quite unexpected. This pressing order had been despatched by Ney immediately previous to the arrival of Colonel Laurent on the heights of Gemioncourt.

If the first appearance of this column had caused alarm and perplexity among the troops of the French left wing, the apprehensions it excited on the Prussian right, when its cavalry was observed to advance and to drive back Colonel Marwitz's brigade, which had been sent towards it *en reconnaissance*, (as already explained,) were still greater; and its equally unexpected disappearance, (with the exception of its cavalry, and a portion of its infantry,) at a moment when it was felt that its vigorous co-operation must have rendered the issue of the battle no longer doubtful, was looked upon as a particularly fortunate turn of affairs; and Blücher's hopes revived as he prepared to carry into effect his meditated attack upon the French left flank.

There did not appear on the part of Napoleon any eagerness to resume the movement of the imperial guard towards the lower extremity of Ligny, but rather an anxiety to await calmly the most favourable moment for his projected attack. Doubtless he had discovered the march of the remaining battalions of Colonel Langen's brigade, from Sombref towards St. Amand, as a further reinforcement to the Prussian right, and calculated upon paralysing the attack which Blücher was evidently preparing against his left flank, by executing a sudden and vigorous assault on the Prussian centre, with a preponderating mass of fresh troops. At length, towards eight o'clock, the Emperor gave the order for the guard and Milhaud's corps of cuirassiers to resume their march. The same precautions were observed as before for masking the movement as much as possible, and so successfully, that Thielemann, on observing a French battery opposite Tongrines entirely withdrawn, and Grouchy's lines of cavalry presenting a diminished extent of front, and conceiving, at the same time, that the contest in Ligny was assuming a change favourable to the Prussians, concluded that the moment had then arrived in which an attack might be made with every probability of success, upon the right flank of the enemy. He had only one brigade remaining of the cavalry of his corps, namely that of Colonel Count Lottum; the other brigade, under Colonel Marwitz, having been, as already explained, for some time detached to the extreme right of the Prussian army. General Hobe, who commanded this cavalry-division, had previously moved forward Count Lottum's brigade and posted it in rear of Colonel Kämpfen's infantry-brigade. Thielemann now desired him to advance with Lottum's brigade and the horse battery No. 19, along the Fleurus high road. In carrying this order into effect, General Hobe posted the battery, in the first instance, close to the 12-pounder battery No. 7, which stood across the Fleurus high road, about midway between the junction of the lattter with the Namur road and the bridge over the Ligny. A cannonade was opened from this point upon the French guns on the opposite height, to which the latter replied with great spirit, and one of the guns of the battery was dismounted. The remaining guns were now advanced rapidly along the high road, preceded by two squadrons of the 7th dragoons: on getting into position, two of the guns continued upon the road itself, on which the French had also posted two pieces, but scarcely had the squadrons formed up, and the battery fired a few rounds, when they were furiously attacked by the 5th and 13th French dragoons of Excelmans' cavalry-corps: in an instant they were thrown into confusion; the two guns upon the road escaped, while the remainder fell into the hands of the French dragoons, who closely pursued the Prussians.

General Borcke (commanding the 9th brigade) observing this mêlée upon the Fleurus road, immediately pushed forward the 1st and 3rd battalions of the 1st Kurmark landwehr, and posted them in rear of the hedges and walls running parallel with the high road, so as to flank the enemy's cavalry; the 2nd battalion of the same regiment followed the movement, and was finally stationed upon the road. In order to support these battalions, and to preserve the communication with Colonel Stülpnagel's brigade (the 12th) on his right, he occupied Mont Potriaux and its outlets with the remainder of his brigade, excepting the 1st and 2nd battalions of the 8th regiment, which he held in reserve.

The 5th and 13th French dragoons finding themselves likely to be thus seriously impeded both in front and on their left, and finally experiencing on their right a cannonade from the two batteries attached to Colonel Kämpfen's brigade, which had moved forward from the height above Tongrines to the rise of ground south of Tongrenelle, retired from this part of the field.

It will be recollected that Colonel Stülpnagel's brigade, on relieving that of Colonel Langen in front of Sombref, had extended a chain of skirmishers along the stream as far as

Ligny: these were now reinforced by both the 3rd battalions of the 31st regiment and the 6th Kurmark landwehr, with the 3rd battalion of the 5th Kurmark landwehr in reserve. The 1st and 2nd battalions of the Kurmark landwehr were posted on the height between Sombref and the Bois-du-loup, having on their right and somewhat in advance, two squadrons from each of the 5th and 6th regiments of Kurmark landwehr-cavalry, together with two guns from the foot-battery No. 12. The remaining four battalions of the brigade were in reserve immediately in front of the inclosures of Sombref.

It was nearly eight o'clock, when General Krafft despatched an aide-de-camp to the rear with a message stating, that it was only by dint of extraordinary efforts that the troops in Ligny could hold out against the enemy, who was continually advancing with fresh reinforcements. General Count Gneisenau, (the chief of staff of the Prussian army), in the absence of the Prince, sent word that the village must be maintained, at whatever sacrifice, half an hour longer.

About the same time, General Pirch II. sent word to Blücher that his brigade, in defending St. Amand-la-Haye, had expended the whole of its ammunition, and that even the pouches of the killed had been completely emptied. To this the Prince replied, that the 2nd brigade must, nevertheless, not only maintain its post, but also attack the enemy with the bayonet.

In fact, the exhaustion of the Prussian troops was becoming more manifest every moment. Several officers and men, overcome by long continued exertion, were seen to fall solely from excessive fatigue. No kind of warfare can be conceived more harassing to the combatants than was the protracted contest in the villages which skirted the front of the Prussian position. It partook also of a savage and relentless character. The animosity and exasperation of both parties were uncontrollable. Innumerable individual combats took place. Every house, every court, every wall, was the scene of a desperate conflict. Streets were alternately won and lost. An ungovernable fury seized upon the combatants on both sides, as they rushed wildly forward to relieve their comrades exhausted by their exertions in the deadly strife—a strife in which every individual appeared eager to seek out an opponent, from whose death he might derive some alleviation to the thirst of hatred and revenge by which he was so powerfully excited. Hence no quarter was asked or granted by either party.

When it is considered that a very great portion of the Prussian army consisted of young soldiers, who were under fire for the first time, their bravery and exertions in maintaining so lengthened a contest of this nature, with the veteran warriors of the French army, cannot fail to be regarded with the highest admiration.

Such were the distribution and the state of the Prussian troops throughout their line, when Napoleon arrived near the lower extremity of Ligny, with a formidable reserve. This consisted of eight battalions of the guard, of Milhaud's corps of heavy cavalry, comprising 8 regiments of cuirassiers, and of the grenadiers à cheval of the guard. It was not, however, his sole reserve, for most opportunely Lobau's corps had just arrived and taken post on the right of Fleurus. The troops which the French Emperor held thus in hand ready to launch as a thunderbolt against the weakened centre of the Prussian line of battle, were perfectly fresh, not having hitherto taken any part whatever in the contest, and they might justly be styled the flower of his army. It was this consciousness of the vantage ground he then possessed which, upon his perceiving the comparatively unoccupied space in rear of Ligny, called forth from him the remark to Count Gérard, "They are lost: they have no reserve remaining!" He saw that not another moment was to be delayed in securing the victory which was now within his grasp, and gave his last orders for the attack at the very time when Blücher, whose right had just been strengthened by the arrival of the remaining three battalions of Colonel Langen's (the 8th) infantry brigade, was making his dispositions for vigorously assailing the French army in its left flank.

The projected movement that was to decide the battle was preceded, at about half-past eight o'clock, by the rapid advance of several batteries of the guard, which opened a most destructive fire upon the Prussians posted within, and formed in the immediate rear of, Ligny. Under cover of this cannonade, Gérard, with Pecheux's infantry-division, reinforced the troops that still maintained that half of the village which lay on the right bank of the rivulet, and pushed forward with a determination to dislodge the enemy from the remaining portion on the left bank. While the Prussian infantry in rear of Ligny were in movement for the purpose of relieving their comrades who were already giving way before this renewed attack, they suddenly perceived, on the French right of the village, a column issuing from under the heavy smoke that rolled away from the well-served batteries which had so unexpectedly opened upon them, and which continued so fearfully to thin their ranks; and, as the mass rapidly advanced down the slope with the evident design of forcing a passage across the valley, they could not fail to distinguish both by its well-sustained order and compactness, and by its dark waving surface of bearskins, that they had now to contend against the redoubted imperial guard. Ligny being thus turned, the Prussian infantry, instead of continuing its advance into the village, was necessitated, by its inferiority of numbers, to confine its operations to the securing, as far as possible, an orderly retreat for the defenders of the place.

Notwithstanding their dreadfully exhausted and enfeebled state, and their knowledge that a body of fresh troops was advancing against them, a body, too, which they knew was almost invariably employed whenever some great and decisive blow was to be struck, they evinced not the slightest symptom of irresolution, but, on the contrary, were animated by the most inflexible courage. The sun had gone down, shrouded in heavy clouds, and rain having set in, the battle-field would speedily be enveloped in darkness; hence the Prussians felt that it required but a little more perseverance in their exertions to enable them to counterbalance their deficiency of numbers upon any point of their line by a stern and resolute resistance, sufficient to secure for the entire of their army the means of effecting a retreat, unattended by those disastrous consequences which a signal defeat in the light of day might have entailed upon them.

The 21st regiment of infantry boldly advanced against the French column, with a determination to check its further progress, but soon found itself charged in flank by cavalry that had darted forward from the head of a column which, by the glimmering of its armour, even amidst the twilight, proclaimed itself a formidable body of cuirassiers. It was, in fact, Milhaud's whole corps of that description of force, which had effected its passage on the other side of the village. The 9th regiment of infantry fought its way through a mass of cavalry, whilst Major Wulffen, with two weak squadrons of the 1st Westphalian landwehr-cavalry, made a gallant charge against the French infantry, which received it with a volley at a distance of twenty paces. The Prussian infantry compelled to evacuate Ligny, effected its retreat in squares, in perfect order, though surrounded by the enemy, bravely repelling all further attacks, made in the repeated but vain attempts to scatter it in confusion.

Blücher, who had arrived upon the spot from his right, having, in consequence of this sudden turn of affairs, been under the necessity of relinquishing his meditated attack upon the French left, now made a last effort to stem the further advance of the enemy, and, if possible, to force him back upon Ligny. The rain having ceased, it became lighter, and the enemy's columns being more clearly discernible, the Prince immediately ordered the advance of three regiments of the cavalry attached to the 1st corps d'armée, namely, the 6th uhlans, the 1st West Prussian dragoons, and the 2nd Kurmark landwehr-cavalry. These regiments, which constituted the only cavalry force immediately at hand, had for some time been posted in reserve, and had suffered severely from their exposure to the fire from the French artillery. Lieut. General Röder directed the 6th uhlans to make the first charge. The regiment was led on by Lieut. Colonel Lützow, to whose brigade it belonged. In the charge which was directed upon the enemy's infantry, Lützow and several of his officers fell under a volley of musketry. The regiment, which was about 400 strong, lost on this occasion 13 officers and 70 men. A second attack, made by the 1st West Prussian dragoons, and supported by the 2nd Kurmark landwehr-cavalry, seemed to offer a fair prospect of penetrating the French infantry, when the former regiment was unexpectedly charged in flank by the enemy's cuirassiers, and completely dispersed. The Westphalian, and 1st Kurmark landwehr-cavalry, with several other squadrons of the landwehr, were collected together, and formed a mass of twenty-four squadrons, with which a further attack was made upon the enemy, but without success.

The cause of this failure is to be attributed not to the want of sufficient cavalry, for indeed there was an ample number for the purpose, but to the confusion and disorder consequent upon the surprise which the enemy's attack had occasioned, and which was augmented by the darkness that had set in upon the field.

Nor was the failure caused by the absence of that most essential requisite in a charge of cavalry, good example on the part of the officers who lead the well-set squadrons into the midst of an enemy's ranks. Blücher himself, seeing that the fate of the day depended solely on the chance of the cavalry at hand succeeding, while there was yet light, in hurling back the French columns into the valley which they had so suddenly and so resolutely crossed, rallied his routed horsemen, and placing himself at their head, charged, in his old hussar style, with the full determination of restoring, if possible, that equal footing with the enemy which had hitherto been so gallantly maintained. The French firmly stood their ground, and the charge proved ineffectual. As Blücher and his followers retired to rally, they were rapidly pursued by the French cuirassiers. At this moment, the Prince's fine grey charger—a present from the Prince Regent of England—was mortally wounded by a shot, in its left side, near the saddle-girth. On experiencing a check to his speed, Blücher spurred, when the animal, still obedient to the impulse of its gallant master, made a few convulsive plunges forward; but on feeling that his steed was rapidly losing strength, and perceiving at the same time the near approach of the cuirassiers, he cried out to his aide-de-camp:—"Nostitz, now I am lost!" At that moment the horse fell from exhaustion, rolling upon its right side, and half-burying its rider under its weight. Count Nostitz immediately sprang from his saddle, and holding with his left hand the bridle of his own horse, which had been slightly wounded, he drew his sword, firmly resolved to shed, if necessary, the last drop of his blood in defending the precious life of his revered general. Scarcely had he done so, when he saw the cuirassiers rushing forward at the charge. To attract as little as possible their attention, he remained motionless. Most fortunately, the rapidity with which the cuirassiers advanced amidst the twilight, already sensibly obscured by the falling rain, precluded them from recognising, or even particularly remarking, the group, although they swept so closely by that one of them rather roughly brushed against the aide-de-camp's horse. Shortly afterwards, the Prussian cavalry having rallied, and re-formed, in their turn began to drive back the French. Again the thunder of their hoofs approached, and again the flying host whirled past the Marshal and his anxious friend; whereupon the latter, eagerly watching his opportunity as the pursuers came on, darted forward, and seizing the bridle of a non-commissioned officer of the 6th uhlans, named Schneider, ordered him and some files immediately following, to dismount and assist in saving the Prince. Five or six powerful men now raised the heavy dead charger, while others extricated the fallen hero, senseless and almost immoveable. In this state they placed him on the non-commissioned officer's horse. Just as they moved off, the enemy was again pressing forward with renewed speed, and Nostitz had barely time to lead the Marshal, whose senses were gradually returning, to the nearest infantry, which gladly received the party, and, retiring in perfect order, bade defiance to the attacks of its pursuers.

The horse-battery No. 2, which had supported these cavalry attacks by directing its fire against the left flank of the enemy, became, all at once, surrounded by French dragoons.

These vainly endeavoured to cut the traces, and the Prussian artillerymen defended themselves so well that they succeeded in effecting the escape of the battery through an opening in the inclosures of Bry. The foot-battery No. 3, however, was overtaken in its retreat by the enemy's cavalry, between the windmill and Bry, and lost one of its guns.

During these cavalry attacks, the Prussian infantry, already exhausted, and broken up into separate divisions by the desperate contest in the valley, had collected together at the outlets of the villages. Some of the regiments presented a remarkable degree of steadiness and good order. At length the cavalry brigade of General Treskow, then comprising the Queen's and the Brandenburg dragoons, and the Brandenburg uhlans, were brought forward, and made several attacks upon the French infantry and cuirassiers. Colonel Langen advanced, at the same time, from near the wind-mill, with the only battalion of his brigade remaining at his disposal, the 2nd of the 23rd regiment, under the guidance of General Pirch I., and covered by the cavalry of General Treskow; but all his efforts proved unavailing. He himself was wounded, and then driven over by a gun. The battalion, however, by continuing in admirable order, enabled General Pirch I., on whom, at this time, the defence of Ligny had devolved, to effect the retreat of the troops from the village. General Jagow retired, with a part of his brigade to Bry, and immediately occupied this point. Some battalions of General Krafft's brigade (the 6th) fell back from Ligny, towards the high road, leaving Bry on their left; others still more to the left towards Bry.

General Pirch II., whose brigade (the 2nd) had been posted by the Prince in rear of St. Amand-la-Haye, preparatory to a renewed attack, was upon the point of proceeding to support the 7th and 8th brigades, then seriously engaged, when he observed the retreat towards Bry. He immediately withdrew his brigade to this point, where he supported and facilitated the retreat of the troops from the village, with the assistance of the 12-pounder battery No. 6, and the foot-battery No. 34, as also of the Westphalian landwehr-cavalry, under Major Wulffen, to which latter corps several dragoons that had become separated from their own regiments, attached themselves.

General Grolman, the Quarter Master General of the Prussian army foreseeing the consequences of the line having been thus broken by the enemy hastened to Bry, and desired General Pirch II. to cover the retreat by means of the troops here collected together. He then proceeded in the direction of Sombref, and finding near this place two battalions of the 9th regiment (6th brigade) he posted them in rear of a hollow-road, leading from Bry towards Sombref. These battalions had, in their retreat from Ligny, defeated several attempts on the part of the enemy's cavalry to break them. Grolman, on perceiving a 12-pounder had stuck fast in this hollow-road, ordered the battalions to advance again in front of the latter, to assist in extricating the battery, and to protect its retreat, which was immediately accomplished within view of the French cavalry.

It was at this critical period of the battle, that the 2nd battalion of the 1st Westphalian landwehr, which still continued in reserve, in rear of Bry, under the command of Captain Gillnhaussen, appeared upon the height in front, where it particularly distinguished itself. In the first place it succeeded in effectually checking, by its vigorous fire, the French cuirassiers, who were in pursuit of the Prussian infantry. Then it drove back French cavalry which was on the point of making a fresh attack upon the Prussian dragoons. Afterwards it successfully withstood three charges by the French cavalry of the guard. General Grolman now ordered this battalion to join the 9th regiment near Sombref, and, with the latter, to take up a position at the junction of the cross-road from Ligny with that from Bry to Sombref. This position, which was in rear of the before-mentioned hollow road, was maintained until past midnight.

Such were the circumstances resulting from the French having forced the Prussian line at Ligny, and pursued in the direction of Bry: it is now necessary to explain what occurred, at that time, at, and in the vicinity of, Sombref.

The first brigade, which had been placed in reserve, was ordered to take post, in squares, upon the high road to Sombref, to check the pressure of the enemy's cavalry. Subsequently, when the direction of the retreat was decided upon, it fell back upon Tilly. The 4th brigade, with the exception of one or two battalions, advanced again through Sombref towards Ligny, just as the French cavalry pushed towards the high road. The battalions of the brigade formed squares, and fell back upon the high road, whence they continued their further retreat.

At the time the French troops were debouching from Ligny, Colonel Stülpnagel's (the 12th) brigade was posted in front of Sombref; and Colonel Rohr had just pushed forward towards Ligny with the 2nd battalion of the 6th Kurmark landwehr, when he perceived three French cavalry regiments advancing against the right wing of the brigade; whereupon he gradually retired, and the whole brigade threw itself into Sombref, just as the French cavalry made an attack at the entrance of the village, and captured the two guns of the battery No. 12, which had been posted there. Major Dorville faced about the rear division of the 6th Kurmark landwehr-cavalry, and gallantly attacked the French cavalry, in the hope of checking their progress, but the lances of his brave followers were shivered against the cuirasses of their opponents, and for a moment the former could only defend themselves with their broken poles. The Prussian infantry, however, hastened forward in support; the French were driven out of the village; and one of the lost guns was retaken.

Every exertion was now made to secure the possession of Sombref. General Borcke (9th brigade) sent thither two battalions of the 1st Kurmark landwehr, which, during this movement, fired upon the flank of the enemy's cavalry as the latter fell back. The defence of the entrance into the village from the side of Ligny was confided to the 2nd battalion of the 6th Kurmark landwehr, under Colonel Rohr.

About this time, General Jürgass received orders to cover with his cavalry (of the 2nd corps) the retreat of the Prussian infantry from St. Amand-la-Haye and Wagnelé. General Brause, perceiving that the enemy had attacked Colonel Marwitz' cavalry-brigade, on his right, and endangered his communication with the rear, hastened with the fusilier battalions of the 22nd regiment (which had continued in reserve in rear of St. Amand-la-Haye) towards the high road, upon which the greater part of the 7th brigade had by this time been collected. The Prussians, on retiring from St. Amand-la-Haye, were closely followed by the French. The 1st battalion of the 14th regiment was still in the hamlet of St. Amand when it received the order to retire. During its retreat it was attacked whilst in a hollow-way. It immediately showed a front on each flank, and succeeded in driving back the enemy. General Jürgass now sent forward the 4th squadron of the Brandenburg hussars to attack the enemy's tirailleurs, who were beginning to advance from out of St. Amand-la-Haye. The latter were immediately forced back upon the village. Somewhat later, however, the French tirailleurs poured forth in greater numbers from out of Wagnelé, and threw themselves upon the right flank of the retreating troops. A mêlée ensued, in which General Jürgass was shot in the shoulder.

When the centre of the Prussian army had been broken by the French cavalry, and the Prussian commander had been placed so completely *hors de combat*, Lieut.-General Count von Gneisenau, the chief of the staff, having undertaken the direction of affairs, ordered the retreat of the 1st and 2nd corps upon Tilly; and despatched Colonel Thile with directions to Thielemann, that if he could not effect a direct retreat upon Tilly, he was to retire upon Gembloux, there to unite with Bülow, and then effect a junction with the rest of the army.

The occupation of Bry by General Pirch II. offered a safe point of retreat to the disordered Prussian battalions; and now that it had become quite dark, Pirch led all the troops from this post towards Marbais, where they re-formed, and whence, soon afterwards, under the command of Lieut. General Röder, they continued the retreat upon Tilly. Marwitz's cavalry-brigade, which was not pursued with much vigour by the enemy, fell back to the rear of the battalions formed up to cover its movement, and now joined the rest of the cavalry of the right wing, in the general retreat.

The 5th infantry-brigade was in full retreat upon Marbais when the 1st and 2nd battalions of the 22nd regiment still continued posted on the high road, not far from the Trois Burettes. The good order and perfect steadiness of these battalions, which were commanded by Major Sack, completely checked the further advance of the French cavalry, and greatly facilitated the retreat of the Prussian troops.

After General Jürgass was wounded, the command of the rear-guard devolved upon Lieut. Colonel Sohr, of whose brigade (the Brandenburg and Pomeranian hussars) it consisted. He executed this duty with great success, falling gradually back upon the cavalry posted in advance of Tilly by Lieut. General Zieten, who then took command of the whole of the cavalry employed in protecting the retreat.

During the retreat of the centre of the Prussian army, which had been effectually broken, and of its right from St. Amand and Wagnelé, which, in consequence of Blücher's previous dispositions for his contemplated attack upon the French left, was better prepared to sustain a reverse of this kind, the left wing, under Thielemann, maintained its position, and contributed not a little, by its firm countenance, in diffusing a considerable degree of caution into the French movements in advance. This was strikingly exemplified by the conduct of the 1st and 2nd battalions of the 30th Prussian regiment. They were posted at Mont Potriaux, and although their knowledge of what was passing on other points of the line was very imperfect, still it sufficed to prompt their commander to cross the rivulet, and undertake, if not a vigorous attack, at least a demonstration, which, now that darkness had almost covered the field, would tend to impede, perhaps to paralyze, the French movements against the Prussian centre. Having effected their passage, they met at first but a feeble opposition from a line of skirmishers: a French regiment of dragoons then advanced very close upon the 2nd battalion, but was driven off; whereupon both these battalions pushed forward, and gained a height which was occupied in force by the enemy. Here they sustained two more cavalry attacks, which proved equally unsuccessful. A mass of infantry belonging to Lobau's corps, having its flanks covered by parties of cavalry, now advanced against the 1st battalion, but having, in the dark, exposed a flank to the battalion, it was also repulsed. Major Dittfurth, however, finding himself in too isolated a position, did not deem it prudent to advance further upon ground which he knew to be in full possession of the enemy, and therefore retraced his steps.

A renewed attempt was made, at the same time, by the French light cavalry-brigade under General Vallin, to push forward along the high road towards Sombref, and gain possession of the barrier; but the attack was as abortive as had been the former one upon this point.

With the darkness of night, now rapidly deepening, the din of battle, which had been terrific and incessant until the last faint glimmering of twilight, became gradually hushed: its expiring sounds still issuing from the heights in front of Bry, whence the flashes from the fire of artillery, and from that of skirmishers along the outskirts of this village, (held by General Jagow with the 1st and 2nd battalions of the 9th regiment, and the 2nd battalion of the 1st Westphalian landwehr,) indicated to the French army the extreme verge of its advance; while the still more vivid flashes emitted from the rattling musketry fire of the two battalions of the 30th regiment, which had so gallantly sallied forth out of Mont Potriaux, under Major Dittfurth, as previously described, as also from the Prussian guns which defended the approach to Sombref, and frustrated the renewed attack along the high road towards that point, plainly intimated that the Prussian left wing (Thielemann's corps) still firmly maintained itself in a position whence it might seriously endanger the flank of any further movement in advance against the centre.

Vandamme's corps (the 3rd) bivouacked in advance of St.

Amand, Gérard's corps (the 4th) in front of Ligny, the imperial guard upon the heights of Bry, Grouchy's cavalry in rear of Sombref, and Lobau's corps (the 6th) in rear of Ligny. This possession of the field of battle, and the capture of 21 pieces of cannon, were the only advantages of which the French could boast as the immediate result of so severe a struggle. With these, however, it would seem that their Emperor was fully satisfied: if he had entertained any idea of pursuit, it was now abandoned; he took no measures for watching the movements and prying into the designs of his adversary; but left his troops resting in their bivouacs, offering no molestation whatever to the Prussians, whilst he in person returned to Fleurus, where he passed the night.

The contrast between the circumstances of the two armies during the night was very striking; for whilst the victors were indulging in perfect repose, the vanquished were completely on the alert, seizing every possible advantage which the extraordinary quietude of their enemies afforded during the precious hours of darkness; and never, perhaps, did a defeated army extricate itself from its difficulties with so much adroitness and order, or retire from a hard-fought field with so little diminution of its moral force. The Prussian commander was carried to Mélioreux, about six miles in rear of Ligny, and the head-quarters were established there for the night. Thielemann still retained possession of his original position in the line of battle; and General Jagow, with several detached battalions belonging to Zieten's corps, occupied Bry and its immediate vicinity. From this position the latter General quietly effected his retreat about an hour after midnight, taking the direction of Sombref, and thence proceeding to Gembloux, presuming, in all probability, that the general retreat would be towards the Meuse. It was not until three o'clock in the morning, when the field of battle had been completely evacuated by the remainder of the Prussian army, that Thielemann commenced his retreat, which he conducted slowly, and in perfect order to Gembloux, near which Bülow's corps d'armée (the 4th) had arrived during the night.

The loss of the Prussian army on the 15th and 16th of June, amounted in killed and wounded* to about 12,000

* In this battle, Colonel Sir Henry Hardinge, K.C.B., of the British army, (now Lieut.-General the Lord Viscount Hardinge, G.C.B.,) who had been attached to the Prussian head-quarters by the Duke of Wellington, received a severe wound, by which he lost his left hand. By the talents which he evinced in the suggestion of several movements which had the effect of checking the successful progress of the French, he deservedly obtained the good opinion and high approbation of

men: that of the French to between 7 and 8,000. But few prisoners were taken on either side.

In consequence of this defeat, Blücher was compelled, in order to maintain and secure his close communication with Wellington, to abandon the line of the Meuse between Namur and Liege; but his orderly and unmolested retreat afforded him sufficient time to remove all his stores and material from these points to Maestricht and Louvain, which now constituted his new base of operations.

It was not, however, a defeat which involved the loss of every advantage previously gained. Blücher was not *driven* from the field, but, on the contrary, he maintained it during the night, with the exception of the villages of Ligny and St. Amand in his front; thus facilitating the orderly retreat of his own army, and, at the same time, affording a considerable degree of security to the direct line of retreat of the Duke of Wellington. The defeat certainly compelled the latter to retire on the following morning, whatever might have been his success at Quatre-Bras; but so long as Blücher had it in his power to fall back in such a manner as to effect his junction the next day with Wellington, the advantage which accrued to the common object of the two commanders was of the highest importance. They would then unite after the concentration of each army had been accomplished; hitherto, they had been compelled to meet their opponents before they had succeeded in collecting their respective forces. If, however, Wellington had been unable to maintain his ground against Ney, and Napoleon had in this manner succeeded in beating both armies in detail, or, if the Prussian defeat had been followed up by a vigorous pursuit, the loss of the battle of Ligny might have placed both armies in a critical position.

The struggle at Ligny was undoubtedly of a most desperate and sanguinary character. It was, almost throughout, one continued village-fight; a species of contest which, though extremely harassing and destructive to both parties engaged, was that most likely to prove of a long duration, and consequently to afford a better prospect of relief by the promised support from Wellington, or by the hoped-for junction of

Prince Blücher, by whose side it was that he was struck by a cannon-ball, which shattered his left hand. After receiving the wound the gallant general had a tourniquet fixed on his arm, and remained on the field until the close of the battle. This incident plainly indicated a man of no ordinary stamp, and subsequent events have proved that it was but the foreshadowing of that principle of action, which, springing from a high sense of honour, and an innate chivalrous devotion to the profession of arms, and combined with his great abilities as a statesman, has so peculiarly distinguished the glorious career of the late Governor-General of India, and covered with imperishable renown the name of Hardinge.

Bülow. It remains a question whether Blücher, had he confined himself during the latter part of the action to the same defensive system he had so successfully carried on up to that time, instead of detaching his reserves to the right, and preparing for an attack upon the enemy's left, might not have fully maintained his original position until dark, and thus have saved his army from defeat. By the arrival of Bülow's corps during the night, he would then have been prepared to meet his opponent on the following morning with a greatly preponderating force, whilst, on the other hand, Wellington, having concentrated a considerable portion of his army, would have been placed in an equally advantageous position as regards the already vanquished enemy in his own front. When it is considered that along the whole extent of Blücher's line, the French had not gained any material advantage upon one single point, and that the Prussians continued to hold their ground with most exemplary firmness, the circumstance of his not having delayed the collecting of his reserves, for a grand attack upon the enemy's left, until actually joined by either the British or Bülow's troops, can scarcely be explained except by a reference to the peculiar character of the Prussian chief, whose natural fiery temperament led him, in all probability, to seize with avidity the first prospect which opened itself of a favourable opportunity of aiming a deadly thrust at his hated foe, rather than to adhere to that comparatively passive kind of warfare which so ill suited his own individual inclination and disposition.

Napoleon had undoubtedly gained the victory from the moment he succeeded in penetrating the Prussian centre, but it was not distinguished by that brilliant success, or by those immediate and decisive advantages, which might have been anticipated from the admirable manner in which the attack had been gradually prepared, and the care with which it was concealed from the Prussians, at a moment when they had no reserve remaining, and when the co-operation of the British on their right, or the arrival of Bülow's corps from Hannut, had become quite impracticable. This appears the more surprising when we reflect that he had a considerable corps of cavalry under Grouchy at hand to support this attack, and that the whole of Lobau's corps was in the field, fully prepared for active operations.

The consequences resulting from the absence of energetic measures on the part of the French Emperor, in following up the defeat of the Prussians, on the evening of the 16th and morning of the 17th, will be fully developed in subsequent chapters.

CHAPTER VII.

The bivouac on the field of Quatre-Bras, during the night of the 16th, continued undisturbed until about an hour before daylight, when a cavalry-patrole having accidentally got between the adverse picquets near Piermont, caused an alarm in that quarter that was quickly communicated to both armies by a rattling fire of musketry, which, rapidly augmenting, extended itself along the line of the advanced posts. Among the first who hastened to ascertain the origin and nature of the engagement was Picton, who, together with other staff-officers, as they arrived in succession, on discovering that no advance had been attempted or intended on either side, soon succeeded in restoring confidence. Similar exertions were successfully made on the part of the French officers, and as day began to break upon the scene, both parties resumed their previous tranquillity. In this untoward affair, the picquets furnished by Kielmansegge's Hanoverian brigade, and by the 3rd Brunswick light battalion were sharply engaged, and a picquet of the field-battalion Bremen suffered considerably.

It was not long before Wellington, who had slept at Genappe, arrived at Quatre-Bras, where he found Major General Sir Hussey Vivian, whose brigade of light cavalry, consisting of the 10th British hussars, (under Colonel Quentin,*) of the 18th British hussars, (under Lieut. Colonel the Hon. Henry Murray,†) and of the 1st hussars of the King's German legion, (under Lieut. Colonel von Wissell,‡) was posted on the left of that point with two strong picquets thrown out; one, of the 18th hussars, under Captain Croker,§ on the Namur road, and the other, of the 10th hussars, under Major the Hon. Frederick Howard,|| in front—with a picquet from the latter, under Lieutenant Arnold,¶ on the right of the Namur road. Vivian, on being asked what account he

* Now Lieut. General Sir George Quentin, C.B., K.C.H.

† Now Major General the Hon. Henry Murray, C.B.

‡ Lieut. Colonel von Wissell, K.C.H., Major General in the Hanoverian service, died on the 30th of May, 1842.

§ Lieut. Colonel Richard Croker, retired from the service in 1844.

|| Major the Hon. Frederick Howard was killed at the battle of Waterloo.

¶ Lieut. Colonel Robert Arnold died, while in command of the 16th Lancers, on the 20th August, 1839.

could give of the enemy, communicated to the Duke the result of his observations, which were necessarily very limited, as, with the exception of the firing that had taken place, as before mentioned, along the line of picquets, the French had continued perfectly quiet, and had as yet given no indication of any offensive movement. The Duke then took a general survey of the field, and while sweeping the horizon with his telescope, he discovered a French vedette on some rising ground, in the direction of Fleurus, and a little to the right of the high road leading to Namur, apparently belonging to some picquet thrown out from Ney's extreme right on the previous night, after the battle had ceased; or to some detached corps placed in that quarter for the purpose of observation, and for the maintenance of the communication between Napoleon and Ney. The Duke had received no intelligence of Blücher; and, probably judging from the advanced position of the vedette in question that whatever might have been the result of the battle of Ligny, the Prussians could not have made any forward movement likely to endanger Ney's right, he came to the conclusion that it was quite possible that, on the other hand, Napoleon might have crossed the Namur road, and cut off his communication with Blücher, with the design of manœuvring upon his left and rear, and causing him to be simultaneously attacked by Ney. His Grace therefore desired Vivian to send a strong patrole along the Namur road to gain intelligence respecting the Prussian army.* A troop of the 10th hussars, under Captain

* In an article of the "Quarterly Review," No. CLI. to (which allusion has already been made—see page 57), the following remarks are made upon the above passage:—

"It is a mistake to suppose, as Captain Siborne does, that on the morning of the 17th (or even on the night of the 16th), the Duke was uninformed of what had occurred on the Prussian field of battle. He had at the Prussian headquarters a staff-officer, the present Governor-General of India, then Colonel Sir Henry Hardinge, who sent him repeated reports during the battle. He had written one after he was himself severely wounded, which was brought to the Duke by his brother, Captain Hardinge of the artillery, with a verbal message given after nightfall. Till nightfall, moreover, the Duke could see; and, need it be added, did see with his own eyes from Quatre-Bras, what passed on the Prussian field of battle. With his glass he saw the charge and failure of the Prussian cavalry, Blücher's disaster, and the retreat of the Prussian army from the field of battle. Captain Wood of the 10th hussars, then at the outposts, pushed a patrole towards the Prussian field of battle at daylight, and ascertained and immediately reported to the Duke that the Prussians were no longer in possession of it. The Duke then sent, as Captain Siborne narrates, with another squadron of the 10th, under Captain Grey, Sir A. Gordon, who had been with his Grace on the Prussian field of battle the preceding day, and therefore knew the ground, in order to communicate with the rear-guard of the Prussian army, and to ascertain their position and designs. Sir A. Gordon found the field of battle deserted,

Grey,* was according despatched on this duty, accompanied by Lieut. Colonel the Hon. Sir Alexander Gordon,† one of

except by a few French vedettes: these were driven in, and Gordon with his squadrons crossed the field of battle unmolested, and communicated verbally with General Zieten, commanding the Prussian rear-guard at Sombref, on the road to Namur, where the Prussian left had rested in the battle of the preceding day. Having accomplished this service, the Duke's aide-de-camp returned as he had gone, unmolested, to Quatre-Bras. If Sir A. Gordon had lived, probably Captain Siborne might have learned the real account of the transaction from him, and would then have known that the patrole moved the whole way to Sombref, and brought back, not a vague report that the Prussians had retreated towards Wavre, but the most positive accounts of their movements and intentions."

Now, with all due deference to the critical knowledge of the Reviewer, but with a thorough consciousness of the all-sufficiency of the means which I possess of disproving his statements, I can unhesitatingly assert that it is *not* "a mistake to suppose that on the morning of the 17th (or even on the night of the 16th), the Duke was uninformed of what had occurred on the Prussian field of battle;" and I do so, not upon hearsay evidence, not upon authority given, either in declining years, or distorted so as to suit a particular object, but mainly upon recollections fresh and clear, dispassionately and deliberately noted down only a few days after the event—noted down, I may observe, by one of "the few officers attached at the time to head-quarters, who," as the Reviewer says elsewhere, "really knew or could know anything of value about the great features of the business." These recollections, I may add, are also fully borne out by a variety of corroborative evidence from other quarters. In order to verify my assertion, it will be necessary, in the first place, that I should state, in detail, from the above mentioned source, circumstances that occurred at head-quarters during the night of the 16th. The distant firing on the Prussian field of battle had ceased, and the Duke, not long after nine o'clock at night, quitted Quatre-Bras for Genappe, where supper had been ordered at the inn. Riding along, and conceiving that Blücher had repulsed the French, the Duke observed "he is a fine old fellow!" Captain Hardinge came to Genappe, about half-past ten, from Blücher's army, for a surgeon to dress the wound of his brother, Sir Henry Hardinge, whose hand had been shot off. The Duke inquired when he had left the ground; he said that it was between eight and nine; at which time he thought the Prussians had suffered severely; that there was considerable confusion; that he saw many Prussian soldiers in small parties of two and three, crossing the corn-fields to the rear; but that he could not affirm the Prussians were defeated, for they still held their position. The Duke did not altogether rely on this information; at least not to its fullest extent; thinking that a young officer, agitated perhaps on account of his brother, might have considered things worse than they really were. Indeed, so little was it conceived that the French had gained any advantage, that Lord FitzRoy Somerset, his Grace's military secretary, at half past ten o'clock, wrote to Lady FitzRoy Somerset, then at Brussels, that "the Prussians and the British had repulsed the French." The Duke went to sleep, at Genappe, between eleven and twelve. The staff were employed, up to a later hour, in despatching letters, by the Duke's orders. About two o'clock in the morning, a courier arrived from Brussels, but with no particular intelligence.

Such was the nature of the verbal message brought by Captain Hardinge; such the degree of uncertainty that existed at the Duke's head-quarters, during the night of the 16th, respecting the result of the conflict at Ligny. Now I proceed to narrate, from the same source, what passed at those head-quarters on the morning of the 17th.

---

* Colonel John Grey died in 1846.

† Lieut. Colonel the Hon. Sir Alexander Gordon was killed at the battle of Waterloo.

the Duke's aides-de-camp. As the patrole advanced along the road, the vedette before mentioned began to circle, evidently

The Duke mounted his horse, about three o'clock in the morning, and proceeded to Quatre-Bras. He immediately despatched Sir A. Gordon with a troop of cavalry to patrole towards the Prussian army, and to ascertain what had really happened. About seven o'clock Sir A. Gordon returned to Quatre-Bras, having seen only a few of the enemy's vedettes, who retired as he advanced; but he brought back information that Blücher had been obliged to retire upon Wavre. Everybody at head-quarters conceived that it was a place a little in rear of the Prussian position—no one at this instant recollecting the precise situation of Wavre, which being really at so great a distance in the rear, it did not occur to any person that the Prussians could have fallen so far back. General Müffling, who had been sent for, was the person that opened the eyes of the Duke; who, upon being told that the Prussians had fallen back upon Wavre, observed, "Ma foi, c'est bien loin." The Duke immediately resolved on making a corresponding movement, and falling back on the road to Brussels.

These details are certainly most contradictory of the statements by the writer in the "Quarterly Review;" but they accord with the accounts given by every historian (including General Müffling) so far as regards the uncertainty in which the Duke remained, until the morning of the 17th, respecting the result of the battle of Ligny; they accord also with the published official despatches transmitted by the foreign officers attached to head-quarters, to their respective governments; they accord also with the information which I have collected concerning the events of the 16th and 17th; above all, they emanate from a source, which admits of no question as to their veracity.

As regards the Reviewer's statement that "till nightfall, (on the 16th) the Duke could see with his own eyes from Quatre-Bras, what passed on the Prussian field of battle," and that "*with his glass he saw the charge and failure of the Prussian cavalry, Blücher's disaster, and the retreat of the Prussian army from the field of battle,*" I must confess that this is a startling assertion; for during the period of 33 years that has elapsed since the events in question, all the world has believed that the field of Ligny was not visible from that of Quatre-Bras. But if the Reviewer be right, and all the world wrong, how extraordinary it is that the Duke should not have communicated to any of his staff on the field, that he could see all that was passing at Ligny; that he should not have alluded to so important a circumstance, when conversing with those who were in the same house with him during the night; that when making the remark, as he was proceeding to his quarters for the night at Genappe, that "he (Blücher) was a fine old fellow," he should have allowed no exclamation to escape him, expressive of regret at the Marshal's "disaster;" and that he should have issued no orders of movement for his troops, consequent upon "the retreat of the Prussian army from the field of battle," until past seven o'clock on the following morning. It is also very extraordinary that, as this "charge and failure of the Prussian cavalry" occurred at a distance of seven miles, long after sunset, about nine o'clock, under a drizzling rain, and beyond the smoke arising from the intermediate right wing of the Prussian army, the Duke should have seen it so clearly as to distinguish a particular individual falling with his horse, and to recognise that individual as the commander of the Prussian army! But the most extraordinary part of all is that the glass which the writer in the "Quarterly" puts into the hands of the Duke, should have been of such a power as to enable his Grace to see all this THROUGH THE INTERVENING HEIGHTS OF MARBAIS AND BRY; by which, and by the features of the country in a direction more to the right, the Prussian field of battle is concealed from the eyes of ordinary mortals striving to obtain a glimpse of it from Quatre-Bras!! Hitherto it has always been considered as a fact, that even the mill of Bry, (or, as it was frequently called, of Bussie), which, if not situated exactly on the most elevated spot, was certainly the highest object of the Prussian position, *cannot be seen* from the field to give notice of the approach of an enemy, and then retired. This induced the patrole to move forward with great caution, so as to guard against the possibility of being cut off. Nevertheless it continued, but with all due precaution, advancing along the road, until after passing a few scattered cottages, comprising a hamlet called Petit Marbais, it reached, about a mile and a half further on, some rising ground, about five miles from Quatre-Bras, and beyond which was another height. A vedette was observed posted upon the latter, but who had evidently not yet discovered the approach of Captain Grey's troop. Down in the intervening hollow was an isolated house, at the door of which stood a dismounted sentry, and some horses were standing in an adjoining yard. Captain Grey directed Lieutenant Bacon,* to patrole towards the house, while he remained with the remainder of the troop, concealed from the enemy's view, a disposition favoured by the nature of the ground, and the trees in the hedges, on both sides of the road. When Lieutenant Bacon's party moved forward, it was discovered by the vedette, who began circling, and fired his carbine. The French picquet posted in the house instantly rushed out; several of the men had their jackets and accoutrements off; and the post could easily have been captured, had

of Quatre-Bras. Some Prussian officers ascended the upper part of the mill, and there can be no doubt that when support from the Duke was so anxiously looked for, they would have gladly availed themselves of the opportunity of distinguishing what occurred at Quatre-Bras. But no one has ever heard of their having done so; nor, until the writer in the "Quarterly" asserted the contrary, has any one ever heard that Ligny could be seen from Quatre-Bras. And it would be most surprising if it were otherwise; since, to assert such a fact, is to assert that which is a *physical impossibility*.

With respect to the latter part of the paragraph which I have quoted from the "Quarterly," I think, with the Reviewer, that if Sir A. Gordon had lived, I might probably "have learned the real account of the transaction from him;" but I also think that this would have been perfectly consistent with my narrative. I am quite certain, however, that he would never have told me that which the Reviewer has, namely, "that Gordon with his squadrons (?) crossed the field of battle unmolested, and communicated verbally with General Zieten, commanding the Prussian rear-guard, at Sombref, on the road to Namur;" for neither during, nor after, the battle, was Zieten at Sombref. He retired, late in the evening of the 16th, to Tilly, where, at the head of the cavalry, he was covering the Prussian retreat. It was there where Gordon found him, and not on the field of battle of the previous day, upon which, indeed, at the time the patrole fell in with the French picquet, there was not a single Prussian soldier.

The Reviewer will perhaps refer me to the Duke's despatch in which his Grace states that he sent a patrole "to *Sombref* in the morning;" (See Appendix XLVIII.) but if he will glance at the Duke's correspondence of that period, he will find that his Grace invariably gave the designation of "Sombref" to the Prussian position; so that sending a patrole to Sombref, no more implied the sending of it to the village of that name, than did Blücher's sending of a patrole to Waterloo on the 18th, presuppose its proceeding to a village considerably in rear of the British position.

* Now General Anthony Bacon in the Portuguese service.

the special duty on which the British patrole was engaged admitted of an attack. The French turned out very quickly and galloped to the rear along the high road, while Bacon's party was recalled. A few French cavalry galloped up to the vedette on the heights, but evinced no disposition to advance. It had now become sufficiently evident that, commencing from this point, the French were in possession of the Namur road; but the principal object which Sir Alexander Gordon had in view was yet to be attained. The patrole now retired a little until it reached a cross-road, which a peasant pointed out as the Prussian line of retreat. Pursuing this track, the patrole within an hour, reached Tilly, where General Zieten, who had been placed in temporary command of the cavalry, was covering the retreat of the Prussian army. After remaining here about a quarter of an hour, during which Sir Alexander Gordon obtained from General Zieten the most ample information respecting the movements of the Prussians, the patrole commenced its return, at a quick pace, striking into a cross-road, which joined the high road at a point nearer to Quatre-Bras, than the one whence it had quitted it. The patrole reached Quatre-Bras at about half-past seven o'clock;* and Sir Alexander Gordon immediately reported to the Duke that the Prussians had retreated towards Wavre, that the French occupied the ground on which the battle had been fought, but that they had not crossed the high road, along which the patrole had proceeded almost into the immediate vicinity of their advanced posts.† This latter circumstance was very remarkable, and

* I have good reason to believe that as soon as the patrole regained the high road, Sir Alexander Gordon quitted it in order to hasten to the Duke. This, moreover, would agree with the fact, which I have from very high and excellent authorities, that Gordon returned about seven o'clock.

† I should be committing an act of injustice to a gallant and estimable officer —Lieut. Colonel Charles Wood, who was a Captain in the 10th hussars at Waterloo—were I to omit mentioning that in the "Naval and Military Magazine" for July, 1841, and for March 1847, he published a statement to the effect that he was sent forward to patrole, previously to the departure of Captain Grey's troop on a similar service; that he fell in with numerous Prussian stragglers, all of whom agreed that Prince Blücher had retired; that on coming to a village on the high road, he found the French vedettes, who retired on his approach; that having determined to seek the Duke, and desired the patrole to return quietly to its squadron, he met the Hon. Sir Alexander Gordon, with Captain Grey's troop, coming in quest of Blücher: that having communicated to them what he had discovered, and suggested that, by leaving the road and bearing to the left, they would be likely to come up with the Prussians, he proceeded to Quatre-Bras, and showed his Grace the village in which he found the French cavalry; that the moment he made his report, the Duke sent directions to the brigades on their march to turn on Waterloo;—further, in the last quoted number of the above Magazine, that Gordon's patrole did not return till about mid-day. This account gave rise to a discussion in the same Magazine for May, June, and July, 1847, between Lieut. Colonel Wood and General Bacon; and I feel myself bound to declare that I find it impossible to reconcile the opposite statements made by

served to satisfy Wellington that, either Napoleon's victory had not been followed up with a vigour and an effect, by which the safety of his own army would have been perilled, or, that it had not been of a character sufficiently decisive to have enabled the French Emperor to avail himself of such a vantage ground. Having ascertained that the contingency for which, as has already been explained, he was fully prepared, had actually taken place, he instantly decided upon retrograding his troops to a position in front of the point of junction of the roads leading from Charleroi and Nivelles upon

these two officers both in that Magazine, and in their several letters to me on the subject, and that the difficulty which I have experienced in this respect, is increased by the fact, that in no single instance of the important evidence which I have collected of the events of the 17th of June, or in the valuable reports made to the late Lieut. General Lord Vivian, only a few years after the battle of Waterloo, by the several officers of his brigade, (to which the 10th hussars belonged), whom he requested, (in consequence of an article which had appeared in the "Quarterly Review," respecting the conduct of the light cavalry), to furnish him with their recollections of all occurrences, from the commencement to the close of the campaign, can I find any mention whatever of the patrole under Captain Wood, although they generally allude to that under Captain Grey; whilst, on the other hand, some of Colonel Wood's statements are at direct variance with the evidence to which I have referred. I deeply regret this circumstance, because, entertaining as I do, great personal regard for Lieut. Colonel Wood, I should have been delighted to have had it in my power to remove the erroneous impressions, and probable misunderstandings, in which the case appears to be involved. As a further proof of these misconceptions, I may add, that in the original edition of Colonel Gurwood's compilation of the Duke of Wellington's Despatches, as also in the "Selection from the Despatches," a note was appended to the Waterloo despatch, stating that Sir A. Gordon was sent "to communicate with the Prussian head-quarters, as to co-operation with the British army, ordered to retire to the position in front of Waterloo." In the new edition of the "Despatches" this note is abandoned, and another substituted, purporting that Captain Wood, having patroled along the road leading to Sombref, and ascertained that the Prussian army had quitted the field of battle the preceding day, hastened to report the circumstance to the Duke, and met Sir A. Gordon's patrole "sent by his Grace to communicate to Marshal Blücher that the British army would proceed to take up the position in front of Waterloo, and co-operate according to previous arrangements with the Prussian army retiring upon Wavre." Now Lieut. Colonel Wood's statement is at variance with *both* these notes, for he declares that the *first* intelligence of the Prussian retreat was given by him to the Duke, who, thereupon, ordered his own troops to retire: further, that, in proceeding with that intelligence, he *met* Sir A. Gordon. If so, how could the latter officer be the bearer of a message connected with the retreat of both armies? On the other hand, the writer in the "Quarterly Review," No. CLI. says that Captain Wood "ascertained and immediately reported to the Duke that the Prussians were no longer in possession of the field of battle;" and that "the Duke *then* sent Sir A. Gordon to communicate with the rear-guard of the Prussian army, and to ascertain their position and designs!" Shortly afterwards the Reviewer states that "as soon as Gordon returned with his patrole, the Duke gave orders for the army to occupy the position in front of Waterloo;" whilst Lieut. Colonel Wood asserts (in the "United Service Magazine," for March, 1847,) that the Duke gave these orders "the moment he (Colonel Wood) made his report," and that Gordon's patrole did not return until "about the middle of the day!" All this confusion arises from the incorrect views which have been put forth respecting the occurrences in question.

Brussels, in which he might rely upon the co-operation of a sufficient portion of Blücher's forces from Wavre with his own, by which he would be enabled to confront Napoleon and his main army with ample means, and thus attain that great aim and end of all strategy, of "operating with the greatest mass in a combined effort upon a decisive point."*

Hence, a change in the direction of the previously ordered movements became necessary, and the following instructions were issued:—

'To General Lord Hill.

'17th June, 1815.

'The 2nd division of British infantry to march from Nivelles on Waterloo, at 10 o'clock.

'The brigades of the 4th division, now at Nivelles, to march from that place on Waterloo, at 10 o'clock. Those brigades of the 4th division at Braine-le-comte, and on the road from Braine-le-comte to Nivelles, to collect and halt at Braine-le-comte this day.

'All the baggage on the road from Braine-le-comte to Nivelles to return immediately to Braine-le-comte, and to proceed immediately from thence to Hal and Bruxelles.

'The spare musket ammunition to be immediately parked behind Genappe.

'The corps under the command of Prince Frederick of Orange will move from Enghien this evening, and take up a position in front of Hal, occupying Braine-le-Château with two battalions.

Colonel Estorff will fall back with his brigade on Hal, and place himself under the orders of Prince Frederick.'†

Shortly after the departure of the before-mentioned patrole of the 10th hussars, along the Namur road, the Duke received some despatches from England, to which he gave his attention; and now that he had satisfied himself as to the real state of things, and issued his orders for the movements of his distant troops, as also for the retreat of those present in the field, he laid himself down on the ground near Quatre-Bras, covered his head with one of the newspapers he had been reading, which had accompanied those despatches, and appeared to fall asleep. After remaining some time in this state, he again rose, mounted his horse, and rode a little distance down the field in front of Quatre-Bras. He then

* Jomini.

† Despatches of Field Marshal the Duke of Wellington, compiled by Colonel Gurwood. Vol. XII., page 475.

looked about through his telescope, and expressed to those about him his astonishment at the perfect stillness of the enemy, remarking at the same time, "What if they should be also retiring? It is not at all impossible."

A second officer, Lieutenant Massow, had been despatched from the Prussian to the Anglo-allied head-quarters, and it was about this time that he reached the Duke, with a verbal communication respecting the retreat upon Wavre, and the position intended to be assumed in that quarter. It was of a nature which, taken altogether, was so far satisfactory, that Wellington immediately sent a verbal message* by this officer to Blücher, acquainting him with his intended retrograde movements, and proposing to accept a battle, on the following day, in the position in front of Waterloo, provided the Prince would detach two corps to his assistance.

The following is the manner in which the retreat of the Anglo-allied infantry, then in full operation, was executed. It was an important matter to mask the retreat as much as possible, so as to gain time for the free and unimpeded movement of the army along the high road leading to the position in front of Waterloo. For this purpose, the light troops continued to maintain the line of outposts, until their respective supports, which had remained stationary sufficiently long to conceal the retreat of the troops in their rear, began also to retire. The 1st and 5th British divisions, and the 2nd Dutch-Belgian division, as also the Brunswick corps, effected their retreat in excellent order, notwithstanding the delay that was created by the narrowness of the bridge and street of Genappe. Their retreat was covered by Alten's division, to which were added for this purpose, the 1st battalion of the 95th British rifles, the 2nd and 3rd Brunswick light battalions, the Brunswick advanced-guard-battalion, and the light companies of Byng's brigade of guards. The main body of Alten's division commenced its retreat about eleven o'clock. Ompteda's brigade of the King's German legion was withdrawn to Sart-à-Mavelines, which it immediately occupied, as also the wood of Les Censes, in its front. Halkett's British brigade then retired secretly until it reached some favourable ground, a little distance in rear of Ompteda's brigade, upon which it was immediately drawn up. Kielmansegge's Hanoverian brigade was withdrawn still further to the rear, and occupied a third position. Thus posted, the division was ordered, in the event of being attacked, to retire by brigades alternately.

* Not a written communication, as stated in former editions of this work.

It was a little before mid-day when the light troops of Alten's division began to retire. They occupied the advanced line, commencing from the southern extremity of the wood of Bossu on the right, extending along Gemioncourt and the inclosures of Piermont, and crossing the Namur road on the left: from which line they gradually and slowly fell back upon Ompteda's brigade, in a manner evincing admirable skill, steadiness, and regularity.

In order more effectually to mask the movements on the Allied side of the Namur road, the whole of the cavalry was drawn up in two lines immediately contiguous to, and in rear of, that road; the heavy cavalry forming the second line, and picquets being thrown out from the first line, to relieve those of the retiring infantry.

The main body of Alten's division now commenced its further retreat; but not by alternate brigades, this mode having been directed only in the event of an attack; the latter retired successively in the order in which they stood, preserving their relative distances, so that they might commence the alternate system of retreat, if attacked. To facilitate the passage of other portions of the army through the narrow defile of the bridge and town of Genappe, this division retired by Bezy, and crossed the Genappe, lower down the stream, by the bridge of Wais-le-Hutte.

In the early part of the morning, Ney had, like his opponent, been ignorant of the result of the battle of Ligny, but he was aware that the Anglo-allied army had been considerably reinforced during the night, principally by the arrival of its cavalry. The Marshal calculated that if Napoleon had gained a victory, and crossed the Namur road, the longer Wellington remained in the position of Quatre-Bras, the greater the danger he incurred of having not only his communication with Blücher effectually cut off, but also his main line of retreat upon Brussels intercepted; and that in such a case it was wiser not to advance against the British General, as the latter might then retire, and thus elude the effect of a combined operation between Napoleon's and his own forces. He also judged that if, on the other hand, the French Emperor had been defeated, an attack made on his own part, upon the Anglo-allied army, might subject himself to the risk of having to contend against a combined operation between Wellington and Blücher, and thus expose both his own and Napoleon's forces to the probability of being defeated in detail. In this uncertainty, Ney sent a message by General Count Flahaut, who happened to be still with him, and who was returning to rejoin the Emperor wherever he might be found, expressive of his anxiety to learn the result of the action of the preceding day. In the mean time, he kept his troops in a state of perfect quietude: his main body was posted in reserve on the heights of Frasne, between which and the outposts there were intermediate columns of support; but no movement whatever was attempted.

Ney at length received the information he had solicited, in a despatch* from Soult, wherein the result of the battle of Ligny was briefly described. It also stated that Napoleon was proceeding, with the principal portion of his forces, to the mill of Bry, close to which the high road leads from Namur to Quatre-Bras, and that therefore it would not be practicable for the Anglo-allied army to act against him (Ney); but that should such a case happen, the Emperor would march directly upon it by that road, while Ney should attack it in front, and in this manner that army would at once be destroyed. The despatch required from Ney a report of the exact position of his forces, and an account of all that was going on in his front. Hence it is evident that Ney's opinion, that a victory at Ligny ought to be followed up by a combined attack upon Wellington, perfectly coincided with Napoleon's views; but while Ney was thus justified in remaining inactive during the early part of the day, the fact of the Emperor's not moving directly upon Genappe with the morning's dawn, and his excessive delay in breaking up his bivouac at Ligny, are inexplicable. A glorious opportunity had presented itself for the attainment of his original design of defeating both armies in detail, but which was completely lost by a most extraordinary and fatal want of energy and vigour in seizing upon the advantages which the victory of Ligny had placed within his reach.

Ney, having ascertained that Napoleon's forces were in motion, had commenced the advance of his own troops, when a second despatch reached him, dated, "in front of Ligny, at noon,"† intimating that the Emperor had just posted a corps of infantry and the imperial guard in advance of Marbais, that he wished him to attack the enemy at Quatre-Bras, and force him from his position; and that his operations would be seconded by the corps at Marbais, to which point his Majesty was proceeding in person.

Upon discovering that the Anglo-allied infantry had retired, and that the troops around, and in rear of, Quatre-Bras, consisted of cavalry covering the retreat, Ney brought for-

* Appendix XXVII. † Appendix XXVIII.

ward his own cavalry in advance, and appeared to regulate its movements so that its attack might be directed against the front of the British simultaneously with that of the cavalry which he now perceived advancing along the Namur road against its flank.

About this time, the 10th hussars were moved across the Namur road, and down the slope in front where they were halted, in echellon of squadrons; and while they were thus posted, Wellington and his staff came to the front of the regiment. From this spot the Duke was attentively watching, through his telescope, the dispositions and movements of the French, whom he could discover as soon as they reached the Quatre-Bras side of Little Marbais; when all at once at a distance of about two miles, masses were seen forming on the side of the Namur road, conspicuously glittering in the sun's rays; by which the Duke was at first induced to believe that they were infantry, whose bayonets were so brilliantly reflected; but it was soon discovered that they were cuirassiers. After a short time, these were observed to advance, preceded by lancers,* and it was not long before the picquet of the 18th British hussars, posted on that road, began skirmishing, as did also the picquet of the 10th British hussars, more in the front of the position, and likewise, still further to the right, in front of Quatre-Bras, a picquet consisting of a squadron of the 11th British light dragoons, detached from Major General Vandeleur's† brigade, which comprised the 11th light dragoons, (under Lieut. Colonel Sleigh,‡) the 12th light dragoons, (under Colonel the Hon. Frederick Ponsonby,§) and the 16th light dragoons, (under Lieut. Colonel Hay.||) The 10th hussars then fell back again into their proper place in the line. Vivian now took up a new alignment, throwing back his left so as to present a front to the enemy's advance, and to protect the left of the position. Vandeleur's brigade was then in right rear of Vivian's and close to Quatre-Bras.

The Anglo-allied infantry having, sometime previously, entirely crossed the Genappe, with the exception of the light companies of the 2nd brigade of guards on the right, and of the 1st battalion 95th British regiment, (rifles,) on the left, which troops had been directed to remain until the last moment, and were now retiring to Genappe, (where they were

* The cuirassiers were those of Milhaud's corps, and the lancers formed part of Subervie's light cavalry-division.

† Now General Sir John Vandeleur, G.C.B.

‡ Now Lieut. General James W. Sleigh, C.B.

§ Major General the Hon. Sir Frederick C. Ponsonby, K.C.B., G.C.M.G., K.C.H., died on the 10th of January, 1837.

|| Now Major General James Hay, C.B.

subsequently drawn up at the entrance of the town,) and the Duke having satisfied himself that a formidable body of the French cavalry was endeavouring to fall upon him and to molest his retreat, it became a question with his Grace, at the moment, how far it might be advisable to offer any serious resistance to the advance of the enemy; but Lieut. General the Earl of Uxbridge, the commander of the Anglo-allied cavalry, having remarked that, considering the defiles in the rear, and the distance to which the great mass of the infantry had already retired, and from which it could offer no immediate support, he did not think the cavalry was favourably situated for making such an attempt, the Duke assented to the correctness of this view, and requested his Lordship at once to carry into effect the retreat of the cavalry.

Uxbridge immediately made the following dispositions for this purpose. The 1st or household brigade of heavy cavalry commanded by Major General Lord Edward Somerset,* and consisting of the 1st life guards, (under Lieut. Colonel Ferrior,†) of the 2nd life guards, (under Lieut. Colonel the Hon. Edward P. Lygon,‡) of the royal horse guards, or blues, (under Lieut. Colonel Sir Robert Chambre Hill,§) and of the 1st (or King's) dragoon guards (under Colonel Fuller,‖) together with the 2nd brigade of heavy cavalry, commanded by Major General the Honorable Sir William Ponsonby,¶ consisting of the 1st, or Royal dragoons, (under Lieut Colonel Clifton,**) of the 2nd Royal North British dragoons, or Scots Greys, (under Colonel Hamilton,††) and of the 6th, or Inniskilling dragoons, (under Colonel Muter,‡‡) formed the centre column, which was to retire by the Brussels high road. Vandeleur's and Vivian's brigades constituted the left column, which was to effect its retreat by a bridge over the Genappe at Thuy, still lower down the stream than that by which Alten's infantry-division had crossed. The right column was formed of part of the 3rd light cavalry brigade, commanded by Major General Sir William Dörnberg, the 1st and 2nd light dragoons of the King's German legion, (under

* General Lord Edward Somerset, G.C.B., died on the 1st of September, 1842.

† Lieut. Colonel Samuel Ferrior, was killed at the battle of Waterloo.

‡ Now Lieut. General the Hon. Edward Pyndar Lygon, C.B.

§ Now Colonel Sir Robert Chambre Hill, C.B., *ret.*

‖ Colonel William Fuller was killed at the battle of Waterloo.

¶ Major General the Hon. Sir William Ponsonby, K.C.B., was killed at the battle of Waterloo.

** Now Lieut. General Sir Arthur Clifton, K.C.B., K.C.H.

†† Colonel James Inglis Hamilton was killed at the battle of Waterloo.

‡‡ Lieut. General Sir Joseph Stratton, (to which this officer's name was subsequently changed,) C.B., K.C.H., died on the 23rd of October, 1840.

Lieut. Colonels Bülow* and de Jonquières,†) while the remaining regiment, which was the 23rd British light dragoons, (under Colonel the Earl of Portarlington,‡) was employed as a portion of the rear-guard of the centre column. The 15th British hussars, (under Lieut. Colonel Dalyrymple,§) belonging to the 5th cavalry-brigade, under Major General Sir Colquhoun Grant,‖ was also attached to the right column; while of the two remaining regiments of the brigade, the 2nd hussars of the King's German legion, (under Lieut. Colonel Linsingen,¶) and the 7th British hussars, (under Colonel Sir Edward Kerrison,**) the former had been left in occupation of a line of posts on the French frontier, extending from Courtrai, through Menin, Ypres, Loo, and Fürnes, to the North Sea, and the latter formed a part of the rear-guard of the centre column. This right column was to pass the Genappe by a ford higher up the stream than the town of Genappe.

These skilful dispositions had scarcely been arranged, when the picquet of the 18th hussars, on the left, came in at a good round trot, followed by two or three squadrons of French cavalry, upon which Vivian's battery of horse-artillery, opened a fire whereby their advanced was checked. The enemy, however, was observed to be very active in bringing up his artillery, which soon opened upon the hussar-brigade. Vivian, having received the Earl of Uxbridge's instructions to retire, accompanied with an intimation that he would be supported by Vandeleur's brigade, then in his rear, and observing that the French cavalry was pressing forward in great numbers, not only in his front, but also on his flank, he put his brigade about, and retired in line, covered by the skirmishers. The French followed, with loud cries of "*Vive l'Empereur!*" and just as the brigade reached a sort of hollow, their guns again opened, throwing shells, which mostly flew over the heads of the 18th hussars, against which regiment they appeared to be principally directed. In the mean time, Vandeleur's brigade had been drawn up in support, on rather a commanding position, and Vivian approached it

* Colonel John Baron von Bülow, C.B., K.H., died on the 29th of July, 1846.

† Major General Charles Frederick de Jonquières, K.H. of the Hanoverian service, died on the 12th of October, 1831.

‡ Colonel the Earl of Portarlington, died in December, 1845

§ Lieut. Colonel Leighton C. Dalrymple, C.B., died on the 15th of June, 1820.

‖ Lieut. General Sir Colquhoun Grant, K.C.B., G.C.H., died on the 20th of December, 1835.

¶ Colonel Augustus Henry von Linsingen, of the Hanoverian service, died on the 12th of December, 1817.

** Now Lieut. General Sir Edward Kerrison, Bart. K.C.B.. G.C.H.

in the full expectation that it would open out for the passing through of his own men, and take the rear-guard in its turn; but on the hussars arriving within fifty or sixty yards of the 4th brigade, Vandeleur put it about, and retired—Vivian not being aware that Vandeleur had previously received orders to retire and leave the road clear for the retreat of the cavalry in his front. Vivian immediately occupied the ground thus vacated, and, with a view to check the enemy's advance more effectually, ordered the 18th hussars to charge, as soon as the French approached within favourable reach.

The weather, during the morning, had become oppressively hot; it was now a dead calm; not a leaf was stirring; and the atmosphere was close to an intolerable degree; while a dark, heavy, dense cloud impended over the combatants. The 18th hussars were fully prepared, and awaited but the command to charge, when the brigade guns on the right commenced firing, for the purpose of previously disturbing and breaking the order of the enemy's advance. The concussion seemed instantly to rebound through the still atmosphere, and communicate, as an electric spark, with the heavily charged mass above. A most awfully loud thunder-clap burst forth, immediately succeeded by a rain which has never, probably, been exceeded in violence even within the tropics. In a very few minutes the ground became perfectly saturated; so much so that it was quite impracticable for any rapid movement of the cavalry. The enemy's lancers, opposed to the 6th British brigade began to relax in their advance, and to limit it to skirmishing; but they seemed more intent upon endeavouring to envelope, and intercept the retreat of, the hussars. Vivian now replaced the 18th hussars by the first hussars of the King's German legion, as rear-guard, with orders to cover well the left flank and left front of the brigade. He had already sent off his battery of horse-artillery, to cross the Genappe by the bridge of Thuy, and despatched an aide-de-camp to Vandeleur, to request he would move his brigade as quickly as possible across that bridge, so that he might meet with no interruption in his retreat, in the event of his being hard pressed.

Of the centre column, the heavy brigades of Lord Edward Somerset and Sir William Ponsonby had retired along the Charleroi road, and were taking up a position on some high ground, a little in rear of Genappe, on either side of that road. The detached squadron of the 11th light dragoons, (under Captain Schreiber,*) was withdrawn and directed to

* Lieut. Colonel James Alfred Schreiber died on the 5th of June, 1840.

retire through the above town. The 23rd light dragoons were also withdrawn, and posted upon the ascent between Genappe and the position occupied by the two heavy brigades. The 7th hussars continued on the south side of Genappe, as rear-guard.

Neither the centre, nor the right, column experienced any serious molestation in its retreat while on the French side of the Genappe: large bodies of cavalry were seen in motion, but their advanced guards limited their attacks to skirmishing.

At length the 7th hussars retired through Genappe, after having thrown out their right squadron, commanded by Major Hodge,* as rear-guard, to cover the retreat of the centre column, regulating its proceedings in conformity with such orders as it might receive from Major General Sir William Dörnberg, who had been desired to superintend the movements of the skirmishers. Major Hodge led out the right troop, under Captain Elphinstone,† to skirmish, while Lieutenant Standish O'Grady,‡ who commanded the left troop, held the high road, from which he had occasionally to send assistance to the former, and frequently to advance, to enable the skirmishers to hold their ground, as their movements were difficult, through ploughed fields so soft that the horses always sank up to their knees, and sometimes to their girths. In this manner, every inch of ground was disputed, until within a short distance of Genappe. Here Dörnberg informed Lieutenant O'Grady, that he must leave him; that it was of the utmost importance to face the enemy boldly at this spot, as the bridge in the town of Genappe was so narrow that the squadron would have to pass it in file; that he was to endeavour as much as possible to obtain time for drawing off the skirmishers, but not to compromise his troop too much. Lieutenant O'Grady then called in his skirmishers, and advanced with his own troop boldly up the road at a trot. The cavalry immediately opposed to him, went about, followed by him for some distance; and he thus continued alternately advancing and retiring, until he saw all the right troop safe on the road in his rear. He then began to retire at a walk, occasionally halting and fronting, until he turned the corner of the town of Genappe: when he filed the men from the left, and passed through the place at a gallop.§

* Major Edward Hodge was killed at Genappe.

† Lieut. Colonel James D. Elphinstone retired from the service in Sept. 1832.

‡ Now Colonel Lord Viscount Guillamore.

§ Dörnberg had been some time time riding about with Lieutenant O'Grady, and on taking leave of him, on the French side of Genappe, shook his hand,

Upon the arrival of the squadron at the opposite entrance of Genappe, it was posted between this point and the main body of the 7th hussars, which had been drawn up on the road in in a column of divisions, prepared to check the advance of the enemy on his debouching from the town.

The British left cavalry column continued its retreat, which was towards the little bridge of Thuy, by deep narrow lanes, converted by the tremendous pour of rain into perfect streams. Vivian withdrew the 10th and 18th hussars from the position he last occupied, but on their approaching the Genappe an interruption occurred in consequence of Vandeleur's brigade not having effected its passage across the bridge; and the delay became so great that he was induced to put about the 18th hussars, with a view to their affording a support to the 1st German hussars, should they require it. In a short time after this, Vandeleur's brigade resumed its progress: the 10th hussars followed; and, as the 1st hussars, with which regiment Vivian himself was at the moment, continued to maintain a vigorous and effective skirmish, he ordered the 18th to resume its retrograde movement; having previously directed that some men of the 10th hussars should be dismounted on reaching the opposite bank of the Genappe, and be prepared with their carbines to defend the passage, should the retreat of the remainder of the brigade be severely pressed. After skirmishing some time, Vivian despatched a squadron of the 1st German hussars to the bridge, and the moment he began to do so, the French cavalry again pushed forward with so much boldness and rapidity as to interpose between the left squadron and the main body of the regiment, and to compel that squadron to pass the Genappe lower down than the bridge over which the brigade passed the little stream. Having ascertained that all was ready, Vivian galloped down the road to the bridge with the remainder of the 1st German hussars. The French followed them, loudly cheering, but as soon as the hussars cleared the bridge, and

while his manner and his observations sufficiently indicated that he considered the service to be one of forlorn hope, and that he did not expect ever to see his young friend again. When the latter rejoined him on the other side of the town, after having so ably executed the duty allotted to him, and reported that he had not lost a man or a horse, Dörnberg exclaimed, "Then Buonaparte is not with them: if he were, not a man of you could have escaped." I have, perhaps, entered rather too much into detail on this point—at least, I anticipate some such remark on the part of the old campaigners—but I could not withhold from the youthful military aspirant, so instructive an example of the important service which may be rendered, and of the great credit which may be gained, by an officer holding even a subordinate rank, when possessing, in an equal degree, the tact, discretion, and gallantry, which distinguished Lieutenant O'Grady's conduct on this occasion.

the enemy's dragoons reached it, some of the dismounted men that had been formed along the top of the opposite bank, in rear of a hedge, overlooking the bridge and a hollow-way, through which the road led from it up the ascent, opened a fire upon the foremost of the French lancers that had come up to the other end of the bridge, while the remainder of the 10th, and the whole of the 18th hussars, were drawn up along the rising ground or bank. The good countenance here shown by Vivian's brigade, combined with the soft and miry state of the ground after the thunder-storm had set in, completely checked the pursuit by the enemy's cavalry, which now turned towards the high road. The left cavalry column, after Vivian's brigade had remained in its position for some little time, continued its retreat without further molestation (the enemy having contented himself with merely detaching a patrole to watch its movements,) along a narrow cross-road, running nearly parallel with the Charleroi high road, and leading through the villages of Glabbaix, Maransart, Aywiers, Frischermont, Smohain, and Verd-cocou. Here Vivian's brigade arrived in the evening, in the vicinity of the Forest of Soignies, and bivouacked; while Vandeleur's brigade passed the night somewhat nearer to the ground which had been selected for the position to be taken up by the Anglo-allied army.

The right cavalry column, consisting only, as previously stated, of the 1st and 2nd light dragoons of the King's German legion, and of the 15th British hussars, effected its retreat in good order, protected by its skirmishers, as far as the ford, which it crossed above Genappe. At this point, the French cavalry suspended its pursuit, and proceeded, in like manner as that on the right had done, to join the main body on the high road; while the British right cavalry column continued its retreat unmolested towards the position of Waterloo, in rear of which it bivouacked.

A large body of French cavalry, consisting of from sixteen to eighteen squadrons, was now entering Genappe by the Charleroi road, followed by the main body of the French army under Napoleon.

The Earl of Uxbridge, who was desirous of checking the enemy's advance, so as to gain sufficient time for the orderly retreat of the Anglo-allied army, and to prevent a compromise of any portion of the rearmost troops, decided upon embracing the advantage which the narrow defile of Genappe seemed to present in aid of his design. The town consists mainly of houses lining the high road, on the Brussels side of the bridge. The road then ascends a ridge, the brow of which is about six or seven hundred yards distant, and here Lord Uxbridge had halted the heavy brigades of Lord Edward Somerset and of Sir William Ponsonby, and posted them so as to cover the retirement of the light cavalry. At first, he formed them in line; Somerset's on the right, and Ponsonby's on the left, of the high road; but observing by the enemy's formidable advance, that the light cavalry would soon be compelled to fall back, his Lordship drew up Somerset's brigade in a column of half squadrons upon, but close to, the right of the road itself, so as to admit of troops retiring by its left; and formed Ponsonby's brigade into a column of half squadrons upon the left of the high road, and somewhat to the rear. The 7th hussars were formed at some little distance in the rear of Genappe, and the 23rd light dragoons were drawn up in support of that regiment, and about midway between it and the heavy cavalry on the height. The squadron of the 7th hussars, under Major Hodge, it will be recollected, was halted between the main body of that regiment and the town of Genappe.

Thus posted, the centre retiring cavalry column remained about twenty minutes, when loud shouts announced that the French had entered the town. Presently a few horsemen appeared galloping out of the street, and dashed at speed into Major Hodge's squadron. They were found, on being taken, to be quite inebriated. In a few moments afterwards, the French column showed its head within the town; the leading troop consisted of lancers, all very young men, mounted on very small horses, and commanded by a fine-looking, and, as it subsequently appeared, a very brave man. The column remained about fifteen minutes within the town, its head halted at the outlet facing the British rear-guard, and its flanks protected by the houses. The street not being straight, and the rear of the column not being aware that the front had halted, continued pressing forward, until the whole mass became so jammed that it was impossible for the foremost ranks to go about, should such a movement become necessary. Their apparent hesitation and indecision induced Lord Uxbridge, who stood upon some elevated ground adjoining the right of the road, to order the 7th hussars to charge. The latter, animated by the presence of the commander of the cavalry, who was also their own colonel, rushed forward with the most determined spirit and intrepidity; while the French, awaiting the onslaught, opposed to them a close, compact, and impenetrable phalanx of lances; which, being securely flanked by the houses, and backed by a solid mass of horsemen, presented a complete *chevaux de frise.* Hence, it is not surprising that the charge should have made no impression upon the enemy; nevertheless, the contest was maintained for some considerable time; the hussars cutting at their opponents, and the latter parrying and thrusting, neither party giving way a single inch of ground; both the commanding officer of the lancers, and Major Hodge, commanding the leading squadron of the hussars, were killed, gallantly fighting to the last. The French had by this time established a battery of horse artillery on the left of Genappe and upon the opposite bank of the river, from which they opened a brisk fire upon the British cavalry in support, and several shot struck the main body of the 7th hussars, upsetting men and horses, and causing great impediments in their rear. The French lancers now advanced, and drove the 7th hussars upon their reserve; but here the 7th rallied, renewed their attack, and forced back the lancers upon the town. The latter having been reinforced, rallied, in their turn, and drove back the hussars. These, however, again rallied, and resolutely faced their opponents, with whom they gallantly continued a fierce encounter for some time longer, when to terminate a conflict which was most obstinate and sanguinary without being productive of any favourable result, but in which the bravery of the 7th hussars shone most conspicuously, and became the theme of admiration of all who witnessed it, Lord Uxbridge decided upon withdrawing that regiment and charging with the 1st life guards. As soon as the hussars went about, in pursuance of the orders received, the lancers followed them. In the mêlée which ensued, the French lost quite as many men as did the hussars; and when at length the latter were able to disengage themselves, the former did not attempt to follow them. The 7th retired through the 23rd light dragoons, took the first favourable turn off the road and re-formed in the adjoining field.

During this contest, the French, having become sensible of the evil that might arise from the closely wedged state of the cavalry in the town, began to clear the rear of the most advanced portions of the column, so as to admit of more freedom of movement in case of disaster. A battery of British horse-artillery had taken post close to a house on the height occupied by the heavy cavalry, and on the left of the road; and it was now replying to the French battery on the opposite bank of the river.

So exceedingly elated were the French with having repulsed the 7th hussars in this their first serious encounter with the British cavalry, that immediately on that regiment retiring, the whole column that was in Genappe raised the war cry, and rent the air with shouts of "*En avant!—En avant!*" evincing the greatest impatience to follow up this momentary advantage, and to attack the supports; for which, indeed, the opportunity appeared very favourable, as the ranks of the latter were suffering considerable annoyance from the well-directed and effective fire of the French guns on the opposite bank of the river. They now abandoned the secure cover to which they had been indebted for their temporary success, and were advancing up the ascent with all the confidence of a fancied superiority, when the Earl of Uxbridge, seizing upon the advantage presented for attacking them while moving up-hill, with their flanks unsupported, and a narrow defile in their rear, and being also desirous of affording the 1st life guards an opportunity of charging, brought forward that regiment through the 23rd light dragoons, who opened out for its passage to the front. The life guards now made their charge, most gallantly headed by Colonel Sir John Elley,* Deputy Adjutant General, who, at the moment of contact with the enemy, began by cutting down two men right and left. It was truly a splendid charge: its rapid rush down into the enemy's mass, was as terrific in appearance as it was destructive in its effect; for although the French met the attack with firmness, they were utterly unable to hold their ground a single moment, were overthrown with great slaughter, and literally ridden down in such a manner that the road was instantaneously covered with men and horses, scattered in all directions. The life guards, pursuing their victorious course, dashed into Genappe, and drove all before them as far as the opposite outlet of the town.

This brilliant and eminently successful charge made a deep impression upon the enemy, who now conducted his pursuit with extreme caution. The 23rd light dragoons, which had supported the 1st life guards in their charge, became again the last regiment in the rear-guard, and continued so during the remainder of the retreat. Ponsonby's brigade had deployed to the right of the high road, and the guns were so disposed as to take advantageous positions, retiring *en échiquier*. The enemy, after quitting Genappe, tried to get upon the flanks of the centre retiring column, chiefly upon the right flank; but the Royals, Greys, and Inniskillings, ma-

* Lieut. General Sir John Elley, K.C.B. died on the 23d of January, 1839.

nœuvred beautifully; retiring by alternate squadrons, and covered by their own skirmishers, who completely beat the French light cavalry in that kind of warfare. Finding that from the deep state of the ground, there was not the least danger of his being turned by the enemy, Lord Uxbridge gradually withdrew Ponsonby's brigade to the high road. He kept the light cavalry, protected by the household brigade, as the rear-guard, and slowly retired into the chosen position in front of Waterloo, the guns and rockets constantly plying the enemy's advance, which, although it pressed forward twice or thrice, and made preparations to attack, never ventured to come to close quarters with its opponents; and the column received from it no further molestation.

On arriving at the foot of the Anglo-allied position, the 23rd light dragoons moved off to the (Allied) right of the high road, and into the hollow in which lies the orchard of the farm of La Haye Sainte. Here they were drawn up, prepared to meet the French advanced guard, should it follow them, or to fall upon its flank, should it venture to continue its march along the road. The latter, however, halted upon the height which intervenes between La Haye Sainte and La Belle Alliance, and opened a fire upon the centre of the Duke of Wellington's line, above the former farm, from two batteries of horse-artillery. Picton, who was then upon the rising ground in rear of La Haye Sainte, and who was intently watching the enemy's advance along the high road, perceived columns of infantry approaching from La Belle Alliance. He immediately took upon himself to unite the two batteries nearest at hand, which were those under Major Lloyd of the British artillery, and Major Cleeves of the King's German legion, (although not belonging to his own division), and to place them in position on the high ground close to the Charleroi road. The guns immediately opened a brisk cannonade upon the French columns, of which they had obtained a most accurate range just as their leading divisions had entered the inclosed space between the high banks which line the high road where it is cut through the height before mentioned as intervening between La Belle Alliance and La Haye Sainte. This mass of the enemy's infantry suffered severely from the fire, to which it stood exposed about half an hour; for the head of the column having been unable to retrograde, in consequence of the pressure from its rear, and prevented by the high bank on either side of the road from filing off to a flank, could not readily extricate itself from so embarrassing a situation. During the whole of this fire, the Allied batteries were replied to, though very ineffectually, by the two batteries of French horse-artillery posted on the height in question.

It was now twilight: the approaching darkness was greatly accelerated by the lowering aspect of the sky. Picquets were hastily thrown forward by both armies, and to so great a height had the mutual spirit of defiance arisen, that the near approach of opposing parties, advancing to take up their ground for the night, led to little cavalry-affairs, which, though unproductive of any useful result to either side, were distinguished, on different points of the lines, by a chivalrous bravery which seemed to require a prudent restraint. In one of these affairs, Captain Heyliger* of the 7th hussars, made a very brilliant charge with his troop, and when the Duke of Wellington sent to check him, his Grace desired to be made acquainted with the name of an officer who had displayed so much gallantry. A very spirited charge was also made by the right troop of the 2nd light dragoons of the King's German legion, under Lieut. Hugo,† who was allowed by his commanding officer to volunteer for that service, and who, from the vicinity of Hougomont, boldly rushed up the height intervening between that point and Mon Plaisir, and gallantly drove back a portion of the French advanced guard of cavalry; recapturing at the same time three carriages filled with British sick and wounded.‡

The manner in which the Duke of Wellington withdrew his army from the position of Quatre-Bras to the one of Waterloo, must ever render that retreat a perfect model of operations of this nature, performed in the immediate presence of a powerful enemy. Those dispositions which have been described as having been made by him for the purpose of masking the retirement of the main body, of affording perfect security to the passage of the defile in his rear, and of ensuring the orderly and regular assembly of the several corps on the ground respectively allotted to them in the new position, evince altogether a degree of skill which has never been surpassed. In such operations, the covering of the army by its cavalry and light troops necessarily forms an important feature; and a glance at the manner in which this duty was fulfilled by the Earl of Uxbridge, with the cavalry, horse-

* Captain Peter Augustus Heyliger retired from the service on the 30th of March, 1820.

† Now Major Ludolph von Hugo, h.p. Hanoverian service.

‡ For return of killed, wounded, and missing, of the British troops and King's German legion on the 17th of June—See Appendix XXIX.

artillery, and a few light battalions, at his disposal, is sufficient to show that the exemplification of such feature on this occasion was exceedingly beautiful. Indeed, so orderly and so perfect were all the arrangements connected with this retreat, from its commencement to its close, that the movements partook more of the appearance of a field-day upon a large scale, than of an operation executed in the actual presence of an enemy; and this was particularly observable as regarded the protection afforded by the cavalry and horse-artillery, which manœuvred to admiration, and in a style that, combined with the brilliant charge by the 1st life-guards at Genappe, evidently impressed the enemy with a due sense of the efficiency of the gallant troops immediately in his front. It may here also be remarked, that the judicious dispositions made by Lord Uxbridge in covering this retreat, and the high degree of confidence with which he inspired the cavalry, afforded well-grounded anticipations of the success likely to attend his measures when conducting that cavalry in the open battle-field, on which, it was foreseen, its prowess would so very soon be tested. The British and German portion of the cavalry was in excellent order, and seemed already to have imbibed, in a high degree, that gallant bearing and chivalrous spirit, which it beheld and admired in its distinguished chief.

In the course of the evening, the Duke received from Prince Blücher a reply to the request he had made for his support in the position he was now occupying. It was highly characteristic of the old man, who had written it, in the following terms, without previously conferring with, or addressing himself to, any one:—"I shall not come with two corps only, but with my whole army; upon this understanding, however, that should the French not attack us on the 18th, we shall attack them on the 19th."*

The Duke, who, as has already been explained, had, from the commencement of the campaign, considered it very possible that Napoleon would advance by the Mons road, still entertained apprehensions of an attempt on the part of his opponent to turn him by Hal, and seize Brussels by a coup de main. For this, however, he was fully prepared, having made his dispositions for the security of that flank, in the manner pointed out in the following instructions, which he issued to Major General the Hon. Sir Charles Colville:—

* The Prussian officer conveying this communication was brought to head-quarters by an escort from a squadron of the 1st hussars King's German legion, which Vivian had detached to the left, with orders to patrole as far as Ohain.

'17th June, 1815.

'The army retired this day from its position at Quatre-Bras to its present position in front of Waterloo.

'The brigades of the 4th division, at Braine-le-Comte, are to retire at daylight to-morrow morning upon Hal.

'Major General Colville must be guided by the intelligence he receives of the enemy's movements in his march to Hal, whether he moves by the direct route or by Enghien.

'Prince Frederick of Orange is to occupy with his corps the position between Hal and Enghien, and is to defend it as long as possible.

'The army will probably continue in its position in front of Waterloo to-morrow.

'Lieut. Colonel Torrens will inform Lieut. General Sir Charles Colville of the position and situation of the armies.'

The respective lines of picquets and vedettes had scarcely been taken up along the low ground that skirted the front of the Anglo-allied position, and the last gun had just boomed from the heights, when "heaven's artillery," accompanied by vivid flashes of lightning, again pealed forth in solemn and awful grandeur; while the rain, pouring down in torrents, imparted the utmost gloom and discomfort to the bivouacs, which the opposing armies had established for the night, upon the ground destined to become celebrated in history, even to the remotest ages.

CHAPTER VIII.

It was not until the night of the 16th, after Zieten's and Pirch's corps d'armée had retired to Tilly and Gentinnes, that it was decided the Prussian army should retreat upon Wavre. This decision was communicated in the orders then transmitted from the Prussian head-quarters to the 1st and 2nd corps d'armée, (Zieten's and Pirch's) directing them to bivouac at Bierge and St. Anne, in the vicinity of Wavre; as also in the orders forwarded, on the next morning, to the bivouacs of the 3rd and 4th corps, (Thielemann's and Bülow's), at Gembloux and Basse Bodecée, directing them to fall back, and bivouac at La Bavette and Dion-le-Mont near Wavre.

Zieten's and Pirch's corps retired by Mont St. Guibert, in rear of which defile the latter corps remained a considerable time as rear-guard, while the former marched on to Wavre, where it arrived about midday, crossed the Dyle, and took up its position at Bierge. Pirch followed the same route, but took post on the right bank of the Dyle, between St. Anne and Aisemont.

With the first glimmering of daylight the troops, which, under the command of General Jagow, had continued in full possession of Bry and its immediate vicinity during the night, began to retire, firstly, in the direction of Sombref, and thence to Gembloux, which they reached before the arrival of Thielemann's corps. After the receipt of the order pointing out the direction of the retreat, Jagow conducted these troops, in the course of the 17th, towards their respective brigades.

Lieut. Colonel Sohr, whose cavalry-brigade with half a horse-battery, formed the rear-guard of the line of retreat of Zieten's and Pirch's corps, received orders to take up a concealed position between Tilly and Gentinnes, thence to watch the movements of the enemy, and, as soon as he found himself pressed by the latter, to fall back upon the defile of Mont St. Guibert.

Thielemann, who, it will be recollected had received a message from Gneisenau, leaving it optional with him to retire by Tilly or Gembloux, according to circumstances, decided on falling back upon the latter point; being well aware that the enemy was in possession of the villages of St. Amand and

Ligny, and of the field of battle to within a very short distance from Sombref.*

He had collected together his widely disseminated brigades, and drawn in his advanced posts; an operation which, executed in the darkness of the night, retarded his departure so much that it was two o'clock in the morning before the reserve-artillery, which formed the head of the column, struck into the road which at Point du Jour, leads from the Namur chaussée to Gembloux. The rear-guard of this line of retreat, which consisted of the 9th infantry-brigade, under Major General Borcke, and the reserve-cavalry, under General Hobe, and was drawn up along the Namur road, having in its front the Fleurus chaussée, leading directly towards the enemy, did not commence its march until after four o'clock, when the sun had risen. The main body of the corps reached Gembloux at six o'clock in the morning. On approaching this place, Thielemann learned that Bülow had posted the 4th corps about three miles in rear of Gembloux, upon the old Roman road; whereupon Major Weyrach, aide-de-camp to Prince Blücher, who had continued with Thielemann during the night of the 16th, (see note), set off to seek out the Field Marshal, and to report to him the position and attendant circumstances of the 3rd and 4th corps d'armée. He soon succeeded in discovering the Prussian head-quarters at Mélioreux, and communicated the above important information to Count Gneisenau. Thielemann gave his own corps a halt on the other side of the town, in order that his troops might obtain rest and refreshment.

The advance of Bülow's corps had reached Basse Bodécée, upon the old Roman road, at nightfall of the 16th of June. Here that General became acquainted with the loss of the battle of Ligny: whereupon he ordered the brigades of his corps to be posted at intervals along this road, with the excep-

* Between seven and eight o'clock in the evening of the 16th, Major Weyrach, aide-de-camp to Prince Blücher, was sent with a message from the latter to General Thielemann. After passing through Sombref, he found the General at some little distance and delivered to him the message. He was then detained by Thielemann who wished him to accompany him along the line of his position, that he might have the opportunity of pointing out to him the spot where, shortly before, a small portion of his cavalry, with a battery of horse-artillery, had advanced across the Ligny rivulet, and, after an engagement which terminated in favour of the enemy, had fallen back again, a circumstance not then known to the Field Marshal. By the time they returned to Sombref, it was dark; and although some scattered French dragoons had ridden up to Sombref, Thielemann was ignorant of the fact of the centre of the Prussian line having been broken. Major Weyrach now started off to join Prince Blücher, but had not proceeded above 800 paces when he was challenged by a French vedette; whereupon he returned to Sombref, and remained with General Thielemann during the night.

tion of the 13th, (under Lieut. General Hake,) which was directed to bivouack more to the rear, near Hottoment, where the same road is intersected by that which conducts from Namur to Louvain.

Both corps remained for some hours in a state of uncertainty as to the direction to be taken for forming a junction with the 1st and 2nd corps. Thielemann wrote to Bülow that he had received no orders from Prince Blücher, but that he presumed the retreat was upon St. Trond. He also stated that he had not been followed by the enemy, but that he had heard distant firing on the right, which he concluded was connected with the Duke of Wellington's army. At length, about half-past nine o'clock, Prince Blücher's aide-de-camp, Major Weyrach arrived at Bülow's head-quarters, and brought the orders for the retreat of the 4th corps to Dion-le-mont, near Wavre, by Walhain and Corbaix. The orders also required that Bülow should post the main body of his rear-guard (which consisted of the 14th brigade) at Vieux Sart; as also that he should send a detachment, consisting of one regiment of cavalry, two battalions of infantry, and two guns of horse artillery, to the defile of Mont St. Guibert, to act, in the first instance as a support to Lieut. Colonel Sohr, who was at Tilly, and then, upon the latter falling back, to act as rear-guard in this direction. Lieut. Colonel Ledebur was accordingly detached upon this duty with the 10th hussars, the fusilier-battalions of the 11th regiment of infantry and 1st regiment of Pomeranian landwehr, together with two guns from the horse-battery No. 12. The corps itself moved directly upon Dion-le-mont, and on reaching the height near that town, on which is situated the public-house of "A tous vents," took up a position close to the intersection of the roads leading to Louvain, Wavre, and Gembloux.

At two o'clock in the afternoon Thielemann commenced his march upon Wavre; where the corps arrived late in the evening, and took up its position at La Bavette, leaving the 9th infantry-brigade (General Borcke) and the cavalry-brigade of Colonel Count Lottum, on the right bank of the Dyle. In this position the corps was now rejoined by Colonel Marwitz's cavalry-brigade, which had retired by Tilly; as also by the 2nd battalion of the 3rd Kurmark landwehr, and the two squadrons of the 6th Kurmark landwehr-cavalry, which troops had been left at Dinant. The squadron of the 7th uhlans that had been detached to Onoz, also joined, but having fallen in with a superior force of the enemy's cavalry, had experienced a great loss. The two squadrons of the 9th hussars, belonging to this corps, had not yet arrived from Ciney.

The Prussian head-quarters were established, early on the 17th, at Wavre. The veteran Field-Marshal, who was still suffering considerably in consequence of his fall, was obliged to seek rest the moment he arrived there, and did not quit his bed during the remainder of the day.

In the course of the forenoon, Lieutenant Massow, who had been despatched with a message to the Duke of Wellington, returned with the one from his Grace, communicating the intention of the latter to fall back upon Waterloo and accept a battle there, provided he received the support of two Prussian corps. (See Page 159). There was every disposition to enter into this proposal, but some degree of uncertainty existed as to whether Bülow's corps would join the army on the 17th, as also a certain misgiving respecting the park of ammunition of both Zieten's and Pirch's corps, which had been directed upon Gembloux, a circumstance that excited apprehensions as to the possibility of furnishing the much needed supply of ammunition to these corps which were at hand. In this state of uncertainty, no other resolution could be adopted than that of holding the position in front and in rear of the Dyle, (with the advanced guard of the 4th corps as far. forward as Mont St. Guibert,) until the required ammunition should be obtained: and Blücher deferred replying to Wellington's communication, in the hope that his army would very soon be relieved from the unpleasant circumstances above mentioned.

While the Prussians were thus effecting their retreat in good order, along the cross roads of that part of the country, (high road there was none,) no corresponding activity manifested itself on the part of the French, whom the morning's dawn found still lying in their bivouac. Their vedettes stood within half a mile of the columns of Thielemann's rear-guard, the retreat of which, not having commenced until after sunrise, might have been easily remarked, and had the French detached but the smallest patrole, they could not have failed to discover the direction of that retreat—whether towards Namur or Gembloux. It was not until after Thielemann had retired a sufficient distance to escape further notice that any disposition for movement occurred to disturb the perfect quietude of their repose. Then, Pajol with a division of his light cavalry-corps, under Lieut. General Baron Soult, consisting of the 1st, 4th, and 5th hussars, was detached in pursuit of the Prussians. He struck into the Namur road, and shortly afterwards Lieut. General Baron Teste's infantry-division of Lobau's corps, (the 6th,) followed in support, and took up a position on the heights of Mazy. Pajol had not proceeded very far when he perceived a Prussian battery retiring upon Namur, which he lost no time in capturing and forwarding to head-quarters; where the circumstance strengthened the belief that Blücher had retreated by that road. It was the Prussian horse-battery No. 14, belonging to the 2nd corps, which, having towards the end of the battle expended every shot, had driven off the field to procure a fresh supply of ammunition, but had not succeeded in falling in with the reserve ammunition-waggons. The battery neither returned to its own corps, nor did it comply with Thielemann's express order to march upon Gembloux, but consumed much time in uselessly driving first in one direction, and then in another. It was accompanied at this moment by a squadron of the 7th Prussian uhlans, which the 3rd corps had neglected to recall from Onoz. The squadron retired on the approach of the French cavalry, and escaped with a loss of 30 men; but all the guns fell into the hands of the enemy. Pajol, feeling at last some reason to doubt that Namur was a point in the Prussian retreat, diverged from the high road, and proceeded to St. Denis, where he was joined by Teste's division. A brigade of Excelmans' cavalry-corps had been detached to offer support to Pajol, should the latter require it, but in consequence of certain information, gained upon the road, it was subsequently directed to proceed towards Gembloux, on approaching which it discovered traces of the Prussian retreat.

Grouchy, who commanded the right wing of the French army in Napoleon's absence, repaired early in the morning to the Emperor's quarters, at Fleurus, for instructions, according to an order he had received to that effect on the previous evening. He was desired to wait and accompany the Emperor, who was going to visit the field of battle. The latter, however, did not start from Fleurus until between eight and nine o'clock, and on reaching St. Amand, he examined the approaches by which this village had been attacked the day before; then, he rode about the field, gave directions for the care of the wounded; and, as he passed in front of different regiments that were falling in without arms, on the ground where they were bivouacked, he was received with loud cheers. He addressed himself to nearly all the corps, and assured them of the lively satisfaction he had felt on witnessing their conduct in the battle. Having dismounted, he conversed freely, and at great length, with Grouchy and Gérard, on the state of public opinion in Paris, the different political parties, and on various other subjects quite unconnected with those military operations upon the successful issue of which depended the stability of his present power.

That Napoleon should have neglected to follow up the advantages which fortune had thrown in his way on the morning of the 17th of June, is quite incomprehensible. With the exception of a Prussian picquet at Gentinnes, his whole front as far as Gembloux, was perfectly clear of an enemy. Wellington was still in position at Quatre-Bras, where his left had become exposed by the retreat of the Prussians, and in rear of which point was the defile of Genappe. There was nothing to prevent Napoleon from marching directly upon that defile, and supporting, by a vigorous attack upon the Anglo-allied left and rear, a simultaneous movement against the front by the force under Ney. Whither had fled the mighty spirit which had shone forth with such dazzling brilliancy in former wars, and which had never displayed the energy of its powers of combination, and activity in following up successes, more eminently than in the campaign of the previous year? When before did he omit pressing every advantage to the utmost, or neglect to seize that moment of time, in which, having defeated one portion of his enemies, he was enabled to fall with combined force upon another? His army was not more fatigued than was that of Wellington, which had arrived at Quatre-Bras by forced marches. The troops which he subsequently did lead upon that point, when it was too late, consisting chiefly of the imperial guard and the 6th corps, were comparatively fresh. The former had not been engaged at Ligny until towards the termination of the action, when they suffered scarcely any loss; the latter, which arrived later, had remained intact. The idea of forming a junction with Ney, with a view of attacking Wellington, was certainly entertained; but its execution was most unaccountably and unnecessarily delayed until its intended effect could not but fall powerless upon a vigilant enemy, fully prepared, by having improved the precious moments of time, thus lost, to detect the purpose of the movement, and to ward off the intended blow.

With an army greatly inferior in numbers to the united forces of his adversaries, Napoleon's prospects of success rested exclusively upon his utmost skill and address, not only in preventing that union of force, but also in so planning, arranging, and executing his combinations, that having succeeded in defeating one opponent with a superior mass, he might then precipitate himself in like manner upon another, at the very moment when the latter might be occupied or engaged with one of his marshals. This would have exacted of him the most untiring energy, the application of all his great resources in strategical science, a lightning-swift decision, and a daring resolution both in adopting and in executing all his movements. It was by the exercise of such powerful mental resources as these, that, unaided by a sufficiently corresponding amount of physical force, he had conducted the campaign of 1814; but the spirit by which they were conceived, and the genius which instinctively seized the means of their execution, seemed to have abandoned him in this, his last, campaign: a faint gleam of the old spirit was visible in its opening movements, but it was now rather a wildfire, dazzling him for a moment, on the downward path to his destiny, than the star which had so often led him to victory. The last flash of his genius was brief, and, on the memorable plains of Fleurus, seemed to disappear, and leave him in utter darkness.

The same fatal inactivity which had marked the French Emperor's proceedings on the evening of the 15th, and during the morning of the 16th,* again manifested itself upon the 17th of June: and it was not until nearly noon of this day, upon receiving a report of a reconnaissance, made in the direction of Quatre-Bras, and upon learning that a considerable body of Prussians had been discovered at Gembloux, that he made any disposition for the movement of his troops, beyond the previous detaching of Pajol's light cavalry in pursuit of the Prussians, along the Namur road. He now ordered the following troops to proceed to occupy a position in advance of Marbais, across the Namur road, facing Quatre-Bras :—Lobau's infantry-corps, (the 6th,) with the exception of the 21st division, under Lieut. General Teste, which had already been detached in support of Pajol; Milhaud's corps of heavy cavalry (cuirassiers); Lieut. General Baron Subervie's light cavalry-brigade, from Pajol's corps; the 3rd light cavalry-division, (belonging to the 3rd corps,) under Lieut. General Baron Domon, and the imperial guard, both cavalry and infantry. To Marshal Grouchy he confided the pursuit of the Prussians, and for this purpose he placed at his disposal as great an extent of force as his limited means would admit: a force, certainly not sufficient to enable that Marshal to confront the whole Prussian army, should the latter, after having rallied and concentrated its strength, make a stand against him, but quite so to enable him to watch its

* See the concluding portion of Chapter IV.

movements, and to manœuvre so as to maintain his communication with the main army, and, if pressed by superior numbers, to effect a junction with Napoleon.

The following were the troops thus detached under Grouchy:—

	Infantry.	Cavalry.	Artillery.	Guns.
3rd corps, General Count Vandamme	14,508	*	936	32
4th corps, General Count Gérard	12,589	2,366	1,538	38
21st division, (6th corps,) Lieut. General Baron Teste .	2,316		161	8
4th division, (1st cavalry corps,) Lieut. General Count Pajol		1,234	154	6
2nd cavalry-corps, Lieut. General Count Excelmans .		2,817	246	12
	29,413	6,417	3,035	96
Deduct loss on 16th .	3,900	800	400	
Total .	25,513	5,617	2,635	96

33,765 men and 96 guns.

The 7th infantry division, under Lieut. General Girard, (belonging to the 2nd corps) having suffered very severely in the battle, was left upon the field.†

Napoleon's instructions to Grouchy were extremely simple and concise: "Pursue the Prussians, complete their defeat by attacking them as soon as you come up with them, and never let them out of your sight. I am going to unite the remainder of this portion of the army with Marshal Ney's corps, to march against the English, and to fight them if they should hold their ground between this and the forest of Soignies. You will communicate with me by the paved road which leads to Quatre-Bras."‡ No particular direction was

* The 3rd light cavalry-division, commanded by Lieut. General Baron Domon, which belonged to this corps was, on the 17th and 18th, with the main army under Napoleon.

† It is very doubtful whether Girard's division was *purposely* left at Ligny. It had not been included among either the troops ordered to Marbais, or those placed under Grouchy's orders; its commander had been mortally wounded; and the corps to which it belonged had been with Ney on the 15th and 16th, and was still at Frasne; which circumstances warrant the probability of its having been forgotten. Besides, Napoleon could very ill spare even the smallest detachment to guard the field of battle and look after the wounded,—the duty stated by certain French historians to have been assigned to this division.

‡ "Observations sur la Relation de la Campagne de 1815 publiée par le Général GOURGAUD; par le Comte de GROUCHY."

prescribed, because the Emperor was totally ignorant of the real line of the Prussian retreat. At the same time he was strongly impressed with the idea that Blücher had retired upon Namur and Liege, with a view to occupy the line of the Meuse, whence he might seriously endanger the right of the French army, as also its main line of operation, should it advance upon Brussels.*

Grouchy did not hesitate to remark to the Emperor, that the Prussians, having commenced their retreat at ten o'clock the previous night, had gained several hours' start of the troops with which he was to follow them; that although the reports received from the advanced cavalry conveyed no positive information as to the direction in which the great mass of the Prussian army had effected its retreat, appearances as yet seemed to justify the supposition that Blücher had fallen back upon Namur; and that as he would thus have to pursue in a direction contrary to that which Napoleon was himself going to take, with very little chance of being able to prevent the execution of any dispositions the Prussians might have resolved upon, when quitting the field of battle, he begged to be allowed to follow the Emperor in his projected movement upon Quatre-Bras. Napoleon declined to entertain this proposition, repeated the order he had already given to him, adding that it rested with him (Grouchy) to discover the route taken by the Prussians, whose defeat he was to complete by attacking them the moment he came up with them; while he himself would proceed to fight the English.†

The order was immediately given for the advance of the troops previously assembled near Marbais, preceded by Subervie's division of light cavalry, as advanced-guard. By

* In the first despatch from Soult to Ney, on the morning of the 17th, the following passage occurs:—"L'armée Prussienne a été mise en déroute. Le Général Pajol est à sa poursuite sur les routes de *Namur* et de *Liège*."—See Appendix XXVII.

† It is worthy of remark that both Napoleon's Marshals, to whom he had confided the command of detached corps, were of opinion that, on the 17th, he should have attacked the Anglo-allied army at Quatre-Bras and Genappe, with his combined force; and there can be no doubt that such opinion was in accordance with the first principles of strategy. It is of course to be understood that in that case, both Pajol's and Excelmans' cavalry-corps would have been left to maintain a vigilant watch upon the Prussian movements, as also an uninterrupted communication with the main army: and another essential point would have been, an earlier co-operation of Napoleon's and Ney's forces. Should this co-operation have led to a complete overthrow of the Anglo-allied army, Napoleon might then have moved again, with his combined mass, upon the Prussians at Wavre, leaving two cavalry-corps, in this case, on his left, to watch the movements of Wellington.

the time they reached Quatre-Bras, which was about two o'clock, the whole of Wellington's infantry had crossed the Genappe, and was retiring along the high road to Brussels, protected by the cavalry, which was now pressed by the French, in the manner described in the preceding Chapter.

The march of the French troops through Bry, in the direction of Quatre-Bras, became known to the Prussians through Lieut. Colonel Sohr, who still held his cavalry-brigade, even at this time, posted in rear of Tilly. Shortly afterwards, some of the French cavalry having approached, he began to retire slowly towards Mont St. Guibert, and, as he frequently formed up, in wait for the enemy, he did not reach that point until the evening of the 17th. Here he found Lieut. Colonel Ledebur, who had arrived with his detachment, and had received orders to maintain the defile.

Upon the departure of Napoleon, Grouchy ordered Vandamme and Gérard to get their corps under arms, and to move them, in the first instance, to the junction of the Gembloux road with that to Namur; and having subsequently received intelligence that a considerable body of Prussians had passed through the former town, he desired that those two corps should continue their movement upon that point. In the mean time he repaired to the advanced posts of Excelmans' dragoons, which were by this time beyond Gembloux. It was part of this cavalry which followed Lieut. Colonel Sohr, on the left. They merely threw out skirmishers against him, and, as night set in, they abandoned the pursuit in this direction.

The corps of Vandamme and Gérard did not reach Gembloux until very late in the evening. The former was posted in advance, the latter, in rear, of the town; near which also, and on the right bank of the Ormeau, was stationed the 6th light cavalry-division, under General Vallin, who succeeded to the command, upon Lieut. General Maurin being wounded at the battle of Ligny. The 1st brigade of Lieut. General Chastel's 10th cavalry-division, consisting of the 4th and 12th dragoons, under General Bonnemain, was pushed on to Sart-à-Wallain, and the 15th dragoons (from General Vincent's brigade of the 9th cavalry-division, under Lieut. General Baron Soult,) were detached to Perwès. From both these points, reports were sent into Gembloux that the Prussians had retired upon Wavre. Pajol, with his light cavalry and Teste's infantry-division, had returned from St. Denis, between Namur and Gembloux, to the original position occupied by the latter in the morning, at Mazy, in the immediate vicinity of the field of Ligny ; a movement for which no satisfactory cause has ever been assigned.

The extent of information obtained by Grouchy concerning the Prussian retreat, and the nature of the dispositions which he adopted in consequence, will be best explained by the following despatch which he addressed to the Emperor :—

'Gembloux, le 17 Juin, à dix heures du soir.

'Sire—J'ai l'honneur de vous rendre compte que j'occupe Gembloux et que ma cavalerie est à Sauveniéres. L'ennemi, fort d'environ trente mille hommes, continue son mouvement de retraite; ou lui a saisi ici un parc de 400 bétes à cornes, des magasins et des bagages.

'Il paraît d'après tous les rapports, qu'arrivés à Sauvenières, les Prussiens se sont divisés en deux colonnes : l'une a dû prendre la route de Wavre, en passant par Sart-à-Wallain, l'autre colonne parraît s'être dirigée sur Perwès.

'Ou peut peutêtre en inférer qu'une portion va joindre Wellington, et que le centre, qui est l'armée de Blücher, se retire sur Liège : une autre colonne avec de l'artillerie ayant fait son mouvement de retraite par Namur, le Géneral Excelmans a ordre de pousser ce soir six escadrons sur Sart-à-Wallain et trois escadrons sur Perwès. D'aprés leur rapport, si la masse des Prussiens se retire sur Wavre, je la suivrai dans cette direction, afin qu'ils ne puissent pas gagner Bruxelles, et de les séparer de Wellington.

'Si, au contraire, mes renseignemens prouvent que la principale force Prussienne a marché sur Perwès, je me dirigerai par cette ville à la poursuite de l'ennemi.

'Les Généraux Thielman et Borstell faisaient partie de l'armée que Votre Majesté a battue hier ; ils étaient encore ce matin à 10 heures ici, et ont annoncé que vingt mille hommes des leurs avaient été mis hors de combat. Ils ont demandé en partant les distances de Wavre, Perwès et Hannut. Blücher a été blessé légèrement au bras, ce qui ne l'a pas èmpêché de continuer à commander après s'être fait panser. Il n'a point passé par Gembloux.

'Je suis avec respect, de Votre Majesté,
'Sire, le fidèle sujet,
'Le Márechal Comte de GROUCHY.'*

Although the information conveyed in this despatch was incorrect on some points, and imperfect on others, inasmuch as it represented that Prussian columns had retired upon Namur and Perwès, which was not the case, and gave no account of the columns (1st and 2nd corps) which had retreated by Tilly and Gentinnes, still it was well calculated to satisfy Napoleon, that at least the spirit of his instructions had been understood by the Marshal. The latter had stated that he suspected a portion of the Prussian troops was pro-

* This despatch is given in the "Dernières observations sur les opérations de l'aile droite de l'armée Française à la battaille de Waterloo, en réponse à M. le Marquis de Grouchy, par le Général Gérard." It is accompanied by the following certificate :—"Certifié conforme à l'original qui nous a été remis par l'Empereur Napoléon, et qui est entre nos mains.

"*Signé*, le Général GOURGAUD."

ceeding to join Wellington, and that, should he ascertain through his cavalry detached to Sart-a-Wallain and Perwès that the great mass of the Prussians was retiring upon Wavre, it was his intention to pursue them in that direction, 'so as to prevent them from reaching Brussels, and to keep them separated from Wellington.' Four hours afterwards (that is, at two o'clock on the morning of the 18th) he sent off another despatch to the Emperor, reporting that he had decided on marching upon either Corbaix or Wavre.

The retreat of the Prussian army, after its defeat at Ligny on the 16th of June, was conducted with great skill, and executed in very good order. By detaining Thielemann's corps upon the field of battle until the morning of the 17th, ample security was afforded to the line of retreat by Gembloux; and by not withdrawing Bülow's corps from that town until Thielemann drew near to it, the distance beween the main bodies of these two corps became so limited as to present the ready means of opposing their combined force to a vigorous pursuit should such be attempted. By the evening of the 17th the entire Prussian army (with the exception of the 9th and 13th brigades, and the reserve-cavalry of the 3rd corps, which arrived by six o'clock on the following morning) had assembled in the immediate vicinity of Wavre—two corps on the right, and the remaining two corps on the left, bank of the Dyle—in perfect order, and fully prepared to resume the offensive. Upon the two lines of retreat, the rear-guards were well disposed at Vieux Sart and Mont St. Guibert; where they continued during that night, and whence they retired leisurely on the following day. On the Prussian left, patroles were despatched towards the main road leading from Namur to Louvain. On the right a detachment was sent from Zieten's corps to Limale, on the left bank of the Dyle, to cover that flank, and patroles were pushed higher up the river, to communicate with the post of Mont St. Guibert. Major Falkenhausen had been detached, during the day, to Seroulx for the purpose of reconnoitring the country in the vicinity of Genappe, and of the high road to Brussels; and he succeeded in discovering, from the wooded tracts beyond Seroulx, the advance of the French army along the chaussée. Patroles were also detached towards Lasne, Couture, and Aywiers, to observe the defiles along the rivulet of the Lasne.

Such were the dispositions of the defeated Prussians on the evening of the 17th, while the victorious French had not advanced beyond Gembloux. The former had fallen back, in good order, upon a line with, and a short distance from, the

Anglo-allied army on their right, while their opponents, though encountering no obstacle of importance, had made but little progress, and were widely diverging from, instead of closely co-operating with, the main army from which they had been detached. These dispositions, so ably planned and so efficiently performed, were well calculated to facilitate the grand operation of the morrow, namely, Blücher's flank movement to the right, to effect a junction with Wellington.

The retreat to Wavre did not in any way incapacitate the Prussian army for the resumption of actively offensive operations. With respect to its material, it so happened that the park of reserve ammunition-waggons had, in the first instance, been directed upon Gembloux; and Colonel Röhl, who superintended the ordnance department of the army, sent his aide-de-camp during the night of the 16th to conduct this reserve to Wavre; whilst he himself hastened to the latter town, for the purpose of putting the whole of the artillery, accordingly as it arrived there, again in a fit state for action. The supply of ammunition, however, was necessarily incomplete; but in order to prevent any failure in this respect, should some mishap occur to the park of reserve ammunition-waggons, a courier was despatched to Maestricht, with directions for the speedy transport of a supply of ammunition from thence to the army, by means of the common waggons of the country. Similar orders were conveyed to Cologne, Wesel, and Münster: and, by way of precaution, an express was sent to Liege for the removal of the battering-train to Maestricht, as also for the destruction, in case of danger, of the iron-foundry in the arsenal of the former place. Fortunately, however, the reserve ammunition-waggons reached Wavre safely at five o'clock in the afternoon of the 17th. The corps and batteries were furnished with a complete supply of ammunition, and the army was thus placed in a perfectly efficient state for commencing another battle. This turn of affairs was most encouraging, and Blücher delayed not another moment in despatching to Wellington the reply to which allusion has already been made. (See page 174.)

As regards the influence which the defeat at Ligny exercised over the *morale* of the Prussian army, its injurious effects were made manifest amongst the newly raised drafts from the Rhenish and Westphalian provinces, and from the duchy of Berg. Of these troops, 8,000 men betook themselves to a flight which admitted of no check until they reached Liege and Aix-la-Chapelle. Among the Rhenish troops, particularly those from provinces which had formerly belonged to

France, there were many old French soldiers; and although several of them fought with great bravery, others evinced a bad disposition, and there were instances in which they passed over to their former companions in arms. Such, however, was not the case with the troops from the other western districts of the Prussian state: there was scarcely a single man amongst the missing, who belonged to any of the old Westphalian provinces, Mark, Cleve, Minden, and Ravensberg, whilst several came from that of Münster.

But the *morale* of the great mass of the Prussian army continued unshaken. The spirit of the troops was neither tamed nor broken; and their enthusiasm, though damped, had not been subdued. Unbounded confidence was placed in the firm decision and restless energy of their aged and venerated chief, who, though suffering from the effects of his fall, by which his whole frame had sustained a severe shock, evinced not the slightest apprehension of fatal consequences to the campaign resulting from this defeat. His unbending nature led him to cast aside for the moment those purely political interests and theoretically strategical principles, by which a more cautious and less enterprising commander might have been induced to secure the line of the Meuse, and to preserve his direct communications with the Prussian states, and thus afford but a doubtful and an inefficient support to his ally. Placing full reliance on the resources of his own mind, and on the stern, warlike character of his troops, he devoted his whole energies to the attainment of the one grand object—that of crushing Napoleon by combining with Wellington. This confidence in himself and in his soldiers was strikingly and characteristically manifested in the concluding words of a general order which he issued to the army on the morning of the 17th. "I shall immediately lead you against the enemy;—we shall beat him, because it is our duty to do so."

Towards midnight of the 17th, a communication reached Blücher from General Müffling (already mentioned as having been attached to the British head-quarters) to the following effect. "The Anglo-allied army is posted with its right upon Braine-la-leud, its centre upon Mont St. Jean, and its left near La Haye; having the enemy in its front. The Duke awaits the attack, but calculates upon Prussian support." This intelligence was forwarded, at midnight, to General Count Bülow, accompanied by the following order:—"You will therefore, at daybreak, march with the 4th corps from Dion-le-Mont, through Wavre, taking the direction of Chapelle

St. Lambert, in which vicinity you will keep your force concealed as much as possible, in case the enemy should not, by that time, be seriously engaged with the Duke of Wellington; but should it be otherwise, you will make a most vigorous attack upon the enemy's right flank. The 2nd corps will follow you as a direct support: the 1st and 3rd corps will also be held in readiness to move in the same direction if necessary. You will leave a detachment in observation at Mont St. Guibert, which, if pressed, will gradually fall back upon Wavre. All the baggage-train, and everything not actually required in the field of action, will be sent to Louvain." Instructions, in conformity with the above, were also forwarded to the commanders of the other corps; and a communication of these arrangements was despatched to General Müffling, with an explanation that the fatigue of the troops could not possibly admit of earlier support. This General was, at the same time, requested to forward timely intelligence of the attack upon the Duke, and of the nature of that attack, that measures might be adopted accordingly.

At five o'clock on the morning of the 18th, Pajol started from Mazy, with Soult's cavalry-division and Teste's infantry-division, marching by St. Denis and Grand-lez, to Tourinnes; where he was to await further orders. At about eight o'clock, Excelmans' corps of heavy cavalry, consisting of eight regiments of dragoons, was put in motion; and at nine o'clock, Vandamme's and Gérard's infantry-corps began their march along one and the same road, by Sart-à-Wallain, upon Wavre. The left of this column was protected, towards the Dyle, by the advance of Maurin's division of light cavalry, under General Vallin.

It was about half-past ten o'clock, when Excelmans' advanced guard came up with the Prussian rear-guard, on the road to Wavre. He immediately formed his troops in position, resting their left upon the wooded ravine near the farm of La Plaquerie, and their right in the direction of Neuf-Sart. While his skirmishers were engaged with those of the enemy, he sent the *chef d'escadron* d'Estourmel, to inform Marshal Grouchy of what was going on in front, and also to make known to him that the Prussian army had continued its retreat upon Wavre during a part of the night and that morning, for the purpose of forming a closer communication with the Duke of Wellington's forces.

The march of the 3rd and 4th corps was greatly retarded by the bad state of the roads, and frequent halts were occasioned by the narrowness and miry nature of the defiles.

Gérard, having preceded the column, reached Sart-à-Wallain at eleven o'clock, where he found Grouchy breakfasting in the house of M. Hollaërt, a notary. In about half an hour after his arrival, Colonel Simon Lorière, who was acting as his chief of the staff, suddenly heard, while walking in the garden of the house, a distant but violent cannonade, of which he immediately went to apprise his General. Grouchy repaired at once to the garden, accompanied by Gérard, Vandamme, Excelmans, and several other officers. He immediately called for M. Hollaërt, and asked him in what part of the country he considered this tremendous cannonade to be going on. The latter, pointing to the Forest of Soignies, replied that it must be in the direction of Planchenoit, Mont St. Jean, and that vicinity.

Gérard then declared his opinion to be in favour of the expediency of marching in the direction of the cannonade, in order to connect the movements of the detached force more closely with Napoleon's operations; and offered to lead his own corps towards the battle. This measure was opposed by the Marshal, as also by General Baltus, of the artillery, who represented the difficulties of a march in which this arm might be compromised. On the other hand, General Valaze, commanding Engineer of Gérard's corps, after having coincided in the opinion expressed by the latter, observed that he had three companies of sappers, by aid of which he could remove many obstacles. Gérard then gave his assurance that he could at all events move on with the gun-carriages and limbers. Grouchy, however, stated his determination to act in conformity with his instructions, which were, to pursue and attack the Prussians, and never to lose sight of them. It had just been intimated to him that his troops had come up with a rear-guard of the enemy's infantry, and he did not consider his information was sufficient to warrant the conclusion that Blücher was drawn up, in expectation of being attacked by him at Wavre; or that he would continue his retreat upon Brussels; or, that if, in manœuvring to effect his junction with Wellington, he would do so in front, or in rear, of the Forest of Soignies. He has since declared,* that he did not deem it his duty to follow the counsel given by Gérard, but to attack the Prussians; that to effect the proposed movement with the whole of his forces would have been acting contrary to his orders;

* "Fragments historiques relatifs à la campagne de 1815, &c. Par le Général Grouchy."

that to have detached only a portion of those forces in the direction of the Forest of Soignies, would have been to separate the two corps of his army by a river, whose waters were swollen by the rain, and whose banks were swampy, and thus have rendered their mutual support impossible, however essential it might have become; finally, that a war of inspiration appertains alone to the General in chief, and that his lieutenants must confine themselves to that of execution. Hence the march to Wavre was continued.

Whilst proceeding to the advanced guard, Grouchy received the despatch, dated from the farm of Caillou, the 18th of June, at ten o'clock in the morning, acquainting him that the Emperor was going to attack the Anglo-allied army, in its position at Waterloo; desiring him to direct his movements upon Wavre in such a manner as to draw his forces nearer to those of Napoleon, and, especially, to keep up a close communication with the latter.* The receipt of these instructions was not followed by any immediate change in Grouchy's dispositions. He despatched no cavalry force—not even a single patrole—to watch any movements that might be attempted, or actually then in course of execution, by the Prussians, towards the field on which the Emperor had intimated to him his intention of attacking the force under Wellington; and hence it is almost needless to add, that he neglected to establish that close and active communication with the main army which was so essentially important for the accomplishment of the object of the general plan of operations, and to which Napoleon had especially directed his attention in the before mentioned despatch. His sole aim seemed to be, a direct advance upon Wavre; and this he carried into execution without at all detaching to, or in any way manœuvring by, his left. On the contrary, upon arriving in person at the position occupied by Excelmans, he desired the latter to move to his right, and take post at Dion-le-Mont; and the ground thus vacated was shortly afterwards taken up by Vallin's light cavalry-division.

At daybreak of the 18th of June, Bülow, in conformity with the order† which he had received during the previous night from Blücher, quitted his position near Dion-le-Mont, to march through Wavre to St. Lambert. This was the commencement of the important flank movement of the Prussians in support of the Anglo-allied army in position in front of Waterloo; and every measure of precaution was

* See commencement of Chapter X. † See Pages 189—190.

adopted with a view to its being carried into effect with certainty and safety. The sun had not yet risen when Major Witowsky was despatched with a detachment of the 2nd Silesian hussars, to Maransart, for the purpose of closely reconnoitring the defiles of the Lasne, which had already been patroled the evening before, and to observe the country in front of those defiles, in the direction of the enemy's position. Major Falkenhausen, previously mentioned as having pushed a reconnaissance beyond Seroulx on the 17th, was now directed also to reconnoitre the Lasne. Scouring parties were sent out, which kept up the communication that had been opened the previous day with Lieut. Colonel Ledebur at Mont St. Guibert: the whole country between the Dyle and the Charleroi high road was carefully explored; and correct intelligence was continually sent to the rear concerning the French army.

By means of this vigilant look-out, the Prussians secured the important advantage of retarding the communications between the French Emperor and his Marshal, since it compelled the bearer of despatches to pursue a very circuitous route.

At half-past nine o'clock, on the morning of the 18th, whilst Bülow's corps was on the march to St. Lambert, the following additional despatch was forwarded to General Müffling:—

"Wavre, 18th June, 1815, at half-past nine o'clock.

"I request you will say to the Duke of Wellington, in my name, that even ill as I am, I shall, nevertheless, put myself at the head of my troops, for the purpose of immediately attacking the enemy's right flank, should Napoleon undertake any thing against the Duke. If however, the day should pass over without a hostile attack, it is my opinion that we ought to-morrow, with our combined forces, to attack the French army. I commission you to communicate this as the result of my inward conviction, and to represent to him that I consider this proposal to be the best and most suitable in our present position.

"Blücher."

The Prussians very soon discovered that the French had made no disposition whatever for the protection of their right flank. Major Witowsky had proceeded as far as Maransart before he fell in with an enemy's patrole; and Major Falkenhausen found the defiles of the Lasne perfectly free and unobserved. Upon receiving this intelligence, Blücher decided upon supporting the Anglo-allied army, by directing the march of his whole force, or at least of three corps, towards the wood of Paris, and debouching from thence upon the flank and rear of the enemy; and Major Lützow was immediately despatched for the purpose of narrowly watching, from the other side of the above wood, the French movements directed against the position of the Anglo-allied army.

No report had as yet been received from the rear-guard, concerning Grouchy's advance, and as Blücher's great object was now to gain the defiles of the Lasne without interruption, and to occupy in force the wood of Paris, he determined to avail himself of the time and opportunity which offered for the projected movement. Being, however, uncertain as to the amount of Grouchy's force, the Prince deemed it advisable that Wavre should not be abandoned until the greater part of the army had passed the defiles of St. Lambert; and with this view, he directed that as soon as Bülow's corps should have proceeded beyond Wavre, Zieten's corps was to commence its march by Fromont and Ohain to join the left wing of Wellington's army near La Haye. Pirch's corps was ordered to follow Bülow's in the direction of St. Lambert; and Thielemann's corps, after retaining possession of the defile of Wavre sufficiently long to render the general movement of the army secure, was then gradually to follow Zieten's corps upon Ohain.

An unfortunate incident occurred during the passage of Bülow's corps, through Wavre, which materially impeded the march of the troops. The advanced guard, consisting of the 15th brigade, (under General Losthin,) with the 2nd Silesian hussars, and a 12-pounder battery, had scarcely passed through the town when a fire broke out in the main street, and extended itself with great rapidity. This not only caused a suspension of the march of the main body of the corps, but created much alarm, in consequence of the great number of ammunition-waggons in the place. Every exertion was made to extinguish the fire. The 1st battalion of the 14th regiment, under Major Löwenfeld, and the 7th pioneer-company, were ordered upon this duty, and after they had encountered considerable difficulty, their efforts were crowned with success.

In the mean time the advanced guard of Bülow's corps had continued its march, and reached St. Lambert by eleven o'clock. The 16th, and then the 13th, brigade arrived much later; and the 14th brigade, which formed the rear-guard, was a long way behind. The advanced guard did not wait the arrival of the other brigades, but proceeded forthwith to cross the defile of St. Lambert. Having effected the passage, which was attended with great difficulty, in consequence of the soft and miry state of the valley, it halted in the wood of Paris, where it continued a considerable time, waiting for the approach of the main body. Patroles, however, from the 2nd Silesian hussars, were immediately sent forward to feel for the Anglo-allied left, and to reconnoitre the French right.

Zieten's corps (the 1st) commenced its march, upon the left bank of the Dyle, towards Ohain, about noon.

Whilst Bülow's reserve-cavalry, following the 13th infantry-brigade, was passing through Wavre, French cavalry had penetrated between the rear-guard of this corps, at Vieux Sart, and the detachment under Lieut. Colonel Ledebur at Mont St. Guibert. The 2nd Pomeranian, and the 1st Silesian landwehr-cavalry were immediately detached from the reserve-cavalry of the corps, to aid in checking the advance of the enemy.

The Prussian Lieut. Colonel Ledebur, who was still at Mont St. Guibert, having received intelligence of the approach of the French, decided on commencing his retreat towards Wavre. Lieut. Colonel Sohr, who had fallen back early in the morning from Mont St. Guibert, sent 150 cavalry and 2 guns of horse-artillery as a reinforcement to Ledebur. The latter now succeeded in forming a junction with the two cavalry regiments detached from the reserve, as also, subsequently, with the cavalry-brigade under Sohr, after a slight affair with the 3rd French corps, (Vandamme's,) whilst making good his retreat to Auzel.

Pirch's corps (the 2nd) broke up from its position between St. Anne and Aisemont, on the right bank of the Dyle, about noon, for the pupose of passing the defile of Wavre. The 1st battalion of the 14th regiment, which occupied this town, was relieved by a battalion of the 30th regiment, belonging to the 3rd corps, (Thielemann's). Pirch had just put his corps in motion, with a view to cross the Dyle by the town of Wavre, when the approach of the enemy was announced. The defile was crowded with the troops; the progress of their march could not be otherwise than slow; and at this moment Lieut. Colonel Sohr, whose brigade formed the rear-guard of the corps, sent in word, that the enemy presented a force of six regiments of cavalry, ten pieces of artillery, and two strong columns of infantry.

The wood of Sarats, close to the farm of Auzel, was now occupied by some battalions of the 8th brigade, the command of which had devolved upon Colonel Reckow. Pirch placed the whole of the rear-guard under the orders of General Brause, the commander of the 7th brigade, and reinforced Lieut. Colonel Sohr with the 11th hussars and four pieces of horse-artillery. Brause posted the remaining battalions of the 8th brigade in rear of the wood, and the three regiments of cavalry on the right, with the foot battery No. 12 in their front. The 7th brigade, deployed into line, remained in reserve.

Lieut. Colonel Ledebur retired slowly before the enemy, and formed a junction with the 8th brigade, under Colonel Reckow, who maintained his position until three o'clock in the afternoon, against the advanced guard of Vandamme's corps. Between three and four o'clock, General Brause ordered the retreat. Lieut. Colonel Sohr crossed the bridge at the mill of Bierge, which was occupied by two companies of the 2nd battalion of the 14th regiment; and then followed the reserve-cavalry of Pirch's corps, to which his brigade belonged, but which he did not overtake until he reached the field of Waterloo. The enemy did not advance with much vigour: the retreat was conducted with perfect order, and the fusilier-battalion of the 1st Pomeranian landwehr, under Major Krüger, distinguished itself on the occasion. After the passage of the river had been effected, the 1st battalion of the Elbe landwehr remained at Bierge until the bridge was destroyed and the mill set on fire. The 11th hussars and the 2nd battalion of the Elbe landwehr were posted in observation of the passages across the Dyle, and did not rejoin the corps before the following day.

Blücher had quitted Wavre before eleven o'clock in the forenoon, and repaired to the vicinity of Limale, in order to make himself acquainted with the nature of the country in the direction of St. Lambert. Whilst here, he received intelligence of the approach of the enemy towards Wavre. Colonel Clausewitz, chief of the staff of the 3rd corps, was immediately made the bearer of an order for Thielemann to defend the position at this place, in the event of the enemy advancing in force; but, should the latter cross the Dyle higher up the stream, or not appear in great strength, (a point concerning which nothing positive was then known,) he was to leave only a few battalions in position at Wavre, and to follow the main army, with his corps, as a reserve, in the direction of Couture.

Grouchy's movements, on the 17th and 18th, form so striking a feature in the history of this campaign, and exercised so important an influence upon the fate of the decisive battle of Waterloo, that it becomes an essential point in the study of that history, to examine how far he complied with, and carried into effect, the instructions received from his master, and to what degree his proceedings, consequent upon his ascertaining the direction of the Prussian retreat, coincided with the general plan and object of Napoleon's operations. On a reference to the account of his transactions during the 17th, given in the despatch written at ten o'clock on that night, it appears he was completely ignorant of the line by which the principal mass of the Prussian army had retreated, namely, that of Tilly and Gentinnes, by Zieten's and Pirch's corps, although his cavalry had driven back the Prussian detachment from the latter place to Mont St. Guibert, but from whence it appears to have been withdrawn in the night. His attention seems to have been much less devoted to this quarter than it was to his right, in which direction he detached as far as Perwès. The main body of his forces did not proceed further than Gembloux on the 17th, that is, about five miles from the field of Ligny. Upon a first consideration, we are strongly impressed by the striking contrast between this march, in pursuit of a defeated army, which had commenced its retreat on the previous night, and which presented no check to the advance, and the march of Napoleon, from the same field, by Quatre-Bras and Genappe, as far as La Belle Alliance, in front of the Waterloo position, a distance of about sixteen or seventeen miles; and this, too, in rear of a victorious army, with a cavalry rear-guard boldly and successfully impeding the advance of its pursuers. It must, however, be taken into account, that in one most important respect Napoleon possessed a decided advantage over Grouchy—an advantage, the magnitude of which increased with every moment that elapsed after the wet weather had set in; for while the former moved the whole distance along a paved high road, the latter had to proceed entirely by cross roads, which may more properly be designated common field-roads. It is to this particular point that both Grouchy and Gérard refer in justification of the late arrival of the infantry at Gembloux. Nevertheless, Grouchy detached considerably to his right, with his cavalry, misled by the same idea which had prevailed with Napoleon, that Blücher had retreated upon the Meuse; and the very circumstance of his dragoons having reached Perwès on the night of the 17th, proves that had he organized a more extended, more combined, and more energetic reconnaissance, with the sixty-five squadrons of cavalry which had been placed under his orders, he might have connected his operations on the right of the Dyle with those of Napoleon on the left of that river, by occupying the line of Nil St. Vincent, Corbaix, Mont St. Guibert, and the bridge of Moustier. The only check he would have experienced would have been at the Prussian post of Mont St. Guibert, which, however, in the case of an active reconnaissance, as above, might have been attacked by a strong detachment in front, and turned by Corbaix on its left. To show the connection which this disposition would have secured with Napoleon's movements, it is only necessaryto state, that the 3rd cavalry-division, under Lieut. General Domon, had been detached from the Emperor's column to reconnoitre the country between the Dyle and the high road to Brussels, and that the 4th regiment of chasseurs à cheval pushed as far as the bridge of Moustier, on which line its skirmishers exchanged a few carbine shots with some Prussian dragoons, who did not, however, appear willing to engage further with them. It was by means of this reconnaissance that Napoleon ascertained the retreat, through Tilly and Gentinnes, of the principal Prussian column, consisting of Zieten's and Pirch's corps, although the line by which they retired was undiscovered by Grouchy, in whose immediate sphere of operations it was situated.

But if such good grounds exist for inferring that, on the 17th, an earlier and a clearer insight into the enemy's movements might have been obtained by the corps detached in pursuit of the Prussians, and that when obtained, it would have rendered the communication with the operations of the main army, on the left of the Dyle, a matter not only important in the highest degree, but also perfectly practicable; and if a failure in this respect be attributable to the absence of sufficient energy and vigour on the part of Grouchy, how much more forcibly does it not expose the extraordinary, the unaccountable, dilatoriness of Napoleon himself during the whole of the precious morning of the 17th! How striking a view it unfolds of what might have been accomplished, had the bivouac at Ligny been broken up a few hours earlier! Then, Wellington's army was still between Quatre-Bras and the narrow defile of Genappe, open to an attack in front by Ney, simultaneously with one in flank by the force collected at Marbais (a part of which might have been detached across the Genappe, towards the rear of the Anglo-allied army, by Villers la Ville and Bousseval, masked by the wood of

Berme); and the rearmost corps of the Prussian army, (Thielemann's,) which was retreating through Gembloux, might have been attacked with effect, by the superior force of all arms under Grouchy.

As regards Grouchy's movements during the early part of the 18th, it is very remarkable, that although he had in his despatch, written at ten o'clock the previous night, communicated to Napoleon his surmises of an intended junction of a portion of Blücher's forces with those of Wellington, and his consequent intention of following the Prussians in the direction of Wavre, "*afin qu'ils ne puissent pas gagner Bruxelles, et de les séparer de Wellington,*" and although he must or ought to have been aware that Wavre was only twelve miles distant from Napoleon's main line of operations, whereas Gembloux was about 15 miles distant from Wavre, he not only delayed his departure from Gembloux until between seven and eight o'clock in the morning, but manœuvred by his right; taking the more circuitous line, through Sart-à-Wallain, and rendering his operations still more dilatory by moving both Vandamme's and Gérard's corps along one and the same road. Had he not, from want of sufficient vigilance, continued ignorant of the fact, that the principal Prussian column, consisting of the 1st and 2nd corps, had retired upon Wavre, at so short a distance from his left as by the line of Tilly, Gentinnes, and Mont St. Guibert, there can be very little doubt that he would have marched upon the latter point, which the Prussians, aware of its importance, had occupied with a rear-guard; but even with the amount of information which he possessed, and with the inference justly impressed upon his mind that a co-operation between Blücher and Wellington was projected, we are at a loss to account for his not having moved upon Mont St. Guibert, and manœuvred by his left. In his despatch, written at two o'clock in the morning, he mentioned to the Emperor his design of marching upon Corbaix or Wavre; a movement of which Napoleon, in his reply, expressed his approval; and if he had directed one of his infantry-corps along the line of Corbaix and La Baraque, and the other by that of Mont St. Guibert and Moustier, there can be no doubt that, even late as was the hour at which he started from Gembloux, he would, in a great measure, have fulfilled the expectations of his imperial master. In this case, he would naturally have so divided his cavalry, that one portion would have scoured the country along the front and right of the column marching by Corbaix and La Baraque, and the other portion would have been employed in a similar manner along the front and left of the column moving upon Mont St. Guibert and Moustier. Both at this point and at Ottignies, about eight hundred yards lower down the stream, there is a stone bridge across the Dyle. There is a direct road from Moustier to St. Lambert, scarcely five miles distant, and another to the field of Waterloo. The cavalry in advance of the left column could not have failed to discover the Prussian troops in march to join the left of Wellington; for they were then passing slowly, and with extreme difficulty, through the defiles of St. Lambert and Lasne. This discovery would have led to the right column being moved by its left, from La Baraque to Moustier, the cavalry attached to it masking the movement as long as possible. The left column would then, in all probability, have followed its advanced cavalry to St. Lambert; and the right corps have either moved upon the same point as a reinforcement, or have diverged upon Lasne as a support, upon which the former might have fallen back, if compelled to effect its retreat towards Planchenoit.

In this manner might Grouchy have so far realized the anxious expectation of Napoleon as to have fallen upon Bülow *flagrante delicto*, and have materially procrastinated the co-operation of Blücher with Wellington on the 18th of June; a co-operation which a contrary proceeding, originating in fatal tardiness of movement, and exhibiting useless manœuvring in a false direction, could not fail to render easy in execution, and successful in result. But beyond such procrastination of the meditated junction of Blücher's and Wellington's forces, Grouchy could have effected nothing. The junction itself could not have been prevented. The tendency of Grouchy's movements had been too narrowly watched; the country between the Dyle and the Charleroi road to Brussels had been too vigilantly explored, and the movements, in succession, of the different Prussian corps had been too nicely calculated and determined, to admit of the possibility of a failure, as regarded the arrival of a considerable portion of the Prussian forces on the left of the Anglo-allied army. Blücher had made so admirable a disposition of his four corps d'armée, that two of them could at any time have combined, and therefore have presented a superior force to Grouchy, at any point between Wavre and Planchenoit, whilst the remainder of the army might have continued its march to the field of Waterloo. Had Grouchy moved by St. Guibert and Moustier upon St. Lambert, Thielemann's corps would then have been on the march towards Couture, according to his original instructions; and, finding Bülow engaged with the enemy, would have joined him. Grouchy might then have contrived to hold both these corps at bay, and thus have reduced the co-operating Prussian force at Waterloo to the two corps under Zieten and Pirch, besides considerably retarding that co-operation, since without having experienced the effects of any such interruption to the progress of the other corps, as we have here supposed, these two Generals did not reach the field of battle until seven o'clock in the evening of the 18th. Such is the extent of the advantage which, under the circumstances, Grouchy would have gained by a march from Gembloux upon St. Lambert; a most important one, no doubt, as time for pushing the struggle with Wellington, with the whole force at his immediate disposal, before the arrival of the Prussians, was of the most vital consequence to Napoleon; and this advantage Grouchy entirely lost by his march upon Wavre—a march which enabled Blücher to appear with three, out of his four, corps d'armée, on the great and decisive field of action; and that in sufficient time to render the victory as complete as could reasonably be desired.

No exertions, however, on the part of Grouchy, after he broke up from Gembloux on the morning of the 18th, could have effectually frustrated the junction of Wellington and Blücher. Two great errors, for which that Marshal was not accountable, reduced the contemplated junction from a measure of calculation to one of certainty. The first and principal of these has already been adverted to at some length, and cannot be too closely kept in view—the fatal neglect of a vigorous pursuit of the defeated Prussians, on the night of the 16th and morning of the 17th, by a detached corps; combined with the extraordinary delay in the attack upon Wellington, at Quatre-Bras, on the latter day. The second error arose from the want of a strong reconnaissance and vigilant look-out on the right of the main French army, on the morning of the 18th, followed up by the occupation of the defiles of the Lasne.

It was nearly four o'clock when Vandamme's corps arrived in front of the position which Thielemann was in the act of quitting, with a view to follow and support the remaining three Prussian corps that were at that moment on the march towards the field of Waterloo; and, with a fire that was opened from the French batteries, commenced the battle of Wavre, which will be described in its proper place in a subsequent Chapter.

CHAPTER IX.

It rained incessantly during the night of the 17th; occasionally in torrents; whilst loud and frequent peals of thunder fell ominously on the ear of the toil-worn soldier, startling him from the fitful slumber, which was all the rest the chill and comfortless bivouac on the field of Waterloo could afford him in that tempestuous night.

Scarcely had the morning dawned when the numerous groups, stretched around the smouldering remains of the bivouac-fires, or couched in the hollows, or lying under such slender cover as the few trees and brushwood within range of the positions of their respective regiments afforded, were seen gradually in motion; and as the eye of an observer wandered along the space which lay between the main bodies of the hostile armies—a space varying in no greater width than from 1000 to 1500 yards—the officers in command of the several picquets might be seen, on either side, withdrawing their vedettes and sentries from the very limited and almost conversational distance that had separated them from their opponents during the night, concentrating their detachments, and establishing their main posts more within the immediate range of the respective positions occupied by the grand armies.

As the morning advanced, the dense vapoury masses which had so long rolled slowly and heavily over the plain, gradually began, as if relieved by the constant discharge of their contents, to soar into a higher region, where, during the whole day, with little or but imperceptible motion, they hung spread out into a broad, expansive vault, through which the rays of the sun were unable fully to penetrate, until just at the moment of its sinking from the scene of strife, when it shed the full blaze of its setting splendour upon the victorious advance of the Anglo-allied army. The drying and cleaning of firearms soon became general, and the continuous discharge of muskets, at rapid and irregular intervals, fell upon the ear like the rattle of a brisk and widely extended skirmish. All at once, the scene became more animated and exciting. Drums, bugles, and trumpets were heard over the whole field, sounding the assembly; and never was the call to arms, in either army, responded to with greater zeal, alacrity, and cheerfulness. While the regimental inspections, tellings-off, and preparatory arrangements of detail were proceeding, staff officers were seen galloping in various directions; and, shortly afterwards, the different brigades, which, by their bivouacs had but faintly and irregularly traced the line of battle taken up by each army, were moved and distributed in the precise order prescribed by the illustrious chiefs who had on that day, and for the first and only time, met to measure swords.

The field of Waterloo is intersected by two high roads (*chaussées*) conspicuous by their great width and uniformity, as also by the pavement which runs along the centre of each. These two roads, the eastern one leading from Charleroi and Genappe, and the western from Nivelles, form a junction at the village of Mont St. Jean,* whence their continuance, in one main road, is directed upon the capital of Belgium. In front of the above junction, and offering, as it were, a natural military position for the defence of this approach to Brussels, a gently elevated ridge of ground is intersected, at right angles, by the Charleroi road, about 250 yards north of the farm called La Haye Sainte, and follows a westerly direction until about midway between the two high roads, whence it takes a south-westerly course, and terminates abruptly at its point of intersection with the Nivelles road, about 450 yards north of Hougomont, a country-seat, with farm, offices, gardens, orchards, and wood. On the east side, the ridge extends itself perpendicularly from the Charleroi road until it reaches a point, distant about 700 yards, where, elevating itself into a mound or knoll, it overlooks the hamlet of Papelotte, and thence, taking a north-easterly course, expands into an open plateau. This ridge constituted the position of the first line of the Duke of Wellington's army, which line is more distinctly defined by a road, entering on the east side, from Wavre, by Ohain, and winding along the summit of the ridge until it joins the Charleroi high road just above La Haye Sainte, from which point of junction a cross road proceeds along the remaining portion of the ridge, and thus connects the two high roads with each other.

The undulations of the ground in rear of this position were admirably adapted to the disposition of the second line and reserves, presenting a gently inclined reverse slope along nearly the whole extent of the ridge, with fine open and con-

* This village does not lie within the extent of ground represented in the plans which accompany this work—the farm only of Mont St. Jean is seen close upon the north boundary—but its situation is at once made known by the direction of the above two roads.

venient stations for cavalry, perfectly concealed from the enemy's observation. The right of the main position is bounded by a valley, which has its source very considerably in rear of the centre of the French position, by which it is intersected, and thence, sweeping round the southern and western inclosures of Hougomont, proceeds in the direction of Merbe-braine. Into this valley a ravine directs its course in rear of, and parallel with, the principal portion of the right wing of the Anglo-allied position, at a distance from the latter varying from 200 to 250 yards; and between this ravine, which is intersected by the Nivelles road, and Merbe-braine, rises a sort of plateau, upon which was posted a portion of the 2nd corps, commanded by Lieut. General Lord Hill, destined to act, as circumstances might require, either in reserve to the first line, or *en potence* to it in repelling any attack upon that flank of the Anglo-allied army.

Upon the extreme left of the first or main line was stationed Vivian's light cavalry-brigade, comprising the 10th and 18th hussars, and the 1st hussars of the King's German legion. The two former regiments were in line, in rear of the Wavre road, and withdrawn a little from the crest of the ridge: the right of the 10th resting upon a lane, which, leading up from Smohain, crossing over the position, and descending along its reverse slope, proceeds in the direction of the village of Verd-cocou. The 1st hussars of the King's German legion were also in line, and formed in reserve. The left of the brigade was completely *en l'air*, upon high, open, and flat ground; the main ridge widening considerably in that direction, as previously explained. A picquet, consisting of a squadron of the 10th hussars, (under Captain Taylor,*) occupied the village of Smohain, down in the valley which, having its source a little to the westward of La Haye Sainte, takes an easterly and therefore parallel course with that part of the ridge which formed the left wing of the British position. The advanced post of this picquet was on the further side of the village, and its vedettes formed a chain on the rising ground beyond, within half-carbine-shot of some French cavalry, standing dismounted in close columns. A party was detached from the picquet as a patrole on the road to Ohain.

The village of Smohain, as also the farms of La Haye and Papelotte, with adjacent houses and inclosures, were occupied by a portion of the 2nd brigade of Perponcher's division of the troops of the Netherlands. The regiment of Orange-

* Now Major General Thomas W. Taylor, C.B.

Nassau, consisting of two battalions, held Smohain and La Haye: while the farm of Papelotte was occupied by the light company of the 3rd battalion of the 2nd regiment of Nassau, which, together with the 2nd battalion of this regiment, and 4 guns of Captain Byleveld's Dutch-Belgian battery of horse-artillery, were posted upon the exterior slope, immediately under the brow of the main ridge, and a little to the westward of the lane leading directly up the slope from the farm of Papelotte.

The advanced posts of these troops were at the foot, and their line of sentries extended along the brow, of the opposite slope of the valley; this line receded towards the western limit of the hamlet of Papelotte, where it joined the general line of picquets along the bottom of the exterior slope of the position of the Anglo-allied left wing.

On the right of Vivian's brigade, and having its own right resting upon a narrow lane, forming a slight hollow-way, lined with hedges, stood Vandeleur's brigade of light cavalry, consisting of the 11th, 12th, and 16th British light dragoons, in columns of squadrons, by regiments, left in front. The lane on which its right rested descending the interior slope of the position, joined the other lane which led from Vivian's right to Verd-cocou.

The extreme left of the infantry of the main line of the position was formed by the 5th Hanoverian brigade, under Colonel Vincke, belonging to Picton's division. It was formed in columns of battalions, those of Hameln and Hildesheim (under Majors Strube and Rheden) in first, and those of Peine and Gifhorn (under Major Count Ludolph von Westphalen, and Major Hammerstein) in second, line; and was posted somewhat under the crest of the ridge, upon the reverse slope, and in rear of the junction of a lane leading up from Papelotte, with the Wavre road.

On the immediate right of Vincke's brigade, and having its own right upon the knoll which presents the highest and most commanding point along the position of the left wing of the Anglo-allied army, the 4th Hanoverian brigade, under Colonel Best, was drawn up. It formed part of the 6th division, and was composed of the landwehr-battalions of Lüneburg, Verden, and Osterode, which were deployed in front line, and of Münden, which was in reserve. A battery of Hanoverian foot-artillery, under Captain Rettberg, was attached to this brigade, and, from the peculiarly favourable circumstances of the ground, which formed a sort of natural fieldwork, was most advantageously placed.

Upon the exterior slope of that portion of the ridge which lies between the before mentioned knoll and the Genappe high road, Bylandt's brigade of Perponcher's division of the troops of the Netherlands was deployed in front line. It consisted of the 27th battalion of Dutch light infantry, the 7th battalion of the Belgian line, and of the 5th, 7th, and 8th battalions, of Dutch militia. Of the above, the 5th battalion of Dutch militia was posted in reserve, along with the remaining 4 guns of Captain Byleveld's battery of horse-artillery attached to this brigade, in rear of the straggling hedge which lines the Wavre road, between the knoll and the Charleroi high road.

Upon the interior slope of the ridge, and at a distance of about 200 yards from the Wavre road, was posted the 9th brigade of British infantry, under Major General Sir Denis Pack, in a line of battalion-columns, at deploying intervals. It consisted of the 3rd battalion 1st royal regiment, the 1st battalion 42nd royal Highlanders, 2nd battalion 44th regiment, and of the 92nd Highlanders. The left regiment, the 44th, was stationed on the knoll, in rear of the right of Best's Hanoverian brigade; and on the right of the 44th stood, in succession, the 92nd, 42nd, and 1st royals. Upon the right, but more in advance, of Pack's brigade, and at a short distance in rear of the hedge along the Wavre road, stood the 8th brigade of British infantry, under Major General Sir James Kempt, also in line of battalion-columns, at deploying intervals, and comprising the 28th regiment, the 32nd regiment, the 1st battalion 79th Highlanders, and the 1st battalion 95th rifles. The right of the 32nd regiment rested upon a high bank of the Charleroi road; on its left stood the 79th Highlanders, and the 28th formed the left regiment of the brigade. In the immediate front of the right of the brigade, and at a distance from the Wavre road of about 120 yards, there was a knoll, having on its right a large sandpit, adjoining the Charleroi road, and partially facing the small garden in rear of La Haye Sainte. On the Allied side of the knoll was a single hedge, extending about 150 yards from the Charleroi road in a direction parallel to the Wavre road. In the sandpit were posted two companies of the 1st battalion 95th British rifles; the knoll and hedge were occupied by another company of the same regiment. These advanced companies had placed an *abatis* across the high road, near that part of it which is joined by the hedge-row. The remaining companies lined a portion of the Wavre road, commencing from the point of its intersection with the Charleroi road.

These two brigades, namely, the 8th and 9th British,

together with the 5th Hanoverian brigade, constituted the 5th division, under Lieut. General Sir Thomas Picton.

Along the continuation of the ridge on the right of the great Charleroi road, the 3rd division, commanded by Lieut. General Sir Charles Alten, was disposed in the following order:—

The 2nd brigade of the King's German legion, commanded by Colonel Ompteda,* which formed the left of the division, consisted of the 1st and 2nd light battalions, (under Lieut. Colonel von dem Bussche,† and Major Baring,‡ and of the 5th and 8th line-battalions of the King's German legion, (under Lieut. Colonels Linsingen§ and Schröder.‖) The 1st light battalion was formed in column of companies at quarter distance, left in front. It stood a little in rear of the cross-road which unites the great Nivelles road with that of Charleroi, on which last its left flank rested. To the right of this column stood the 5th line-battalion, formed in column at quarter distance upon one of its centre companies. In rear of these two columns, and fronting the deploying interval between them, stood the 8th line-battalion, in second line, in column of companies, at quarter distance, upon one of its centre companies. The 2nd light battalion under the command of Major Baring, occupied the farm of La Haye Sainte.

The buildings of this farm are so disposed as to form three sides of a square, the north side comprising the farm-house itself, with a portion of the stabling; the west side the remainder of the stables and cow-houses; and the south side principally a large barn: a brick wall, extending along the great road, unites the north and south buildings, and thus forms the fourth boundary of the large quadrangular farm-yard. On the south, or French, side of the farm, and down in the valley, which here separates the Allied and French positions, lies an orchard, about 240 yards long and 80 wide, having for its eastern boundary the great road, in direct prolongation of the wall which incloses the farm-yard on that side. This orchard is inclosed within a hedge-row, as is also a kitchen-garden, on the north side of the farm, excepting the

* Colonel Christian Ompteda was killed in this battle.

† Now Lieutenant General Lewis von dem Bussche, G.C.H., C.B., in the Hanoverian service.

‡ Major General Baron Baring, K.C.H., C.B., in the Hanoverian service, died in February 1848.

§ Now Lieut. General William von Linsingen, K.C.H., C.B., h-p. Hanoverian service.

‖ Lieut. Colonel John Christian von Schröder, was mortally wounded in this battle.

boundary of the latter, along the road-side, which is a continuation of the eastern wall. A large gate and a door-way, the former almost facing the east end of the barn, and the latter quite close to the east end of the dwelling-house, lead from the yard into the great road; another gate, at the south end of the stabling which forms the western side, as also a large door from the west end of the great barn, lead both into a small, narrow portion of the orchard, whence there is an outlet into the open fields on the right. From the front door of the dwelling-house, which faces the farm-yard, there is a passage to the back or north side of the house, whence a door opens into the kitchen-garden.

Since day-break, the little garrison, amounting to scarcely 400 men, had been busily engaged in strengthening their post to the fullest extent of the means within their reach, which, however, were extremely limited. Among the difficulties which they had to overcome, it may be remarked that, on the preceding evening, immediately after taking possession of the farm, the soldiers had broken up the great barn door, on the west side, for fire-wood; and that, about the same period, the carpenters of the regiment were detached to Hougomont, in compliance with an order received to that effect. Unfortunately, also, the mule laden with the regimental trenching tools, had been lost the day before, so that not even a hatchet was forthcoming. Loop-holes were pierced through the walls, and a barricade was thrown across the high road, in prolongation of the south wall. The battalion was composed of six companies, of which Major Baring posted three in the orchard, two in the buildings, and one in the garden.

On the right of Ompteda's brigade stood the 1st Hanoverian brigade, under Major General Count Kielmansegge, consisting of the field-battalions of Bremen, Verden, Duke of York, Grubenhagen, and Lüneburg. The last mentioned battalion was formed in column, at quarter distance, upon one of its centre companies; the head of the column in line with, and at a deploying interval from that of the right column of Ompteda's brigade. Next, on the right, at the proper interval for deployment, stood the two battalions Verden and Bremen, in contiguous columns of companies, at quarter distance; the former right in front, the latter left in front. The two battalions York and Grubenhagen were formed in second line, in rear of the centre of the interval between the battalions Lüneburg and Verden, in contiguous columns of companies at quarter distance, York right, and Grubenhagen left, in front.

On the right of Kielmansegge's Hanoverian brigade, was posted the 5th British brigade, commanded by Major General Sir Colin Halkett, and comprising the 2nd battalion 30th, the 1st battalion 33rd, 2nd battalion 69th, and 2nd battalion 73rd British regiments. Its position was more forward than that of the other portion of Alten's division, with which its front was in an oblique direction, its right shoulders having been brought forward so as to preserve the parallelism between the general line and the crest of the main ridge. The 2nd battalions 73rd and 30th regiments formed contiguous columns of companies, at quarter distance, the former right, the latter left, in front, and at a deploying interval for two battalions from the head of the column formed by the Bremen battalion. The other two battalions of this brigade, the 1st battalion 33rd and 2nd battalion 69th regiments, were formed in contiguous columns of companies, at quarter distance, in second line, and in right rear of the 73rd and 30th regiments; the 33rd right, and the 69th left, in front.

In rear of the centre of the interval between the right of Kielmansegge's, and the left of Halkett's brigade, was posted, in second line, the 1st battalion of the 1st regiment of Nassau, forming part of the Nassau brigade, commanded by Major General Kruse. The battalion was in column on a central company. The remainder of this brigade, consisting of the 2nd and 3rd battalions of the same regiment, was formed in contiguous columns, in a third line, as a reserve.

On the right of Halkett's brigade, the 1st British division, commanded by Major General Cooke, was posted. It consisted of the 1st and 2nd brigades of guards, and was disposed in the following manner:—The 1st brigade commanded by Major General Maitland, and comprising the 2nd and 3rd battalions of the 1st regiment of foot guards, formed the left brigade of the division. The 3rd battalion stood in columns of companies, at quarter distance, on the crest of the ridge; and between it and the head of the right column of Halkett's brigade, there was a deploying interval for one battalion. The 2nd battalion was placed in right rear of the 3rd, also in column of companies, at quarter distance: it was on the reverse slope, and immediately under the crest of the ridge.

The 2nd brigade, comprising the 2nd battalion of the 2nd or Coldstream regiment, and the 2nd battalion of the 3rd regiment of foot guards, and commanded by Major General Sir John Byng, was posted on the crest of the ridge, between the 1st brigade and the Nivelles road. The 2nd battalion 3rd foot guards was on the left, the 2nd battalion of the Coldstream guards on the right, and more in advance on the brow of the hill; and the disposition was such, that the four battalions of the division were placed *en échiquier*. The buildings of Hougomont, its gardens and orchards, were completely overlooked from the commanding ground occupied by the 2nd brigade, which formed the reserve to the troops therein posted, consisting (including those in the wood) of the four light companies of the division, the 1st battalion of the 2nd regiment of Nassau, a company of Hanoverian field-riflemen, and a detachment of a hundred men from the field-battalion Lüneburg, of Kielmansegge's brigade.

The principal dwelling-house or château of Hougomont was a substantial brick building, of a square form. Adjoining its north-east angle was the farmer's house, the east end of which abutted on the great garden; and in the angle between this house and the château was a narrow tower, of the same height as the latter, to which its interior served as a staircase. At the south-east corner of, and communicating with, the château, stood a very neat little chapel. On the north, or British side of the château, was a spacious farm-yard, bounded on the west by a large barn, and a shed, and on the east by cow-houses and stabling adjoining the garden. There was a continuation of the stabling along the north side, and a gateway; and near the centre of the yard there was a draw-well of which the superstructure formed a dove-cot. On the south, or French side of the chateau, and inclosing the latter, was the court-yard, of which a barn on the west, the gardener's house, some stables, and other offices, on the south, and the garden-wall on the east, formed the boundaries. There was a communication between the court and the farm-yard, by means of a doorway in the small portion of wall connecting the château with the great barn, and through the whole length of the latter building there was also a carriage-way leading from the one court into the other. A gateway, passing through a portion of the gardener's house, led out from the court-yard to the south or French side, and from this gate a narrow road conducted across the open space between the buildings and the wood, through which it took its course in the same direction until it gained the fields beyond the inclosures. There was also a pathway from this road, commencing at the corner of the little garden, and traversing the wood in the direction of the south-east angle of the general boundary of the inclosures, whence it continued towards La Belle Alliance. The approach to Hougomont from the Nivelles road was lined, nearly as far as the château, by fine tall elms; it conducted to the gate of the farm-yard facing the British line, and, sweeping along the west side, it led also to the south gate of the court-yard. On the east side of the buildings was a large garden, laid out with all the formality which characterises the Flemish style. It was inclosed on the south and east sides by a high brick-wall, and on the north side, facing the British line, by a hedge. Adjoining the east side of the garden, but considerably wider and longer than the latter, was the large orchard, and along the north side was the smaller orchard—the latter bounded by a hedge and hollow-way, and the former inclosed within high and compact hedges, partially lined by a ditch on the inner side. A prolongation of the southern hedge of the great orchard formed the boundary of the wood facing the south garden-wall, and in the narrow space between these two boundaries was a row of apple trees, which, together with the hedge, served to conceal, in a great measure, the garden-wall from the view of an enemy, approaching through the wood. There was a small garden in front of the gardener's house, formed by the continuation of the south garden-wall until it met another wall issuing perpendicularly from the south gateway leading out of the court-yard. There were two inclosures on the west side, of which one served as a kitchen-garden. The wood extended in length, southwards, about 350 yards, and its greatest width was about 280 yards. It was bounded on the west by another orchard, and on the east by two large inclosures, of which the one nearest the great orchard was a grass-field fenced with hedges, and lined by a ditch on the inner side.

Although the site of the buildings of Hougomont was but slightly elevated above the valley, which, as already remarked, winds along the south and west inclosures, there was a gradual but uninterrupted ascent of the ground from thence as far as the eastern portion of the fence which divides the two inclosures, beyond the great orchard, where it attained a height not much inferior to that of either the French or Allied front lines, between which it was centrically situated. On the south or French side of that hedge, the ground inclined at first gently, and then rapidly, into the valley; but on the west, throughout the extent of the wood, and on the north of the Allied side, across the great orchard, the descent was everywhere very gradual.*

* I have been induced to enter so fully into detail in this description of Hougomont in order to convey a correct notion of its great value and importance, when considered in relation to the Anglo-allied and French positions, as a military post, to whichever army might succeed in maintaining it, and thus to account for the powerful and repeated efforts made by the French to secure so valuable a vantage-ground.

Such was Hougomont—a decidedly important point in the field of battle, from its prominent position in the immediate front of the right of the British line, and rendered ever memorable by the truly heroic and successful stand maintained throughout the day by the troops allotted for its defence.*

From the first moment of the occupation of this post, measures were concerted and adopted for strengthening the means of defence which it presented. During the night, the garden-walls were pierced with numerous loop-holes; and, in order to enable the men to fire down from the tops of the walls upon their assailants, platforms, constructed out of such materials as the place afforded, were raised wherever the depth of the wall on the inner side rendered such a measure desirable. In many places, however, and especially on the eastern side, the ground formed embankments against the wall, sufficiently elevated to obviate the necessity of any additional aid for such purpose. The outer gates were closed up, with the exception of the one from the farm-yard, which faced the Anglo-allied position, and which was left open in order to facilitate the communication with the latter. The different flanking fires which were offered by the relative

* There is not, perhaps, at the present day, any single feature of the field of Waterloo so well calculated to excite the interest of visitors as Hougomont, which still continues what it was reduced to on the day of battle—a heap of ruins. The barn in the court-yard, has, indeed, been again roofed, and the gardener's house is now occupied by the farmer; but the château itself, and the buildings surrounding the old farm-yard, present to the eye nothing more than crumbling walls, scattered stones, bricks, and rubbish. A portion of the tower, with its winding staircase, still exists. But the attention of the visitor is most naturally and strongly arrested by the chapel, which, though it immediately joined the burning château, survives the wreck around it, and inclines him to listen without a sneer to the guide, when, pointing to the scorched feet of the wooden figure of the Saviour of mankind, in the interior, over the entrance, he ascribes the preservation of the sanctuary to the miraculous interposition of Providence. A sanctuary indeed it proved to such of the wounded as took refuge within its walls, who were thus spared from the agonizing death that befel their suffering comrades in the other buildings, which became a prey to the devouring flames, and from which it was impossible, under the circumstances of the moment, to extricate but a small proportion. In the great garden it is not easy to trace its original design: grass, weeds, and wild flowers now luxuriate where neat and gay parterres, redolent with nature's sweet perfumes, were wont to tempt the seigneur of the château to the enjoyment of a contemplative lounge within the walls of this retired spot; while the wilderness at the east end of the garden is more appropriately designated by that term than when it was intersected by its straight and formal, though smooth and neatly trimmed walks. The garden-walls, too, on which, from outspread branches once hung the clustering fruit, now bear nothing but tokens of the deadly strife of which they were the scene. The identical loop-holes with the innumerable marks of shot indented around them, are still permitted to remain as they were left by the brave defenders of the place. The wood, however, has altogether vanished, and the ground on which the beech and elm by their countless shot-holes told a fearful tale, now yields its surface to the harrow and the plough. This constitutes the only material deviation; the orchards, and remaining inclosures, continue unaltered, and retain the self-same aspect.

situations of the garden-walls, and the fences of the orchards, wood, and other inclosures, imparted to the post, a strength, of which, in the course of the action, due advantage was taken. In short, every precaution was adopted which the means at hand suggested for contributing to the security of the place; and the preparations that were in progress indicated, on the part of the troops stationed in this quarter, an intention to give the enemy a warm reception, and a resolution to maintain a vigorous defence.

When, on the previous evening, the light companies of the division were thrown into Hougomont, it was so arranged that those of the 2nd brigade, under the command of Lieut. Colonel Macdonell, should occupy the buildings and the gardens, and that those of the 1st brigade, under Lieut. Colonel Lord Saltoun, should hold the great orchard and the wood; in which latter the Hanoverians and Nassauers were principally stationed.

The abrupt termination of the ridge along which the Allied front line was posted, at its point of junction with the Nivelles road, was in the direct rear of the buildings of Hougomont. On the other side of the road, this termination presented a sudden and bold, though short, slope down into the long valley which, after sweeping by Hougomont, proceeds in the direction of Merbe-braine. A portion of the slope, including the summit, was covered with brushwood, and its base was bounded by a horse-path, partially lined with a stunted hedge, forming, altogether, excellent cover for light-infantry.* On the other side of the valley the ground ascends, at first abruptly, and then gradually, to the summit of that portion of the main ridge upon which the left of the French army rested; and from the point of junction of the avenue conducting to Hougomont with the great Nivelles road, a narrow road leads directly up the opposite slope, and stretches across the ridge or plateau in the direction of Braine-la-leud. Along a portion of this road, principally consisting of a hollow-way, were posted in advance, some light troops of the Anglo-allied army. They formed a part of the 4th brigade of the 4th division, (under Colonel Mitchell,†) attached to the 2nd corps, commanded by Lieut. General Lord Hill. The brigade consisted of the 3rd battalion of the 14th British regiment,

* This spot of ground, bounded by the Nivelles road, the horse-path, and, on the north, by a hollow-way, was once entirely covered with brushwood, which has been gradually cleared away by poor people, to whom small portions were allotted for cultivation, so that at the present day no vestige of the brushwood remains.

† Colonel Hugh Henry Mitchell, C.B., died on the 20th of April, 1817.

(under Lieut. Colonel Tidy,*) of the 23rd fusiliers, (under Colonel Sir Henry Ellis,†) and of the 51st British light infantry, (under Lieut. Colonel Rice,‡) which troops were disposed in the following manner. Along that portion of the Hougomont avenue which is nearest to the Nivelles road was extended the light company of the 23rd regiment. On its right was an *abatis*, which had been thrown across the great road, and close upon the right of this artificial obstacle, a company of the 51st regiment was posted. Four more companies of this regiment, and the light company of the 14th, were extended along the hollow-way alluded to as stretching across the ridge, on the extreme left of the French position. The remainder of the 51st stood in column of support, about two hundred yards in rear of the hollow-way. The 23rd regiment was stationed on the left of the Nivelles road, on the reverse slope, and immediately under the crest of the main ridge, in rear of the 2nd brigade of guards. The 14th regiment was posted in column on the southern descent from the plateau, on which was assembled the 2nd British division, and from the view which it possessed of the ground occupied by the 51st, it was well placed as a reserve to the light infantry. In a ravine, descending from the immediate right of the skirmishers of the brigade down into the valley, was posted a squadron of the 15th British hussars, (under Captain Wodehouse,§) from which a picquet was detached to the right of the *abatis*, as also an intermediate one for keeping up the communication, and some vedettes were thrown out to the right, having in their front a continuation of the ravine, possessing a more marked and distinct character.||

The troops posted upon the plateau already described as situated on the west of the Nivelles road, and in front of the village of Merbe-braine, and which, together with Colonel Mitchell's brigade, constituted the extreme right of the Anglo-allied army, under the command of Lord Hill, were available either as a reserve to the main line of battle, or as a defence against any hostile attempt upon the right flank.

* Colonel Francis Skelly Tidy, C.B., died on the 9th of October, 1835.

† Colonel Sir Henry Walton Ellis, K.C.B., was killed in this battle.

‡ Colonel Samuel Rice, C.B., K.H., died on the 7th of March, 1840.

§ Colonel Philip Wodehouse died in December 1847.

|| It will scarcely escape the eye of an accurate observer of the features of ground, that this ravine, or rather passage, throughout its course from over the opposite ridge, down into the valley, and through the brushwood, and across the plateau eastward of Merbe-braine, inclining towards the Nivelles road, betrays an artificial origin; and he will thus readily comprehend its being the track of the old road to Nivelles, which existed previously to the construction of the present excellent *chaussée*.

They consisted of the main body of the 2nd infantry-division, commanded by Lieut. General Sir Henry Clinton. This was composed of the 3rd British light brigade, under Major General Sir Frederick Adam,* of the 1st brigade of the King's German legion, under Colonel du Plat,† and of the 3rd Hanoverian brigade, under Colonel Halkett.‡ Adam's brigade, consisting of the 52nd regiment, (under Colonel Sir John Colborne,§) of the 71st regiment, (under Colonel Reynell,||) of the 2nd battalion of the 95th regiment, (under Lieut. Colonel Norcott,¶) and two companies of the 3rd battalion of the latter corps, (under Lieut. Colonel Ross,**) was, previously to the commencement of the battle, posted between the village of Merbe-braine and the Nivelles road, near where the latter is intersected by the cross-road leading to Braine-la-leud; but as soon as the first attack was made upon Hougomont, (with which the battle opened,) it was advanced beyond this cross-road, and stood, in battalion-columns of companies, at quarter distance, on the plateau, whence it overlooked the Nivelles road, and had a full view of that portion of the main front line to which the troops of Clinton's division formed a reserve. Du Plat's brigade of the King's German legion, consisting of the 1st line-battalion (under Major Robertson††), of the 2nd (under Major Müller,‡‡) of the 3rd (under Lieut. Colonel Wissell,§§) and of the 4th (under Major Reh||||), stood in open column, near the foot of the slope descending towards the Nivelles road. Halkett's brigade, consisting of the landwehr-battalions Bremervörde (under Lieut. Colonel von der Schulenburg), Salzgitter (under Major Hammerstein), Osnabrück (under Major Count Münster), and Quackenbrück (under Major von dem Bussche Hünefeld), was posted in contiguous close columns of battalions, on the north side of the plateau, near the village of Merbe-braine.

The second general line of the Anglo-allied army consisted

* Now Lieut. General the Right Hon. Sir Frederick Adam, G.C.B., G.C.M.G.

† Colonel Charles du Plat was mortally wounded in this battle.

‡ Now Lieut. General Hugh Halkett, C.B., in the Hanoverian service.

§ Now Lieut. General Lord Seaton, G.C.B., G.C.M.G., G.C.H.

|| Lieut. General Sir Thomas Reynell, Bart. K.C.B., died on the 1st of February, 1848.

¶ Major General Sir Amos Godsill Norcott, C.B., K.C.H., died on the 8th of January, 1838.

** Major General Sir John Ross, K.C.B., died on the 21st of April, 1835.

†† Now Lieut. Colonel William von Robertson, C.B., K.C.H.

‡‡ Now Major General George Müller, C.B., K.C.H., in the Hanoverian service.

§§ Colonel Frederick von Wissell, C.B., K.C.H., in the Hanoverian service, died on the 16th of December, 1820.

|||| Lieut. Colonel Frederick Reh, C.B., K.C.H., died on the 24th of July, 1829.

entirely of cavalry, British and German. Posted partly on the reverse slope of the main ridge, and partly in the hollows in rear, it was entirely screened from the enemy's observation. The brigades were formed, for the most part, by regiments, in close columns of squadrons, at deploying intervals.

Commencing from the right, near to the Nivelles road, stood the 5th brigade, under Major General Sir Colquhoun Grant, consisting of the 7th and 15th hussars, and of the 13th light dragoons,* (under Colonel Doherty.†)

On the left of Grant's brigade was posted the 3rd brigade under Major General Sir William Dörnberg, consisting of the 23rd light dragoons, and of the 1st and 2nd light dragoons of the King's German legion. The Cumberland Hanoverian hussars (under Lieut. Colonel Hake) were attached to, and formd in rear of, this brigade. They properly belonged to Colonel Estorff's Hanoverian cavalry-brigade, as did also the Prince Regent's hussars (under Lieut. Colonel Ferdinand Count Kielmansegge), and the Bremen and Verden hussars (under Colonel August von dem Bussche), which regiments were detached with the force at Hal.

Still more to the left, and in rear of the right of Alten's division, stood the 3rd hussars of the King's German legion, under Colonel Sir Frederick von Arentsschildt.‡

Immediately on the right of the Charleroi road, and in rear of Alten's division, the first or household brigade, under Major General Lord Edward Somerset, was drawn up. It comprised the 1st and 2nd life guards, the royal horse guards (blue), and the 1st dragoon guards.

On the left of the Charleroi road, and in rear of Picton's division, stood the 2nd brigade, under Major General Sir William Ponsonby; consisting of the 1st dragoons (royals), the 2nd dragoons (Scots Greys), and the 6th dragoons (Inniskillings.)

The 4th and 6th brigades, under Major Generals Sir John Vandeleur and Sir Hussey Vivian, were posted upon the

* This regiment did not properly belong to Grant's brigade, but was taken from Colonel Arentsschildt's brigade, to replace the 2nd hussars of the King's German legion, which was still upon the frontier, as explained at page 164.

† Colonel Patrick Doherty, C B., K.C.H., retired from the service on the 8th December, 1818.

‡ This officer was in command of the 7th cavalry brigade, consisting of the 13th light dragoons, and the 3rd hussars of the King's German legion; but the former having been removed to supply the place of the 2nd hussars of the King's German legion, in Grant's brigade, he had now only the 3rd hussars, which regiment, however, was of considerable strength. Major General Sir Frederick Levin August Arentsschildt, K.C.B., K.C.H., of the Hanoverian service, died on the 10th of December, 1840.

extreme left of the main line of the position, as previously explained.

The reserves consisted of the Dutch-Belgian cavalry-division, under Lieut. General Baron Collaert; of the Brunswick corps, comprising both cavalry and infantry, the command of which, since the fall of the Duke, had devolved upon Colonel Olfermann, and of the 10th British brigade, under Major General Sir John Lambert. The latter formed part of the 6th division, commanded by Lieut. General the Hon. Sir Lowry Cole, and had only just reached the field, after having performed forced marches from Ghent.

Collaert's division was stationed in rear of the centre, and within the angle formed by the junction of the high roads leading from Charleroi and Nivelles. It comprised the 1st brigade, commanded by Major General Trip, and consisting of the 1st Dutch carabiniers, the 2nd Belgian carabiniers, and the third Dutch carabiniers; the 2nd brigade, commanded by Major General Ghigny, and consisting of the 4th Dutch dragoons, and the 8th Belgian hussars: and the 3rd brigade, commanded by Major General van Merlen, and consisting of the 5th Belgian light dragoons, and the 6th Dutch hussars.

The Brunswick corps was posted between the northern portion of the village of Merbe-braine and the Nivelles road, on which its left rested; and comprised the following troops: —a regiment of hussars, a squadron of lancers, the advanced guard-battalion (which was at this time detached to the right of Merbe-braine); a light infantry brigade, under Lieut. Colonel Buttlar, consisting of the guard-battalion, and the 1st, 2nd, and 3rd light battalions; and an infantry brigade, under Lieut. Colonel Specht, consisting of the 1st, 2nd, and 3rd line-battalions.*

Lambert's brigade was posted near the farm of Mont St. Jean, and consisted of the 4th regiment (under Lieut. Colonel Brooke†), of the 27th regiment (under Major Hare‡), and of the 40th regiment (under Major Heyland§).

In order to afford greater security to the right flank of the Anglo-allied army, and also to keep open the communication with the detached forces near Hal, and at Tubize, namely, the

* In order to include these troops in the Plan representing the armies in position before the commencement of the battle, they have been placed somewhat more in advance, and as having taken up the ground previously occupied by Adam's brigade, which has been moved into the position it proceeded to take up as soon as the battle began.

† Lieut. Colonel Francis Brooke, C.B., retired from the service on the 3rd of August, 1820.

‡ Now Major General John Hare, C.B., K.H.

§ Major Arthur Rowley Heyland was killed in this battle.

corps of Prince Frederick of Orange, and the 6th British and 6th Hanoverian brigades, under Lieut. General Sir Charles Colville, it was deemed essential to occupy the small town of Braine-la-leud, about three-quarters of a mile westward of Merbe-braine: and whence a road leads to Tubize, which is distant between eight and nine miles.

With this view, the 3rd division of the Netherlands, commanded by Lieut. General Baron Chassé, was placed under the orders of General Lord Hill, a part of whose corps, as previously explained, formed the extreme right of the Anglo-allied position. The 1st brigade, under Colonel Ditmers, occupied the town itself. It consisted of the 35th battalion of Belgian light infantry, the 2nd battalion of the Dutch line, and of the 4th, 6th, 17th, and 19th battalions of Dutch militia. The 17th battalion, detached a little to the left, kept up the communication with Clinton's British division. The 2nd brigade, under Major General d'Aubremé, occupied a good position about half a mile in advance of Braine-la-leud, upon a height on which stood the farm of Vieux Foriez.

It was at a very early hour of the 18th that Lieut. Colonel Torrens, Deputy Quarter Master General, reached Braine-le-Comte, and delivered to Sir Charles Colville the order (see page 175,) for his falling back upon Hal. That General immediately put in motion his two brigades. These consisted of the 6th British brigade, under Major General Johnstone, and the 6th Hanoverian brigade, under Major General Sir James Lyon, accompanied by Major Brome's British foot-battery. The remaining brigade, (the 4th British, under Colonel Mitchell,) as also the other foot-battery, belonging to the 4th division (Captain Rettberg's Hanoverian), were on the field of Waterloo. On reaching Tubize, Colville fell in with the advance of Prince Frederick's corps, and as that was the point of junction with the road leading by Braine-le-château and Braine-la-leud to the position in front of Waterloo, he halted there, and despatched Lieut. Colonel Woodford,* Assistant Quarter Master General to the division, to report his proceedings to the Duke. His Grace expressed himself perfectly satisfied, and desired Lieut. Colonel Woodford to remain upon the field of Waterloo, in order that he might be prepared to return to Sir Charles Colville with any instructions which circumstances might induce the Duke to transmit to him.†

* Now Major General Sir John George Woodford, K.C.B., K.C.H.

† Lieut. Colonel Woodford was detained on the field during the whole of the battle, and did not rejoin the 4th division until the following morning. It is

The artillery of the Anglo-allied army, commanded by Colonel Sir George Wood, was distributed in the following manner:—On the extreme left was a British horse-battery* of 6 guns, under Lieut. Colonel Sir Robert Gardiner,† with Vivian's hussar-brigade. Upon the exterior slope of the main ridge, and above the hamlet of Papelotte, were 4 guns of Captain Byleveld's Dutch-Belgian horse-battery, attached to Perponcher's division. The remaining 4 guns of this battery were on the crest of the main ridge, in rear of that division. On the highest point of the position of the left wing, and in front of the right of Best's Hanoverian brigade, was posted Captain Rettberg's Hanoverian foot-battery of 6 guns. In front of Kempt's brigade stood Major Rogers's British foot-battery of 6 guns. Major Lloyd's British, and Captain Cleeves's King's German, foot-batteries, of 6 guns each, were with Alten's division. Major Kuhlmann's King's German horse-battery, and Captain Sandham's‡ British foot-battery, of 6 guns each, were attached to Cooke's division. All the above batteries were posted in front line; as was also Lieut. Colonel Sir Hew Ross's§ British horse-battery, (from the reserve,) of 6 guns, which was posted on the height immediately in rear of La Haye Sainte, and near the intersection of the Wavre road with the Charleroi high road, in which latter 2 of its guns were stationed. Major Sympher's|| King's German horse-battery, and Captain Bolton's¶ British foot-battery, of 6 guns each, were attached to Clinton's division. The remaining horse-batteries were with the cavalry. They were (exclusive of Lieut. Colonel Sir Robert Gardiner's

singular that, notwithstanding the tremendous and continuous cannonade, nothing was heard of the battle by these detached troops, although at so short a distance from the field. They remained on the open ground, with piled arms, during the whole day and night, without knowing anything of the momentous affair at Waterloo, until Sir Charles Colville received, through the medium of an officer of Belgian gens d'armerie, a letter from Colonel Felton Hervey,[1] of the Quarter Master General's Staff, announcing to him the glorious victory, and directing him to march immediately to Nivelles.

* For the sake of uniformity, and to prevent misconception, I have adopted, throughout this work, the terms "horse-battery" and "foot-battery," employed in all the continental armies, although in the British service the distinction is better known by the terms "troop" and "brigade."

† Now Major General Sir Robert Gardiner, K.C.B., K.C.H.

‡ Now Major Charles Freeman Sandham, h.p. Royal Artillery.

§ Now Major General Sir Hew Dalrymple Ross, K.C.B.

|| Lieut. Colonel Augustus Sympher, C.B., K H., of the Hanoverian artillery, died on the 11th of December, 1830.

¶ Captain Samuel Bolton was killed in this battle.

1 Colonel Sir Felton E. B. Hervey, Bart. C.B., died in 1819.

already mentioned) Major Bull's* of 6 howitzers; Lieut. Colonel Webber Smith's† of 6 guns; Major Whinyates's‡ of 6 guns, and provided with rockets; Captain Mercer's§ of 6 guns; and Major Ramsay's|| of 6 guns. Captain Petter's Dutch-Belgian horse-battery of 8 guns, was attached to Collaert's cavalry-division. The Dutch-Belgian horse-battery under Captain van der Smissen, and foot-battery under Captain Lux, of 8 guns each, were with Chassé's division, at Braine-la-leud. The Brunswick horse-battery, under Captain Heinemann, and foot-battery, under Major Moll, of 8 guns each, were with the Brunswick corps. The British horse-battery under Major Beane,¶ and foot-battery under Captain Sinclair,** (belonging to the 6th division,) as also the Hanoverian foot-battery under Captain Braun,†† all three having 6 guns each, were in reserve near Mont St. Jean. The whole of the batteries were engaged in the front line, more or less, during the course of the battle.

This disposition of Wellington's forces, so completely in accordance with the general features of the ground which he had selected with consummate judgment as the field on which he was prepared to give battle to his imperial rival in the great art of war, was admirably calculated for either offensive or defensive measures. The opposite line of heights, which the enemy would naturally crown with the main line of his forces, was fully within the effectual range of cannon-shot; and no hostile movement could be made against any part of the position, that would remain undiscovered within the range of musketry. The formation of the ground in rear of the ridge, along the brow of which his front line was posted, was such as effectually to screen from the enemy's observation any movements of the supports and reserves, preparatory to either a contemplated attack, or to the assembling of the necessary means of resistance at any threatened point. In rear of the main front line the ground was practicable for the movements of all arms, the country was perfectly open, and the two high roads added still further to the facility of communication between the front and rear.

* Lieut. Colonel Robert Bull, C.B., K.H., died on the 17th of April, 1835.

† Now Major General James Webber Smith, C.B.

‡ Now Colonel Whinyates, C.B.

§ Now Colonel Alexander Cavelie Mercer.

|| Major William N. Ramsay was killed in this battle.

¶ Major George Beane was killed in this battle.

** Now Lieut. Colonel James Sinclair, *ret.*, h.p. Royal Artillery.

†† Now Lieut. Colonel William Braun, K.H., of the Hanoverian Artillery.

The occupation of the posts of Hougomont and La Haye Sainte presented important advantages in aid alike of offensive and defensive operations. The right flank was rendered secure, not only by the position of Clinton's division, commanding the valley skirting the village of Merbe-braine, but also by the occupation of the town of Braine-la-leud, whence Chassé's division could co-operate so as to render any attempt of the enemy to turn that flank a most hazardous experiment. Although the left of the main front line rested upon an open plain or elevated plateau, and was therefore completely *en l'air*, yet the village of Smohain, the farms of La Haye and Papelotte, together with the scattered houses and numerous enclosures on the abrupt slope descending into the valley in front, by being well garnished with infantry, offered the means of protracted resistance; while cavalry was at hand, on the high ground, to cover the latter if forced to retire, and to frustrate the complete development of the enemy's disposition of attack. The latter description of force was also available in maintaining a vigilant look-out for any direct flank attack, which, however, was the less to be apprehended in consequence of the preconcerted Prussian co-operation in that quarter.

The position also afforded ample security for a retreat. The two broad high roads uniting at a point in rear of the centre, greatly facilitated the retirement of unbroken masses upon Mont St. Jean, while the village itself, and the numerous buildings and inclosures which lined the great road as far as the forest of Soignies, presented the ready means of securing the further retreat of those masses, which, it may be assumed, would have constituted a main central column. On the right, the villages of Merbe-braine, Le Mesnil, and L'Estraye, connected with Braine-la-leud and with one another, as also with the forest, by several cross-roads, and intersected by numerous inclosures, were well calculated for the retirement of the extreme right of the army, by the advantages which they afforded for covering such retreat with light troops. On the left the ground was more open, but the distance between the position and the forest was infinitely less, the latter stretching southward to the village of Verd-cocou; and the troops retiring in this direction, being much closer to the high road, would have their right in a great measure protected by the well defended retreat of the central column. The forest itself, consisting almost entirely of tall trees, unaccompanied by underwood, was passable for all arms; it was intersected by numerous roads and lanes in every direction; and its southern extremity, adjoining the high road, was thickly skirted with houses and gardens, adding considerably to its capabilities for a vigorous stand against the further advance of an enemy. The retrograde march of the detached forces from Tubize and Hal upon Brussels, and their junction with the remainder of the Anglo-allied army in the position of Uccle, between that capital and the forest of Soignies, will readily present itself to the minds of military men studying the dispositions and movements to which a retreat would have probably given rise; but this is a subject which, embracing as it naturally would, the consequent operations of the Prussians, opens a wide field for discussion, into which it is unnecessary to enter.

The general direction of the front line of the French army was nearly parallel with that of the Anglo-allies. The high road from Charleroi to Brussels, which intersected the Allied position near its centre, also passed through the centre of the French line. The point of this intersection was La Belle Alliance,* a small farm-house and inn; and the distance from the one position to the other, taken along the high road between those two points was 1400 yards. About 200 yards in the French rear of this house is a summit, the altitude, of which exceeds, by about 13 feet, that of any point along the Anglo-allied position. A ridge issuing from it, and extending in a north-easterly direction towards Frischermont, formed the position of the right wing of the front line of the French army. On the west side, a road leading from the summit, descends rather rapidly as a hollow-way down into and across the long valley that takes its course towards Hougomont, then ascends until it reaches another ridge, along which it winds round that post, at a distance varying from 300 to about 440 yards, until it joins the Nivelles chaussée; and that winding road indicates pretty

* The origin of this appellation is not a little curious, and in order to explain it, it is necessary to remark that, on the other side of the road, and commencing opposite the end of the garden of La Belle Alliance, stands the farm-house of Trimotion; and about three hundred yards further on the road is a house, the same that was occupied in 1815 by Jean Baptiste de Coster, who, during the battle, served Napoleon in the capacity of *guide du pays*. Upon the death of a former landlord of this public-house, his widow married the farmer of Trimotion; but losing him shortly afterwards, she consoled herself by taking for her third husband a peasant who lived in the other house alluded to as since occupied by de Coster; but here again death interrupted her happiness, when she once more embraced the married state, and espoused the *aubergiste* of her first house, which from that time, obtained among the neighbouring peasantry the title it now bears—*la belle alliance*.

nearly the ground occupied by the left wing of the French front line.

The right wing of this line consisted of the 1st corps d'armée, commanded by Lieut. General Count d'Erlon, comprising four divisions of infantry, and one of light cavalry. Its left division, which was the 2nd, commanded by Lieut. General Baron Donzelot, rested its left upon La Belle Alliance. The 1st brigade of this division, under General Baron Schmith, consisted of the 13th regiment of light infantry and the 17th regiment of the line, the former comprising three, and the latter, two battalions. The 2nd brigade, under General Aulard, consisted of the 19th and 51st regiments of the line, each comprising two battalions. These brigades were deployed in two lines, the second at a distance of 60 yards in rear of the first. On the right of the 2nd division was the 1st, commanded by Lieut. General Alix. Its 1st brigade, under General Baron Quiot, consisted of the 54th and 55th regiments of the line, each comprising two battalions. Its 2nd brigade, under General Baron Bourgeois, consisted of the 28th and 105th regiments of the line, each comprising two battalions. The brigades were deployed in two lines, the second at a distance of 60 yards in rear of the first. On the right of the 1st division stood the 3rd, commanded by Lieut. General Baron Marcognet. Its 1st brigade, under General Noguès, consisted of the 21st and 46th regiments of the line; and its second brigade, under General Grenier, of the 25th and 45th regiments of the line; all four regiments comprising two battalions each. These two brigades were, in like manner, deployed in two lines, the second at a distance of 60 yards in rear of the first. On the right of the 3rd division, nearest to the extremity of the ridge, and immediately opposite the farms of Papelotte and La Haye, was posted the 4th division, commanded by Lieut. General Count Durutte. Its 1st brigade, under General Chevalier Pegot, consisted of the 8th and 29th regiments of the line; and its 2nd brigade, under General Brue, of the 85th and 95th regiments of the line; all four regiments comprising two battalions each. These two brigades were also deployed in two lines, the second at a distance of 60 yards in rear of the first. The cavalry attached to this corps, which was the 1st division, commanded by Lieut. General Baron Jaquinot, was posted in a valley, on the right of the infantry; having in its front the village of Smohain, which it held in observation, as also the château of Frischermont, on the right of the valley; at the same time throwing out patroles in the direction of Ohain. It was deployed in three lines. Its 1st brigade, under General Bruno, consisting of the 3rd and 7th chasseurs; and its 2nd brigade, under General Gobrecht, of the 3rd and 4th lancers. The artillery attached to the infantry-corps, consisting of 5 batteries of 8 guns each, (including a reserve-battery of 8 twelve-pounders,) was ranged along the front of the different divisions respectively; and the battery of horse-artillery—6 guns—attached to the 1st division of cavalry, was posted on the right of the latter.

The left wing of the front line of the French army was formed by the 2nd corps, commanded by Lieut. General Count Reille, comprising three divisions of infantry and one of light cavalry. Its right division, which was the 5th, commanded by Lieut. General Baron Bachelu, rested its right upon La Belle Alliance, and was ranged along the descent from thence down into the valley, which, more westward, winds past Hougomont. The 1st brigade of this division, under General Husson, consisted of the 2nd regiment of light infantry and the 61st regiment of the line, the former comprising two, and the latter, three, battalions; and the 2nd brigade, under General Baron Campy, of the 72nd and 108th regiments of the line, the former comprising two, and the latter, three, battalions. The brigades were deployed in two lines, the second at a distance of 60 yards in rear of the first. On the left of the 5th division, and upon the height facing the southern boundary of Hougomont, stood the 9th division, commanded by Lieut. General Count Foy. Its 1st brigade, under General Baron Gauthier, consisted of the 92nd and 93rd regiments of the line, comprising two battalions each. Its 2nd brigade, under General Baron Jamin, consisted of the 4th regiment of light infantry, and of the 100th regiment of the line, each comprising three battalions. These two brigades were, in like manner, deployed in two lines, the second at a distance of 60 yards in rear of the first. On the left of the 9th division, and along the ridge of the western boundary of Hougomont, stood the 6th division, commanded by Prince Jerome Napoleon. Its 1st brigade, under General Baron Bauduin, consisted of the 1st regiment of light infantry and of the 3rd regiment of the line, the former comprising three, and the latter, two, battalions. Its 2nd brigade, under General Baron Soye, consisted of the 1st and 2nd regiments of the line, comprising three battalions each. These two brigades were also deployed in two lines, the second at a distance of 60 yards in rear of the first. On the left of the infantry was posted the light-cavalry, attached to the corps, namely, the

2nd cavalry-division, commanded by Lieut. General Baron Piré. Its 1st brigade, under General Baron Hubera, consisted of the 1st and 6th chasseurs; and its 2nd brigade, under General Mathieu, of the 5th and 6th lancers. It stood across the Nivelles high road, in three deployed lines, rather under the crest of the ridge, on its reverse slope, and threw out picquets in the direction of Braine-la-leud, as also more to its left, thus keeping up a vigilant look-out around this flank of the army.

The second general line of the French army was formed in the following manner:—

In the centre, close along the west side of the Charleroi high road, stood the 6th corps, commanded by Lieut. General Count Lobau. Only two of its divisions, the 19th and 20th, were present; the 21st was with the army under Marshal Grouchy. Each of the two divisions formed a close column of battalions by grand divisions; the head of the column of the 19th division being distant about 100 yards in rear of the right of the 2d corps, and an interval of about 200 yards was preserved between the rear of the 19th division and the head of the column of the 20th division. The former was commanded by Lieut. General Baron Simmer, and its 1st brigade, under General Baron de Bellair, consisted of the 5th and 11th regiments of the line, the former comprising two, the latter, three battalions. Its 2nd brigade, under General Simmer, consisted of the 27th and 84th regiments of the line, comprising two battalions each. The 20th division was commanded by Lieut. General Baron Jeannin: its 1st brigade, under General Bony, consisted of the 5th regiment of light infantry, and of the 10th regiment of the line; and its 2nd brigade, under General Tromelin, of the 107th regiment of the line;* all three regiments comprising two battalions each. There were three batteries of foot artillery, of 8 guns each, attached to the divisions, including one of reserve; as also a horse-battery of 6 guns; they were posted on the left flank of the corps.

On the right of these two divisions of the 6th corps, and separated from them by the high road only, were stationed the 3rd light cavalry-division, commanded by Lieut. General Baron Domon, and the 5th light cavalry-division, commanded by Lieut. General Baron Subervie (belonging to the 1st cavalry corps, commanded by General Count Pajol). They were formed in close column of regiments by squadrons. The first brigade of the former, under General Baron Dommanget,

* The 47th regiment, belonging to this brigade, was in La Vendée.

consisted of the 4th and 9th chasseurs; and the 2nd brigade, under General Baron Vinot, of the 12th chasseurs. The 1st brigade of the 5th division, under General Count Colbert, consisted of the 1st and the 2nd lancers; and the second brigade, under General Merlin, of the 11th chasseurs. The two batteries of horse-artillery attached to these two divisions, comprising 6 guns each, were posted on the right flank of the column.

The right wing of the second French general line was composed of the 4th cavalry-corps, commanded by Lieut. General Count Milhaud, which was posted on a parallel ridge, in rear of the two central divisions of the 1st infantry-corps, and distant from them about two hundred yards. It was deployed in two lines, the second at a distance of sixty yards in rear of the first. The corps consisted of two heavy cavalry-divisions —the 13th, commanded by Lieut. General Wathier St. Alphonse, and the 14th, under Lieut. General Baron Delort. The 1st brigade of the 13th division, under General Dubois, consisted of the 1st and 4th cuirassiers; the 2nd, under General Baron Travers, of the 7th and 12th cuirassiers. The 1st brigade of the 14th division, under General Baron Farine, consisted of the 5th and 10th cuirassiers; and the 2nd, under General Baron Vial, of the 6th and 9th cuirassiers. The two batteries of horse-artillery attached to this corps, comprising 6 guns each, were stationed, one in the centre, and the other on the left flank.

The left wing of the French second general line, composed of the 3rd cavalry-corps, commanded by Lieut. General Kellermann (Count de Valmy), was posted about 200 yards in rear of the centre of the 2nd infantry-corps. It was deployed in two lines, the second at a distance of 60 yards in rear of the first. The corps consisted of two heavy cavalry-divisions; the 11th, commanded by Lieut. General Baron L'Héritier, and the 12th, under Lieut. General Roussel d'Hurbal. The 1st brigade of the 11th division, under General Baron Picquet, consisted of the 2nd and 7th dragoons; and the 2nd, under General Gniton, of the 8th and 11th cuirassiers. The 1st brigade of the 12th division, under General Baron Blancard, consisted of the 1st and 2nd carabiniers; and the 2nd, of the 2nd and 3rd cuirassiers. The two batteries of horse-artillery attached to this corps, comprising 6 guns each, were posted one upon each flank.

The 3rd general line, forming the grand reserve of the whole line of battle, and comprising the entire force of the imperial guards, cavalry and infantry, under the command of Lieut. General Count Drouot,* was thus formed.

The infantry of the imperial guard constituted the centre of the reserve. It consisted of four regiments of grenadiers, four regiments of chasseurs, two regiments of tirailleurs, and two regiments of voltigeurs; each regiment divided into two battalions. The 1st and 2nd regiments of grenadiers, and the 1st and 2nd of chasseurs, formed the old guard, under Lieut. General Count Friant; the 3rd and 4th regiments of grenadiers, and the 3rd and 4th of chasseurs formed the *moyenne*, or middle guard, under Lieut. General Count Morand; the four regiments of tirailleurs and voltigeurs constituted the young guard, under Lieut. General Count Duhesme. This force was posted somewhat in advance of the farm of Rossomme, in six lines of four battalions each, at a distance of 20 yards from one another, and so disposed that the Charleroi high road alone separated the two right, from the two left, battalions of each line. To each description of the infantry of the imperial guard, the old, the middle, and the young guard, two batteries, of 8 guns each, were attached. These were stationed on either flank, and the reserve-artillery of the guard, consisting of 24 guns, was posted in rear of these lines. The right wing of the third line, or reserve, consisted of the light cavalry of the imperial guard, commanded by Lieut. General Lefebvre-Desnouettes, namely the chasseurs and lancers of the guard. It was posted at a distance of about 200 yards in rear of the 4th cavalry-corps and deployed in two lines, the second at a distance of 60 yards in rear of the first. The two batteries of horse-artillery belonging to the corps, comprising 6 guns each, were posted in its centre. The left wing of the third line, or reserve, consisted of the heavy cavalry of the imperial guard, commanded by Lieut. General Count Guyot, namely, the grenadiers and dragoons of the guard. It was stationed in rear of the 3rd cavalry-corps, and deployed in two lines, the second at a distance of 60 yards in rear of the first. Its two batteries of horse-artillery, comprising 6 guns each, were posted in the centre.

This admirable order of battle, at once grand, simple, and imposing, and presenting to its skilful designer the most ample means of sustaining, by an immediate and efficient support, any attack, from whatever point he might wish to direct it, and of possessing every where a respectable force at

* He was Major General of the Staff of the Guards, and commanded in the absence of Marshal Mortier, Duke of Treviso, who was left sick at Beaumont.

hand to oppose any attack upon himself, from whatever quarter it might be made, was no less remarkable for the regularity and precision with which the several masses, constituting thirteen distinct columns, advanced to their destined stations, than for the unusual degree of warlike pomp and high martial bearing with which the lines drew up in this mighty battle-array. The movements throughout were executed under the cheering and spirit-stirring sounds of bugles, drums, and trumpets, sending forth the long-cherished national military airs of the republic and of the empire. The weather had cleared up a little, and to the Anglo-allied army, the crowning of the opposite heights by the French lines, with all its accompanying circumstances, presented a magnificent spectacle.

Napoleon has frequently been blamed for having thus consumed some very precious time in a mere ostentatious display of his forces. Public opinion, however, should not suffer itself to be too easily influenced by the apparent justness of such censure, and it would be ungenerous to the established renown of the French leader not to attach due weight to the following circumstances. In the account of the battle attributed to the Emperor's own dictation, one cause of delay in commencing offensive operations, is represented to have been the soft and miry state of the ground after the excessive rain which had fallen during the night, in consequence of which it was found impossible to manœuvre the artillery and the cavalry, and it was considered advisable to wait until the ground had, in some degree, resumed its natural consistency. When, therefore, the manœuvring of these two arms was pronounced to be practicable, though attended with some difficulty, which, however, it was added, would gradually disappear, the employment of the interval in an orderly and a deliberate formation of a well-defined order of battle, was a measure scarcely questionable *at the moment*, however much the *subsequent* course of events may have proved that it militated against the chances of success on the part of the French. The additional impulse which this imposing spectacle was calculated to impart to the moral force of his troops, is also well worthy of consideration. His soldiers, as they contemplated the extended double front line of infantry, disposed as if about to enfold the enemy in a deadly embrace, and the fluttering of gay lance-flags on either extremity, indicating that its flanks were duly protected; as they glanced at the second general line, a double one of cavalry, superbly mounted, and proudly mailed in glittering helmet and cuirass; and, as they scanned the well-disposed reserves and serried centre, their reliance on their own strength and in the resources of their leader was unbounded, their anticipations of success were heightened, and their eager longing for the contest was greatly augmented. And while adverting to the grand spectacle in a moral point of view, it would be well to consider whether it may not have also been designed to exert a powerful influence on that portion of the Anglo-allied forces with which the Emperor was tampering, in the full expectation of seeing them again range themselves under his victorious eagles, but which Wellington, with judicious foresight and prompt address, broke up as a united body, and distributed among his British troops; thus securing himself against the possible enactment of a scene similar to that which so powerfully contributed to Napoleon's disaster on the plains of Leipzig.

But supposing it to be admitted upon these grounds that the delay of the attack, having once been determined, was judiciously and advantageously employed, we ought also to consider whether the delay itself may not have been superinduced by motives of far higher import.

Although the miry state of the ground has been put forward as the ostensible cause, can we for a moment imagine that Napoleon was the man to have allowed himself to be deterred by such an obstacle from commencing the attack at an earlier hour, had he, at the moment, been sufficiently acquainted with the actual state of things to foresee that the delay, together with the possibility of a lengthened contest, and of the approach of aid to the British General from the Prussian side, tended to render his situation one of extreme peril? May we not rather be justified in inferring, that his object was to gain time for the due execution and succesful development of Grouchy's operations! The despatch which the Emperor had received from Grouchy, dated Gembloux, 17th June, at 10 P.M., (see page 186,) clearly explained that General's intentions, which were, that should the mass of the Prussian forces retire upon Wavre, he would follow them in that direction, as to prevent them from either reaching Brussels or forming a junction with Wellington; but that if, on the other hand, they should fall back upon Perwès, he would advance towards that town in pursuit of them. In the former case, Napoleon's delay was likely to facilitate the combined operation, because in order to prevent the junction with Wellington, Grouchy required sufficient time to throw himself between the Prussians and the Emperor, and, in the latter case, the delay would be immaterial, because then the Prussian co-operation with Wellington was not to be apprehended, and the battle with the Anglo-allied army would have to be fought by the Emperor, unsupported by Grouchy. It may, perhaps, be argued that Napoleon, by commencing his attack much earlier, would not have been under the necessity of employing a considerable portion of his reserve against the Prussians, in defence of his right flank, at a time when he so urgently needed them for following up and strengthening his attacks upon the Duke of Wellington's line. There existed, however, no such striking disparity, in point of numbers, between Wellington's forces, and his own, as to warrant his throwing away a chance amounting, according to the information he had already received, almost to a certainty, of being enabled to bring his greatest mass to bear against each army separately; and which would doubtless have been the case as regards the Anglo-allied army, had Grouchy, by the adoption of more vigorous and energetic measures, manœuvred in such a manner as to sufficiently impede the Prussian co-operation by posting one of his corps so as to command the defiles of St. Lambert and Lasne, and holding the other in reserve, to be employed by either the Emperor or himself, according to circumstances.

Whether Napoleon was really actuated by any such motives, must remain a doubtful point. These remarks, however, are offered for the consideration of those who censure him for his delay in commencing the battle of Waterloo.

The strength of the Anglo-allied army in the field was as follows:—

	Infantry.	Cavalry.	Artillery.	Guns.
British	15,181	5,843	2,967	78
King's German Legion . .	3,301	1,991	526	18
Hanoverians	10,258	497	465	12
Brunswickers	4,586	866	510	16
Nassauers	2,880			
Dutch-Belgians	13,402	3,205	1,177	32
Total . .	49,608	12,402	5,645	156

GRAND TOTAL.

Infantry . . .	49,608
Cavalry . . .	12,408
Artillery . . .	5,645
Total . .	67,661 men, and 156 guns.*

* For detailed return—See Appendix XXX.

The French army consisted of:—

Infantry . . .	47,579
Cavalry . . .	13,792
Artillery . . .	7,529
Total . .	68,900 men, and 246 guns.*

The martial sounds already adverted to as having accompanied the march of the French columns into position, had scarcely been wafted towards the Anglo-allied army, when mounted officers were discerned galloping along the opposite heights, and taking up the necessary alignments; and, presently, the simultaneous flashing of bayonets over dark masses, on various points, and the roll of drums, now become more distinctly audible, announced the arrival of the heads of the columns destined to constitute the front line. As this gradually developed itself, and was seen extending on either side, from La Belle Alliance, and apparently almost overlapping both flanks of the Allies, the scene became truly imposing and highly exciting. The two armies were now fairly in presence of each other, and their mutual observation was governed by the most intense interest, and the most scrutinizing anxiety. In a still greater degree did these feelings actuate their commanders, while watching each other's preparatory movements, and minutely scanning the surface of the arena on which tactical skill, habitual prowess, physical strength, and moral courage, were to decide, not alone their own, but in all probability, the fate of Europe. Apart from national interests and considerations, and viewed solely in connection with the opposite characters of the two illlustrious chiefs, the approaching contest was contemplated with anxious solicitude by the whole military world. Need this create surprise when we reflect, that the struggle was one for mastery between the far-famed conqueror of Italy, and the victorious liberator of the Peninsula; between the triumphant vanquisher of Eastern Europe, and the bold and successful invader of the South of France! Never was the issue of a single battle looked forward to as involving consequences of such vast importance—of such universal influence.

* For detailed return—See Appendix XXXI.

CHAPTER X.

While the preparatory dispositions, alluded to in the preceding chapter, were in progress, Napoleon ordered the following despatch to be addressed to Grouchy:—

'En avant de la ferme de Caillou,
le 18 juin, à 10 heures du matin.

'Monsieur le Maréchal,

'L'Empereur a reçu votre dernier rapport daté de Gembloux.* Vous ne parlez à sa Majesté que des deux colonnes prussiennes qui out passé à Sauvenières et Sarra-Walin; cependant des rapports disent qu'une troisieme colonne, qui était assez forte, a passé à Gery et Gentinnes, se dirrigeant sur Wavres.

'L'Empereur me charge de vous prévenir, qu'en ce moment S.M. va faire attaquer l'armée anglaise qui a pris position à Waterloo, près de la forêt de Soignes; ainsi S.M. désire que vous dirigiez vos mouvemens sur Wavres,† afin de vous rapprocher de nous, vous mettre en rapport d'opérations et lier les communications, poussant devant vous les corps de l'armée prussienne qui ont pris cette direction et qui auraient pu s'arrêter à Wavres, où vous devez arriver le plus tôt possible. Vous ferez suivre les colonnes ennemies qui ont pris sur votre droite par quelques corps légers, afin d'observer leurs mouvemens et ramasser leurs fuyards; instruisez-moi immédiatement de vos dispositions et de votre marche, ainsi que des nouvelles que vous avez sur les ennemis, et ne négligez pas de lier vos communications avec nous; l'Empereur désire avoir très souvent de vos nouvelles.

'le Major Général Duc de Dalmatie.'

It will thus be seen that Grouchy's report, despatched from Gembloux on the previous night, was well calculated to inspire the Emperor with great confidence as to the result of his present plan of operations, notwithstanding the very little progress that had hitherto been made in that quarter, and which, as already remarked, must be ascribed principally to his own inactivity during the early part of the 17th. He approved of the movement upon Wavre, in pursuit of the great mass of the Prussian army, but at the same time ex-

* See page 186.

† In the "Fragments historiques relatifs à la campagne de 1815," published by Marshal Grouchy, the latter has referred, in justification of his having moved his whole force upon Wavre, to the above passage in Napoleon's despatch. It must, however be borne in mind, that in the verbal instructions given by Napoleon to Grouchy, on the field of Ligny, no mention whatever was made of Wavre, and that the indication of that direction, to which allusion was made for the first time in the above despatch, resulted solely from Grouchy's own suspicion, expressed in his report, to which the above letter was a reply, that a portion of the Prussians would endeavour by retiring on Wavre, to join Wellington's forces, and his intention, should such appear to be the case, of following them in that direction, so as to prevent the threatened junction.

pressed his desire that it should be executed in such a manner as to draw the detached force more within the sphere of the operations of the main French army; and above all, he enforced the necessity of maintaining a close communication with the latter.

Some time before the battle commenced, a Prussian patrole reached the village of Smohain, in which was posted the picquet of the 10th British hussars, under Captain Taylor,* whom the officer accompanying the patrole desired to report to the Duke of Wellington that General Count Bülow was at St. Lambert, and advancing with his *corps d'armée*. Captain Taylor immediately despatched Lieutenant Lindsey,† of the 10th, with the intelligence to head-quarters, as directed. The Prussian officer was certainly ignorant of the very slow progress made by the main body of Bülow's corps, and the information which he thus conveyed to the Duke, before the battle had commenced, naturally led the latter to calculate upon a much earlier arrival of the Prussians than could possibly take place; for, in point of fact, it was only Bülow's advanced guard which had then reached St. Lambert.

The formation of the French lines was scarcely completed when the magnificent and animating spectacle which they presented was heightened in an extraordinary degree by the passing of the Emperor along them, attended by a numerous and brilliant staff. The troops hailed him with loud and fervent acclamations. There was depicted on their brows a deep-rooted confidence in his ability, with such an army, to chain victory to the car in which he had already advanced in triumph to within a few miles of the capital of Belgium. They exulted in the idea that they were now fairly ranged in battle-array, under the chief of their choice, and the idol of their devotion, against the army of that nation which of all others had proved the most inveterate and the most enduring in its hostility to France; a nation which had not only by its wealth cemented and held together the great European league which had once precipitated that idol from the throne, but had also flung into the scale her own native strength and valour, by which the fleets of the Empire had been destroyed, its armies driven out of the Peninsula, and the sceptres of Spain and Portugal wrested from its grasp. They appeared as if excited by the assurance, that the hour had arrived in which the disasters of the Nile and Trafalgar, of Salamanca and Vittoria,

* See page 204.

† Lieutenant William H. B. Lindsey died on the 1st of June, 1822.

were to be cast into the dark shade of oblivion, by the dazzling splendour of the triumph about to be achieved.

Never throughout the whole of his career had Napoleon received from his soldiers more unequivocal demonstrations of attachment to his person, of unlimited confidence in his power, of complete devotion to his cause, and of absolute submission to his will, than were manifested in this short and fatal campaign, by which that career was terminated. With an army thus animated by one sentiment, and presenting in appearance and material all that his practised eye could desire, it may readily be conceived that he fully participated in the general confidence of a signal victory.

Wellington's dispositions remained as previously described. Shortly before the action commenced, he rode down to Hougomont, and, proceeding by the lane which crosses the wood in the direction of La Belle Alliance, remained a few minutes at the point where the lane reaches the eastern boundary of the wood. Having made his observations upon that portion of the enemy's line which came under his view, he ordered the light companies of the British guards that were in the wood to be relieved by the Nassau battalion and the Hanoverian light infantry. The former were then withdrawn to the great orchard, where the light companies of the 1st brigade remained, while those of the 2nd brigade moved on, along the rear of the enclosures, to the lane which passes between the right of the buildings and the kitchen-garden, and leads into the wood on that side. The Duke next rode up to the high ground on the Nivelles road, unaccompanied by his staff, to reconnoitre the enemy's left. He then rode along to the left of his own line as far as La Haye. When the action began, he was in front of the left of the 1st brigade of guards.

Napoleon, having completed the inspection of his troops, proceeded to take up his own station upon the height in rear of La Belle Alliance, which afforded him a commanding view of the whole field. The infantry-brigades speedily formed lines of battalion-columns respectively. The state of the ground was reported practicable for the movements of artillery. All was in perfect readiness.

The anxiously-looked-for moment had now arrived. The Emperor sent an order to Reille to begin the battle by an attack upon Hougomont; and it was about half-past eleven o'clock when, from the right of Prince Jerome's division, a column, advancing towards the south-western boundary of the wood, rapidly extended itself into a strong line of skirmishers. As they approached the wood, a few straggling shots from behind the outermost trees and hedges gave warning that the defenders were prepared for resistance, and announced to both armies that the battle had actually commenced. The French, hastening their advance, to obtain a better view of their opponents, began to single them out; and the shots from both sides, quickening in succession, speedily increased into a brisk and well-sustained fire of musketry. Jerome's supporting columns had not advanced far when the Duke of Wellington, with his staff, galloped up to the spot on which the Coldstream guards were formed, and having directed his glass upon the French columns, the guns of Captain Sandham's foot-battery, attached to Cooke's division, were ordered to the front. They instantly unlimbered and opened the cannonade from the Anglo-allied position. The first discharge was from a howitzer, the shell of which burst over the head of a column moving towards the Hougomont inclosures. The shots from the remaining guns in succession, also took effect, and the battery was soon in full play. It was immediately followed up by an equally well-directed fire from Captain Cleeves's foot-battery of the German Legion, in front of Alten's division. The batteries of Reille's corps now opened in their turn, to draw off the fire from their columns. Napoleon sent an order to Kellermann to push forward his twelve pieces of horse-artillery into the front line, facing Hougomont. The intervals between the reports from the guns on either side rapidly diminished: in a brief space of time no intervals could be distinguished; and the cannonade, increasing in violence every moment, now thundered forth in one continual roar.

> " ——— deep-throated engines belch'd, whose roar
> Imbowel'd with outrageous noise the air."

The French columns, as they moved towards Hougomont, were twice checked by the fire from the British batteries, which, having been given with remarkable precision, appeared to cause considerable loss and disorder among them. At length they effected their advance. The French skirmishers, followed by fresh supports, had, in the mean time, made good their entrance into the wood, and such was the boldness of their advance that they soon drove the Nassau battalion and Hanoverian riflemen before them. They were also pushing forward in considerable force, across the inclosures adjoining the left of the wood. At this moment Wellington gave orders, in person, to Major Bull's British howitzer horse-battery, which had just been drawn up on that part of the main ridge which was immediately in rear of the great orchard of Hougomont, to dislodge the enemy's infantry from those inclosures by means of shells. This service, which, considering the proximity of the Allied troops in the wood, was of a very delicate nature, was executed with admirable skill, and attended with the desired effect. The enemy was forced to abandon the fields in front of the great orchard; from which the light companies of the first brigade of guards now moved on, as did also those of the 2nd brigade, from the lane and kitchen-garden on the right, to relieve the Nassauers and Hanoverians in the wood. They dashed forward with the most determined resolution, blazing away in the very faces of their opponents, whose further advance they completely checked; and then gallantly pressing on, they gradually succeeded in clearing the wood of the French skirmishers.

With the exception of the cannonade maintained between the French left and the Anglo-allied right wing, and which was gradually extending towards the opposite extremities of the hostile lines, the action was as yet confined to the post of Hougomont. About this time, a body of French cavalry, issuing from the low ground near Papelotte, approached that part of the Anglo-allied left wing which was occupied by Best's Hanoverian infantry-brigade, and Captain Rettberg's Hanoverian foot-battery. It was a strong *reconnaissance*, made by the French to ascertain whether the summit on which the above battery was posted had really been intrenched, its appearance, as viewed from the opposite heights, having induced a supposition that such was the case. Best expecting to be attacked, immediately formed his brigade into battalion-squares, but the French cavalry speedily retired.

Jerome now moved down fresh columns to reinforce his skirmishers. They were directed more against the Allied right of the wood, while a part of Foy's division was ordered to support the attack by a simultaneous advance against the front. The descent of Jerome's troops was observed from the position of the extreme right of the Allied second line, which afforded a partial view up the valley on that side of Hougomont. Two guns were therefore detached, under Captain Napier,* from Captain Bolton's battery, to open a fire upon the advancing columns, but they were instantly cannonaded by the batteries on the French extreme left,

* Major Charles George Napier retired from the service in 1827.

particularly by the horse-battery of Piré's light cavalry, on the height intersected by the Nivelles road. The remaining guns of the battery were brought into action, as were also those of Major Sympher's Hanoverian horse-battery; and a vigorous fire was now maintained against both the attacking troops and the French guns. Lieut. Colonel Webber Smith, whose British horse-battery was also with Clinton's division, but lower down the slope, commenced firing up the valley, across the Nivelles road, at one of Jerome's columns, but on ascertaining that the latter was somewhat beyond the effectual range of his 6-pounders, he detached an officer to the right of the front line in rear of Hougomont, to discover whether a more commanding position could be obtained for his battery on that part of the field.

In the mean time, Jerome's skirmishers, having been very strongly reinforced, renewed their attack upon the wood, in conjunction with Foy's infantry on their right. The light companies of the British guards presented a stout and desperate resistance, but were forced to yield to an overwhelming superiority of numbers. Retiring from tree to tree, and frequently hazarding a bold and obstinate stand, by which they suffered most severely, they at length withdrew from the unavailing contest: those of the Coldstream and 3rd regiment seeking shelter partly in the lane adjoining the right of the château, and partly behind a haystack which fronted the wood near the south-west angle of the buildings; while those of the 1st regiment fell back into the great orchard, on the left. The French skirmishers, finding themselves relieved for the moment from any immediate pressure upon their front, now rapidly advanced towards the buildings and garden. The hedge which lined the wood on this side appeared to them, as it gradually presented itself to their view, to form also the boundary of the great garden. In the full confidence that this important post was now within their grasp, they rushed forward at the *pas de charge* to force an entrance. They were instantly and fatally undeceived. A deadly fire bursting forth from the loop-holes and platforms along the garden-wall, which was parallel to, and about 30 yards distant from, the hedge, laid prostrate the leading files. Those which came up in rapid succession were staggered by the sudden and unexpected appearance of this little fortress. Not venturing upon an escalade, they were forced to take advantage of such cover as was afforded by the hedge and trees, whence they kept up a popping fire, though at fearful odds with opponents so well concealed by the wall, as also by a row of apple-trees which ran along its exterior.

The French infantry were pushing forward through the wood in support of this attack, when Major Bull's horse-battery re-commenced its fire, and a shower of howitzer-shells fell amongst them, causing the greatest destruction and confusion in their ranks. Again the defenders dashed forward from the flanks, and regained a considerable portion of the wood; whereupon Major Bull ceased firing in that direction, and pointed his guns on strong columns of French infantry in support, which he succeeded in causing to retrograde, notwithstanding the very galling fire to which he was himself at that time exposed, not only from the batteries in his front, but also from Piré's horse-battery on the French height adjoining the Nivelles road, by which his own battery was completely enfiladed. The French that were in the wood having rallied, and obtained a vast preponderance of force, now advanced in a most determined manner against the light infantry of the British guards, and compelled the latter to retire to their former posts on the flanks of the château and gardens. At the same time, Jerome's light troops were advancing rapidly, and in great force, against the right of the buildings. That portion of the light companies of the Coldstream and 3rd regiment of guards which was outside the farm made a gallant stand, under cover of the haystack, and from the lane before mentioned. The haystack itself was set on fire by the French in one of their attacks, and was now in full blaze. These guardsmen held their ground with the greatest bravery until they saw themselves completely outflanked, and in danger of being cut off from all retreat. They then hastily withdrew into the great court-yard by the gate which faces the Allied position, and which they instantly closed and endeavoured to block up with ladders, posts, barrows, or whatever was nearest at hand. The French, however, succeeded in forcing the gate; but the defenders betook themselves to the nearest cover, whence they poured a fire upon the intruders, and then rushing forward, a struggle ensued which was distinguished by the most intrepid courage on both sides. At length, Lieut. Colonel Macdonell, Captain Wyndham,* Ensigns Gooch† and Hervey,‡ and Serjeant Graham,§ of the Cold-

* Now Lieut. General Wyndham.

† Lieut. Colonel Henry Gooch retired from the service on the 11th of June, 1841.

‡ Captain James William Hervey retired from the service in October, 1837.

§ This individual deserves honourable mention, having greatly distinguished himself during the memorable defence of Hougomont. At a later period of the day, when in the ranks along the garden-wall facing the wood, and when the struggle was most severe in that quarter, he asked Lieut. Colonel Macdonell's

stream guards, by dint of great personal strength and exertions, combined with extraordinary bravery and perseverance, succeeded in closing the gate against their assailants. Those of the latter who had entered the courtyard fell a sacrifice to their undaunted and conspicuous gallantry. The remainder of the French skirmishers, passing on by the left and to the rear of Hougomont, and, crossing the avenue leading to it from the Nivelles road, and the adjacent rivulet, spread themselves over some broken ground partially covered with brushwood. They were now immediately under the position to which Lieut. Colonel Smith had moved his battery from its former station on the other side of the Nivelles road, and which was in front of the extreme right of the first line of the Anglo-allied army. This battery had just been hotly engaged with, and had suffered severely from, the horse-battery posted in front of Piré's light cavalry-brigade, which had previously directed its fire upon Bull's guns, and which maintained the cannonade with Lieut. Colonel Smith's battery, for the purpose of covering the advance of these light troops. Smith had succeeded in silencing the fire of his opponent, when the French skirmishers, taking advantage of both the broken ground and the high corn beyond it, suddenly opened upon his battery a popping fire so destructive in its effects, that in a few moments several of the gunners and horses were killed, and so much

permission to fall out. The Colonel, knowing the character of the man, expressed his surprise at the request made at such a moment. Graham explained that his brother lay wounded in one of the buildings then on fire, that he wished to remove him to a place of safety, and that he would then lose no time in rejoining the ranks. The request was granted: Graham succeeded in snatching his brother from the horrible fate which menaced him; laid him in a ditch in rear of the inclosures, and, true to his word, was again at his post.

Early in August of that year, and while the Anglo-allied army was at Paris, the Duke of Wellington received a letter from the Rev. Mr. Norcross, rector of Framlingham, in Suffolk, expressing his wish to confer a pension of £10 a-year, for life, on some Waterloo soldier to be named by His Grace. The Duke requested Sir John Byng (now the Earl of Strafford) to choose a man from the 2nd brigade of guards, which had so highly distinguished itself in the defence of Hougomont. Out of the numerous instances of good conduct evinced by several individuals of each battalion, Serjeant James Graham, of the light company of the Coldstream, was selected to receive the proffered annuity, as notified in brigade-orders of the 9th of August, 1815. This was paid to him during two years, at the expiration of which period it ceased, in consequence of the insolvency of the benevolent donor. Graham is now an inmate of the Royal Hospital of Kilmainham; and amongst the gallant veterans who enjoy the comforts afforded to them, in their declining years, in that venerable institution, there are few who, in the course of their service, have acquired such honourable distinction.

Since the above was written Graham has been borne to the grave by his comrades of Kilmainham Hospital, with all the military honours to which he was so deservedly entitled.

damage was sustained by the limbers, that it became absolutely necessary to withdraw the guns into a little hollow-way that led from the rear of the battery into the Nivelles road, and in which it remained some time for the purpose of refitting and getting into order. This daring onset of the French skirmishers was checked by the advance of four companies of the Coldstream regiment of guards, under Lieut. Colonel Woodford.* They then fell back to the wall of the farm-yard, near which they collected a considerable force, when Colonel Woodford charged them. They gave way immediately, and withdrew from the contest, which afforded Colonel Woodford an opportunity of entering the farm with a part of the re-inforcement by the side door in the lane. The remainder of the detached force occupied the inclosures between the château and the Nivelles road.

During this advance of the French skirmishers against the extreme right of the Allied front line, the troops which formed their support attempted again to force open the rear gate of Hougomont. The individuals before mentioned as having closed the gate, were, at the time, occupied in rendering it more secure by placing against it some pieces of ash timber that lay in the yard. The French failing in their endeavours to push in the gate, a brave grenadier volunteered to climb over and open it from the inside. Captain Wyndham, on perceiving the latter at the top of the gate, instantly desired Serjeant Graham, whose musket he was holding whilst the latter was bringing forward another piece of timber, to drop the wood, take his firelock, and shoot the intruder. The order was instantly obeyed; and the intrepid assailant, who for any useful result, ought to have been accompanied by a score of his comrades, fell beneath Graham's deadly aim. It was at this moment that the French skirmishers who had advanced against the main position, were falling back upon their support, and the whole of these troops were driven off by the advance of the four companies of the Coldstream guards, detached from the main position, as previously described.

In the mean time, the French infantry in the wood, finding their advance against the garden so suddenly checked, endeavoured to turn it by its left. With this view they were debouching through a large gap in the fence, forming an outlet from the wood into the orchard, when Lieut. Colonel Lord Saltoun, seizing the favourable opportunity, made a most gallant charge upon the head of the column with

* Now Lieut. General Sir Alexander Woodford, K.C.B., G.C.M.G.

the light companies of the 1st brigade of guards, and succeeded in driving the enemy back into the wood.

Shortly afterwards a large body of the enemy's light troops began to advance stealthily along the eastern hedge of the Hougomont inclosures, communicating at the same time with the infantry in the wood on their left. This was immediately followed by a direct front attack upon the orchard, which compelled Lord Saltoun gradually to withdraw his greatly reduced force, from tree to tree, until he reached the hollow-way in rear of that inclosure.

The light troops in front of Alten's division, having perceived the French creeping along the hedge so as to turn the left flank of Hougomont, were on the point of forming to oppose them, but on the latter being pointed out to the Prince of Orange, who had just come to the front to make his observations, he coolly remarked:—"No, don't stir—the Duke is sure to see that movement, and will take some step to counteract it." He had scarcely spoken, when two companies of the 3rd regiment of British guards, detached from the Allied line, were seen advancing along the same hedge, in an opposite direction, to meet them.* Lord Saltoun being thus reinforced upon his left, and the French skirmishers in his front having become exposed to a sharp flanking fire from the guards lining the eastern garden-wall, he resumed the offensive; cleared the orchard of the enemy, and re-occupied its front hedge; while the detachment on the left drove the French along the outer hedge, and down into the hollow whence they had debouched, and then joined the troops in the great orchard. The front hedge of the orchard, the front wall of the garden, with the lane and avenue on the right, constituted at this time the outer line of the defence of Hougomont.

During the progress of the contest of Hougomont, Ney had been occupied in making his preparatory dispositions for carrying into execution Napoleon's intended grand attack upon the centre and left of the Anglo-allied line.† The troops destined for this service consisted of the whole of d'Erlon's corps d'armée, and of Roussel's division of Kellermann's cavalry-corps. Their advance was to be covered

* During the earlier period of the battle, the Duke frequently gave orders to the Prince of Orange in person, for the movement and formation of the troops; but subsequently he gave these orders himself wherever they were required.

† Napoleon had given orders that the battle should commence with the above attack; but this disposition was subsequently altered, and Reille was directed to begin by attacking Hougomont.

and supported by no less than ten batteries, which were now brought forward and posted along a ridge that intervened between the French right and the Allied left wing, affording the guns a range of from 600 to 800 yards of the Duke's line. These batteries consisted of the three 12-pounder batteries of the 1st, 2nd, and 6th corps, drawn up with their left close upon the Charleroi road; of the four divisional foot-batteries; of the horse-battery belonging to Jaquinot's light cavalry-brigade; and of the two horse-batteries of Milhaud's corps of cuirassiers, which stood in second line, in rear of d'Erlon's corps—altogether 74 guns.

This imposing force of infantry, cavalry, and artillery, exclusive of the ample cavalry-reserves at hand, was not more than commensurate with the importance of the object which Napoleon had in view. His aim was not only to turn the Allied left, but also to force the centre of the position, and, by gaining possession of the farms of La Haye Sainte, and Mont St. Jean, to cut off Wellington's main line of communication by the high road to Brussels, and, at the same time, to prevent any contemplated junction of the Prussian and Anglo-allied armies. This appeared to him preferable to any plan of operation against the Allied right, where the skilful dispositions made by the Duke would require such a plan to embrace the attack and repulse of the troops occupying Braine-la-leud, and the post of Vieux Foriez, as well as the forcing of the position, *en potence*, held by Lord Hill; a consideration which, combined with a knowledge of the existence of a considerable body of Allied troops near Hal, and the fear of allowing himself to be induced into too great an extension of his own force towards his left, caused him to resign all idea of attempting any movement of importance in that quarter. He felt, moreover, that even a successful attack upon the right would, in all probability, induce the Duke to fall back upon the Prussians, and thus effect that junction which it was his great object to frustrate; whereas, an attack upon the Anglo-allied left, which was not so strong, if successful, held out to him the prospect of his being enabled, by aid of the presumed vigorous co-operation on the part of Grouchy, and the momentarily expected arrival of a portion of that Marshal's forces on his own right, to defeat both armies in detail.

The batteries had been regularly posted and fully prepared for action, and the infantry columns had advanced to the inner brow of the intervening ridge, when Ney sent word to the Emperor that the preliminary arrangements were completed, and that he only waited His Majesty's orders to commence the attack. Napoleon immediately took a general view of the field of battle, and continuing his observations beyond his right, in order to discover, if possible, any indication of the approach either of Grouchy, or of a hostile force, he perceived in the direction of St. Lambert an indistinct mass, having the appearance of a body of troops; and pointing out the object to Soult, who was near him at the time, asked his opinion; whereupon the Marshal observed, that he really conceived it to be a column on the march, and that there was great reason to believe it was a detachment from Grouchy. All the staff directed their telescopes upon the point indicated; and, as the atmosphere was not very clear, different opinions were entertained: some asserting that what had been taken for troops were trees; others that they were columns in position; whilst several agreed with Soult, that they were troops on the march. In this state of uncertainty and suspense, the Emperor sent for General Domon, and desired him to proceed instantly with a strong reconnoitring party to the right, and procure correct intelligence; to put himself quickly in communication with the troops approaching from St. Lambert; to effect a junction with them, if they belonged to Marshal Grouchy, and to impede their advance if they proved to be enemies. At the same time, the two light cavalry-divisions of Domon and Subervie proceeded some distance in the direction of the wood of Paris, and were then drawn up *en potence* to the right of the French army.

Not long after Domon's departure, Napoleon's impatience to ascertain the precise character of the distant column was relieved by the arrival of an officer of chasseurs with a Prussian hussar, who had just been taken prisoner, and who was the bearer of a letter, addressed by the Prussian General Bülow to the Duke of Wellington, to acquaint the latter with his arrival at St. Lambert. The prisoner stated that the column which was perceptible in the vicinity of this village, was the advanced guard of Bülow's corps, which had not been engaged at Ligny; that he had been in the morning at Wavre; that the three other Prussian corps were stationed close to that town, and had passed the previous night there, without perceiving any indication of an enemy in their front; and that a patrole of his own regiment had advanced, during the night, as far as two leagues from Wavre without encountering any body of French troops.

Soult who had just at that moment written the following

letter to Grouchy, in reply to his second report from Gembloux, immediately added a postscript, referring to the above intelligence, and sent off the despatch, accompanied by the intercepted communication and the hussar's report.

'Du champ de battaille de Waterloo,
le 18, à une heure après midi.

'Monieur Le Maréchal,

'Vous avez écrit ce matin, à deux heures, à l'Empereur que vous marcheriez sur Sart-à-Wallain; donc votre projet était de vous porter à Corbaix ou à Wavres: ce mouvement est conforme aux dispositions qui vous out été communiquées: cependant l'Empereur m'ordonne de vous dire que vous devez toujours manœuvrer dans notre direction; c'est à vous à voir le point où nous sommes pour vous régler en conséquence et pour lier nos communications, ainsi que pour être toujours en mesure pour tomber sur quelques troupes ennemies qui chercheraient à inquiéter notre droite, et les écraser. En ce moment la bataille est engagée sur la ligne de Waterloo. Le centre de l'armée anglaise est à Mont-Saint-Jean, ainsi manœuvrez pour joindre notre droite.

'Le Duc de Dalmatie.'

'P.S.—Une lettre qu'on vient d'intercepter porte que le Général Bulow doit attaquer notre flanc. Nous croyons apercevoir ce corps sur les hauteurs de Saint-Lambert; ainsi ne perdez pas un instant pour vous rapprocher de nous et nous joindre, et pour écraser Bulow que vous prendrez en flagrant délit.'

The above letter is of much historical importance. Although conveying Napoleon's approval of Grouchy's movement upon either Corbaix or Wavre, it clearly indicates the commencement of that anxiety and uneasiness of mind which the Emperor experienced through the fear of even the possibility of a want of just conception on the part of the Marshal, of the true spirit in which the combination of his movements with those of the main army should be carried on. He draws the Marshal's attention to the necessity of his manœuvring so as to prevent the execution of any hostile design against the right flank of the main army, which is then engaged with Wellington's forces, and names Mont St. Jean, the centre of the Duke's position, as a guiding point. This anxiety was naturally augmented very considerably by the discovery of Bülow's troops, and the postscript accordingly enjoins still more urgently, the necessity of a close and active co-operation.

Very shortly after the officer who was the bearer of this despatch had started, a message was sent in by General Domon to the effect that his scouts had fallen in with detachments from the enemy in the direction of St. Lambert, and that he had just sent out patroles towards other points to obtain intelligence of Marshal Grouchy, and to communicate with him, if practicable.

It is to be observed, however, that the troops discovered by the French cavalry did not belong to Bülow's main body, but merely to his advanced guard. The former was the mass first seen from La Belle Alliance, when it was moving across the heights of St. Lambert, on the right or opposite bank of the Lasne, but as explained in a preceding Chapter, it encountered great obstruction and much delay during its march towards the field; whilst the latter, awaiting its arrival, rested concealed in the wood of Paris, near Lasne. Thus it appears that both commanders were deceived as to the proximity of any considerable body of Prussians, at this period of the day.* Nevertheless, the conviction of such a proximity, while it imparted increased confidence to Wellington, in regard to the speedy execution of the plan of combined operation which he had preconcerted with Blücher, compelled Napoleon to employ additional vigilance and circumspection upon his right flank. Great, however, as was the necessity for such vigilance, the measures that were adopted were lamentably deficient in energy, vigour, and judgment. Considering that the main body of Bülow's corps was on the point of entering the defile of St. Lambert, in which it had to overcome the greatest difficulties, it appears unaccountable that the officer employed in reconnoitring and patroling beyond the extreme right of the French army should not have urged the occupation of the wood of Paris with a detached body of infantry, with a view to impede Bülow's advance, and compel him to take a more circuitous route. In this manner the Prussian co-operation might have been so far obstructed or delayed as to secure to Napoleon the power of advancing against Wellington with almost the entire of his force, and of thus, perhaps, accomplishing his grand object of defeating both armies in detail. No disposition of this kind was made, but, in place of it, Domon's and Subervie's light cavalry-divisions were moved to the right, *en potence* to the front line, their picquets not extending beyond the plateau in front of the wood of Paris.† Whether this culpable neglect arose from

* See page 233.

† It is even doubtful if the whole of this cavalry moved off so early as above stated. In the "Mémoires historiques de Napoléon, Livre ix." it is asserted that Domon was despatched *with* these two divisions when the distant column was first seen; but, according to the observations made by the Prussian advanced parties in front of the wood of Paris, it would appear that the cavalry in question marched off at a later period. It is further asserted by the same authority that shortly afterwards, Lobau was ordered to march with his corps to the support of the light cavalry in the vicinity of St. Lambert. This is decidedly incorrect. The advance of Lobau's corps to the right was distinctly observed from the extreme left of the Duke of Wellington's army, and from the Prussian side of the field, at a much later period of the day.

the want of due penetration and foresight on the part of General Domon, or from this officer having been instructed not to act as if in command of a detached corps, but only to take up a position, within a prescribed distance, *en potence* to the general front line, or, from an over-confident expectation on the part of Napoleon of approaching aid from Grouchy, are points not easily determined; but there can be no doubt that the error of not occupying the wood of Paris with a strong body of infantry, flanked and supported by the cavalry, was fatal to the development of Napoleon's original design. One infantry-division, combined with Domon's and Subervie's cavalry-divisions, would have sufficed for obstructing the debouching of Bülow's corps from the almost impassable defile of St. Lambert, and compelling it to move by its right, into the line of march of Zieten's corps, which did not reach the field before seven o'clock in the evening. To move by its left, along the deep and miry valley of the Lasne, would have been impracticable so long as the wood of Paris and its vicinity continued to be occupied by the French. In short, the importance of seizing upon the means that presented themselves for materially retarding, if not of completely frustrating, the co-operation of the principal portion of the Prussian forces, was of so vital a nature, that the French Emperor would have been justified in detaching the whole of Lobau's corps, along with the cavalry already mentioned, under an experienced and enterprising General, such as Lobau himself, to operate against the Prussians whilst these were occupied in passing the defiles which led to his right flank. None of those troops were engaged with the Anglo-allied army during any part of the day, so that, without diminishing the numbers actually opposed to the latter, they might have been detached in the manner suggested, instead of remaining, as was the case, drawn up *en potence* on the immediate field of action, to be attacked by the Prussians, who were permitted to pass the defiles without interruption, to collect their forces under cover of the wood of Paris, to debouch from the latter successively and at their leisure, and to organize their movements of attack in perfect security, and with the most systematic order and regularity.

CHAPTER XI.

Napoleon, having taking the precaution of posting a cavalry corps of observation upon his right flank, no longer delayed sending the order to Ney for the commencement of the grand attack upon the centre and left wing of the Anglo-allied army. About the same time, Wellington, considering that some of the battalions along the right wing of his front line were too much exposed to the enemy's cannonade, which had from the commencement been principally directed against them, and which was now conducted with increased vigour, withdrew them more under shelter of the crest of the ridge. It might then be about half-past one, or perhaps a quarter before two o'clock. The simultaneous advance of d'Erlon's four divisions of infantry, amounting to more than 16,000 men, was grand and imposing. As the heads of the columns cleared their own line of batteries ranged along the crest of the intervening ridge, and as the points on which they were directed for attack opened out to their view, loud and reiterated shouts arose from their ranks of "*Vive l'Empereur!*" which, as the masses began to descend the exterior slope of their position, were suddenly drowned in the roar produced by the discharge of seventy-four pieces of French cannon over their heads. The effects of the latter upon Picton's division, and upon Bylandt's Dutch-Belgian brigade, which, as before stated, was deployed upon the exterior slope of the Anglo-allied position, were severely felt. Light troops now issued forth from each column, and soon spread out into a line of skirmishers extending the whole length of the valley. As Donzelot's division, which was on the left, approached La Haye Sainte, one of its brigades moved out to attack that farm, while the other continued its advance on the right of the Charleroi road; and it was not long before a sharp fire of musketry along and around the hedges of the orchard of La Haye Sainte announced the first resistance to d'Erlon's formidable advance. Shortly afterwards a dropping fire commenced among the hedges and inclosures of Papelotte, La Haye, and Smohain, which were occupied by the Nassau battalions under Prince Bernhard of Saxe Weimar. The right brigade of Durutte's division was thrown out against the troops defending these inclosures, while the left brigade continued to advance across the valley, so as to form a support to Marcognet's division on its left, and, at the same time, to connect this attack with the advance of the latter against the main front line of the Allied right wing.

Durutte's skirmishers pressed boldly forward against those of Prince Bernhard's brigade; and it was not long before they succeeded in gaining possession of the farm-house of Papelotte, driving out the light company of the 3rd battalion of the 2nd regiment of Nassau, commanded by Captain Rettberg; but the latter, on being reinforced with four additional companies, resumed the offensive, and gallantly retook the farm. The contest in this quarter was now limited to a persistent skirmish, which extended itself along La Haye and Smohain, occupied by the regiment of Orange-Nassau. With this tiraillade on either flank of d'Erlon's corps, the central columns pursued their onward course, and began to ascend the exterior slope of the Allied position.

Immediately on the departure of d'Erlon's corps from the French position, Bachelu's infantry-division, which constituted the right of Reille's corps, was moved forward to the immediate height between La Bella Alliance and La Haye Sainte, (where it is intersected by the hollow-way formed by the Charleroi road,) in order to maintain that point, to be at hand as a reserve to the attacking force, and to keep up the connection between the right and left wings of the front line of the French army.

The three central columns continued their advance up the exterior slope of the Allied position. The nature of the ground still admitted of the play of the French batteries over their heads, and great was the havoc produced by this fire upon Picton's devoted ranks. As the heads of the columns neared the deployed line of Bylandt's brigade, the shouts of "*Vive l'Empereur!*" were renewed. The skirmishers in advance had scarcely opened their fire upon the brigade, in order to prepare for, and give increased effect to, the succeeding charge of the columns, when the Dutch-Belgians, who had already evinced a considerable degree of unsteadiness, began firing in their turn, but with very little effect: immediately after which they commenced a hurried retreat, not partially and promiscuously, but collectively and simultaneously—so much so, that the movement carried with it the appearance of its having resulted from a word of command. The disorder of these troops rapidly augmented; but, on their reaching the straggling hedge along the crest of the position, an endeavour was made to rally them upon the 5th battalion of Dutch militia. This attempt, however, notwithstanding the most strenuous and praiseworthy exertions on the part of the officers, completely failed. The reserve battalion and the artillerymen of Captain Byleveld's battery, though they seemed to stem the torrent for a moment, were quickly swept away by its accumulating force. As they rushed past the British columns, hissings, hootings, and execrations, were indignantly heaped upon them; and one portion, in its eagerness to get away, nearly ran over the grenadier company of the 28th British regiment, the men of which were so enraged, that it was with difficulty they could be prevented from firing upon the fugitives. Some of the men of the 1st, or Royal Scots, were also desirous of shooting them. Nothing seemed to restrain their flight, which ceased only when they found themselves completely across and covered by the main ridge along which the Anglo-allied army was drawn up. Here they continued, comparatively under shelter, during the remainder of the battle, as a reserve, in which capacity alone, considering their losses and their crippled state, they could now be rendered serviceable.

Picton, who had been calmly watching the French movements, and whose quick and practised eye detected the increasing unsteadiness and wavering disposition of the Dutch-Belgians, appeared to expect but a feeble resistance on their part; and upon his aide-de-camp, Captain Tyler,* remarking to him that he was sure they would run, he said, "Never mind; they shall have a taste of it, at all events." He had certainly not anticipated the possibility of their retiring so precipitately as they did, the moment the French came within musket-range of their ranks.†

* Lieut. Colonel John Tyler, K.H., died on the 4th June, 1842.

† The Dutch-Belgians having been posted in line on the exterior slope, where, from the circumstance of their having been the only troops of the Anglo-allied left wing so distinctly visible to the enemy, they became exposed in an especial manner to the destructive effects of the formidable array of French batteries, which continued playing over the heads of the attacking columns. The losses of Bylandt's brigade on the 16th had already thinned, and in a measure disorganised, its ranks, but those which it suffered on this occasion were terrific, and the numerous gaps that so rapidly presented themselves along the line, as well as the number of superior officers that were observed to fall, could scarcely fail to produce a prejudicial effect among these raw troops. Their confidence in their own power of resistance had also been very considerably shaken, by the circumstance of their having been deployed in a two-deep line, instead of having been allowed to assume the three-deep formation to which they had previously been accustomed. In this affair, Perponcher had two horses shot under him, Bylandt was wounded, as were also Colonel Van Zuylen van Nyefelt, Lieut. Colonel Westenberg, who commanded the 5th battalion of Dutch militia, and several other officers.

Had the British soldiers been fully aware of all these circumstances, their

Now, however, that these troops had completely cleared away to the rear, and left him no other means wherewith to brave the coming storm than could be afforded by the shattered remnants of Kempt's and Pack's brigades which had survived the sanguinary fight of Quatre-Bras, Picton immediately deployed his force, and assumed an attitude of patient but determined resistance. When the disparity in relative numbers of the assailants and defenders is considered, the attempt to make head with such odds, against the advancing masses of an enemy elated by his triumphant progress, was, it must be admitted, a daring and critical undertaking. Each brigade presented a thin two-deep line. Their united strength did not amount to more than about 3,000 men; whilst of the French force, the central attacking columns alone, which were now advancing directly upon these two brigades, consisted of nearly 12,000 men. Picton had, moreover, no infantry-reserve whatever, from which he could obtain support in case of success, or upon which he could fall back in case of disaster. He was not, however, one to be daunted by the approach of heavy columns, formidable as they might appear in point of numbers, when he could meet them with a well trained British line, though it should be but two deep, and present but a fourth of the numerical force of its opponents. It is true, that nearly all the regiments in Kempt's and Pack's brigades had lost half their numbers in the battle of the 16th; but Picton well knew that they had not lost that indomitable spirit, which, under his guidance, had immortalized them on that memorable field of battle. There, he had triumphantly led them both in line against heavy columns of infantry, and in squares against charging squadrons of cavalry. What, then, might not be achieved by such innate valour—by such consummate discipline? The entire confidence which he reposed in his men was warmly reciprocated on their part. With such a chief to lead them, they would have bravely confronted the whole French army, had it been moving in mass against them. The flight of the

feelings would assuredly not have been so greatly roused against the Dutch-Belgians as they were on this particular occasion. But they had neither time nor opportunity for reflection. They only saw the hurried and confused retreat, and this, at such a moment, would have equally exasperated them, had the troops so retiring been British. That Picton, who could perceive all that was passing along the exterior slope, should have given vent to his irritation, in the remark he made to Captain Tyler, is more surprising; but it must be borne in mind, that his habitual reliance upon his own British infantry, with which he felt that he could attempt anything, usually led him to make but little allowance for the failure or discomfiture of troops in general under almost any circumstances.

panic-stricken Dutch-Belgians produced no effect upon them beyond that of exciting their derision and contempt.

The 28th, 32nd, and 79th regiments of Kempt's brigade, when deployed, occupied a line parallel to, and about fifty yards distant from, the hedge along the Wavre road, its right resting on a high bank lining the Charleroi road, and its left terminating at a point in rear of that part of the Wavre road which begins to incline for a short distance towards the left rear. In their right front, immediately overlooking the intersection of the Charleroi and Wavre roads, stood (as before stated)* the reserve of the first battalion 95th rifles; they had two companies, under Major Leach,† posted in the sand-pit adjoining the left of the Charleroi road; and one company, under Captain Johnston,‡ at the hedge on the knoll in rear of the sand-pit. Their commanding officer, Colonel Sir Andrew Barnard, and Lieut. Colonel Cameron,§ were with these advanced companies, watching the enemy's movements. Pack's line was in left rear of Kempt's brigade, and about 150 yards distant from the Wavre road. Its left rested upon the knoll between the Wavre road and a small coppice on the reverse slope of the position; but the centre and right extended across a considerable hollow which occurs on the right of that coppice. The front of the interval between the two brigades became, after the retreat of the Dutch-Belgians, completely exposed and uncovered.

The French left central attacking column had continued its advance in a direction contiguous to, and parallel with, the high road, until the skirmishers in front were suddenly checked by the companies of the 95th British rifles posted in the sand-pit, which obstacle had hitherto been in a great measure concealed from their view by the particular formation of the ground, combined with the height of the intervening corn. Influenced by the discovery of this impediment, and by the appearance of the *abatis* upon the high road, the column inclined to the right so as to clear the sand-pit; and as their skirmishers were pressing on in that direction, the companies of the 95th became turned, and were forced to fall back upon the other company stationed along the little hedge in rear of the pit. So vigorous and effective was the fire maintained from this hedge by the British riflemen, both upon the skirmishers and upon the column itself, that the

* See page 206.

† Now Lieut. Colonel Jonathan Leach, C.B.

‡ Major William Johnston died in April, 1836.

§ Now Major General Sir Alexander Cameron, K.C.B.

latter was induced to swerve still further to the right, out of its original direction. The retreat of Bylandt's brigade having removed all impediment to the advance of the central attacking columns, the three companies of the 95th soon found themselves outflanked by the French skirmishers, and gradually retired upon their reserve. The light companies of the other regiments of Kempt's brigade, which had moved out to skirmish, fell back in like manner, accordingly as the French columns advanced. With a view to secure the left flank of the attacking force, and at the same time to connect the movements with those on the opposite side of the high road, the French presented a strong line, or rather a mass, of skirmishers, in the interval between that road and the left central column.

As the columns now rapidly approached the crest of the Anglo-allied position, the greater part of the batteries along the French ridge—that is, all those which had been cannonading that portion of the line embraced by the attack—gradually suspended their fire. The partial cessation of their thunder was immediately succeeded by loud and reiterated shouts from the columns of "*Vive l'Empereur!*" whilst at short intervals were heard the cheering exhortations of "*En avant! en avant!*" mingled with the continued roll of drums beating the "*pas de charge.*" The left central column was advancing in a direction which would have brought it in immediate contact with the right of the 28th British regiment and the left of the 79th Highlanders, and had arrived within about forty yards of the hedge lining the edge of the Wavre road, when Picton moved forward Kempt's brigade close to the hedge, where it was joined by its light companies, who came running in, followed by some of the most daring of the French skirmishers, who, however, were quickly driven back. Suddenly the column halted, and commenced a deployment to its right, the rear battalions moving out rapidly to disengage their front. Picton, seizing upon the favourable moment, ordered the brigade to fire a volley into the deploying mass, and its brief but full and condensed report had scarcely died away, when his voice was heard loudly calling "Charge! charge! Hurrah!" Answering with a tremendous shout, his devoted followers burst through the nearest of the two hedges that lined the Wavre road. In doing this their order was in some degree broken; and, when making their way through the further hedge, a fire was poured into them by such of their opponents as had their front uncovered. The enemy's skirmishers that had previously fallen back upon the flanks of the column instantly darted forward, and by their rapid and close-telling fire assisted in the endeavour to augment the apparent disorder of Kempt's line. The 79th Highlanders suffered greatly, and experienced some delay in clearing the hedges. The Ensign (Birtwhistle*) carrying the regimental colour of the 32nd, was severely wounded. Lieutenant Belcher,† who commanded the left centre subdivision, took the colour from him. In the next moment it was seized by a French officer whose horse had just been shot under him. A struggle ensued between him and Lieutenant Belcher; but, while the former was attempting to draw his sword, the covering colour-sergeant (named Switzer) gave him a thrust in the breast with his halbert, and the right-hand man of the subdivision (named Lacy) shot him, just as Brevet Major Toole,‡ commanding the right centre subdivision, called out, though too late, (for the French officer fell dead at Lieutenant Belcher's feet,) "Save the brave fellow!" The delay in crossing the hedges was but momentary; order was speedily restored; and then, levelling their bayonets, the brigade disclosed to view the glorious sight of a British line of infantry at the charge.

It was during this brief struggle that a severe and irreparable blow was inflicted upon the entire British army, and a whole nation plunged into grief and mourning for the loss of a chief, the brilliancy of whose career had so excited her admiration, and the fame of whose exploits had so exalted her pride.§ The truly brave and noble Picton was struck by a musket-ball on the right temple. His death, which was instantaneous, was first observed by the Earl of Uxbridge's aide-de-camp, Captain Horace Seymour,‖ whom he was, at the moment, desiring to rally the Highlanders. Captain Seymour, whose horse was just then falling, immediately called the attention of Picton's aide-de-camp, Captain Tyler, to the fact of the General having been wounded, and, in the next moment, the hero's lifeless corpse was, with the assistance of a private soldier of the nearest regiment, borne from off his charger by that officer. Thus fell the gallant soldier, who, as the leader of the 3rd or "fighting division" in the Peninsular

* Now Major John Birtwhistle, Unatt.

† Captain Robert Tresillian Belcher retired ftom the service on the 13th May, 1842.

‡ Major William H. Toole died on the 17th of August, 1831.

§ It is said that one of Napoleon's first inquiries, on the morning of this day, was, "*Ou est la division de Picton?*"

‖ Now Colonel Sir Horace B. Seymour, K.C.H.

war, had already acquired an imperishable renown in the history of the British army. As his life was spent in fighting the battles of his country, his death was an end suited to his stirring career. His brave spirit passed away amidst the roar and din of the bloody conflict, and his eyes closed on his last of fields in the very moment of the advance of his troops to victory.*

The French column, surprised in the midst of its attempted deployment, and appalled by the bold and determined onset of Kempt's line, appeared as if struck by a panic, fell into irremediable confusion, and fled with precipitation from its pursuers. Just as the British brigade bore down the slope, its front was partially crossed from the right by French cuirassiers, followed by the 2nd British life guards; the former, dashing in amongst their own thickly-scattered infantry-skirmishers, who threw themselves down to allow both fugitives and pursuers to ride over them, and then, in many cases, rose up and fired after the latter. But although the greater part of the cuirassiers turned about and boldly faced their opponents, whereby several isolated individual contests occurred, the 2nd life guards soon obtained the mastery, and compelled them to resume their flight, whilst the 95th rifles speedily closed upon the disordered mass of infantry through which this portion of the cavalry had passed, and amongst which the greatest confusion and consternation prevailed. Many flew wildly they scarcely knew whither; others delivered themselves up; and several were seized as prisoners.

On its right, the brigade was supported in the charge by the 1st light battalion of the King's German legion, which crossed over for that purpose from the opposite side of the high road.

Immediately after passing through the hedge, the extreme left of the 28th regiment had unexpectedly found itself almost in contact with a well-formed French column still advancing

* What nobler instance of patriotism could be afforded than the fact, that in order to secure his being present at the great battle which he foresaw would take place, he concealed from every one the circumstance of his having been wounded at Quatre-Bras. This was not discovered until his corpse was laid out at Brussels, shortly after the action. It then appeared that the skin, on one side, just above the hip, was raised into a very large bladder, and distended with a mass of coagulated blood, unaccompanied by any abrasion. It had evidently been occasioned by the action of a round shot, causing extensive contusion, and its very dark colour showed that the wound must have occurred previously to the 18th of June. Such was Picton; such his stern sense of duty; such his boundless zeal for the honour of his profession; such his complete devotion to the cause of his sovereign and country!

against the Allied position. The right wing of the regiment was too deeply engaged with the column directly before it to admit of its attention being drawn off to any other quarter; but the left wing, having a clearer front, boldly brought forward its right shoulders, thus detaching itself from the right wing, and fired into the left flank of the advancing column at the very moment when the head of the latter was charged by the right regiment (the Royals) of Ponsonby's brigade of heavy cavalry. Kempt, becoming aware of the prolongation of the French attack along the line to his left, and of the consequently exposed state of this flank, and possessing no infantry-support or reserve of any kind, felt himself under the necessity of restraining his men from further pursuit, and ordered the brigade to halt and re-form. The left wing of the 28th, however, having its whole attention fixed upon the column charged by the Royals, followed these dragoons some distance down the slope, and assisted them in securing a great number of prisoners, after which it fell back, and rejoined the right wing of the regiment. The 95th rifles continued advancing, and driving the French skirmishers before them, beyond the knoll by the sand-pit.

From this extremely gallant and most decisive attack by Kempt's brigade, we must proceed to describe the no less brilliant charges performed by both Somerset's and Ponsonby's cavalry-brigades; but to afford a more ready comprehension of this period of the action, it will be necessary, in the first instance, to revert to the attack and defence of La Haye Sainte.

The French skirmishers thrown out by the left brigade of Donzelot's division advanced boldly and resolutely against the orchard of La Haye Sainte. The first shot tore away the bridle of Major Baring's horse close to his hand, and the second killed Major Bösewiel, the next in command. The three companies of the 2nd light battalion of the King's German legion, which, as before stated, were posted in the orchard, together with two companies of the 1st light battalion of the King's German legion under Captains Wynecken* and Goeben,† and a company of Hanoverian riflemen under Major Spörken, which were extended on the right of the farm, presented a gallant resistance to the enemy; but the latter continued to press forward with superior force, and the main body of the French brigade having formed two columns of attack, which were rapidly advancing, one into the orchard,

* Now Lieut. Colonel Christian Wynecken, K.H. in the Hanoverian service.

† Captain Augustus Alexander von Goeben was killed in this battle.

and the other towards the buildings, Major Baring fell back with his men upon the barn. At this moment, Colonel Klencke reached the farm with the Lüneburg field-battalion, which Wellington, on observing the French advance, had detached from the left of Kielmansegge's brigade as a reinforcement to the troops at La Haye Sainte. Baring immediately endeavoured to recover the orchard, and had already made the enemy give way, when he perceived a strong line of cuirassiers forming in right front of the inclosure. At the same time, Lieut. Meyer* came to report to him that the enemy had surrounded the garden in which his company was posted, and that it had become no longer tenable. Baring ordered him to fall back into the buildings, and to assist in their defence. The skirmishers upon the right, on the sudden appearance of the cavalry, ran in upon the orchard to collect together, but coming in contact with the newly-arrived Hanoverians, the latter got into disorder; and the effect produced by the sight of the advancing line of cuirassiers in their front, as also by the shouts of the French infantry gaining possession of the garden in their rear, was such, that notwithstanding all Baring's exertions to halt and collect his men, the whole of these troops betook themselves to an indiscriminate flight towards the main position of the Allied army, a course which they seemed to imagine constituted their only chance of safety. They were speedily undeceived. The cavalry overtook them in the midst of their confused retreat, rode over, sabred, and still further dispersed them; whilst, to add to the severity of their loss, they became exposed, after the cavalry had passed on, to a flank fire from the enemy's infantry lining the hedge of the garden. A portion of them succeeded in gaining the main position, whilst the remainder, securing themselves in the buildings, augmented the little garrison under Lieuts. Carey† and Græme,‡ and Ensign Frank,§ who bravely and successfully maintained possession in defiance of the vigorous attacks on the part of the French light troops. The Lüneburg Hanoverian battalion, however, suffered most severely: many were killed and wounded; among the latter was the commanding officer, Lieut. Colonel Klencke, and among the prisoners

* Now Captain Charles Meyer, in the Hanoverian service.

† Now Captain Thomas Carey, K.H., on the retired list of the Hanoverian service.

‡ Now Major George Drummond Græme, K.H., in the Hanoverian service.

§ Now Captain George Frank, K.H., on the retired list of the Hanoverian service.

taken was Major Dachenhausen. Some on the left saved themselves by a precipitate retreat into the high road. The few that were collected together again during the remainder of the day constituted but a very insignificant portion of the original strength of the battalion.

The Earl of Uxbridge, on perceiving the advance of the French cavalry by La Haye Sainte, on the British right of the Charleroi road, (the same alluded to as having dispersed the Hanoverian Lüneburg battalion and Baring's skirmishers of the legion,) as also the approach of the infantry-columns which constituted the attack upon the Allied left wing on the opposite side of that road, decided upon a simultaneous charge by the heavy cavalry-brigades of Lord Edward Somerset and Sir William Ponsonby; the former against the enemy's cavalry, the latter against his masses of infantry. The resolution was scarcely formed when he proceeded to carry it into instant execution. Riding up to Lord Edward Somerset, he ordered him to prepare to form line, keeping the Blues in support: and galloping on to Ponsonby's brigade on the opposite side of the high road, he ordered that officer to wheel into line as soon as he saw the other brigade do so, and to hold the Scots Greys in support. He then returned to the household-brigade, and immediately put the whole in motion.

As this was the first grand attack made by the French on that day in fair open field, Lord Uxbridge felt very desirous, in meeting it, to establish, if possible, the superior prowess of the British cavalry, and thus to inspire it with confidence, and cause it to be held in respect by its opponents. He, therefore, with a view to excite the courage and heighten the enthusiasm of his followers, led the advance in person, placing himself in front of the left of Somerset's brigade, so as to be at about the centre of the line when the brigades should unite, on the continuation of the advance, in front of the Allied position. Nobly and faithfully did these brave dragoons fulfil his anxious expectations.

For the purpose of ensuring efficient support to his cavalry attacks, Lord Uxbridge had, before the commencement of the battle, intimated to the generals of brigade that as he could not be present everywhere to give orders, he expected they would always take upon themselves to conform to, and support, offensive movements in their front; and having on this occasion light cavalry-brigades on either flank of the charging force, he felt in a great degree justified in placing himself in front line, particularly as he had assigned to each of the advancing brigades its own immediate support. Though greatly palliated by the adoption of these precautionary measures, this was perhaps not altogether a prudent act on the part of the commander of the entire cavalry of an army; since, in the charge of an extended line of cavalry against an enemy close at hand, the *carrière* once begun, the leader becomes so completely identified and mixed up with that line itself, that his virtual command is rapidly limited to that of a squadron-officer; whereas, when accompanying a *second* line, he is enabled to draw off, or reinforce, as circumstances may render expedient. His eager desire, however, to render this first charge a brilliant affair, combined with his own chivalric nature, led him to assume the post of honour and of danger, in order to animate by his example as a bold and determined soldier. At the same time, he trusted to the dispositions he had already made, and to the alertness of his brigadiers, for due support to his attack, but which, from fortuitous circumstances, as will be seen by the sequel, was not forthcoming at the moment it was most urgently required.

The French line of cavalry, as it advanced, presented an imposing appearance. These veteran warriors bore with them an air of confident superiority and anticipated triumph, joined with a sort of *gaieté de cœur*, inspired no doubt by the reflection that they were about to encounter and overthrow their most implacable enemies, the British. Their advance, like that of the infantry on their right, had been to a certain extent triumphant; and, as the flight of the Dutch-Belgians had led that infantry to imagine that victory was already within its grasp, so the dispersion of the Hanoverians was hailed by these dragoons as a happy prelude to their grand attack. They had now ascended the brow of the ridge on which the Anglo-allied infantry was posted, prepared for their reception: a vigorous fire was opened upon them by the four guns of Ross's British horse-battery on the right of the high road, as also by Lloyd's British foot-battery still further to the right; but a few seconds sufficed to restore the order of their advance: in the next moment their trumpets sounded the charge; when, amidst shouts of "*Vive l'Empereur!*" this gallant line, glittering in all the splendour reflected from burnished helmet and cuirass, rushed on to the attack. On the other hand, the British household-brigade, presenting a beautiful line, and animated by an equal degree of enthusiasm, had already been put into charging speed; and just as the cuirassiers came close upon the squares, and received a fire from their front faces, the two lines dashed into each other with indescribable impetuosity. The shock was terrific. The British, in order to close as much as possible upon the cuirassiers, whose swords were much longer, and whose bodies were encased in steel, whilst their own were without such defence, seemed for a moment striving to wedge themselves in between the horses of their infuriated antagonists. Swords gleamed high in air with the suddenness and rapidity of the lightning-flash, now clashing violently together, and now clanging heavily upon resisting armour; whilst with the din of the battle-shock were mingled the shouts and yells of the combatants. Riders vainly struggling for mastery quickly fell under the deadly thrust or the well-delivered cut. Horses, plunging and rearing, staggered to the earth, or broke wildly from their ranks. But desperate and bloody as was the struggle, it was of brief duration. The physical superiority of the British, aided by transcendant valour, was speedily made manifest; and the cuirassiers, notwithstanding their most gallant and resolute resistance, were driven down from off the ridge, which they had ascended only a few minutes before with all the pride and confidence of men accustomed and determined to overcome every obstacle. This first collision at the charge did not occur, however, throughout the entire extent of the opposing lines. Somerset's line was not parallel to that of the cuirassiers, and as its right was thrown somewhat forward, this came first in contact with the enemy, and the collision, in consequence of the rapidity of the charge on both sides, followed in instantaneous succession in the direction of the Allied left until intercepted in its further progress by a natural obstruction consisting of the hollow-way through which the cross-road leads into the Charleroi road. The cuirassiers on the right of the French line were suddenly thrown out of their speed by coming unexpectedly on this hollow-way, into which they consequently descended abruptly and confusedly; and as they began to urge their horses up the opposite bank, they beheld the 2nd British life guards, which formed the left of Somerset's brigade, in full speed towards them. All idea of resistance, in such a situation, was abandoned as hopeless. They immediately filed away down this hollow-way to their right, and struck across the Charleroi road into the field in front of the 95th British rifles, followed by the 2nd life guards, who were in equal disorder from having to pick their way as they best could down the steep banks adjoining the intersection of the two roads. These cuirassiers, after having rushed in upon the French infantry-skirmishers, thickly and confusedly congregated in that quarter, reined in their steeds, and fronting their pursuers, engaged them individually in hand to hand combat.* They were soon, however, made sensible of their inferiority in this species of contest, and either submitted to the victors, or fled with precipitation; whilst at the same time, Kempt's brigade was charging gloriously down the exterior slope of the Allied position, and closing upon the infantry with which these horsemen had become intermingled, in the manner previously described.†

No sooner did Ponsonby perceive the household-cavalry in motion, than in pursuance of the orders he had received, he led on his own brigade; but not being sufficiently aware of the state of affairs on the opposite side of the Wavre road, and not wishing to launch his line against the enemy's masses until the favourable moment had arrived, he commanded a temporary halt, and rode up to the hedge, in order that he might, by personal observation, ensure the correct timing of the charge. He was accompanied by Colonel Muter, commanding the Inniskilling dragoons, whom he desired to return, and place himself in front of the centre squadron, and to order and conduct the movement, the moment he should observe him hold up his cocked-hat as a signal. It is necessary to remark that the Scots Greys, who stood in support some short time previously to this advance, just where the enemy's round shot, after passing over the ridge in front, descended in quick succession and occasioned some losses in their ranks, were ordered to some lower ground in left rear of the other two regiments, which new position they had scarcely reached when the latter were advanced, as above, and the Greys immediately conformed to this movement.

During the advance of Alix's French division, (the 1st,) its rear brigade, which consisted of the 54th and 55th regiments,

* Among the combatants on this part of the field was one whose prowess acquired for him considerable reputation. This was Corporal Shaw, of the 2nd life guards, a noted pugilist, possessing great physical strength, combined with the most resolute courage. When in the midst of the cuirassiers, he rendered himself conspicuous by the bold and dexterous manner in which he encountered all who came in his way. Rapid and deadly were the blows which he dealt around him, and it is said that no less than nine of his opponents were laid prostrate within an incredibly short space of time. His career, however, was suddenly cut short. A cuirassier, who had proceeded some little distance, so as to clear the left of the 2nd life guards, turned round, and taking a very deliberate aim with his carbine, deprived Shaw of that life which his powerful arm and gallant daring had made proof against the swords of all who ventured to approach him.

† See p. 254.

inclined to its right, moved out of the mass, and formed two columns, of two battalions each, in support, *en échelon* to the leading brigade, consisting of the 28th and 105th regiments. In like manner, the rear brigade of Marcognet's division, (the 3rd,) consisting of the 21st and 46th regiments broke into two columns of two battalions each, in support, *en échelon* to, but more immediately in rear of, the leading brigade, consisting of the 25th and 45th regiments.

While Kempt's brigade was bravely charging down the slope on the right, the heads of the leading brigades of Alix's and Marcognet's divisions, with conspicuous gallantry, and amidst shouts of triumph, crowned the crest of the Allied position on the left, crossing the Wavre road and the straggling hedge, by which their order had been in some degree disturbed. Alix's leading brigade, having passed clear of Kempt's left, found itself unopposed by infantry, in its front, but the head of Marcognet's column, after passing close by the right of Captain Rettberg's Hanoverian foot-battery, from which it had received a very destructive fire, during its advance, beheld a short but compact line of Highlanders directly in its front. This was the remnant of the 92nd regiment, which had so gallantly fought, and so greatly suffered, at Quatre-Bras. It did not at that moment consist of more than 230 men, whilst the opposing column numbered about 2000. Pack, who was in front of the 92nd, on seeing the head of the French column making its way through the hedge, resolved in his own mind that not a moment must be allowed to it for observation and reflection, as otherwise the French would succeed in establishing themselves in great force on the summit of the British position. He instantly decided upon a measure, which, in daring and determination, was fully commensurate with the emergency of the occasion. Addressing himself to the Highlanders, he said, in an energetic tone, "92nd, you must charge—all in front of you have given way!" With loud cheers, and under the animating sounds of their native pibroch, the 92nd moved steadily on with the noble mien and gallant bearing of men bent upon upholding at any sacrifice, the honour and glory of their country. That portion of the French column which had by this time crossed the hedge was in perfect order, and presented a bold and determined front. As the 92nd approached the column, it received from it a fire, which, however, it did not return, but continued to advance steadily until it had arrived within twenty or thirty yards distance, when the head of the French column appeared panic-struck, and facing about in the greatest confusion, endeavoured to escape; the Highlanders, at the same moment, throwing into the mass a concentrated fire, most destructive in its effects. The 92nd immediately charged; but at this very moment Ponsonby's brigade came up. Colonel Muter had just before perceived the raised cocked-hat,* when he instantly ordered and conducted the advance of the brigade. It will be recollected that the Scots Greys had been ordered to support the Royals and Inniskillings; but having as was before explained, moved down into lower ground on the left, to get more under cover from the enemy's cannonade, and subsequently advanced in left rear, of those two regiments, they beheld in their direct front the head of Marcognet's division establishing itself on the height. Their course from that moment was obvious. They soon got up into line, or nearly so, with the remainder of the brigade, and joined in the general charge. Upon Ponsonby's brigade coming up with the infantry, it passed through the latter as well and as quickly as it could: in some instances intervals were made for the dragoons by the wheeling of companies; in others, by that of subdivisions or of sections: but generally the passage was effected in rather an irregular manner; and under the circumstances this was unavoidable. Of the remaining regiments of Pack's brigade, the 44th, which formed the left, having its front covered by Best's Hanoverians, remained in support, on the summit or knoll, immediately above, and on the left of, the hollow in which the rest of the brigade had been posted. The 1st Royal Scots, and the 42nd Highlanders on the right of the 92nd, moved forward immediately after the advance by the latter, and crossing the hedge, assisted Ponsonby's cavalry in securing prisoners.

As the Scots Greys passed through, and mingled with the Highlanders, the enthusiasm of both corps was extraordinary. They mutually cheered. "Scotland for ever!" was their war-shout. The smoke in which the head of the French column was enshrouded had not cleared away, when the Greys dashed into the mass. So eager was the desire, so strong the determina-

* This signal was not made by Sir William Ponsonby himself, but by his aide-de-camp Major Evans, (now Major General Sir De Lacy Evans, K.C.B.; Lieut. General in the Spanish service.) The former was mounted on a secondary untrained horse, which became restive, and startled by the fire and noise that prevailed at the very moment the general had decided upon advancing the brigade. His cloak being loose, flew off; and he dismounted for an instant for the purpose of restoring it to its place, and it was while he was thus engaged that he directed Major Evans to make the signal in question.

tion, of the Highlanders to aid their compatriots in completing the work so gloriously begun, that many were seen holding on by the stirrups of the horsemen, while all rushed forward, leaving none but the disabled in their rear. The leading portion of the column soon yielded to this infuriated onset; the remainder, which was yet in the act of ascending the exterior slope, appalled by the sudden appearance of cavalry at a moment when, judging by the sound of musketry-fire in front, they had naturally concluded that it was with infantry alone they had to contend, were hurled back in confusion by the impetus of the shock. The dragoons, having the advantage of the descent, appeared to mow down the mass, which, bending under the pressure, quickly spread itself outwards in all directions. Yet, in that mass were many gallant spirits, who could not be brought to yield without a struggle; and these fought bravely to the death; not that they served to impede, but only to mark more strongly the course of the impetuous torrent as it swept wildly past them, presenting to the eye of the artistic observer those streaks which, arising incidentally from such partial and individual contests, invariably characterize the track of a charge of cavalry. Within that mass too, was borne the imperial eagle of the 45th regiment, proudly displaying on its banner the names of Austerlitz, Jena, Friedland, Essling, and Wagram—fields in which this regiment had covered itself with glory, and acquired the distinguished title of "The Invincibles."* A devoted band encircled the sacred standard, which attracted the observation, and excited the ambition of a daring and adventurous soldier, named Ewart, a serjeant of the Greys. After a desperate struggle, evincing on his part great physical strength combined with extraordinary dexterity, he succeeded in capturing the cherished trophy. The gallant fellow was directed to proceed with it to Brussels, where he was received with acclamations by thousands who came forward to welcome and congratulate him.†

Without pausing for a moment to re-form, those of the Greys who had forced their way through, or on either flank of, the mass, rushed boldly onward against the leading supporting column of Marcognet's right brigade. This body of men, lost in amazement at the suddenness, the wildness, of the charge, and its terrific effects upon their countrymen on the higher ground in front, had either not taken advantage of

* This eagle now adorns the chapel of Chelsea Hospital.

† Early in the following year, Serjeant Ewart was appointed to an Ensigncy in the 3rd Royal Veteran battalion.

the very few moments that had intervened, by preparing an effectual resistance to cavalry, or, if they attempted the necessary formation, did so when there was no longer time for its completion. Their outer files certainly opened a fire which proved very destructive to their assailants; but to such a degree had the impetus of the charge been augmented by the rapidly increasing descent of the slope, that these brave dragoons possessed as little of the power as of the will to check their speed, and they plunged down into the mass with a force that was truly irresistible. Its foremost ranks driven back with irrepressible violence, the entire column tottered for a moment, and then sank under the overpowering wave. Hundreds were crushed to rise no more; and hundreds rose again but to surrender to the victors; who speedily swept their prisoners to the rear, while the Highlanders secured those taken from the leading column.

Along the remainder of the line, the charge of the "Union brigade" was equally brilliant and successful. On the right, the Royal dragoons, by inclining somewhat to their left, during the advance, brought their centre squadron to bear upon the head of the leading column of Alix's division, which had crossed the hedges lining the Wavre road, and being unchecked, was rapidly advancing across the crest of the ridge. Suddenly its loud shouts of triumph ceased as it perceived the close approach of cavalry up the interior slope of the Anglo-allied position. Whether it was actuated by a consciousness of danger from the disorder necessarily occasioned in its rear by the passage through the banked-up hedges, by a dread of being caught in the midst of any attempt to assume a formation better adapted for effective resistance, or of being entirely cut off from all support, it is difficult to decide, but the head of this column certainly appeared to be seized with a panic. Having thrown out an irregular and scattering fire, which served only to bring down about twenty of the dragoons, it instantly faced about, and endeavoured to regain the opposite side of the hedges. The Royals, however, were slashing in amongst them before this object could be effected. The rear ranks of the column, still pressing forward, and unconscious of the obstruction in front, now met those that were hurled back upon them, down the exterior slope, by the charge of the Royals, who continued pressing forward against both front and flanks of the mass. The whole was in a moment so jammed together as to have become perfectly helpless. Men tried in vain to use their muskets, which were either jerked out of their hands, or discharged at random, in the attempt. Gradually, a scattering flight from the rear loosened the unmanageable mass, which now rolled back helplessly along its downward course. Many brave spirits, hitherto pent up in the midst of the throng, appeared disposed to hazard a defiance; and amongst these the swords of the Royals dealt fearful havoc: many threw down their arms, and gave themselves up in despair, and these were hurried off by the conquerors to the rear of the British line.

The 28th French regiment,* which formed a direct support to the 105th regiment,* comprising the column thus attacked, though astounded by the scene before it, and almost driven back by the panic-stricken fugitives, still retained a considerable semblance of order. Amidst the crowd that was now precipitating itself on this supporting column, to seek its shelter and protection, was an officer, the bearer of the eagle of the 105th regiment. This standard, on which were inscribed the victories of Jena, Eylau, Eckmuhl, Essling, and Wagram, was accompanied at the moment by a party apparently forming a guard for its defence. Captain Clark,† commanding the centre squadron of the Royals, on discovering the group, instantly gave the order "Right shoulders forward—attack the colour!" and led directly upon the eagle himself. On reaching it, he ran his sword through the body of the standard-bearer, who immediately fell, and the eagle dropped across the head of Captain Clark's horse. He endeavoured to catch it with his left hand, but could only touch the fringe of the colour, and it would probably have fallen to the gruond, and have been lost in the confusion of the moment, had it not been saved by Corporal Stiles, who, having been standard-coverer, and therefore posted immediately in rear of the squadron-leader, came up at the instant, on Captain Clark's left, and caught the colour as it struck, in falling, against his own horse's neck.‡

So great were the confusion and dismay created in the

* These two regiments, consisting of two battalions each, constituted the left brigade of Alix's division, commanded by General Quiot.

† Now Colonel Alexander Kennedy Clark Kennedy, C.B., K.H., Unatt.

‡ As a reward for this distinguished service, Lieut. Colonel Clark has since been appointed a Companion of the Order of the Bath. Upon receiving the eagle from Corporal Stiles, he vainly endeavoured to break it off from the pole, with the intention of placing it in the breast of his coat, in order to secure it, whilst in the midst of the enemy's troops. Seeing this, Corporal Stiles remarked, "Pray, sir, do not break it;" whereupon Colonel Clark said, "Very well, carry it to the rear as fast as you can—it belongs to me." This eagle has also been deposited in Chelsea Hospital.

Corporal Stiles was appointed, in the following year, to an Ensigncy in the 6th West India regiment.

second column by the rush towards it of the disorganized remnant of the leading body, mixed up as it were with the dragoons, still pressing eagerly forward, as also by the signal overthrow of the columns on their right by the Inniskillings, that the entire mass speedily yielded to the pressure, and commenced a disorderly flight, pursued by the Royals to the foot of the valley by which the two positions were divided.

The Inniskillings, forming the centre regiment of the brigade, did not come quite so soon into contact with the French infantry as did the flank regiments. The columns in their immediate front were the two formed by the 54th and 55th French regiments, of two battalions each, which as previously explained, advanced in support, and in right rear, of Alix's leading brigade. Only the left, and part of the centre, squadron of the Inniskillings had to pass through British infantry as they advanced; the front of the right squadron was clear. The Irish "*hurrah!*" loud, wild, and shrill, rent the air, as the Inniskillings, bursting through the hedge and bounding over the road, dashed boldly down the slope towards the French columns, which were about a hundred yards distant; an interval that imparted an additional impetus to their charge, and assisted in securing for it a result equally brilliant with that obtained by the other two regiments. The right and centre squadrons bore down upon the 55th French regiment; while the left squadron alone charged the 54th regiment. These two columns, like those on their right and left, were not allowed time to recover from their astonishment at the unexpected, sudden, and vehement charge of cavalry launched against them. A feeble and irregular fire was the only attempt they made to avert the impending danger. In the next instant the dragoons were amongst them, plying their swords with fearful swiftness and dexterity, and cleaving their way into the midst of the masses, which, rolling back, and scattering outwards, presented an extraordinary scene of confusion. In addition to the destruction effected by this regiment, the number of prisoners which it secured was immense.*

* Just as the Inniskillings were on the point of advancing across the Wavre road to charge, an individual in plain clothes, on their left, called out, "Now's your time!" This was the late Duke of Richmond, who was induced by his intimacy with the Duke of Wellington, and the interest which he naturally felt in the progress of the campaign, to repair to the field of battle; not in a military capacity, for he held no rank in the army, but merely *en amateur*. He was accompanied by his son, the present Lord William Lennox, then a Cornet in the Blues, and extra aide-de-camp to Major General Maitland. Lord William had,

The household-brigade continued its charge down the slope on the right, and partly on the left, of La Haye Sainte, with the most distinguished gallantry and success; and bringing their right shoulders forward, the 1st life-guards pressed severely on the rear of the cuirassiers, as a very considerable portion of them rushed tumultuously towards that part of the high road beyond the orchard of La Haye Sainte which lies between high banks, and which was thus completely choked up with the fugitives. Many of those who found their retreat so seriously impeded, again faced their opponents, and a desperate hand-to hand contest ensued, which, however, was suddenly terminated by a destructive fire, poured down upon the 1st life-guards from the top of the banks, by the light troops of Bachelu's division, that crowned the heights through which the road has been excavated. The King's dragoon guards, leaving this struggle on their right, and rattling across the *pavé*, boldly ascended the enemy's position. They were joined on their left, by the 2nd life-guards, whose course had been by the left of La Haye Sainte. With these were now mingled Royals and Inniskillings, while further to the left were the Greys—the whole line, without even any semblance of regularity, madly pursuing their wild career, as if intoxicated with the excess of triumph. Then it was that Lord Uxbridge, who had so gallantly led the charge in person, and incited all by his example, eagerly sought for the support on which he had confidently calculated, when, to his great surprise and mortification, he discovered that there was none at hand. Ponsonby's own immediate support, which Lord Uxbridge himself had ordered to be

a few days before the battle, met with a violent accident, by a fall from his horse in the park of Enghien: his right arm was severely fractured, the sight of his right eye destroyed, and his life despaired of; but hearing, when on the sick list at Brussels, that his brother aide-de-camp, Captain Lord James Hay, had been killed at Quatre-Bras, he decided on accompanying his father to the field on the 18th. Here he presented himself to General Maitland, who, however, would not permit his lordship to remain with him, deeming a boy of fifteen, with a maimed arm, bandaged eye, and weak frame of body, but ill calculated to prove an efficient aide-de-camp. Lord William then joined his father, who rode about the field, unmindful of the frequently heavy fire to which he became exposed, conversing with his friends, and passing his remarks as if on actual service. After witnessing the brilliant cavalry-charge on the left, his Grace proceeded towards the right, but finding the fire had become very heavy, and the ground strewed with the slain, he and his son returned leisurely to Brussels. Two other members of the noble house of Lennox were present on the field, and distinguished themselves by their zeal and efficiency as staff-officers—Captain the Earl of March, (the present Duke of Richmond,) who was extra aide-de-camp to his Royal Highness the Prince of Orange, and Lieutenant Lord George Lennox, who was aide-de-camp to the Duke of Wellington (retired from the service, as Lieut. Colonel, in July, 1832.)

formed by the Greys, had necessarily been employed in front line, on the left, in the manner described; a fact of which, from his own position as leader of that line, he had been quite unaware. The direct support of Somerset's brigade, consisting of the Blues, had, during the charge, come up with, and joined, the front line. The regiment was kept well in hand, and, by its comparatively good order, facilitated the drawing off of the remainder of that brigade from further pursuit. But it was on the left of the high road, in rear of Ponsonby's line, that support was most needed. His Lordship could not account for the circumstance of neither of the light cavalry-brigades, posted on the extreme left, having come up in support of Ponsonby's advance, in conformity with the general instructions conveyed to his brigadiers on the subject of affording mutual support. The fact is, that Vandeleur's brigade, which was the nearest, was then in motion for the purpose of affording its aid, but its progress was unfortunately impeded by its having previously to make a retrograde movement in order to pass a hollow-way which separated it from the troops on the right. In vain did Lord Uxbridge sound to halt and rally—neither voice nor trumpet was heeded. In a few seconds more, the advanced line was seen crowning the enemy's position. The King's dragoon guards were suddenly exposed to a severe fire from the batteries and from Bachelu's columns of infantry on their right; and perceiving a strong and well formed body of cuirassiers on the point of advancing from the hollow beyond the ridge they had so rashly ascended, they, with such of the Royals and Inniskillings as had joined them, at length commenced a hasty retreat. The Greys, along with many of the Royals and Inniskillings, dashed in amongst the batteries, and then, wheeling sharply to their left, rode along the line of cannon in that direction, sabring the gunners and stabbing the horses, until they became sensible of the approach of a body of French laucers moving down obliquely from the left upon the arena of this memorable conflict. They now fell back, but, with their horses blown amd exhausted, it was not long before they were overtaken by the lancers. These formed the advance of Jaquinot's light cavalry-brigade, which had been unaccountably remiss in not having afforded a prompt and close support to the attacking columns of infantry.

Both the British heavy cavalry-brigades were now in full retreat. Somerset's regained the position without any serious molestation, but Ponsonby's dragoons, particularly the

Greys, who were upon the extreme left, suffered severely from Jaquinot's lancers and chasseurs, the greater part of them being in a state of the utmost confusion and exhaustion, whilst the latter were infinitely superior in numerical force, were in good order, and mounted on horses perfectly fresh. On their right the lancers charged in open column; the remainder, extending in open lancer-order towards their left, rapidly spread over the plain, darting upon the stragglers and wounded of the British cavalry who came within their reach; and, at the same time, giving confidence to such of their own scattered infantry as were still retreating in disorder and confusion.

At length, the support so greatly needed by Ponsonby's brigade arrived upon its left flank. Vandeleur, having passed the hollow-way and ravine which intercepted his progress towards the scene of action, had reached that part of the crest of the position occupied by Best's Hanoverian brigade, through which it now advanced to the front in open column of divisions. The 12th light dragoons, being the leading regiment, moved quickly down the slope: the 16th regiment remained higher up the acclivity; while the 11th were drawn up in reserve upon the brow of the hill. The 12th and 16th wheeled into line to their right. Lieut. Colonel the Hon. Frederick Ponsonby, who commanded the 12th, perceiving the confusion that prevailed amidst the French infantry in the valley, as also the extremely critical situation of a great number of scattered red-coated dragoons nearly on the crest of the French position, instantly charged a mass of unsteady infantry which intervened between him and these dragoons. This infantry comprised the rearmost supporting column of Marcognet's division, and was the only one of the attacking columns yet intact. It was now destined to share their fate. Already alarmed by the disorder into which the entire of the infantry on its left had been thrown, and now attacked so suddenly and unexpectedly on its right, it was penetrated by the charge of the 12th. These dragoons having forced their way through the column, whereby their order was naturally much broken, came upon the right flank of the lancers who were in pursuit of Ponsonby's brigade. Quickening their speed, they dashed in amongst the French cavalry, and acting almost perpendicularly upon their flank, they 'rolled up' such as were immediately in their front. The 16th light dragoons, with Vandeleur at their head, very gallantly charged obliquely upon the front of the lancers, whose further advance was completely checked by this double attack. On their extreme right, the 16th rather clashed with some of the retiring dragoons, but the two regiments, carrying every thing before them, succeeded in driving the French light cavalry down again to the foot of the valley, which they had been ordered, previously to their charge, not to pass. Some few of both the 12th and 16th did, nevertheless, madly rush up the opposite height, where, by this time, fresh troops had arrived, who made them suffer for their temerity.

Ghigny's Dutch-Belgian light cavalry brigade, which had, at the commencement of this cavalry-attack, crossed the Charleroi road, came up, in the mean time, to the brow of the main position, on the left of Vandeleur's brigade. One of its regiments, the 4th light dragoons, went down the slope, following the 12th light dragoons; and after experiencing the effects of a brisk fire which was kept up by Durutte's skirmishers from behind a bank and hedge, low down the slope, and from which the 12th light dragoons had previously suffered, it assisted in completing the dispersion of the French infantry. The other regiment (the 8th hussars) remained a few minutes upon the height, and then advanced to draw off the retiring cavalry.

Vivian, who had come forward in person from the extreme left, and proceeded some way down the slope for the purpose of making his observations, upon perceiving Ponsonby's brigade charging in disorder up the French heights, immediately sent back word for the 10th and 18th British hussars to move through the hollow-way to their right, leaving the remaining regiment of his brigade, the 1st hussars of the King's German legion, to keep a look-out to the left. Very shortly afterwards, two guns detached in advance from his horse-battery, drew up on the brow of the main ridge, but had scarcely opened a fire when a well-directed shot from one of the French batteries passed through the ammunition-boxes of one of the limbers, causing an explosion, which drew forth a shout of triumph on the part of the French artillerymen. The charge of Vandeleur's brigade having succeeded, without the active aid of even its own immediate support, the 11th light dragoons, the further advance of the 10th and 18th hussars was not required, but they continued in their new position, on the right of the lane leading to Verd-cocou, and the two guns rejoined their battery.

Major Whinyates's rocket-troop, having been brought up to the crest of the main ridge, from its previous position in reserve near Mont St. Jean, its rocket-sections were moved down to the foot of the exterior slope, whence they discharged several rockets at the French troops then formed, or in the act of re-forming, upon the opposite heights. Immediately after the execution of this service, which was gallantly and skilfully conducted, the troop rejoined its guns on the crest of the position.

In the general mêlée which resulted from the charge of the British heavy dragoons, and the overthrow of such masses of infantry, augmented as it was by the subsequent charges of, firstly, the French lancers, and, then, the two regiments of British light cavalry, severe losses were sustained on both sides; and the British army was deprived of some of its brightest ornaments. The gallant leader of the "Union brigade," when endeavouring to return to the Allied position, after using the most strenuous but fruitless exertions to restrain his men in their wild pursuit, and to withdraw them from a contest in which they had already gained undying fame, became a sacrifice to his chivalrous and patriotic zeal. Intercepted by a party of the lancers in the soft ground of a newly ploughed field, out of which his exhausted steed had not the power to extricate itself, he fell beneath their deadly thrusts. Sir William Ponsonby had highly distinguished himself as a cavalry officer in Spain; and, independently of his merits as a soldier, which were justly appreciated by the whole service, his amiable disposition and private virtues endeared him to all his brother officers. His equally gallant namesake, Colonel the Hon. Frederick Ponsonby, immediately after his brilliant charge with the 12th light dragoons, first through a column of infantry, and then upon the right flank of the lancers, was endeavouring to withdraw his regiment from further pursuit, when he was disabled in both arms, and carried by his horse up to the crest of the French position, where, receiving a sabre cut, he was struck senseless to the ground; and it was very generally supposed at the time that he had been left dead on the field.* Lieut. Colonel Hay,

* Upon recovering, some time after his fall, and raising himself up a little to look around him, he was observed by a lancer passing by, who, in a savage and cowardly manner, struck his lance through his back, exclaiming "*Ah! coquin, tu n'est pas mort!*" Not long afterwards he was plundered by a *tirailleur*: but the latter was no sooner gone than he was accosted by a French officer, who had just brought up and halted some troops near the spot. He experienced great kindness from this individual, who, upon his complaining of thirst, held his brandy-bottle to his lips, directing one of his men to lay him straight on his side and place a knapsack under his head. He then passed on into the action, and Sir Frederick Ponsonby never knew to whom he was indebted, as he believed, for his life. Late in the day he was passed over by two squadrons of Prussian cavalry, in full trot, whereby his sufferings were much increased. On the following morning he was discovered by some English, and removed to the village of

who commanded the 16th light dragoons, was desperately and dangerously wounded. Colonel Hamilton, the commanding officer of the Scots Greys, after gallantly leading his regiment through the enemy's columns, across the valley, and up the opposite heights, was last seen far in advance, where it is presumed, from his never having again appeared, he fell in the midst of the French lines, a sacrifice to his distinguished but indiscreet valour. Colonel Fuller, who commanded the 1st, or King's, dragoon guards, was killed when pursuing the cuirassiers, he boldly led his regiment up the French height immediately upon the Allied left of the Charleroi road. In addition to the above mentioned, the British cavalry engaged in this affair sustained a very heavy loss in both officers and men.

With the exception of the bodies of the slain, of such of the wounded as were too far from their respective lines to be removed, of loose horses, some wildly careering about, others quietly grazing, and many staggering, plunging, or convulsively pawing the ground around them, from the agony of their wounds, the arena of this terrible conflict, which had ceased but a few minutes before, was now perfectly clear. The retiring crowds of French infantry had disappeared behind the foremost ridge of their position, to collect and reform their scattered remnants. The British cavalry were similarly employed—Somerset's brigade on the right of the Charleroi road, near the orchard of the farm of Mont St. Jean; Ponsonby's on the opposite side of the road, in rear of a coppice bordering the hollow below that farm; and Vandeleur's on the interior slope of the position, more to the right than where it had been posted during the earlier part of the day. Pack's and Best's brigades closed to their right upon Kempt, so as to fill up the interval occasioned by the retreat of Bylandt's Dutch-Belgian brigade; and the knoll in front of Kempt's brigade was again occupied by three companies of the 95th regiment; as was also the farm of La Haye Sainte by the 2nd light battalion King's German legion, reinforced by two companies of the 1st light battalion of that corps. Major General Sir John Lambert's infantry-brigade, which had been kept in reserve near Mont St. Jean, was put in motion at the time Ponsonby's dragoons advanced to the charge, and it was now placed on the left of the Charleroi

Waterloo. To the inexpressible delight of his corps, and of all who enjoyed his acquaintance and friendship, he gradually recovered from his dreadfully severe wounds, notwithstanding their great number, as well as their extremely critical and almost hopeless nature.

road, in column, at quarter distance, in rear and in support of the 5th division.

The importance of the result of this signal defeat of the French attack was fully commensurate with the glory by which its achievement was distinguished. The object of that attack, which was to force the centre and left wing of the Anglo-allied army, and to establish a very considerable body of troops in the vicinity of Mont St. Jean, was completely frustrated: 3,000 prisoners were taken; 2 eagles were captured; and between 30 and 40 pieces of cannon were put *hors de combat* for the greater part of the remainder of the day.

Thus terminated one of the grandest scenes which distinguished the mighty drama enacted on the ever-memorable plains of Waterloo; a scene presenting in bold relief, genuine British valour crowned with resplendent triumph; a scene, which should be indelibly impressed upon the minds as well of living British warriors, as of their successors in ages yet unborn. Britons! before other scenes are disclosed to your view, take one retrospective glance at this glorious, this instructive spectacle. Let your imagination carry you to the rear of that celebrated position, and a little to the left of the Charleroi road. Behold, in the foreground, on the right, a British line of cavalry advancing to the charge, exulting in the consciousness of its innate courage, indomitable spirit, and strength of arm. Whilst you are admiring the beautiful order and perfect steadiness of their advance, your eyes are suddenly attracted by the glittering splendour of a line of horsemen in burnished coats of mail, rising above the brow, and now crowning the summit of the ridge. They are the far-famed cuirassiers of France, led on by a Kellermann; gallant spirits, that have hitherto overcome the finest troops that could be brought against them, and have grown grey in glory. Trumpets sound the charge; in the next instant your ears catch the low thundering noise of their horses' hoofs, and your breathless excitement is wound to the highest pitch as the adverse lines clash together with a shock, which, at the moment, you expect must end in their mutual annihilation. Observe the British, how they seem to doubt, for a second, in what manner to deal with their opponents. Now they urge their powerful steeds into the intervals between the necks of those of the cuirassiers. Swords brandished high in air, gleam fitfully in rapid succession throughout the lines, here clashing together, there clanging against helmets and cuirass, which ring under their redoubled strokes. See! the struggle is but a moment doubtful—the cuirassiers, seemingly encumbered by their coats of mail, are yielding to superior strength, dexterity, and bravery combined—men and horses reel and stagger to the earth—gaps open out in their line—numbers are backing out—others are fairly turning round—their whole line now bends, and breaks asunder into fragments—in the next moment they appear, as if by a miracle, to be swept from off the crest of the position, and being closely and hotly pursued by the victors, the whole rushing down the other side of the ridge, are snatched from your view. Your attention is now irresistibly drawn to that part of the foreground immediately facing you; where you have barely time to catch sight of a line of British infantry just as it forces its way through the hedge that runs along the crest of the ridge, to charge a column advancing up the other side. At the moment the shouts that proclaim its triumph reach your ear, you are struck by the majestic advance, close to your left, of another line of British horsemen. These halt just under the brow of the ridge. In their left front your eye now also embraces a line of British infantry; whilst at the same time you see the heads of two hostile columus, issuing through the hedge, and crowning the ridge amidst shouts of "*Vive l'Empereur!*" The one nearest to you, finding no immediate opposition to its further advance, is rapidly establishing itself on the height: the other is instantly met by a small but daring band of Scotch Highlanders. A struggle ensues; the furthest column is concealed from your view by the smoke in which it is suddenly enshrouded; but at the very moment when doubts arise in your mind as to the result, the cavalry rushes forward, and, passing through intervals opened out for it by the infantry, which immediately follows in pursuit, charges both these heads of columns, cutting them up, as it were, root and branch; and then bounding through the hedge, the whole disappear as if by magic. Now let your imagination, keeping pace with the intensity of feeling excited by such a scene, carry you up to the summit of the ridge. Behold, at once, the glorious spectacle spread out before you! The dragoons are in the midst of the enemy's columns—the furious impetuosity of their onslaught overcomes all resistance—the terror-stricken masses, paralyzed by this sudden apparition of cavalry amongst them, have neither time nor resolution to form squares, and limit their defence to a feeble, hasty, straggling fire from their ill-cemented edges—a flight, commencing from the rearmost ranks, is rapidly augmented by the outward scattering occasioned by the continually increasing pressure upon the front—the entire slope is soon covered with the dispersed elements of the previously attacking force—parties of infantry are hurrying over the brow of the ridge to aid others of the cavalry in securing the prisoners—3,000 of these are swept to the rear, and 2 eagles are gloriously captured. From the momentary contemplation of these trophies, your eyes instinctively revert to the course of the victors, whom you now perceive in the middle distance of the view—a broken line of daring horsemen, rushing up the opposite heights. Their intoxicating triumph admits of no restraint. They heed not the trumpet's call to halt and rally, but plunging wildly amidst the formidable line of batteries ranged along the French position, they commence sabreing the gunners, stabbing the horses, and seem to clear the ground of every living being. But physical efforts, however powerfully developed and sustained, have their limit: exhausted nature yields at length; and their fiery steeds, subdued, not by force but by exhaustion, retire with lagging, faltering pace. You look in vain for a support—there is none—but your eye is suddenly caught by the fluttering lance-flags of a column of the enemy's cavalry, approaching from the left, and you become nervously alive to the danger that awaits the valiant band of heroes, who are only now made sensible of the necessity of retiring to collect and rally their scattered numbers. Seeing no support ready to receive them, and becoming aware of the near approach of hostile cavalry, they make a last and desperate effort. Those who are best mounted, and whose horses are least blown, succeed in regaining the allied position unmolested; but a very considerable number are overtaken by the lancers, with whom they now contend under a fearful disadvantage in point of speed and order. But mark! a rescue is at hand—a gallant line of friendly cavalry throws itself against the right flank of the lancers, the further portion, or left, of that line first dashing through and scattering an unsteady mass of infantry, the sole remaining column out of the entire attacking force that has yet kept together. The tide of destruction now sets in strongly against the lancers. Their pursuit is checked. The heavy dragoons are relieved from the pressure. A mêlée ensues: but you are not kept long in suspense; for in another moment this newly-arrived force, making good its way, succeeds in driving the lancers in confusion down to the foot of the valley. The arena in your front is speedily cleared of both friends and foes—the discharge of rockets, which now attracts your attention, appears like a display of fire-works in celebration of the glorious triumph—the affair has terminated. But stay to witness the concluding part of the scene. Observe the splendidly attired group entering upon the right, just above La Haye Sainte. It is headed by one whom you cannot for a moment mistake—the illustrious Wellington. Lord Uxbridge, returning from his brilliant charge, now joins the Duke, while the whole *corps diplomatique et militaire* express in the strongest terms their admiration of the grand military spectacle of which they have been spectators. Among them are representatives of nearly all the continental nations, so that this glorious triumph of your valiant countrymen may be said to have been achieved in the face of congregated Europe. Honour, imperishable honour, to every British soldier engaged in that never-to-be-forgotten fight! When Britain again puts forth her strength in battle, may her sovereign's guards inherit the same heroic spirit which animated those of George, Prince Regent, and inspire them with the desire to maintain in all their pristine purity and freshness the laurels transmitted to them from the field of Waterloo; and when the soldiers of the three united kingdoms shall again be found fighting side by side against the common enemy, may they prove to the world that they have not degenerated from the men of the "Union brigade,"* who by their heroic deeds on that great day, so faithfully represented the military virtues of the British empire!

* Sir William Ponsonby's brigade was thus designated from the circumstance of its having consisted of an English regiment—the Royals,—a Scotch regiment —the Greys,—and an Irish regiment—the Inniskillings.

CHAPTER XII.

MUCH as the attention of both commanders had been absorbed by the contest described in the last Chapter, the attack and defence of Hougomont had nevertheless been renewed and maintained with unabated vigour. The assailants, who continued in possession of the wood, having been strengthened by powerful reinforcements from both Jerome's and Foy's divisions, now opened so rapid and indiscriminate a fire upon the garden wall that it might almost be supposed they entertained the hope of battering it down with their shower of bullets. They failed to make any impression upon the little garrison; though they obtained partial successes on the flanks, which again were counteracted on the part of the defenders by the aid of detachments from the main body of Byng's brigade of guards, as also by the natural advantages of the localities. Thus, upon the right, a retreat of the guards from the hedge which lines the avenue and road leading to the château, if followed up by the French, would draw upon the latter a murderous fire from the banks, brushwood, and other cover, in rear of the avenue, together with a flank fire from behind the buildings; and, upon the left, if they succeeded in forcing back the defenders from the front to the rear hedge of the orchard, their left flank became exposed to a severe fire from the troops lining the eastern garden-wall, while they suffered at the same time from the new fire directed against their front by the retreating party, formed under cover of the hollow-way by which that rear hedge is bounded.

It was about two o'clock when Byng, perceiving the increased pressure upon the troops in the orchard, and the great diminution which had taken place in their numbers, desired Colonel Hepburn,* who commanded the 2nd battalion of the 3rd foot guards, to move down the slope with the remainder of his men as a reinforcement. Colonel Hepburn on reaching the hollow-way found it occupied by Lord Saltoun with a very small force, and his Lordship having scarcely a man remaining of his own battalion, gave over to the Colonel the command of that part of Hougomont, and rejoined Maitland's brigade. After a short time, Hepburn and his battalion made a sudden and vigorous rush into the great orchard from the hollow-way

* Major General Hepburn, C. B., died in June, 1835.

in its rear. The French skirmishers gave way; and, as they crowded together while retreating through the gap that leads into the wood, they suffered severely from the concentrated fire poured upon them by the guards; who quickly established themselves along the front hedge of the orchard.

This happened nearly at the same time in which the French were repulsed in their grand attack upon the centre and left of the Duke of Wellington's line. It might be about half-past two o'clock. The battle was then limited to a general cannonade, the roar of which was incessant, and its effects, now that the range on both sides had been very accurately obtained, were most galling and destructive to the troops posted along the interior slope of either position. Alten's light troops again spread themselves out to the front as soon as Kellermann's cuirassiers had been swept from off the exterior slope of the Anglo-allied position. They had not been out long before their attention was directed to a heavy column of infantry, apparently advancing from the vicinity of La Belle Alliance towards La Haye Sainte. It was Bachelu's division, which had fallen back a little after the failure of d'Erlon's attack, to which it had acted as a reserve. Lieut. Colonel Vigoureux,* of the 30th British regiment, who commanded these light troops of Alten's division, immediately threw them forward to meet the column. They poured a well concentrated and most galling fire upon the mass, which immediately brought its right shoulders forward, and took the direction of Hougomont, either in consequence of that fire, or in accordance with orders previously given. The ground over which it wound its course descended sufficiently to render the movement indistinct to the British batteries on the position; but the circumstance having been communicated to Captain Cleeves, whose foot-battery of the King's German legion was posted on the most commanding point of the ridge on the right of the Charleroi road, this officer lost not a moment in making his arrangements. He permitted the column to continue its march unmolested until it reached a point immediately in his front, on which he had directed his guns so as to concentrate upon the mass, at the proper moment, the whole fire of his battery. The column continued its march, and had cleared more than two-thirds of the distance between La Belle Alliance and Hougomont, when, having well entered within Captain Cleeves's line of fire, three rounds from each gun were thrown into it with astonishing rapidity, and awful effect. In a moment the greater portion of the column ap-

* Colonel Charles A. Vigoureux, C.B., died on the 25th of February, 1841.

peared to be dispersed, and flying back in confusion towards the lower ground for shelter; leaving an immense number of dead and dying to attest the fatal accuracy of the fire from the battery. As no hostile force of either cavalry or infantry appeared in its immediate vicinity, Bachelu soon succeeded in rallying his division, and renewing the advance. A similar result followed; whereupon all further attempt to effect the contemplated movement was abandoned; and thus a most serious flank attack upon Hougomont was completely frustrated by the skilfully managed fire of a single battery. Bachelu now took post again, upon the right of Foy, leaving a considerable interval between his division and the Charleroi road.

Foiled in his varied and repeated attacks upon Hougomont, Napoleon had now recourse to incendiary projectiles. For this purpose he had ordered a battery of howitzers to be formed, from which shells were thrown so as to descend into the buildings. The great barn, the outhouses on the north side of the château, the farmer's house, and finally the château itself, were speedily set on fire. Dense volumes of smoke, enveloping the whole post and its defenders, were wafted slowly towards the Anglo-allied line; the roofs of the buildings soon fell in; and, shortly before three o'clock, the flames burst forth with great brilliancy. Many of the wounded had been carried, or had crawled, into the buildings; but although their comrades entertained the most distressing apprehensions for their safety, the stern sense of duty and of honour prescribed that of the post itself as paramount to every other consideration. Invested as the place was by an enemy so overwhelmingly superior in numbers, and so unceasingly on the alert to seize upon any advantage that might offer, not a man could be spared to assist in extricating the sufferers from their perilous situation. Obedience to the natural dictates of humanity was necessarily sacrificed to that which was due to the severe demands of discipline. Thus several perished in the flames. Others, who had contrived to crawl into the open courts, could scarcely breathe in the scorching and suffocating atmosphere. Many who had sought shelter, or had been laid, in the chapel, and whose terrors were excited as they heard the crashing fall of burning timbers, or the frequent explosion of shells around them, at length beheld the flames penetrating the door of the sanctuary. The prayers that had been fervently, though silently, offered up from that holy place, had surely been accepted—the fire, reaching the feet of the wooden image of the

Saviour of mankind, that stood above the entrance, seemed to feel the sacred presence; for here its progress terminated; and this, without the aid of human efforts.*

The conflagration did not occasion a moment's relaxation in the heroic exertions of the brave defenders of Hougomont. The courage and devotedness of the men kept pace with the zeal and intelligence of their officers; and no sooner did new difficulties arise than they were met and overcome by the most judicious arrangements, combined with the most consummate gallantry.

It was now about half-past three o'clock. The Anglo-allied line continued compact and unshaken in its original position. Its advanced posts of La Haye Sainte and Hougomont had successfully resisted the most formidable assaults. The left wing had sustained considerable loss in meeting and repelling the French right wing, but the losses endured by the latter in that attack were infinitely more severe: whole columns of infantry had been completely overthrown and dispersed; squadrons of the most splendid and most devoted cavalry, had shared a similar fate; whilst from thirty to forty pieces of cannon had been rendered useless for nearly the remainder of the day. Hence, the French Emperor, did not deem it advisable to renew, at least so soon, an attack upon the left of the Anglo-allied army. He decided on forming a grand attack upon its right and centre; and since Reille's infantry had already suffered very considerably in its assaults upon Hougomont, he determined upon employing his cavalry for that purpose; more especially as the ground in front of that part of the Allied line appeared well adapted for the movements of this description of force. To gain possession of La Haye Sainte and Hougomont, as a preliminary step, was undoubtedly the most judicious course; but hitherto his endeavours to obtain that vantage-ground had altogether failed, and he was now compelled to limit his plan, combining with the projected attack, renewed assaults against those posts, which, even if again unsuccessful, would at least serve to divert in some degree, the enemy's attention. Napoleon also contemplated a more important diversion, by causing a demonstration to be made with Piré's light cavalry against Wellington's right flank.

In pursuance of this plan, renewed efforts were made by the attacking force against Hougomont; and two columns from Donzelot's division descended upon La Haye Sainte.

Meanwhile Major Baring having applied for a reinforce-

* See note at page 212.

ment, two companies were detached to his post from the 1st light battalion of the King's German legion. To these and a part of his own battalion, he intrusted the defence of the garden; and, abandoning altogether the orchard, he placed the remainder of his force in the buildings, distributing their defence among the three officers who had so courageously maintained them during the previous attack. The French columns advanced against this post with the most undaunted resolution and the most conspicuous gallantry. The well-aimed bullets of the German rifles, though they told quickly and fearfully amidst their masses, arrested not their progress for a moment. They rushed close up to the walls, and, seizing the rifles as they protruded through the loop-holes, endeavoured to wrest them from the hands of the defenders. They also made a most furious assault against the gates and doors, in defence of which many lives were sacrificed. The greatest struggle was at the western opening to the large barn, the door of which was wanting. The French, determined to make good an entrance, encountered the brave Germans, equally resolute to prevent them. The foremost Frenchmen, dashing boldly on to force their way, were struck down by the deliberate fire from the rifles the instant they reached the threshold, and seventeen of their dead bodies already formed a rampart for those who continued to press forward to carry on the struggle.

It was nearly four o'clock when certain movements made by the lancers on the French extreme left, led the Duke to suspect an attack from that quarter; and which, considering the almost isolated position of his detached force at Braine-la-leud and Vieux Foriez, might, if successful, be attended with very serious consequences to himself. He drew Lord Uxbridge's attention to that point; and the latter immediately despatched Grant, with the 13th light dragoons and the 15th hussars of his brigade to attack the lancers, detaching at the same time the 2nd light dragoons of the King's German legion, from Dörnberg's brigade, towards Braine-la-leud, for the purpose both of facilitating the attack, by manœuvring on the left of the lancers, and of watching the enemy's dispositions in that direction.

The fire of artillery along both lines had been maintained with the utmost vigour. At this moment, however, a most furious cannonade was directed against that part of the Anglo-allied line which was situated between the two high roads. While some of the French light batteries took post in advance, others of the imperial guard, comprising 12-pounders, opened a fire from the heights in rear of, and above, La Belle

Alliance; and as the batteries upon the main French line were ranged along the arc of the chord formed by the Allied line, the French artillery was enabled by its very great numerical superiority in guns to concentrate an overwhelming fire upon any part of the Duke's position. The Allied infantry posted in columns along the interior slope of the ridge, were entirely screened from the observation of the French, who could not distinguish any portion of their enemies beyond the devoted British and German artillerymen at their guns, which, despite the severity of the fire from their opponents, were worked with the most admirable coolness and intrepidity, and with a precision beyond all praise.

The thunder of the artillery continued pealing forth in an uninterrupted roll, and the scene became awfully grand. The guns having once obtained the required range, were fired without intermission. Instantaneous flashes met the eye, all along the heights, succeeded by volumes of smoke bounding forth along the ground in front, and enveloping the batteries in clouds. The earth trembled beneath the dread concussion. The oldest soldiers had never witnessed a cannonade conducted with such fury, with such desperation. The Allied columns of infantry were lying down upon the ground to shelter themselves as much as possible from the iron shower that fell fast and heavily—round shot, tearing frightful rents directly through their masses, or ploughing up the earth beside them; shells, bursting in the midst of the serried columns, and scattering destruction in their fall, or previously burying themselves in the soft loose soil to be again forced upwards in eruptions of iron, mud, and stones, that fell among them like volcanic fragments.

During this terrible conflict of artillery, Ney was making his preparatory dispositions with the cavalry which Napoleon had desired him to launch against the Anglo-allied right wing. He first formed for attack, Milhaud's corps of cuirassiers, consisting of 24 squadrons, and directed Lefebvre-Desnouette's light cavalry-division of the guard, comprising 7 squadrons of lancers and 12 squadrons of chasseurs, to follow and support—in all 43 squadrons—constituting a magnificent array of gallant horsemen. As they began to advance, the first line, of cuirassiers, shone in burnished steel, relieved by black horse-hair crested helmets; next came the red lancers of the guard, in their gaudy uniform, and mounted on richly caparisoned steeds, their fluttering lance-flags heightening the brilliancy of their display; whilst the third line, comprising the chasseurs of the guard, in their rich costume of green and gold, with fur-trimmed pelisses *à la hussard*, and black bear-skin shakos, completed the gorgeous, yet harmonious, colouring of this military spectacle. Though formed in successive lines of columns, in the hollow space on the immediate left of La Haye Sainte, where they were sheltered in some degree from the cannonade that raged so furiously above them, the rear lines obliqued to their left, on the advance, and became echelonned to the first line, so as to present a general front, extending from the Charleroi road on their right, to the Hougomont inclosures on their left. As they ascended the ridge, the French artillery suspended their fire, and the Allied batteries commenced pouring a destructive shower of grape-shot amidst their devoted ranks. Fiercely and fatally did this iron hail rattle against the helmed and steel-clad cuirassiers, here glancing off, there penetrating the armour, wounding or laying prostrate many a gallant warrior, at the very moment when the brightest visions of glory had opened on his ardent imagination. This iron sleet, however, caused no perceptible check to their progress; and, with shouts of "*Vive l'Empereur!*" they accelerated their pace until, having arrived within about forty yards of the guns, they received the last and well-prepared discharge. Its effects were terrific: but though their order was somewhat broken, their courage was not shaken. The charge was sounded; a cheer followed; and, in the next instant, they rushed up to the very cannon's mouth. In accordance with previous instructions given by the Duke of Wellington himself, the artillerymen withdrew, upon the close approach of the cavalry, and sought shelter either beside, or in rear of, the infantry-squares; or, where occasion required, they threw themselves under the projecting bayonets of the outer kneeling ranks for protection. The cuirassiers, on crowning the crest of the ridge, and finding themselves so unexpectedly in possession of a line of batteries, shouted loudly forth their triumph; and, then renewing their onward charge, were, in a moment, lost to the view of the lancers and chasseurs of the guard. These troops, carried away by the enthusiasm of the moment, and the eager desire to share in the fancied victory, advanced with the same fiery impetuosity, and the whole force was now fairly across the ridge. The Allied infantry, distributed in chequered squares along the interior slope, were fully prepared to meet the attack. Some little apprehension had been entertained for the safety of the right of the front line, where the Brunswickers, who, as before remarked, were mostly young, raw troops, had taken up the ground previously occupied by Byng's brigade of guards, which had been entirely absorbed by the defence of Hougomont, with the exception of two companies which, with the colours, had been withdrawn, as a reserve, to a more sheltered position on the right of the Nivelles road. As the French cavalry advanced, the 23rd British regiment of infantry was led up to the front line, and into an interval between the Brunswick squares. This regiment had nearly reached the brow of the ridge when it was suddenly ordered to halt and prepare to receive cavalry; and the chasseurs of the guard appearing the next moment in its front, a fire from this face was opened so hastily that scarcely a shot could have told upon the enemy. It instantly recovered this somewhat nervous precipitation, and presented a bold and determined stand, as did also the Brunswickers, who acted on this occasion in a manner that would have reflected credit on the most experienced veterans.

The cannonade had necessarily ceased along the right wing of the Anglo-allied front line, and along the French batteries to which it was opposed. Hence the vehement cheering on the part of the French cavalry became the more distinctly audible and the more highly exciting. A sullen silence was maintained throughout the Allied squares, which were all at the "prepare,"—front ranks kneeling, and the second at the charge,—thus forming a *chevaux-de-frise*, over which the rear ranks were ready to fire, as occasion might demand. As the cavalry now rushed down upon the squares, the front faces of the latter opened their fire when the former had approached within about thirty paces of them. The effect of this fire was to create disorder and confusion in the leading squadron or half-squadron (as the case might be), which would then open out from the centre, and obliquing to the right and left respectively, pass on by the flanks of the square attacked, to the fire from which it would consequently become completely exposed. The succeeding, repeated the manœuvre of the leading, divisions; and their disorder became greater and greater as the continually augmenting obstacles in their front, the upset riders and horses, increased in multitude. Here, as at Quatre-Bras, the French cavalry did not rush to the shock against a single British square. The horsemen of the leading divisions who escaped the opposing fire, failed to maintain the direction of their speed with unabated vigour, and to dash against the square, heedless of personal danger, and intent only upon securing the sole chance that offered for the success of their immediate followers. That portion of the cavalry which passed through the intervals between the foremost squares, directed their advance upon those that were in rear, and the squares being generally *en échiquier*, the opening out and dividing of the attacking squadrons in the manner described, soon commingled the horsemen of different regiments, and added considerably to the disorder already caused by the dropping fire which assailed them in all directions. The Anglo-allied cavalry, having the advantage of perfect order, now advanced to the charge, and after encountering some little resistance on different points, speedily succeeded in relieving the squares from the presence of the enemy, whom they pursued over the crest of the ridge and down the exterior slope. No sooner was Ney's cavalry driven from the position, than the Allied artillerymen flew from their shelter to their guns, and the French batteries recommenced their fire. The former dealt destruction amidst the retiring masses, as soon as, and wherever, they were uncovered by the Allied cavalry; but some of the British regiments, giving too much rein to their ardour, carried their pursuit rather too far; particularly the 23rd British light dragoons; who, having attacked the flank of a column of cuirassiers whilst the latter was advancing against the 1st regiment of Dutch carabiniers, by which it was then attacked in front—Trip himself leading—drove both the cuirassiers and a body of lancers across the hollow on the right of La Haye Sainte, back upon their own batteries on the heights beyond, and thus created confusion amongst the French gunners; who, however, made them pay for their temerity as they withdrew again towards their own position.

Towards the Allied right, the lancers, pursued by the 1st light dragoons of the King's German legion, instantly reformed, and, resuming their charge, became themselves the pursuers; but on advancing over the ridge, they were not only exposed again to the fire from the squares, but were at the same time most unexpectedly assailed by a brisk discharge of round-shot from Captain Bolton's British foot-battery, which had just been rapidly advanced to its left front, and very judiciously posted on some favourable ground close to, and on the right of, the Nivelles road, and in direct rear of the main ridge. Its fire was directed with great precision at the French cavalry in the intervals between the squares in its front, and by its valuable assistance the enemy was soon compelled to retire again across the ridge. It will be readily conceived that such assistance was most essential, when it is recollected that, at this time, the 7th hussars, the 1st light dragoons of the King's German legion, the Brunswick hussars, and the squadron of Bunswick lancers, were the only cavalry-regiments posted in rear of that portion of the front line extending from the Nivelles road on the right, to the position of Halkett's British infantry-brigade on the left, in rear of which latter stood the 23rd light dragoons. The manner in which those regiments charged and repelled the French cavalry opposed to them, merits the highest commendation.

The French cavalry evinced the greatest alacrity, nay, impatience, in again getting into order—actuated, no doubt, by a sense of shame and indignation at finding its efforts frustrated, and its valour fruitless, although in possession of the enemy's guns, and at liberty to act at its own discretion against his squares. The advance was speedily renewed, but evidently conducted with more caution, though not with less enthusiasm. Again did this brilliant array of horsemen boldly face the iron shower of grape, and gallantly crown the crest of the Anglo-allied right wing. But now, instead of attacking indiscriminately, as before, one portion was allotted to that service, whilst the remainder was kept in more compact order to stem the onset of the Allied cavalry, by which, on the former occasion, they had been so signally repulsed. The charges were repeated against the squares, in the same style, and upon the same system, as before, and with an equally fruitless result. This portion of the attacking force became gradually exhausted and out of order, but the remainder appeared well formed up, and moving forward to charge the second line comprising Allied cavalry, which, however, did not wait for the attack, but instantly advanced to meet it. The latter consisted of Somerset's brigade on the left, (greatly diminished by the effects of its former charge, on the occasion of the French attack of the Allied left and centre,) of the 23rd British light dragoons, in rear of Halkett's British infantry-brigade, of Trip's Dutch-Belgian carabinier-brigade, in rear of the 23rd, of the Brunswick hussars and lancers, more to the right, of the 1st light dragoons of the King's German legion, close to the Nivelles road, and of the 7th British hussars, on the interior slope of that portion of the ridge which was immediately in left rear of Hougomont—a force scarcely amounting to half the number of squadrons with which the French cavalry had commenced this attack. The charge was executed under great excitement, and with the utmost steadiness and gallantry. The struggle was desperate and sanguinary, but the French cavalry, assailed in front, by the same description of force, and on their flanks, by the fire from the squares, at length went about, and were followed, as before, over the ridge and down the exterior slope. In rear of the right of the Anglo-line, where, as previously observed, the cavalry was then so very weak in numbers, the 1st light dragoons of the King's German legion had deployed into line, in order to occupy more ground and show a greater front. As the French lancers were attacking the squares, and advancing through the intervals between them, notwithstanding the renewed fire from Bolton's battery, the regiment hastened forward to charge them. The Germans had not proceeded far when it was discovered that a body of the enemy's cavalry had penetrated to the open space on their left. With great presence of mind and admirable promptitude, Major Reizenstein,* who perceived the danger to which the regiment was exposed by the already meditated attack upon its left flank, drew off a great part of it, and, with a right-shoulder-forward movement, advanced to meet these new assailants who were now coming on at full speed. The mutual impetuosity of the charge, and violence of the shock, were terrific. The two lines dashed at and through each other, and those of the horsemen that were yet firm in their saddles, wheeling sharply round, again rushed to the fierce encounter with the most resolute bravery; and the dispersed riders, after rapidly exchanging cuts and thrusts, *en passant,* sought out their respective corps.

As the cavalry retired, the infantry that had attacked La Haye Sainte desisted from their fruitless endeavours to force the gallant little garrison. Not long afterwards, Major Baring, on finding that the ammunition of his men had, by the constant firing, been reduced to less than one-half, became apprehensive of its speedy exhaustion; and despatched an officer to request a supply, which was promised to him. In the mean time, the Germans set about diligently repairing the injuries they had sustained, and making the best preparation in their power to meet the next attack.

Upon the first advance of the French cavalry, by the Allied left of Hougomont, a body of infantry skirmishers crept along the boundary hedge of the great orchard on that side, and by thus turning the flank of the 3rd guards, who were at the same time assailed with renewed vigour in front, compelled them to retire into the hollow-way in rear of the inclosure; but, as the cavalry withdrew, so did the light troops on the left of the orchard, and Lieut. Colonel Hepburn, advancing his men from their cover, drove back the

* Colonel Augustus Reizenstein, C.B., K.C.H., of the Hanoverian service, died on the 6th of November, 1830.

French skirmishers in the orchard, and again occupied its front hedge.

The contest at this time, between the Allied left, and the French right, wing, was limited to a continued cannonade, with light troops skirmishing in the valley which separated the two positions. The Nassau troops, under Prince Bernhard of Saxe-Weimar, maintáined their ground with great spirit along the villages and inclosures upon the extreme left of the Anglo-allied army.

Grant, who, it will be recollected, had been detached with the 13th light dragoons and the 15th hussars, to attack the 5th and 6th French lancers, upon the extreme left of the French line, in consequence of certain menacing dispositions on their part, was first made aware that these had been merely a diversion, to draw off a portion of the Allied cavalry from the real point of attack, by the shouts which suddenly proceeded from their ranks, when, on turning round to ascertain the cause, he perceived the French in possession of the batteries along the crest of the position, and charging the squares posted on the interior slope. Observing a repetition of the attack, and the want of cavalry on that part of the position which he had quitted, he most judiciously took upon himself to return to it with both regiments ; and, as will appear in the sequel, he arrived there at a most critical moment, when his absence might have produced the most fatal consequences. As a precautionary measure, the right squadron of the 15th hussars, under Captain Wodehouse, was left in its original position, to observe the extreme left of the French line; and the second light dragoons of the King's German legion continued to keep a look-out between that point and Braine-la-leud.

Napoleon, perceiving the necessity of affording an immediate support to Ney's attack sent an order to Kellermann to advance for that purpose, with his corps of heavy cavalry, consisting of the two divisions commanded by L'Heritier and Roussel-d'Urbal, and comprising (at the commencement of the battle) 7 squadrons of dragoons, 11 squadrons of cuirassiers, and 6 squadrons of carabiniers. In the mean time, Ney, with a similar object in view, had ordered forward Guyot's heavy cavalry-division of the guard, comprising 6 squadrons of horse-grenadiers, and 7 squadrons of dragoons. These 37 squadrons, combined with the force which had already attacked, and which had originally consisted of 43 squadrons,* constituted a stupendous array of cavalry, in comparison with

* See page 282.

that which was then posted in rear of the right wing of the Anglo-allied army, and which received no accession beyond the 5 squadrons that Grant was in the act of withdrawing, as before explained, from the extreme right. Guyot's division of the guard having been placed by Napoleon at Ney's disposal, when he first desired him to form the grand cavalry-attack, the Marshal was entitled to employ it if he thought proper; but it is doubtful whether Napoleon, after having sent forward Kellermann's corps, was desirous that the combined force should be thus prematurely engaged, since it would deprive him of his only cavalry-reserve. Still, when we consider the limited extent of the field of battle, and the consequent facility with which he might have either suspended the employment of the heavy cavalry of the guard, or countermanded Kellermann's advance, it is reasonable to infer that the French Emperor was not altogether displeased with the grand experiment which was about to be made, and which encouraged the most sanguine expectations of a glorious triumph.

The coming attack was, like the former one, preceded by a violent cannonade. As before, the French batteries concentrated their fire upon the Allied artillery and squares. The entire space immediately in rear of the crest of the ridge that marked the front line of the Duke's right wing, was again assailed with a tempest of shot and shell. Again were whole files torn away, and compact sections rent asunder.

But the extraordinary skill and the untiring energies of the British and German gunners, combined with the heroic forbearance and the admirable steadiness of the squares, fully impressed upon the mind of Wellington the conviction that, however formidable and disproportionate the force that his powerful adversary could wield against him, it might yet be made to suffer an exhaustion, moral as well as physical, that would render it totally unavailable and helpless at the moment when its extremest tension and fullest application would be so urgently required to extricate the Emperor from that perilous crisis which, by his Grace's masterly arrangements, was gradually approaching its consummation. To act exclusively on the defensive, to maintain his ground in defiance of every assault and every stratagem, and yet to harass and weaken his enemy to the extent of his power, constituted the grand point on which hinged the practical development of those arrangements. A defeat and dispersion of his army before the arrival of the Prussian troops, would lead to new measures, to additional sacrifices—perhaps to irretrievable disasters. But his resolve was fixed and irrevocable; for he knew that he could fearlessly rely upon the devotion, the endurance, and the valour, of his British and German soldiers. And this implicit confidence was nobly reciprocated; for as the troops remarked the serenity of his countenance and demeanour when rectifying any confusion or disorder, or felt as if spell-bound by the magic influence of a few simple and homely words from his lips, they entertained no doubts as to the result of their glorious exertions.

When the tremendous cavalry force which Ney had thus assembled, moved forward to the attack, the whole space between La Haye Sainte and Hougomont appeared one moving glittering mass; and, as it approached the Anglo-allied position, undulating with the conformation of the ground, it resembled a sea in agitation. Upon reaching the crest of the ridge, and regaining temporary possession of the batteries, its very shouts sounded on the distant ear like the ominous roar of breakers thundering on the shore. Like waves following in quick succession, the whole mass now appeared to roll over the ridge; and as the light curling smoke arose from the fire which was opened by the squares, and by which the latter sought to stem the current of the advancing host, it resembled the foam and spray thrown up by the mighty waters as they dash on isolated rocks and beetling crags; and, as the mass separated and rushed in every direction, completely covering the interior slope, it bore the appearance of innumerable eddies and counter currents, threatening to overwhelm and engulph the obstructions by which its onward course had been opposed. The storm continued to rage with the greatest violence; and the devoted squares seemed lost in the midst of the tumultuous onset. In vain did the maddening mass chafe and fret away its strength against these impregnable barriers, which, based upon the sacred principles of honour, discipline, and duty, and cemented by the ties of patriotism and the impulse of national glory, stood proudly unmoved and inaccessible. Disorder and confusion, produced by the commingling of corps, and by the scattering fire from the faces of the chequered squares, gradually led to the retreat of parties of horsemen across the ridge; these were followed by broken squadrons, and, at length, the retrograde movement became general. Then the Allied dragoons, who had been judiciously kept in readiness to act at the favourable moment, darted forward to complete the disorganization and overthrow of the now receding waves of the French cavalry.

The Allied artillery had barely time to fire a few rounds into the retiring masses, when the enemy's formidable support rapidly advanced to renew the attack; and, as if it had been made aware that the right of the Anglo-allied line was the weakest part, from the want of a sufficient cavalry-support, its efforts appeared particularly directed to that point. A body of heavy dragoons was drawn up in line, and advanced up the ridge leaving the Hougomont inclosures immediately on its left. At this moment, however, Grant had most opportunely returned with the 13th light dragoons and 15th hussars from the extreme right; and instantly forming the 13th, which was the leading regiment, in line to the front, moved it up to the crest of the ridge, over which it gallantly charged and routed the French dragoons, driving them about three hundred yards down to the low ground near the north-east angle of the great orchard of Hougomont. The 15th hussars were also formed to the front, on the left of the 13th light dragoons, and charged a mass of cuirassiers, which was driven back a like distance, upon large bodies of cavalry. As these were observed commencing offensive operations, both in front and on the flank, the two regiments, first the 13th, and then the 15th, were compelled to retreat to the main position, and take post in rear of the squares; but this they did with so much order and regularity that their presence and example imparted new life and confidence to the young Brunswickers, whose steadiness, on the right of the line, had been severely tested in the course of the grand cavalry attack. Notwithstanding these reverses, and the decided failure of their former attempts, the French horsemen most gallantly and resolutely renewed their advance, and again plunged in masses, amidst the Allied squares. Failing in their direct attack, they rode through the intervals between the squares in all directions, exhibiting extraordinary coolness and intrepidity. Some of the most daring approached close up to the ranks, to draw forth the fire from a square, and thus secure a better chance of success for the squadron prepared to seize the advantage and to charge. Small parties of desperate fellows would endeavour to force an opening at some weak point, by cutting aside the bayonets and firing at the defenders with their pistols. But the squares were proof against every assault and every stratagem. More cavalry crossed over the summit of the ridge; and the greater part of the interior slope occupied by the Allied right wing seemed covered with horsemen of all kinds—cuirassiers, lancers, carabiniers, chasseurs, dragoons, and horse-grenadiers. The French, enraged at their want of success, brandishing their swords, and exciting one another by shouts of "*Vive l'Empereur!*" reiterated their attacks with redoubled but fruitless vigour. Like the majestic oaks of the forest, which are poetically said to strike their roots deeper and more tenaciously into the earth as the fury of the storm increases, so stood the Anglo-allied squares, grand in the imposing attitude of their strength, and bidding defiance to the tempestuous elements by which they were assailed on every side. At length the attack evinced symptoms of exhaustion: the charges became less frequent and less vigorous; disorder and confusion were rapidly augmenting; the spirit of enthusiasm and the confidence of superiority, were quickly yielding to the feeling of despondency, and the sense of hopelessness. The Anglo-allied cavalry again advanced, and once more swept the mingled host, comprising every description of mounted troops from off the ground on which they had so fruitlessly frittered away their strength.

On this occasion, a body of cuirassiers, having been intercepted in its direct line of retreat by a party of British light dragoons, was induced to surrender; but taking advantage of the weakness of their escort, they suddenly broke away, and galloped down the Nivelles road, by which they hoped to return to the French lines. They were fatally deceived. As they passed the high bank, covered with brush-wood, on the right of the road, where a detachment of the 51st regiment was stationed as one of the supports to the light troops extended in front of the extreme right, they were fired upon, though but partially, in consequence of their close pursuit by the light dragoons. This attracted the attention of Captain Ross* of that regiment, who was posted with his company more in advance, and close to the *abatis* which had been thrown across the road near the head of the avenue leading to Hougomont. Captain Ross, being thus prepared, also fired upon the cuirassiers, whereupon their commanding officer, finding all further retreat effectually cut off by the *abatis*, surrendered to Captain Ross, declaring that he would not give himself up to the dragoons. At this spot eighty of the cuirassiers and twelve of their horses were killed; and the remainder, about sixty, were dismounted, taken, or dispersed.

* Now Colonel John Ross, Commanding the St. Helena Regiment.

Shortly before this, Ney, perceiving the ill success of his cavalry attacks, determined on combining them with such infantry as he had at his disposal. Between d'Erlon's and Reille's corps there was now a great interval, and the only troops of which he could make use for the above object, consisted of Bachelu's division, on the right of the latter, as Donzelot's division, on the left of the former, was still required for the attack upon La Haye Sainte, and which he now ordered to be vigorously renewed, whilst he advanced a heavy column of Bachelu's infantry towards the centre of the Allied right wing. Wellington, who had, from the first, anticipated that the attacks of cavalry would be followed up by others, in which that arm would be combined with infantry, was fully prepared to meet this contingency, having as soon as he had ascertained that the enemy was not disposed to attempt any serious movement against his right flank, despatched an order to Chassé to evacuate Braine-la-leud and its vicinity, and to proceed with his Dutch-Belgian division, towards the principal scene of action, along the low ground through Merbe-braine. By this means, his Grace, who contemplated reinforcing his first line with troops from his second, would be enabled to supply their place in the latter, with others of equal strength. Chassé's movement, executed with much judgment, was in a great measure, if not entirely, concealed from the enemy's observation, and was very skilfully covered by the 2nd light dragoons of the King's German legion, who continued hovering near the left flank of the French army.

In the mean time, the attack upon La Haye Sainte had been renewed with the same fury as before. Major Baring on perceiving the advance of the enemy's columns, sent an officer to the position with this intelligence, and repeated his request for ammunition. The light company of the 5th line-battalion of the King's German legion was sent to his assistance, but the supply of ammunition, of which he stood so much in need, was not forthcoming; and he therefore, after waiting half an hour longer, during which the contest was uninterrupted, despatched another officer on the same errand. This application proved equally unsuccessful. He received, however, a reinforcement of two flank companies from the 1st regiment of Nassau. The great struggle was again at the open entrance to the barn, and the French, finding all their efforts to force an entrance so obstinately and successfully frustrated, had recourse to the expedient of setting the place on fire. A thick smoke was soon observed issuing from the barn. The greatest consternation pervaded the little garrison, for although there was a pond in the yard, there were no means at hand for conveying the water to the point of danger. Major Baring, whose anxiety was extreme, glancing his eye at the large camp-kettles borne by the recently-arrived Nassauers, instantly pulled one from off a man's back: several officers followed his example, and filling the kettles with water, carried them in the face of almost certain death, to the fire. The men hesitated not a moment. Every kettle was instantly applied to the same good office, and the fire was fortunately extinguished, though at the sacrifice of many a brave soldier. Several of the men, although covered with wounds, rejected all persuasion to retire. Their constant reply was, "So long as our officers fight, and we can stand, we will not stir from the spot."* At length the enemy, wearied out by this most resolute and gallant defence, once more withdrew.

At the commencement of this attack, while one portion of the enemy's force was principally directed against the western entrance of the great barn, the other, leaving the buildings on its right, advanced higher up the slope, as if intending either to penetrate the farm by the garden, or to cut off its communication with the main position. The Prince of Orange, conceiving this to be a favourable opportunity for attacking the French column, ordered the 5th and 8th line battalions of Ompteda's brigade of the King's German legion to deploy and advance. The line was quickly formed, and the battalions, bounding across the narrow sunken road, rushed forward, at a charging pace, driving the enemy before them. But a body of cuirassiers, that had unsuccessfully charged the left squares of Kielmansegge's Hanoverian brigade, whilst those battalions were advancing, came upon the right flank of the latter, unexpectedly for both parties. The 5th line battalion, which was on the right, having been supported in sufficient time by Somerset's heavy cavalry-brigade, suffered little loss; but the 8th line battalion—being on the left, and more in advance, in the act of charging when the cuirassiers appeared—was completely surprised, and its right wing cut down and dispersed.

* One of the men, named Frederick Lindau, bleeding from two wounds in his head, and carrying in his pocket a large bag full of gold, which he had taken from a French officer, stood at the small barn-door facing the yard, defending from thence the open western entrance. Major Baring, observing that the cloth bound round his head did not suffice to stop the strong flow of blood, called out to him to withdraw; but the latter, as heedless of his wounds as of his gold, replied, "None but a scoundrel would desert you so long as his head remains upon his shoulders!" This brave fellow was afterwards taken prisoner, and lost his treasure.

The commanding officer of the battalion, Colonel Schröder, was mortally wounded: several other officers fell: Ensign de Moreau,* who carried and defended the King's colour, having been severely wounded, as also the serjeant who afterwards held it, the enemy succeeded in carrying off the prize. Major Petersdorf,† the next in command, collected the scattered remnant of the battalion, and posted it in rear of the hollow-way.

The moment the Anglo-allied right wing became cleared of the presence of the French cavalry, it was again exposed to a furious cannonade. Several of the guns along the main ridge were by this time disabled. Major Bull, who had been obliged at an earlier period to withdraw his howitzer-battery to the second line, for the purpose of repairing casualties and completing ammunition, advanced again to his former post in the front line, along with Major Ramsay's horse-battery, during the second general charge of the French cavalry. These batteries suffered severely from Piré's guns, stationed on the extreme left of the French line. Bull directed Lieutenant Louis‡ to turn his two right guns towards them, and it was not long before this officer succeeded in silencing them; a service which, as they enfiladed the Allied right flank, was of considerable advantage, during the remainder of the battle, to all the batteries and troops in this part of the field. The Duke, considering that a reinforcement of artillery was particularly required in front of Cooke's division and the Brunswick infantry, against which the enemy was evidently preparing fresh attacks, ordered up Lieut. Colonel Dickson's British horse-battery, commanded by Major Mercer, and Major Sympher's horse-battery of the King's German legion, into the front line; the former, to the left of Lieut. Colonel Smith's horse-battery, in front of the Brunswickers, and the latter further to the left. Major Mercer's battery had barely time to get into action, when a heavy column of cavalry, composed of horse-grenadiers and cuirassiers, was seen ascending the ridge, and advancing at a rapid rate directly towards the spot upon which it had taken post. The guns, which were 9-pounders, were each loaded with a round and a case shot; and were run close up to a bank of two or three feet in height, which descended from the narrow cross-road along the ridge,

* Now Captain William de Moreau, K.H., on the retired list of the Hanoverian army.

† Lieut. Colonel Charles von Petersdorff, C.B., K.C.H., in the Hanoverian service, died on the 13th March, 1834.

‡ Now Lieut. Colonel Matthew Louis, Royal Artillery.

and which thus formed a sort of *genouillère* to the battery. In front, the summit of the ridge consisted of a flat surface, of forty or fifty yards in width, whence the ground descended rapidly towards the plain that divided the two armies. The column continued to advance until it came quite close upon these guns, the muzzles of which were nearly on a level with the cross-road, when it suddenly recoiled from the very destructive fire with which it was received. The horsemen of the leading squadrons faced about, and endeavoured to force their way to the rear; confusion ensued, and the whole mass broke into a disorderly crowd. Several minutes elapsed ere they succeeded in quitting the summit of the ridge, during which the fire from the battery was incessant; and, from the shortness of the distance, the size of the objects, and the elevation of the ground on which they stood, the consequent carnage was truly frightful. Many, instead of seeking safety in retreat, dashed through the intervals between the guns, and surrendered; but the greater part, rendered desperate at finding themselves held, as it were, in front of the battery, actually fought their way through their own ranks; and, in the struggle, blows were exchanged on all sides. At length, the wreck of this formidable column gained shelter under the slope of the ridge, leaving the summit encumbered with its killed and wounded.

About the same time, a strong column of French infantry, supported by cavalry, was advancing against the centre of the Anglo-allied right wing. Whilst the opposed batteries were concentrating upon it a vigorous fire, Lord Uxbridge brought forward Somerset's heavy cavalry-brigade from its position on the right of the Charleroi road, for the purpose of attacking this column, and also ordered up, in support, Trip's Dutch-Belgian carabinier-brigade. The attack was made with great gallantry by the household cavalry, which succeeded in checking the advance of the enemy; but, having been so much reduced in numbers, it was unable to penetrate the column, which received it with a heavy fire. As Somerset retired, the French cavalry by which the column had been supported, prepared to advance. Trip's Dutch-Belgian cavalry was now at hand. Uxbridge, pleased with their fine appearance, and desirous of exciting in them a courageous enthusiasm, placed himself conspicuously in their front, and ordering the "charge," led them towards the enemy. He had proceeded but a very short distance, when his aide-de-camp, Captain Horace Seymour, galloped close up to him, and made him aware that not a single man of them was following him. Turning round his horse, he instantly rode up to Trip, and addressed himself to this officer with great warmth. Then, appealing to the brigade in terms the most exhorting and encouraging, and inciting them by gestures the most animated and significant, he repeated the order to charge, and again led the way in person. But this attempt was equally abortive; and Uxbridge, exasperated and indignant, rode away from the brigade, leaving it to adopt any course which its commander might think proper; and as the French cavalry, to which this hesitation was but too manifest, was now advancing rapidly to the attack, the Dutch-Belgians went about, and retired in such haste and disorder that the two right squadrons of the 3rd hussars of the King's German legion experienced the greatest difficulty in maintaining their ground, and avoiding being carried along to the rear by these horsemen in the wildness of their flight. The 3rd hussars had just moved up into the second line, in rear of Kruse's Nassau brigade, when this occurred, and the left squadron, being free from any interruption of the kind, gallantly charged and completely overthrew that portion of the cuirassiers which was in its immediate front. As soon as the other two squadrons had recovered their order, which had been so unexpectedly disturbed by the fugitive Dutch-Belgians, the whole regiment advanced to the crest of the position, where it received from Lord Uxbridge, in person, the order to charge a line of French cavalry, distant about a hundred and fifty yards, and consisting of about three squadrons of cuirassiers and three squadrons of heavy dragoons. Commencing the charge with a steady trot, and then plunging into a gallop, they broke through the enemy's line, which was advancing at a short trot, or almost at a walk, but became so completely turned and hemmed in upon their flanks and rear, that a vast proportion of them was cut off. The remainder, dispersed, and pursued by the French cavalry, rode back to the infantry-squares, in rear of which the regiment re-formed. Here the great loss which it had suffered in these two attacks became manifest. It was reduced to between sixty and seventy files, which were formed into two squadrons, and posted in rear of Kielmansegge's Hanoverian brigade.

About this time, the Earl of Uxbridge, on examining the state of his cavalry, perceived the Cumberland regiment of Hanoverian hussars at some distance in the rear, on the Brussels road. He immediately ordered them forward, and on their coming up, he posted them where they were by no means much exposed, but where they would at least *appear* to fill a gap occasioned by the severe losses experienced by Somerset's and Ponsonby's brigades, for the manner of their commanding officer, whilst being thus posted, rendered his Lordship doubtful of their continuing there if attacked. That he had reason to apprehend something of this kind, was subsequently proved, for Colonel Hake, on finding the shot flying about him a little, took himself and his regiment out of the field; on discovering which, Lord Uxbridge despatched his aide-de camp, Captain Horace Seymour, with an order for his return. When Captain Seymour delivered this order, the Colonel remarked that he had no confidence in his men, that they were volunteers, and that their horses were their own property. The regiment continued moving to the rear, notwithstanding Captain Seymour's repeating the order to halt, and asking the second in command to save the honour and character of the corps, by placing himself at its head and fronting the men. Finding his remonstrances produced no effect, he laid hold of the bridle of the Colonel's horse, and commented upon his conduct in terms such as no man of honour could have been expected to listen to unmoved. This officer, however, appeared perfectly callous to any sense of shame, and far more disposed to submit to those attacks upon his honour than he had been to receive those of the enemy upon his person and his regiment. Upon rejoining the Earl of Uxbridge and relating what had passed, Captain Seymour was again directed to proceed to the commanding officer, and to desire that, if he persevered in refusing to resume his position in the line, he would, at least, form the regiment across the high road, *out* of fire. But even this order was disregarded, and the corps went altogether to the rear, spreading alarm and confusion all the way to Brussels.*

In front of the right of the Anglo-allied line, the French column of horse-grenadiers and cuirassiers which had met with so disastrous a repulse from Major Mercer's horse-battery, was reformed for another attack, to meet which the British gunners were fully prepared, for the French horsemen had not retired so far down the hill but that the high caps of the horse-grenadiers of the leading squadrons, were visible above the brow of the exterior slope. The second attempt was preluded by a cloud of skirmishers, who, advancing to within a very short distance of the front of the battery, did considerable mischief to the gunners with their

* As might have been expected, Colonel Hake was tried by a General Court Martial for this conduct and sentenced to be dismissed from the profession of arms, of which he had proved himself so unworthy a member.

carbines and pistols; but their intention being evidently to draw forth their fire, no notice was taken of them. Then the column again ascended the ridge, and advanced to attack the battery, but on this occasion their pace scarcely exceeded a walk, or at most a gentle trot, too many obstacles lying in their way to admit of more rapid movement without confusion. Experience having shown the gunners the destructive effects of a close fire, they allowed the leading squadrons to attain about half the distance between the brow of the slope and the narrow road in their front before they commenced. The result as may be readily imagined, was precisely similar to that of the former attack, which has already been detailed. Again the French horsemen fell into confusion, and again for several minutes were they exposed to a deliberate and an unerring fire of case-shot, within a distance of not more than twenty yards, so that the pile of killed and wounded, left on the ground immediately in front of the battery, before great, was now enormous.

Other batteries along this part of the position were equally successful in repelling the attacks of the enemy's cuirassiers, who were assembling in considerable numbers at the foot of the exterior slope, close to the Hougomont inclosures, apparently with the object of cutting off the direct communication with that post, and forcing the right of the Allied front line. The moment seemed favourable for such a project. Several of the Allied guns had by this time become completely disabled; the 2nd battalion of the 3rd British guards, awfully reduced, had been driven into the hollow-way in rear of the orchards of Hougomont; the young Brunswick infantry had suffered severe losses; and the supporting cavalry had become greatly exhausted by its repeated charges. But Wellington, foreseeing the probability of a serious attempt upon this weakened point of his line, and perceiving the approach of Chassé's division, (see page 293,) supplied the required remedy by desiring Lord Hill to bring forward troops from the second line. The zeal, intelligence, and activity which had ever characterized the hero of Almaraz and Arroyo del Molino when carrying out the designs of the Chief under whom he had acquired a lasting fame, seemed but to wait this summons to the more immediate scene of action, to appear again in all their accustomed vigour. He immediately put in motion, du Plat's infantry-brigade of the King's German Legion. As the latter advanced across the Nivelles road, from its left, the 2nd line battalion became the leading column. It was followed by the 4th, then by the 3rd, and lastly by the 1st line battalion. As the 2nd approached the crest of the ridge, several gunners ran in upon it for shelter from the enemy's cuirassiers, whose main body was now advancing against this battalion. The four light companies of the brigade, however, had just posted themselves close to the three small trees near this part of the crest of the ridge, and being armed with rifles, they delivered so destructive a fire into the cavalry as to compel it to withdraw. Some of the Allied cavalry then moved forward in pursuit, and du Plat's brigade continued its advance until the 2nd line battalion had approached close to the hedge of the great orchard of Hougomont, whence a dropping fire was opened upon the Germans by the French skirmishers. The dragoons made a sudden and rapid retreat through the intervals of the columns, in left front of which a fresh line of hostile cavalry now presented itself. Captain Sympher, who, with his horse-battery of the legion, had accompanied du Plat's advance, instantly unlimbered, and poured round shot through the intervals of the columns, the latter maintaining, at the same time, a very effective independent file-fire. The cuirassiers gallantly advanced, notwithstanding this formidable resistance. They first became exposed to a flank fire from the left face of the 4th line battalion-square, and then again to that from the left face of the 3rd line battalion: nevertheless, they resolutely attacked the battery, the gunners of which either flew to the last mentioned square for protection, or sought shelter under the carriages. At length, after having suffered severe losses by the unremitting fire from the nearest squares, the French cavalry retired in disorder, receiving a renewed discharge from the battery, which was again in full play. When du Plat's brigade moved down the slope, the 2nd and 3rd light, and 2nd line, battalions of the Brunswickers, advanced a short distance over the crest of the ridge, in left rear of the former. Here they became exposed to a destructive fire of both artillery and musketry, the latter from the French skirmishers that had crept from along the eastern hedge of Hougomont, close under the brow of that part of the Anglo-allied position. They withstood this heavy fire, as also the subsequent charges of cavalry, with great steadiness and courage; but as soon as the French horsemen were driven back by a portion of the Allied cavalry, consisting of the 23rd British light dragoons, the 1st light dragoons of the King's German legion, and the Brunswick hussars and lancers, the above-mentioned battalions withdrew from their exposed situation to the interior slope.

The French skirmishers, who had, during this last attack by their cavalry, pushed forward a very considerable force through the great orchard of Hougomont, and along its eastern boundary, now concentrated a most galling fire upon the squares of the legionary brigade, whose commander, du Plat, was mortally wounded: several officers fell, and all those that were mounted had their horses shot under them. The fire ceased; and in the next moment the cuirassiers, having rallied, renewed their charge, but with no greater success than before; and a third charge proved equally ineffectual against the determined bravery and patient endurance of the soldiers of the legion.

About the time that du Plat's brigade moved into the first line, a considerable body of French cuirassiers, which still remained in the hollow westward of La Haye Sainte, exposed to a fire from one or two of the Allied batteries, advanced at a walk, to make another effort to break the right centre of Wellington's line. This proved as unsuccessful as the previous attacks. The squares, reserving their fire until the close approach of the hostile cavalry, and then directing it against the latter in the most cool and deliberate manner, which the absence of all impetus in an attack at a walk enabled them to do with unerring effect, soon compelled the shattered squadrons once more to withdraw from a contest which the unexampled steadiness of the Allied infantry had rendered almost hopeless on their part.

The French cavalry that attacked the squares of du Plat's brigade, immediately in rear of Hougomont, had no sooner been driven off by the gallant resistance of the Germans, than the skirmishers, who, as before observed, had advanced in such numbers along the eastern inclosures of that post, crept close up under the brow of that part of the ridge on the interior slope of which was posted the main body of the Brunswick infantry. At this time, however, Lord Hill was bringing forward Adam's British light infantry-brigade, having directed it to cross the Nivelles road, and to advance in columns up the slope, in rear of the Brunswickers. (The brigade had, some time before, been moved from the plateau on the right, close to the edge of the Nivelles road, in which position it had continued in immediate reserve.) Suddenly the summit in its front was crowded with the French skirmishers, who were almost as quickly concealed by the smoke from the rattling fire which they opened upon the Allied artillery and the squares. The gunners, whose numbers were fearfully diminished, were speedily driven back from their crippled batteries upon the nearest infantry, upon which the concentration of this galling fire threatened the most serious consequences. But succour was at hand. Wellington, in the midst of the shower of bullets, had galloped to the front of Adam's brigade, ordered it to form line, four deep, and then, pointing to the daring skirmishers on the height, called out, with perfect coolness and unaffected assurance, "Drive those fellows away!" With loud cheers, the brigade moved rapidly up the slope, eager to obey the Duke's commands. From the want of sufficient space, the 52nd regiment was not formed in line with, but in rear of, the 71st, and 2nd battalion of the 95th regiment, to which it consequently served as a support. The French skirmishers began to give way as the firm and intrepid front of the brigade presented itself to their view. Adam continued his advance, driving the French infantry before him. On crossing the ridge, the brigade brought forward its right shoulders, and, when halted, it stood in a slight hollow, which, commencing in front of the right of the position occupied by Maitland's brigade of guards, descends towards the north-east angle of the great orchard of Hougomont. At the former point the 2nd battalion of the 95th regiment formed the left, and at the latter, the 71st regiment with the two companies of the 3rd battalion of the 95th regiment formed the right, of this line. The enemy's cavalry having been perceived preparing for attack, the battalions of the brigade formed squares; and as the interval between the 71st and the 2nd battalion 95th regiment, in this new position, was larger than was desirable, Colonel Sir John Colborne moved down the 52nd regiment, in squares of wings of battalions, to fill up the space, which he reached just in time to throw a most effective oblique fire upon the cavalry which was in the act of attacking the 71st regiment.

The French carabiniers and horse-grenadiers of the guard made some gallant attacks upon the brigade. They generally advanced by *their* right of the Hougomout inclosures, then fell upon the 71st regiment, by which their charge was invariably broken, when such portions of them as continued in any degree of order, rushed onward in apparent infatuation upon the right wing-square of the 52nd regiment; from the front and right faces of which they received a close, well-directed fire, which completed their disorder and confusion. In one of these attacks, Major Eeles,* whose company of the 3rd battalion 95th rifles, was attached to the 71st regi-

* Colonel William Eeles, K.H., of the Rifle Brigade, died on the 11th October, 1837.

ment, upon observing the approach of the carabiniers towards the right angle of the front face of the square, moved his company to the right, in line with the rear face, and, placing himself in its front, prevented his men from firing until the carabiniers approached within thirty or forty yards of the square, when he ordered a volley, which, combined with the cross-fire from the 71st, brought down so many horses and men to the ground, at the same moment, that the further progress of the charge was most effectually frustrated. In an instant, one half of the attacking force was on the ground; some few men and horses were killed; more were wounded; but by far the greater part were thrown down over the dead, the dying, and the wounded. These, after a short interval, began to extricate themselves from the mass, and made the best of their way back to their supports, some on horseback, but most of them on foot.

Adam's brigade, by means of the advanced position which it thus occupied, along the space between the Hougomont inclosures and the right front of Maitland's brigade, presented an effectual barrier to the advance of French cavalry against that portion of the Allied front line which was situated upon the right of the latter point. In the intervals between the charges of cavalry, it suffered severely from the enemy's artillery, more particularly the 71st regiment, and 2nd battalion 95th rifles, the position of these regiments being somewhat more exposed than that of the 52nd.

Halkett's Hanoverian brigade had moved from its previous position, near Merbe-braine, into the space within the angle formed by the Nivelles road and the hollow way which leads from the right of the front line down into the low ground below Hougomont; and it was shortly after Adam had moved into his forward position, that Halkett advanced, with the landwehr-battalions Osnabrück and Salzgitter, and took post on the exterior slope of the main ridge, in rear of du Plat's brigade.

It was now about six o'clock. The formidable attacks made by the French, along the entire line of the Anglo-allied army, had been productive of no positive advantage: the advanced posts of Hougomont and La Haye Sainte had successfully resisted the furious assaults which had hitherto been directed against them; and the forward position taken up by Adam's British brigade, made it manifest to the French Emperor that, notwithstanding the gallantry, enthusiasm, and devotion displayed in those attacks, by the finest troops he had ever assembled together, headed, too, by generals of the highest celebrity, still greater efforts, and still greater sacrifices must be made, if he hoped to drive the British lion from the position which it yet proudly retained with so firm a footing, before the Prussian eagle, which, for some time past, had hovered over, and was at this moment darting at, his extreme right, should alight, in the plenitude of its force, to satiate its thirst for vengeance in the fierce and sanguinary struggle.

Napoleon sent an order to Ney, to renew the attack upon the centre. To execute this with effect, however, fresh infantry was requisite, and the Marshal had none at his disposal. He therefore despatched his first aide-de-camp, Colonel Heymés, to represent to the Emperor the exhausted condition of his troops, half of which were placed *hors de combat,* and the other half overcome by fatigue, and failing in ammunition; and to request he would send him reinforcements. At this moment, however, Lobau's corps and the young guard were required for the security of the French right flank against the offensive operations of the Prussians; consequently, the battalions of the old guard, which constituted the only remaining reserve of infantry, could not be spared. To Ney's demand for fresh troops, Napoleon therefore replied,—"*Où voulez-vous que j'en prenne? Voulez-vous que j'en fasse?*" Ney, on being made acquainted with the manner in which his request had been received, saw very plainly that the battle was far from being gained; and darted off to animate, by his presence, the attack which was now renewed upon La Haye Sainte, and which was covered by a vigorous fire from the French artillery against that portion of the Anglo-allied line immediately in rear of this post, in order to disturb any attempt to relieve or assist its defenders. The united remains of Somerset's and Ponsonby's brigades, which were on the reverse slope, behind Ompteda's brigade of the King's German legion, and which were extended in single file for the purpose of making a *show* of force, suffered much from this cannonade. On perceiving its effects, Lord Uxbridge sent an aide-de-camp to recommend Lord Edward Somerset to withdraw his men from the range of the enemy's guns. The latter sent back word that, were he to do so, the Dutch-Belgian cavalry, who were in support, would immediately move off the field! Somerset retained his position until the end of the battle.

Shortly before the columns from Donzelot's division advanced to this attack of La Haye Sainte, a party of horse-artillery, which had been detached from Whinyates's rocket-battery, proceeded, under Captain Dansey,* along the Charleroi road, to the front of the centre of the Anglo-allied line, and came into action with rockets, near that farm, leaving its two guns in the rear, under Lieutenant Wright.† Captain Dansey very soon received a severe wound, which obliged him to retire; and the party, after firing a few rockets, fell back a little, to where its horses were standing. It was then commanded by a Serjeant, (Daniel Dunnett,) who, on perceiving the advance of the nearest French column towards the farm, dismounted his men as coolly and deliberately as if exercising on Woolwich Common, though without any support whatever; laid rockets on the ground, and discharged them in succession into the mass—every one of them appearing to take effect. The advance of the column was checked, and was not resumed until Sergeant Dunnett, having expended all his rockets, retired with his party to rejoin the guns in rear.

Major Baring's detachment, after its extraordinary and successful exertions in repelling the previous assaults, was fearfully reduced in numbers; but its excellent spirit and conspicuous bravery remained unshaken. One circumstance, however, could not fail to render unavailing all their efforts, their courage, and their endurance. Notwithstanding Major Baring's urgently repeated applications for a supply of ammunition, his men were still left without the means of adequately defending their post against the host of enemies by which they were successively assailed.‡ They cheerfully repaired, as

* Now Colonel Charles C. Dansey, C.B., Royal Artillery.

† Major Amherst Wright, Royal Artillery, died on the 27th September, 1840.

‡ Two different causes have been assigned for the non-compliance with Major Baring's requisitions for ammunition; namely, theinterception of the communication between the post and the main line, and the difficulty in procuring *rifle* ammunition. The first appears scarcely tenable; for, although the communication was frequently cut off by the French, as they passed by the farm when attacking the main position, it was as frequently open and available. This is sufficiently proved by the different reinforcements that were sent into the farm: ammunition might have been escorted thither with equal facility; and yet Baring had made three distinct applications for a supply *before* the Nassau detachment was added to his force. The difficulty of procuring *rifle* ammunition certainly appears a more probable cause; but, even in this case, it is impossible to overlook the circumstance that the post in question was immediately in front of the brigade to which its defenders belonged, and of which two out of the four battalions composing it were armed with rifles.

Since the above was written it has been communicated to me from Hanover, upon excellent authority, that the cause of Major Baring not having been supplied with ammunition arose from the circumstance, that there existed only one cart far as practicable, the gaps made in the walls by the French artillery, and betrayed no despondency as they looked upon the sad and numerous proofs that lay around them of the immense sacrifices they had already made. But when, upon counting the cartridges, they discovered that they had not, upon an average, more than from three to four each, their consciousness of the desperate situation to which they were reduced, and of the impossibility of holding out under such circumstances, led to remonstrances, which their gallant commander could not but admit to be reasonable. Yet no sooner did the latter, upon perceiving two French columns again advancing towards the farm, exhort them to renewed courage, and also to a careful economy of the ammunition, than he received the unanimous reply,—" No man will desert you,—we will fight and die with you !"

The French, exasperated by the protracted resistance of this handful of brave defenders, now came on with redoubled fury. The open end of the great barn was first assailed. Again they succeeded in setting the building on fire ; but the Germans, having recourse to the same expedient as on the previous occasion, again contrived to extinguish the flames. Baring's anxiety and uneasiness increased with every shot that was fired by his men ; and he again sent to the rear for ammunition, coupling his demand with a distinct report, that he must and would abandon the place should no supply be forthcoming. This message, however, proved equally ineffectual. The fire of the garrison was gradually diminishing: perplexity was depicted in every countenance: many of the men now called out urgently for ammunition, adding,— " We will readily stand by you, but we must have the means of defending ourselves !" Even their officers, who during the whole day had displayed the greatest courage, represented to their commander the impossibility of retaining the post under such circumstances. The French, who failed not to observe the distressing situation to which the defenders were reduced, now boldly broke in the door at that end of the long western building which is nearest to the entrance of the great barn, already so frequently assailed. The passage from the door through the building into the farm-yard having been barricaded, but few of the enemy could enter at a time. These were instantly bayoneted, and the rear hesitated to follow. They now climbed up the outer wall of the long

with rifle ammunition for the two light battalions of the King's German legion, and that this cart was involved in the precipitate retreat of a great part of the baggage, &c. and thrown into a ditch.

building, and mounted the roof, from which they easily picked off the defenders, who, not possessing the means of retaliation, were completely at their mercy. At the same time, they pressed in through the open barn, which it was impossible to defend any longer. Baring was now reduced to the painful necessity of abandoning the place, and gave the order to retire through the dwelling-house into the garden. Many of the men were overtaken in the narrow passage through the house by the victors, who vented their fury upon them in the lowest abuse and most brutal treatment.*

Baring having satisfied himself that the possession of the dwelling-house by the enemy must render the garden quite untenable, and finding that his officers fully agreed with him on this point, he made the men retire, singly, to the main position. The greater part of them, accompanied by their brave but disconsolate commander, descended into the high road by an opening in the bank adjoining the north-east angle of the garden, and retired along the opposite side of the chaussée. Baring sent back to their respective regiments the remains of the reinforcements he had received, and, with the few men that were left of his own battalion, he attached himself to two companies of the 1st light battalion of the King's German legion, which were then posted in the hollow-way close to the right of the high road.

The surrender of La Haye Sainte, under the circumstances which have been described, was as purely honourable, as its defence against an overwhelming and furious host had been heroically brave. A thorough conviction that further re-

* The passage through the farm-house to the garden in the rear was narrow, and here the officers endeavoured to halt the men, and make one more charge, but as the French had already commenced firing down the passage, this was found impracticable. Ensign Frank, on perceiving a French soldier levelling his musket at Lieutenant Græme, called out to the latter to take care; but, as he was still trying to rally his men, he replied, "Never mind, let the rascal fire!" At this instant the piece was levelled, but it fell to the ground with its owner, whom Ensign Frank had stabbed in time to save his friend. The French were now rushing into the house, and the foremost of them having fired at Ensign Frank, his arm was shattered by the bullet. Nevertheless he contrived to obtain shelter in a bed-chamber, and succeeded in concealing himself under the bed. Two of the men also took refuge in the same room; but the French followed close at their heels, crying, "Pas de pardon à ces coquins verds!" and shot them dead close to Ensign Frank, who had the well-merited good fortune of remaining undiscovered until the house again fell into the hands of the Allies. Lieutenant Græme, who had continued in the passage, was suddenly seized by the collar by a French officer, who exclaimed to his men, "C'est ce coquin!" Their bayonets were immediately thrust at him, but he managed to parry them with his sword, and as the officer for a moment relinquished his grasp, Græme darted along the passage, the French firing two shots after him, and calling out, "Coquin!" but they did not follow him, and he succeeded in rejoining the remnant of his battalion.

sistance must have been marked by the sacrifice of the entire remnant of his courageous band, at once suggested to the mind of a commander like Baring, gifted with the requisite discernment and forethought of a true soldier, the reservation of such gallant spirits for some other part of the great contest, in which they might yet face their enemies, if not on equal terms, at least in a manner that would render their bravery and devotion not altogether unavailable in the general struggle for victory.*

Loud and reiterated shouts of triumph having announced to the French Emperor the capture of La Haye Sainte, he immediately ordered it to be followed up by a vigorous attack upon the centre of the Anglo-allied line, and by a simultaneous renewal of the assault upon Hougomont.

It was quite evident to Ney, that without an additional force of infantry, it would be impossible for him to follow up, with effect, the advantage which he anticipated from the capture of La Haye Sainte. The cavalry which Napoleon had placed at his disposal, had been nearly annihilated in the course of its numerous attacks upon the Anglo-allied line,—attacks executed throughout with the greatest gallantry, but unproductive of any solid or decisive result upon a single point of that line. If this arm, comprising the flower of the chivalric cavalry of France, had failed him when it sallied forth, gaily exulting in the freshness of its vigour, proudly conscious of the imposing attitude of its masses, and unrestrainedly impatient for the onslaught which was to exalt still more its already high renown, how could he calculate upon its efficacy, now that it was comparatively paralyzed? The state to which his infantry was reduced presented a prospect almost as cheerless. D'Erlon's corps, severely crippled by its signally unsuccessful attack upon the Anglo-allied left wing and centre, had still further exhausted its force by repeated assaults against La Haye Sainte, on its left; and, since the arrival of Bülow, it had been compelled to resort to active precautionary measures on its right. On the other hand, Reille's corps had suffered immense losses in its incessant, yet unavailing efforts to gain possession of the important post of Hougomont. But Ney, "*le plus brave des braves,*" in whose character, resolution and perseverance were preeminent, was not to be deterred by this discouraging aspect, from fulfilling, to the best of his abilities, the task imposed

* For a nominal list of the officers who were present at La Haye Sainte, in the glorious defence of that farm on the 18th of June, see Appendix XXXII.

upon him by his imperial master. There can be but little doubt that at the time he made his urgent demand upon the Emperor for a fresh supply of infantry, he had projected an assault upon the Anglo-allied right wing, in accordance with that prominent feature in the tactics of the empire,—the column of attack in mass of battalions—to be supported by his cavalry, whilst this arm still continued vigorous and effective. Now, however, his exhausted means precluded the execution of such a plan of attack, and he therefore had recourse, as far as was practicable with his reduced extent of force, to another system, which had been attended with so much success in the time of the republic, and which had always found great favour with the French soldiery—the grand attack *en tirailleurs.* In this way he would be better enabled to conceal the weakened condition of his troops, and he might also succeed in making such an impression upon some important point of the Allied line, as would induce the Emperor to seize upon the advantage gained, and, launching forth his reserve, strike the decisive blow.

The whole of Donzelot's division, supported by a part of Alix's division, as also a considerable body of cuirassiers, forming the gallant remnants of entire regiments, were put in motion against the centre of the Anglo-allied line; whilst fresh reinforcements were poured down from Reille's corps into the Hougomont inclosures.

The first disposition made by the captors of La Haye Sainte, was to avail themselves of the advantage which the possession of the farmhouse, the garden, and the adjacent high bank, afforded them for pouring a commanding fire upon the two companies of the 95th British rifles, which occupied the knoll by the sandpit, on the opposite side of the road; when these, being at the same time pressed in front, finding their post no longer tenable, retreated upon their main body in the Wavre road. The French at the same time contrived to push two guns round by the garden-hedge to the bank of the high road, and immediately opened a fire of grape upon Kempt's brigade, posted along, and in rear of, the Wavre road, on the opposite side of the chaussée; but this was speedily silenced by the 1st battalion of the 95th British rifles, who, taking a deliberate aim at the artillerymen, destroyed them before they could discharge a second round. There then issued from under cover of the farm, a large body of infantry, which, as it ascended the main ridge, spread out into a very close line of skirmishers, who pressed boldly forward against the left of Alten's division.

Their concentrated fire was telling fearfully upon the devoted squares. Alten sent an order to Ompteda to deploy one of his battalions, if practicable, and advance against the enemy. Ompteda, as brave and high-minded a soldier as ever graced the profession of arms, was quite prepared to execute the order, but being fully aware, from previous observation, that in the hollow behind the curtain formed by the *tirailleurs* there lay in wait a body of the enemy's cavalry, he felt it his duty to represent the imminent risk which was likely to attend such a movement. At this moment of hesitation, the Prince of Orange rode up to Ompteda and ordered him to deploy. The latter respectfully submitted the same opinion he had before expressed to Alten's messenger; whereupon his Royal Highness became impatient, repeated the order, and forbade further reply. Ompteda, with the true spirit of a soldier, instantly deployed the 5th line battalion, placed himself at its head, and gallantly led it against the mass of *tirailleurs*, who had continued to crowd forward, and under whose teazing fire the Germans displayed the greatest steadiness and bravery. The French gave way as the line advanced at the charge; and as it approached the garden of La Haye Sainte, they suddenly and rapidly sought shelter along the hedges. In the next moment, the battalion was furiously assailed by a regiment of cuirassiers, who, taking the line in its right flank, fairly rolled it up. This cavalry-charge, pre-concerted with great skill, and executed with amazing rapidity, proved awfully destructive to the courageous but unfortunate Germans ; and fully, and fatally, confirmed the truth of the unheeded prediction of their intrepid commander. So severe was the loss sustained, that out of the whole battalion, not more than about 30 men with a few officers were gradually collected in the hollow-way that lay along the front of the left of the brigade. Amongst the slain was Ompteda himself, who, with his followers, thus fell a sacrifice to the absence of that precaution, the necessity for which he had vainly endeavoured to impress upon his superior officer.

Whilst the French cuirassiers were cutting and stabbing in all directions, and completing their work of destruction amidst the unfortunate Germans, the 95th British rifles, who, from the other side of the high road, had been attentive observers of the scene, had already taken aim at the cuirassiers, but had refrained from firing, fearing to injure their friends, at length poured in amongst them a terrific volley, just at the very moment when the 3rd hussars of the King's

German legion advanced to the rescue of their compatriots, which sent both sides flying, and completely cleared the front of Ompteda's brigade. Shortly afterwards the 3rd hussars again advanced, but the support of the cuirassiers having, in the mean time, ascended the slope, the former, so inferior in numbers, were brought to a stand, and, after a brief struggle, were compelled to withdraw.

A mass of *tirailleurs* now ascended by their left, from the hollow westward of La Haye Sainte, (in which hollow they could assemble in comparative security since the capture of that post by the French) and pushed forward with great boldness against the advanced square of Maitland's British brigade, formed by the 3rd battalion of the 1st foot guards. Their fire, concentrated upon the square, and maintained with astonishing rapidity and vigour, was most galling to the British guards. Also upon their left, another portion of their numbers poured a destructive fire upon the left square of Adam's brigade, formed by the 2nd battalion of the 95th rifles. Maitland, perceiving the serious annoyance which his 3rd battalion experienced from the fire of the French skirmishers, directed Lieut. Colonel D'Oyley, who commanded it, to advance for the purpose of dislodging them, and being well aware that some of the enemy's cavalry were drawn up near the foot of the slope, he threw the flank faces of the square into sections, in which order the battalion moved forward, being thus prepared to re-form square with the greatest expedition. Under a tremendous fire from the opposite French batteries, which had perceived this movement, the guards gallantly drove the skirmishers down the slope, and so marked was their steadiness on this occasion, that a body of French cavalry, which was now observed approaching, struck with the promptitude and precision with which the gaps caused in their ranks by the round shot were closed, neither assaulted them in their advance nor molested them in their retreat to their position on the brow of the hill, which was effected in perfect order. The cavalry, though it refrained from attacking, received the fire of, the guards, and then, dashing along the front of the 52nd regiment, it exposed itself to another vigorous fire by which it was nearly destroyed.

Of all the troops comprising the Anglo-allied army at Waterloo, the most exposed to the fierce onslaught of the French cavalry, and to the continuous cannonade of their artillery, were the two British squares posted, during a very great portion of the battle, in advance—at times, considerably so—of the narrow road which ran along the crest of the Duke's position. They consisted of the 3rd battalion of the 1st guards, belonging to Maitland's brigade, and of the 30th and 73rd regiments acting together as one corps,* belonging to Halkett's brigade. It was upon these troops that fell the first burst of the grand cavalry attacks; and it was upon these troops, also, that the French gunners seldom neglected to pour their destructive missiles, so long as they continued to constitute, by their exposed position, such prominent marks for their fire. An attack upon the square of the guards by skirmishers has just been described; and it was not long after this that the square of the 30th and 73rd was attacked by some French artillery, which trotted boldly up the slope directly in the front of those regiments, and having approached within a fearfully short distance, unlimbered two of its guns, from which several rounds of grape were discharged in rapid succession, into the very heart of the square. Awful gaps were made in its devoted ranks; but the readiness and alacrity with which they were filled up, at the commands of their officers, by men prepared to share the same fate as that which had befallen their predecessors, was truly heroic. That an occasional murmur broke forth, cannot be denied—not, however, at their exposed situation, but at the stern refusal to allow them to charge the guns, near which the French cavalry was hovering, ready to take advantage of any such attempt.

The Duke was frequently an eye-witness of this devotedness of his soldiers, but when asked for support, his reply was that there was none to spare; or, if for permission to attack, that this could not be granted; and, if any intimation were made to him that it might become necessary to fall back a little out of fire, it was met, in a cool and decided tone, that every man must stand his ground, and that there must not even be a semblance of retreat.

The reinforcements from Reille's corps having moved to Hougomont, the skirmishers in and around this post were relieved upon all points. The wood, as also the fences on either flank, soon swarmed with *tirailleurs;* and the brisk rattle of musketry that followed, intermingled with shouts of "*En avant!*" seemed to betoken a determination on the part of the French that the capture of La Haye Sainte should not be their only triumph achieved in front of the Anglo-allied army. Everywhere the assault was bravely met by the gallant

* It is affirmed, and very currently believed, that this square was charged *eleven* times by the French cavalry.

defenders of the post. The flank companies of the guards, within the walls and buildings, held at defiance every attempt of their assailants to dislodge them from their cover. By this time, all the outhouses were on fire, with the exception of those that fronted the wood. The roof and upper story of the château had fallen in, and flames continued bursting forth on all sides with the greatest fury. The heat had become so intense as to produce upon the men whose duty brought them within its influence, a feeling of suffocation; while the frequently emitted volumes of thick smoke gave an indistinctness to every object around them. Yet so admirable was the system of defence, so perfect were the discipline and the order, maintained throughout this trying scene, by the devoted garrison, that the enemy completely failed in forcing an opening at any one point. The well maintained fire from the walls was such as to deter the French from attempting an escalade. Whilst the central portion of the *tirailleurs* kept up an incessant fire from behind the hedge and trees facing the south buildings and the gardens, the remainder pressed on in crowds against the inclosures by which the post was flanked. On the right, the 2nd battalion of the Coldstream guards, lining the hedge that bordered the main approach to the château, successfully withstood this furious onset. On the left, the 2nd battalion of the 3rd guards, in the orchard, having suffered such frightful losses, found it impossible to stem the overwhelming torrent, and speedily fell back upon its friendly hollow-way. The French *tirailleurs*, pushing forward in pursuit, were staggered by the sudden and vigorous fire opened upon them by the troops within the eastern garden-wall; and the 3rd guards having, in the mean time, been reinforced by the 2nd line battalion and the light companies of du Plat's brigade, drove the enemy back to the front hedge of the orchard; whence, however, they were shortly, in their turn, compelled to retire. Again the flank fire from the eastern garden-wall, combined with that in front from the defenders of the orchard, as they reached the rear hedge, compelled the enemy to fall back. The 3rd guards once more lined the front hedge, and also, in conjunction with the light troops of du Plat's brigade, and the remains of both the Brunswick advanced-guard-battalion, and the 1st battalion of the 2nd regiment of Nassau, forced the entrance into the wood near the south-east angle of the garden-wall, and firmly established themselves in that quarter.

At the commencement of this last mentioned attack upon Hougomont, the right of Adam's brigade was considered too near the inclosures of that post, and exposed to be taken from thence in flank. It was therefore withdrawn further up the slope, towards the crest of the main position; and after a brief interval, it retired to the reverse slope in order to be covered from the enemy's cannonade which had been directed against it.

It was now nearly seven o'clock. The troops defending Hougomont and its inclosures had succeeded in repelling the last assault, and the contest in and around this post again degenerated into a *tiraillade,* kept up with more or less vigour on all points. Along the front of the extreme right of the Anglo-allied line, the skirmishers from Mitchell's British infantry-brigade maintained their ground with great steadiness and gallantry. The main body of the Brunswick infantry stood on the interior slope, in rear of Adam's brigade; and Chassé's Dutch-Belgian infantry-division, which had arrived from Braine-la-leud, was deployed along, and in rear of, the Nivelles road, its centre intersected by the narrow road leading from the chaussée to the village of Merbe-braine, which position it had taken up on the advance of Adam's brigade to the general front line. In front of the Anglo-allied left, the skirmishers of both armies were continually engaged; and upon the extreme left the troops in Smohain, La Haye. Papelotte, and adjacent inclosures, successfully resisted all attempts of the enemy to dislodge them. The attack upon the centre of the Anglo-allied line had been incessant from the moment La Haye Sainte fell into the possession of the French. On their left of the Charleroi road, they debouched from that farm, and ascended the position in clouds of skirmishers. One portion of them crowded upon the artificial mound which abutted upon the high bank of the road, and was situated about sixty yards only in front of the hollow-way occupied by Ompteda's brigade. On the opposite side of the Charleroi road, the fire from the French troops on the knoll above the sand-pit was maintained with remarkable rapidity and perseverance. They continued, as before, to conceal themselves as much as possible under the brow of the knoll, exposing only so much of their bodies as was necessary to enable them to fire over its crest, in a kneeling position. This fire was replied to with the greatest spirit and determination on the part of Kempt's and Lambert's brigades. On the allied right of the high road, the exhausted remnant of Ompteda's brigade was no longer a match for the daring *tirailleurs* that crowded together in its front. Its stock of ammunition had begun to fail: many who had not a cartridge left fell to the rear, and more than the usual number assisted the wounded out of action.

Exposed as Alten's division had been to the most furious assaults of artillery, cavalry, and infantry, the British and German brigades of which it was composed had become awfully diminished; and the facility which the possession of La Haye Sainte now afforded the French for continuing their desperate endeavours to force that part of the Allied line, rendered the situation of these troops extremely critical. Alten, who had throughout the day displayed the same coolness, intrepidity, and skill, which had characterized his career in the Peninsular war, and who, by his presence and example, had so powerfully sustained the energies of his men, was not permitted to witness the closing scene of their glorious exertions; for about this time he was wounded, and compelled to quit the field, leaving the command of the division to his gallant countryman Kielmansegge.

At a short distance in rear of Lambert's brigade stood that of Pack, (with the exception of the 1st Royal Scots, then in front line,) in contiguous columns at quarter distance, its right resting on the high road, while further to the rear, as a reserve, was posted Vincke's Hanoverian brigade, having two of its battalions, Hameln and Gifhorn, in contiguous close columns on the left of the road, and the other battalions, Peine and Hildesheim, in a similar formation, on the right of the road, near the farm of Mont St. Jean.

The pertinacity and zeal displayed by the French in their attacks upon the centre of the Anglo-allied line, and the indications now manifested of following them up with increased force, were in accordance with Napoleon's great object of breaking that centre, and overthrowing the right wing, of the Duke's army; and for the execution of this latter part of his plan, he was preparing to strike another formidable blow, even now that the Prussians were fairly *aux prises* with the troops constituting the extreme right of his army in and around Planchenoit. But previously to entering into the subject of the concluding scene of the struggle between the Anglo-allied and French armies, it will be necessary to revert to the operations of the Prussian forces, in order to arrive at a full and comprehensive development and due interconnection of all the leading features and various bearings of the great battle, the result of which was to determine the issue of the campaign in Belgium.

CHAPTER XIII.

Blücher's dispositions for the grand flank movement of his army towards the field on which Wellington had announced to him his intention of accepting battle from Napoleon, provided he might calculate on the Marshal's assistance, were fully described in Chapter VIII. Reconnoitring parties and patroles had been pushed forward, early in the day, to feel for the left of the Anglo-allied army, the communication with which was successfully established. It then became desirable to explore the ground that lay more to the right front of the Prussians, in the direction of the right flank of the main French army, in order to ascertain the nature of any precautionary measures adopted by Napoleon to impede the junction of the Allied commanders. Major Lützow, of the Staff, was sent upon this duty, with a detachment of the 2nd Silesian hussars; and on reaching the wood of Paris, he not only found this unoccupied, but discovered that no steps whatever had been taken by the French to cover and secure their right flank. A Prussian troop of hussars advanced beyond the wood of Paris, to a point near Frischermont, whence it had a good view of both the French and Allied dispositions and movements; and where it was not even menaced by the approach of any hostile party.

As Major Lützow, fully alive to the importance of speedily occupying the wood of Paris, was returning to communicate the above intelligence to the Prince, he met General Grolman, the quarter master general of the army, to whom he immediately represented how matters stood; when this officer directly pushed forward the Silesian hussars and two battalions of infantry from Bülow's advanced guard, to take possession of the wood, these troops having fortunately just crossed the defile of St. Lambert. Grolman at the same time sent a message to the Prince, suggesting that the 15th and 16th brigades should be ordered to follow the advanced guard, as soon as they should be collected on the French side of the defile.

Great as had been the difficulties hitherto encountered along the Prussian line of march, the passage of the defile of St. Lambert seemed to present an almost insurmountable obstacle. The rain which had set in during the afternoon of the 17th, and had continued without cessation the entire night, had transformed the valley of the Lasne into a perfect swamp. The miry and watery state of the roads between Wavre and St. Lambert, had caused so many stoppages and breaks in the columns that they were frequently lengthened out for miles. Blücher showed himself on every point of the line of march, encouraging his exhausted soldiers, and inciting them to renewed efforts. The troops, after a short halt to collect their scattered ranks, entered the defile. As the ground yielded to their pressure, both cavalry and infantry became dispirited; and when the artillery were fairly checked, by the guns sinking axle-deep, and the men, already worn down by fatigue, were required to work them out, their murmurs broke forth in exclamations of—"We *cannot* get on." "But we *must* get on," was old Blücher's reply; "I have given my word to Wellington, and you will surely not make me break it: only exert yourselves a few hours longer, children, and certain victory is ours." This appeal from their venerated chief was not made in vain: it served to revive the drooping energies of the wearied, and to stimulate still further to successful exertion the more robust and able-bodied.

At length, after considerable delay and constant difficulty, the passage of the 15th and 16th brigades, as also of the reserve of both cavalry and artillery, was accomplished, and by four o'clock these troops had ascended the opposite slope of the valley, and reached the plateau of the ridge which, constituting the narrow interval between the Lasne and the Smohain, with a rapid fall on either side towards those streams, presented a comparatively dry and firm soil, favourable for the further operations of the Prussian forces in this direction.

As the troops reached the wood of Paris, they were disposed, with a considerable front, and in a close compact order, on each side of the road leading from Lasne towards Planchenoit. The artillery kept the road itself; and the cavalry was drawn up in rear of the wood, ready to follow the infantry.

The 13th and 14th brigades were expected to join in a short time; and Pirch's corps was following along the same line. It had been Blücher's intention to await the arrival of these troops, and then to debouch with the assembled force; but having watched the progress of the battle, he became apprehensive, on perceiving the tremendous cannonade, and the renewed attack after four o'clock, that the enemy might direct a still greater force against Wellington's line, and succeed in breaking the latter before he commenced the attack on his side of the field. He could clearly distinguish Napoleon's reserves, in rear of La Belle Alliance, evidently prepared, for being launched against the Anglo-allied line, which had already sustained the most desperate attacks. The frequent and pressing communications he had received from the Duke, also showed how anxiously the latter relied on his support. These considerations satisfied the Prince, that the moment had arrived in which his appearance on the field would be productive of consequences the most favourable to the views of his ally, and the most influential on the development of their combined exertions; and he now gave the order for the attack to commence, even with the small amount of force then at his disposal, as also for the hastening of the march of the troops still in the rear.

It was half-past four o'clock when the 15th and 16th brigades debouched from the wood of Paris; the former on the right, the latter on the left; and each in the usual brigade-formation for advance peculiar to Prussian tactics. The direction of the attack was perpendicular to the right flank of the French army, and consequently, also, to the Charleroi road, which constituted the French main line of operation.

In order to cover the left flank, Colonel Hiller, commanding the 16th brigade, detached both the 3rd battalions of the 15th regiment and the 1st Silesian landwehr, under Major Keller, to keep a look-out in that direction as far as the rivulet of the Lasne; beyond which, Major Falkenhausen was scouring the country with 100 horsemen of the 3rd regiment of Silesian landwehr-cavalry. General Losthin, commanding the 15th brigade, detached three battalions towards Frischermont and Smohain, to cover the right flank. They were the 2nd battalion of the 18th regiment, and the 3rd battalion of the 3rd Silesian landwehr, followed by the 1st battalion of the former regiment.

Domon's cavalry continued drawn up *en potence*, and was at a considerable distance from the Prussian advance, when Blücher ordered a cannonade to open upon it, more with a view to make known his arrival to the Anglo-allied army, and to induce the French to withhold the employment of a still greater force against the latter, than from any motive affecting his own immediate operations at the moment.

Domon now sent forward a regiment of chasseurs à cheval to attack the Prussian column, whilst he followed with his whole line. Hereupon the 2nd Silesian hussars, and the 2nd Neumark landwehr-cavalry, moved through the intervals of the infantry, and formed up in front, the hussars to the left, and the landwehr to the right. They then advanced, followed by the 3rd Silesian landwehr-cavalry in support, and drove back the French chasseurs; but becoming menaced in flank, and observing Domon's whole line advancing, they were, in their turn, compelled to retire. This movement was covered by the horse-battery No. 11, and more particularly by Captain Schmidt's foot-battery of the 15th brigade, which drew up to oppose the pursuit of the French cavalry. The vigorous fire which continued to be maintained by both these batteries, combined with the advance of the Prussian infantry-columns, induced Domon to decline following up his attack at the moment.

The three battalions already mentioned as having been detached to the right, had, by this time, reached Smohain. Their advance in that direction had been conducted with so much caution, that they debouched from the south-eastern inclosures of the village most unexpectedly for both the Allied troops in that vicinity, and the infantry forming the extreme right of the French front line. The Prussians continued to advance; crossed the principal fence which separated them from the French extreme right, and drew up in line almost at right angles with the direction of the enemy's front—two battalions in line, with the third in support. It was half-past five o'clock when this took place. The French at once advanced against them, whereupon the Prussians retired, and after regaining the hedges in the valley, lined the latter as skirmishers, and maintained a vigorous and successful *tiraillade* with their opponents.

In the mean time Napoleon, judging from the boldness of the Prussian advance, that considerable support was at hand, and apprehensive, no doubt, of the evil consequence likely to arise from that advance, if not promptly and effectually checked, had ordered the 6th corps, under Count Lobau, to move forthwith to the right from its reserve-station in rear of La Belle Alliance, and, in conjunction with Domon's cavalry, to take up a position favourable for repelling the attack by which he was menaced on that side of the field. Blücher, observing this disposition, the execution of which was effected with great rapidity and in good order, proceeded to give a broader and more imposing front to his own troops. He extended his right flank to the wooded heights of Frischermont, and rested his left upon a ravine descending to the Lasne, close to the wood of Virère. The reserve-cavalry, under Prince William of Prussia, was put in motion in two columns, towards the left flank, on which it was subsequently formed up.

When Lobau's corps moved off to the right, the regiments of the old and middle guard advanced and took up the position, in reserve, which it had occupied on the heights in rear of La Belle Alliance.

As Lobau's corps advanced and passed Domon's cavalry, the latter was disposed as a support. Having crossed the valley which, commencing from the ridge above Planchenoit, on the north side of the village, descends towards Smohain, he opened a brisk fire from his guns upon Bülow's line. A spirited cannonade ensued, in the course of which the Prussian foot-battery No. 14 had three guns disabled. It was not long, however, before the remaining brigades of Bülow's corps, the 13th and 14th, came up. Their batteries hastened to the front, and materially increased the force of the Prussian fire.

Blücher, who had now the whole of Bülow's corps at his disposal, was bent upon following up his original intention of directing his attack against the enemy's rear. With this view he made the 16th brigade take ground to its left, and brought up the 14th brigade in its rear, as a support; whilst at the same time he supplied the place of the former in the line by posting the 13th brigade on the left of the 15th. General Hacke, who commanded the 13th brigade, detached the 1st and 3rd battalions of the 2nd Neumark landwehr to the right, in support of the troops in Smohain. A portion of this detachment occupied Frischermont, thus obtaining an *appui* for the Prussian right flank, and securing the communication with the Prince of Saxe-Weimar's brigade, posted along the inclosures in front of the extreme left of the Anglo-allied army. This flank was also covered by the West Prussian uhlans and the 2nd Neumark landwehr-cavalry, that had been detached from the reserve-cavalry of the 4th corps, under Prince William of Prussia, which was following, as a support, the left wing of Bülow's line, now advancing in the direction of Planchenoit. The artillery along the Prussian line had by this time assumed a formidable appearance, the following batteries of the corps having come successively into action,—the 12-pounder batteries Nos. 3 and 5, the 6-pounder batteries Nos. 2, 13, 14, and 21, and the horse-batteries Nos. 11 and 12—comprising altogether 64 guns.

The ground over which Bülow's corps was now in the act

of advancing, was highly favourable for the development of a force destined to attack the flank of an army, the front of which was so completely *aux prises* with the enemy as was that of the French at this moment. Nearly at all points it commanded the position occupied by the French right *en potence*; the line was remarkably well *appui'd* on the flanks; and its front was parallel with the enemy's main line of operation.

The force which Lobau had at his disposal was greatly inferior to that of the corps he was sent to oppose. The former amounted to 15 battalions, 21 squadrons, and 42 guns—the latter (exclusive of the six battalions and eight squadrons detached to the right) consisted of 30 battalions, 27 squadrons, and 64 guns. He could not present a front sufficiently extensive and compact that would secure him from being turned in either flank. Hence, when he perceived that the principal force in this well-planned attack was advancing from the Prussian left, in the direction of Planchenoit, which then lay in his right rear, unoccupied by any French troops, he felt the necessity of retiring towards the Charleroi road, which he did by withdrawing his brigades *en échiquier*.

It was not long before several round shot from the Prussian batteries reached the Charleroi road; some of them falling both in front and rear of La Belle Alliance, where Napoleon was then stationed. It was evident to the latter that, unless reinforcements were despatched in support of Lobau, his right flank, already so seriously menaced, would speedily be turned. His trusty guard, with which, in former campaigns, he had so frequently succeeded in stemming the current that had suddenly set in against him from some previously hidden source, and threatened to overwhelm him, constituted the sole reserve at his disposal. Engaged during so many hours in carrying on a desperate attack along his whole front, without having as yet secured one single point of vantage-ground, he clearly foresaw that without some vigorous effort, by aid of a powerful reserve, no ray of victory would ever gleam upon his arms on that side of the field. But now that he was also engaged in defensive operations, along his right, against another enemy, by whom even his rear, and the main line of his retreat became endangered, the necessity of employing a portion of this reserve in a direction different from that which he had contemplated, was alike obvious and urgent. The appearance of Bülow's left bearing down upon Planchenoit, turning Lobau's right, and the powerful batteries along the Prussian front, admirably disposed in accordance with the favourable nature of the ground, over which the whole line was gradually approaching, distinctly indicated the immediate possession of that village in force, as the true and only measure that could be adopted for averting the impending danger. The two divisions of the young guard, posted on the plateau on the right of the chaussée close to Rosomme, and consisting of four battalions of voltigeurs, and four battalions of tirailleurs, were the nearest at hand for the occupation of Planchenoit, and Napoleon accordingly desired General Duhesme instantly to march thither with that force, accompanied by 24 pieces of cannon of the guard, and place himself on the right of Lobau's corps.

It was about this time (six o'clock) that Napoleon replied to Ney's demand for fresh infantry, "*Ou voulez-vous que j'en prenne? Voulez-vous que j'en fasse?*"* an expression, the force of which is rendered sufficiently obvious by the critical circumstances of his position.

It was also at this period that Blücher received intelligence that Thielemann was attacked by a superior force at Wavre, and that it was doubtful whether he would be able to maintain his ground. But the determination of the Prince to carry out his present plan of attack was fixed and irrevocable. He saw clearly that it was on the field where he himself stood, that the fate of the campaign must be decided; and that by giving the fullest effect in his power to the combined operation which he had preconcerted with Wellington, and which was already developing itself with so fair a prospect of success, he was pursuing the right and only course, by which the main army of Napoleon could be overthrown—a course founded upon the leading principle of all strategy, that of bringing the greatest mass to bear upon the decisive point. He immediately gave orders that Thielemann should be directed to hold out as well as he could, and to dispute every inch of ground with his opponents. At the same time he desired Bülow to continue pressing forward with his left, and to gain possession of the village of Planchenoit.

Colonel Hiller, who commanded the 6th brigade, formed the latter into three columns of attack. Two battalions of the 15th regiment, under Major Wittig, marched on the right against the village; two battalions of the 1st Silesian landwehr, under Major Fischer, in the centre; and two battalions of the 2nd Silesian landwehr, under Lieut. Colonel Blandowsky, formed the left column. The 14th brigade followed as a reserve, sending forward the 1st battalions of the

* See page 304.

11th regiment and 1st Pomeranian landwehr, as a support to the columns of attack.

In the mean time the troops of the young guard had occupied Planchenoit, and made their dispositions for its defence. As the skirmishers that preceded the Prussian columns approached the eastern inclosures of the village, they were received with a most destructive fire by the French tirailleurs. Some pieces of artillery were also brought to bear directly upon the columns, which, nevertheless, advanced with great bravery and steadiness, captured a howitzer and two guns, and gained possession of the churchyard. The occupation of this spot, which is naturally strong, being inclosed within a low stone wall, strengthened nearly all round by a steep outer bank, and commanding by its elevated position a very considerable portion of the village, appeared to offer great security to the Prussian troops, but the young guard, evidently prepared for this contingency, flew to the surrounding houses and gardens, whence they opened a concentrated fire upon the possessors of the churchyard. To this the latter replied with great spirit, and as the distance by which the hostile parties were separated was extremely limited, numbers fell in rapid succession on both sides. At length the French supports having come up and joined in this contest, and one of the columns having shown itself in rear of the Prussians, the latter were compelled to abandon the advantages they had acquired, and to withdraw altogether from the village. They were followed by some of Lobau's cavalry, which, however, having fallen into the line of fire of the Prussian battery, No. 2, was forced to retire.

The Prussian troops that had been driven out of Planchenoit immediately rallied and re-formed. The 2nd battalions of the 11th regiment and 1st Pomeranian landwehr now joined their respective 1st battalions, which had previously acted in support of the attacking columns, and advanced to a second assault, followed by the 15th regiment.

Napoleon, perceiving the determination of the Prussian commander to persevere in his attack upon Planchenoit, as also his dispositions for completely turning the French right, ordered General Morand, colonel-in-chief of the chasseurs à pied of the old guard to march to the village with a battalion from each of the second regiments of grenadiers and chasseurs. These battalions reached the scene of action just as the Prussians had re-entered the village; and taking the lead in the contest, succeeded in driving them out of the place, pursuing them as far as their main position on the opposite heights.

Here the French skirmishers penetrated amongst the Prussian batteries, but were overthrown and cut up by the 4th squadron of the 2nd Silesian hussars. The French cavalry now showed a disposition to advance, and it was not long before a regiment of lancers, which took the lead, was attacked and defeated by the 8th Prussian hussars. In following up the pursuit, however, after their charge, the hussars were suddenly involved in the fire from a battalion of French infantry, and were forced to fall back. On the other hand, a regiment of French chasseurs á cheval was driven off in a similar manner by a Prussian battalion.

By the advance of the 16th and 14th brigades against Planchenoit, a vacant space had been created in the Prussian line between those troops and the 13th and 15th brigades, which still maintained their ground with great gallantry, in the open field on the right. This vacant space was now covered by the main body of the reserve-cavalry of Bülow's corps, commanded by Prince William of Prussia, which by its perfect steadiness and good countenance, not only induced the enemy to confine himself to the defensive, but advanced in support of the Prussian infantry, even into the midst of the opposing musketry-fire, and here occupied the place which, had the line been complete, would have been held by infantry. On this occasion, the loss of the Prussian cavalry was considerable. The brigadiers, Colonel Count Schwerin, and Lieut. Colonel Watzdorf, were killed. The latter although previously wounded, would not quit the field, and was soon afterwards struck by a shot which deprived the Prussian army of a very distinguished officer.

Napoleon, observing preparatory dispositions for a renewal of the attack on Planchenoit by Bülow, who was only waiting for the co-operation and support of Pirch's corps which was now rapidly approaching, deemed it advisable to send a further reinforcement to the troops in the village. This consisted of the 1st battalion of the 2nd regiment of the chasseurs of the guard, under General Pelet, to whom he represented the great importance of maintaining possession of Planchenoit. At the same time orders were sent to the 1st battalion of the 1st regiment of the chasseurs of the guard, which was with the Emperor's baggage at Caillou, to march to the wood of Chantelet, for the purpose of covering the right of Planchenoit, and securing the village from being turned.

The situation of Napoleon had become critical in the extreme. The Prussian attack seemed to be checked for the moment, and the occupation of Planchenoit in sufficient force held out the prospect of a protracted, if not a successful, struggle in that quarter, should the attack be renewed. Still it must have appeared sufficiently evident to the Emperor that Blücher was but awaiting either the arrival of an additional portion of his army, or the favourable moment when he might combine his attack with a simultaneous one by Wellington. Should the Prussian general succeed in defeating the troops comprising the French right *en potence*, Napoleon's line of retreat by the Charleroi road would be completely intercepted, and his main front line being thus taken in flank and rear, would become an easy prey to the Anglo-allied army. He might yet attempt a skilful retreat upon Nivelles, but with an army so exhausted by its repeated and ineffectual attacks upon Wellington's unshaken line, this would have been a hazardous operation. It is, moreover, very questionable whether the idea of retreat ever entered into his views; for a retreat, after such sacrifices had been made, harassed and interrupted as it undoubtedly would be by the two hostile armies, which had succeeded in effecting a junction, must prove no less disastrous than a signal defeat, and equally involve the downfall of his military and political power. Hence his desperate resolve to peril the fate of his brave army and of his resuscitated empire upon another and a final struggle for victory over Wellington, whose troops had with such truly heroic courage, and such inflexible endurance, successfully withstood the most furious attacks which he had repeatedly launched against them during the whole day. By a victory alone, no matter how dearly purchased, could he hope to keep alive the national enthusiasm which he had again awakened, but which would assuredly relapse into irrecoverable apathy, should the *prestige* of returning glory be torn from the idol of the military portion of his subjects, and the empire become again exposed to be overrun by those foreign legions that had once more taken up arms with a firm resolve finally to crush a power, the existence of which was incompatible with the security and independence of the states of Europe.

As the prospect of the consequences of failure thus flashed across his mind, Napoleon, like a desperate gambler, driven to his last stake, determined to risk his *all* upon another venture. The meditated blow was to be struck against his bold antagonist, Wellington, whose line was to be attacked along its entire front by a simultaneous effort, while its right and centre were to be forced at all hazards. He immediately ordered General Count Druot to collect all his battalions of the guard that were still in reserve, in front of La

Belle Alliance. These were accordingly moved forward from their position near the house of De Coster; and the two battalions of the 1st regiment of grenadiers, which had previously been stationed on the height in rear of La Belle Alliance, were now destined to form a reserve to the attacking columns. D'Erlon and Reille were at the same time ordered to advance the whole of the remaining disposable force against the enemy, with a view to second the main attack. The centre of the Anglo-allied line, immediately in rear of La Haye Sainte was not to be allowed a moment's respite from the attacks which continued to be made against it by the troops occupying, and debouching from, that farm. These were also to carry the centre by assault, as soon as the guard should reach the height.

Wellington, who seemed to have acquired a thorough insight into his opponent's designs, having satisfied himself that his position was destined shortly to be again assailed by a formidable force, became anxious for the arrival of the Prussian troops expected on his extreme left. He desired his aide-de-camp, Lieut. Colonel Fremantle,* to proceed immediately in that direction, to hasten the advance of any corps he might fall in with, and to represent to its commander that if he would supply him with the means of strengthening those points along his line which had been so seriously weakened by repeated attacks, he entertained no doubt of not only maintaining his ground, but of also gaining the victory.

Although the Duke was fully aware that Bülow's corps was in active operation against the extreme right of the French army, the ground upon which that operation was mainly carried on was too remote from his own immediate sphere of action to admit of his calculating upon support from it, beyond that of a diversion of the enemy's forces; and it was only from the high ground on which the extreme left of the Anglo-allied line rested, that a general view could be obtained of the Prussian movements As regards, however, the village of Planchenoit itself, the spire of the church was all that could be seen even from the point alluded to, so that it was scarcely possible to distinguish which was the successful party in that quarter. Napoleon might (as he really did) present an efficient check to the Prussian attack, and at the same time retain sufficient force wherewith he might make another vigorous assault upon the Anglo-allied army. When, therefore, the Duke beheld his line so fearfully reduced in numbers,

* Major General John W. Fremantle, C.B., died in April, 1845.

which he had no means of replacing, and which the indomitable courage of his British and German troops alone had hitherto been able to supply, it is not surprising that he should have manifested some little impatience for the arrival of that portion of the Prussian forces which was to co-operate more immediately with his own army. The latter, with the exception of the Dutch-Belgian troops, which still continued in reserve, for it was useless to place them where they would be exposed to the brunt of the battle-shock, presented but a mere wreck of that proud array which it had displayed in the morning. But, if the vain confidence of strength had departed, the more noble pride of unflinching bravery still remained unshaken. Exposed, however, as they had been for so many hours to a tremendous cannonade, which only ceased at times but to give place to attacks of cavalry and musketry, their exemplary passive forbearance seemed, in some instances, to be approaching its utmost limits. Frequent messages reached the Duke from commanding officers, soliciting reinforcements and support, since their corps were reduced to skeletons; but the only reply they received was, that no reinforcements could be granted, and that they must hold their ground to the last man. Occasionally too, as he rode along the line, a murmur would reach his ear, indicative of impatience to be led against the enemy. This would draw from him some encouraging appeal, such as "Wait a little longer, my lads, and your wishes shall be gratified."

In all three arms of the service the losses had been awfully severe. Battalions, dwindled to mere handfuls of men, were commanded by either captains or subalterns. A vast number of guns along the whole extent of the line had been disabled. The British and German cavalry-brigades, with the exception of Vivian's and Vandeleur's on the left, were reduced to less than the ordinary strength of regiments—Somerset's and Ponsonby's brigades united did not comprise two squadrons. Many, it is true, had quitted the ranks to assist the wounded, and to convey prisoners to the rear; but if amongst these were to be found the weak and faint-hearted, the brave spirits that remained nobly represented the valour and devotion which, under the guidance of a master-hand, were destined to be crowned with lasting triumph. Familiarized as the men had become with scenes, in rapid succession, of violent death, under almost every variety of aspect, from the sudden gush of life to the slow and lingering anguish—from the calm and tranquil sleep "that knows no waking," to the ghastly writhings of convulsive death-throes, the short and frequent command of "Close up!" as their comrades fell around them, was as mechanically obeyed as would have been any common parade order in a barrack-square.

Such was the situation of the troops against which Napoleon was meditating an assault with all the force he could collect, in the hope—his last and only hope—of seeing his eagles soaring in triumph over those heights upon which the British standard continued to wave in proud defiance.

The battalions of the imperial guard which had been collected in front of La Belle Alliance, and which were to constitute the leading feature in the general attack upon the Anglo-allied line, consisted of nine battalions, exclusive of the two battalions of the 1st regiment of grenadiers, destined, as previously observed, to remain as a reserve. These nine battalions were formed into two columns of attack. The first comprised four battalions of the middle guard, namely, the 1st and 2nd battalions of the 3rd regiment of grenadiers, and the 1st and 2nd battalions of the 3rd regiment of chasseurs. It was formed in mass of battalions, and destined to advance against the centre of the right wing of the Anglo-allied army. The second column of attack consisted of the three remaining battalions of the middle guard—namely, the 1st battalion of the 4th regiment of grenadiers, and the 1st and 2nd battalions of the 4th regiment of chasseurs—and of two battalions of the old guard, namely, the 1st and 2nd battalions of the 1st regiment of chasseurs. These five battalions were moved down into the hollow adjoining the south-eastern angle of the inclosures of Hougomont, and there formed into a column in mass, which was to support the first column, and to direct its advance somewhat more to the left.*

In rear, and on the right and left, of these columns, stood the remains of that splendid cavalry, with which Wellington's line had been so furiously and so perseveringly assailed, occupying the interval that had been continually augmenting between d'Erlon's and Reille's corps. They formed the last and only cavalry-reserve remaining at Napoleon's disposal for following up the attack by the guard, should the latter

* At this time a French officer of cuirassiers galloped up to the Allied line, as a deserter, and joining Lieut. Colonel Sir Augustus Fraser, (commanding the British horse artillery,) and Major Blair, brigade major to Major General Adam's brigade,) who were together in rear of the 52nd regiment, he announced to them that the line would be attacked, within half an hour, by Napoleon with the imperial guard. Sir Augustus, after having requested Major Blair to look to the deserter, rode off to communicate this information to the Duke. Blair sent the French officer to the rear, in charge of a serjeant of the 52nd regiment.

prove successful, or for covering its retreat, in the event of failure.

It was shortly before the columns of attack were put in motion that Vivian, whose hussar-brigade it will be recollected, was posted upon the extreme left of the Anglo-allied line, was informed by patroles which he had detached to look out to his left for the expected arrival of the Prussians, that the latter were advancing in force along the road from Ohain. Having satisfied himself as to the fact, and perceiving their advanced cavalry coming on, Vivian felt that there could be no longer any apprehension of the left of the army being turned; and, having previously understood from Sir William Delancey* and other staff officers, that fresh cavalry was much wanted in the centre, he proposed to Vandeleur, who was on his right, and who was his senior officer, that the two brigades should move towards the centre, where they might be of service. Vandeleur declined to act without orders; whereupon Vivian put his own brigade in motion, passing along the rear of Vandeleur's, and soon after having commenced his march he met Lord Uxbridge, who was much pleased to find that the Duke's wishes had thus been anticipated, and sent orders to Vandeleur to follow, accompanying the former brigade himself towards the centre, passing along the foot of the slope in rear of the position of the left wing of the Anglo-allied line.

The Prussian troops, whose advance had thus induced Vivian to quit the extreme left, were the advanced guard of Zieten's corps, and consisted of a part of the 1st infantry-brigade, namely, the 3rd battalion 12th regiment, the 1st and 2nd battalions 24th regiment, the 3rd battalion 1st Westphalian landwehr, and the 1st and third Silesian rifle companies; as also of a part of the reserve-cavalry, namely, the 1st Silesian hussars, the Brandenburg uhlans, the Brandenburg dragoons, and the 2nd Kurmark landwehr cavalry. They had already been joined by Lieut. Colonel Fremantle, who delivered to Zieten the Duke's message,† in reply to which that general remarked that he did not feel himself authorised to detach his corps in the manner proposed, adding, however, that the great mass of the Prussian army was arriving upon the field.

The remainder of the reserve-cavalry which was commanded by Lieut. General Röder, together with the main body of the corps, were still considerably in the rear. They were met by

* Colonel Sir William Delancey, K.C.B., Deputy Quarter Master General, was mortally wounded in this battle.

† See page 326.

Captain Jackson* of the British staff-corps, who had been sent to look for them. These troops did not reach the field of battle until after the victory had been decided.†

Wellington, finding that there was no chance of his shattered line being strengthened by the arrival, in sufficient time, of a Prussian force from his left, to support his weak points of defence, and that he must therefore depend solely on his own resources for the means of warding off the desperate blow which Napoleon was about to strike, immediately made such dispositions as the circumstances of the moment appeared to him to demand. The incessant attacks made by the French light-troops debouching from La Haye Sainte, from the moment that farm fell into their possession, had caused great havoc in the centre of his line, where the want of reinforcement became most apparent. To meet this deficiency, he ordered the Brunswick battalions, which stood at this time in rear of Maitland's and Adam's brigades—namely, the 2nd and 3rd light, and the 1st, 2nd, and 3rd line, battalions, to move by their left into the interval between Halkett's British, and Kruse's Nassau, brigade. To occupy the ground thus vacated by the Brunswickers, he put in motion d'Aubremé's Dutch-Belgian infantry-brigade from its recently-assumed position in rear of the Nivelles road; whence the other brigade of Chassé's Dutch-Belgian division, under Major General Ditmer, was shortly afterwards ordered to move in the direction of the left of Maitland's British brigade. The remains of his cavalry stood in rear of the centre, towards which Vivian's and Vandeleur's brigades were now moving from the left, as previously explained.‡

Whilst the imperial guard was forming for attack, the French troops in possession of La Haye Sainte and its inclosures, now consisting of the entire of Donzelot's division,

* Now Lieut. Colonel Basil Jackson, h.p. Royal Staff Corps.

† The effective strength of the Prussian troops on the field of Waterloo, is given in Appendix XXXIII.

‡ It was about this time that the Duke, having observed six foreign guns on the right of Captain Bolton's battery, abandoned by their gunners, desired Colonel Sir George Wood (who commanded the artillery) to have them withdrawn from the front line to the rear, a duty which was immediately assigned to, and executed by, Lieutenant Anderson,[1] and a party of the before-mentioned battery, with the exception of one gun, which being more in advance, and the French columns approaching, covered by their skirmishers, could not be removed with safety. (In communicating to me this information, Major Anderson stated that these foreign guns were Belgian; but, as no Belgian battery had stood on the ground in question, he must have been mistaken. They probably belonged to the Brunswick artillery, which had suffered very severely in that exposed position.)

[1] Now Lieut. Colonel William C. Anderson, Royal Artillery.

from the left of d'Erlon's corps, renewed, with redoubled vigour, their assault upon the centre of the Allied line; the object being evidently either to force that point previously to the arrival of the guard on its left, and thus facilitate the assault to be made by the latter, or to harass it in such a manner that, should the effort of the guard prove successful, they would be enabled completely to overthrow the Allied centre. The fire from the skirmishers that had located themselves between the farm and the position, and from those on the knoll by the sandpit, on the opposite side of the high road, had been incessant since the capture of that post. Ompteda's brigade of the King's German legion, which had hitherto occupied the hollow-way that descends into the chaussée, was reduced to a mere handful of men: the two squares in which Kielmansegge's Hanoverian brigade, the next on the (Allied) right, had stood its ground so many hours, were fearfully diminished; Kruse's Nassau brigade, still further to the right, formed in three contiguous columns, (two in front and one in rear,) began to evince symptoms of hesitation; and the interval between this and Halkett's British brigade had become much greater than was consistent with the due security of this part of the line. So weakened indeed was the latter at this period, that, to remedy the evil in some degree, it had been deemed advisable, with a view rather of giving it the appearance of greater strength than of affording any very active support, to draw close up in its rear, the skeleton remains of the Scots Greys and of the 3rd hussars of the King's German legion. On the Allied left of the high road, an unremitting fire was maintained against their opponents by the 95th and 4th British regiments in extended order along the front hedge of the Wavre road, commencing from the Charleroi chaussée, as also from the 40th, 79th, 1st, and 28th British regiments, deployed behind the embanked hedge on the rear side of that road. The 27th British regiment had been brought up by Lambert, and posted in square, in the angle formed by the junction of the above roads, having one face parallel with, and close to, the chaussée, for the purpose either of throwing a flank fire upon the French troops on the opposite side, should these succeed, as appeared very probable, in compelling Ompteda's and Kielmansegge's brigades to retire, or, of pouring a close, deadly volley upon any column endeavouring to penetrate along the high road itself. The artillery on the Allied right of the high road, in front of these brigades, was at this moment completely disabled. Two British artillerymen were observed vainly endeavouring to serve a couple of guns, but were compelled to desist from the want of all material for loading.

Such was the state of things in the centre of the Anglo-allied army, when the continued popping fire from the French skirmishers suddenly quickened into a fierce tiraillade, which threatened to bear down every thing opposed to it. The bank along the high road, beyond the garden of La Haye Sainte, and the mound adjoining it, which latter was quite close to the Allied position, became all at once thickly crowded with skirmishers. Those that lined the banks seemed intent upon keeping down the fire from the British regiments of Kempt's and Lambert's brigades, along the Wavre road, while those under cover of the little mound in advance, as if aware of the object of the formation of the 27th British regiment, and sensible of the necessity of securing their right flank in their meditated forcing of the position, opened such a close, sharp, fire upon that regiment, that, within the brief space of a few minutes, it lost more than half of its numbers. At the same time, taking advantage of the crippled state of the Allied artillery in this quarter, the French brought up two guns in advance of the north-western angle of the garden of La Haye Sainte, in which position they were covered from any fire from the opposite side of the high road, by the skirmishers occupying the bank and the mound. From these guns a smart fire of grape was opened, and maintained without intermission, upon the left square of Kielmansegge's brigade, (consisting of the field-battalions Grubenhagen and York,) at the short distance of 150, and afterwards of scarcely 100, paces. The square manifested the most exemplary submission and forbearance, notwithstanding the ravages that continued to be made in its ranks; not venturing to reply to the fire, by the apprehension of cavalry being under the brow of the position, prepared to take instant advantage of any favourable opportunity for a charge. The right square (consisting of the field-battalions Bremen and Verden) also suffered most severely. Some other guns, which had accompanied the columns in rear of the French skirmishers, were suddenly brought forward, and opened so destructive a discharge of grape upon this latter square, that one of its sides was literally completely blown away; the remainder being left standing in the form of a triangle. The commander, and many other officers, were wounded. The ammunition was failing rapidly. The combined fire of grape and musketry continued to increase in violence; and the square finally dwindled into a mere clump of men. The French *tirailleurs* continued pressing forward in a very compact line, whilst the sound of drums beating the *pas de charge* announced the advance of the columns immediately in their rear. The Prince of Orange, perceiving the probability of the centre of the Allied line being forced, unless some great effort were made to check the enemy's advance, ordered the 1st and 2nd Nassau battalions of Kruse's brigade to charge, gallantly placing himself at their head. His Royal Highness was soon struck by a bullet in the left shoulder;* the attack failed; and the Nassauers were falling back, when the reinforcement which Wellington had provided for this part of the line, consisting of five battalions of Brunswick infantry, moved rapidly into the interval between Kruse's Nassau, and Halkett's British, brigade.† But so unexpectedly did the Brunswickers find themselves placed under a most destructive fire, and so suddenly were the heads of their columns assailed, that they were unable, in the midst of the thick smoke in which they became involved, to recover from the partial irregularities by which, under such circumstances, their advance was accompanied, and to form up in sufficient order, before they came in close contact with the enemy, whose vigorous attack compelled them, as also Kruse's, Kielmansegge's, and Ompteda's brigades, to fall back about a hundred paces.

At this critical moment, Wellington hastened to the spot in person, to avert so alarming a catastrophe as that of having

* On receiving his wound, His Royal Highness immediately dismounted, and staggered towards the rear. A Nassau officer accosted him, but apparently without recognizing him, and returned to his post. A second officer from the Nassau regiment advanced towards the Prince, who had become exhausted by loss of blood, and who now leaned for support against this officer's horse. In the next moment, a Dutch-Belgian staff officer, Captain Baron Jules de Constant Rebecque de Villars—perceiving the close approach of the enemy, rode up to the Prince, dismounted, and begged His Royal Highness to accept his horse. The Prince made no reply, and nearly fainted in the Baron's arms. After several attempts to get his foot into the stirrup—the horse having become fidgetty by a brisk cannonade and the whistling of balls—His Royal Highness, notwithstanding the pain which he suffered, made a great effort, and succeeded in mounting. His thoughts were still upon the battle, and he wished to give orders respecting it; but his great loss of blood prevented him. Several officers, British and Belgian, as also his aides-de-camp returning from the delivery of orders, now hastened to the Prince, who was conducted to the rear by the Earl of March and others, from the murderous fire to which His Royal Highness had continued to be exposed.

Throughout the whole of the two great battles of the 16th and 18th of June, the Prince of Orange had displayed the greatest gallantry and the most ardent devotion to his country. His conduct was the admiration of all, and the whole Anglo-allied army rejoiced to find that the life which he had so freely exposed, had been spared for the future benefit and service of his native country, over which he now reigns in the hearts of his people.

† See page 330.

his centre broken, at a time, too, when he was preparing to receive a formidable attack, directed against another point of his line, situated at but a short distance on the right of that centre. He addressed himself to the Brunswickers, and succeeded, by the electrifying influence of his voice, gesture, and presence, in rallying the discomfited columns. The 3rd line-battalion, under Major Normann, was the first to re-form in good order: it then boldly stood its ground; and, when the enemy's infantry approached, received it with so destructive a fire as completely to check its further advance.

By dint of example and encouragement on the part of all the commanding officers, the brigades on the left of the Brunswickers were also rallied and formed up: upon seeing which, the Duke galloped off to the right.

Just at this time, Vivian's hussar-brigade drew up immediately in rear of these troops—relieving the exhausted remains of the Scots Greys and 3rd hussars of the King's German legion—the 10th and 18th British hussars in front, and the 1st hussars of the King's German legion in second line. The presence and appearance of this fresh cavalry tended very considerably to restore confidence to that part of the line. The brigade had previously, in consequence of a mistake in the transmission of orders, been halted on the left of the high road about midway between the front line and the farm of Mont St. Jean; whence, however, it was speedily brought forward, and posted as above, by Lord Uxbridge.*

* To the troops comprising Vivian's and Vandeleur's brigades, as they arrived quite fresh from the extreme left, the air of ruin and destruction which met their view in rear of the centre of the line—the desperate struggle which appeared to be carried on upon the crest of the main ridge by a single line of infantry, evidently exhausted by the continuous fight—the almost total absence of *British* cavalry in support of that line—the numbers of wounded retiring both singly and in groups—the whole scene was calculated to inspire them with thoughts by no means akin to anticipations of victory. They quickly partook of the feeling of extreme doubt and uncertainty which pervaded the rest of the army as to the result of the contest, and many imbibed the idea that they had been brought from the left for the purpose of covering a contemplated retreat. "Where is your brigade?" said Sir Hussey Vivian to Lord Edward Somerset. "Here," replied his lordship, as pointing firstly to a small band of horsemen, amounting to little more than a squadron, and then to the ground covered with dead and dying, clad in red, and with mutilated horses, wandering or turning in circles, he displayed to him the wreck of what had been the household and union brigades of cavalry combined—a force amounting at the commencement of the action, to upwards of 2000 dragoons. Sir Denis Pack, whose brigade consisted altogether of a mere handful of men, posted with its right resting on the Charleroi road, rode up to Sir John Vandeleur, and having told him he had received orders to hold his ground to the last, consulted him as to the most advisable course to be pursued in case of a retreat. But, notwithstanding the gloomy appearance

The Prince of Orange, Alten, and almost all the superior officers of the 3rd division, had been wounded. But Kielmansegge, who now commanded in this part of the field, was fully alive to the critical circumstances under which the 3rd division was placed, and exhibited great ability, coolness, and determination, by the manner in which he succeeded in restoring it to order. Still, the persevering and incessant *tiraillade* kept up against these troops by the French was such, that the fire thrown out from their shattered and enfeebled ranks was quite inadequate to repress it. The French skirmishers again crowded close up to the line; maintaining a most rapid and destructive fire. The Allied infantry was once more on the point of giving way. One battalion of the Brunswickers was retiring in close column, but in good order, having totally exhausted its ammunition. The Nassauers were falling back *en masse* against the horses' heads of the 10th hussars, who, keeping their files closed, prevented further retreat. Vivian and Captain Shakespeare* of the 10th, (acting as his extra aide-de-camp,) rendered themselves conspicuous at this moment by their endeavours to halt and encourage the Nassauers. The Hanoverians and the German legion on the left, led by Kielmansegge, now resolutely dashed forward, at the double quick—their drums rolling. The enemy fell back. The Brunswickers took up the movement, as then did also the Nassauers—Vivian and his aide-de-camp cheering them on; whilst the hussars followed in close support. In this manner, Kielmansegge succeeded in leading back the shattered remnants of the division to the place they had so long and so honourably occupied on the ridge.

Vivian's brigade, by its proximity to these troops, against which so close and unremitting a fire of musketry was maintained, was placed in a very trying situation for cavalry,

which affairs had assumed, no despondency was perceptible on the part of that portion of the army whose fate it was to bear the whole brunt of the battle; and which, firmly relying on its own indomitable courage, and on the oft-proved skill of its chief, still cherished the hope that by persevering a little longer in those mighty efforts by which the enemy had, during so many hours, been kept at bay, such heroic exertions, though unaided by those on whose effective support they had calculated, would yet be crowned with success. This feeling was aptly expressed by Colonel Sir Felton Harvey, of the Duke's staff, who having ridden to the 18th British hussars, to change his wounded charger, exclaimed as he was in the act of mounting a troop-horse belonging to that regiment—" The Duke of Wellington has won the battle if we could but get the d——— ——— to advance."

* Captain Arthur Shakespeare, of the 10th hussars, afterwards on half-pay of the 99th regiment, retired from the service on the 11th July, 1826.

and suffered much in consequence. As soon, however, as the infantry had rallied and resumed their former position in the line, Vivian withdrew his brigade under the crest of the ridge, a distance of not more than thirty yards, to place his men a little out of fire; and when thus posted, he was better prepared to make an attack if required.

The fire from the enemy's infantry in front of this part of the line suddenly slackened; and it was soon manifest that they were falling back: the change arose out of occurrences on their left, which will be explained in the next Chapter.

CHAPTER XIV.

It was during the fierce and desperate conflict just described as having taken place in the centre of the Anglo-allied line, that the French imperial guard moved forward to the attack; and this was the signal for the simultaneous advance of all the disposable battalions of d'Erlon's and Reille's corps. In the preliminary pause which occurred in the fire from the French batteries, from the first moment of the advance until the columns had sufficiently descended from the heights to be below the range of their guns, the thunder of Bülow's artillery upon the French extreme right, and of the guns brought to bear against it, was so distinctly audible that Napoleon, apprehending its evil effects upon the troops, on whose bravery, discipline, and devotion, his fate now hung, despatched aides-de-camp along the line, to spread the false intelligence of the arrival of Grouchy, and to declare that it now required but a little firmness to secure the victory to which they were advancing. The loud shouts with which this announcement was received by the troops, who had then descended below the range of the guns, were speedily drowned in the roar that burst forth from the entire line of the French batteries. The effects of this terrific cannonade upon the skeleton ranks of the Allied front line, combined with the aspect of the advancing hosts, tended not in the slightest degree to shake that noble and unequalled courage with which the British and German troops had hitherto sustained every assault. The scene of havoc and devastation which met their view as they looked around them, the constant ravages which they had been destined passively to endure for so many hours, their ranks repeatedly torn open, and their files scattered asunder, as shot and shell plunged in amongst them,—all conduced to excite in the breasts of men of such impenetrable mould, a feeling of exultation and relief, as they observed the approach of the enemy's infantry, and panted for the long-wished-for moment when they might grapple with their deadly foe at close quarters, in a hand-to-hand encounter. Most fully did they realise the expectations entertained of them by their enemy, but admirer, the brave General Foy, who had felt it his duty, prior to the commencement of the battle, to declare to the Emperor, that his Majesty had an infantry opposed to him which he had never known to yield.

The French troops, perceiving their whole front line in motion, felt conscious that the final struggle was at hand, and assured that the varied fortunes of the day were to be wound up by some splendid triumph. The guard proudly took the lead in this grand attack—that sacred cohort, whose glory had ever shone conspicuously when a great crisis summoned forth those energies by which its valour and its prowess had acquired for it imperishable renown. The greatest enthusiasm reigned amidst the devoted defenders of the imperial diadem, which was now to be strengthened by the fame of their renewed successes, and adorned with fresh wreaths of never-fading laurels.

Napoleon, nervously anxious to strain to its utmost tension, the daring spirit and high resolve which animated his troops, galloped forward to the inner gentle slope of the eminence on the left of the Charleroi road, which, overlooking the farm of La Haye Sainte, formed the most prominent point of his whole line, and by which was to pass the leading column of the guard, there to strengthen, by the magic spell of his immediate presence, the link which bound their fortunes to his own fate, and to the destiny of the empire. As they approached, he pointed significantly to the Allied position; a gesture which drew forth renewed shouts of "*Vive l'Empereur!*" The fond regards which he seemed to cast upon these, his old and tried campaigners, and the air of confidence he assumed, as he contemplated their advance, rivetted upon him the affectionate gaze of the devoted band, to hundreds of whom it proved the last look upon the idol for whom they were to sacrifice their lives.

At this time, d'Erlon's corps presented an advance of columns in *échelon* between the Charleroi road and its right flank, which was engaged with the Prussians; whilst Reille's corps, descending in columns, some into the wood, others into the inclosures on the right, and some also still more to the right, outside of Hougomont, and close upon the centre of the line, seemed bent upon carrying that post by main force, and upon seconding, with one mighty effort, the main attack by the imperial guard. This general advance of columns was preceded by a host of skirmishers, whose line spreading along the valley in front of d'Erlon's corps, gradually became engaged with the light troops of the left wing of the Anglo-allied army, and the sudden impulse given to the rattle of musketry in the wood of Hougomont, betokened that the brave defenders of this post were already engaged in a renewed and desperate struggle for the maintenance of its possession. The French skirmishers between the wood of Hougomont and the extreme left of their army, continued to maintain a desultory warfare with the Allied light troops in the front, consisting of the 3rd regiment of British guards, the light companies of the 14th and 23rd British regiments, and six companies of the 51st British regiment. Piré's light cavalry-brigade was still in the position it had occupied upon the extreme left of the French front line, having a few vedettes thrown out, which were narrowly watched by those belonging to Captain Wodehouse's squadron of the 15th British hussars.*

As the leading column of the imperial guard began to ascend the slightly inclined tongue of ground that projects from that part of the ridge of the Duke's position in rear of the crest of which Maitland's brigade of guards was lying down at the time, it became very much exposed to the concentrated fire from nearly all the batteries of the Anglo-allied right wing, by which the most frightful havoc was dealt amidst its devoted ranks. The line of skirmishers which preceded it, now pushed rapidly and boldly forward up to the very summit of the Duke's position, for the purpose both of concealing by their veil of smoke the precise direction of the advance of the columns, and of driving away the artillerymen from their guns, by the fire of which the guard was suffering so severely.

Notwithstanding the terrible havoc made in the ranks of the leading column of the imperial guard, it continued its advance in admirable order, and with the greatest enthusiasm. Several of its superior officers placed themselves at its head. Ney's horse having been shot under him, he drew his sword, and chivalrously led the way on foot, sustaining to the last his appropriate and well-earned *nom de guerre*—"*le plus brave des braves.*" General Friant, who commanded the grenadiers, fell severely wounded. General Michel, colonel *en second* of the chasseurs, was killed a few moments afterwards. The fall of the latter occasioned some hesitation—the 1st battalion of the 3rd regiment of grenadiers halted; but at the call of General Poret de Morvan, who commanded it, it renewed its advance at the *pas de charge*, amidst loud shouts of "*Vive l'Empereur!*" As the column neared the rise of ground which constituted the highest point of the ridge occupied by the right wing of the Duke's line, it gradually passed the line

* See page 228.

of fire hitherto directed upon it by the greater portion of the batteries on the British right of that point. Wellington rode up to the British foot-battery posted on the immediate right of Maitland's brigade of guards, with its own right thrown somewhat forward, and addressing himself to an artillery officer, (Lieutenant Sharpin,*) hastily asked who commanded it. The latter replied that Captain Bolton, having just been killed, it was now under the command of Captain Napier. The Duke then said, "Tell him to keep a look-out to his left, for the French will soon be with him." The message had scarcely been communicated when the bear-skin caps of the leading divisions of the column of the imperial guard appeared just above the summit of the hill. The cannonade hitherto directed upon this point from the distant French batteries, now ceased, but a swarm of skirmishers opened a sharp and teasing fire among the British gunners. In the next moment, however, they were scattered and driven back upon the main body by a sudden shower of canister, grape, and schrapnel shells, poured forth from Napier's guns, which now kept up a terrific fire upon the column, within a distance of forty or fifty yards. Nevertheless the French guards continued to advance. They had now topped the summit. To the astonishment of the officers who were at their head, there appeared in their immediate front no direct impediment to their further advance. They could only distinguish dimly through the smoke extending from Napier's battery, the cocked hats of a few mounted officers, little imagining, probably, that the most prominent of these was the great Duke himself. Pressing boldly forward, they had arrived within fifty paces of the spot on which the British guards were lying down, when Wellington gave the talismanic call—"Up, guards; make ready!" and ordered Maitland to attack. It was a moment of thrilling excitement. The British guards springing up so suddenly in a most compact four-deep line, appeared to the French as if starting out of the ground. The latter, with their high bonnets, as they crowned the summit of the ridge, appeared to the British, through the smoky haze, like a corps of giants bearing down upon them. The British guards instantly opened their fire with a tremendous volley, thrown in with amazing coolness, deliberation, and precision. An oblique fire was also poured in among them from the 33rd and 69th British regiments, which Halkett had most promptly and judiciously pushed forward to the immediate left of the guards at this critical moment. The head of the column

* Now Lieutenant William Sharpin, h. p. Royal Artillery

became, as it were, convulsed by the shock, and nearly the entire mass staggered under the effect. In less than a single minute more than three hundred of these brave old warriors fell, to rise no more. But the high spirit and innate valour which actuated the mass were not to be subdued by a first repulse. Its officers, placing themselves conspicuously in its front and on its flanks, called aloud, waved their swords, and, by encouraging words and gestures, commenced a deployment in order to acquire a more extended front. But the head of the column being continually shattered and driven back upon the mass, by the well-sustained and rapidly destructive fire by which it was assailed within so extremely limited a space, this attempt altogether failed. The front of the column was becoming momentarily more disordered and broken up; men were turning round and disappearing by the flanks, whilst others in the rear began firing over the heads of those before them. The confusion into which the French guards had now been thrown became manifest. The Duke ordered Maitland to charge; whilst, at the same instant, the gallant Lord Saltoun, equally alive to the real situation of the column, called out, "Now's the time, my boys!" The brigade sprang forward, with a loud cheer, to the charge. Numbers of the French guards nearest to the British, threw down their arms and knapsacks, and dispersed. The flanks began rapidly to spread out; and then the mass partaking more generally of the panic, appeared as if rent asunder by some invisible power.

During the advance of the attacking column of the imperial guard, one of its battalions had moved out from the mass to its right (probably for the better security of that flank from any attempt that might be made to molest it from the dip or hollow on that side of the projecting tongue of ground along which the main attack had proceeded), and took a direction which brought it immediately in front of Halkett's left wing, consisting of the shattered remnants of the 30th and 73rd British regiments, formed in a four-deep line, scarcely exceeding, if equalling, in extent (such had been their losses), the front of the approaching column. The order in which this column advanced was admirable. Its formation was undisturbed by the fire of artillery, of which arm there was none in this part of the field in working condition; and, as it pressed on with the compactness and regularity of a parade movement, it appeared at the same time to be animated with the best spirit. Presently the column halted and fired, and, in return, received a well-directed volley, after delivering which, the 30th and 73rd regiments ported arms, and, with a loud cheer, dashed forward at the charge. On reaching the ground where they expected to meet the French guards, they were greatly astonished at discovering, through the clearing smoke, that their recent opponents were flying in a mass. At this moment, Major van der Smissen's Dutch-Belgian horse-battery, which had just come up by the right of Halkett's brigade, opened upon them a terrific fire from which they suffered immensely.

The British guards had continued their charge some distance down the slope of the hill, when Maitland perceived the second attacking column of the imperial guard advancing on his right, and exposing his brigade to the imminent risk of being turned on that flank. He accordingly resolved to face about the right wing of his brigade, and to give the words, "halt, front," as soon as he had got his line parallel with the front of the advancing column. This manœuvre was executed with great regularity and precision by the right wing, with which Maitland was immediately present, and which he had well in hand. But amidst their victorious shouts, and the noise of the firing of cannon and other arms, the command was imperfectly understood by the left wing, and the first sense of danger led to a cry of "Form square" being passed along their line, it being naturally assumed that the enemy's cavalry would take advantage of their isolated position; which, however, was not the case. The flanks of the 3rd battalion, of which this left wing was composed, gave way as if to form square. Saltoun conspicuously exerted himself in endeavouring to rectify the mistake, but in vain; and the whole of the battalion went to the rear. The confusion in which they retired was unavoidable; but it was not the confusion consequent upon either defeat or panic: it resulted simply from a misunderstanding of the command; and no greater or more distinguished proof could be afforded of the excellent order, cool self-possession, and admirable discipline of these troops, than the steadiness, alacrity, and intelligence with which, upon regaining the crest of the ridge, they obeyed the command then given of "Halt, front, form up;" mechanically resuming their four-deep formation, and instantly darting forward at the double-quick, to their proper place on the left of the 2nd battalion, so that the whole brigade was now in one steady and compact line; parallel with the front of the advancing second attacking column of the imperial guard.*

* In connexion with the momentary confusion of the left wing of Maitland's brigade, may be mentioned a somewhat similar occurrence in Halkett's brigade.

How marked a contrast did such conduct on the part of the British guards, who thus, in the battle's front, so gloriously upheld their country's honour, offer to that of a considerable body of the Allied troops then posted in second line as their support! D'Aubremé's infantry-brigade of Chassé's Dutch-Belgian division, which, as before stated, had been moved into the space in rear of Maitland's brigade, previously occupied by the Brunswickers, was now formed into three large squares, of two battalions each. These troops, on hearing the loud shouts of the second advancing column of the French imperial guard—of that very column which had been moving in rear of the British guards while the latter were retiring from their triumphant charge towards their original position—became so unsteady, and evinced so decided a disposition to quit their ranks, that Vandeleur, whose brigade of British light dragoons was at this time drawn up in their rear, deemed

on its left wing returning to its former position, after having advanced to charge the imperial guard. Whilst thus retiring, the 30th and 73rd regiments suffered most severely from the enemy's fire. Presently they found themselves commingled with the 33rd and 69th regiments. This put an end to all order, and the brigade became a confused mass. The exertions of the officers, whose number was awfully diminished, were ineffectual in extricating their men from this confusion; but, all at once, a shout was raised, which was immediately responded to by the whole brigade. Every man halted and fronted, and order was quickly restored; whilst skirmishers were thrown out to repel the close-telling fire of Donzelot's light troops. The Duke having observed the confusion above described, said to some of his staff, "See what's wrong there." Major Dawson Kelly,[1] of the quarter-master-general's department, immediately rode up to the brigade, and while addressing himself to Sir Colin Halkett, the latter, at the instant, received a wound in the face, a ball passing through his mouth, and he was consequently obliged to retire to the rear. Lieut. Colonel Elphinstone, commanding the 33rd regiment, then ran up, and asked Major Kelly if he had any orders. The latter replied, "None, beyond enquiring into the cause of the confusion." Lieut. Colonel Elphinstone then stated that they were much pressed, and the men exhausted; that Colonel Harris of the 73rd had been severely wounded, and that the command of the brigade had devolved upon him. At this period, the attacking column was again retiring, and Major Kelly, having observed that the different battalions had got intermixed, from the frequent formations of squares, he advised Lieut. Colonel Elphinstone to direct both officers and men to resume their respective stations, and get into order, covering themselves as well as they could by lying down, and to prepare to meet the next attack. At the same moment, one or two serjeants of the 73rd came up and told Major Kelly that they had no one to command them, their officers being all killed or wounded. It being his own regiment, he considered it his duty to remain with them, and upon his saying so, they cheered, and instantly got into order. This was probably the cheer which was so readily caught up by the remainder of the brigade in the manner already stated, and had been the means of restoring their order, which for a few minutes had been so unexpectedly disturbed. Scarcely had this been effected, when Donzelot's columns again pressed boldly forward, and renewed their assault, as the second attacking column of the imperial guard approached the Allied line.

[1] Colonel Dawson Kelly, C. B., on half pay of the 73rd regiment, died in March, 1837.

it advisable to close his squadron-intervals, the better to impede their contemplated retreat; and was induced, along with his Major of brigade, Major Childers* of the 16th light dragoons, Captain Tomkinson† of the same regiment, and several of his officers, on perceiving that the squares were on the point of giving way, to dart forward and endeavour, partly by menaces, and partly by exhortations, to induce them to maintain their ground. The Dutch-Belgian officers exerted themselves in restoring order and confidence, but their men were evidently bent upon abandoning their position in this part of the field. Between them and the attacking column intervened the crest of the main ridge, occupied by the Duke's first line; the latter holding out to them a bright example of perfect discipline, of unflinching steadiness, and patient endurance. Of the attacking column itself they could see absolutely nothing; but its shouts alone seemed sufficient to scare them off the ground! Besides, they had but just entered the immediate field of action, and had not hitherto been engaged with the enemy, whereas the British brigade of guards had been exposed during eight hours to an incessant cannonade, and to numerous and desperate attacks of both cavalry and infantry. Of such materials was composed the Duke's second line in rear of the main point of attack by the French army at this, the most critical moment of the whole battle!

The second attacking column of the French imperial guard, which, as before explained, had been formed in the hollow adjacent to the south-east angle of the Hougomont inclosures, advanced in a line parallel with, and at a very short distance from, the hedge forming the eastern boundary. On reaching the foot of the British position, however, the column diverged a little to its right, either to take advantage of a slight undulation of the ground which seemed to offer a partial cover from the tremendous fire of artillery that continued to pour upon it, or solely for the purpose of directing its advance upon the point at which it perceived the first attacking column was engaged, and at which it might be better enabled to follow up any success that column might obtain. Between the heads of the two attacking columns there was a distance, during their advance, of from ten to twelve minutes' march. Whether this difference in the time of their movement was intentional, or arose from a misunderstanding in the con-

* Now Colonel Michael Childers, C.B.

† Now Lieut. Colonel William Tomkinson, h.p., 24th dragoons.

veyance of orders, or from any other accident, is uncertain, but it is quite evident that by forming two separate attacks, they subjected themselves to the imminent risk of being defeated in detail—a risk which, as will be presently shown, was speedily converted into a reality.

The second, like the first, column of attack, advanced with great boldness, and in excellent order, and appeared animated by the best possible spirit. Its left front was covered by a cloud of skirmishers, in order to conceal its movement as much as possible from the view of the British line. The battalions of Adam's brigade threw out each a company for the purpose of checking them. During the advance of the column, and more especially as it descended the gentle declivity eastward of the great orchard of Hougomont, it suffered severely from the British cannonade. So destructive indeed had been the fire from some of the British batteries on the right of Maitland's brigade, from the commencement of the advance of the imperial guard, that the French were at length induced suddenly to push forward a body of cuirassiers to endeavour to silence these guns. In this they partially succeeded; the cuirassiers having gallantly charged one of the batteries, and forced the gunners to seek shelter in the rear of the infantry—driving in, at the same time, the skirmishers of the 2nd battalion of the 95th regiment, and those of the 52nd regiment. They were checked, however, by the to them sudden and unexpected appearance of Adam's brigade, which had just been moved, in its four-deep line, close up to the narrow road that runs along the summit of the ridge. The 52nd regiment, which was more directly opposed to them, came down to the "Prepare for cavalry!" As a renewal of the attack seemed probable, a squadron of the 23rd British light dragoons, under Captain Cox,* was detached across the ridge, down the outer slope, towards the great orchard; from the rear of which it charged the cuirassiers as they advanced again towards the guns, overcame them, and pursued them across the plain, far in rear of the second attacking column of the imperial guard, until it fell into a fire thrown out upon it from the head of French column of infantry, by which its files were scattered, and the whole compelled to make a hasty retreat towards the Allied position.†

* Captain Philip Zachariah Cox, 23rd Light Dragoons, retired from the Service on the 24th January, 1818.

† This isolated charge, carried into the rear of the attacking columns of the imperial guard, and continued until checked by the French reserves, was gallantly executed under Lieutenant Banner,[1] the squadron having scarcely crossed the

[1] Major John Banner, 93rd Highlanders, died on the 24th December, 1837.

Had the second column of attack continued in the original direction of its advance, it would have come upon the centre of Adam's brigade, but having, as it began to ascend the exterior slope of the main ridge of the Allied position, slightly diverged to its right, as before observed, by following the direction of a very gentle hollow, constituting the re-entering angle formed by the tongue of ground that projected from the front of Maitland's brigade, and that part of the ridge occupied by Adam's brigade, it, in some degree, lent its left flank to the latter. This circumstance was not only observed, but had been in a great measure anticipated by Lieut. Colonel Sir John Colborne, commanding the 52nd regiment, an officer of great repute in the British army. He had been watching with intense anxiety, the progress of the enemy's column, and, seizing the most favourable moment, he, without orders, and upon his own responsibility, wheeled the left company of the 52nd to the left, and then formed the remainder of the regiment upon that company, for the purpose of bringing its front nearly parallel with the flank of the French column. At this moment Adam rode up, and asked Colborne what he was going to do, to which the latter replied, "to make that column feel our fire." Adam, approving of this, ordered Colborne to move on, and galloped off to bring up his right regiment, the 71st. The Duke, who had just seen Maitland's brigade re-formed and posted in the best order, parallel with the front of the attacking column, was at this moment stationed on the right of Napier's battery. He despatched an aide-de-camp (Major the Hon. Henry Percy*) to direct Sir Henry Clinton to advance and attack the imperial guard; but a single glance at Colborne's forward movement satisfied him that his intention had been anticipated; and he immediately pushed forward the 2nd battalion of the 95th regiment to the left of the 52nd. The head of the French column had by this time nearly reached the brow of the ridge, its front covering almost the whole of Napier's battery, and a portion of the extreme right of Maitland's brigade. It was still gallantly pressing forward, in defiance of the most galling fire poured into its front by the battery

ridge when Captain Cox was obliged to leave the field from the effects of a severe stun in a previous charge, occasioned by his horse falling upon him. At the time the squadron was detached on this duty, the remainder of the 23rd light dragoons proceeded to the centre, where it was attached to the remnant of the household brigade of cavalry.

* Lieut. Colonel the Hon. Henry Percy, C.B., retired from the service in September, 1821.

and by the British guards, when the sudden and imposing appearance of the four-deep line of the 52d regiment bearing directly towards its left flank, in the most admirable and compact order imaginable, caused it to halt. In the next instant, wheeling up its left sections, it opened a rapid and destructive fire from the entire length of its left flank against the 52nd regiment. Colborne, having brought his line parallel to the flank of the imperial guard, also halted, and poured a deadly fire into the mass; and, almost at the same moment, the rifles of the 2nd battalion 95th regiment, then coming up on the left, were levelled and discharged with unerring aim into the more advanced portion of the column. The 71st regiment was, at this time, rapidly advancing, on the right, to complete the brigade-movement. Colborne, eager fully to carry out his projected flank attack upon the enemy's column, caused his men to cease firing, and then gave the command, "Charge! charge!" It was answered by three hearty British cheers that rose distinctly above the shouts of "*Vive l'Empereur!*" and the now straggling and unsteady fire from the column. The 2nd battalion 95th regiment hastened to join in the charge on the left. The movement was remarkable for the order, the steadiness, the resoluteness, and the daring, by which it was characterized. The column of the imperial guard, which already seemed to reel to and fro under the effect of the front and flank fire which had been so successfully brought to bear upon it, was evidently in consternation as it beheld the close advance of Adam's brigade. Some daring spirits—and it contained many within its ranks—still endeavoured to make at least a show of resistance; but the disorder, which had been rapidly increasing, now became uncontrollable; and this second column of the imperial guard, breaking into the wildest confusion, shared the fate of the first; with this difference, however, that in consequence of the combined front and flank fire in which it had been so fatally involved, and of the unrestrained pursuit which deprived it of the power of rallying its component parts, it became so thoroughly disjointed and dispersed, that with the exception of the two rear battalions, which constituted the 1st regiment of chasseurs (old guard), it is extremely doubtful whether any portion of it ever re-united as a regularly formed military body, during the brief remaining period of the battle —certainly not on the Allied side of La Belle Alliance, towards which point it directed its retreat. It is necessary to remark that this regiment of the old guard, which was commanded by General Cambronne, formed a separate column of support in *échelon* to, and immediate left rear of, the three battalions of the middle guard; but so close to each other were the two columns, that although an interval was observed between them by Adam's brigade when the latter stood in the general front line of the Allied position, they appeared to it but as one column, when charged in flank, and may, to all intents and purposes, be considered as having formed one general column of attack. Cambronne's battalions, however, forming the rear of the column, did not become exposed to the fire from Adam's brigade, inasmuch as neither the 71st regiment nor the 3rd battalion 95th regiment, could complete the brigade flank movement in time to open a fire upon the mass before the actual charge was commenced. Hence, although they turned, along with the rest of the column, yet, unlike the latter, they retained a considerable degree of order.

Troops could scarcely be placed in a more critical situation than was this second attacking column of the imperial guard from the moment it came to a halt. With its front immediately facing a battery within sixty or seventy yards' distance, the double-shotted guns of which continued ploughing through the mass, and tearing up its ranks; with its left flank faced outwards to repel a formidable attack on that side, and its right flank partially exposed to the oblique fire from the greater portion of the line of British guards; the interior of the mass, enveloped in smoke, feeling a pressure from both front and flank, and yet perceiving no indication of the means of extricating itself from so perilous a position, it was truly a most trying moment even to such veteran warriors as those which constituted the renowned imperial guard of France. Any attempt at deployment to its right, while thus attacked on its left, was of course out of the question. Had it continued to advance until Adam's brigade had approached quite close to its left flank, the charge of the latter must have brought it to a stand, and rendered the efforts of the head of the column abortive. If, on the other hand, after having faced altogether to the left, and converted that flank into a compact line, it had advanced to meet the 52nd regiment when it first became aware of this attack, it would still have been exposed on the right (its previous front) to the havoc created by Napier's guns, as also to a charge by Maitland's brigade, which by bringing forward its left shoulders, might have rendered the situation of the column so hopeless, as probably to have led to its immediate and unqualified surrender on the spot. The dilemma into which these veterans were thus thrown was mainly attributable to the fatal neglect of not accompanying the column with an effective support of cavalry. A strong body of the latter on each flank, or in its immediate rear, would have secured the column from any such flank attack as that which so successfully arrested its progress, and so completely effected its dispersion.

The direction given to Adam's line by its "right-shoulder-forward" movement having brought it perpendicular to the general front of the French position, that officer became naturally anxious for support upon his right flank, to secure the latter from the enemy's cavalry, which, it was to be presumed, would now be brought forward from his reserve, since none of it had been employed in immediate support of the last attack. He urgently requested for this purpose, the aid of troops from the other part of Clinton's division, and Lieut. Colonel Halkett, seeing what was required, immediately advanced with the nearest battalion of his Hanoverian brigade, the Osnabrück landwehr, in column at quarter distance, and close up in right rear of the 71st regiment.* Thus Adam's brigade, maintaining its four-deep line, and being flanked by the Hanoverian battalion which could form square at any moment, was secured against cavalry.

The confused and disordered mass of the imperial guard, from the first impulse given to it by the flank charge, hastened a short distance in a direction parallel with that of the Anglo-allied line, and then naturally inclining towards the French position, it fell into nearly the same track of retreat as that pursued by the first attacking column, namely towards the first rise of ground intersected by the Charleroi road, a little beyond the southern extremity of the orchard of La Haye Sainte. As it approached the rear of those columns of d'Erlon's corps, which had been so desperately opposing Alten's division, the latter became infected with the panic, and commingled with the flying guard. Adam's brigade continued its triumphant advance, at first parallel, for a short distance, to the Allied line, and then, bringing forward its left shoulders, swept proudly onward in the direction of the French height before-mentioned; crowds of fugitives hurrying along and striving to escape from the pursuing wave that seemed every instant on the point of engulphing them.

During its advance, the front of Adam's brigade was partially crossed by the squadron of the 23rd light dragoons,

* During the advance, Halkett sent his brigade-major, Captain von Saffe, to bring up the two battalions of his brigade that were posted in rear of Hougomont; but that officer having been killed on his way, the message was not delivered, and the Osnabrück battalion continued to be separated from the rest of the brigade during the remainder of the battle.

under Lieut. Banner, retiring in disorder from its charge.* Mistaken for hostile cavalry, these dragoons were unfortunately fired upon by the 52nd regiment, and it was not until the foremost of them had fallen close upon the bayonets, that the error was discovered. Immediately after this incident, a fire of grape was opened upon the 52nd by three French field pieces in the prolongation of its right flank. This enfilading of the regiment in its four-deep line was a judicious measure on the part of the French artillery, and well calculated to derange the advance of Adam's brigade. It was however, very gallantly and speedily checked by the wheeling up and advance of the right section of the 52nd, under Lieutenant Gawler,† who succeeded in driving off the guns, whilst the rest of the regiment continued its pursuit.

Wellington, as soon as he saw that the success of the charge by Adam's brigade was so decisive, requested Uxbridge immediately to launch forward some fresh cavalry to check the probable advance of that of the enemy, and to second the efforts of the infantry in front, by boldly attacking the French reserves, which appeared collected in front of La Belle Alliance, the critical point of Napoleon's line. Lieut. Colonel Lord Greenock,* Assistant Quarter Master General of the cavalry, was despatched to Vivian with orders for him to move his hussar-brigade to its right from its position in rear of Alten's division, so as to get clear of the infantry, and then to advance directly to the front by the right of Maitland's brigade of guards. At the same time, the Duke turned round to order up the nearest supports to the space which had been vacated in his front line by the advance of Adam's brigade. But what a spectacle met his view! The three Dutch-Belgian squares, into which d'Aubremé's brigade had been formed, and whose unsteadiness, previously described, had greatly augmented as the firing and shouting on the exterior slope of the ridge, of which they could see nothing, became more continuous and intense, were now in a state bordering on dissolution. The faces of the squares were already broken at intervals by groups in the act of abandoning their ranks; whilst several officers of Vandeleur's brigade, which, as before observed, (see pages 343-344) was drawn up in their rear, were zealously exerting themselves in endeavouring to induce these troops to stand fast. The Duke, observing this, called out, "That's right; tell them the French are retiring." This intelligence, quickly caught up and spread

* See note at page 345.
† Now Colonel George Gawler, K.H., Unatt.
‡ Now Lieut. General Earl Cathcart, K.C.B.

through their ranks, had the desired effect of restoring them to order. They shortly afterwards formed into columns, and advanced to the front line.

In order to preserve a distinct and connected view of the combined operations against Napoleon, it will be necessary, previously to describing the general advance of the Allied line, consequent upon the failure of the attack by the French imperial guard, to revert to the movements of the Prussians.

It will be recollected that Vivian's, and subsequently, Vandeleur's brigade, quitted the left of the Anglo-allied line, on the approach of the advanced guard of Zieten's corps towards that point. Shortly before the arrival of these troops, the French skirmishers in front of Durutte's division, which constituted the angle of the *potence* on which stood the extreme right of Napoleon's army, having been considerably reinforced, were pushed forward for the purpose of establishing themselves in the houses and inclosures in the valley below them, and of impeding, by this means, the connection between Bülow's corps and the Anglo-allied left. The Nassauers, of Prince Bernhard of Saxe-Weimar's brigade, fell back from the houses of the hamlet of Papelotte, but firmly maintained their ground on the Allied side of the valley, retaining possession of the farms of Papelotte and La Haye. The French skirmishers, passing further to their right, pressed on to the village of Smohain, where they became warmly engaged with the Prussian troops that had been so judiciously posted in that quarter. Blücher, perceiving the infantry of the advanced guard of Zieten's corps upon the height above Smohain, sent an order for its moving by the shortest way to engage the enemy in the valley. The Prussian General Müffling, attached to the head-quarters staff of the Duke of Wellington, was at that moment in this vicinity, and gave the requisite instructions to the staff officer sent forward from Zieten's corps.

About this time, the 5th and 6th infantry-brigades, as also the reserve-cavalry of Pirch's corps, reached the field, in rear of Bülow. Pirch, placing himself at the head of his leading brigade (the 5th), immediately conducted it in the direction of Planchenoit; and, on coming up with the 14th and 16th brigades, he began, in conjunction with Colonel Hiller, to make the necessary dispositions for the third attack upon that village. The 6th brigade was ordered to follow as a reserve; and the attack was to be supported by a simultaneous advance of the right wing of Bülow's corps against

Lobau's line, which was exceedingly well drawn up, and exhibited every indication of making a determined stand. Blücher had despatched an order to the 7th brigade (of Pirch's corps) to move together with the 4th Kurmark landwehr-cavalry, upon Maransart, on the south side of the Lasne, for the purpose of covering his left flank. The remaining brigade (the 8th) of Pirch's corps, which had been detained in consequence of the rear-guard affair near Wavre, received orders from Pirch to quicken its advance. The reserve-cavalry of Pirch's corps was deployed in three lines on the right of the cavalry of the 4th corps. The first line consisted of the Pomeranian hussars and the Brandenburg hussars; the second, of the Silesian uhlans, two squadrons of the 6th Neumark dragoons, and the Queen's dragoons; and the third, of the 5th Kurmark and Elbe landwehr-cavalry. These lines of cavalry thus occupied the interval between the wings of Bülow's corps, and, at the same time, served to impose, by their display of force, upon the French cavalry, under Domon, which was then in reserve.

Blücher, judging the re-capture of Planchenoit to be a most essential aid in the general operations against the French, as affording the means not only of turning the right of Lobau's corps, but also of molesting the rear of the French army, and of endangering its main line of retreat, ordered the immediate advance of the troops destined for the third attack upon that village. They were formed in the following order:—The second and third battalions of the 2nd regiment (5th brigade) made the attack in the direction of the church; the first and second battalions of the 5th Westphalian landwehr, formed into one, were directed upon the French left of the village; the first battalion of the 2nd regiment followed in rear of the central space between these two columns; Major Witzleben led the third battalion of the 25th regiment (5th brigade) towards the heights on the (French) right of the village; and the remainder of this regiment, which had occupied the outer edge of the wood of Virère on the left, also advanced. The 11th regiment and the 2nd Pomeranian landwehr, belonging to the 14th brigade, and the first and second battalions of the 15th regiment, with the first and second battalions of the 1st Silesian landwehr, belonging to the 16th brigade, followed in support of this attack. The whole force was disposed in chequered columns, preceded by a strong line of skirmishers. and covered by the Prussian batteries on the heights in rear. The horse-battery, No. 6, posted on the high ground upon the right of the wood of Virère, was principally occupied in diverting the fire from a horse-battery of the reserve-artillery of the French imperial guard, which had one half of its guns above the hollow-way formed by the road leading down into Planchenoit from La maison du Roi, and the other half detached to an elevated spot in the south part of the village, whence it had a commanding view of a considerable portion of the advancing columns.

Simultaneously with this third attack upon Planchenoit, the 13th and 15th brigades, which constituted Bülow's right wing, advanced against Lobau's line, covered by a force of artillery much superior to that which the French could bring to bear against them. They were disposed in chequered columns of battalions, in the following manner:—In front line were the second battalion of the 18th regiment and the third battalion of the 3rd Silesian landwehr; in the second line were the first and third battalions of the 18th regiment, the first and second battalions of the 3rd Silesian landwehr, and the first battalion of the 10th regiment; in the third line were the three battalions of the 4th Silesian landwehr, and the second battalion of the 10th regiment. The three battalions of the 3rd Neumark landwehr followed in reserve. The right of this advance was supported by the West Prussian uhlans and the second Neumark landwehr-cavalry.

In the meantime, the first infantry-brigade of Zieten's corps, having continued its descent into the valley, passing Hacke's infantry in and about Smohain, on its left, advanced upon La Haye and Papelotte, and mistaking the Nassauers for French, through the similarity of uniform, opened a sharp fire upon them, and drove them from their post. The latter at first replied to this fire, which was kept up for some minutes, killing and wounding on both sides, until the error was discovered. These troops then began pressing forward, conjointly with those from Smohain, against the French skirmishers.

The advanced cavalry of Zieten's corps which had been seen approaching the left of Wellington's line, had now joined. The Brandenburg dragoons and Brandenburg uhlans, drew up in line in rear of the Wavre road, and on the immediate left of Best's Hanoverian infantry brigade. The 1st Silesian hussars formed upon the outer slope of the ridge, in rear of the lane leading from the Wavre road down to Papelotte. The 2nd Kurmark landwehr-cavalry drew up in the hollow in the rear of the interval between the landwehr-battalions Osterode and Verden of Best's brigade. It was on the ground immediately in front of this interval that Captain

Rettberg's Hanoverian foot-battery had been posted throughout the day, and as the latter had expended the whole of its ammunition, it withdrew to the rear as the Prussian horse-battery, No. 7, came up, by which it was then relieved, and the Prussians opened a cannonade from this point upon the opposite heights.* The Prussian foot-battery, No. 7, quitting the Wavre road, proceeded some way down the outer slope of the ridge to seek a favourable point whence it could by its fire cover the advance of the infantry in the valley.

Such was the general disposition of Blücher's forces relatively with that of Wellington's army at the time when the latter had defeated the attacking columns of the French imperial guard; and was following up its triumph by boldly assailing the very centre of Napoleon's position, at which point the latter had collected his sole remaining reserves. Perhaps a more comprehensive view of this relative disposition of the Prussian troops may be afforded by simply stating, by way of a summary, that the advanced portion of Zieten's corps had joined the left of the allied line, that part of Pirch's corps (including his reserve cavalry,) had joined Bülow; and that the latter was on the advance—his right to attack Lobau, and his left to make a third assault upon Planchenoit—the French opposed to them evincing, at all points, every indication of making a firm and determined stand.

We must now resume the detail of the brilliant and decisive dispositions of the Duke of Wellington, whom we left triumphantly defeating the French imperial guard, and requesting the Earl of Uxbridge to bring forward fresh cavalry, to aid the advancing infantry in taking immediate advantage of the disorder and confusion into which the enemy had been thrown by the failure of his last grand attack.

There is not, perhaps, an instance in modern history, in which the threatening tide of battle, has, through the lightning-like promptitude of decision, and the energetic application of yet remaining resources, been so suddenly and powerfully controlled, and so majestically and irresistibly hurled back, overwhelming all and every thing that, in the previous

* Captain von Rettberg was occupied with his ammunition-waggons immediately in rear of the knoll on which his battery was posted, and on the right of a patch of brushwood, when his attention was arrested by trumpet sounds with which his ear was unacquainted, and he perceived the advance of the Prussian cavalry. Lieut. General von Zieten was at the head of the latter, and asked Captain von Rettberg the shortest way to the high road that passes by La Haye Sainte; whereupon Captain von Rettberg conducted him to the point at which that road is intersected by the one from Wavre. It was shortly after this that the general advance of the Allied line took place.

plenitude of its force, it had borne aloft, with buoyant hopes, and carried along exultingly in its course, as it was by the immortal Wellington in this his last, his crowning victory. Never did a battle-field present so complete, so magical a transition of scene as that which succeeded the defeat of the imperial guards of France by the guards of the sovereign of England and the British light infantry-brigade. The state of the Duke's army at the time of Napoleon's last grand attack has already been adverted to, but let us glance again, for a moment, at the awfully diminished numbers, and almost exhausted energies, of those heroic bands which, in front line, had been exposed to the incessant and concentrated cannonade from a range of batteries forming almost the entire arc of which that line was the chord; subjected to repeated and vigorous attacks of all arms during so many hours; and now called upon to resist "to the death" another assault more fierce and determined than any they had yet encountered—look at the rear of that line, and observe the palpable defection in the ranks of an ally, whose contingent, whilst it constituted so great a proportion of the Duke's entire force, had already afforded too evident proofs that in a calculation of available resources, its services must be thrown entirely out of the scale—see, too, at increased intervals, the wrecks of the British and German cavalry, with, however, the fortunate exception of the two light brigades so opportunely brought from the extreme left to the rear of the menaced point of attack—how discouraging an aspect, when compared with that of the French army advancing to its last grand attack! Is it to be wondered that at that moment, doubts as to the issue of the great contest should have prevailed in the minds even of those who were prepared to support their noble chief to the last drop of their blood? And yet, with such apparently inefficient elements, the bare contemplation of which might have both weighed down the energies, and altered the purpose, of another general, did the British chief not only successfully defeat this most formidable assault, but finally gain a signal and resplendent victory. It would, however, be unjust to the abilities, and to the fame of the Duke, to ascribe such victory solely to his defeat of the attacking columns of the imperial guard upon his own position; though such, no doubt, was the foundation upon which he erected the structure of his final triumph. The nine battalions of the guard, of which the attacking columns had been composed, were defeated; but these, it must be borne in mind, constituted but the *van* of the attacking force, which comprised no less than the whole front line of the French army. D'Erlon's corps from the right, and Reille's corps from the left, were pouring forth their numerous columns, the principal portion of which had already reached more than midway towards the Allied position, and presented a formidable array, whilst from the heights which they had quitted, their artillery thundered forth as vigorously over their heads, upon the exhausted line of the Allies, as at any previous period of the battle. The four battalions of the first attacking column of the guard had been rallied with great rapidity by Napoleon, and posted on a commanding eminence, intersected by the Charleroi road in front of his centre. Near La Belle Alliance, reserves had been collected, principally of cavalry; and though the latter consisted entirely of the remains of corps that had previously suffered great losses, they might have been wielded with powerful effect against any point at which the advancing infantry should succeed in making an impression. Besides these, there stood on the French extreme left, a brigade of light cavalry, which had not been engaged during any part of the day, and had never yet moved out of its position. On the other hand, too, however glorious the result of the struggle with the imperial guard, it could not but tend to cripple still further the slender physical means which the Duke yet retained at his disposal. Victory, hovering over the brave conquerors of the imperial guard, alighted for a moment at the feet of Wellington, and ere the goddess could be scared away by the still threatening countenance of the enemy, Britain's hero secured her favour by the display of that extraordinary foresight, prompt decision, and unflinching determination, which, though at all times his distinguishing characteristics, now shone forth with more than ordinary brilliancy. His perfect knowledge of the character and composition of the French army plainly told him that a signal defeat of the imperial guard, a force employed only on occasions of great and critical emergency, would be certain to exercise a powerful influence upon the *morale* of the enemy's troops; but it also told him that, unless instant advantage were taken of that defeat, unless it were followed up in such a manner as to render the incipient panic which it had created, general and uncontrollable, that same army might, through the powerful influence and indefatigable exertions of such men as Napoleon and Ney, rapidly recover the shock; d'Erlon's and Reille's columns, although faltering for a moment, might pursue their advance with determined efforts to regain the footing which the guard had lost; the veterans composing the latter force, resolved to avenge their defeat, might speedily rally, and, with deperate resolution, renew their attack, aided by a more direct and effective support by the cavalry-reserves collected in front of La Belle Alliance. This view had scarcely passed across the mind of the Duke, when his decision was fully made. With those critically slender means, to which allusion has more than once been made, and which in the hands of many a commander would have been deemed totally inadequate for even the maintenance of the position, at such fearful odds, Wellington determined to compensate for the awfully reduced and exhausted state of the fighting portion of his troops, and the utter want of confidence in the remainder, by one of those bold and daring acts, which, when hazarded at the right moment, carry with them the *prestige* of conscious superiority, and allow an enemy no time to discover deficiencies, or to calculate mischances. No sooner was the second attacking column of the imperial guard defeated and dispersed, than he ordered it to be vigorously pursued, and the rallied force of the first column to be attacked, by Adam's brigade; whilst at the same moment he launched forth Vivian's hussar-brigade against the cavalry-reserves near La Belle Alliance, before these had made their dispositions for attack, and even before they had recovered from the surprise and hesitation which prevailed amongst them on witnessing the discomfiture of the guard.

Vivian, the moment he received the order to advance, wheeled his brigade, half-squadrons to the right. Thus the 10th hussars became the leading regiment, the 18th hussars followed, and the 1st hussars of the German legion, which had stood in second line, moved off, as soon as its front was clear, in rear of the latter corps. The brigade proceeded, at a trot, a short distance in rear of the infantry, and parallel to the crest of the position; and, as it approached the right of Maitland's brigade of guards, Vivian, ordering the leading half-squadron to wheel to the left, through Napier's battery, led it perpendicularly to the front. As the column thus advanced across the ridge, in left front of Vandeleur's light cavalry-brigade, it was saluted by the latter with cheers of encouragement; and in a similar manner by Maitland's brigade of guards as it passed their flank. The smoke lay heavily along the entire position, and especially, at this moment, over that part of the exterior slope of the ridge on which the struggle with the French imperial guard had taken place, and across which Vivian was now leading his brigade. On advancing further, and getting clear of the smoke, he obtained a more distinct view of the dispositions of the enemy's forces in his direct front. A very considerable portion appeared in great confusion; disordered columns of infantry were hurrying back to the main position, up the slope, on which were numerous stragglers of all arms, and in various uniforms, mixed together and retiring in crowds. Guns were firing from different points to cover the retreat, and the discharge of musketry in and about Hougomont continued very brisk. On arriving about midway towards the enemy's position, well formed bodies of troops were observed on the French left of La Belle Alliance, posted as if fully prepared to resist the threatened attack. They consisted of two squares of infantry, with cavalry and guns formed on the flanks and between them. The cavalry on their left was somewhat advanced, comprising separate bodies, partially covering one another, but presenting a general front, and posted on some rising ground about 200 yards on the Allied left of the south-east angle of the Hougomont inclosures. The two squares here alluded to were the two battalions of the grenadiers of the old guard, which had been placed in reserve of the main attack by that force as previously explained.* The cavalry on the left was thus disposed—first, on the slope of the little eminence, a portion of the lancers of the imperial guard; then, in left rear of the latter, on lower ground, were two squadrons of the dragoons of the guard, and, in their right rear, two more squadrons of the same corps; in right rear of these again, and on the summit of the eminence, stood the brigade of carabiniers. In rear of these, and of the squares themselves, as also on the right of the latter, were collected the remainder of that portion of the French cavalry which had made such repeated attacks upon the Duke's line during the day. All these different bodies of cavalry were but mere wrecks of their former selves—regiments, and, in many instances, entire brigades, were diminished to less than squadrons. In the morning, as they came fresh into the field, they constituted the flower of the French cavalry; now, so severe had been their losses, they presented a mere phantom of their former splendour.

Vivian, as soon as he perceived this disposition of the enemy's forces in his immediate front, decided upon forming a front line with the 10th and 18th British hussars, and upon holding the 1st hussars of the German legion in second line, in support. For this purpose, and also with a view to oppose,

* See pages 326 and 328.

and, if possible, to turn, the left of the enemy's cavalry, he made the leading regiment, the 10th hussars, incline to its right. Shortly afterwards, Vivian was joined by Colonel Sir Colin Campbell* of the staff, who brought him an order from the Duke that he was not to attack before the infantry came up, unless he felt confident of success. Vivian remarked that as the Allied infantry in its anxiety to get on, was probably not in compact order, its safety might be seriously endangered should it be exposed to a cavalry-attack; and that, in his opinion, it would be better that not a moment should be lost on his part in driving off the cavalry which appeared in his front. Sir Colin Campbell coincided in this opinion, and returned to the Duke. After the very short pause at the head of the column, consequent upon this little discussion, Vivian, continuing the advance, ordered the 10th hussars to form line on the front half-squadron, and, at the same time, sent orders to his two other regiments also to form line on their leading half-squadrons respectively, but then to remain in support. The rapid pace which had been maintained by the head of the column, and the incline to the right which had been given to it, required great activity on the part of the left half-squadrons to get up into line; and as Vivian ordered the charge as soon as the first squadron was formed, it was executed not in line but rather in *échelon* of squadrons, which, under the circumstances of the moment, as will presently be seen, was the preferable and more desirable formation. Just as the charge was ordered, the 2nd light dragoons of the King's German legion, in a column of squadrons, which had been detached from the main position, almost simultaneously with the advance of Vivian's brigade, came up on the right of the 10th hussars, and in a direction rather crossing the front of the latter regiment, which had its left thrown somewhat forward whilst the Germans were moving straight to their front, and directly upon the French dragoons of the guard before mentioned as posted in the hollow on the Allied right of the eminence on which stood the French cavalry about to be charged by Vivian's brigade. The dragoons at first appeared disposed to resist the Germans, and received them with a tolerably effective carbine-fire from their rear ranks, but the former charged home, cut down several of the enemy's horsemen, and made some prisoners. In following up the charge, however, the regiment exposed its right flank to a body of cuirassiers, by which it was thrown into

* Lieut. General Sir Colin Campbell, K.C.B., died on the 13th June, 1847.

disorder. Lieut. Colonel de Jonquières, the commanding officer, ordered the halt and rally to be sounded, but in the next moment he was wounded, as was also Lieut. Colonel Maydell.* Major Friedrichs,† who was next in command, highly distinguished himself on this occasion by the spirited manner in which he rallied several of his men together; and as those that had been dispersed, rapidly placed themselves on his flanks, and thus extended his new line, he made another charge, which sent the enemy's cavalry about, and put it to flight. The regiment then continued moving forward, with proper caution, along the base of the higher ground on the left, over which the 10th British hussars were also charging and advancing.

In the mean time, the latter regiment made its charge: the right, centre, and left squadrons, in rapid succession, dashed in amongst the French cavalry posted as before mentioned. The left squadron of the 10th had scarcely closed with the enemy, before the whole of the cavalry on the (French) left of the squares of the guard, was in full flight. Vivian, perceiving the complete success of this brilliant charge, ordered a halt; and then returned as quickly as possible to the 18th hussars.‡ After the 10th hussars had pursued the French cavalry about two hundred yards, a body of cuirassiers charged their right squadron, on its right flank, and forced it about a hundred yards away to the left, whilst the centre and left squadrons not being aware of Vivian's order to halt continued their pursuit, inclining to their right, under Lieut. Colonel Lord Robert Manners,§ then commanding the 10th. Previously to describing the subsequent proceedings of this brigade, it is necessary to revert to other matters in order to connect them with the general disposition of the main army.

Adam's light infantry-brigade had, in the mean time, been steadily advancing from the moment of its charge upon the left flank of the second attacking column of the French imperial guard, sweeping along the front of the right centre of the Anglo-allied position, and bringing forward its left shoulders as

* Lieut. Colonel Charles von Maydell retired from the King's German legion in 1826.

† Now Colonel Augustus Friedrichs, C.B., K.H., on the Hanoverian retired list.

‡ On his way to the 18th hussars, Vivian was attacked by a cuirassier. His right hand was in a sling, in consequence of a wound received at Croix d'Orade, near Toulouse. Taking the reins in this hand, which was barely capable of holding them, he contrived to give the cuirassier a thrust in the neck with his left hand, whilst at the same moment he was joined by his German orderly, who cut the Frenchman off his horse.

§ Major General Lord Robert Manners, C.B., died on the 15th of November, 1835.

it neared the Charleroi road, so that its left skirted the orchard of La Haye Sainte. It had now reached the hollow immediately under the nearest French height which was intersected by that road, and upon which the troops that had composed the first attacking column of the guard had been rallied by Napoleon, and formed into three squares. The 2nd regiment of chasseurs of the old guard having formed the extreme left of the attacking force had been closely observed by Lieut. Colonel Halkett, who continued to follow it very steadily with the Osnabrück landwehr-battalion as it retired towards the high road, inclining to La Belle Alliance.

Wellington, perceiving the confusion in which the columns of the French imperial guard fell back after the decided failure of their attack—a confusion which was evidently extending itself with wonderful rapidity to a vast portion of the troops in their vicinity who witnessed their discomfiture; remarking also the beautiful advance of Vivian's hussar-brigade against the French reserves posted close to La Belle Alliance, and in the very heart of Napoleon's position; as well as the steady and triumphant march of Adam's brigade, which, driving a host of fugitives before it, had now closely approached the nearest rise of the French position contiguous to the Charleroi road; finally, observing that Bülow's movement upon Planchenoit had begun to take effect, perceiving the fire of his cannon, and being also aware that part of a Prussian corps had joined his own left by Ohain,—he ordered a general advance of the whole of his line of infantry, supported by the cavalry and artillery.

As this long-wished-for command rapidly passed along the line, loud and joyous were the shouts with which it was received. The passive endurance, not unaccompanied by murmurs, with which the Allied troops had, during so many hours, withstood the incessant attacks of cavalry, infantry, and artillery, to which so vast, so awful a proportion of their comrades had fallen a sacrifice, now gave place to feelings of intense exultation, of intoxicating triumph. At the same time, when they saw that the advance was general, that the enemy had retired in confusion from his last grand attack, and that the brigades detached to the front were boldly assailing his reserves, the conviction flashed across their minds that if the Duke had hitherto resisted their demands to be led to the attack, his consummate and unerring judgment had caused him to defer the advance until that attack could be undertaken with every probability of success.

Just as this decisive moment, the faint rays of the setting

sun shone forth, and as they struggled to penetrate the almost universal haze created by the hitherto unremitting volumes of smoke which a close, dense atmosphere appeared incapable of altogether dissipating, they cast upon the varied and multitudinous objects on the field, a lurid light, imparting to them a colouring so strikingly impressive, as can never be effaced from the memories of those who witnessed that magnificent battle-scene. In front of the line, on the rise occupied by Maitland's brigade of guards, stood prominently in view, the great and noble Duke himself, his hat raised high in air, as the signal for the commencement of the general advance; leaders in front of their divisions and brigades, appearing, by their animated gestures, to take their tone from their great chieftain; unfurled colours raised aloft, proudly displaying their shattered remnants; drums, bugles, trumpets, sending forth their warlike sounds to commingle with the enthusiastic and tumultuous cheering of the troops; artillerymen occupied in working out their guns from the soft soil in which they had become so deeply imbedded; squadrons and supports pressing forward to gain the ridge, as this became vacated by the first line, to behold, and participate in, the glorious triumph; numerous isolated soldiers, hurrying on, wherever they could be spared from attending the wounded, to join their ranks, and share in the inspiring excitement of such a moment; in the distance, in front, the retiring masses of the French, intermingled with crowds of fugitives of all arms, mounted and dismounted; far away to the left, the dark columns of the Prussians, and the smoke ascending from their batteries; on the right, and somewhat in advance, the dense vapour still slowly circling upwards from the glowing embers of Hougomont, assuming a reddish glare as it floated over the heads of the brave defenders of that post of honour;—all appeared to the eyes of the beholder illumined, as it were, by a light partaking rather of the supernatural, than of the ordinary effects of sunshine. It was of brief duration. The sun sank rapidly below the horizon, and if the gorgeous colouring which departed with it had been congenial to the exhilarated feelings of the victors, so, in an equal degree, must the succeeding twilight, rendered still more gloomy by a clouded sky, have toned in with the dejected and gloomy spirits of the vanquished. With these there prevailed no other sentiments than those of a vexed and mortified perplexity, or an extreme dismay. The panic which had set in was extending itself widely and speedily throughout the line, and despondency was depicted in every countenance.

The Duke galloped off to Adam's brigade, which was then in the valley immediately below the height on which the three squares of the French guard were posted; and as these appeared inclined to make a stand, he ordered Adam to attack them. The latter, however, suggested to his Grace that as the brigade, in consequence of its rapid advance over the heavy soil in the valley, encumbered as the latter was with dead and dying men and horses, both singly and in heaps, had become somewhat loose in its formation, it might be advisable to halt it, to allow the files to close in. This was accordingly done. But after a few moments only had elapsed, the Duke said, "They won't stand—better attack them;" and being at the time close to the colours of the centre regiment, (the 52nd,) he called out, "Go on, Colborne, go on!"

Colonel Sir Colin Campbell now rejoined the Duke, and explained the grounds upon which Vivian had decided upon attacking the French cavalry-reserves; on learning which Lord Uxbridge, who was present,* determined upon personally leading the attack with the hussars, and participating in the final and decisive triumph of the British cavalry; and was on the point of darting off to that part of the field, when his intentions were suddenly frustrated by a grape-shot from a battery on the height above him striking and severely wounding his right leg. Reluctantly compelled to desist from further exertion, this gallant and noble warrior, who had so bravely, so chivalrously, so skilfully, and so successfully, led the British cavalry throughout the day, had still the satisfaction of feeling and knowing that although not permitted to witness the closing triumph of that branch of the service of which he was at once the chief, the ornament, and pride, he had well and truly performed his duty to his sovereign and his country. He was supported for some moments by Sir Colin Campbell, and shortly afterwards, with the assistance of a party of the 23rd light dragoons, carried into the high road, along which he was borne to Waterloo; and, when subsequently undergoing, at that village, the necessary operation of amputation, so great were the satisfaction

* Previously to this, and at the time when his lordship ordered forward Sir Hussey Vivian's brigade, he rode up to Major Latour,† then commanding the 23rd light dragoons, on the left of the household cavalry, and asked him for a troop-horse, his own charger being tired or wounded. Major Latour immediately dismounted Serjeant Major Stride, and gave his mare to Lord Uxbridge, who proceeded to the front, and rejoined the Duke.

† Now Major General Peter Augustus Latour, C.B., K.H.

and contentment which had been wrought in his mind as he calmly reflected on the brilliant exploits that had marked the arduous and varied struggle, that observing the anxious and compassionate looks of his friends around his couch, he exclaimed, "Who would not lose a leg for such a victory?" Seldom indeed has a cavalry-chief more distinguished himself in the field than did the Earl of Uxbridge on this great day. As he flew from one point to another, now boldly rushing into the fight at the head of a glorious charge, then skilfully covering a retreat under the pressure of overpowering numbers; here zealously endeavouring by his own personal example to stimulate and rouse into action the lukewarm energies of an ally; there collecting and rallying, for further high emprize, the remnants of the devoted bands of his own nation; restlessly vigilant in watching and preparing for the manœuvres of a renowned and powerful cavalry, admirably appointed and equipped, and led by a Kellermann, a Guyot, and a Lefebvre-Desnouettes; evincing the most cool and resolute confidence in the prowess of his followers, as he dashed forward either to break asunder the combined advance of the enemy's masses, or to follow up the advantage already gained by the Allied infantry—he seemed to blend and embody in his own character, in a pre-eminent degree, the heroic valour of ancient chivalry, with the skilled address of modern cavalry tacticians.*

As Adam's brigade ascended the hill, in compliance with Wellington's orders, to charge the French squares, it was received with a heavy fire from their front and flanks. The Duke being at this time close to the centre of the advancing line, against which point this fire was principally directed, incurred great personal risk; and as the shot flew fast and thick about him, Sir Colin Campbell said to him, "This is no place for you—you had better move." To this the Duke replied, "I will when I see those fellows off." On the near and imposing approach of the brigade, in the attitude of charging, the imperial guard ceased firing, faced to the rear, and commenced a retreat by word of command. As they withdrew, his Grace rode up the valley in the direction of his right front, and came upon the plain, on which Vivian was successfully attacking the French reserves.

The gallant charge made by the 10th hussars upon the

* In consideration of his distinguished services, the Prince Regent was pleased to grant him the dignity of a Marquess, by the name, style and title of "Marquess of Anglesey."

French cavalry posted in its right front, has already been described. After ordering the halt and rally, Vivian galloped towards the 18th hussars, which regiment he found well formed in line, and in perfect order. In its front stood the two squares of the grenadiers of the old guard; in its left front, and much nearer to it, were posted artillery and cavalry, in advance of the proper right of the squares. This cavalry consisted principally of cuirassiers—the wrecks of entire brigades. Nearer to, and partly in rear of, the squares, stood the chasseurs, and grenadiers à cheval, of the imperial guard, greatly diminished in numbers. It was immediately evident to Vivian that the attack must in the first instance be directed against the advanced cavalry and artillery; and having put the line in motion, he placed himself in front of the centre, beside Lieut. Colonel the Honorable Henry Murray, the commanding officer, for the purpose of putting the regiment into the required direction. This having been effected, he ordered the charge; when the hussars dashed forward with the greatest impetuosity, and, at the same time, with as much steadiness and regularity as if they had been at field-day exercise on Hounslow heath. Thus, the direction of the charge by the 18th diverged as much to the left, as that by the 10th had inclined to the right. Just as the charge commenced, some French artillery coming from their right, and slanting towards the right of the 18th, made a bold push to cross the front of the latter at a gallop. But the attempt failed, and the hussars were instantly among them, cutting down the artillerymen and drivers, and securing the guns. In the next moment they fell upon the advanced cavalry, which they completely dispersed, and then, bringing forward their left shoulders, they attacked the cavalry and guns that stood more to the right front, and near to the right square, which was now retiring. This cavalry appeared, at first, determined upon making a stand; and an officer in its front dashed forward, and fired at Lieut. Colonel Murray; but, in another moment, the 18th were fiercely and dexterously plying their swords amongst them. They were forced to give way, the artillerymen were driven from their guns, and the whole fled in disorder. The charge then ceased to be compact, for the assailants and the flying were intermingled pell-mell; all riding as fast as the confusion of the mêlée would permit; a part of them along the high road, but the principal portion on the Allied right of the latter; the whole, however, passing by La Belle Alliance, and leaving the two squares of the guard on their right.

Vivian, satisfied with the complete success of the charge, ordered the regiment to halt and re-form; whilst he proceeded himself to bring up the 1st hussars of the legion, which corps he had left in reserve. On his way he found Major the Honorable Frederick Howard, with the right squadron of the 10th hussars, which, as before stated, (See page 360), had been driven to the left by a charge of cuirassiers. This squadron stood forward within a short distance of the left square of the grenadiers of the guard, from the fire of which it was losing men fast. Vivian doubted for a moment how far it might be advisable to attack the square, but perceiving an infantry-regiment in red advancing on his left, and calculating on its immediately charging the face and angle of the square next to it, he ordered Major Howard to charge the face and angle to which he was opposed. This was executed with the greatest gallantry and determination. Vivian himself joined in the charge, on the right of the squadron. The hussars charged home to the bayonets of the French guard, and a fierce conflict ensued. Major Howard was killed at the head of his men. He was shot in the mouth, and fell senseless to the ground, when one of the imperial guard stepped out of the ranks, and brutally beat his head with the butt-end of his musket.* Two other officers, Lieutenants Arnold and Bacon, were wounded. Lieutenant Gunning was killed immediately previous to the attack. The regiment of infantry, however, did not charge, as Vivian had expected, but continued pursuing a separate column in its own immediate front on the high road.

Although the square, a very strong one, cannot be said to have been broken by the shock, for the veteran soldiers of

* This officer was highly esteemed, not only by his own regiment, but by all who knew him. One of my informants, who was a brother-officer of his, says—"I never knew Howard do or say a thing one could wish otherwise. He was an excellent officer too; and, I know, a sincerely attached husband." Byron's lines are as just to the memory of the chivalrous soldier, as they are honourable to the feelings of the noble bard:—

"And his was of the bravest, and when shower'd
The death-bolts deadliest the thinn'd files along,
Even where the thickest of war's tempest lower'd,
They reach'd no nobler breast than thine, young, gallant Howard."

The same brother-officer, above mentioned, has favoured me with some lines which he wrote, in 1822, upon his friend's death, when in a transport (not, as he humorously related to me, a *poetical* one, but a *troop-ship*,) crossing to Ireland with the regiment. This effusion, whilst it breathes the outpourings of a generous heart and noble mind, presents so truly graphic a description of that part of the closing scene of Waterloo, connected with the proceedings of Vivian's hussar-brigade, that I have been induced to append it to this work.—See Appendix XXXIV.

whom it was composed knew too well their power of resistance against such a handful of horsemen, still the manner in which the latter, notwithstanding the rapid diminution of their number, continued cutting at the ranks, parrying bayonet-thrusts, and pertinaciously pressing on, reflects the highest credit on the 10th British hussars. The men fought with desperation; maddened probably by the fall of their officers. The square, yielding to the pressure, continued to fall back until it reached the hollow-way formed by the narrow road that leads from the chaussée in rear of La Belle Alliance, towards the left of the French position. Into this the guard hastily descended in confusion, and escaping by either outlet, mingled with the host of fugitives hurrying along the general line of retreat of the French army.

In the mean time, the remainder of the 10th hussars, consisting of the left and centre squadrons, that had, in the course of the first charge, crossed over to the right of the rise of ground on which the French reserve-cavalry had been posted, had continued its course, under Lord Robert Manners, down into the valley, south-east of the Hougomont inclosures. The routed cavalry spread out in the utmost confusion—cuirassiers, of an almost gigantic size, galloped as hard as they could; and numbers tumbled off their horses to save themselves. The hussars now came upon retiring infantry, that appeared seized with a panic as their routed cavalry dashed past them—the large bear-skin caps, worn by several of them, betokened a portion of the imperial guard—they commenced throwing down their arms, numbers of them loudly calling out "*Pardon!*" Then, crossing the same narrow road, before mentioned as leading from La Belle Alliance to the left of the French position (but on the Allied right of the hollow-way by which the square of the guard effected its escape), the hussars brought up their right shoulders, and ascended the height in rear of the hollow-road. Upon the slope of the hill, about half a battalion of the French guard had rallied and formed, with some cavalry close behind them, and opened a sharp fire upon the 10th. Part of the 18th hussars, at this time, reached the hollow-way, an obstacle, however, which rendered *their* attack wholly impracticable. Lord Robert Manners halted for a minute, when within about forty paces from them, to allow his men to form up. He then gave a cheer and charged; when the imperial guard and the cavalry instantly turned and fled; the greater portion of the former throwing themselves down, and many of the latter tumbling off their horses. The hussars pursued up to the brow of the hill; on the further or south side of which was a deep hollow, and beyond this a knoll, (on the Allied right of the Charleroi road and nearly opposite De Coster's house,) upon which another square of infantry had formed, and appeared very steady. At this time a party of the 18th hussars—not more than from 30 to 35 men—continuing the charge, before described, close along the right of La Belle Alliance and Trimotion, and crossing the narrow road near its junction with the Charleroi road, dashed down the hollow, and ascending the height above mentioned, charged the square in most gallant style; but, as might have been expected, was checked and turned by the latter. Lord Robert Manners and Captain Taylor had rallied a party of the 10th hussars, with a view to support the 18th, should these be charged in their turn, which however did not occur.

The two last mentioned regiments had, by this time, been thrown so much into disorder by their charges, that it became necessary to check their further advance, in order to gain time for collecting and re-forming their ranks. Although this measure was supported by the coming up of the 1st hussars of the legion to take post in front of the brigade, and was also rendered secure by the advance, on the right, of Vandeleur's brigade, (which had come up on Vivian's right, and between him and the inclosures of Hougomont, in column of squadrons, at the moment he was preparing to charge the square of the imperial guard with the party of the 10th hussars under Major Howard,) still the rallying and re-forming of those two regiments was attended with considerable difficulty, inasmuch as they had become completely intermingled with the fugitives.

It is now necessary to recur to Adam's brigade, which we left advancing, and driving before it, near the Charleroi road, the three squares of the guard that had retired as it approached to charge them. It will be recollected that upon the brigade first advancing from the Allied position Lieut. Colonel Halkett, followed it in immediate rear of its right flank, with the Osnabrück battalion of Hanoverian landwehr. When Adam reached the three squares above mentioned, Halkett, having the shortest space of ground to move over, soon came up in line with the brigade, still pursuing the column formed by the two battalions of chasseurs of the old guard. The Osnabrückers having then become much annoyed by a fire that opened upon them obliquely from a French battery within a very short distance of their right, their 1st company broke into subdivisions and, supported by the sharpshooters of the battalion, made a dash at the artillery, and captured six guns. During the greater part of the advance, they had been in almost close contact with the column formed by the two battalions of chasseurs of the old guard; and Halkett frequently called out to them to surrender. Having for some short time fixed his eye upon an individual whom he took to be the general-officer in command of the guard, from his being in full uniform, and from the animation he displayed in his endeavours to induce his men to stand their ground, and observing that the column, after receiving the fire of the Osnabrückers, left the general with two officers in its rear, he ordered the sharpshooters to dash on, whilst he, at the same time darted forward at full gallop to attack the general. When he had come up with him, and was about to cut him down, the latter called out that he would surrender. Cambronne, for he it was, then preceded Halkett as he returned to the Hanoverian battalion, but had not gone many paces, before Halkett's horse was wounded, and fell to the ground. In a few seconds, however, Halkett succeeded in getting him on his legs again, when he found that his prisoner was escaping in the direction of the French column; he instantly overtook him, seized him by the aiguilette, brought him to the battalion, and gave him in charge to a serjeant of the Osnabrückers who was to deliver him to the Duke.*

Adam's brigade had by this time crossed to the opposite

* I have entered somewhat into detail concerning the capture of General Cambronne, in consequence of the statements put forth by several French writers that, when the imperial guard was called upon to surrender, this officer replied, "*La garde meurt et ne se rend pas,*" an expression which the author of "*L'histoire de l'ex-garde,*" who insists upon its veracity, has affixed as a motto to his work. But even this writer is compelled to admit the difference of opinion that exists as to whether Cambronne really uttered the words imputed to him. Doubts are also entertained on this point by the authors of the "Victoires, conquêtes et désastres des Français," and no mention is made of the matter in the "Mémoires historiques de Napoléon, Livre IX." There can be no doubt as to the identity of the French general, as Cambronne declared himself to Lieut. Colonel Halkett, his captor, and was afterwards, along with Count de Lobau and other prisoners, sent to Ostend.

Since writing the above, I have learned that when it was proposed, during the summer of 1844, to erect a monument, at Nantes, to the memory of Cambronne, for which a subscription had been raised in all the towns of La Loire Inférieure, the committee appointed to superintend the design decided that on one face of the pedestal should be inscribed, in letters of bronze, the words "La garde meurt et ne se rend pas." Much, however, to the surprise and embarrassment of the Prefect of that department and of the committee, an energetic protest, supported by memoirs and other documentary evidence, was made against the decision of the latter by the family of General Michel, for whom is now claimed the honour of having uttered those remarkable words, while commanding one of the divisions of the imperial guard, and who was killed in the attack upon the British line, as stated at page 339. How the matter was settled I know not.

side of the Charleroi road, and, bringing forward its left shoulders, was continuing its advance, in pursuit of the defeated squares, in a direction parallel with that road; whilst Halkett, by continuing on the inner flank, and following the battalions of the chasseurs of the old guard, had got somewhat in advance, or rather, in right front of that brigade; and had, shortly before, reached the immediate vicinity of that part of the field on which Vivian was in the act of preparing to charge the square of the grenadiers of the old guard with the squadron of the 10th hussars under Major Howard. The Osnabrückers will here be recognised as the regiment of Allied infantry already alluded to in the description given of that charge.

Adam, after his repulse of the three squares of the imperial guard, perceiving that he was so much in front of the main line of the Anglo-allied army, and not being aware of Vivian's advance, had become apprehensive of an attack upon his right flank; and he therefore desired his brigade-major, Major Blair,* to proceed in the prolongation of his right flank, and observe whether there was any threatening appearance of the enemy's cavalry in that quarter. The latter, pursuing his errand, met the Duke of Wellington moving at a quick pace, followed by a single individual, to whom Major Blair addressed himself, but who immediately checked him by remarking, "*Monsieur, je ne parle pas un seul mot d'anglaise!*" Major Blair then explained to him, in French, the order he had received, to which he replied, *Le Duc lui-même a été voir; il n'y a rien à craindre;*" whereupon the former returned to Adam, with this satisfactory information.

Here, then, was the great chieftain himself, still in the battle's front, vigilantly watching, and eagerly seizing advantage of, the course of events; braving every peril, and acting solely upon his own personal observation; his staff, and even orderlies, almost all killed or wounded; the very few that remained untouched, carrying messages; his only attendant, a foreigner, (Major Count de Sales,† a Sardinian officer,) attached to his suite! It is impossible not to recognise in the extraordinary degree of security with which this great man so fearlessly exposed himself throughout the entire day, the protecting interposition of an all-wise and merciful Providence. At this moment, too, he was not only upon the track of his great antagonist, but, in all probability, within the shortest distance that ever separated these

* Now Colonel Hunter Blair, C.B., Unatt.

† Now his Excellency Lieut. General Count Paul François de Sales, the Sardinian Ambassador in Paris.

wonderful men from each other; the one, alone, and in front of his advancing line, borne forward on the wings of victory, and upheld by the knowledge of his might and the fulness of his glory; the other, seeking shelter amidst his devoted, yet broken and dispirited cohorts, abandoning himself to despair, and flying from the fatal field on which the sceptre he had usurped was signally and irrecoverably struck from his iron grasp.

CHAPTER XV.

THE very forward movement of Vivian's brigade, and the vigorous attack which it made against the centre of the French position, having rendered obvious the necessity of an immediate support, Vandeleur's brigade was despatched across the ridge in column of half squadrons, right in front, at the moment of the general advance of the line. It proceeded at a smart trot along the east side of the Hougomont inclosures, and then descended into the valley in rear of the latter, passing Vivian's brigade on its left. Here it fell in with disordered columns of the French infantry in full retreat, as also cavalry of all kinds mixed together, the cuirassiers throwing off their armour to facilitate their flight. In the midst of this confusion, however, there stood higher up the valley a large column on the opposite side of the road which connects the centre with the left of the French position, forming square, and seemingly determined to oppose the further advance of the brigade. The latter, receiving the fire from the column, charged, and the French giving way, the whole of them were taken or destroyed. In this charge the 11th light dragoons, forming the right of the brigade, captured a battery on the height to which the before-mentioned road ascends. It was the last which had maintained the cannonade from the French left wing. Vandeleur's brigade continued to press forward, driving a host of fugitives before it. It was by this time in advance, and rather in right front, of Vivian. Colonel Sir Felton Harvey, of the staff, came up to its then commander, Lieut. Colonel Sleigh, of the 11th light dragoons,—Vandeleur having taken the command of the cavalry upon the fall of Lord Uxbridge,—and informed him that a French cavalry-brigade was moving along the heights on the right (or western) side of the valley. This cavalry did not, however, venture to descend into the lower ground, where it might have fallen upon Sleigh's right flank, but continued its course along the high ground towards some point on the Charleroi road, quite in rear of the main French army, apparently with the intention of protecting the retreat and rallying the fugitives. It was Piré's light cavalry-brigade, that had been stationed throughout the day on the extreme left of the French line.

In this manner, Vivian's brigade, which had not only broken, but completely pierced, the centre of the French position, had its right effectually protected, and due advantage was promptly taken of the disorder into which its bold and successful advance had thrown those French troops that had been moving in that quarter. At the same time, Vivian's left was secured by the advance of Adam's brigade, which continued to drive before it, along the left side of the Charleroi road, the squares of the guard, as also the cuirassiers by whom the latter were supported. These cuirassiers, it should be observed, had fronted, and evinced a disposition to charge as the brigade crossed the high road. Adam, however, feeling secure in his four-deep formation, continued pressing towards them; and when, along that part of his line against which the attack was threatened, the British bayonets were lowered, the cuirassiers declined the contest.

Having thus detailed the brilliant successes of these three British brigades, with which Wellington had so boldly assailed the centre, and effectually destroyed the last reserves, of the enemy, it is now time to consider their important consequences in conjunction with the general advance of the Anglo-allied army; and for this purpose it will be necessary to take a more extended view of the prominent features which the field of battle presented at this period of the day.

On no part of the French army, beyond the immediate sphere of action of the above brigades, did the advance of the latter exercise so powerful an influence as on d'Erlon's corps, which constituted its right wing. The defeat of the second attacking column of the imperial guard, it will be recollected, involved in it the retreat of Donzelot's division of that corps, which, from the cover afforded it by the possession of La Haye Sainte, and from the hollow on its left of that farm, had so furiously assailed the central portion of the Duke's line, occupied by Alten's division. On the opposite side of the Charleroi road, from the knoll above the sand-pit, part of Alix's division was still maintaining a most destructive fire upon the remains of Picton's division and of Lambert's brigade posted along the Wavre road. The remainder of this division, as well as that under Marcognet, were advancing across the valley which separated the Anglo-allied left, from the French right, wing, and presented an array of columns between the knoll on the left of La Haye Sainte and the left of Durutte's division, which latter was now operating in concert with Lobau's corps in maintaining a defensive position against the advance of the Prussians. When, therefore, Wellington so suddenly launched forth Vivian's hussar-brigade against Napoleon's reserves, then posted close to La Belle Alliance, in the very centre of the French army, and also pushed forward Adam's light infantry-brigade past the farm and orchard of La Haye Sainte towards the eminence on which stood the three rallied squares of the imperial guard, he completely turned the left of d'Erlon's corps, and by means of the brilliant success which attended these movements, he gradually established himself in rear both of d'Erlon and of Lobau; the latter of whom was still defending himself against Blücher's advance. In like manner, the columns of Reille's corps, comprising the left wing of the French army, and which were advancing through, and contiguously to, the Hougomont inclosures, were turned in their right flank.

Thus, by this bold and masterly manœuvre, the whole front line of the French army, which, a short time before, had presented so menacing an appearance, was thrown into disorder and confusion; and supported as that manœuvre was by the advance, at the right moment, of the Duke's entire line, any attempt, on the part of the French, to rally and resume the offensive, was entirely frustrated. The firm, decided, and determined attitude which Wellington had assumed, had, in fact, struck terror and dismay into the ranks of his opponent, who, perceiving the hasty and confused retreat of his troops, as also the extreme pressure upon his right by the formidable and now more general attack on the part of Blücher, became completely paralyzed; and conscious of the utter futility of attempting to stem the torrent, he threw himself for temporary shelter into the square of the second battalion of the 2nd regiment of chasseurs of the guard.

The Anglo-allied line continued its magnificent advance, which was in truth a march of triumph, not of attack, since all fled before its approach. In the centre, Lambert's brigade, together with the 1st or royal Scots, crossed to the Charleroi road, and took possession of La Haye Sainte, which was found entirely abandoned to the wounded and the dying, who constituted its sole but numerous occupants. The troops that had stood in rear of Hougomont, now poured into its inclosures, aiding and supporting those who had so bravely maintained that important post,* in completely clearing it of its assailants, as many of the latter in the wood, ignorant of what was passing in the open field, still endeavoured to hold their ground. The light troops on the right of Hougomont crossed the Nivelles road without opposition, not only the infantry in their front having retired, but Piré's light cavalry-brigade, which had formed the extreme left of the French army during the whole day, having been ordered to proceed to the

* A list of the British officers who were present at the defence of Hougomont is given in Appendix XXXV.

rear of the centre to cover the general retreat. The extreme left of the line was flanked by the Prussian regiments of cavalry, belonging to Zieten's corps, previously mentioned as having joined shortly before the general advance; and the battalions of the first Prussian infantry-brigade, together with the Nassau brigade under Prince Bernhard of Saxe-Weimar, were pressing up the heights against the left of Durutte's division, posted at the apex of the angle of *potence* on which stood the extreme right of the French army. As the Allied left descended the outer slope of the position, those columns of d'Erlon's corps which had advanced to attack it, were hastily retiring; part of them, indeed, along and near the Charleroi road, had already fallen back in disorder the moment they became aware of the defeat of the troops on the other side of that road, and of the advance of Adam's brigade, by which their left flank was completely turned, and their rear most seriously endangered. Durutte's division, forming, as before observed, the right of d'Erlon's corps, and posted in the angle of *potence*, perceiving in its direct rear, the retreat of the imperial guard, followed by British infantry, as also that of the columns of its own corps on its left, followed by the Anglo-allied line, besides the attack of the Prussians in its front and on its right, and which was increasing every moment in vigour and effect, at once saw the certainty of its being cut off if it remained in its present attitude, and, hence, aware of its own helplessness, it took to flight.

In the next moment the renewed cheering along the Anglo-allied left wing, announced that it had reached and captured the strong line of batteries, by the fire of which, maintained during the entire day, its ranks had been so awfully diminished. Zieten's battalions took possession, also, of the batteries which had protected the apex of the angle of *potence*, and which had been covered by Durutte's division. Notwithstanding the confused retreat of the flank columns of d'Erlon's corps, those which constituted the central portion of his line had hitherto retired in some little degree of order, but now they began rapidly to dissolve as the Allied line approached, and, soon spreading out, they broke forth into one general crowd of fugitives. The flight of these troops immediately along the rear of Lobau's line, at the very moment of its being most vigorously assailed by the 13th and 15th infantry-brigades of Bülow's corps, covered by an overpowering cannonade, involved its ranks in the general panic which had become uncontrollable. The whole corps rushed wildly into the stream of fugitives which, with overwhelming force, had set in towards Rossomme and Maison du Roi, on the Charleroi road, the direct line of retreat.

By this time, (about a quarter past eight o'clock,) Adam's brigade, pursuing its course on the left side of the high road, was ascending the higher ground in rear of La Belle Alliance. Here it fell into the line of fire of one of Bülow's batteries, which had immediately followed up the retreat of Lobau's corps, and opened a cannonade from the previous position of the latter, at a distance of about 700 yards. Wellington, perceiving that this fire might occasion serious injury to his advancing troops, directed Count de Sales (who was still his sole attendant*) to proceed to the Prussian battery, and cause it to cease firing, its commanding officer not being aware that its shot were falling among British troops. Bülow, on becoming acquainted with this circumstance, immediately checked the fire of his artillery, and, at the same time, ordered the infantry of his right to refrain from firing during its forward movement.

The road which leads from the chaussée across the height in rear of La Belle Alliance, towards Planchenoit, becomes, after a distance of about a hundred yards, a complete hollow-way. As it was approached by Adam's brigade, a column of artillery and infantry, from the French right, was hastily retreating up that part of it which was in front of the 52nd regiment, quite unaware of its having fallen into the immediate vicinity of British infantry. Astonished by the sudden appearance of the latter along the bank, the column hesitated for a moment what course to adopt. The infantry at first presented some little show of defence, but soon threw down their arms, dispersed and escaped as best they could. The artillery made a dash at the opposite bank, but some of the horses of each gun were instantly brought down by a fire from the British, and the attempt failed. The commanding officer of the battery, as if in a fit of desperation, standing in the centre of his guns, waved his sword above his head in defiance. A soldier from the 52nd regiment sprang forward, parried his thrust, closed with him, threw him on the ground, and bayoneted him. The guns were immediately abandoned. On the right of the brigade, the 71st regiment having gained the height on which a reserve-battery of the imperial guard had been posted the entire day, and had just made an attempt to draw off into the high road, was captured by that corps; when some men of the right flank company of the latter (Captain Reed's),†

* See page 370.

† Lieut. Colonel Samuel Reed, h.p., 71st regiment, died on the 13th of July, 1842.

under Lieutenant Torriano,* immediately turned round one of the guns, which was then discharged into the retiring columns of the imperial guard by Captain Campbell, aide-de-camp to Major General Adam, and was, there is reason to believe, the last French gun fired on that day.

Lieut. Colonel Halkett, who, with the Hanoverian battalion Osnabrück, had entered the Charleroi road, near La Belle Alliance, continued to press before him the two battalions of the chasseurs of the old guard, under the protection of which, Napoleon with several of his principal staff officers were retiring from the field. Halkett soon found himself in the midst of a great but disordered mass of the enemy's cavalry, which menaced the battalion in a most vociferous manner, but, after receiving the fire from the latter, it went off in all directions. Further on, perceiving several guns in full retreat, he sent the sharpshooters of the battalion, supported by a company, amongst them, who, by their fire, increased the confusion, and then made many prisoners, and cut the traces of the horses from the leading guns.

The regiments of Prussian cavalry belonging to Zieten's corps, before mentioned as having joined the left of the Anglo-allied army, after crossing the valley and ascending the French position, had got somewhat in advance of the left of the Anglo-allied infantry, taking the direction of Rossomme, but they soon found their progress most seriously obstructed and retarded by the vast crowds of fugitives of all arms intermingled in the wildest confusion. Such was also the case with the much more advanced British light cavalry-brigades under Vandeleur and Vivian on the right of the Charleroi road. In fact, the cavalry thus situated in the van of the Duke's victorious army, had now become almost helpless: it seemed as if carried aloft on the billows of the agitated sea, yielding rather to its impulses than controlling the angry element. As might have been expected, there were innumerable instances in which the rage and disappointment of the conquered foe gave rise to covert assaults, which, however, were speedily repressed, more especially by the Prussians, against whom a word or look sufficed to draw down their vengeance upon an enemy whom they held in detestation. The 10th and 18th British hussars of Vivian's brigade, whilst endeavouring to re-form between La Belle Alliance and Rossomme, found themselves in the midst of an immense crowd, composed partly of defeated soldiers of the imperial guard, who could but ill conceal their mortification, and who

* Lieutenant William Torriano, 71st regiment, retired from the service in May, 1824.

seized every opportunity that afforded to gratify their hatred and revenge. Lieut. Colonel the Hon. Henry Murray, commanding the 18th, was very nearly bayoneted by one of them; and his orderly was compelled, for the security of his master, to cut down five or six in rapid succession.

A remarkable exception to the general disorganization of the French army was manifested about this time in front of Vandeleur's brigade, which was the furthest in advance of any of the Allied troops. In the midst of the crowd of fugitives which impeded the progress of the brigade, there appeared a regiment of cavalry, moving at a walk, in close column, and in perfect order, as if disdaining to allow itself to be contaminated by the confusion that prevailed around it. It was the "*grenadiers à cheval.*" The 12th British light dragoons were the nearest to it, having got in advance of the rest of the brigade, and were opposite the right flank of the column, whence a few pistol or carbine shots were fired at them. The 12th made a partial attack, but they were so much inferior in numbers, (being very weak at this period,) and were so greatly obstructed in their movements by the crowd, that they were unable to produce any impression upon so compact and steady a body of cavalry; which literally walked from the field in the most orderly manner, moving majestically along the stream, the surface of which was covered with the innumerable wrecks into which the rest of the French army had been scattered. As Napoleon and his staff were at this time retiring along the high road, on the right flank of this cavalry of the guard, it is reasonable to infer that the latter was therefore induced to maintain the admirable order in which it was thus seen, to secure the Emperor's retreat.

Whilst the great mass of the French army, in a state of thorough disorganization, was thus driven by Wellington's victorious troops across the whole extent of ground which had constituted its general position, as also, on its right, by that portion of the Prussian troops consisting of part of Zieten's, and of the right wing of Bülow's, corps, the battalions of the French imperial guard in Planchenoit were maintaining a most desperate and obstinate contest with Bülow's left wing, aided by a part of Pirch's corps, to which the attack of the village had been confided. The principal force of the imperial guard having taken post within the central portion of the village, and strongly occupied the church-yard, the headmost columns of this third Prussian attack met with a most destructive fire as they pressed forward through the lanes that led towards the eastern side of the church. The supporting columns now came up, and joined in the *fusillade* that was maintained with the French in the church-yard, the stone wall encircling which, lined with troops, gave to it the appearance of a little fortress. The Prussians, extending their front so as to envelope a considerable portion of the church-yard, and taking advantage of the houses and inclosures which they had reached on their own side, maintained a terrific fire upon their opponents, and as the latter appeared resolved to keep them at bay to the last, a great loss of life occurred on both sides. The soldiers of the imperial guard fought desperately, and so greatly was their animosity excited, that some officers of the 15th Prussian regiment, and of the Silesian landwehr, who had been made prisoners in the previous attack, were with difficulty saved by General Pelet's personal exertions from becoming a sacrifice to their fury. Reinforcements were moved into the church-yard from the reserves on its western side, and the pertinacity with which the attacks upon it were repelled showed very plainly that other means than that of a front assault must be resorted to for forcing the French from a post which afforded them such superior advantages in the defence of the village. If the Prussians attempted to outflank the church-yard by advancing along the low open space on its right, they became exposed to the commanding fire from its walls, to that from the opposite houses, and in front, to the reserves. If they ventured to pass close by its left they had but a narrow road open to them, bounded by the church-yard wall on one side, strongly lined by the defenders, and by houses on the other, which the enemy still occupied, and presenting also at its further extremity a farm house and its offices in flames, situated so close to the church-yard as to conceal by its smoke any column of reserve that might be posted in that quarter. Hence it was determined to act upon a broader extent of front, and to turn the entire village on both flanks, so as either to force or to intercept the retreat of the enemy from his stronghold in the church-yard. On the Prussian left, Major Witzleben, with the fusilier-battalion of the 25th regiment, had already crossed the rivulet which divides the village into two nearly equal parts, and was attacking that portion of the French guard which was posted upon the narrow ridge which lies between that rivulet and the Lasne. His skirmishers were joined upon their left by those that had preceded the 1st and 2nd battalions of this regiment, and which latter having pushed through the wood of Virère, were now following close up in support of the attack on this part of Planchenoit. These skirmishers were also connected on their left with those of the fusilier-battalions of both the 15th regiment and the 1st Silesian landwehr, under Major Keller, who was advancing along the right bank of the Lasne. Along the crest of this ridge runs a narrow road, with several cottages on either side of the latter: the ground is throughout intersected with hedges, and studded with trees; and altogether admirably adapted for a protracted defence by light troops. Every house, every lane, and every hedge was gallantly contested. The Prussians not only boldly attacking in front, but skilfully and gradually turning the ridge on both sides, at length gained possession of all this portion of the village, and thus outflanked the troops in the church-yard, who maintained to the last the most desperate defence. In the meantime, the houses and inclosures on the left of the church had also been turned on that side by the right of the Prussian attack, and principally by the 5th Westphalian landwehr, the skirmishers of which had beaten back their opponents close under the walls of the burning buildings; the bright flames from which, gleaming upon the combatants, who rent the air with their shouts, gave a peculiar wildness to this scene of mortal strife. But still more wild and awful must have been the scene within the church, as the red flood of light which they poured through the windows of the aisles, fell upon the agonized and distorted features of the wounded and the dying, with which that sacred edifice was at this moment filled. The Prussians continued pressing forward along both flanks of the village, driving the imperial guard from house to house, from hedge to hedge, and from tree to tree, until at length it became obvious to the French that their rear would soon be intercepted. The latter were also by this time fully aware of the *déroute* of the main army, and, giving up all for lost, as they fell back upon the western portion of the village, they made a hasty and disorderly retreat towards Maison du Roi. The chasseurs of the old guard were the last to quit the church-yard, and suffered severely as they retired. Their numbers were awfully diminished, and Pelet, collecting together about 250 of them, found himself vigorously assailed by the Prussian cavalry from the moment he quitted the confines of Planchenoit and entered upon the plain between the latter and the high road. At one time, his ranks having opened out too much, in the hurry of their retreat, some of the Prussian troops in pursuit, both cavalry and infantry, endeavoured to capture the eagle, which, covered with black crape, was carried in the midst of this devoted little band of veterans. Pelet, taking advantage of a spot of ground which afforded them some degree of cover against the fire of grape by which they were constantly assailed, halted the standard-bearer, and called out, "*A moi, chasseurs! sauvons l'aigle ou mourons autour d'elle!*" The chasseurs immediately pressed around him, forming what is usually termed the rallying square, and, lowering their bayonets, succeeded in repulsing the charge of cavalry. Some guns were then brought to bear upon them, and subsequently a brisk fire of musketry, but notwithstanding the awful sacrifice which was thus offered up in defence of their precious charge, they succeeded in reaching the main line of retreat, favoured by the universal confusion, as also by the general obscurity which now prevailed; and thus saved alike the eagle and the honour of the regiment.

The reserve-cavalry of the 2nd and 4th Prussian corps received orders to pass to the front through the infantry: that of the 4th corps, under Prince William of Prussia, moved by the right of Planchenoit, as also through the village itself; but its progress was greatly impeded by the fugitives that crowded towards Maison du Roi.

In the mean time, the Prussian battalions that had been detached for the protection of the left of the attack upon Planchenoit, namely the fusilier-battalion of the 15th regiment, and that of the 1st Silesian landwehr, under Major Keller, as also that of the 25th regiment, under Major Witzleben, had turned the village, and followed the enemy nearly in the direction of Maison du Roi. They met with some resistance on the part of the battalion of the grenadiers of the imperial guard, which had advanced from Caillou, in pursuance of the orders it had received, into the wood of Chantelet; but they soon forced their way to the high road, and by their presence added greatly to the disorder in which the enemy was flying from the field. Major Falkenhausen, having remarked the retreat of the French, as he stood on the height of Seroulx, to which he had been detached with 100 horsemen of the 3rd Silesian landwehr-cavalry, also moved down upon the high road, and charging the flank of the flying foe, tended still further to augment the alarm and confusion that prevailed.

When the French imperial guard was falling back from Planchenoit in disorder and confusion, towards the high road between Rossomme and Maison du Roi, Wellington's advanced brigades had reached the former place. It was about half-past eight o'clock—perhaps somewhat later—and the darkness, which had been rapidly setting in, had become so great as to render it difficult to distinguish one particular body of troops from another. Some little time before this, one of the Prussian advanced regiments of cavalry, suddenly entering the high road between La Belle Alliance and Rossomme, came into partial collision with the 18th British hussars, who, not anticipating the presence of any other foreign troops in that vicinity than those of the French army, commenced an attack upon them: cuts were exchanged, and some few lives lost, before the error was corrected. The 1st hussars of the German legion, while advancing along the right of the high road, came upon the rear of Vandeleur's brigade, and were all but in collision with the 11th and 16th British light dragoons, which regiments, having previously ascertained that a brigade of French cavalry (Piré's) was on their right, and perceiving, though but dimly, in the dark, the approach of a strong body of horsemen towards their rear, concluded that an attempt was made to intercept their retreat. They immediately went "threes about," and struck into a charge. On the other hand, the 1st German hussars, not being aware that any British cavalry was in their front, and misled in a great measure by the sudden clamour of French voices proceeding from the numerous fugitives who, taking the alarm, were endeavouring to get out of their way, prepared to charge, and gave a loud cheer. This cheer was fortunately recognized by the British dragoons, when in the act of charging, as that of the 1st German hussars, and was thus the means of preventing a rencontre that might have been productive of the most fatal consequences to the parties concerned.

Wellington had, previously to this, given orders that the main body of his army should halt upon what had been the French position, in the line of La Belle Alliance; having arranged, by communication with Blücher, that the latter, whose troops were comparatively fresh, should take up the pursuit: and, as the Prussians continued moving forward in great force towards the high road, he directed his own troops to proceed to the right of the latter, so as to leave it clear for their advance. The Prussian regiments, on passing the British, caused their bands to play the national anthem, "God save the King," a compliment which was greeted, on the part of the latter, by hearty and friendly cheers.

The Duke now stood with his advance of both infantry and cavalry, on the elevated ground beyond Rossomme, overlooking Maison du Roi. The moon had risen, and by the light it gradually spread over the field, as also by the objects set fire to at intervals along the high road, the retreating line of his vanquished foe became sufficiently perceptible to satisfy him that the brilliant victory he had gained was rendered secure beyond a doubt. Having ordered his advanced brigades to take up their bivouacs for the night, he returned from this distant part of the field, and proceeded leisurely along the Charleroi road back towards Waterloo. Adam's brigade bivouacked on the spot it had reached;* Vandeleur's, on the right, near the wood of Callois, in which stood the observatory; while Vivian, inclining somewhat to his right, led his hussars much further in advance of the army, on the French side of the observatory, and established his bivouac close to the hamlet of Hilaincourt. On approaching La Belle Alliance, Wellington ordered the whole of his army to bivouac on the field of battle. On reaching that point, he met Blücher, and mutual congratulations took place between them on the splendid victory achieved. The latter, taking advantage of the designation of the house as felicitously applicable to the meeting of the two commanders, and considering also that it had constituted the direction-point for the advance of the main portion of his troops, styled this glorious contest the Battle of La Belle Alliance. With the promise of vigorously following up the pursuit, and allowing the enemy no opportunity of rallying within a march from the field, he took his leave of the Duke; who then continued to ride leisurely towards Waterloo, where he passed the night. The circumstance of the Duke having established his head-quarters in this village, and the name of the latter being more consonant to English pronunciation than that of any other place nearer to the field, acquired for this ever-memorable struggle, the designation, by the British, of the Battle of Waterloo.

Blücher, determined to allow no breathing-time to the flying enemy, and to deprive him of all power of rallying, at least on this side of the French frontier, gave orders that Bülow's corps should undertake the pursuit along the Charleroi road; that Zieten's corps should follow in support of Bülow; and that Pirch's corps should march by Aywiers, and cross the Dyle, for the purpose of intercepting Grouchy's troops, which, it was presumed, would soon be retreating from Wavre towards the Sambre.

The Prussian battalions, already mentioned as having turned the village of Planchenoit, and entered the high road near Maison du Roi, accompanied by only three squadrons of uhlans, formed the advance of the pursuing army. Gneisenau, placing himself at their head, proceeded to carry into effect

* Lieut. Colonel Halkett, with the Hanoverian battalion of Osnabrück landwehr, having continued in advance of Adam's brigade, along the high road, and having received no order to halt, moved on with the Prussians, until he reached some houses on the left of the chaussée, near Genappe; when, finding his men fatigued, and perceiving no British troops in his rear, he halted, and occupied those houses during the night, after having detached the Major of the battalion with a company into Genappe, to see what was going on in that place.

the commands of his veteran chief and friend. The cavalry, under Prince William, followed; and then the infantry of the two corps.

At Genappe, the first important defile through which the main French army retired, an immense number of carriages and waggons of all kinds had been collected together—some having been withdrawn from the field, and others, such as those of the commissariat or ordnance departments, having come up to join, or to follow in the track of the French army. By judicious management, these materials, combined with a suitable defence, would have afforded the means of seriously impeding the further pursuit by the victors. Some intention of this kind appeared to have been entertained, as several waggons had been upset, so as to obstruct the crossing of the bridge, a narrow passage only being left to admit stragglers. But no sooner did the Prussian advance appear, in the moonlight, descending from the heights overlooking Genappe, with drums beating and bugles sounding, than the rearmost of the French troops, (for rear-guard there was none to an army from which all semblance of order and regularity had vanished,) immediately after firing a few shots, fled from the place. This was at about eleven o'clock. The quantity of baggage that was collected here presented a rich booty to the Prussians; but the most valuable and most interesting object consisted of Napoleon's travelling carriage, which, with all its contents, fell into the hands of the fusilier-battalion of the 15th regiment. The infantry of Bülow's and Zieten's corps halted at Genappe, but as soon as the Prussian advance, including the cavalry under Prince William, had succeeded in forcing its way through the immense mass of waggons and carriages of all kinds with which this defile had been blocked up, Gneisenau, moving the infantry along the road, and flanking it on each side by the cavalry, continued the pursuit. He succeeded in driving the French from not less than seven bivouacs, which they had taken up in succession, but each of which they abandoned the moment they heard the sounds of the Prussian drums or bugles.

It was an hour after midnight when Napoleon reached Quatre-Bras, whence he despatched several officers to make known to Grouchy the loss of the battle, and to order him to retire upon Namur. The officers whom he had previously detached from Genappe to Ligny, for the purpose of moving Girard's division, which had been left there, into position at Quatre-Bras, now brought him word that they had not succeeded in finding it. There appeared to be no possibility of presenting, at this point, any effectual check to the Prussian pursuit. General Nègre of the artillery was here with the parks of reserve, but accompanied by a very feeble escort. The soldiers of the 1st and 2nd corps, who, during the advance of the 15th, had crossed the Sambre by the bridge of Marchiennes, had quitted the high road, both at Quatre-Bras and at Gosselies, to proceed in the direction of that point, and with so much precipitation that they could not be halted for the purpose of forming something like a rear-guard. The 6th corps, the imperial guard and part of the cavalry, retreated upon Charleroi, whither Napoleon himself proceeded, after having sent his brother Jerome to Marchiennes, with orders to rally the troops between Avesne and Maubeuge.

In the mean time, Gneisenau continued his wild nocturnal chase, which was truly "*Lützow's. wilde verwegene Jagd.*" His followers, however, having been on the march or in action, since daybreak, were becoming weary, especially the infantry; besides which, several, impelled by hunger, stopped on the way to plunder provision-waggons; so that their numbers had greatly diminished But Gneisenau, who was the life and soul of the pursuit, and who seemed bent on pushing forward whilst a man and horse remained, now had recourse to a stratagem, which, as regarded its effect upon the enemy, fully compensated for the exhaustion of his infantry. Observing that the fugitives always took alarm at the sound of the drum, which announced the presence even of infantry, thus far in pursuit, and close upon their rear, ordered the last remaining drummer, who was unable to proceed further on foot, to mount one of the horses that had been disengaged from Napoleon's travelling-carriage, and then to keep up with the cavalry, and beat the drum without intermission. In this manner Gneisenau passed through Quatre-Bras, which had been abandoned on his approach; and even the heights of Frasne were left free to him; whilst the affrighted foe, completely scattered and dispersed, endeavoured to escape by Gosselies, Marchiennes, and Charleroi. Upon reaching the inn of "*à l'Empereur,*" on the high road, beyond Frasne, this favoured companion of Blücher halted his followers, who then consisted but of a few squadrons, and a party of the 15th regiment, and allowed them to take rest, satisfied with having thus, by mere beat of drum and shouts of triumph, succeeded in scaring the remnant of the French army across the Sambre.

Such was the termination of this ever-memorable battle—a battle, remarkable for the spectacle it afforded, on the one hand, of a bravery the most noble and undaunted; of a passive endurance, the most calm, dignified, and sublime: of a loyalty and patriotism, the most stern and inflexible: and on the other, of a gallantry in assault the most daring and reckless; of a devotion to their chief, the most zealous and unbounded; and, lastly, of a physical overthrow and moral annihilation unexampled in the history of modern warfare. Such was the consummation of a victory, the most brilliant in its development, the most decisive in its operation, and the most comprehensive in its result, of any that had occurred since the commencement of that revolution which it was thus the instrument of bringing to the termination so long and so ardently desired by the suffering and indignant nations of Europe.

From the contemplation of the triumph, the glory, and the result, of such a battle, we are impelled to turn our thoughts upon the melancholy spectacle of the awfully severe losses sustained by both the victors and the vanquished; whose heroic exertions and noble endurance could not but be attended with immense sacrifice.

The following table shows the losses sustained by the troops composing the Anglo-allied army:—

	KILLED.			WOUNDED.			MISSING.		
	Officers.	Non-com. Officers, Trumpeters, Drummers, and Privates.	Horses.	Officers.	Non-com. Officers, Trumpeters, Drummers, and Privates.	Horses.	Officers.	Non-com. Officers, Trumpeters, Drummers, and Privates.	Horses.
*British† . .	85	1334	1319	365	4560	719	10	582	708
*King's German Legion	27	335	194	77	932	144	1	217	54
*Hanoverians . .	18	276	..	63	1035	..	3	207	..
*Brunswickers .	7	147	77	26	430	..	..	50	..
*Nassauers . .	5	249	..	19	370	..	..	..	..
Total	142	2341	1590	550	7327	863	14	1056	762

* For detailed returns of the losses of these troops, see Appendix XXXVI., XXXVII., XXXVIII., XXXIX., and XL. The Hanoverian return, in Appendix XXXVIII. has been furnished by Major Benne, K.H., of the Hanoverian staff, (see p. 17.) It embraces the casualties from the 16th to the 18th of June, inclusive; but in order to obtain the numbers in the above table, the Hanoverian losses incurred on the 16th, as stated in the "London Gazette" of the 8th July, 1815, have been deducted. A List of all British officers who were present in the actions of 16th, 17th, or 18th of June, distinguishing those who were killed, wounded, or missing, is given in Appendix XLI. Lists of the King's German legion, Hanoverian, and Brunswick officers, killed, wounded, and missing, are given in Appendix XLII., XLIII., and XLIV.

† The above numbers are taken from the official returns transmitted by the Duke of Wellington to the British Government on the 30th June, 1815, and

If to this loss be added that of the Dutch-Belgian troops—about 4000*—the total number of non-commissioned-officers, trumpeters, drummers, and privates, killed, wounded, and missing, amounted to 14,728.

The losses of the Prussian army in the battle were as follows:—

	KILLED.			WOUNDED.			MISSING.		
	Officers.	Under-Officers, Trumpeters, Drummers, and Privates.	Horses.	Officers.	Under-Officers, Trumpeters, Drummers, and Privates.	Horses.	Officers.	Under-Officers, Trumpeters, Drummers, and Privates.	Horses.
Zieten's corps .	—	34	18	8	164	21	—	111	2
Pirch's do .	1	36	9	3	192	7	4	93	9
Bülow's do. .	21	1133	259	151	3869	328	35	1143	89
Total	22	1203	286	162	4225	356	39	1347	100

Total under-officers, trumpeters, drummers, and privates, killed, wounded, and missing, 6,775.†

In the absence of all returns it is difficult to estimate the losses of the French army. They were, however, immense; besides which, the whole of their artillery, ammunition-waggons, and baggage, fell into the possession of the victors. Of the French generals, Michel and Duhesme were killed; Prince Jerome, Friant, and several others were wounded; and Lobau, Compans, and Cambronne, were taken prisoners.

The minuteness of detail with which the foregoing history of the battle of Waterloo has been written, the gradual development which has been presented of the motives and dispositions of the commanders, and the circumstantial

published in the "London Gazette" of the 8th July, 1815. There can no doubt, however, that the casualties given in those returns are very much underrated, and at variance with the regimental records. As a proof of this, I may mention that according to the "London Gazette" the whole number of killed and wounded of the 2nd Life Guards, amounted to only 58, and those of the 1st Dragoon Guards to 147; whilst, according to the "Regimental Records" they amounted, the former, to 156, and the latter, to 263! Similar discrepancies are numerous.

* A detailed return of the losses of the Dutch-Belgian troops on the 16th, 17th and 18th of June, will be found in Appendix XLV.

† A detailed return of the losses of the Prussian troops at the battle of Waterloo is given in Appendix XLVI; and a list of the Prussian officers killed, wounded, and missing, at this battle, in Appendix XLVII.

description which has been afforded of the movements of the troops engaged—of the working, as it were, of the machinery in the hands of the three most renowned captains of the age —obviate the necessity of further comment upon those points; but it would be unjust to the honour, the fame, and the glory, of the actors in that memorable scene, to omit putting forth certain important considerations which are essential to enable an impartial public, and an unprejudiced posterity, to arrive at correct and satisfactory conclusions upon other points, hitherto involved in doubt and obscurity.

These refer chiefly to the relative numerical strength of the combatants, the relative proportions in which the troops of the Anglo-allied army were actively engaged with the enemy, the conduct of these troops respectively, while so engaged, and, lastly, the extent of the actual share taken in the battle by the Prussians.

The most simple, and at the same time the most rational, mode of computing the relative strength of armies is by placing in juxta-position their respective numbers of battalions, squadrons, and guns. According to this rule, the Anglo-allied and French armies, as they stood in front of each other at the commencement of the battle, were constituted as follows:—

	Battalions.	Squadrons.	Guns.
Anglo-allied army	73	98	140
French	103	127	246

Napoleon having, about one o'clock, detached the light cavalry-divisions of Domon and Subervie, as a corps of observation upon his right flank, the opposed forces, from that hour until about six o'clock, stood as follows:—

	Battalions.	Squadrons.	Guns.
Anglo-allied army	73	98	140
French	103	106	234

During this period of the battle, the Anglo-allied army was thus composed:—

	Battalions.	Squadrons.	Guns.
British	26	49	78
King's German Legion	8	16	18
Hanoverians	18	*	12
Brunswickers	8	5	16
Nassauers	3	.	.
Dutch-Belgians	10	28	16
Total	73	98	140

* The Cumberland hussars not having been engaged, but, on the contrary, withdrawn from the field by their commanding officer, who was subsequently cashiered and degraded for such conduct, are not included in the above table.

Almost all these battalions were at one time or another in the front line, and all conducted themselves in the most courageous and exemplary manner, with the exception of five of the Dutch-Belgian battalions, which hastily retreated as the French approached, when making their first grand attack upon the Anglo-allied centre and left wing, and took no further active part in the battle. The remainder of the above 10 battalions in the service of the King of the Netherlands, were three battalions forming the 2nd regiment of the Nassau contingent, and two battalions of Orange Nassau, under Prince Bernhard of Saxe Weimar, and occupied the houses and inclosures in the valley in front of the extreme left of the Allied line.* These troops behaved extremely well.

Of the squadrons above mentioned, a large proportion, nearly one third, consisted of the Dutch-Belgian cavalry; but although their numbers serve to augment the amount of the Anglo-allied cavalry, *on paper*, the actual value of their services in the battle was by no means commensurate with their display of strength, and hence it was that the brunt of the cavalry contest devolved almost exclusively upon the British and German dragoons. The same observation applies in an equal degree to the artillery.

About six o'clock the relative strength of the contending forces was altered, on the part of the French army, by the detaching of Lobau's corps and the young guard to oppose the Prussians, and on that of the Anglo-allied army, though somewhat later, by the bringing into the field of Chassé's Dutch-Belgian division; so that they stood about that time as follows:—

	Battalions.	Squadrons.	Guns.
Anglo-allied army . .	85	98	156
French army . . .	80	106	186

Of the assistance derived by the Duke of Wellington from this augmentation of the 12 Dutch-Belgian battalions, a sufficient estimate may be deduced from the foregoing history of the battle—one half of them were with great difficulty prevented from abandoning the field, although, at the moment, they were not in contact with, nor did they even see, the enemy; and the other half only joined the front line (on the left of Maitland's brigade) at the time of the general advance.

Whatever may have been the cause of the comparative supineness of the Dutch-Belgian troops; whether produced by dislike entertained towards recent political arrangements, which

* Excepting the 1st batt. 2nd regt. of Nassau, which was at Hougomont.

alienated each party from its native country, without securing to either its national independence, or, by predilections imbibed for the chief against whose arms they were now opposed, and in whose ranks they had formerly served; the fact of such supineness is too well attested to admit of any doubt respecting the value to be attached to their co-operation in the great struggle, so courageously and resolutely sustained by the remainder of the Anglo-allied army: and becomes a most important point for consideration in any calculation of the relative strength of the combatants, when taken into conjunction with the actual proportion of the entire Dutch-Belgian force brought into the field to that of each of the Allies, as appears by the followng table:—

Amount of the effective Strength of the Anglo-allied Army at the Battle of Waterloo.

	Infantry.	Cavalry.	Artillery.	Total Men.	Guns.
British . . .	15,181	5,843	2,967	23,991	78
King's German Legion .	3,301	1,997	526	5,824	18
Hanoverians . . .	10,258	497	465	11,220	12
Brunswickers . .	4,586	866	510	5,962	16
Nassauers . . .	2,880	. .	. .	2,880	. .
Dutch-Belgians . .	13,402	3,205	1,177	17,784	32
Total* .	49,608	12,402	5,645	67,661	156

Hence it appears that the Dutch-Belgian contingent, compared with the British troops alone, consisted, in infantry, as 13,402 to 15,181; in cavalry as 3,205 to 5,843; and, in guns, as 32 to 78. It is needless now to speculate upon what might have been the result, had this large proportion of force been replaced by a corresponding number of either British or German troops. The fact testifies abundantly, in addition to what has been already related, as to the heroic firmness and enduring courage with which the brave British and Germans stood the brunt of that remarkable contest; and this, too, be it remembered, with unquestionably the finest army which even Napoleon had ever collected together, formed exclusively of one nation—of that nation whose legions had at one time subjugated nearly the whole of Europe—imbued with inve-

* See Appendix XXX.

terate hatred against its foes, cherishing the most enthusiastic devotion to its chief, and filled with the ardent desire of restoring the fallen glory of the Empire.*

* As in no former history of the battle, the conduct of the Dutch-Belgian troops has been so fully developed, my remarks may be considered by some unduly severe; but I have advanced nothing beyond the limits of the most ample testimony, which has been afforded me by eye-witnesses: and, in a work designed to furnish the fullest details respecting all the dispositions and movements that were made by the respective chiefs, it would have been utterly impossible for me to have fulfilled my task without entering into the explanation which that conduct rendered requisite for such a purpose. I have suggested as the probable cause of this comparative apathy, the dislike which they entertained towards those political arrangements by which Holland and Belgium had been incorporated in a Kingdom of the Netherlands; but it is not for me to inquire more particularly into the cause, whatever it may have been; it is with *facts* which I have to deal, and considering the important proportion which the number of these troops bore to the amount of the remainder of the Duke of Wellington's forces, I could not have omitted facts such as have been detailed, without inflicting a gross injustice both upon the merits of the other troops engaged, and upon the skill of him who fought the battle under so great a disadvantage. 'Magna est veritas et prevalebit;' and a period of twenty-eight years may surely be considered a lapse of time sufficient for the subsidence of private feelings, in favour of historical truth. One great step has already been taken towards this desideratum by the gallant compiler of the Duke of Wellington's despatches, in the last volume of which we learn that the Duke, with unexampled modesty and forbearance, endeavoured to dissuade a certain literary gentleman from writing a history of the battle, evidently from a feeling that the real history could not be told without an exposure of the want of due zeal displayed on the part of a portion of his troops, as may be seen by the following remarks:—

"Then the faults or the misbehaviour of some gave occasion for the distinction of others, and perhaps were the cause of material losses; and you cannot write a true history of the battle without including the faults and misbehaviour of part at least of those engaged."[1] Again, the following significant postscript is appended to the Duke of Wellington's letter, transmitting to the King of the Netherlands his Grace's report of the battle:—

"P.S.—J'ai marqué au crayon des paragraphes dans mon rapport que je prie votre Majesté de ne pas laisser publier."[2]

That there were many honourable exceptions to the general lukewarmness on the part of these troops is perfectly true. Their officers appeared, for the most part, well disposed, and were frequently seen endeavouring to rouse into action the apparently dormant energies of the men; and the circumstance of a Dutch major, with a squadron of hussars, having voluntarily followed Vivian's brigade when it advanced to attack the centre of the enemy's position, shows that the Dutch-Belgian army contained within its ranks those who were willing and even eager to prove themselves brave and gallant soldiers.

Since the above was written, a Pamphlet has been published in Holland, by Captain Knoop, in the Dutch, German, and French languages, entitled "Upon Siborne's History of the War in France and Belgium in 1815." In this abusive

[1] Despatches, &c., vol. xii. page 590.
[2] Despatches, &c., vol. xii. page 501.

Of the conduct of the British infantry, of its heroic valour, its indomitable resistance, its proud defiance, and its admirable discipline, the history of the battle affords abundant testimony: further comment is superfluous The superior prowess of the British cavalry also shone most conspicuously on this great day. The combined charge of the two heavy brigades against the French cavalry and infantry which attacked the centre and left wing of the Anglo-allied army between one and two o'clock, whether we regard the brilliancy of its execution, or the magnitude of its success, is perhaps without a parallel in the last war; and when we consider the preponderance of the enemy in this arm, the frequency of his charges, and the masses with which he advanced, it is impossible to advert to the heroism of Britain's cavalry, without at the same time according the praise so pre-eminently due to the skill of the noble and gallant chief who was the life and soul of its movements throughout the arduous and desperate struggle, and who so judiciously economised its strength, that when at the critical moment its services were required for securing the victory, he was enabled to bring forward two fresh brigades, which fulfilled those services in a style the most brilliant that can be conceived, and with a success, which commanded the admiration of all who witnessed it.* The British artillery,

publication I am denounced as a "liar" and "slanderer;" and every fact which I have stated, conveying the slightest reflection upon the Dutch-Belgian troops is stigmatized as a falsehood. My work is pronounced worthless in every point of view as a military history, and is, in short, declared to be *not* a history but an eulogium of the Duke of Wellington (whom the author places in the "*second* rank of commanders") and of the British army. ("Ce livre n'est pas une composition historique. Pour cela le jugement porté sur Wellington comme général est entr'autres trop exagéré, trop exclusivement louangeur.")

The author is most fully entitled to pass whatever judgment he pleases upon my work: I would merely remind him that the constant accusations which he makes against me of stating that which is false, cannot apply to myself individually, but to the several British and German officers who have narrated to me the facts of which they were eye-witnesses; and I feel confident that the combined testimony of gentlemen universally acknowledged to possess high and honourable principles—of men who would scorn the bare idea of mis-stating or distorting facts for the purpose of throwing discredit upon their foreign allies and thereby endeavouring to raise their own merits—cannot fail to exercise an infinitely greater influence on the opinion of the public, than Captain Knoop's bold and unqualified denials of the accuracy of such testimony.

I have already declared, and I now repeat, upon my word of honour, as a British officer and a gentleman, that as regards the conduct of the Dutch-Belgian troops at Waterloo, I have not stated a single fact for which I have not received the most clear and positive evidence.

* The French historians invariably attribute the final *déroute* of their army to the charges made by the British light cavalry launched against it immediately after the attack by the imperial guard.

which had to contend against an immense preponderance of metal, evinced during the whole day, a degree of bravery, zeal, activity, and intelligence, which can never be surpassed; and nobly sustained its long and honourably acquired pre-eminence.

Of the troops of the King's German legion, whether cavalry, infantry, or artillery, it is impossible to speak in terms of too high praise; suffice it to remark that their conduct was, in every respect, on a par with that of the British.

Of the four Hanoverian infantry-brigades, that of Kielmansegge, and a part of Halkett's, were the most actively engaged: Best's stood almost the entire day on the extreme left of the front line of the Anglo-allied infantry; and Vincke's, in reserve in front of Mont St. Jean. They had been but recently and hastily raised; and yet the manner in which such raw soldiers withstood, as Kielmansegge's brigade did, for so great a length of time, the most furious assaults made by the gallant and well disciplined troops of France, would have conferred honour on long-tried veterans.

The Brunswickers, who were also composed of young soldiers, performed a glorious part in the battle, and amply avenged the death of their Prince. Some of their battalions were much shaken at the moment Alten's division was driven back a short distance, but they speedily rallied, and resumed their lost ground. Altogether, their bravery, which was frequently called into action, and their endurance, which was severely tested, merited the strongest commendation.

The troops constituting the Nassau brigade under Kruse, (or more properly the 1st regiment of the Nassau contingent,) were attached to Alten's division. They were consequently, often in the thick of the fight; and though, on the occasion above alluded to, they were thrown into disorder and driven in by a furious onset of the enemy, they conducted themselves generally throughout the day with great steadiness and bravery.

It is impossible to allude in terms of adequate praise to the services of that most important branch of the army, the general staff; the officers of which distinguished themselves no less by the zeal, the daring, and the activity, with which they carried into execution the commands of their respective chiefs, than by the alacrity and intelligence which they evinced in catching and imparting the true spirit of their instructions. The constant exposure to which their peculiar duties necessarily subjected them could not but entail upon them severe losses.* Few indeed were those who escaped unhurt throughout this arduous conflict.†

* As far as the French accounts would lead us to infer, it appears that the losses among Napoleon's staff were comparatively trifling. On this subject, perhaps, the marked contrast afforded by the following anecdotes, which have been related to me on excellent authority, may tend to throw some light. At one period of the battle, when the Duke was surrounded by several of his staff, it was very evident that the group had become the object of the fire of a French battery. The shot fell fast about them, generally striking and turning up the ground on which they stood. Their horses became restive, and "Copenhagen" himself so fidgety that the Duke, getting impatient, and having reasons for remaining on this spot, said to those about him, "Gentlemen, we are rather too close together —better to divide a little." Subsequently, at another point of the line, an officer of the artillery came up to the Duke, and stated that he had a distinct view of Napoleon attended by his staff; that he had the guns of his battery well pointed in that direction, and was prepared to fire. His Grace instantly and emphatically exclaimed, "No! no! I'll not allow it. It is not the business of commanders to be firing upon each other."

† The Duke's feelings on the loss of so many friends, to whom he was warmly attached, as also on that sustained by his gallant troops, by whose heroic exertions his plans were carried out with such signal success, are beautifully expressed in the following letters:—

To the Earl of Aberdeen, K.T.

'Bruxelles, 19th June, 1815.

'My dear Lord,

'You will readily give credit to the existence of the extreme grief with which I announce to you the death of your gallant brother,[1] in consequence of a wound received in our great battle of yesterday.

'He had served me most zealously and usefully for many years, and on many trying occasions; but he had never rendered himself more useful, and had never distinguished himself more, than in our late action.

'He received the wound, which occasioned his death, when rallying one of the Brunswick battalions which was shaking a little; and he lived long enough to be informed by myself of the glorious result of our actions, to which he had so much contributed by his active and zealous assistance.

'I cannot express to you the regret and sorrow with which I look round me, and contemplate the loss which I have sustained, particularly in your brother. The glory resulting from such actions, so dearly bought, is no consolation to me, and I cannot suggest it as any to you and his friends; but I hope that it may be expected that this last one has been so decisive, as that no doubt remains that our exertions and our individual losses will be rewarded by the early attainment of our just object. It is then that the glory of the actions in which our friends and relations have fallen will be some consolation for their loss.

'Believe me, &c.

'Wellington.'

To the Duke of Beaufort, K.G.

'Bruxelles, 19th June, 1815.

'My dear Lord,

'I am very sorry to have to acquaint you that your brother Fitzroy[2] is very severely wounded, and has lost his right arm. I have just seen him, and

[1] Lieut. Colonel the Honorable Sir Alexander Gordon.
[2] Now Lieut. General Lord Fitzroy Somerset, G.C.B.

The co-operation of the Prussians in this battle has been gradually developed and fully detailed. That the communications which Wellington received from Blücher led him to expect that co-operation at a much earlier period, is beyond a doubt; but setting aside all consideration of the causes of the delay which attended the arrival of the Prussian forces, it is equally doubtless that the tardiness of that co-operation had a more decided influence on the general result of the battle than if they had reached the field at an earlier period. For, supposing the Prussians to have arrived in force before the French had become so seriously and desperately engaged with the Anglo-allied army, Napoleon was too much a master of his art to have risked a decisive battle with the combined forces of his antagonists. In this case he would, in all probability, have fallen back upon his frontier, have called in all available reserves from the interior, and by means of his triple line of fortresses, as well as by skilful manœuvring, have endeavoured to separate once more the opposing armies, and to obtain another chance of beating them in detail. As it happened, however, he was too deeply involved in the contest with Wellington, he had suffered too severely in his repeated attacks, to admit of a retreat, under such circumstances, being looked upon, even by his friends in Paris, in any other light than that of a defeat; and he knew too well that with a defeat, however it might be produced, would vanish the only tie which yet bound him to the nation—the implied belief in his invincibility, and the firm reliance on his ability to re-establish and maintain the military glory of France. It is to this conviction alone that we can attribute the desperate resolve with which he risked the fate of the empire and his own political existence, upon the issue of his final attack upon Wellington's line, at a moment when the armies opposed to him had effected their junction; and which, by calling the whole of his force into requisition, deprived him of an adequate reserve, by aid of which he might have succeeded in effecting an orderly and honourable retreat.

he is perfectly free from fever, and as well as any body could be under such circumstances. You are aware how useful he has always been to me; and how *much* I shall feel the want of his assistance, and what a regard and affection I feel for him: and you will readily believe how much concerned I am for his misfortune. Indeed the losses I have sustained have quite broken me down; and I have no feeling for the advantages we have acquired. I hope, however, that your brother will soon be able to join me again; and that he will long live to be, as he is likely to become, an honour to his country, as he is a satisfaction to his family and friends.

'Believe me, &c.

'WELLINGTON.'

Had the Prussians succeeded in driving the French out of Planchenoit half an hour earlier, such a circumstance, combined with the general advance of the Anglo-allied line, would no doubt have caused the whole of Lobau's corps, and perhaps also d'Erlon's, to lay down their arms and surrender at discretion, since their retreat towards Maison du Roi would thus have been cut off, whilst the British advance would have frustrated any attempt to retire across the Charleroi road. On the other hand, a similar result might have ensued, at least as regards Lobau's corps, had that general advance occurred half an hour earlier, while the French right was engaged with the Prussians at a greater distance from the Charleroi road. In the former case, however, the final attack was judiciously delayed until, by the arrival of the additional force which was fast approaching, such a simultaneous attack could be made along the whole of the French right as would insure most decided success: and in the latter case, the final attack could not have been made at a more opportune moment, and with a greater prospect of success, than immediately after the signal defeat of the French imperial guard upon the Anglo-allied position. Indeed, contingencies of this kind might be brought forward with reference to any battle whatever, and when it is considered that there exists no example in modern warfare of so complete a victory, the result must appear as glorious as decisive, and as comprehensive as the most stern and rigid calculator of the chances of battle could have desired.

As regards the actual share which the Prussians had in the battle, it may be truly affirmed that the contest maintained between Bülow's corps and Lobau's troops in conjunction with a portion of the imperial guard, was most obstinate and sanguinary. In the three successive struggles for the possession of Planchenoit, especially, the deadly animosity mutually cherished by the troops of both nations, was fearfully exemplified, and the losses sustained by the Prussians in the comparatively brief period during which they were engaged, afforded ample proof of the value of their co-operation. It is undeniably true that the blow which decided the victory was that given by Wellington, when, after having completely defeated the grand attack, by the French imperial guard, he instantly followed up that defeat by boldly attacking and penetrating the centre of the enemy's lines, and sustaining this movement by the general advance of his whole army; but it is at the same time, equally true, that the powerful diversion effected by the Prussians diminished the strength of those French lines by the corps of Lobau, which had not hitherto fired a single shot in this campaign, by twelve battalions of the imperial guard, which had suffered scarcely any loss at Ligny, and, finally, by eighteen squadrons of cavalry. The vigorous attack which was made by Bülow upon Lobau's line simultaneously with the last assault upon Planchenoit, contributed most materially to the general and fatal panic which seized upon the whole of the French army. The Prussians too, by the energetic pursuit which they kept up during the night, under the guidance of the indefatigable Gneisenau, rendered the victory still more complete and decisive, and effectually deprived the enemy of every opportunity of recovering himself on the Belgian side of the frontier. In short, both armies admirably and honourably performed the parts respectively assigned to them—the one, holding its defensive position with unparalleled bravery, and unmitigated perseverance, until the moment when its chief, having defeated the last desperate attempt of his opponent to force his line, leads it on to victory; the other, operating a powerful diversion, by which the effect of that advance is made still more decisive, and rendering the victory complete by a harassing and vigorous pursuit—and thus was consummated the tactical solution of the plan which had been, with so much skill and foresight, strategically preconcerted by the Allied commanders.

The Duke, when writing his despatch descriptive of the battle, in which he stated that his own army "never, upon any occasion, conducted itself better," was not unmindful of the important aid he had derived from the Prussians. "I should not," he said, "do justice to my own feelings, or to Marshal Blücher and the Prussian army, if I did not attribute the successful result of this arduous day to the cordial and timely assistance I received from them. The operation of General Bülow upon the enemy's flank was a most decisive one; and, even if I had not found myself in a situation to make the attack which produced the final result, it would have forced the enemy to retire if his attacks should have failed, and would have prevented him from taking advantage of them if they should unfortunately have succeeded."

On the other hand, the Prince, although, as is manifest upon a perusal of a similar despatch on his part, was not aware of the circumstances under which Wellington had attacked the very centre of the French lines, and had pushed his advanced brigades along the rear of those troops to which he himself had been exposed, nevertheless did ample justice to the bravery of the British army, which, he remarked, "fought with a valour which it is impossible to surpass."*

* The description given, in the present work, of the distribution of the Prussian troops at the moment of the defeat of the attacking columns of the French imperial guard by Maitland's and Adam's British brigades, being at variance with the representation of those troops upon the Model of the Battle of Waterloo when the latter was *first* submitted to the public, some explanation of the grounds upon which this deviation from my original arrangement is founded, appears to be requisite.

Having applied to the Prussian government for the information I required concerning the disposition of their troops at that particular moment represented on the model, it was most readily and liberally supplied to me by the officers of the head-quarters staff in Berlin, at the instance of the Prussian minister of war. This information, which was given with minute detail, was rendered more complete by the distribution of the troops having been laid down upon a plan, drawn on a large scale. On comparing these data with the evidence I had collected from officers of rank and intelligence, posted, some throughout the greater part of the battle, and others, during the whole day, on the left of the Anglo-allied line, whence the Prussian movements could be distinguished, I felt perfectly satisfied that there could be no doubt as to their accuracy on certain points, whilst upon others, this evidence was of too vague a nature, as regarded *time* and *situation*, to enable me either to corroborate or to rectify the details with which I had been furnished by the Prussian authorities. Thus, for instance, the junction of the leading column of Zieten's corps with the left of the Anglo-allied line, the forming up of the cavalry of that column on the flank, and in the rear, of Best's Hanoverian brigade, the relief of a Hanoverian battery by a Prussian battery upon the summit or knoll on which the Anglo-allied left rested, as also the previous conflicts in and about both Planchenoit and Smohain, upon the extreme right of the French army, are facts satisfactorily confirmed by coroborative evidence. But, as regards the disposition of the Prussian troops between the extreme left of the Anglo-allied line and the immediate vicinity of Planchenoit, I feel equally satisfied, after a most careful and diligent investigation of the whole question of the Prussian co-operation, in all its bearings, that, according to the *original* arrangement of the figures upon the model, the Prussian troops distributed along that intervening space, immediately in front of Lobau's corps, were represented in too forward a position. It was only subsequently, when collecting that further information which has enabled me in the present work to describe with such minuteness of detail those brilliant dispositions of the Duke of Wellington, by which he not only defeated the French imperial guard upon his own position, but secured the victory, that I discovered the error into which the Prussian authorities had been unconsciously but naturally led, when laying down for me the distribution of their troops along that part of the field to which I have particularly adverted, and which distribution gave the appearance of a much greater pressure upon the French right flank than could have occurred at the *moment* represented on the model. The cause of this error is very simple, and is easily explained. All the Prussian accounts of the battle, more especially those two which have appeared "under authority,"—I allude to that published in 1825, by Colonel Wagner, of the Prussian staff, and to the more recently published history by Major von Damitz of the same staff, founded upon materials furnished by General von Grolman, who was employed in the capacity of quarter-master-general of the Prussian army during the campaign of 1815—concur in representing the Duke of Wellington's defeat of the attacking columns of the imperial guard, and the advance of his whole line, as happening *at one and the same moment;* whereas, in reality, there was an interval of *at least* twelve minutes between these two incidents. The Prussian authorities have not hitherto been cognizant of the fact that when the British line advanced,

Long may Great Britain and Prussia cherish that mutual amity which was engendered by the zealous and successful co-operation of the armies of these two great nations in bringing to so prompt and satisfactory a termination a war, which, originating in the re-assumption of the throne of France by that ambitious soldier and extraordinary man, who had once already overrun the continent with his legions, subjugating

Vivian's light cavalry-brigade was attacking and dispersing Napoleon's last reserves of both cavalry and infantry posted on the French left of La Belle Alliance, the very centre of the enemy's lines; that Adam's light infantry-brigade was attacking and defeating the rallied force of the first attacking column of the imperial guard upon the height situated midway between La Belle Alliance and La Haye Sainte; and that Vandeleur's light cavalry-brigade was pushed forward in support of Vivian. These attacks, planned with consummate judgment and electric decision, and carried into execution with perfect order and unequalled gallantry, could not, from the configuration of the ground, be observed by the Prussian army; to which circumstance may be attributed the origin of that miscalculation concerning the actual disposition of the Duke of Wellington's forces at the moment of the general advance of his line, which induced the Prussian authorities to confound that advance with the defeat of the attacking columns of the imperial guard. When, therefore, those authorities, with a liberality and good feeling for which I can never feel sufficiently grateful, furnished me with the information I solicited relative to the distribution of the troops "at the moment of the defeat of the imperial guard upon the crest of the British position," they did so under the impression that that event and the general advance of the Anglo-allied line were *coincident*. Hence the fact of the Prussian troops, along the central portion of their line, having continued advancing against the French right up to the moment of the general forward movement of the Anglo-allied line, has rendered it necessary, in order to afford a more correct representation, to make such alteration upon the model in the dispositions and movements of those troops as shall accord in point of *time* with the defeat of the attacking columns of the imperial guard, instead of their being made to conform, as they previously did, with the moment of the general advance of the Duke of Wellington's army; which advance, it should be remembered, was made by his Grace to follow up a victory he had *already* secured, and, in conjunction with the Prussian attack, to render the overthrow of the enemy complete in every respect. This arrangement, which has been observed upon the illustrative plan accompanying the present work, will, I feel persuaded, present the nearest attainable approximation to truth, and I trust, at the same time, prove satisfactory, by means of the foregoing explanation, to those of either nation who have shared in, or studied, the memorable events of the glorious 18th of June.

I may take this opportunity of remarking that notwithstanding the complicated details which must necessarily be comprised in a modelled representation of a battle, like that of Waterloo, at so late a period of the action, only one single instance of inaccuracy has been pointed out to me as occurring in the distribution of the Anglo-allied troops—namely, the posting of the 3rd battalion of the 1st or royal Scots, in second, instead of front, line—an error which has been duly corrected. Such a result has indeed exceeded my most sanguine expectations, and I feel perfectly confident that my amended arrangement of the model offers a true and faithful representation of the battle at the most critical moment of the day.

It may not be out of place to mention that the model is about to be deposited in the United Service Institution, where it will be open to the inspection of the public.

emperors and kings to the influence of his mighty will, threatened once more to involve the nations in all the calamities and horrors which before had followed in the train of his triumphant but desolating career. The general peace, which was the ultimate result of their united efforts, still happily continues, and on every successive anniversary do the British and German troops commemorate their glorious and crowning victory; and Europe, grateful for the lasting and inestimable blessings conferred upon her, emblazons forth in the pages of her history, the heroic deeds of the defenders of her liberty and independence.

———————— "thou fatal Waterloo!
Millions of tongues record thee, and anew
Their children's lips shall echo them, and say—
Here where the sword united nations drew,
Our countrymen were warring on that day!
And this is much, and all which will not pass away."

CHAPTER XVI.

It was explained at the conclusion of the eighth Chapter that Thielemann, who had been ordered by Blücher to defend the position of Wavre in the event of the enemy advancing in force, or, if otherwise, to follow the main army in the direction of Couture, was on the point of fulfilling the instructions appertaining to the latter contingency, when Vandamme's corps arrived in front of that position, about four o'clock in the afternoon, and its artillery immediately opened a cannonade upon the Prussian troops.

All the brigades (the 9th, 10th, 11th, and 12th) of Thielemann's corps, had, at that time, received the order to commence the general movement to the right. A detachment of only two battalions, (the fusilier-battalions of the 30th regiment and of the 1st Kurmark landwehr,) under Colonel Zepelin, from the 9th brigade, which had not yet crossed the Dyle, was to be left in occupation of Wavre. The 12th brigade was already in full line of march, and the 11th had been just put in motion.

When General Borcke, who commanded the 9th brigade, fell back upon Wavre, for the purpose of carrying out his instructions, he found the bridge already barricaded, and therefore proceeded with his brigade to Bas Wavre; and having crossed the Dyle at this point, left a detachment there, consisting of the sharpshooters of the fusilier-battalion of the 8th regiment, and of those of the 1st battalion of the 30th regiment, under Major Ditfurth, whom he directed to destroy the bridge immediately. He then detached the 2nd battalion of the 30th regiment and his two squadrons of the 3rd Kurmark landwehr-cavalry, as a reinforcement to Colonel Zepelin at Wavre; and, with the remainder of his brigade, continued his march.

In the mean time, French tirailleurs were observed extending along the opposite heights, and, in their rear, considerable masses of the enemy's troops appeared advancing. It soon became manifest that they contemplated forcing the passage of the river. Thielemann, judging by the want of vigour displayed in the French pursuit, and by the enemy not having attempted to secure the passages of the Dyle at Moustier, Limelette, and Limale, that it was only a weak detachment of the enemy that was advancing upon Wavre, confining itself to the design of creating some little uneasiness by its movement along this road to Brussels, had hitherto been of opinion that the occupation of Wavre by a few battalions, as directed by Blücher, would be quite sufficient; but he now plainly saw that the moment had arrived which required him, in pursuance of his instructions, to maintain the position at Wavre, and he accordingly ordered the halt of his whole corps for this purpose.

The town of Wavre is situated on the left bank of the Dyle; having a suburb on the opposite side of the river, with which it is connected by two stone bridges, the principal one leading towards the middle, and a small one towards the upper end, of the town. Higher up the stream, at the mill of Bierge, at Limale, and at Limelette, as also below the town, at Bas Wavre, there are wooden bridges. The river is not deep, but at the period of the battle it was swollen by the recent heavy rain. The low range of heights on either side of the valley is covered in many places with wood. The heights on the right bank are generally more elevated, but those on the left have steeper declivities, and offer a greater command of the river and its passages. The shortest road from Namur to Brussels passes through the town, besides which there are numerous cross roads practicable for the movements of all arms. The great number of hollow-ways forms a prominent feature in the vicinity, and these, being in a miry state from the rain, were unfavourable to the progress of troops passing through them.

The position was thus occupied:—the 12th brigade (Colonel Stülpnagel,) with the horse-battery No. 20, was posted on the height in rear of Bierge. The bridge in front of this village was barricaded, and the mill occupied for the defence of the bridge. The 10th brigade (Colonel Kämpfen) stood upon the height in rear of Wavre, its right resting on a wood which lay between it and the 12th brigade. The 11th brigade (Colonel Luck) was formed across the Brussels road. The reserve-cavalry was drawn up, near La Bavette, in columns of squadrons. The artillery was distributed along the heights. The horse-battery No. 18 remained in reserve. That part of the town of Wavre which lies on the right bank, or, more properly, the suburb, was occupied by light troops only. The great bridge was barricaded as well as time and circumstances would admit. The houses adjoining the left bank of the river were hastily loop-holed. The smaller bridge was left perfectly open. A detachment of two companies of light infantry, under Major Bornstädt was detached to reinforce the troops at the bridge of Bas Wavre.

Thielemann intended that the 9th brigade should be posted in rear of this general disposition of his troops, so that its services might be made available according as circumstances might require; but through some misunderstanding in the transmission of the order, General Borcke was induced, after having moved along the Brussels road until near La Bavette, thence to turn off to his left, and continue his march, according to his original instructions, in the direction of Fromont, Bourgeois, and St. Lambert, towards Couture; being under the impression that the whole corps had already commenced this march, in pursuance of the general plan, and that his brigade was destined to cover the movement. The departure of the brigade was not immediately discovered, and thus, by this misunderstanding, Thielemann's force suffered an unexpected reduction of six battalions and the foot-battery No. 18; and consisted, therefore, of only 15,200 men, with which number he had now to contend against Marshal Grouchy's force, amounting altogether to 33,765 men.

Thielemann's position was certainly a very favourable one, and the occupation of it was arranged with great skill. As it was impossible to foresee in what manner the attack upon it would be conducted; whether it would be directed against one particular bridge, or against all the bridges, with the design of carrying the whole line by storm, Thielemann limited the occupation of the town and of the line of the river, to the number of light troops which might be sufficient for sustaining any sudden assault; taking care to have supports close at hand for that purpose, but disposing his reserves, which comprised his main force, so that they might become available at any point which might be pressed, or, should the enemy develope greatly superior numbers, as was subsequently the case, serve to guard against any flank attack.

As before explained, it was Vandamme's corps which arrived in front of Wavre between three and four o'clock. Two batteries, of which one consisted of 12-pounders, were drawn up on the right of the road overlooking the valley, and opened the cannonade. These were subsequently reinforced by a third battery, posted on the left of the road. Excelmans' cavalry-corps was posted in right rear of Vandamme. Gérard, with the 4th French corps, was still in the rear on the march; and Pajol, with his light cavalry, had only just passed through Tourrines, situated scarcely half-way between Gembloux and

Wavre. Marshal Grouchy sent word to both these officers to accelerate their march.

Whilst the French skirmishers were gradually forcing back the Prussian light troops into the valley, Grouchy, hearing a powerful cannonade in the distance to his left, rode off a little way in that direction, and concluding that Napoleon was closely engaged with Wellington, conceived that as he had now reached the Prussians, he would best fulfil his instructions by vigorously attacking them, so as to prevent their detaching reinforcements to the Anglo-allied army. He was quite ignorant as to the strength of the enemy in his front, and was in doubt whether the whole Prussian army was before him, or merely a strong detachment. Of the fact that three Prussian corps were on the march to co-operate with Wellington's forces, he of course knew nothing. In this state of uncertainty, and with his troops *aux prises* with the Prussians, he was fearful of detaching to his left, since by so doing, he would expose himself to the risk of his main force becoming overpowered by superior numbers, and his detachment cut off.

Independently of other considerations which might have assisted in dissuading Grouchy from detaching a portion of his force at this period, such as the length of time his troops had been upon the march, along bad and miry roads, he was perfectly justified, under all the circumstances of his then position, in adopting this course of proceeding. And even if he had been fully cognizant of the actual disposition of the Prussian army, he could at this time have rendered no essential service to Napoleon; the opportunity for doing so had been suffered to pass by, as was fully explained in Chapter VIII. His total ignorance, however, of Blücher's proceedings, and of all that was then taking place between Wavre and the field of Waterloo, afforded undeniable proof of his having completely failed in acting up to the spirit of the instructions he had received, not to lose sight of the Prussians, and in exercising that degree of enterprise, energy, and decision, which Napoleon had so naturally anticipated from a general of Grouchy's note and experience, especially when entrusted with so important a command, under such highly critical circumstances.

A message having reached Grouchy from Pajol, communicating his having fallen into the Marshal's line of operation, he directed that general to move upon Limale, His right flank, however, continued to be protected by the 17th dragoons, detached from General Berton's cavalry-brigade (of

Excelmans' corps) *en reconnaissance,* towards the high road leading from Namur to Louvain.

In the mean time, a vigorous cannonade was maintained between Vandamme's and the Prussian batteries across that part of the valley in which lay the town of Wavre. Under cover of the French guns, the skirmishers pressed down upon that portion of the town situated upon the right bank of the river, and of which they soon gained possession, the Prussians having previously decided upon not making any effort to retain it. On reaching the river, however, they were met by a most destructive fire of musketry from the opposite houses and the bridge. The contest now became desperate, and the defence of the Dyle was obstinately maintained by the Prussians. The skirmishers rapidly extended on either flank along both banks of the river from Bierge as far as Bas Wavre. All the Prussian brigades pushed forward their sharpshooters. Those of the 4th Kurmark landwehr took up the line between the town and Bas Wavre, those of the 3rd Kurmark landwehr took post in the town, between the two bridges; on the right of the latter stood the sharpshooters of the 10th brigade; and those of the 12th brigade formed the right wing of the whole line at Bierge.

This tiraillade had continued about an hour, when General Hulot's division of Gérard's corps d'armée reached the field, and received orders to take possession of the mill at Bierge, and to cross the Dyle at that point. A battalion of Vandamme's corps was at the time vainly attempting to effect a passage. Upon the height opposite Bierge were several guns of the 3rd corps, endeavouring to keep down the fire from the Prussian batteries on the other side of the valley. Grouchy desired Gérard to relieve the battalion attacking the mill at Bierge by one of his own corps, whereupon the latter directed General Hulot to push forward with a battalion of the 9th light infantry for that purpose. The battalion descended into the valley, covered by the fire from the guns on the height. Its advance was much impeded by the swampy nature of the ground at the foot of the declivity, and by the numerous broad and deep drains by which the valley is intersected; and its order was still further deranged by the fire from the artillery on the opposite heights, as also by that of the Prussian skirmishers posted along the left bank of the river, and strongly occupying the mill. The banks of the river at this part, more particularly the left bank, are mostly lined with trees, which tended still further to increase the means of resistance on the part of the Prussians to the advance of the French troops. The latter on reaching the mill, and relieving Vandamme's troops, made an attack, but without success.

Grouchy was on the point of ordering this attack to be renewed, when he received, between six and seven o'clock, Soult's despatch, addressed to him from the field of Waterloo at one o'clock in the afternoon;* and desiring him to manœuvre always in that direction, to maintain a close communication with the main army, and to lose not a moment in joining the latter, and attacking Bülow's corps d'armée, which, it added, could then be seen upon the heights of St. Lambert.

The circumstances in which Grouchy found himself at the time this despatch reached him, held out no prospect of his being able to fulfil, even partially, the instructions which it contained. Vandamme's efforts to force the bridges of Wavre, and to capture the town were completely frustrated by the most gallant defence maintained on the part of the Prussians. The issue of the attack upon the mill of Bierge appeared very doubtful. Neither the main body of Gérard's corps, nor General Teste's division of the 6th corps, nor even Pajol's light cavalry, had as yet arrived. Grouchy, becoming impatient, rode hastily towards la Baraque, accompanied by Gérard, to meet the first mentioned force; and on coming up with the columns, directed their march upon Limale, his object now being to turn the right of Thielemann's position, and to prevent the retreat of the latter upon Brussels, and at the same time open his direct road to St. Lambert. This he might succeed in effecting, but it is sufficiently evident from the above view of his position, at so late an hour of the day, that any important diversion on his part in favour of Napoleon, was quite out of the question.

On returning with Gérard to Wavre, Grouchy found that notwithstanding the furious assaults that were made in rapid succession upon the bridges, supported by the vigorous cannonade from the heights, and the incessant fusillade along the banks of the river, no further progress was effected. As if determined that the passage should be forced, he dismounted from his horse, and placing himself at the head of a battalion, led on another attack upon the mill of Bierge. But the bravery of the troops, though so strongly excited by the noble example of the marshal, could avail nothing against the indomitable resistance of the Prussian defenders of this

* See pages 243—244.

important post. Gérard, who had accompanied the Marshal in this attack, fell severely wounded by a shot which struck him in the breast.

Grouchy now decided upon leaving Vandamme's corps and Excelmans' cavalry in front of Wavre and Bierge, and proceeding himself with that portion of Gérard's troops which was at hand, along the right bank of the Dyle, towards Limale, and uniting them to the remainder of the corps which had been ordered to march in the direction of that point from la Baraque. This movement occupied considerable time, in consequence of the difficulties opposed to the march of troops along the side of the river. At length, having arrived in front of Limale, and formed a junction with Pajol's cavalry, preparations were made for an attack.

Limale was at that time occupied by Lieut. Colonel Stengel with the three battalions of the 19th Prussian regiment, two squadrons of the 6th uhlans, and one squadron of the Westphalian landwehr-cavalry. It was the detachment left by Zieten for the purpose of covering the right flank of the 3rd corps d'armée. It had unaccountably neglected to adopt any measures for barricading the bridge, the defence of which, if conducted with the same energy and resolution by which that of the bridges lower down the stream had been distinguished, might have been the means of preventing the French from crossing the Dyle at all on that day.

Pajol having reconnoitred the place and discovered this neglect, succeeded in gaining possession of the bridge by means of a brisk cavalry attack. Hulot's infantry-division of Gérard's corps reached it shortly afterwards, and it was soon made manifest to Lieut. Colonel Stengel that he was attacked by a force much superior to his own. Nevertheless he continued to fall gradually back, in good order, until Thielemann pushed forward the 12th brigade to his support. Three battalions of the 10th brigade moved into the position thus vacated by the 12th; and a general movement was made to the right by all the troops that could be spared from the defence of Wavre and Bierge. The 4th Kurmark landwehr, belonging to the 11th brigade, crossed the Brussels road. The reserve-cavalry was ordered to move upon Limale, in support of the 12th brigade.

When Colonel Stülpnagel was ordered to move his brigade (the 12th) upon Limale, he left three battalions for the defence of Bierge. With the remaining six battalions he came up close to the enemy, who was posted on a height in advance of Limale, his left thrown considerably forward and covered by his cavalry, and his right resting upon some houses which he had occupied with infantry. This line, which was perpendicular to the direction of the original position of the Prussians, had been taken up with great skill by Grouchy, notwithstanding the difficulties with which the movement had been attended. His troops had to ascend the heights during the obscurity of the night, in rear of Limale, by a narrow, rugged road, in the immediate proximity of the Prussians, whose fire reached the head of the defile, and he was fully occupied until a very late hour, in posting the battalions in their proper places, as they filed out of the road, on reaching the height; whilst, in the mean time, Pajol's light cavalry pushed rapidly round by the left.

Colonel Stülpnagel posted the fusilier-battalion of the 5th Kurmark landwehr, and his battery, in reserve, in rear of the small wood on the right of Bierge, and advanced to the attack, late as it was, with his five remaining battalions, having Lieut. Colonel Stengel with his detachment on the right. The darkness of the night prevented the Prussians from correctly ascertaining the position and strength of the French, but nevertheless it was decided that an attempt should be made to regain Limale, and drive back the enemy across the Dyle. The attack was thus formed. Two battalions in front, closely followed by the remaining three battalions. Both the brigade-squadrons joined the three squadrons under Lieut. Colonel Stengel; and the whole of the reserve-cavalry formed in support. In this movement, however, the mutual connection of the advancing troops was greatly impeded by the darkness of the night. The two battalions in front line were on the point of passing a hollow-way when they received a volley from two French battalions on the opposite side, by which their further advance was checked. The three battalions of the second line had inclined too much to the left, where they became engaged with French tirailleurs. Lieut. Colonel Stengel's detachment, in attempting to push forward, was checked by the French cavalry, and as the latter made a disposition which menaced his right flank, that officer fell back with his detachment as far as the wood near Point du Jour.

The decided failure of the attack induced Colonel Stülpnagel to withdraw all his troops to the wood, leaving only the first battalion of the 6th Kurmark landwehr in support of the chain of advanced posts. The reserve-cavalry bivouacked in rear of the wood. Thus ended the contest on this part of the field. The Prussian and French picquets were so close to one another during the night, that the patroles were constantly clashing, and the whole line kept upon the *qui vive*.

Upon the Prussian left, the conflict for the possession of the town and bridges of Wavre continued to be carried on with unabated fury on both sides until late in the night. Vandamme devoted the whole of his corps to the attack; constantly pushing forward fresh troops to relieve those who had failed in their attempts to dislodge the Prussians. The latter, who exhibited on this occasion an extraordinary degree of bravery and resolution, succeeded in repelling no less than thirteen different assaults, and even dislodged, in five instances, the French from the houses they occupied, from the commencement, on the right bank of the Dyle. At one time the French had already gained possession of the great bridge and some houses on the left bank, when they were driven back again to their own side of the river by the Prussian reserves—these having advanced to the relief of their comrades. The struggle was desperate, and apparently interminable. When the French attacked the houses nearest the bridge they succeeded in bursting open the doors, and by superiority of numbers, in possessing themselves of the ground floors. But even this did not induce the heroic defenders to relax their exertions; on the contrary, with increased fury, they defended the upper stories of the houses, and held out most gallantly until relieved by the arrival of their supports.

This brilliant defence of Wavre was distinguished, on the part of the Prussians, not only by the unflinching bravery of the troops, but also by the judicious disposal of the reserves, by means of which the enemy was foiled in every attempt to gain a permanent footing in the town. While the skirmishers and their supports were posted along the Dyle and the adjacent houses, the reserves were concealed in the nearest streets, that lay in a direction parallel with that of the river: and at the moment the French columns of attack, already crippled by the fire concentrated from the skirmishers, endeavoured to force the bridge, these reserves rushed forward from their cover in the side streets, and presenting themselves in mass before the enemy, invariably drove them back with great slaughter. It was in this manner that the fusilier-battalion of the 30th regiment, under Major Sprenger, and the 3rd battalion of the 1st Kurmark landwehr, under Major Bornstädt, constantly repulsed, with admirable bravery, the attacks made with such superior numbers during the earlier part of the contest. One of these attacks having been attended with a somewhat favourable result, the second battalion of the 30th regiment, under Major Beaufort, was brought forward: and, at a similarly critical moment, the first battalion of the 4th Kurmark landwehr, under Major Grolman, came up, when both battalions succeeded in compelling the enemy to retire. These battalions then took post in the streets lying parallel with the river, in the manner before explained, and, with heroic courage, overcame every renewed attempt on the part of the French to establish themselves in the town. When, finally, it is considered that from four o'clock until night, four Prussian battalions successfully maintained their ground against a whole corps d'armée, with which they were constantly and desperately engaged during the whole of that period, the merits of Colonel Zepelin and his brave troops are beyond all praise, and present one of the brightest examples of the defence of a town and of the passage of a river, recorded in military history.

Both the bridges of Wavre remained in the possession of the Prussians, and the smaller one was barricaded during the night. At a late hour, as the fire on both sides began to slacken, the combatants bivouacked on their respective sides of the river. Upon the Prussian extreme left, at Bas Wavre, the French had only shown one battalion. This occupied an isolated building, and was supported by two squadrons and a piece of artillery. Several unsuccessful attempts were made to gain the bridge, which, at nightfall, continued in the possession of the Prussians.

Grouchy was occupied late in the night in making his preparations for renewing the attack on the following morning. General Teste's division of the 6th corps having at length arrived, his left wing, which was thus considerably reinforced, bivouacked upon the height westward of Bierge, separated by this village and the Dyle from his right wing which lay in front of Wavre. He had not yet received any intelligence of Napoleon's signal defeat at Waterloo, and was therefore resolved upon following up, at daybreak, the advantages he had already gained, by forcing back the Prussian right flank. Thielemann, on the contrary, having despatched an officer of Marwitz's cavalry-brigade *en reconnaissance* to the right, ascertained through this means that the Allied armies had gained a complete victory, and he therefore fully expected that Grouchy would be compelled to effect an immediate retreat.

With the first dawn of the 19th of June, Colonel Stengel, whose detachment was posted on the extreme right of Thielemann's corps, took upon himself to march off by St. Lambert, to join his corps d'armée (the 1st), the grounds for which proceeding remain to the present time as unaccountable as his neglect on the previous day to secure the bridge of Limale. In consequence of this movement, the 12th brigade was necessitated to extend its line too much to the right and to retain a reserve of only three weak battalions upon the road leading through the wood to Point du Jour. The wood to the right was occupied by a battalion and two companies from each of the remaining regiments of the 12th brigade. The left wing of this line, which rested upon Bierge, was formed by six battalions of the 10th brigade.

Colonel Luck, commanding the 11th brigade, was directed to support this division, which was much too weak, with the three battalions of the 3rd Kurmark landwehr; but to leave the two battalions of the 4th Kurmark landwehr, as also the brigade-squadrons, in rear of Wavre, in a hollow near the windmill, where they served to cover the 12-pounder battery No. 7.

The mill of Bierge was occupied by two battalions of the 12th brigade: Wavre and Bas Wavre were held by the same troops which defended those points on the previous day. The barricades and preparations for defence were rendered more complete.

Lieut. Colonel Ledebur, whose detachment, consisting of the 10th hussars, a squadron of landwehr-cavalry, and two guns from the horse-battery No. 12, had formed on the 18th the advance of the rear-guard which Thielemann's corps was considered to constitute, having reached St. Lambert before Grouchy's attack became so decided, remained there during the night. Early on the 19th, Grouchy sent off three cavalry-regiments to his left to watch these troops. They showed no indication of an intention to attack, and when, later in the day, they retired and disappeared from Ledebur's view, the latter passed the defile, for the purpose of proceeding to join his corps d'armée (the 4th), which, however, he did not reach before the 20th.

This, as well as Colonel Stengel's detachment, thus withdrew from the field, without any apparent necessity, reducing Thielemann's numbers, already too weak, and taking up a line of march, along which their services were comparatively useless.

Thielemann, concluding from the account that he had received of the defeat of Napoleon, that the French would commence a retreat, renewed the combat at daybreak by an attack with his cavalry. Colonel Marwitz was sent forward with the 8th uhlans and two squadrons of the 6th Kurmark landwehr-cavalry, towards the plateau above Limale, occupied by Grouchy's left wing; whilst General Hobe followed this movement with the 5th and 7th uhlans, and formed up on the left of the advanced cavalry. The 5th uhlans were immediately afterwards advantageously posted in a hollow in support of Colonel Marwitz.

The horse-battery No 20, subsequently reinforced by the foot-battery No. 18, opened a cannonade upon the enemy's columns at the plateau, which displayed a great superiority of numbers, and were supported by a considerable force of cavalry. The preponderating number of guns in the enemy's line answered the fire of the Prussians with great vigour, and as the intervening space was very limited, the numbers of killed and wounded were very great. The Prussian artillery lost five guns on this occasion.

Grouchy delayed not a moment in making dispositions for an attack on his part. His force on this side of the field consisted of the three divisions of Gérard's corps, and of Teste's division of the 6th corps. The latter and two of the former were posted in front line; the remaining division, in reserve. He formed three columns of attack. That on the right consisted of Teste's division, and was directed upon Bierge; the central column was put in motion against the Prussian centre; and that on the left against the right of the Prussian formation.

The head of each column was accompanied by a battery, and preceded by a swarm of skirmishers. At the same time, Pajol put his cavalry in motion, and threatened to turn the Prussian right.

Thielemann resolved upon not only offering to the enemy a vigorous opposition, but also upon assuming the offensive himself, and immediately gave the necessary orders for that purpose. He also reinforced his right with two more companies, and his left with an additional battalion. It was soon made manifest, however, that this attack failed to check the forward movement of the enemy. The ten Prussian battalions were forced to give way to the advance of twenty-two French battalions, which were followed by six more in support. The French gained possession of that part of the wood of Rixansart which was on the right of the Prussian position, and drove back the 12th brigade. The battalions of the latter collected again immediately in rear of the wood, under the protection of the three beforementioned battalions of the 11th brigade and of a battery of fifteen guns.

General Teste's division had in the mean time attacked Bierge, which was bravely defended by the two battalions of the Kurmark landwehr. Whilst the engagement continued at this point, Thielemann took up a second position in rear of the first, with four battalions of the 10th brigade, and occupied the small wood in rear of Bierge. The Prussian cavalry-brigade, under Colonels Marwitz and Count Lottum, comprising 12 squadrons, secured the right towards Chambre.

About eight o'clock, just as this position had been taken up, Thielemann received, through General Pirch, the decisive and authentic intelligence that a great victory had been gained by the Allies on the previous day, as also a communication of the fact of the 2nd corps d'armée having marched to intercept Grouchy's retreat upon the Sambre. Advantage was immediately taken of these joyful tidings to raise the spirits of the troops, and to excite them to a renewed attack. With loud cheers the Prussian batteries advanced to the attack, which was attended with complete success, and even the wood of Rixansart was again taken.

The enemy appeared irresolute, and as if impressed with the idea that Thielemann had received reinforcements; but observing that no further progress was made, he renewed the attack, on his part, and re-took the wood of Rixansart.

It was not until about this time—towards nine o'clock—that Teste's division gained possession of the village of Bierge, on which occasion General Penne, an officer of considerable distinction in the French army, was killed. The French were prevented for some time from debouching from the place, by the determined opposition of the tirailleurs of the 31st Prussian regiment, under Major Natzmer.

Thielemann had now done all which could possibly have been expected from any general under similar circumstances —with a force not equal to one half of that of the enemy, he had endeavoured, whenever an opportunity offered, and in defiance of superior numbers, to force back the French left wing upon the Dyle; but now that he had failed in effecting this object, and that Bierge, the key of his position, had been taken from him, whilst the French left was pressing forward with increased numbers, to gain the Brussels road, he saw very plainly that to attempt to maintain his ground any longer would be, to expose himself to the imminent risk of total overthrow, and that no other course was left for him but to order a general retreat.

It was about ten o'clock in the morning when the Prussian troops began to retire from the field. The town of Wavre had not been attacked on the 19th, and Colonel Zepelin abandoned it without being much pressed upon his line of retreat. Colonel Marwitz was ordered to form the rear-guard, which was furnished from the 7th and 8th uhlans, and the 3rd and 6th Kurmark landwehr-cavalry. It was accompanied by three batteries of horse, and one of foot, artillery. With these troops Colonel Marwitz took post, at first, in front of the Brussels road; placing three batteries on his left, and the remaining one in reserve. Thielemann gave the rear-guard an express order not to march off until Wavre had become completely evacuated.

In the mean time, Gérard's corps d'armée had crossed the Dyle both at Bierge and at Wavre. The two battalions of the 4th Kurmark landwehr, which had been posted in the hollow in rear of the town, for the protection of the 12-pounder battery, became closely pressed in consequence of this movement. One of the battalions under Major Schmade, had advanced against an enemy's column near the Brussels road, when it unexpectedly received the fire of three French battalions, which were pushing forward under cover of an eminence, and followed by some cavalry. The battalion succeeded in reaching the small wood near la Bavette, and as the enemy attempted to turn the latter, it suddenly attacked and drove him back, after which it came up with the rear-guard. The other battalion, commanded by Major Schwerin, attacked a French battalion which was advancing against it, threw it back in confusion, and then continued its retreat. The gallantry and steadiness displayed in this affair by the Kurmark landwehr, acquired for the latter great and well-merited renown.

The French cavalry debouched from the wood of Rixansart and drew up, with its left resting upon Chambre. Vandamme now advanced the columns of his corps towards the heights of la Bavette, and pushed forward some cavalry along the high road. The latter, however, was driven back by Colonel Marwitz.

It has been explained that General Borcke, instead of posting his remaining six battalions in rear of the position at Wavre, as intended by Thielemann, proceeded on his march to Couture, by St. Lambert. This place he reached about nightfall, when he despatched an officer to Blücher to report his arrival. The latter, in reply, desired him to bivouac on the spot where he was, and to await further orders on the following morning. The brigade was still in its bivouac at seven o'clock the next morning, when Colonel Stengel passed through St. Lambert with his detachment.* The latter informed General Borcke that he had defended the bridge of Limale, and had been

* See pages 410, 411.

followed by the enemy's troops. Borcke, on hearing this, immediately broke up his bivouac, and decided upon securing the wood which extends from St. Robert as far as Rixansart. He deployed two battalions of the 8th regiment along the edge of the wood, and held the remaining four battalions of his brigade, then with him, in reserve. Perceiving the French cavalry, at the time of their first attack, marching into the wood of Rixansart for the purpose of advancing through it upon Chambre, he opened a fire upon them from his battery, with the hope of checking their movement. The only effect it produced was that of their detaching three regiments of cavalry towards his brigade. These, however, contented themselves with watching his movements. It is curious that the 9th brigade, as if bent upon continuing the blunder committed the previous day of detaching itself from its corps, should not have attempted, with its six battalions, to effect a more important diversion upon the enemy's extreme left, from which it was not more than 3,000 paces distant. It was then eight o'clock, and the battle was maintained until about eleven, and yet General Borcke allowed the three cavalry-regiments to move off and join the remainder of the French cavalry, towards ten o'clock, at Chambre, without even attempting to molest their movement,

Thielemann effected his retreat, in several columns, by Ottenburg and St. Achtenrode, at which latter place (about half-way to Louvain) he took up a position. The French cavalry followed as far as the Brussels road, and the infantry occupied the heights of la Bavette.

Between Wavre and Louvain the country assumes a new character, being covered with hedges, hollow-ways, ditches, and gardens, and is altogether much intersected. From Ottenburg as far as St. Achtenrode, there is almost one continued defile. In this, cavalry cannot act with advantage, and it was therefore fortunate for the Prussian cavalry that it was followed but slowly by the French.

The loss experienced by Thielemann's corps d'armée in this battle of the 18th and 19th of June, amounted to 2,476 men.* No returns whatever of the losses sustained by Grouchy's army are forthcoming, but they could not have been less than those of the Prussians.

Such was the battle of Wavre; a battle the result of which was of no advantage to Napoleon on the 18th, and of positive disadvantage to him on the 19th. On the former day it did not prevent the march of the great mass of the Prussian army

* There does not appear to be any *detailed* returns extant of these losses.

towards the field of Waterloo, and, on the 19th, the continuance of the contest, while Napoleon was in full flight, exposed this, the only remaining intact portion of the French army, to the imminent risk of being completely cut off from all retreat. Nor can this defeat of Thielemann be looked upon as having shed additional lustre upon the French arms, when it is considered how long and successfully the Prussians battled against them with less than half their strength. The errors which led to the circumstance of the force under Grouchy—constituting, as Napoleon himself has been pleased to term it, the right wing of the French army—becoming exclusively occupied in attacking a single corps of the Prussian army, whilst the remaining three corps of the latter were wending their way unmolested towards the decisive field of battle, have already been sufficiently discussed; and now that their result has been fully exhibited, it is scarcely necessary to draw attention to the proof which the latter affords of the entire ignorance of each other's proceedings which characterized the conduct of Napoleon and Grouchy, great generals as they were, in this memorable campaign. The former received intelligence, before he began the battle with Wellington, that the right wing was to follow the Prussians to Wavre, and to act in such a manner as to prevent these from detaching towards the Anglo-allied army, and therefore felt satisfied that his general plan of operations was in successful progress. But in less than two hours from the commencement of the battle, the fatal consequence of both generals having unaccountably neglected to maintain a vigilant reconnaissance and an uninterrupted communication, was made manifest, and the first intimation Napoleon received of the advance of the Prussians towards La Belle Alliance was the distant view which he himself had, from his own field, of Bülow's corps descending the heights of St. Lambert, at about one o'clock.

The leading principle of the French Emperor's plan was to endeavour, by all means in his power, to beat the armies opposed to him *in detail*. It was therefore incumbent on him, in order to insure the success of that plan, to adopt such precautionary measures as should procure for him the earliest and the clearest information concerning the movements of his enemies. If he found it necessary temporarily to divide his force, and act upon two lines, those measures became still more indispensable, and at the same time admitted the greater facility of execution. Several reconnoitring parties, both upon the flanks of the army and in front of the interval between the two lines of operation, under the guidance of experienced, active and intelligent officers, would have obtained for both generals that insight into the movements and designs of their opponents which was so essential for the attainment of their common object, whilst parties detached from each wing, for the sole purpose of maintaining a close and direct communication between them, would have afforded the ready means of regulating each other's proceedings according to the circumstances under which they might have found themselves respectively placed. That there should have been so total a disregard of any measure of the kind, appears almost incredible; yet such was the fact; and hence it came to pass that the despatch sent to Grouchy, at one o'clock, from the heights in rear of La Belle Alliance did not reach him until seven in the evening, at which time, as before explained, it was too late to admit of the instructions it conveyed being fulfilled; and hence, also, Grouchy was left battling with his entire force—not less than a third of the whole French army—against a single incomplete Prussian corps, under Thielemann, from daybreak until about eleven o'clock in the forenoon of the 19th, when he was first made acquainted with the fact that during the whole of that time the army under Napoleon, having been most signally defeated and completely scattered on the preceding evening, was flying across the frontier in the wildest confusion.

On receiving this latter intelligence, Grouchy's first idea was to march against the rear of the main body of the Prussian army; but, calculating that his force was not adequate for such an enterprise, that the victorious Allies might detach to intercept his retreat, and that he should be closely followed by that portion of the Prussians which he had just defeated, he decided on retiring upon Namur, where he would regulate his further operations according to the intelligence he might gain in that quarter concerning the real state of affairs.

CHAPTER XVII.

It would be difficult to discover, in the whole history of the wars of modern times, an instance in which so fine, so splendid, an army as that of Napoleon, one composed almost exclusively of veterans, all men of one nation, entirely devoted to their chief, and most enthusiastic in his cause, became so suddenly panic-stricken, so completely disorganized, and so thoroughly scattered, as was the French army when it lost the battle of Waterloo. A defeated army usually covers its retreat by a rear-guard, but here there was nothing of the kind: and hence that army cannot be said to have retreated, but truly to have fled from the field of battle. No attempt to rally was made on the Belgian soil, and it was not until some of the scattered fragments of the immense wreck had been borne across the French frontier that their partial junction on different points indicated the revival of at least some portion of that mighty mass of warriors, who, but three days before, had marched across this same frontier in all the pride of strength, and in all the assurance of victory.

The rearmost of the fugitives having reached the Sambre, at Charleroi, Marchienne, and Châtelet, by daybreak of the 19th, indulged themselves with the hope that they might then enjoy a short rest from the fatigues which the relentless pursuit by the Prussians had entailed upon them during the night, but their fancied security was quickly disturbed by the appearance of a few Prussian cavalry, judiciously thrown forward towards the Sambre from the advanced guard at Gosselies: they resumed their flight, taking the direction of Beaumont and Philippeville.

It had been arranged by Wellington and Blücher, on the field of Waterloo, that the Prussian army, not having been so much crippled and exhausted by the battle, should undertake the further pursuit, and proceed by Charleroi towards Avesnes and Laon, whilst the Anglo-allied army, after remaining during the night on the field, should advance by Nivelles and Binch towards Peronne. On the following morning, the pursuing cavalry belonging to the 1st, 4th, and partly to the 2nd Prussian corps d'armée, reached the vicinity of Frasne and Mellet. The 4th corps marched at day-break from Genappe, where it collected together the brigades which had been so much broken up by the continued pursuit. The 8th Prussian hussars, under Major Colomb, were detached from this corps towards Wavre, to observe Marshal Grouchy. They were supported by the 1st Pomeranian landwehr-cavalry, and, shortly afterwards, the 2nd Silesian landwehr-cavalry, under Lieut. Colonel Schill, also followed in the same direction.

After some hours rest, the 4th corps d'armée marched to Fontaine l'Evéque, where it bivouacked. It had received orders to communicate from this place with Mons. The advanced guard, under General Sydow, was pushed forward, as far as Lermes, on the road to Thuin, it being intended that this corps should proceed by the road to Maubeuge, along the Sambre.

The 1st corps d'armée, which had from the beginning followed the 4th as a reserve, now advanced in pursuit of the enemy by the direct road to Charleroi. The light cavalry at the head of the column reached the passages of the Sambre at Châtelet, Charleroi, and Marchienne, without meeting any sort of opposition or impediment; nor did it perceive any thing of the enemy on the other side of the river. The corps halted for the night at Charleroi; having its advanced guard at Marchienne, and its outposts occupying the line from Montigny by Louverval, as far as Châtelet. Detachments from the reserve-cavalry were sent in the direction of Fleurus, to secure the corps from any molestation on the part of Grouchy, of whose proceedings nothing positive was then known at the Prussian head-quarters.

It was not until nearly five o'clock in the evening of the 19th, that General Borcke, whose brigade, the 9th, was still in the vicinity of St. Lambert, discovered the retreat of Grouchy's troops. He immediately communicated the fact to General Thielemann, who ordered him to cross the Dyle the next day (the 20th) and march upon Namur. The French rear-guard of Gérard's corps-de-armée continued to occupy Limale until nightfall. Thielemann remained posted, during the night of the 19th, at St. Achtenrode, having his advanced guard at Ottenburg.

On the evening of the 18th, Pirch received orders to march from the field of Waterloo with his corps d'armée (the 2nd) in the direction of Namur, for the purpose of turning Marshal Grouchy's left flank and intercepting his retreat upon the Sambre. Pirch made this movement during the night, passing through Maransart, where he was joined by his 7th brigade, and crossing the Genappe rivulet at Bousseval, as also, subsequently, the Dyle, on his way to Mellery, which place he reached at eleven o'clock in the forenoon of the following day. His corps was much divided on this occasion. He had with him the 6th, 7th, and 8th, infantry-brigades, and 24 squadrons of cavalry; but the 5th infantry-brigade, and the remaining 14 squadrons, were with that portion of the Prussian army which was pursuing the enemy along the high road to Charleroi. The corps being greatly fatigued by the night march and its exertions on the previous day, Pirch ordered the troops to bivouack and to betake themselves to rest.

During this march, Lieut. Colonel Sohr had pushed on with his cavalry-brigade, as an advanced guard; and now he was required to gain intelligence concerning the enemy's movements, and to seek a communication with Thielemann. He found the defile of Mont St. Guibert strongly occupied by the enemy, but could obtain no information respecting Thielemann's corps.

When it is considered how very near to Mellery Gérard's corps d'armée must have passed, in order to fall into the Namur road at Sombref, it seems extraordinary that Pirch, who reached that place at eleven o'clock in the forenoon of the 19th,—the same hour at which Grouchy, then beyond Wavre, received the first intimation of the defeat of Napoleon, —should have permitted Gérard to continue his retreat unmolested. His troops required rest, it is true, but had he maintained a good look-out in the direction of Gembloux, he would, in all probability, after the lapse of a few hours, have been enabled to fulfil his instructions so far as to have completely intercepted the retreat of a considerable portion of Grouchy's army. That part of the enemy's force which Lieut. Colonel Sohr observed at Mont St. Guibert, was probably the advanced guard only of Gérard's corps d'armée, since its rear-guard remained at the bridge of Limale until nightfall. Taking all the circumstances into consideration, more especially the express object of the detached movement of the 2nd Prussian corps d'armée, it must be admitted that, on this occasion, there was a want of due vigilance on the part of General Pirch.

It was on the 19th, also, that Prince Blücher issued, whilst at Genappe, a proclamation to his army, in which he thanked the troops for their conduct during the recent struggle.

At daybreak of the 19th, that portion of the Duke of Wellington's army which had fought the battle of Waterloo, broke up from its bivouack, and began to move along the high road to Nivelles. Those troops which had been posted in front of Hal during the 18th, consisting of Stedman's Dutch-Belgian division, Anthing's Dutch-Belgian Indian brigade, and Colonel Estorff's Hanoverian cavalry-brigade, under Prince Frederick of the Netherlands, as also of Johnstone's British infantry-brigade, and Lyon's Hanoverian infantry-brigade, under Lieut. General Sir Charles Colville were likewise directed to march upon Nivelles. The army occupied Nivelles and the surrounding villages during the night of the 19th, in the course of which the Duke arrived from Brussels, and established his head quarters in the town.

An hour's rest was all that the harassing pursuit by the Prussians permitted Napoleon to enjoy at Charleroi; and he was compelled to fly across the Sambre, without the slightest chance of being enabled to check that pursuit on the Belgian side of the frontier.

The following inscription, which has been cut over the centre of the archway of the Charleroi gate, is singularly appropriate to the flight of Napoleon on this memorable occasion:

'ABIIT . EXCESSIT . EVASIT . ERVPIT'

The circumstances, however, under which the flight of Cataline, here described, and that of Napoleon, took place, form a strange contrast. The former, subdued in the senate by the indignant philippics and burning eloquence of Cicero, escaped from Rome to the rebel camp of Manlius, to take up arms against his native city for the purpose of satisfying the cravings of his profligate ambition; and the latter, defeated in the battle-field, fled to the capital, in the vain hope of obtaining from the senate of his country further means of waging war against the legitimate sovereign.

From Charleroi, Napoleon proceeded to Philippeville, whence he hoped to be able to communicate more readily with Grouchy. He continued here four hours, which he employed in expediting orders to Generals Rapp, Lecourbe, and Lamarque, to advance with their respective corps d'armée by forced marches to Paris; and also to the commandants of fortresses, to defend themselves to the last extremity. He desired Soult to collect together all the troops that might arrive at this point, and conduct them to Laon, for which place he himself started with post-horses, at two o'clock in the afternoon.

The general disposition of the respective armies on the evening of the 19th, was as follows:—

The Anglo-allied army, which constituted the right wing of the advancing forces, was at Nivelles and in its vicinity.

The Duke of Wellington's head-quarters were at Nivelles.

Of the Prussian army, which formed the left wing, its 1st corps d'armée was at Charleroi;

2nd corps on the march to Mellery;

3rd corps at St. Achtenrode;

4th corps at Fontaine l'Evêque;

5th brigade of the 2nd corps at Anderlues, near Fontaine l'Evêque.

Prince Blücher's head-quarters were at Gosselies.

The disorganized force of the main French army was in the vicinity of Beaumont, Philippeville, and Avesnes.

Napoleon was posting towards Laon.

The detached portion of the French army under Grouchy was on the march to Namur.

The Duke of Wellington, in whose character the highest military talents of the warrior, were so intimately blended with the most comprehensive views of the statesman, did not allow the dazzling allurements which beset the path of a conqueror, to divert him for a single moment from that fixedness of purpose, or to dim that penetrating foresight, which so peculiarly distinguished his proceedings on all great occasions of a similar nature, involving the peace, the honour, and the security of not only his own sovereign and country, but also of all the Allied powers, in whose interests he was so actively engaged. He did not view the great battle he had gained in the light of an event to be followed up by an irruption into the enemy's country, conducted in such a manner as to humble to the dust the national pride of the French people, and to impose upon them the whole weight and bur then of the oppressions, ravages, and horrors which generally follow in the train of a victorious and lawless soldiery over the face of an enemy's country. His sole aim was directed to the carrying out of the great object of the war, which comprised not only the annihilation of the power of Napoleon and of the adherents to his cause, but also the restoration of the legitimate sovereign to the throne of France. With the latter sovereign he had been in constant communication, devising means for his protection during his temporary exile in the Netherlands, and now that the armies were on the point of crossing the frontier, counselling him to hasten forward and show himself in the midst of his people, in order that by identifying his cause with the common object of the Allied powers he might avail himself of all the influence and advantages to be derived from the recent victory, and become, as it were, a participator in the brilliant successes which attended their arms on the glorious 18th of June. In proof of the sincerity of his intentions, and as a first step towards securing the good will, if not the friendly disposition of the French people, more especially of the legitimists and the well and peaceably disposed, the Duke issued the following general order to the whole of the troops under his command:—

Nivelles, 20th June, 1815.

General Order.

1. As the army is about to enter the French territory, the troops of the nations which are at present under the command of Field Marshal the Duke of Wellington, are desired to recollect that their respective sovereigns are the Allies of His Majesty the King of France, and that France ought, therefore, to be treated as a friendly country. It is therefore required that nothing should be taken either by officers or soldiers, for which payment be not made. The commissaries of the army will provide for the wants of the troops in the usual manner, and it is not permitted either to soldiers or officers to extort contributions, The commissaries will be authorized either by the Field Marshal or by the generals who command the troops of the respective nations, in cases where their provisions are not supplied by an English commissary, to make the proper requisitions for which regular receipts will be given; and it must be strictly understood that they will themselves be held responsible for whatever they obtain in way of requisition from the inhabitants of France, in the same manner in which they would be esteemed accountable for purchases made for their own government in the several dominions to which they belong.

2. The Field Marshal takes this opportunity of returning to the army his thanks for their conduct in the glorious action fought on the 18th instant, and he will not fail to report his sense of their conduct in the terms which it deserves to their several sovereigns.

WELLINGTON.

On the same day, the Duke, in consequence of a report received by him from Lieut. General Lecoq, and of a previous communication made to him by the King of Saxony, consented to take command of the Saxon corps d'armée, amounting to nearly 17,000 men. He directed the above general to march these troops to Antwerp, and there await further orders.

The Anglo-allied army marched this day to Binch and Mons. The British cavalry moved into villages between Roeulx and Mons. Vivian's hussar-brigade took the outpost duties on the Sambre. The Hanoverian cavalry furnished outposts towards Maubeuge. The Duke fixed his head-quarters at Binch.

Blücher, having secured the passage of the Sambre in the neighbourhood of Charleroi, continued his pursuit of the enemy, and crossed the French frontier on the 20th. He directed Zieten to march the first corps d'armée from Charleroi to Beaumont, to throw forward his advanced guard as far as Solre le Château, to detach a party of observation to the left, towards Florenne, and to watch the road from Philippeville to Beaumont.

As the 1st corps d'armée advanced, it discovered at every

step fresh proofs of the extreme disorder in which the French army had retreated, and found twelve pieces of artillery which they had hitherto contrived to save from the great wreck at Waterloo, but had now abandoned to their pursuers. On arriving at Beaumont, the corps took up a bivouack. Its advanced guard, under General Jagow, consisting of the 3rd infantry-brigade, the 1st Silesian hussars, and a horse-battery, reached Solre le Château upon the road to Avesnes.

The Prince, at the same time, ordered Bülow to move the 4th corps d'armée as far as Colleret, where the road to Thuin intersects the high road from Beaumont to Maubeuge, and to push on the advanced guard to Beaufort. Bülow accordingly directed General Sydow to proceed with an advanced guard, consisting of a cavalry-brigade, a horse-battery, and two battalions of infantry, which had the day before reached Lermes on the road to Thuin, and to ascertain very particularly whether the French had established themselves on the Sambre, to secure the bridges both here and at Lobbes, and further, to restore these passages, should they have been destroyed by the enemy. Another detachment, under Colonel Eicke, consisting of two fusilier-battalions, the two squadrons attached to the 13th brigade, and of the 2nd Silesian hussars, was sent forward to take possession, in the first instance, of the passages of the Sambre, and then to join General Sydow, who, proceeding by Colleret towards Beaufort, was to form both detachments into an advanced guard on reaching the latter place. In the mean time, the mass of the 4th corps, headed by the reserve-cavalry under Prince William of Prussia, followed in one column.

The progress made by this portion of the Prussian army on the 20th was not so rapid as was desirable. Considerable delay arose in consequence of the degree of caution imparted to the movements, by the impression which Bülow entertained that the enemy would defend the passages, and endeavour to maintain himself along the opposite side of the river. Hence the advanced guard of the corps only reached Ferrière la petite; part of the main body proceeded as far as Montignies, and the remainder with the reserve-artillery, did not get farther than the bridges across the Sambre.

The 5th brigade (belonging to the 2nd corps d'armée) had started at daybreak from its bivouack at Anderlues, near Fontaine l'Evêque, and directed its march, by Binch, upon Villers, towards Maubeuge. The brigade was reinforced by 100 dragoons under Major Busch, and half a horse-battery, which detachment arrived at Villers at five o'clock in the afternoon. This cavalry was employed in observing the fortress of Maubeuge, from the Mons road, as far as the Sambre, and the brigade bivouacked at Villers. A Hanoverian regiment of hussars also observed the fortress on the right of the Prussian cavalry upon the Bavay road.

The left wing of the Prussian army, comprising the 3rd, and part of the 2nd, corps d'armée, came into collision with the enemy, this day, when pursuing that part of the French army which was under Grouchy. Thielemann, having learned that the latter had commenced his retreat upon Gembloux, marched at five o'clock in the morning from St. Achtenrode to Wavre, where he further ascertained that already on the afternoon of the 19th, the French had effected their retreat across the Dyle, leaving only a rear-guard on the left bank of the river.

Grouchy, when he decided on retiring upon Namur, ordered General Bonnemains to move on rapidly, by Gembloux, with the 4th and 12th dragoons, as an advanced guard, and to reach that town as soon as possible, and secure the passage of the Sambre. They were followed by the remainder of Excelmans' cavalry, and the reserve artillery, together with the wounded. The infantry was put in motion in two columns; the one, consisting of the 3rd corps d'armée, proceeding by Gembloux, and the other, comprising the 4th corps, passing more to the right, and falling into the Namur road in rear of Sombref. The light cavalry was principally with the rear-guard. To deceive Thielemann, Grouchy left his rear-guard in Wavre and Limale, with cavalry picquets thrown out towards the Prussians, until near evening, when it followed the main body to Namur.

Thielemann, having placed the whole of his cavalry, with eight pieces of horse-artillery, at the head of his column, now ordered them to move on at a trot, for the purpose of overtaking the enemy; but it was not until they had passed Gembloux that they discovered the rear of Grouchy's force, consisting of a few regiments of cavalry. These, however, now made so rapid a retreat, that it was impossible to bring them to action. At length, on arriving near the village of Fallize, within about three miles from Namur, the Prussians found Vandamme's rear-guard posted on the brow of the declivity at the foot of which lay the town, in the valley of the Meuse. It presented about two battalions of infantry, three regiments of cavalry, and four guns, and was formed to cover the retreat of the French troops.

The Prussian battery immediately opened a fire, during

which Colonel Marwitz, moving out to the right, with the 1st cavalry-brigade, and Count Lottum to the left, with the 2nd, turned the enemy in both flanks. The latter brought forward a reserve of cavalry, when the 8th Prussian uhlans, under Colonel Count Dohna, at the head of the column that turned the enemy's left, made a most gallant attack upon the French dragoons, who met it with a volley from their carbines, but were overthrown. The 7th uhlans and a squadron of the 12th hussars also charged on this occasion, and captured three pieces of French horse-artillery, which were in the act of moving off, as also fifty cavalry-horses. The enemy's infantry now threw itself into the adjacent wood, with which the declivities that here lead down into the valley of the Meuse are covered, and thus succeeded in preventing the Prussians from following up their success.

At this moment, intelligence was received that General Pirch was pursuing the enemy with the 2nd corps d'armée upon the high road leading from Sombref to Namur, whereupon the cavalry of the 3rd corps was moved into this direction. A French column, consisting of about 12 battalions and 2 batteries, but without any cavalry, was perceived marching along that road. They belonged to Gérard's corps d'armée, which had effected its retreat by Limale, through Mont St. Guibert. Upon the height on which the château of Flavinnes is situated, was posted a detachment from Vandamme's corps, consisting of from 4 to 5 battalions with a battery, and a regiment of cavalry, for the purpose of receiving Gérard's column as it fell back, and of protecting its retreat. As the enemy continued its retrograde march in close column and in good order, it was not deemed advisable to undertake an attack with the two Prussian cavalry-brigades of the 3rd corps, which were much fatigued; but the horse-battery was drawn up, and discharged several rounds of shell and grape at the French troops during their retreat upon the town. The latter, therefore, quitted the high road, and moved along the adjacent heights until they reached the battalions which had been drawn up in support, and which now opposed the further advance of Pirch's corps d'armée. At this time, Thielemann's cavalry withdrew, leaving the fnrther pursuit of the enemy to the latter corps—to the movements of which it is now necessary to recur.

It was not until five o'clock in the morning of the 20th that Pirch received intelligence that the enemy was retiring by Gembloux upon Namur. Lieut. Colonel Sohr was immediately detached, in all haste, to Gembloux with his cavalry-brigade, a battery of horse-artilley, and the fusilier-battalions of the 9th, 14th, and 23rd regiments, as an advanced guard. On approaching that town, Lieut. Colonel Sohr ascertained that Thielemann's cavalry was pursuing the enemy along the high road from Gembloux to Namur. He therefore decided upon marching by the narrow road on the right of the chaussée leading from Sombref, in full trot, covered by the wood, to overtake the French troops in retreat. At Temploux, the latter presented a force of two battalions, some cavalry, and four pieces of artillery, in position, prepared to cover the retreating column. Lieut. Colonel Sohr immediately attacked with both the regiments of hussars, supported by the battery of horse-artillery, and defeated this portion of the enemy's forces. It was at this moment, too, that a cannonade was opened upon the latter by the horse-battery, before mentioned, of Thielemann's corps, whereupon it fell back upon the favourable position taken up near Flavinnes, and in which the enemy appeared determined to make a stand.

Pirch immediately ordered the attack, and directed that it should be supported by Major General Krafft with the 6th brigade, which had closely followed the advanced guard, and had come up with the latter at four o'clock in the afternoon. Three columns of attack were formed. The 1st consisted of the 1st battalion of the 9th regiment, the fusilier-battalion of the 26th regiment, and the 1st battalion of the 1st Elbe landwehr. It was under the command of Major Schmidt, and detached to the left of the road, to drive back the enemy's troops posted in the wood and upon the heights. The second consisted of the 1st and 2nd battalions of the 26th regiment and the 2nd battalion of the 9th regiment, under Colonel Reuss, and of the 2nd and 3rd battalions of the Elbe landwehr, under Colonel Bismark. This column, which advanced partly on the right, and partly on the left, of the road, was supported by the battery No. 5, and led by Major General Krafft in person. The third column comprised the fusilier-battalions which had constituted the infantry of the advanced guard, and was detached more to the right, towards the Sambre, to support the general advance upon Namur.

General Krafft, after having kept up a fire, for a short time, upon the enemy with his artillery, ordered the attack with his infantry. Colonel Reuss threw out his skirmishers, who were quickly followed by the columns of attack. The enemy, after some little resistance, was fairly driven into Namur by a charge with bayonets, and suffered much loss.

In the mean time, Major Schmidt, with his column of three battalions, had turned the enemy's right flank on the Louvain road; and the French were now limited to the defence of the suburb, which, however, was maintained with great obstinacy. The Prussian columns of attack, advancing at the *pas de charge*, drove the enemy out of the suburb, and endeavoured to gain possession of the gates of the town. Colonel Zastrow, the second in command of the 6th brigade, wished to burst open the gate which leads to the Louvain road, but was repulsed by a most murderous fire of musketry and grape, directed upon the assailants from the walls of the town. On repeating the attempt, the Prussian battalions fought with distinguished bravery, but with a great sacrifice of life. Colonel Zastrow was killed at their head; Colonel Bismark also fell; Colonel Reuss was wounded: and the 6th brigade alone lost 44 officers, and 1274 under-officers and privates.

The main body of Grouchy's army was at this time in full retreat upon Dinant, along the defile of the Meuse. The troops left in Namur to keep the Prussians at bay as long as possible, consisted of General Teste's division. They carefully barricaded all the gates, lined the walls facing the Prussians, and made a most gallant resistance. The officers, finding that their men continued so perfectly steady as not to require their attention, armed themselves with the muskets of the wounded, and assisted in maintaining the fire from the walls. The greatest order prevailed in the town. The wounded, the provisions, and ammunition, had already been removed, and were on the line of march.

General Pirch was well aware that the French defended the town solely for the purpose of covering their retreat, and had therefore no intention of undertaking any serious attack; he wished simply to possess himself of the suburbs, and to hold the enemy in check by detaching troops to the Porte de Fer and the St. Nicholas gate. He thought that a demonstration against the latter gate would raise apprehensions in the minds of the French, respecting the security of the bridge over the Sambre. With this view, he ordered General Brause to relieve, with the 7th brigade, the troops then engaged, and together with the advanced guard under Lieut. Colonel Sohr, to blockade the town. At the same time he directed the remainder of the corps to bivouack near Temploux.

General Brause proceeded to post the fusilier-battalion of the 22nd regiment in the direction of the Porte de Fer, and the fusilier-battalion of the 2nd Elbe landwehr towards the

Brussels gate. The main body of the 7th brigade, under Colonel Schon, was stationed in rear of the suburb. The first mentioned battalion stood, under cover, at 400 paces distance from the Porte de Fer, having its tirailleurs in the avenue near the gate. Just as General Brause rode up to examine its formation, an alarm was spread in front that the enemy was making a sortie. The general desired the commanding officer, Major Jochens, to lead his battalion quickly against the defenders, to overthrow them, and then, if possible, to penetrate into the town along with the retreating troops. As Major Jochens approached the gate, he found in its immediate vicinity the tirailleurs of the 6th brigade, still maintaining the contest in that quarter. The attacking column and the tirailleurs now rushed towards the gate and the walls, which the French, probably not deeming themselves strong enough to resist this pressure, abandoned in the greatest haste. General Teste had, in fact, prepared every thing for his retreat, and had so well calculated the time which the enemy would require in forcing an entrance by the Porte de Fer, that he succeeded in filing his battalions along the parapets of the bridge, which had been barricaded, and thus withdrew them to the south bank of the Sambre. The Prussians found it impossible to force open the gate. The windows of the adjoining house of the *douaniers* were therefore driven in, and a small iron door which led from the interior of the house into the town was opened, and, in this manner, an entrance was effected for the assailants, who were conducted by Major Jochens, of the 22nd, and Major Luckowitz, of the 9th regiment, across the market-place, and as far as the bridge over the Sambre, which the French had barricaded, as before stated, and behind which they had again established themselves. These troops were closely followed by Major Schmidt, with the 9th regiment, and lastly by the 2nd Elbe landwehr, in close column, under Majors Mirbach and Lindern.

The Prussians immediately occupied the captured portion of the town; posted a column of reserve on the market-place, and, with loud cheers, made themselves masters of the bridge over the Sambre. An attempt had been made to gain the enemy's rear, by means of a ford in this river, but it proved unsuccessful. The French were driven with so much impetuosity towards the gate leading out to Dinant, that there appeared every probability of a considerable number of them falling into the hands of the Prussians. The former, however, had heaped up large bundles of wood, intermingled with straw and pitch, against the gate, and set them on fire on the approach of the Prussian troops. The gate and the street were soon in flames, and the pursuit was thus obstructed; but even had this not occurred, the great fatigue of the troops, who during the previous sixteen hours, had been either marching or fighting, was sufficient to deprive them of the power of following the retreating enemy with any degree of vigour.

After nine o'clock in the evening, the town was in the possession of the Prussians. Major Schmidt took the command at the Dinant gate and Major Jochens at the bridge over the Sambre. The remaining troops of the 7th, and some battalions of the 6th, brigade, were posted by General Brause upon the market-place. The fusilier-battalions of the advanced guard, which had supported the attack, more to the right, had also advanced into the town, towards the bridge over the Sambre. They had been sharply cannonaded by the enemy from the right bank of the Sambre. A small party of cavalry, under Captain Thielemann, of the Pomeranian hussars, was sent forward a short distance on the road to Dinant, to form the advance of the troops destined to pursue the enemy at daybreak.

General Teste's division retired slowly, and in good order, by the Dinant road, as far as Profondeville, where it took up a position during three hours. At midnight it resumed its march, and arrived at Dinant at four o'clock on the following morning.

This retreat of Grouchy by Namur upon Dinant was executed in a skilful and masterly manner; and the gallant defence of the former town by General Teste's division, unaided by artillery, merits the highest commendation.

In this action the Prussians suffered a loss, including that already mentioned as having occurred to the 6th brigade, of 1,500 men; and the French are supposed to have lost about the same number. In the last attack, the latter abandoned 150 prisoners they had previously taken from the Prussians.

The 2nd Prussian corps d'armée occupied Namur during the night. The cavalry of the 3rd corps bivouacked at Temploux; the infantry of the latter, (which had been rejoined on the march from Wavre by the 9th brigade,) near the town of Gembloux.

The circumstances under which the French army, generally, was placed on the 19th of June rendered it sufficiently obvious that Grouchy would be compelled to effect his retreat by Namur, and further, that whatever show of resistance he might offer on that point would be solely intended to gain time for the security of his troops whilst retiring in one column only, by the long and narrow defile of the Meuse which leads to Dinant. Aware that Napoleon's defeated army was retiring along the direct line of operation, the Charleroi road, he immediately saw the imminent risk of his own retreat becoming intercepted, and the consequent necessity of his effecting the latter in a parallel direction, with a view to his rejoining the main army as soon as practicable. To retire, therefore, by Gembloux upon Namur, and thence along the line of the Meuse, by Dinant and Givet, naturally presented itself as the true and proper course to be pursued. To generals in command of corps d'armée, such as Thielemann and Pirch, a little reflection upon Grouchy's critical position must have led to a similar conclusion. The inactivity of the former, during the afternoon and evening of the 19th, is probably to be explained by his having satisfied himself that the longer Grouchy continued in the vicinity of Wavre, the greater became the chance of his retreat being cut off by a portion of the Allied armies, which, in their advance, would reach the Sambre much sooner than it would be in the power of the French marshal to do, and that, therefore, it would be injudicious on his part to attempt to force the latter from the position which appearances induced him to believe he still occupied with his entire force, on the Dyle. He may also have been strengthened in this opinion by the circumstance of his not having received any positive instructions as to his future dispositions, or any reinforcements to secure for him a preponderance over Grouchy. With Pirch, however, the case was very different. He received distinct orders, on the evening of the 18th, to march at once from the field of Waterloo, and continue his movement during that night, so as to cut off Grouchy's retreat upon the Sambre. It has already been explained, that on reaching Mellery, at eleven o'clock on the following morning, he halted to give his troops rest; that he subsequently ascertained, through Lieut. Colonel Sohr, who had been despatched, during the march, with his cavalry-brigade to reconnoitre on the left, that the French occupied the defile of Mont St. Guibert in force. This intelligence might have satisfied him that Grouchy had not yet reached Namur; but, if he entertained any doubts on that point, these could easily have been settled by means of a reconnoitring party, detached from Mellery, by Gentinne, and St. Géry, to Gembloux, a distance of seven miles. He would then have learned, that no portion whatever of Grouchy's force had hitherto crossed this line, in retreat; that he had, consequently, gained considerably on his rear, and had it in his power, after allowing a few hours rest to his troops, to march them by the high road which leads directly from Mellery into the high road near Sombref, and to anticipate Grouchy in the possession of Namur. In this case, Grouchy, on pproaching the latter place, and finding it occupied by Pirch, would, in all probability, have hesitated to risk the loss of so much time as an attempt to force the town and the Pont de Sambre would necessarily incur, and have preferred endeavouring to pass his troops across the Sambre by some of the bridges and fords between Charleroi and Namur, and retire upon either Philippeville or Dinant; but, with a Prussian corps d'armée at each of these points, and another in his rear, this would have been, to say the least of it, a most hazardous undertaking; and if he attempted to cross the Meuse below Namur, his chance of regaining Napoleon's army would have been still more remote.

But setting aside the circumstance of Pirch's not having, in this manner, taken due advantage of the position in which he stood relatively with Grouchy during the 19th, and passing to the fact, that he first learned, at five o'clock on the morning of the 20th, whilst still at Mellery, that the enemy was retiring along the high road from Gembloux to Namur, pursued by Thielemann's cavalry, it seems strange that, inferring, as he must naturally have done, that Grouchy would only endeavour to hold out long enough at Namur to effect his passage by the Pont de Sambre, and to cover his retreat to Dinant, he did not immediately move off by his right, and push his troops across the Sambre by some of the bridges and fords higher up the stream, and then, marching in the direction of Profondeville, under cover of the wood of Villers within the angle formed by the confluence of the Sambre and the Meuse, intercept Grouchy's retreat through the long and narrow defile in which the road to Dinant winds by the side of the last mentioned river. The situation in which Grouchy would have been placed by a movement of this kind—his troops in a long, narrow, precipitous defile, obstructed in front by Pirch, and attacked in rear by Thielemann—would have been perilous in the extreme. Pirch probably felt that his corps d'armée, part of which was then attached to the army pressing the enemy by the Charleroi road, was not equal to cope with Grouchy's troops; but in the case here supposed, by judiciously disposing his force then present so as to command the defile at some favourable point in its course, he would have secured for himself an advantage which, under such circumstances, would have fully compensated for his deficiency in regard to numbers.

The scattered remnants of the main French army continued to be hurried forward in wild confusion across the frontier. Some of the fugitives hastened towards Avesnes, others to Philippeville, whilst a very great proportion of them sought no temporary rest of this kind, but, throwing away their arms, fled into the interior, to return to their homes; the cavalry, in many instances, disposing of their horses to the country people. Several of the superior officers hastily collected such of the troops as appeared better disposed, and conducted them in the direction of Laon. Napoleon reached the latter town in the afternoon of the 20th. After conferring with the *préfet*, he desired M. de Bussy, one of his aides-de-camp, to superintend the defence of this important place, and despatched General Dejean to Avesnes, and General Flahaut to Guise. In the mean time, a body of troops had been discerned in the distance, moving towards the town. Napoleon sent an aide-de-camp to reconnoitre it; when it proved to be a column of about 3000 men, which Soult, Jerome, Morand, Colbert, Petit, and Pelet, had succeeded in rallying and preserving in order. Napoleon now appeared intent upon remaining at Laon until the remainder of the army had re-assembled; but he subsequently yielded to the force of the arguments expressed in opposition to this determination by the Duke of Bassano and others who were present; and took his departure for Paris, purposing, at the same time, to return to Laon on the 25th or 26th of the month.

The following was the general disposition of the respective armies on the evening of the 20th:—

The Anglo-allied army had its right at Mons, and its left at Binch.

The British cavalry was cantoned in the villages of Strepy, Thieu, Boussoit-sur-Haine, Ville-sur-Haine, and Coegnies; Vivian's brigade in those of Merbes-Ste. Marie, Bienne-le-Hapart, and Mont: and the Hanoverian cavalry in those of Givry and Croix. The reserve was at Soignies.

The Duke of Wellington's head-quarters were at Binch.

The Prussian army had its 1st corps d'armée at Beaumont: 4th corps at Collerets: 2nd corps at Namur, with the exception of the 5th brigade, which was on the march to blockade Maubeuge, and bivouacked at Villers: 3rd corps was at Gembloux, with its cavalry bivouacked at Temploux.

Prince Blücher's head-quarters were at Merbes le Château.

The French army under Napoleon was completely dispersed. A few of the troops took refuge in Avesnes, others in Guise, and the principal body of them, evincing any kind of order, but not exceeding 3000 men, reached Laon.

The French forces under Grouchy were at Dinant. Napoleon quitted Laon for Paris.

On the 21st, the Duke of Wellington crossed the French

frontier, moving the principal portion of his army to Bavay, and the remainder from Mons upon Valenciennes, which fortress was immediately blockaded, and established his head-quarters at Malplaquet, celebrated as the scene of the glorious victory gained by the Duke of Marlborough and Prince Eugene over the French under Marshals Villars and Boufflers, on the 11th of September, 1709. Both the Allied commanders had now reached the triple line of fortresses, which, until the campaign of 1814 proved the contrary, had been considered by so many military men as presenting an insurmountable barrier to the advance of hostile armies into France by its north-eastern frontier. It was most essential that some of the principal fortresses should be secured, and made to constitute a new basis whence to direct the operations now contemplated against the interior. The following, which first presented themselves on the respective lines of advance of the two commanders, were destined to be immediately blockaded:—Valenciennes, Lequesnoy, and Cambray, by the Anglo-allied army; and Maubeuge, Landrecy, Avesnes, and Rocroi, by the Prussians. The general arrangements for the besieging of the fortresses, and the planning of the further operations, above alluded to, were to form the subject of a conference to be held very shortly between the chiefs.

Prince Blücher having, on this day, received reports from Pirch and Thielemann, detailing their proceedings during the two previous days, and showing that Grouchy had succeeded in effecting his escape by Dinant, immediately ordered that the 2nd corps d'armée should move upon Thuin, and place itself under the orders of Prince Augustus of Prussia, who was to undertake the besieging of the fortresses to be left in rear of the Prussian army; and that the 3rd corps should march by Charleroi, and follow the 1st and 4th corps as a reserve.

It will be recollected that Captain Thielemann was sent forward, from Namur, with a party of the Pomeranian hussars, on the night of the 20th, a short distance along the road to Dinant. He was joined at daybreak of the 21st by Lieut. Colonel Sohr, with the fusilier-battalions of the 14th and 23rd regiments, the Brandenburg and Pomeranian hussars, and five pieces of horse-artillery; when the whole force followed the enemy towards Dinant. The latter had, during his retreat, seized every favourable opportunity in narrow and rocky parts of the defile, to barricade the road, and offer every obstruction to the pursuit; by means of which precaution, and the previous night-march, the French contrived to gain so considerably in advance, that Lieut. Colonel Sohr deemed it prudent when near Dinant, to forego all further pursuit, and to endeavour to effect a junction with the main body of the Prussian army, by moving upon Florennes and Walcour. At the former place he halted his detachment during the night of the 21st, and, in this manner, covered the left flank of the main army.

Anxious to gain intelligence concerning the assembling and marching of the French troops on the left of the Allied armies, Prince Blücher despatched Major Falkenhausen, with the 3rd regiment of Silesian landwehr-cavalry, to scour the country in the vicinity of the road by Rettel to Laon. A detachment of 50 dragoons was posted at Bossule le Valcourt, in observation of Philippeville.

The 4th corps d'armée was ordered by the Prince to advance, this day, as far as Maroilles, upon the road from Maubeuge to Landrecies. Its advanced guard, under General Sydow, was directed to proceed still further, and to blockade the latter fortress.

Zieten, in pursuance of orders which he had received the night before, marched with the 1st corps d'armée upon Avesnes; which fortress the advanced guard, under General Jagow, was directed to blockade on both sides of the Helpe. The march of the corps was made in two columns: the right, consisting of the 1st and 2nd brigades, proceeded by Semonsies, and halted at the junction of the road from Maubeuge with that from Beaumont to Avesnes; the left, comprising the 4th brigade, the reserve-cavalry, and reserve-artillery, marched by Solre le Château towards Avesnes, and bivouacked near the 1st and 2nd brigades. Two companies of the 4th brigade, with 20 dragoons, were left to garrison Beaumont; but after the capture of Avesnes, they were ordered to move on to the latter place.

It was between three and four o'clock when the advanced guard of the 3rd brigade, consisting of the 1st Silesian hussars, two rifle companies, and a fusilier battalion, arrived in front of the fortress of Avesnes. The commandant having rejected Zieten's summons to surrender, the latter ordered the bombardment to be commenced forthwith. Ten howitzers, of which six were 10-pounders, and four 7-pounders, drew up on the flank of the cavalry, and fired upon the town. The houses of the latter being all strongly built, the shells failed in setting any part on fire; and a 12-pounder battery produced no great effect upon the firm masonry of the works. At nightfall the bombardment was suspended, with the intention, however, of resuming it at midnight. When it ceased, a sortie was made by the French tirailleurs; but these were immediately encountered and gallantly driven in by the Silesian rifles, who lost ten men on this occasion. Immediately after midnight the Prussian batteries re-commenced their fire. At the fourteenth round, a 10-pounder shell struck the principal powder-magazine, when a tremendous explosion ensued, by which forty houses were involved in one common ruin; but it occasioned no damage whatever to the fortifications. The panic, however, which it created amidst the garrison was such as to induce the latter to express its desire to capitulate. Such a desire could only have proceeded from the want of sufficient energy on the part of the commandant, or from a bad disposition evinced by the garrison, for when the Prussians subsequently entered the place, they found in it 15,000 cartridges for cannon, and a million musket-ball cartridges. There were also in the fortress 47 pieces of artillery, mostly of heavy calibre, which were now made available in the besieging of the remaining fortresses. The garrison, comprising three battalions of national guards, and 200 veterans, were made prisoners of war. The national guards were disarmed, and sent off to their respective homes; but the veterans were conducted to Cologne.

The possession of Avesnes, gained too with so little sacrifice of life, and with none of time, was of essential importance to the Prussians; offering as it did a secure depôt for their material and supplies, upon their new line of operation. It also served for the reception of their sick, and all who had been rendered incapable of keeping up with the army.

On the 21st, the French army continued collecting its scattered remnants between Avesnes and Laon.

The following was the general disposition of the respective armies on the evening of the 21st:—

The Anglo-allied army had its principal force at Bavay, and its right at Valenciennes, which it blockaded.

The Duke of Wellington's head-quarters were at Malplaquet.

The Prussian army had its 1st corps d'armée near Avesnes.

The 4th corps at Maroilles; its reserve cavalry blockading Landrecy.

The 2nd corps at Thuin, except the 5th brigade which blockaded Maubeuge.

The 3rd corps at Charleroi.

Prince Blücher's head-quarters were at Noyelles sur Sambre.

The defeated portion of the French army lay between Avesnes and Laon.

Grouchy's force was at Philippeville.

The Duke of Wellington, steadfastly pursuing that line of policy which led him to constitute as an important feature of his plan, the practical assurance to the French people, that, although entering their country as a conqueror, he did so in hostility to none, save the usurper and his adherents, issued the following proclamation, previously to his quitting Malplaquet:—

PROCLAMATION.

'Je fais savoir aux Français que j'entre dans leur pays à la tête d'une armée deja victorieuse, non en ennemi (excepté de l'usurpateur, prononcé l'ennemi du genre humain, avec lequel on ne peut avoir ni paix ni trève), mais pour les aider à secouer le joug de fer par lequel ils sont opprimés.

'En consequence j'ai donné les ordres ci-joints* à mon armée, et je demande qu'on me fasse connaître tout infracteur.

'Les Français savent cependant que j'ai le droit d'exiger qu'ils se conduisent de manière que je puisse les protéger contre ceux qui voudraient leur faire du mal.

'Il faut donc qu'ils fournissent aux réquisitions qui leur seront faites de la part des personnes autorisées à les faire, en échange pour des reçus en forme et ordre; et qu'ils se tiennent chèz eux paisiblement, et qu'ils n'aient aucune correspondence ou communication avec l'usurpateur ennemi, ni avec ses adhérens.

'Tous ceux qui s'absenteront de leur domicile après l'entrée en France, et tous ceux qui se tronveront absens au service de l'usurpateur, seront considérés comme ses adherens et comme ennemis; et leurs propriétés seront affectées à la subsistance de l'armée.

'Donné au Quartier Général à Malplaquet, ce 22 de juin, 1815.

'WELLINGTON.'

No proclamation of a similar nature was issued by Prince Blücher, nor were any direct orders given by the latter to remind his troops that France was "to be treated as a friendly country," or to forbid them taking anything "for which payment be not made."† Hence, in the advance to Paris a marked contrast was observed between the conduct of the Prussian, and that of the Anglo-allied, army: the troops of the former committing great excesses and imposing severe exactions along their whole line of march; whilst the British and German troops under the Duke of Wellington acquired from the outset the good will and kindly disposition of the inhabitants of the country through which they passed. The Anglo-allied troops inspired the people with confidence: the Prussians awed them into subjection. Much of the cause of all this may be traced to the different views entertained by the two great commanders. Blücher's extreme hatred of the French would not allow him to modify, still less to abandon, the opinion which he had imbibed from the first moment he heard of the escape of Napoleon from Elba, that they ought not only to be thoroughly humbled, but also severely pun-

* The orders in question are given in p. 423.
† See General Order, p. 423.

ished. Neither he nor his soldiers could ever forget the monstrous cruelties and grinding extortions which their own country had been compelled to endure when overrun by the French; and now that they were once more brought into the land of their bitterest enemies, and another period of retribution had arrived, but one sentiment pervaded the whole Prussian army—that those who had not scrupled to inflict the scourge of war throughout the whole continent, should, in their turn, be made duly sensible of its evils. A contrary train of ideas, or a different course of proceeding, on the part of the Prussians, was scarcely to be expected. Hence the value of the excellent and orderly conduct of the British troops operating as a salutary counterpoise to the domineering and revengeful spirit which actuated the Prussians. Blücher felt equally with Wellington that the advance upon Paris before the approach of the Allied armies, which were then only crossing the Rhine, was a departure from strictly military principles, and that this could only be justified by the extraordinary moral effect which would be produced by the signal defeat of Napoleon. But his views were limited to the military part of the plan, which was to make a dash at the capital, and, if possible, to intercept Grouchy whilst endeavouring to rejoin the routed force under Soult. Wellington's admirable policy embraced a wider field. He invariably kept in view the great object for which the war had been undertaken. The information which he contrived to obtain relative to the effect which Napoleon's disaster produced upon the minds of the leading men of the great political parties by which France was then agitated, and upon the members of the two chambers of parliament generally, combined with the knowledge he had already acquired of the disposition of the inhabitants of the department of the North, which, in fact, had not evinced that enthusiasm attendant upon the return of Napoleon from Elba that was manifested throughout the greater part of the nation, convinced him that by adopting measures calculated to impress upon the French people that the Allies were friendly towards them, though inveterately hostile to Napoleon, and by seizing every advantage afforded by the presence and the influence of their legitimate monarch, he was, by such means, insuring the security of the operations upon Paris more effectually than could have been accomplished by additional military force applied under different circumstances.

The aid which such a line of conduct, on the part of the Duke, gave to the cause of Louis XVIII. was immense.

The people of the northern departments, who, in general, were wearied by the continuance of wars undertaken for the sole purpose of aggrandizing and upholding the power of Napoleon, and who now longed to enjoy the blessings of peace, saw in the friendly disposition of the Allies, and the support which these yielded to the King's authority, a pledge of their determination to crush the war-party, and, at the same time, to cement their alliance with the legitimate sovereign. The white flag was soon seen to wave from countless steeples. The tide of royalty, favoured in no small degree by the versatile nature of the French character, was already setting in fast, and as it rolled steadily on towards the capital, the Duke's customary foresight and good tact gave it an impulse, which not only bore him along with it in easy triumph, but, when it subsequently reached the goal, swept away every vestige of the government usurped by Napoleon and his adherents.

CHAPTER XVIII.

On the 22nd of June, the 2nd and 4th British divisions, as also the cavalry, of the Anglo-allied army marched to Le Cateau and its vicinity. The 1st and 3rd British divisions, the divisions of Dutch-Belgian infantry attached to the 1st corps, the Nassau troops, and the Dutch-Belgian cavalry were encamped near Gommignies. The 5th and 6th British divisions, the Brunswick corps, and the reserve-artillery, were encamped about Bavay. The advanced guard (Vivian's brigade) was at St. Benin. Troops of the corps under Prince Frederick of the Netherlands blockaded Valenciennes and Le Quesnoy.

The Duke of Wellington's head-quarters were at Le Cateau.

Prince Blücher being desirous of bringing his different corps d'armée into closer connection, moved the 1st and 4th only half a march this day. The former proceeded from Avesnes to Etroeung, sending forward its advanced guard to La Capelle, and patroles as far as the Oise: the latter marched along the road leading from Landrecy towards Guise, as far as Fesmy; pushing forward its advanced guard to Henappe, and detachments to Guise. Scouring parties of cavalry were also detached from the 1st corps, in the direction of Rocroi.

The 3rd Prussian corps d'armée advanced from Charleroi to Beaumont, detaching towards Philippeville and Chimay, for the security of its left flank.

The 2nd Prussian corps, which was destined to operate against the fortresses, moved from Thuin. It was disposed in the following manner:—The 5th and 7th brigades, with the cavalry, blockaded Maubeuge; the 6th brigade was on the march to Landrecy; and the 8th brigade was moving upon Philippeville and Givet.

Prince Blücher's head-quarters were at Catillon sur Sambre.

Grouchy's troops, on this day, reached Rocroi.

The remains of the vanquished portion of the French army continued retiring upon Laon, and collecting in its vicinity. Soult had established the head-quarters at this place. The men and horses of the artillery-train were moved on to La Fère, to be supplied with new ordnance; and every means was adopted to replace this branch of the service on an efficient footing. Grouchy was effecting his retreat upon Soissons, by the line of Rocroi, Rethel, and Rheims; and it was considered, that as soon as the latter should be able to unite his force to the remains of the army collecting under Soult, it would yet be found practicable, with the additional aid of reserves, to stem the advance of the Allies. But where was the chief whose presence had heretofore been the spell by which a turbulent and restless soldiery was wont, when subdued by the *fortune de la guerre*, to be restored to its former self, and to be imbued with new life and renovated strength by the prospect of acquiring fresh glory in retrieving a great national disaster? Had he flown towards the nearest corps d'armée of Rapp and Lecourbe, to lead them, along with all the reserves that he could possibly collect together, including the regimental depôts, the gensd'armerie, and even the douanerie, against the flank of the victorious armies of Wellington and Blücher, during their hazardous advance upon the capital, and, in combination with Soult and Grouchy, to effect their separation, perhaps, their destruction? No! The sword by which the empire had been raised and held in subjection, by which Europe itself had been enthralled and all but conquered, had fallen powerless from his grasp. In him were no longer centred the might and the will of imperial France. These had been delegated through the constitution, to the organs of the nation, the elected representatives of the people. He no longer possessed, in his own person, the administrative and the executive; but was under the control of that power which, as before observed, when he quitted Paris to join the army, he dreaded more than the enemy he was going to confront—the power of public opinion legitimately expressed. If he had so keenly felt its force before his downfall on the battle-field, how great, nay, how hopeless, must have appeared to him the task of endeavouring to soothe its excitement, and to obtain its sanction to renewed sacrifices, when suddenly appearing in Paris on the afternoon of the 21st of June—but one short week from the time of his assuming the command of his army—himself to announce the disastrous result of his enterprise. The imperialists in the capital, who had indulged in the most extravagant hopes, engendered by the news of the victory at Ligny, had scarcely manifested their exultation, when sinister rumours began to spread of some sudden reverses which had befallen the cause of Napoleon; and presently all doubts and suspense were removed by the unexpected appearance of the Emperor himself, which gave rise to the most gloomy anticipations.

Napoleon immediately summoned a cabinet council. He frankly explained to his ministers the critical state of affairs; but, at the same time, with his usual confidence in his own resources, declared his conviction, that if the nation were called upon to rise *en masse*, the annihilation of the enemy would follow; but that if, instead of ordering new levies and adopting extraordinary measures, the chambers were to allow themselves to be drawn into debates, and to waste their time in disputation, all would be lost. "Now that the enemy is in France," he added, "it is necessary that I should be invested with extraordinary power, that of a temporary dictatorship. As a measure of safety for the country, I might assume this power, but it would be better and more national that it should be conferred upon me by the chambers." The ministers were too well acquainted with the general views and disposition of the chamber of representatives to pronounce a direct approval of this step; but Napoleon, perceiving their hesitation, called upon them to express their opinion upon the measures of public safety required by existing circumstances. Carnot, the minister of the interior, conceived it to be essential that the country should be declared in danger; that the *fédérés* and national guards should be called to arms; that Paris should be placed in a state of siege, and measures adopted for its defence; that at the last extremity the armed force should retire behind the Loire, and take up an intrenched position; that the army of La Vendée, where the civil war had nearly terminated, as also the corps of observation in the south, should be recalled, and the enemy checked until sufficient force could be united and organised for the assumption of a vigorous offensive, by which he should be driven out of France. Decrès, the minister of the marine, and Regnault de Saint-Jean-d'Angely, the secretary of state, supported this opinion; but Fouché, the minister of police, and the remaining ministers, remarked that the safety of the state did not depend upon any particular measure which might thus be proposed, but upon the chambers, and upon their uniting with the head of the government; and that by manifesting towards them confidence and good faith, they would be induced to declare it to be their duty to unite with Napoleon in the adoption of energetic measures for securing the honour and independence of the nation.

This advice on the part of Fouché was an artful piece of dissimulation. No man in France possessed so intimate a knowledge of the secret workings of the public mind; he knew precisely the dispositions and views of the different factions, as also the character and temperament of their leaders. He knew also that the great parties in the chambers, with the exception of the imperialists, who were in the minority, but whom he secretly flattered with the prospect of a Napoleon II., were fully prepared to depose the Emperor, in favour of full constitutional freedom, and liberal institutions. This knowledge, obtained with an adroitness and a precision quite peculiar to this celebrated minister of police, he made completely subservient to his own personal views. These had been, from the commencement of Napoleon's second reign, to coquet with the factions in such a manner as to induce each to consider him an indispensable instrument in the realization of its hopes, and to exert this extraordinary influence either to support or to undermine the power of Napoleon, according as the fortunes of the latter might be in the ascendant or on the decline. The resolute attitude assumed by the Allies soon satisfied him that, although the Emperor might once more dazzle the world with some brilliant feat of arms, he must eventually succumb to the fixed determination of the sovereigns to crush his usurped authority, and to the overwhelming masses with which Europe was preparing to subjugate the country. He had been, and was still, in secret communication with the ministers and advisers of Louis XVIII. and was consequently in full possession of the general plans and intentions of the Allies. When, therefore, Napoleon's enterprise had so signally failed, and the re-occupation of Paris appeared to be its necessary consequence, Fouché foresaw clearly, that were the proposed dictatorship to be assumed by means of a sudden and forced dissolution of the chambers, implying that the recent reverses had been produced by treachery on the part of the representatives, and were new levies to be raised *en masse*, in support of the force that yet remained available, the result would inevitably be anarchy and confusion in the capital, disorder and excesses throughout the whole country, renewed disasters to the nation, together with an awful and useless sacrifice of life. To prevent such a catastrophe, it was necessary to lull Napoleon's suspicions of the intentions of the chambers, with which, at the same time, Fouché was fully acquainted. Hence it was, that to gain sufficient time for the developement of these intentions, Fouché gave to the council the advice before mentioned. He strongly expressed his disapproval of the projected dissolution of the chambers, and assumption of the dictatorship, declaring that any measures of that kind would only tend to create distrust, and, not improbably, a general revolt. But, at the same time, his agents were making known throughout Paris the fullest extent of the disasters that had befallen Napoleon, and which had caused his sudden and unexpected return; and the deputies were assembling in all haste, and in great numbers, to take a bold and decided step in this great national crisis.

In thus dissembling from his master the real disposition of the great political parties, and the true state of the public mind, Fouché, no doubt, betrayed the trust reposed in him; but, setting aside the question whether he was really influenced by patriotic motives, or merely acting upon a system of deep duplicity and time-serving expediency, there can also be no doubt that, by pursuing the line of conduct which he did on this important occasion, he became the means of preserving his country from the infliction of a still further accumulation of evils.

The cabinet council continued in discussion; some supporting, and others disapproving, the propositions of Napoleon, who, at length, yielding to the arguments of Fouché and Carnot, declared he would submit himself to the loyalty of the chambers, and confer with them as to the measures which the critical position of the country might render necessary. In the mean time, the deputies had met, and commenced their deliberations on the existing state of affairs. M de la Fayette, the acknowledged leader of the liberal party, having received intelligence of the subject of discussion in the council, and aware that not a moment was to be lost in averting the blow with which their liberties were menaced, ascended the tribune, and thus addressed the chamber, amidst the most profound silence, and breathless suspense:—

'Representatives! For the first time during many years you hear a voice, which the old friends of liberty will yet recognize. I rise to address you concerning the dangers to which the country is exposed. The sinister reports which have been circulated during the last two days. are unhappily confirmed. This is the moment to rally round the national colours—the tri-coloured standard of 1789—the standard of liberty, equality and public order. It is you alone who can now protect the country from foreign attacks and internal dissensions. It is you alone who can secure the independence and the honour of France. Permit a veteran in the sacred cause of liberty, in all times a stranger to the spirit of faction, to submit to you some resolutions which appear to him to be demanded by a sense of the public danger, and by the love of our country. They are such as, I feel persuaded, you will see the necessity of adopting:—

'I. The chamber of deputies declares that the independence of the nation is menaced.

'II. The chamber declares its sittings permanent. Any attempt to dissolve it, shall be considered high treason. Whosoever shall render himself culpable of such an attempt, shall be considered a traitor to his country, and immediately treated as such.

'III. The army of the line, and the national guards, who have fought, and still fight, for the liberty, the independence, and the territory of France, have merited well of the country.

'IV. The minister of the interior is invited to assemble the principal officers of the Parisian national guard, in order to consult on the means of providing it with arms, and of completing this corps of citizens, whose tried patriotism and zeal offer a sure guarantee for the liberty, prosperity, and tranquillity of the capital, and for the inviolability of the national representatives.

'V. The ministers of war, of foreign affairs, of police, and of the interior, are invited to repair immediately to the sittings of the chamber.'

No one ventured to oppose these bold resolutions, and, after a brief discussion, in which their instant adoption was urged in the strongest manner, they were carried by acclamation, with the exception of the fourth, which was suspended on account of the invidious distinction which it appeared to convey between the troops of the line and the national guards. They were then transmitted to the chamber of peers, where, after a short discussion, they were adopted without amendment.

The message from the chambers, conveying these resolutions, reached the council in the midst of its deliberations. Napoleon was staggered by an act which he looked upon as an usurpation of the sovereign authority. To him, who had so long exercised an almost unlimited control in the state, who had led mighty armies to victory, and who had subjected powerful nations to his despotic sway, this sudden and energetic voice of the people, conveyed through the medium of their representatives, aroused him to a full sense of the wonderful change which had been effected in the public mind, and in his own individual position, through the intervention of a constitution. He was alike indignant at what he conceived to be a daring presumption, and mortified at his own miscalculation in having convoked the chambers. "J'avais bien pensé," he remarked, "que j'aurais dû congédier ces gens-là avant mon départ." After some reflection, he determined, if possible, to temporize with the chambers. He sent Regnault de Saint-Jean-d'Angely to the chamber of deputies, in his capacity of member, to soothe the irritation that prevailed, to relate that the army had been upon the point of gaining a great victory, when disaffected individuals created a panic; that the troops had since rallied, and that the Emperor had hastened to Paris to concert, with the ministers and the chambers, such measures for the public safety as circumstances seemed to require. Carnot was directed to make a similar communication to the chamber of peers. Regnault vainly endeavoured to fulfil his mission: the deputies had lost all patience, and insisted upon the ministers presenting themselves at the bar of the house. The lätter at length obeyed the summons, Napoleon having consented, though with great reluctance, to their compliance with the mandate. He required them, however, to be accompanied by his brother Lucien, as an extraordinary commissioner, appointed to reply to the interrogatories of the chamber.

At six o'clock in the evening, Lucien Buonaparte and the ministers made their appearance in the chamber of deputies. Lucien announced that he had been sent there by Napoleon as a commissioner extraordinary, to concert with the assembly measures of safety. He then placed in the hands of the president the message of which he was the bearer from his brother. It contained a succinct recital of the disasters experienced at Mont St. Jean; and recommended the representatives to unite with the head of the state in preserving the country from the fate of Poland, and from the re-imposition of the yoke which it had thrown off. It stated, also, that it was desirable that the two chambers should appoint a commission of five members, to concert with the ministers the measures to be adopted for the public safety, and the means of treating for peace with the Allied powers.

This message was far from being favourably received. A stormy discussion ensued, in the course of which it was soon made manifest that the deputies required a more explicit declaration of Napoleon's opinions and designs; one, in fact, more in accordance with the views which the majority of them evidently entertained, and was apparently determined to enforce. One of their number significantly remarked, as he addressed himself to the ministers, "You know as well as we do, that it is against Napoleon alone that Europe has declared war. From this moment, separate the cause of Napoleon from that of the nation. In my opinion, there exists but one individual who stands in the way between us and peace. Let him pronounce the word and the country will be saved!" Several of the members spoke in a similar strain, and the debate was kept up with great animation, until at length it was agreed, that in conformity with the terms of the imperial message, a commission of five members should be appointed, consisting of the president and vice-presidents of the chamber, to collect, in concert with the cabinet and with a committee from the house of peers, the fullest information upon the state of France, and to propose suitable measures of safety. The committee consisted of Messrs. Lanjuinais, La Fayette, Dupont de l'Eure, Flangergues, and Grenier.

Lucien now presented himself in the same capacity of commissioner extraordinary, to the chamber of peers. After hearing the message, the latter also appointed a committee, which consisted of Generals Drouot, Dejean, Andreossy, and Messrs. Boissy d'Anglas and Thibaudeau.

Napoleon, being fully informed of the proceedings of the chamber of deputies, and of the general tenor of the debates, hesitated a long time whether to dissolve the assembly, or to abdicate the imperial crown. Some of his ministers, on perceiving the direction of his views, assured him that the chamber had acquired too firm a hold of the public opinion to submit to any violent *coup d'état*, and expressed their opinion, that by withholding the act of abdication, he might eventually deprive himself of the power of vacating the throne in favour of his son. Nevertheless he appeared determined to defer this step to the very last moment, trusting in the mean time some favourable event might occur, tending to modify the present disposition of the chamber.

The deputies again met, at an early hour on the following morning. The utmost impatience was manifested for the report of the committee. Two hours having elapsed, the members became greatly excited. Some of them proposed that the exigencies of the state were such, that it was their duty to adopt immediate and decisive measures, without waiting for the report. At length, in the midst of the agitation and tumult which prevailed, General Grenier, the reporter of the committee, suddenly made his appearance. He stated that, after a deliberation of five hours, the committee had resolved:—

'That the safety of the country required that the Emperor should consent to the nomination, by the two chambers, of a commission, charged to negotiate directly with the coalesced powers; stipulating only that they should respect the national independence, the territorial integrity, and the right which belongs to every people, of adopting such constitutions as it may think proper; and that these negotiations should be supported by the prompt development of the national force.'

This statement excited general murmurs of disapprobation. But the reporter, aware of the expectations of the chamber, proceeded:—

'This article, gentlemen, appears to me insufficient. It does not fulfil the object which the chamber proposes to itself, because it is possible that your deputation may not be admitted. I would not, therefore, urge the adoption of this measure, had I not reason to believe that you will soon receive a message, in which the Emperor will declare his wish, that the effect of this should first be tried, and that, should he then prove an insuperable obstacle to the nation being permitted to treat for its independence, he will be ready to make whatever sacrifice may be demanded of him.'

This produced an extraordinary sensation in the assembly. It was looked upon as an artful design upon the part of Napoleon to create delay by proposing to the chambers a proceeding which he was well aware would prove unsuccessful, and to seize the first favourable opportunity of destroying their independence, and re-establishing his despotism—to re enact, in short, the eighteenth of Brumaire. The tumult had reached a fearful height. Many members exclaimed vehemently against the report. At length, one of them, M. Duchesne, ascended the tribune, and spoke in the following energetic and decided manner:—

'I do not believe that the project proposed by the committee is capable of attaining the desired end. The greatness of our disasters cannot be denied: they are sufficiently proved by the presence of the chief of our armies in the capital. If there are no bounds to the energies of the nation, there are limits to its means. The chambers cannot offer negotiations to the Allied powers. The documents which have been communicated to us demonstrate that they have uniformly refused all the overtures which have been made to them; and they have declared that they will not treat with the French, as long as they shall have the Emperor at their head.'

The speaker was here interrupted by the president, who announced that the message to which the reporter had referred would speedily be received. The interruption, however, at this most important point of the debate, renewed the tumult in the chamber. Some exclaimed, "It is a concerted plan to make us lose time." Others cried out, "Some plot is concerting;" and the majority vociferated, "Proceed, proceed; there is no middle course."

Duchesne continued:—

'It is necessary that we should be certain of finding in the development of the national force, a defence sufficient to support our negotiations, and to enable us to treat with success, concerning our honour and independence. Can that force be developed with sufficient rapidity? May not circumstances again lead victorious armies to the capital? Then, and under their auspicies, will re-appear the ancient family.' ("Never! never!" exclaimed several voices.) 'I freely express my opinion. What may be the consequences of these events? We have only *one* certain means left, which is, to engage the Emperor, in the name of the safety of the state, in the sacred name of a suffering country, to declare his *abdication*.'

No sooner was this word pronounced than the entire assembly rose; and amidst the clamour that ensued were heard a hundred voices exclaiming, "Seconded! seconded!" When, at length, the president succeeded in restoring some degree of order, he said—

'I cannot hope to arrive at any result, unless the agitation of the assembly be repressed. The safety of the country depends on the decision of this day. I entreat the chamber to wait for the Emperor's message.'

The proposition of Duchesne was instantly supported by General Solignac, an officer who, during the last five years, had been made to suffer the severest mortifications, arising from the hatred entertained towards him by Napoleon, in consequence of his refusal to be the servile instrument of his ambition; and, therefore, the curiosity of the chamber was naturally excited to hear what course he was about to adopt.

'And I also,' said the general; 'I share in the uneasiness of him who has preceded me at this tribune. Yes! we ought to consider the safety of the empire, and the maintenance of our liberal institutions; and, while the government is inclined to present to you such measures as tend to this end, it appears important to preserve to the chamber the honour of not having proposed an object which ought to be the free concession of the monarch. I move that a deputation of five members shall be appointed to proceed to the Emperor, which deputation shall express to His Majesty the urgency of his decision. Their report will, I trust, satisfy at once the wish of the assembly, and that of the nation.'

This proposition was most favourably received, and the president was on the point of putting it to the vote, when Solignac again appeared in the tribune.

'I wish,' said he, 'to propose an amendment to my motion. Several persons have intimated to me that we shall soon be informed of His Majesty's determination. I consequently think it necessary that we should wait for *one hour*, to receive the message, which it seems is to be addressed to the chambers. I therefore move that we adjourn for that time.' (This part of his speech was met with great disapprobation on the part of the chamber.) 'Gentlemen!' continued the general, 'we all wish to save the country; but can we not reconcile this unanimous sentiment with the laudable desire that the chamber should preserve the honour of the chief of the state?' (Cries of "Yes! yes!") 'If I requested that we should wait until this evening or to-morrow, some considerations might be opposed—but, one hour'—("Yes! yes! To the vote!" was the general exclamation; and the chamber adjourned.)

In the mean time, Napoleon had been made acquainted with the disposition of the chamber of representatives, by Regnault de Saint-Jean-d'Angely, who hastened to warn him that if he did not immediately abdicate, his deposition would, in all probability, be declared. He was enraged at the idea of this contemplated violence. "Since that is the case," he said, "I will not abdicate at all. The chamber is composed of a set of jacobins, impracticables, and intriguers, who are seeking for disorder, or for place. I ought to have denounced them to the nation, and given them their dismissal. The time that has been lost may yet be recovered." Regnault, however, urged him in the strongest manner to yield to imperious circumstances, and to renew the noble and generous sacrifice he made in 1814. He assured him that if he did not take this step, he would be accused by the chamber, and even by the whole nation, of having, out of personal considerations alone, prevented the possibility of obtaining peace. Solignac and other deputies were then announced. They boldly declared to him that he had no other course open to him but that of submission to the desire entertained by the representatives of the nation. Solignac described to him the scene in the chamber of deputies, and the difficulty he had experienced in inducing the latter to suspend, even for one hour, their decision, which, if not anticipated by a voluntary abdication, would entail upon him the disgrace of forfeiture. Even his brothers, Lucien and Joseph, now gave their opinion that the moment for resistance had passed. When the paroxysm of rage, to which these representations gave rise, had subsided, Napoleon announced his determination to abdicate in favour of his son; and, desiring his brother Lucien to take a pen, he dictated to him the following declaration:—

'Frenchmen! In commencing the war for maintaining the national independence, I relied on the union of all efforts, of all desires, and the concurrence of all the national authorities. I had reason to hope for success, and I braved all the declarations of the powers allied against me.

'Circumstances appear to be changed. I offer myself a sacrifice to the hatred of the enemies of France. May they prove sincere in their declarations, and have really directed them solely against my power. My political life is terminated; and I proclaim my son, under the title of NAPOLEON II., Emperor of the French.

'The present ministers will form provisionally the council of the government. The interest which I take in my son induces me to invite the chamber to form the regency by a law without delay.

'Unite all for the public safety, in order to remain an independent nation.

'NAPOLEON.'

This was the last great act of his political life. Defeated and humbled by foreign enemies, subdued and controlled by the representatives of the nation, he was forced to descend from a throne whence he had at one time swayed the destinies of sovereigns rendered dependent on his mighty will. Almost all the previous changes and gradations in his extraordinary career had been preluded or accompanied by some magnificent scene of dramatic effect, or a violent *coup d'état;* but, in this instance, the transition was attended by no circumstance more remarkable than the quietude with which it was effected. The cessation of the political existence of such a man would have been most naturally looked for as an event coincident only with the termination of a life which, if not closed upon the pinnacle of glory, would be sought for amidst the shock of battle, or in the vortex of a state convulsion. That he meditated a second 18th of Brumaire, there can be no doubt; but the decided tone of the debates in the national assembly, the solicitations of his friends, and the hope of securing the throne to his family, induced him to abandon all idea of such a project. It is, besides, more than probable that, aware as he was of the bad feeling that existed, to a great extent, both in the chambers and in the country, towards the Bourbons, as also of the conflicting principles of the different factions, he calculated upon the chances of a revolution, productive of anarchy and confusion, which he might yet be called upon to reduce to order and submission.

When it is considered that the great mass of the army of the line was devoted to Napoleon, that the rallied army of the North was falling back upon Paris, where it would concentrate its strength and be reinforced from the regimental depôts, and, further, that the armies on the Eastern frontier were still holding their respective positions, and that even in La Vendée the imperial troops had succeeded in quelling the insurrection,—when, in addition to all this, it is considered how great, how extraordinary, was the influence induced by the *prestige* of Napoleon with the majority of the nation, dazzled as the latter had been by countless victories, that outweighed, in its estimation, those fatal disasters which it ascribed solely to the united power of the great European league established against France,—it is impossible not to be struck by the firm, bold, and determined attitude assumed by the French parliament. France, on this critical occasion, displayed one of the brightest examples the world has yet beheld of the force of constitutional legislation. Under all the attendant circumstances, it was a remarkable triumph of free institutions over monarchical despotism.

It is now necessary to revert to the operations of the Allied armies.

On the 23rd of June, Wellington and Blücher gave to the great mass of their troops a halt, not merely for the sake of affording them rest, but also for the purpose of collecting the stragglers, and bringing up the ammunition and the baggage.

The only movement made on the part of the Anglo-allied army, on this day, was that by Major General Lyon's 6th Hanoverian brigade, which, together with Grant's hussar-brigade, Lieut. Colonel Webber Smith's horse-battery, Major Unett's and Major Brome's foot-batteries, marched, under the personal command of Sir Charles Colville, to attack Cambray, the garrison of which the Duke had been led to believe, had abandoned the place, leaving in it at most 300 or 400 men. Colville was furnished with a letter from the Duke to the governor, summoning him to surrender, as also with some copies of his Grace's Proclamation of the 22nd to the French. The 1st Brunswick light battalion was sent forward from the reserve at Bavay, to watch Le Quesnoy, which fortress was still occupied by the enemy.

The 3rd Prussian corps d'armée was pushed forward to

Avesnes, by which means the three corps destined to advance upon Paris were so placed that they could form a junction, with only half an ordinary march, and this relative position was maintained throughout the remainder of the line of advance.

The Allied Commanders had an interview on this day at Catillon, for the purpose of arranging their plan of combined operations. The intelligence they had procured having satisfied them that the enemy was collecting his forces at Laon and Soissons, they decided upon not pursuing him along that line, since their progress towards the capital might, in that case, be impeded by affairs of advanced and rear-guards, but upon moving by the right bank of the Oise, and crossing this river at either Compiegne or Pont St. Maxence. By thus turning the French left, they hoped to intercept the enemy's retreat, or at all events to reach Paris before him; and in order to deceive him as to these intentions, he was to be followed by Prussian cavalry, assuming to be the advanced guard of the Allied armies. It was also settled, that as they might find it necessary to throw bridges across the Oise, the British General should bring forward his pontoon train, that possessed by the Prussians being inadequate for the purpose. In order to secure a good base whence to conduct these operations, it was further arranged that the corps under Prince Frederick of the Netherlands should remain, for the purpose of besieging the fortresses situated on the Scheldt, and between that river and the Sambre; and that the following corps should undertake the besieging of the fortresses on the Sambre, and between this last river and the Moselle, namely, the 2nd Prussian corps d'armée, commanded by General Pirch, the corps d'armée of North Germany,* commanded at first by General Count Kleist von Nollendorf, and subsequently by Lieut. General Hacke, as also a portion of the garrison-troops of Luxemburg, commanded by Lieut. General Prince Louis of Hesse Homburg,—the whole of these German forces being placed under the chief command of Prince Augustus of Prussia.

This plan of operations was such as might have been expected from the combined councils of such leaders as Wellington and Blücher, and was undoubtedly the one best calculated to attain the object they had in view; and it was

* This corps had crossed the Rhine at Coblence and Neuwied on the 12th of March, and taken up a position on the Moselle and the Sarre; in which it remained until the 16th of June, when, in consequence of the repulse of the army under Blücher, it received orders to fall back upon St. Vith. From this point it was now pushed forward across the French frontier by Bastogne and Neufchateau, to attack Bouillon and Sedan.

carried into effect with all that mutual cordiality and good fellowship which had invariably characterized their proceedings.

On the morning of the 24th, the Duke of Wellington, in consequence of a report which he had received from Sir Charles Colville, directed Lord Hill to march the two brigades of the 4th division then at Le Cateau, towards Cambray, where they would join the other brigade of the division, and also to send with them a 9-pounder battery.

On the arrival of these troops, Colville made his preparations for the attack, which took place in the evening, in the following manner. Three columns of attack were formed. One commanded by Lieut. Colonel Sir Neil Campbell, (Major in the 54th regiment,) escaladed at the angle formed by the Valenciennes gateway and the curtain of the body of the place. A second, commanded by Colonel Sir William Douglas, of the 91st regiment, and directed by Lieut. Gilbert of the royal engineers, escaladed at a large ravelin near the Amiens road. A third, consisting of Colonel Mitchell's brigade, and directed by Captain Thompson of the royal engineers, after having forced the outer gate of the Couvre Port, in the hornwork, and passed both ditches, by means of the rails of the drawbridges, attempted to force the main Paris gate, but not succeeding in this, it escaladed by a breach on that side, which was in a state of reparation. The three batteries of Lieut. Colonel Webber Smith, and Majors Unett and Brome, under the direction of Lieut. Colonel Hawker, rendered the most essential service in covering these attacks, which having succeeded, the town speedily fell into the hands of the assailants. The citadel continued to hold out, but the governor solicited a suspension of hostilities which, however, could not be granted.*

Of the Anglo-allied army, the 1st and 3rd British divisions,

* The facility with which the noted fortress of Cambray was captured, is thus commented upon by the late Major General Sir James Carmichael Smyth, Bart., (then Commanding Officer of Engineers in the Duke of Wellington's army,) in his instructive account (published in 1817) of the Attacks upon the Fortresses by the British and Prussian Armies in the Campaigns of 1814 and 1815 :—'The easy capture of Cambray affords another lesson to statesmen and military men, (in addition to the many with which both ancient and modern history abounds,) not to suffer the fortresses of a state to be neglected or to fall into disrepair. The boar in the fable is represented as whetting his tusks, although no enemy was in sight; well knowing that he would have no time to spare, when he might require them. Had the escarp of Cambray been in order, or the ditch near the Paris gate been kept clear of mud and reeds, the place could not have been carried by assault in the easy manner it was. The escarp of Cambray is from 40 to 70 feet high, where the ditch is dry; and from 30 to 40 where the ditch is wet. Such an escarp, if in order, it is evident is not to be despised.'

the Dutch-Belgian infantry attached to the 1st corps, and the Dutch-Belgian cavalry, were moved this day from Gommignies to Forest, upon the road to Le Cateau, and then encamped between the villages of Croix and Bousies.

The 2nd British division continued at Le Cateau.

The Duke made no movement in advance, having found it necessary to afford additional time for the coming up of the pontoons and supplies. The reserve, consisting of the 5th and 6th divisions, of the Brunswick corps, and the reserve-artillery, was moved nearer to the main body, and cantoned and encamped in and about the villages of Engle-Fontaine, Rancour, and Préau au Bois.

On this day proposals were made to the advanced posts of this corps under Prince Frederick of the Netherlands, near Valenciennes, as also to those of the 1st Prussian corps d'armée, for a suspension of hostilities, upon the grounds that Napoleon had abdicated in favour of his son, that a provisional government had been appointed, consisting of Fouché, Caulincourt, Grenier, and Quinette, and that these persons had sent ministers to the Allied powers to treat for peace. Both Wellington and Blücher considered that they would not be acting in accordance with the spirit and intentions of the alliance of the powers of Europe were they to listen to such proposals, and therefore peremptorily refused to discontinue their operations. Those which were addressed to the Prussian commander emanated from General Count Morand, who commanded the rear-guard of the French army at Laon, and to whom Blücher replied, that no armistice could be entered into, except in the case of Napoleon being delivered up, and the fortresses in rear of the armies being abandoned, and conceded as guarantees for its fulfilment.

Louis XVIII., acting on the advice so urgently tendered to him by the Duke of Wellington, arrived at Le Cateau late in the evening, followed by a numerous train; and only awaited the surrender of the citadel of Cambray to fix his temporary residence in the latter town.

The Prussian army renewed its operations on the 24th, according to the plan agreed upon the day before by the Allied commanders. At break of day, Lieut. Colonel Schmiedeberg was despatched with the Silesian regiment of uhlans, and some horse-artillery, towards Laon, for the purpose, in conjunction with the detachments already sent from the 1st corps d'armée, of watching and deceiving the enemy. Blücher disposed his three corps d'armée in two columns. The left column, which was the one nearest to the enemy, consisted of the 1st and 3rd corps, and was to move close along the Oise—the third corps remaining half a march in rear of the 1st. The right column, formed by the 4th corps d'armée, was to advance along a parallel road, keeping on a line with the former, and at the distance of about half a march. The left column moved upon Compiegne, the right upon Pont St. Maxence.

At nine o'clock, the 1st corps d'armée (Zieten's) commenced its march from Etroeung towards Guise. The advanced guard, under Major General Jagow, to which were attached the 8th foot-battery, and two 10-pounder howitzers, halted when opposite to St. Laurent, a suburb of Guise, in order to observe the fortress on this side; whilst Zieten sent an infantry-brigade, a regiment of cavalry, together with a horse, and a foot, battery, by St. Germain and La Bussière, across the Oise, to menace the place from the other side.

The enemy, on finding himself completely invested, withdrew his troops into the citadel, whereupon preparations were immediately made by the Prussians to open their batteries against that part, but previously to giving the order to commence the cannonade, Zieten sent a summons to the commandant to surrender; with which the latter did not hesitate to comply. The garrison, consisting of 18 officers and 350 men, laid down their arms on the glacis, and were made prisoners of war. The Prussians found in the place, 14 pieces of cannon, 3,000 muskets, 2,000,000 musket-ball cartridges, a quantity of ammunition, and considerable magazines; and gained, what was of more importance, another strong point in their new base of operations, without having fired a single cannon-shot. Major Müller, with the two weak fusilier-battalions of the 28th regiment, and of the 2nd Westphalian landwehr, remained to garrison the place.

As soon as the remainder of Zieten's corps arrived near Guise, which was before the place surrendered, the advanced guard, consisting of the 3rd brigade, moved on, but did not reach Origny before nine o'clock in the evening. The 1st regiment of Silesian hussars pushed on as far as Ribemont. Parties were also detached from the reserve-cavalry towards Crecy, Pont à Bussy, and La Fère, to observe the Serre.

Thielemann, with the 3rd corps d'armée, moved from Avesnes upon Nouvion, which he reached about four o'clock in the afternoon. The detachments of observation which had been previously sent out to the left from this corps, to endeavour to gain intelligence concerning Grouchy's army, reached Hirson and Vervin in the evening. Scouring parties were also sent towards the road leading from Mezières by Montcornet towards Laon.

Bülow, with the 4th corps d'armée, which formed the right Prussian column, marched from Femy to Aisonville and Bernonville. Parties of cavalry, detached from the corps, reached Chatillon sur Oise, and found St. Quentin unoccupied. This circumstance having been made known to General Sydow, upon his arrival at Fontaine notre Dame, with the advanced guard, he pushed on, and took possession of that important town. A detachment of from 500 to 600 French cavalry had marched from this place on the previous day towards Laon. The troops which had been employed in the investment of Landrecies rejoined the 4th corps on this day.

By means of these movements, and of the halt of the Duke of Wellington at Le Cateau, the Prussians were a day's march in advance of the Anglo-allied army.

Grouchy's troops this day reached Réthel.

The positions of the respective armies on the evening of the 24th were as follows:—

The 1st, 2nd, and 3rd divisions of the Anglo-allied army were in and around Le Cateau Cambresis: the 4th division at Cambray; the 5th and 6th divisions, the Brunswick corps, and reserve-artillery, at, and in the vicinity of, Engle-Fontaine.

The Duke of Wellington's head-quarters were at Le Cateau Cambresis.

The 1st Prussian corps d'armée was at Guise, the 3rd at Muvion, and the 4th at Aisonville and Bernonville.

Prince Blücher's head-quarters were at Henappe.

The French troops under Soult were at Laon; those under Grouchy at Réthel.

On the 24th, the Provisional Government in Paris, which had been appointed on the previous day, after a stormy discussion in both chambers on the subject of the recognition of Napoleon II., and which consisted of the Duke of Otranto (Fouché), minister of the police; the Duke of Vicenza (Caulincourt), minister of foreign affairs; Carnot, minister of the interior; General Grenier; and M. Quinette; issued the following proclamation:—

'Frenchmen!

'Within the period of a few days, brilliant successes and dreadful reverses have marked your destinies.

'A great sacrifice appeared necessary to your peace and that of the world; and Napoleon abdicated the imperial throne. His abdication forms the termination of his political life. His son is proclaimed.

'Your new constitution, which possesses as yet only good principles, is about to undergo its application, and even those principles are to be purified and extended.

'There no longer exist powers jealous of one another. The space is free to the enlightened patriotism of your representatives; and the peers feel, think, and vote, as they are directed by the public opinion.

'After twenty-five years of political tempests, the moment has arrived when every thing wise and sublime that has been conceived respecting social institutions may be perfected in yours. Let reason and genius speak, and from whatever side their voices may proceed, they shall be heard.

'Plenipotentiaries have been despatched, in order to treat in the name of the nation, and to negotiate with the powers of Europe that peace which they have promised on one condition, which is now fulfilled.

'The whole world will, like you, be attentive to their reply. Their answer will make known whether justice and promises are accounted any thing on earth.

'Frenchmen! be united! Let all rally under circumstances of such vast importance. Let civil discords be appeased. Let dissensions be silent at this period, in which the great interests of nations are to be discussed. From the northern frontier to the Pyrenees, and from La Vendée to Marseilles, let all France be united.

'Who is the man, that, born on the soil of France, whatever may be his party or political opinions, will not range himself under the national standard, to defend the independence of the country?

'Armies may in part be destroyed, but the experience of all ages, and of all nations, proves that a brave people, combating for justice and liberty, cannot be vanquished.

'The Emperor, in abdicating, has offered himself a sacrifice. The members of the government devote themselves to the due execution of the authority with which they have been invested by your representatives.

'The Duke of Otranto,

'June 24th, 1815.' 'T. Berlier, Secretary.'

On the 25th, Louis XVIII., at the suggestion of the Duke of Wellington, despatched an officer, Le Comte d'Audenarde, with a summons, in His Majesty's name, for the governor, Baron Roos, to surrender the citadel of Cambray. The summons was obeyed, and the garrison capitulated; when the Duke immediately gave over the fortress entirely to His Majesty.

The main body of the Anglo-allied army advanced this day to Joncour. The 4th division continued at Cambray. The reserve moved on to Marets.

The 1st Prussian corps d'armée marched this day from Guise to Cérisy, on the road from St. Quentin to La Fère: its advanced guard pushed on to Fargnières, near the latter place. An officer and thirty dragoons were detached across the Oise, to cut off the communication between this fortress and Laon, by which means the investment of the place was effected. Along the right bank of the Oise, La Fère was protected by inundations, and no favourable points presented themselves for the establishment of batteries. On this account, preparations were made in the night to cross the river below the place, and gain the heights which command the fortress on the Laon side.

During the march of the advanced guard, Major General Jagow, who commanded it, sent a detachment of the 1st Silesian hussars to Chauny, which communicated by its left, through St. Gobain, with Captain Goschitzky in Crespy, and by its left, with the outpost at Jussy, of the advanced guard of the 4th corps. The parties detached on the previous day to Crecy, Pont à Bussy, and along the Serre, were now called in.

The 3rd Prussian corps d'armée marched from Nouvion to Homblières and its vicinity. Two of its brigades occupied passages across the Oise, namely, the 9th at Origny, and the 12th at Neuvillette. The 11th brigade bivouacked at Marey, and the 10th at Homblières and Menil St. Laurent. The detachments sent out from this corps on the previous day towards the road leading from Mezières to Laon, brought in word that at eleven o'clock on the forenoon of the 24th, the French troops had abandoned Aubenton, and marched off to Monternet; also that Grouchy's army had reached Rocroi on the 23rd, and Réthel on the 24th; and it was presumed that his next march was to be on Soissons. On the receipt of this intelligence these detachments were drawn back, and their observation limited to the ground nearest to the left bank of the Oise.

The advanced guard of the 4th Prussian corps d'armée was closely followed by the reserve-cavalry, and all these troops were placed under the command of Prince William of Prussia. The cavalry marched along the road leading to Chauny, as far as Montescour, where it bivouacked. The main body of the corps reached Essigny le grand.

At St. Quentin, Prince Blücher received a letter from Laon addressed to the Allied commanders by the commissioners sent from the two chambers of the French parliament; in which they communicated the fact of Napoleon's abdication, and of the elevation of his son to the throne, and stated that they had been deputed by the provisional government to negotiate an armistice. To this the Prince replied verbally, by an aide-de-camp, that he would suspend hostilities on arriving at Paris, provided Buonaparte was given up to him, and several fortresses on the frontiers delivered up as sureties; and provided, also, that the Duke of Wellington should agree to what might be proposed.

According to the accounts which were this day received from Lieut. Colonel Schmiedeberg it was presumed that the enemy was still at Laon. The reports from the detachments of the 3rd corps d'armée also confirmed this view, and intimated that Grouchy's troops were yet two marches distant from Laon. This intelligence, combined with the attempts made by the French to induce the Allies to enter into negotiations, clearly shewed the importance of endeavouring, by means of a forced march, to gain the passages of the Oise, and then to intercept the enemy's line of retreat by Soissons upon Paris. In the night of the 25th, however, decided information was received that the French army had marched from Laon to Soissons, a fact from which it was naturally concluded that the enemy was no longer deceived as to the advance of the Prussians towards Laon, and that he was therefore bent upon effecting his further retreat, or, perhaps, even of anticipating their movements towards the Oise, and detaching towards Compiegne. Hence, not a moment was now to be lost in securing the points of passage, particularly that at Compiegne, to which Prince Blücher attached so much more importance from the circumstance that his army had no pontoons; and that the British pontoon-train was still far behind, and not to be calculated upon. The Prince decided upon moving his left column (the 1st and 3rd corps) on Compiegne, and his right column (the 4th corps) upon Pont St. Maxence; the latter to secure the passage both at this place and at Creil, lower down the Oise.

Soult, who had been indefatigable in collecting at Laon the remains of the defeated portion of the French army, marched the latter, on the 25th, to Soissons, where it was to be joined by the force under Grouchy, who, having preceded his troops, which were yet a march and a half distant, had arrived in that town, to take the command of the whole army, according to instructions conveyed to him from the Provisional Government. Soult, as soon as he found himself thus superseded in the command, quitted the army, and repaired to Paris, disgusted with the abrupt and uncourteous manner in which he had been treated.

The positions of the respective armies, on the evening of the 25th, were as follows :—

Of the Anglo-allied army, the advanced guard (Vivian's brigade) was at Crisour, near St. Quentin.

The 2nd division, the Nassau troops, and the British cavalry, were encamped in the vicinity of Joncour.

The 1st and 3rd divisions, the Dutch-Belgian infantry attached to the 1st corps, and the Dutch-Belgian cavalry, were encamped near Serain and Premont.

The 4th division, with Grant's light cavalry-brigade, was at Cambray.

The 5th and 6th divisions, the Brunswick infantry and cavalry, and the reserve-artillery, were encamped at, and in the vicinity of, Marets.

The Duke of Wellington's head-quarters were at Joncour.

The 1st Prussian corps d'armée was at Cérisy; the 3rd at Homblières; and the 4th at Essigny le grand.

Prince Blücher's head-quarters were at St. Quentin.

The right wing of the French army, led by Vandamme, was at Rheims; the left, with Grouchy, at Soissons.

On the 25th, Napoleon withdrew from the capital to the country palace of Malmaison, whence he issued the following address to the army:—

'SOLDIERS!

'While obeying the necessity which removes me from the French army, I carry with me the happy assurance that it will justify, by the eminent services which the country expects from it, the praises which our enemies themselves have not been able to refuse it.

'Soldiers! I shall follow your steps, though absent. I know all the corps; and not one of them will obtain a single advantage over the enemy, but I shall give it credit for the courage it may have displayed. Both you and I have been calumniated. Men, very unfit to appreciate your labours, have seen in the marks of attachment which you have given me, a zeal of which I was the sole object. Let your future successes convince them that it was the country, above all things, which you served in obeying me; and that if I had any share in your affection, I owe it to my ardent love for France—our common mother.

'Soldiers! Some efforts more, and the coalition will be dissolved. Napoleon will recognise you by the blows which you are about to strike. Save the honour, the independence, of France! Be, unto the last, the same men which I have known you for these twenty years, and you will be invincible.

'NAPOLEON.'

'De la Malmaison, le 25 juin, 1815.

CHAPTER XIX.

On the 26th the Duke of Wellington marched the main body of his army to Vermand and its vicinity. Major General Sir John Byng, who was now in command of the 1st corps, having heard, on passing that village, that the Duke himself was there, immediately waited upon His Grace for any orders he might wish to give him. The Duke, on seeing him, said, "You are the very person I wish to see—I want you to take Peronne. You may as well take with you a brigade of guards, and a Dutch-Belgian brigade. I shall be there almost as soon as yourself." Byng having given the necessary orders for Maitland's brigade, and a Dutch-Belgian brigade of Chassé's division attached to his corps, to proceed on this duty, the former was immediately put in motion. The Duke, on reaching Peronne just as these troops arrived there, summoned the garrison, and then proceeded, in person, to reconnoitre that fortress; and perceiving the possibility of taking it by storm, gave orders to prepare for an assault. His Grace then directed the attack to be made upon the horn-work which covers the suburb on the left of the Somme. Lieut. Colonel Lord Saltoun immediately led on the light troops of Maitland's brigade, stormed, and carried the out-work, with but little loss; on observing which, the Duke, being satisfied the place would prove an easy capture, returned to Vermand. Some pieces of Dutch artillery were now brought into the horn-work, and a cannonade was opened upon the town, but the fire kept up on both sides was trifling, and of short duration, for Byng having sent forward his acting Assistant Quarter Master General, Lieut. Colonel the Hon. J. Stanhope,* with a white flag, the civil authorities interfered, and urged the garrison to capitulate; whereupon the maiden fortress of Peronne surrendered on the condition that its defenders should lay down their arms, and be allowed to repair to their homes. Byng,† on return-

* Lieut. Colonel the Hon J. Stanhope, h.p., Portuguese service, died in March, 1825.

† In the course of the battle on the 18th, this officer, (the present Earl of Strafford,) experienced a hair-breadth escape, of a very singular nature. It was with him a habit, when tired with long sitting on horseback, to raise and extend an arm by way of temporary relief. He had just raised his right arm in this manner, when a round shot, grazing his right breast, entered the folds of his cloak, immediately under the shoulder of that arm, and tore its way through the

ing to Vermand, to report the capture of the fortress to the Duke, met the Dutch-Belgian brigade, which had been ordered to move to Peronne at the same time as the guards, about half way towards that place!

Colville's division rejoined the main body of the army from Cambray, which place was handed over to the troops of the King of France, under the Duke of Berry.

The reserve moved on to Bellicourt and Belle Englise.

Upon returning in the night to his head-quarters at Vermand, the Duke of Wellington found a note from Prince Blücher, forwarding to him the letter from the French commissioners, before referred to,* and to which his Grace immediately replied as follows:—

'Head Quarters, 26th June, 1815.—10 P.M.

'As Field Marshal the Duke of Wellington has only at this moment returned to his quarters, he has only now received from Marshal Prince Blücher the letter of their Excellencies, and which their Excellencies had sent to the Prussian outposts.

'When the Field Marshal last heard from the head-quarters of the Allied Sovereigns, the 21st instant, their Majesties were at Heidelberg, and they must still be in that direction. It must be obvious to their Excellencies that the Field Marshal can neither prevent nor aid their Excellencies in reaching their Majesties; but if he has it in his power, or if their Excellencies think proper to pass through the countries in which the troops are under his command, the Field Marshal begs they will let him know in what manner he ean facilitate their journey.

'The Field Marshal was not aware that any officer commanding an advanced post had agreed verbally, or in any other manner, to a suspension of hostilities.

'Since the 15th instant, when Napoleon Buonaparte, at the head of the French armies, invaded the dominions of the King of the Netherlands, and attacked the Prussian army, the Field Marshal has considered his Sovereign, and those Powers whose armies he commands, in a state of war with the Government of France; and he does not consider the abdication of Napoleon Buonaparte of his usurped authority, under all the circumstances which have preceded and attended that measure, as the attainment of the object held out in the declarations and treaties of the Allies, which should induce them to lay down their arms.

'The Field Marshal cannot consent therefore to any suspension of hostilities, however desirous he is of preventing the further effusion of blood.

'As the only object on which their Excellencies desired to converse with the Field Marshal was the proposed suspension of hostilities, they will, probably, after the perusal of his sentiments and intentions, as above declared, consider any interview with him an useless waste of time; but, if their Excellencies should still do him the honour to desire to have an interview with him, the Field Marshal will be ready to meet them at the time and place they shall appoint.

'The Field Marshal begs their Excellencies will receive the assurance of his high consideration. WELLINGTON.'†

From the moment that Prince Blücher had become aware of the retirement of the French troops from Laon upon Soissons, he was most anxious to secure the passage across the

cloak, behind his back, towards his left. The gallant general was thrown from his horse by the concussion, and remained insensible for a short time; after which he re-mounted, and continued at the head of his division.

* See page 458.

† Despatches, vol. xii. p. 512.

Oise at Compiegne, Verberie, Pont St. Maxence, and Creil. In the middle of the night of the 25th, he therefore sent an order for the advanced guard of the 1st Prussian corps d'armée to proceed on the following day, from Fargnières, by forced march, as far as the first named place. In the afternoon of the 26th, it reached Noyon, where it halted for a rest, having marched five leagues, and having nearly an equal distance before it to Compiegne. The 12-pounder battery and the four 10-pounder howitzers which had been attached to this advanced guard (the 3rd brigade under Major General Jagow) were, by Zieten's order, left under the protection of a battalion, to be employed with the 1st brigade, which was directed to make an attempt upon the fortress of La Fère. The advanced guard, after having sent on a squadron of the 1st Silesian hussars, under Major Hertel, to Compiegne, with orders to push forward a detachment thence upon the road to Soissons, resumed its march in the evening. It was still in movement about midnight, when Major General Jagow received a communication from the front that Major Hertel had, with his squadron, entered Compiegne at eight o'clock, in the evening, and had learned from the mayor that a French corps was on the march from Soissons to that town, in which it had already bespoken 10,000 rations. Jagow immediately communicated this importaut circumstance to Zieten, and ordered his troops, after another short but indispensable halt, to continue their toilsome march.

On the morning of this day, the 1st brigade of Zieten's corps d'armée completed the investment of La Fère. The troops that had been previously detached to this point by General Jagow were moved off to follow this officer's brigade on the road to Compiegne. Notwithstanding the vigorous bombardment which the Prussians maintained against the fortress until noon, and by which several buildings were set on fire, they failed to induce the garrison to surrender. As it was not intended, however, to attempt any more serious attack, the brigade, after leaving the fusilier-battalion of the 12th regiment and a squadron of the Brandenburg uhlans to watch the fortress, followed the corps d'armée, which had marched to Noyon, but it did not even reach Chauny, scarcely seven miles from La Fère.

Zieten, on arriving at Chauny at eight o'clock in the evening, with the remainder of his corps—the 2nd and 4th brigades, the reserve-artillery, and a reserve cavalry-brigade—considered his troops too much fatigued to fulfil Blücher's intentions that they should march as far as Noyon, and he therefore ordered them to bivouack at Chauny.

The 3rd Prussian corps d'armée marched from the vicinity of Homblières to that of Guiscard; partly by Jussy, and partly by St. Quentin and Ham. It was only the 11th brigade, with the greater portion of the reserve-cavalry and artillery that took the latter road. These troops on reaching the fortified town of Ham, found it occupied by the enemy, who seemed prepared to oppose their passing through the place. General Hobe, who commanded them, summoned the commander of the garrison to open the gates and allow the troops to march through, and on perceiving that this summons was disobeyed, he tried the effect of a few cannon-shot, which quickly procured a free passage for his force. No further notice was taken, and no further use was made, by the Prussians of this otherwise insignificant place. A detachment of the reserve-cavalry of this corps was sent to Chauny, from which it pushed forward a small party along the road towards Soissons, which the latter pursued until on arriving at about a league beyond Coucy, it came upon an enemy's outpost, consisting of a regiment of dragoons and a battalion of infantry.

The 4th corps d'armée was also required to make a forced march on this day—namely, from Essigny le grand as far as Lassigny, and its advanced guard was to reach Gournay, and thence push forward detachments to Clermont, Creil, and Pont St. Maxence, for the purpose of securing and examining the bridges across the Oise, and of preparing all that was requisite for effecting a passage for the troops. Bülow, in his brigade-orders, drew the attention of his troops to the necessity which had arisen for those forced marches on the part of the Prussian army with a view to obtain a decisive result. The advanced guard started at four o'clock in the morning from Jussy, and proceeded by Lassigny to Gournay, situated upon the road from Peronne to Pont St. Maxence; but the detachments which it sent thence towards Clermont, Creil, Pont St. Maxence, and Verberie, did not reach those places until the following day. The reserve-artillery of the 4th corps commenced its march at five o'clock in the morning, following the advanced guard, and reached Ressons late in the evening; where it bivouacked, as did also, subsequently, the main body of the corps, after a march of about twenty-five miles.

Whilst the Prussians were thus, on the 26th, hastening towards Compiegne, the French General, Count d'Erlon, was, on this very day, also marching upon that point from Soissons, with the remains of his corps d'armée—about 4,000 men—having succeeded, through his urgent representations of the expediency of such a movement, in obtaining Grouchy's assent to its execution.

The troops of the 3rd and 4th French corps d'armée moved this day from Rheims towards Soissons, a distance which they could not, however, accomplish in one day's march.

The positions of the respective armies on the evening of the 26th, were as follows :—

Of the Anglo-allied army, the advanced guard (Vivian's hussar-brigade) was at Mattignies, near the Somme, having its picquets on that river.*

The 2nd division, the Nassau troops, and the British cavalry, were encamped near Beauvois and Lanchy.

The 1st and 3rd divisions, the Dutch-Belgian infantry attached to the 1st corps, and the Dutch-Belgian cavalry, were encamped near Caulaincourt and Martin de Des Près.

The 4th division was encamped at Gouay.

The 1st British brigade of guards was at Peronne.

---

* Vivian had on this day sent forward Lieutenant Slayter Smith,[1] of the 10th hussars, *en reconnaissance*, as far as Nesle, with directions to proceed, if practicable, to Roye, and gain information concerning the movements of the French army. Lieutenant Smith, having reached the latter place, ascertained that French troops had left the town the night before, and that a body of *Gensd'armerie* had marched out at one end of the town, whilst he and his party had entered by the other. On returning from Nesle, he had proceeded but a short distance, when he perceived a carriage moving rapidly, and coming from a cross road. He ordered the driver to halt, and found in the carriage a military-looking man, who, after some evasive answers to his questions, acknowledged himself to be General Lauriston, aide-de-camp to Napoleon; and stated that he was going, in the first instance, to his country-seat at Vœux, near Le Cateau, and then to join the King, Louis XVIII. He added that he had gone to Paris to raise a party for His Majesty, that he had not only failed in the attempt, but had narrowly escaped being arrested. Having given this explanation, he entreated Lieutenant Smith to allow him to continue his route, but the latter, considering it his duty to make him a prisoner, took him that night to Sir Hussey Vivian, who then desired Lieutenant Smith to proceed with the general to the Duke of Wellington. On reaching his Grace's quarters at one o'clock in the morning, and intimating his errand, a curious incident occurred. There was no guard at the house, not even a sentry, and Smith had some difficulty in rousing a sleepy servant from amongst his fellows, to announce him. The Duke was engaged in conversation with a Frenchman. On a table in the room appeared the *débris* of a repast. Having explained to the Duke the name and rank of the individual he had brought with him, his Grace said, "Bring him in." On hearing the name of Lauriston, the Frenchman before mentioned, who had been sent to the Duke by Fouché, to treat for a cessation of hostilities, became greatly alarmed, and begged to know how he might escape without being recognised. His Grace remarked, "There is but one door and one window—take your choice." He preferred the door, and escaped by passing behind the Duke's back as Lauriston entered. An animated conversation ensued between the two generals, and an hour had elapsed in this way, when the Duke gave his orders to Lieutenant Smith for the disposal of the General; whom he subsequently sent to the King, much to his annoyance, since he was thus obliged to appear before His Majesty as a prisoner instead of a volunteer.

1 Now Captain William Slayter Smith, h.p. 72nd regiment.

The reserve, consisting of the 5th and 6th divisions, the Brunswick troops, and the reserve-artillery was encamped near Nourois, Magny, and Bellenglise.

The pontoon-train was at Estrées.

The Duke of Wellington's head-quarters were at Vermand.

The 2nd and 4th brigades of the 1st Prussian corps d'armée were at Chauny, not far from which was also the 1st brigade. The 3rd brigade, forming the advanced guard, was on the march to Compiegne.

The 3rd corps was at Guiscard.

The 4th corps was at Ressons.

Prince Blücher's head-quarters were at Genvry, near Noyon.

The French troops under d'Erlon were not far from Compiegne, on the road from Soissons. Those of the 3rd and 4th corps, under Vandamme, were at some point between Rheims and Soissons.

Grouchy's head-quarters were at Soissons.

It was half-past four o'clock in the morning of the 27th, when the advanced guard of the Prussian corps d'armée, (the 3rd brigade,) after a forced march of about 25 miles, reached Compiegne. General Jagow immediately posted his troops, in the most advantageous manner, in and about the town, so as to be prepared to meet any attack that the enemy might make, and detached three squadrons of the 1st Silesian hussars upon the Soissons road, and the remaining squadron upon the Paris road, in observation. About five o'clock, by which time he had scarcely completed his arrangements, information reached him from the hussars on the Soissons road that the enemy was advancing. This was, as before remarked, Count d'Erlon, with the remains of his corps d'armée, from which circumstance it will be seen that if Zieten's advanced guard had arrived but a single half hour later, the French would have anticipated the Prussians in securing the bridge of Compiegne.

From along the edge of the extensive wood which adjoins this town, a fire was quickly opened by the French skirmishers against the Prussian picquets. Very shortly afterwards a column of infantry appeared advancing from their rear. A half-battery of Prussian horse-artillery, which had been posted on the Soissons road, in front of the gate on that side of the town, having allowed the column to approach within a suitable range, directed a fire upon it with such vigour and precision, that in a few moments more the mass rushed for shelter into the wood. Four French guns were now brought forward, and these replied to the Prussian artillery; during which the enemy moved through the wood to his left. The Prussians concluded from this movement that he contemplated abandoning the attack in this quarter, for the purpose of assailing the lower and weaker side of the town, by the Crespy and Paris roads; but on renewing his advance, he soon showed that he was only masking his retreat; whereupon the 1st

Silesian hussars advanced along the road to Soissons in pursuit.

By the result of this affair, which lasted an hour and a half, but was limited to a cannonade and mutual tiraillade, the French were foiled in their attempt to cover their retreat by securing Compiegne, and checking the advance of the Prussians along the Oise. The 3rd Prussian brigade, however, which had continually formed the advanced guard of the 1st corps d'armée since the battle of Waterloo, was too much exhausted by its efforts during the previous day and night, to attempt seriously to molest the enemy during his retreat; a circumstance of which the latter failed not to take advantage. Zieten decided upon relieving these troops from the duties of an advanced guard by the 2nd brigade, which, however, had not yet come up: and hence the French gained some valuable time.

The main body of Zieten's corps did not reach Compiegne until mid-day. Blücher, who had already arrived there, ordered that the advanced guard (now consisting of the 2nd brigade) and the reserve-cavalry, preceded by 100 riflemen, should march through the wood, towards Villers-Cotterets, followed by the main body of the corps, it having been his intention to throw these troops upon the enemy's line of retreat, in the event of the advanced guard falling in with French troops at or near that point. This order, however, was not strictly followed by Zieten, who marched the main body of his corps, including the reserve-cavalry, and the reserve-artillery, through the wood of Compiegne, to Gillicourt, detaching only his 2nd brigade, reinforced by the Brandenburg dragoons and five pieces of horse artillery, towards Villers-Cotterets. The 1st Silesian hussars were pushed forward upon the road from Compiegne to Soissons, to cover the left flank during this movement. The reserve-cavalry, in front of the column of the main body, reached Gillicourt just as the enemy (under Count d'Erlon) had crossed the defile formed by a tributary stream of the Oise, in which that place is situated. The 1st West Prussian dragoons and the Brandenburg uhlans, together with a horse-battery, went on in pursuit; and the 3rd brigade was ordered to follow the latter in support. The 4th brigade was directed to maintain the defile of Gillicourt.

The enemy's rear-guard was overtaken on this side of Crespy by the two regiments of cavalry, which threw it back in disorder upon that town. The French quickly retired from the place, whereupon the 3rd brigade, with a cavalry-brigade, bivouacked there, throwing out parties of dragoons in the direction of the enemy's retreat.

The 4th brigade, the other cavalry-brigade, and the reserve-artillery, bivouacked at Gillicourt. The 2nd brigade, with the additional force attached to it, as before mentioned, reached Longpré, not far from Villers-Cotterets, in the middle of the night. The long march which the troops of the 1st corps d'armée made this day from Noyon, and the probability of their coming into collision with the enemy on the following day, rendered a few hours' rest absolutely necessary.

Separated from one another as Zieten's brigades thus were, a strong support was essentially requisite, and this was supplied in good time by the 3rd Prussian corps d'armée which marched on this day from Guiscard to Compiegne. Prince Blücher directed its commander, Thielemann, to detach strongly towards Soissons, for the purpose of observing the enemy, and of molesting him should he be retiring. The cavalry thus detached presenting the means of covering Zieten's left flank, the 1st Silesian hussars, which had been previously posted on the Soissons road, were directed to rejoin their own corps. The 3rd corps bivouacked on the left bank of the Oise, with the exception of the 12th brigade, which remained on the right bank, at Venette.

On the same day, the 4th Prussian corps d'armée, forming the right column, marched from Ressons and its vicinity, with orders to cross the Oise lower down the stream, at Verberie, Pont St. Maxence, or Creil. Bülow formed his advanced guard with the 3rd Neumark landwehr, a battalion of the 1st Silesian landwehr, the 8th hussars, the 1st Pomeranian landwehr-cavalry, and half the horse-battery No. 12, and desired General Sydow, who commanded the advanced guard, to move off with a detachment, at the first break of day, and secure the bridge over the Oise at Creil. This general, aware of the importance of attaining the object in view, proceeded himself, at the head of a squadron of the 8th hussars, and of 100 infantry, the latter being transported in carts, and reached Creil with this small detachment just as the French were on the point of entering the place. The latter were immediately attacked and repulsed, and the Prussian infantry occupied the bridge, which, on the arrival of the advanced guard, was given over to the first Silesian landwehr, whilst the remainder of the troops, after a short halt, commenced their march upon Senlis.

Another striking instance was thus again afforded of the

vast importance of a correct calculation of time in military operations. The Prussians, on this morning, reached the bridge of Compiegne only half an hour before the French approached it, and had they arrived at Creil but a few minutes later, they would have found the French in possession of the bridge at this point.

Major Blankenburg was detached in advance, with the 1st Pomeranian landwehr-cavalry, from Creil towards Senlis. They had but just reached this town, and had begun to bivouack on the great market-place, when, towards nine o'clock in the evening, Kellermann, with the 1st cuirassier-brigade of French cavalry, approached on the opposite side, and made a dash at the very spot occupied by the Prussians. Major Blankenburg had barely time to mount: nevertheless, with such of his men as were accoutred and prepared, he attacked the French horsemen, and drove them back to the gates of the town. The latter, however, collecting their strength, renewed their attack, overpowered the Prussians, and forced them to retire along the road to Pont St. Maxence. Kellermann's brigade then resumed its march along the prescribed line of retreat. In the mean time, his 2nd cuirassier-brigade, and d'Erlon's French corps d'armée, were retiring along the same road towards Senlis. Upon this point also General Sydow was moving from Creil, with the advanced guard of the 4th Prussian corps, following, as it was supposed, the detached 1st Pomeranian landwehr-cavalry. On reaching Senlis at ten o'clock in the evening, with the head of the column, consisting of the 8th hussars and the 3rd battalion of the 3rd Neumark landwehr, and finding the place unoccupied, he took possession of it. The French troops had already approached close to the town, from the side of Crespy. The Prussian infantry were immediately posted in the houses nearest to the gate, and as soon as the enemy's cavalry came fully within the effective range of musketry, they suddenly opened upon the latter a sharp fire, which compelled it to go about. The head of d'Erlon's corps now came up, but was forced, along with the cavalry, to take another direction. Sydow, having collected the whole of the advanced guard, followed the French some little distance, and bivouacked, about midnight, somewhat in advance of Senlis. The latter, however, reached, next morning, the road leading through Gonesse to Paris.

During the operation of the advanced guard of the 4th Prussian corps d'armée, another detachment of the latter was sent to occupy Pont St. Maxence and Verberie. The French having partially destroyed the bridge at the former point, the 2nd Pomeranian landwehr-cavalry were ferried to the opposite bank of the river, and detachments were immediately pushed on to Verberie and Senlis. The 14th brigade followed the cavalry, and was passed over the river in a similar manner, after which it occupied the heights on both sides of the great Paris road. These troops bivouacked for the night on their position; whilst the main body of the corps, on reaching Pont St. Maxence, remained on the right bank of the river. The greatest activity was used in repairing the bridge sufficiently for the passage of artillery.

In this manner Blücher had effectually secured the line of the Oise, and by pushing forward his advanced troops as far as Villers-Cotterets, had closed so much upon the flank of the retiring enemy, that he had every reasonable expectation of succeeding in cutting off the line of retreat of the latter upon the capital.

Grouchy, on discovering that the detachments he had thrown out to gain the passages of the Oise, on his left, had been thwarted by the rapidity of the Prussian movement, and had been compelled to fall back, now employed them in covering his retreat by means of partial combats. Hence arose the engagements at Compiegne, Crespy, and Senlis; but such was the feebleness of the French resistance, and so frequent were the desertions of the soldiers, who threw away their arms, and fled to their homes, that it was evident the re-organization of the army, and the re-animation of its former spirit, were far from having been thoroughly effected. It has been said that a cry of alarm spread through its ranks of, "Our retreat is cut off!" as soon as it was known that the Prussians were upon its left flank. At all events it appears tolerably certain that the army was not in that state which would have warranted Grouchy in risking any serious stand against the Prussians. To succeed in reaching the capital, by means of forced marches, and to secure his troops, as far as practicable, from molestation, was all that he could hope to accomplish.

On the 27th, the main body of the Anglo-allied army, crossing the Somme at Willecourt, marched through Nesle upon Roye.

The 4th division marched through Peronne, towards Roye.

Two battalions of the Dutch-Belgian brigade at Peronne were ordered to remain in occupation of that place: the remainder of the brigade, and the brigade of guards at Peronne, marched through Nesle to the village of Crescy, and joined the 1st corps.

The 5th division, the Brunswick cavalry, and the reserve-brigade of howitzers, moved upon Ham.

The 6th division, the Brunswick infantry, and the reserve-artillery, encamped between the villages of Douilly and Villers.

Notwithstanding the precautions which the Duke of Wellington had taken to ensure the orderly conduct of his troops, and to conciliate in their favour the good disposition of the inhabitants along the line of march, it being his anxious desire that they should be considered as being on a friendly footing, and as acting on behalf of the legitimate sovereign, there was one portion of his army which committed the greatest excesses: these were the Dutch-Belgian troops, who set his orders on this head completely at defiance. They pillaged wherever they went, not even excepting the head-quarters, the house which he himself occupied: they forced the safeguards, and rescued, at the point of the bayonet, the prisoners from the gensd'armerie which the Duke had formed for the police of the army. Two of the officers had just rendered themselves conspicuous by participating in, and actually encouraging, these disorders, which had arisen to such a height as to arouse his Grace's just indignation and severe censure. He desired the general officer then in command of that part of the army to put in full force his general order of the 26th of June, to cause a roll-call of companies to be made every hour, and to see that every officer and soldier was present. He also directed him to place the two officers before alluded to in arrest, and to send them to the Hague, to be disposed of by the King of the Netherlands, to whom he forwarded a copy of the letter containing these instructions. This letter, which strongly evidenced the feelings of annoyance, under which the Duke wrote it, concluding with the following cutting reproof:—"Je ne veux pas commander de tels officiers. Je suis assez longtemps soldat pour savoir que les pillards, et ceux qui les encouragent, ne valent rien devant l'ennemi; et je n'en veux pas."

The following were the positions of the respective armies on the evening of the 27th:—

The 1st Prussian corps d'armée had its main body at Gillicourt; its 2nd brigade at Longpré, about half a league from Villers-Cotterets; and its 3rd brigade at Crespy.

The main body of the 3rd Prussian corps d'armée was at Compiegne: it had strong detachments in the direction of Soissons.

The main body of the 4th Prussian corps was at Pont St. Maxence: it had its advanced guard at Senlis, and detachments at Creil and Verberie.

Prince Blücher's head-quarters were at Compiegne.

Of the Anglo-allied army, the 2nd division, the Nassau troops, and the British and Hanoverian cavalry, were in the vicinity of Roye.

The 3rd division, one brigade of the 1st division, the Dutch-Belgian infantry attached to the 1st corps, and the Dutch-Belgian cavalry were encamped near the villages of Crescy, Billencourt, and Bereuil.

The 4th division was at the village of Puzeaux, on the road to Roye.

The brigade of guards was at Crescy.

The 5th division and the Brunswick cavalry were at Ham.

The 6th division, the Brunswick infantry, and the reserve-artillery, were between the villages of Douilly and Villers.

The Duke of Wellington's head-quarters were at Nesle.

The remains of the 1st and 2nd French corps d'armée, detachments from which had this day been defeated at Compiegne, Crespy, Creil, and Senlis, were in full retreat, partly upon the Senlis, and partly upon the Soissons, road.

The imperial guards and the 6th corps were at Villers-Cotterets.

The 3rd and 4th corps were at Soissons.

Grouchy's head-quarters were at Villers-Cotterets.

General Pirch II. having learned, upon his arrival at one o'clock of the morning of the 28th, with the advanced guard of the 1st Prussian corps d'armée, at Longpré, near Villers-Cotterets, that the latter place was not occupied by the enemy in any force, determined to capture the place forthwith by a surprise. The troops detached to the front on this service (the fusilier-battalion of the 6th regiment and the Brandenburg dragoons) favoured by the darkness, (which as yet was scarcely relieved by the approaching dawn), as also by the wood through which they advanced, fell upon a detachment that was moving by a by-road through the wood, consisting of a French horse-battery of 14 guns, 20 ammunition-waggons, and an escort of 150 men. The whole vicinity of Villers-Cotterets was, in fact, filled with French troops, thus dispersed, that they might sooner obtain refreshment after the long march, and be prepared to start again at two o'clock in the morning. Thus they were all in motion at the time of this capture. General Pirch now pushed on to Villers-Cotterets, where the Prussians made many prisoners. Grouchy himself narrowly escaped being taken as he was mounting his horse and hastening out of the opposite side of the town. On reaching the windmill height, upon the road to Nanteuil, he succeeded in collecting together and forming his troops. Pirch, after detaching cavalry in pursuit of the enemy, as also towards Longpré to cover his right, and towards Soissons to protect his left, took up a defensive position. He deployed his infantry, with the foot-battery, upon the height at the garden of the château, posted two battalions at the point of a wood that jutted out on his right, and was still occupied in making his arrangements, when a cavalry-detachment, on the Soissons road, sent in word that a hostile corps was to be seen approaching from Soissons. Another report was received immediately afterwards, that the enemy showed much cavalry on that side, and was already detaching two regiments of the latter arm towards the

Prussian left flank, as also another cavalry-force, along with from 20 to 25 pieces of artillery, against the right flank. In the mean time, the French Marshal had collected about 9,000 men on the height before mentioned, near the road to Nanteuil, one third of whom had already constituted the rear-guard, and the remainder was composed of troops that had halted during the night in the vicinity, as at Vauciennes, Coyolles, and Pisseleux. With these troops, Grouchy showed every disposition to accept an engagement.

General Pirch II., finding himself thus critically situated between two separate and overpowering hostile forces, prepared to effect his retreat. This was facilitated in a peculiar manner. The troops of Vandamme's corps, perceiving the Prussians thus posted on the high road to Paris, and imagining their force to be greater than it really was, fell into the greatest disorder, and with loud cries of "Into the woods on the left, towards La Ferté Milon—we are cut off from Paris!" they all rushed in that direction, with the exception of 2,000 men and some guns conducted by Vandamme himself by the way of Pisseleux, leaving Villers-Cotterets on their right, and masking the movement by a vigorous attack upon this place. The 6th Prussian regiment was driven back by the enemy's superior numbers, and Pirch, after having kept up a brisk cannonade, gradually withdrew the regiment from Villers-Cotterets, for the purpose of moving upon Crespy, the direction previously laid down for him, with a view to the concentration of the corps. As Grouchy was moving by the Soissons road towards Nanteuil, Pirch was desirous of proceeding in a parallel direction, through Longpré, but he was subsequently induced, on consideration of the defiles in that direction, and which he did not deem it prudent to pass so near to the enemy, to prefer retiring along the Compiegne road, as far as where it is joined by the one leading from Viviers, and where, for the covering of the left flank and rear, a squadron of the Brandenburg dragoons had already been posted. From this point he struck into the road leading by Buts, and reached, towards mid-day, Frenois la Rivière, where he gave his troops a few hours' rest, and then proceeded by Crespy to Nanteuil, which place he reached about nine o'clock in the evening, having marched 21 leagues within the last 38 hours, during 6 of which he had also been engaged with the enemy. He had succeeded in creating confusion in one portion of the retiring French force, and in impeding the retreat of that which was with Grouchy himself sufficiently long to enable Zieten to anticipate the latter in his arrival at Nanteuil.

It has already been explained, when describing the proceedings of the 27th, how much separated the brigades of the 1st Prussian corps d'armée were from one another. The 1st was still on the march from La Fère (it rejoined on the afternoon of this day); the 2nd, with the Brandenburg dragoons, was near Villers-Cotterets; the 3rd, with a cavalry-brigade, was at Crespy; and the 4th, with the other cavalry-brigade was at Gillicourt. Hence Zieten was desirous, on the morning of the 28th, to concentrate his corps at Crespy, leaving only a strong cavalry-detachment at Villers-Cotterets. But whilst despatching the order to Pirch to move upon Crespy, he received a report from this general, that he had fallen upon the French troops retreating through Villers-Cotterets, and was upon the point of being driven back by superior numbers. Zieten, considering that the Prussian troops at Crespy, the nearest to Villers-Cotterets, were nearly three leagues distant from the latter point, decided upon not attempting to give any direct support to Pirch, but to advance with the 3rd brigade, together with the reserve-cavalry and artillery, towards Levignon, on the great Paris road, between Villers-Cotterets and Nanteuil, and, if possible, occupy that point before the French could reach it. He found the latter in the act of marching through the village, and immediately ordered a howitzer-battery to be drawn up, which commenced throwing shells into the place. He also ordered the 1st West Prussian dragoons, and the 1st Silesian hussars, with a horse-battery, to attack the enemy. The French, however, retired in such haste, that they were not overtaken until about midway between Levignon and Nanteuil, when they halted their rear-guard, which made front against the Prussians. They comprised the 2nd corps d'armée, under Reille, who had with him several regiments of cavalry, and continued their march, supporting, however, the rear-guard. On coming up with the latter, two squadrons of the 2nd West Prussian dragoons charged; but they were repulsed, and attacked in flank by a French regiment of lancers. The enemy now advanced, with the hope of completely routing the Prussian cavalry. This attempt failed in consequence of a most successful attack by the 1st Silesian hussars, by which the French were put to flight, and two of their guns captured. The horse-battery drew up, at the same time, on the left of the high road, and, by its effective fire, committed great havoc amidst the flying enemy, who was pursued by the Prussian cavalry even beyond Nanteuil. During the movement upon Levignon, General Hobe came up with a cavalry-brigade from the 3rd corps d'armée. It advanced by the right, along the road from Crespy to Nanteuil, with the design of intercepting a portion of the enemy's retreating columns; but the French, in the mean time, fled in such haste, that only a few prisoners were made.

Notwithstanding the pressure thus made upon the French line of retreat, Count Reille succeeded in uniting the remains of his corps d'armée with those of Count d'Erlon's corps, which had escaped through Crespy and by the left of Senlis.

The French imperial guards, and the 6th corps d'armée, which were under the more immediate orders of Grouchy, and had formed the column that retired through Villers-Cotterets in the morning, reached Levignon after Zieten had passed through it in pursuit of Reille's troops to Nanteuil; and becoming acquainted with the danger of their proceeding further on that road, they turned off to their left, to make their retreat through Assy, Meaux, Claye, and Vincennes.

General Vandamme, who, with the 3rd and 4th French corps d'armée was most in the rear, and had withdrawn from the high road at Villers-Cotterets on perceiving the Prussian brigade in possession of that place, took the direction of La Ferté Milon, Meaux, crossing the Marne to L'Agny, to Paris.

Bülow, who had been directed to move the 4th corps d'armée from Pont St. Maxence to Marly la Ville, on the 28th, deemed it advisable to augment his advanced guard, and therefore added to it the 14th brigade and the reserve-cavalry, and placed the whole under the command of Prince William of Prussia. In the afternoon Prince William fell upon detachments of d'Erlon's, and also upon Reille's corps d'armée, which latter was retreating from Nanteuil. He immediately attacked the enemy, dispersed a great number of his troops, and took more than 2,000 prisoners. It was evening before the advanced guard reached Gonesse, where it bivouacked. Detachments were pushed on to the front as far as le Bourget and Stains, which points were occupied by the enemy. The main body of the corps arrived at Marly la Ville in the evening, and halted there for the night.

Thielemann, having been directed to proceed with the 3rd corps d'armée from Compiegne to Senlis, should its support not be required by the 1st corps, marched his infantry and artillery upon Crespy, and sent the reserve-cavalry by Verberie; but on hearing that the 1st corps was engaged with the enemy, he drew in his cavalry towards Crespy, from Verberie, as soon as it arrived there. The 1st cavalry-brigade, with six pieces of horse-artillery, was pushed on from Crespy, along the road to Nanteuil, where it joined the reserve-cavalry of the 1st corps d'armée, but not in time to take any active part in the engagement at that place. The 2nd cavalry-brigade was detached towards Villers-Cotterets. The main body of the 3rd corps d'armée bivouacked for the night at Crespy and its vicinity.

Prince Blücher deemed it advisable to send, on this day, a strong detachment of cavalry, consisting of the Queen's dragoons, under Lieut. Colonel Kamecke, beyond the left of the 1st Prussian corps, towards the Marne, for the purpose of gaining intelligence of the enemy's movements in that direction. Lieut. Colonel Kamecke was instructed to act discretionally; and to proceed, subsequently, by Meaux, or Chateau Thierry, and endeavour to open a communication with the advance of the Bavarian army.

Thus it will be seen that, on the 28th, the Prussian army succeeded in cutting off the line of retreat of the French troops by the Soissons high road, compelling the greater portion of them to seek, along cross-roads, the line of the Marne, by Méaux and L'Agny. It had, since it crossed the Oise, created great disorder and confusion in the French ranks, captured 16 pieces of cannon, and made, altogether, 4,000 prisoners. The Prussians now occupied both the high roads leading from Senlis and Soissons, and had their advanced posts (those of the 4th corps d'armée) within five miles of Paris. The sound of their cannon was already heard in the capital, where the greatest consternation prevailed amongst the citizens, whose fears had been previously excited by the most exaggerated reports brought in by fugitives from the retreating army. The fortified works that had been thrown up on the north side, appeared sufficient to check the progress of the Allied armies, and to secure Paris from a *coup de main;* but time was essential for the organization of of the defence, for the recovery of the exhausted remains of the army of the north, expected to arrive on the morrow, and for the collection of every available defensive means. It was only by the assumption of a sufficiently respectable, if not an imposing, attitude, that they could hope to succeed in negotiating for the preservation of the capital and the establishment of their own prescribed form of government—perhaps, by some extraordinary effort, to disconcert the plans of their enemies, and obtain a triumph under the walls of Paris. Actuated by these considerations, the provisional government was desirous of inducing the victorious commanders of the Allied armies to enter into negotiations. Another commission was appointed, the members of which were Messrs. Andréossy, Valence, Boissy d'Anglas, Flangergues, and la Benardière. They were directed to proceed to the head-quarters of the Allied field marshals, again to solicit a suspension of hostilities, and to negotiate an armistice.

During these proceedings in Paris, a renewed application had been received by Prince Blücher, on the 27th, and by the Duke of Wellington on the 28th, from the first named commissioners, for a suspension of hostilities, as also a request that a passport and assurances of safety might be accorded to Napoleon and his family, to enable them to pass to the United States of America, the provisional government having previously succeeded, through the medium of representations made to the ex-Emperor by some of his friends, in persuading the latter to consent to this step. Prince Blücher declined taking any notice of the application, conceiving his former verbal reply quite sufficient. The Duke of Wellington referred the commissioners to his note of the 26th, on the proposed suspension of hostilities, and stated that, with regard to the passport for Napoleon, he had no authority from his government, or from the Allies, to give any answer to such demand.

The Anglo-allied army advanced this day from Nesle, so as to bring its right in rear of St. Just, and its left in rear of La Taulle, where the high road from Compiegne joins the high road from Roye to Paris.

The 2nd corps, under Lord Hill, as also the British and Hanoverian cavalry, marched by Montdidier to Petit Crevecœur.

The 1st corps, under Sir John Byng, marched upon Couchy.

The reserve, under Sir James Kempt, marched upon Roye.

The following were the positions of the respective armies on the evening of the 28th:—

The 4th Prussian corps d'armée, which was the nearest to Paris, was posted at Marly la Ville; having detachments pushed forward close to le Bourget and Stains.

The 1st Prussian corps d'armée stood in rear of Nanteuil; having its advanced guard at le Plessis, Belleville, and Dammartin.

The 3rd corps d'armée was at Crespy and in its vicinity.

Prince Blücher's head-quarters were at Senlis.

The Anglo-allied army had its right behind St. Just and its left behind La Taulle.

Its reserve was at Roye.

The advanced guard (Vivian's hussar brigade) was at Antheuil.

The 2nd and 4th divisions, the Nassau troops, and the Hanoverian cavalry, were encamped at Petit Crevecœur, on the road to St. Just.

The British cavalry was encamped near La Taulle and Ressons.

The 1st and 3rd divisions, and the Dutch-Belgian troops, were encamped near Couchy.

The 5th and 6th divisions, the Brunswick troops, and reserve-artillery, were encamped near Roye.

The Duke of Wellington's head-quarters were at Orvillé.

The remains of the 1st and 2nd French corps d'armée, after forming a junction at Gonesse, where the high roads from Nanteuil and Senlis unite, reached the suburbs of Paris. The imperial guard and the 6th corps, immediately under Grouchy, were in full retreat from Meaux by Claie and Vincennes. The 3rd and 4th corps, under Vandamme, having crossed the Marne at Meaux, were retreating by Lagny and Vincennes.

Blücher having issued orders, during the night of the 28th, for the continuation of the advance upon Paris, the advanced guard of the 4th Prussian corps d'armée moved on the morning of the 29th, from Gonesse to le Bourget, which place it found abandoned by the enemy, who, however, was strongly posted at St. Denis, towards which point therefore, some battalions were pushed forward in observation. The enemy having been driven out of Stains, this post was occupied by two fusilier-battalions and a regiment of cavalry, under Lieut. Colonel Schill, for the purpose of securing the right flank of the corps. La Cour neuve, between St. Denis and le Bourget, was also occupied. The main body of the corps broke up from Marly la Ville at seven o'clock in the morning, and on reaching le Bourget, bivouacked in its vicinity.

The advanced guard of the 1st Prussian corps d'armée pushed on, at day-break, from Dammartin to Blanc-Mesnil, whence, immediately on its arrival, it sent detachments beyond the wood of Bondy, to reconnoitre the enemy's preparations of defence. The main body of this corps took up a position, having its right resting on Blanc-Mesnil, and its left on Aulnay. It sent out infantry-detachments towards Livry, and along the Ourcq canal, towards Bondy and Pantin, and cavalry-parties towards Grande-Drancey and Baubigny. Zieten also occupied Nonneville with the 7th regiment of infantry; and the 6th uhlans furnished outposts at the Ourcq canal, communicating with those of the 4th corps.

The 3rd Prussian corps d'armée marched from Crespy as far as Dammartin, in the vicinity of which it was bivouacked. The reserve-cavalry was sent forward as far as Tremblay, in direct support of the 1st corps d'armée.

The 1st and 2nd French corps d'armée had reached the suburbs of Paris on the Gonesse road, during the night, and held possession of le Bourget until the morning of the 29th. The imperial guard and the 6th corps, as also the reinforcements that had arrived from the interior, were, during the forenoon of the 29th, on the high road by Claie and Pantin, under the command of Grouchy, and were directed to occupy several defensive points on that side. The 3rd and 4th corps d'armée, under Vandamme, reached Paris at noon on the 29th, by the Lagny road: they passed through the capital, and occupied the heights of Montrouge on the south side.

The Anglo-allied army arrived, on the 29th, at different points on the road between Gournay and Pont St. Maxence.

The advanced guard, consisting of Vivian's light cavalry-brigade, supported by that of Arentschild, crossed the Oise at Pont St. Maxence, and reached Senlis.

The British cavalry moved from La Taulle to Pont St. Maxence.

The 2nd corps, under Lord Hill, moved from Petit Crevecœur to Clermont.

The 1st corps, under Sir John Byng, moved from its camp, near Couchy, by Estrée St. Denis, along the high road to St. Martin Longeau.

The reserve, under Sir James Kempt, moved from its camp, near Roye, to Gournay, on the road to Pont St. Maxence.

The following were the positions of the respective armies on the evening of the 29th :—

The 1st Prussian corps d'armée had its advanced guard and reserve-cavalry at Aulnay and Savegny; with detachments of the latter at Serran, Livry, Bondy, and Baubigny. The fusilier-battalion of the 7th regiment stood at Nonneville. The 6th uhlans and the 1st Silesian hussars, with two horse-batteries, were posted along the Ourcq canal. The corps itself rested its right on Blanc-Mesnil, and its left on Aulnay.

The 3rd corps d'armée was at Dammartin and in its vicinity. Its reserve-cavalry stood at Tremblay, in support of Zieten.

The 4th corps had its advanced guard between le Bourget and St. Denis which it invested. Lieut. Colonel von Schill, with the 1st Silesian landwehr-cavalry and two battalions of infantry, was posted at Stains. The corps itself was at le Bourget.

Prince Blücher's head-quarters were at Gonesse.

The advanced guard of the Anglo-allied army was at Senlis.

The British cavalry was at Pont St. Maxence.

The 2nd and 4th divisions, the Nassau troops, and Estorff's light cavalry, were at Clermont.

The 1st and 3rd divisions, and the Dutch-Belgian troops, were at St. Martin Longeau.

The 5th and 6th divisions, the Brunswick troops, and the reserve-artillery, were at Gournay.

The pontoon-train and hawser-bridges were at Estrée St. Denis.

The Duke of Wellington's head-quarters were at Le Plessis Longeau.

The French troops comprising the army of the North had entered the capital.

The French force in the capital, after the arrival of the army that had been defeated in Belgium, consisted as follows:— The troops under Grouchy, including the depôts that had come up from the district of the Loire, and from other parts of the interior, amounted to 60 or 70,000 men. They were reinforced, also, by a very considerable amount of field-artillery. One portion of these troops was posted at Montmartre, at St. Denis, and in rear of the Ourcq canal: the remainder, under Vandamme, occupied the heights of Montrouge, on the opposite side, with the exception of the cavalry, which lay in the wood of Boulogne. The national guards amounted to about 30,000 men; their disposition, however, was very doubtful, and, in general, they were considered as but little disposed to offer any resistance to the Allied armies. There was another description of force, called the federal tirailleurs, raised in the suburbs, and consisting chiefly of veterans: they amounted to 17,000 men. Hence, setting aside the national guard, there remained, for the defence of Paris, a disposable force of about 80, or 90,000 men, besides a numerous artillery. Marshal Davoust, Prince of Eckmühl, was appointed to the chief command of the French army, and his head-quarters were fixed at la Villette.

The measures which had been adopted for taking advantage of the local capabilities of defence which the capital afforded, consisted in the intrenchments that had been raised around the heights of Montmartre, Monfauçon, and Belleville. An advanced line of defence was presented by the Ourcq canal, which, proceeding through the wood of Bondy and contiguously to the high road from Meaux, has an arm that branches off from Pantin towards St. Denis. This canal, which was 30 feet wide but not entirely completed, had been filled with water. Along its inner bank ran a high dam, forming an excellent parapet, in which embrasures were cut to admit heavy ordnance; and St. Denis, which formed the *point d'appui* of this line of defence on the Seine, was strongly fortified. The ground on the north side of this town, too, had been inundated by means of the little rivers Rouillon and la Vieille Mer. The village of Aubervilliers, which formed an advanced post at musket-shot distance from the line, was occupied: and in rear of it the canal was covered by a sort of *tête de pont,* which secured the communication between both banks. The barriers to the several approaches to Paris were covered by works with strong batteries. Vincennes had been strengthened, and covered by the works which defended la Pissotte. A strong *tête de pont* was also constructed upon the left bank of the Marne, to cover the bridge of Charenton. All ferries and boats upon the Seine and the Marne were transported to the left bank. The bridge of Neuilly had been partially destroyed, and the wooden bridge at Bessons, over the Seine, had been burned. Several villages, parks, and gardens, on the right bank of the Seine and the Marne, were rendered defensible by the walls being crenelated, the approaches barricaded, and the gates blocked up. Upon the left bank of the Seine, on the south side of the capital, preparations for defence were comparatively neglected; they were limited to the heights of Montrouge.

For the defence of the principal works, 300 guns oflarge calibre were supplied, and for the manning of these, 20 companies of marine artillery which had been brought into the capital. The line between St. Denis and Vincennes was defended by the 1st, 2nd, and 6th corps d'armée. The imperial guard formed the reserve, and was posted at Menil montant. The cavalry was stationed in the Bois de Boulogne. The 3rd and 4th corps d'armée under Vandamme, defended the south side of Paris, and occupied Montrouge.

In the midst of all these preparations, the Provisional Government, the majority of which, under the influence of Fouché, was most desirous of effecting a cessation of hostilities, though acting ostensibly upon the grounds of a necessity of gaining time for the completion of the measures of defence, and of securing the capital from an assault, could not be otherwise than convinced, from the tenor of the replies made by the Allied commanders to all its propositions, that the presence of Napoleon in Paris was the chief obstacle to any satisfactory arrangement. General Becker had been appointed to attend the latter at Malmaison, to watch over his safety, to insure him that respect to which he was so eminently entitled, and to prevent the ill-disposed from making use of his name for purposes of excitement and tumult. Symptoms of a rising among the Buonapartists in Paris had been manifested on the 28th, a circumstance naturally consequent upon the re-union in the capital, of so many regiments of the line, as also of the imperial guard, whose excitement, devotion, and enthusiasm, had Napoleon placed himself once more at their head, might have been such as to have brought them into hostile and fierce collision with the other great parties of the state, and thus have led to scenes of the wildest anarchy and confusion within the walls, whilst the enemy was thundering at the gates from without. Hence every effort was employed to induce the ex-Emperor to quit the capital. The fact of the arrival of the Prussians in front of St. Denis, and the possibility of an attempt being made to carry him off from Malmaison, were explained to him with much earnestness. He immediately referred to the map, and on perceiving the practicability of this coup de main, he adopted precautionary measures of defence. He also offered to the government his services in the capacity of General only, remarking, that he was prepared to march against the enemy, and frustrate his bold and hazardous attempt upon the capital. This proposal was sternly rejected. Fouché declared that to accede to it would be to remove every chance of arrangement with the Allied powers, to create fresh troubles and disorders throughout the country, and, though a temporary success might be gained, to bring down eventually the concentrated force of the immense European armament upon the devoted capital. The commissioners appointed by the government to communicate its wishes to Napoleon, no longer hesitated in arranging his departure. The minister of the marine, and Count Boulay, repaired to his residence, and explained to him that the Duke of Wellington and Prince Blücher had refused to give him any safeguard or passport, and that he had now only to take his immediate departure. Napoleon at length yielded to what he considered to be his destiny, and the preparations for travelling having been completed, he entered his carriage about five o'clock in the afternoon of the 29th, accompanied by Generals Bertrand, Gourgaud, and other devoted friends, and took the road to Rochefort, whither two frigates had been ordered for the embarkation of himself and suite for America.

Napoleon narrowly escaped falling into the hands of the Prussians, whilst at Malmaison. Blücher hearing that he was living there in retirement, had despatched Major Colomb, on the 28th, with the 8th hussars and two battalions of infantry to secure the bridge of Chatou, lower down the Seine, leading directly to the house. Fortunately, however, for Napoleon, the Prince of Eckmühl, when he ascertained that the Prussians were nearing the capital, had desired General Becker to cause this bridge to be destroyed. Hence Major Colomb was much disappointed at finding there was no passage at this point, which in fact was not more than 800 yards distant from the palace, in which Napoleon was yet remaining at the time of the arrival of the Prussians.

On the 29th, the new commissioners appointed by the French government waited upon the Duke of Wellington at Etrées, for the purpose of negotiating a suspension of hostilities. In the course of the discussion which took place on this occasion, the Duke declared that he had nothing to add to the communication he had made to the former commissioners, that he could not but consider the abdication as a deception, and would not feel himself justified in suspending his operations on such a pretext, which was by no means calculated to fulfil the object the Allies had in view. He explained that, besides Napoleon, there were his adherents, who were the declared enemies of the Allies, and stated that before he could agree to any suspension he "must see some steps taken to re-establish a government in France which should afford the Allies some chance of peace." Upon this point his Grace was pressed to give some explanation as to what would satisfy the Allies. He replied that he had no authority from his own government, much less from the Allies, to enter upon the subject, and that all he could do was to give them his private opinion, which he should certainly urge upon the Allies with all the influence he might be supposed to possess, unless otherwise instructed by his own government.

This opinion was a remarkable illustration of the sound judgment, straight-forward policy, and unerring foresight, which are so pre-eminently characteristic of the career of this great man. Subsequent events proved its correctness to the letter. It was in strict accordance with the design traced out and enforced by the united diplomacy of Europe. It is best expressed in the Duke's own words:—

'I then told them that I conceived the best security for Europe was the restoration of the King, and that the establishment of any other government than the King's in France must inevitably lead to new and endless wars; that Buonaparte and the army having overturned the King's government, the natural and simple measure, after Buonaparte was prisoner or out of the way, and the army defeated, was to recall the King to his authority, and that it was a much more dignified proceeding to recall him without conditions, and to trust to the energy of their constitutions for any reforms they wished to make either in the government or the constitution, than now to make conditions with their Sovereign; and that, above all, it was important that they should recall the King without loss of time, as it would not then appear that the measure had been forced upon them by the Allies.

'The Commissioners professed, individually and collectively, their earnest desire to see the King restored in the manner I had mentioned, which they said was likewise the desire of the Provisional Government. —— —— was, however, of opinion that the two chambers could not be brought to recall the King without conditions; and he mentioned, as those upon which they would probably insist, and upon which it was desirable the King should give way, the responsibility of the administration and the alteration of the constitution, so far as that the initiative in making the laws should be vested in the assemblies, and not in the King.

'I told them regarding the first point, that I had every reason to believe that the King had determined to form a ministry which should be individually and collectively responsible for all the acts of the government; and that I did not doubt that His Majesty would not oppose himself to the wishes of the French people, if it was desired that the initiative in framing the laws should be invested in the assemblies: that, however, I had no authority to speak on this subject, and recommended to them not to look after little points of difference, and if they really wished to restore the government of their King, to do it at once and without any conditions.

'In the course of this conversation they stated that the assemblies had proclaimed Napoleon II. as emperor, only to conciliate the officers and soldiers of the army, who had come into Paris in such numbers after the battle, that they had been apprehensive of a civil war in Paris if this measure had not been adopted.

'While we were discussing the conditions to be proposed to the King, and the evils and inconveniences which the mode of making the laws, and the want of responsibility and power in the ministers had occasioned, I received from Sir Charles Stuart, the King's declaration of the 28th, countersigned by M. de Talleyrand, which I immediately communicated to the French Commissioners, and pointed out to them the King's promise, to make the alteration in his administration, which they had proposed to be made in the constitution.

'They objected to certain paragraphs in the declaration referable to the exclusion of certain persons from the King's presence, to the intention announced to punish some of those concerned in the plot which had brought back Buonaparte, and to that of calling together the old houses of legislature, upon which, at their desire, I wrote to M. de Talleyrand, a letter, of which Sir Charles Stuart will probably have sent to England a copy, which I communicated to the Commissioners before I sent it.

'I then told them I could not talk more upon the suspension of our operations, which they urged in the most earnest manner, in order to give them time to take their measures to recall the King, until I should see Marshal Blücher, to whose head-quarters I promised to go that evening.

'Before I set off, the Commisioners asked me whether the appointment of a regency to conduct the affairs of the government in the name of Napoleon II. was likely to satisfy the Allies, and would be such an arrangement as would induce me to stop my operations. I answered, certainly not; that I conceived the Allies, after their declaration, would never treat with Napoleon or any of his family; that the appointment of Napoleon II. was to be attributed to Napoleon I., and the acknowledgment of him to the desire to conciliate the army, and that I should not stop my operations in consequence of such an arrangement.

'They then asked me what would be the case if any other prince of a royal house were called to the throne of France? To which I said it was impossible for me to answer such loose questions; that, as an individual, I had made them acquainted with my opinion of what it was best for them to do, and it rested with them either to follow this opinion or not.

'One of the Commissioners, before I went away, took occasion to tell me that he wished I had given a more positive answer to this last question, and I determined to take another opportunity of doing so before the Commissioners should report this conversation to Paris.

'I left them at Etrées, and went to the head-quarters at Le Plessis, to give the orders for the movement of the troops in the morning, and I overtook them again in the night at Louvres. I then told them I had considered their last question since I had last seen them, and that I felt no objection to give them my opinion on it as an individual; that, in my opinion, Europe had no hope of peace if any person excepting the King were called to the throne of France; that any person so called must be considered an usurper, whatever his rank and quality, that he must act as an usurper, and must endeavour to turn the attention of the country from the defects of his title towards war and foreign conquests; that the powers of Europe must, in such a case, guard themselves against this evil, and that I could only assure them that, unless otherwise ordered by my government, I would exert any influence I might possess over the Allied Sovereigns to induce them to insist upon securities for the preservation of peace, besides the treaty itself, if such an arrangement as they had stated were adopted.

'The Commissioners replied that they perfectly understood me, and some of them added—"*Et vous avez raison.*"'*

---

* Despatches of Field Marshal the Duke of Wellington, compiled by Colonel Gurwood, C.B.—vol. xii. p. 534.

CHAPTER XX.

PRINCE Blücher had satisfied himself, by means of the reconnaissances made during the 29th, that very considerable pains had been taken by the enemy to oppose a serious obstruction to the farther advance of troops marching against the north side of Paris. He was now desirous of ascertaining whether the disposition and spirit of the enemy's troops were at all commensurate with the extent of the works which he saw before him; and, with this view, he directed Bülow to make an attack, in the night of the 29th, with part of his corps d'armée, upon Aubervilliers. He also desired Zieten to support this attack, by raising as much alarm as possible in the villages of Bondy and Pantin.

Before the attack commenced, Blücher was joined by Wellington in person, who communicated to him the proposals which had been made by the French commisioners. Being already engaged in an important operation, he could not consent to suspend hostilities; and the two commanders agreed in opinion that, as long as Napoleon remained in Paris they could not arrest their operations without insisting upon his being delivered up to them. Accordingly, the Duke wrote a letter immediately to the commissioners to this effect.

Blücher confided the attack upon Aubervilliers to General Sydow, with the 13th brigade (9 battalions), together with one battalion of the 14th brigade, and two regiments of cavalry. The remainder of the 4th corps d'armée was held under arms, in readiness to follow up any acquired advantage. Four battalions advanced in column, under Colonel Lettow, supported by the remaining five battalions. The arrangements, being made during the night, occupied some little time, so that twilight had set in when the attack commenced. Colonel Lettow penetrated the extensive village on three sides, forced the barriers, and carried every thing before him with the bayonet. The place had been occupied by 1,000 of the enemy's best troops, of whom 200 were made prisoners, and the remainder pursued as far as the canal of St. Denis.

General Sydow, accompanied by Major Lützow, of the staff, immediately made a reconnaissance of the canal, and soon discovered that its opposite bank was lined with infantry in great force, and that the different points of passage were defended by batteries. Nevertheless he made the attempt to advance; but the troops were received with a vigorous fire of both artillery and musketry; and it soon became evident, that the enemy's fortified position could not be taken except at a great sacrifice of both time and men. Sydow, therefore, limited his operations to the occupation of the captured village.

A simultaneous advance towards the canal was made, on the left of Aubervilliers, by the 3rd battalion of the 1st Pomeranian landwehr, and the 10th regiment of hussars, which maintained the communication with the 1st corps. A sharp tiraillade took place, which terminated in the withdrawal of these troops to their former position.

By means of this reconnaissance it was made sufficiently manifest that the line of the canal of St. Denis could not be carried without a serious assault, preluded by a heavy cannonade. It then became a question with the Allied commanders, who had thus, most fortunately, the opportunity of concerting measures in person, whether it would not be advisable to endeavour to turn the enemy's strongly fortified lines of St. Denis and Montmartre, by masking those lines with one army, whilst the other should move off to the right, and cross to the left bank of the Seine, lower down the stream. Although this movement would have the effect of extending and dividing the Allied forces, and consequently of augmenting the chances of success on the part of the enemy, should the latter possess the disposition and the means, not only of acting determinedly on the defensive, but also of assuming the offensive, accordingly as circumstances might favour the attempt, still any defeat of this kind was fully counterbalanced by the advantages which the plan presented. It cut off the entire communication with Normandy, from which Paris derived its chief supplies; whilst the approach of the Bavarian army towards the opposite side was gradually limiting the resources of the capital in that quarter. It enabled the commanders to present their forces simultaneously at different points, and thus, by continuing that display of vigour which had characterized their advance, they were far more likely to impose upon the *morale* of both the defeated army and the citizens, than by limiting their combined operations to the attack of the stronghold presented by the lines of St. Denis; for to do this, would, in all probability, require time, and it was evident from the repeated proposals made by the French government for a suspension of hostilities, that time was their great object, whether for the purpose of facilitating the collection and organization of their resources, or in the hope of obtaining more favourable terms from the Allies. It had also been tolerably well ascertained that, although fortified works had been thrown up on the right bank of the Seine, the defence of the left bank had been comparatively neglected. A further inducement towards the adoption of this plan arose from a report which was now received from Major Colomb, stating that although he had found the bridge of Chatou, leading to Malmaison, destroyed, he had hastened to that of St. Germain, on hearing that it had not been injured, and succeeded in gaining possession of it, at the very moment the French were on the point of effecting its destruction. The bridge of Maisons, still lower down the stream, was also taken and occupied.

No time was lost by the Prussian commander in taking advantage of the captured bridges across the Seine. Lieut. Colonel Sohr received an order that night to move, with his cavalry-brigade (the Brandenburg and Pomeranian hussars), from the vicinity of Louvres, and to regulate his march so that he might cross the Seine at St. Germain on the following morning. Thence he was to proceed so as to appear, with his brigade, on the 1st of July, upon the Orleans road from Paris, where he was to interrupt this communication, and increase the confusion already produced in that quarter by the fugitives from the capital. Altogether, he was to act independently and discretionally, and, as far as practicable, to impede the supplies of provisions from the western and southern provinces.

It was arranged that the Prussian army should move to its right for the purpose of crossing the Seine, and, in order to mask the operation as much as possible, the advanced posts of the 1st and 4th corps d'armée were to remain in their present position until the arrival of the Anglo-allied army, which was expected to take place on the evening of the 30th. The 3rd corps was directed to resume, at five o'clock in the morning of the 30th, its march upon Gonesse: and thence to proceed to St. Germain, but in such a manner as to conceal its movements by means of the valley of Montmorency, and not to reach the more open ground about Argenteuil until darkness should have completely set in. From the latter point it would then complete its march to St. Germain. The 1st corps was ordered to break up from its bivouac at ten o'clock in the evening, and march southward of Gonesse, by Montmorency, Franconville, Cormeille, and Maisons, at which latter point it was to cross the Seine, and immediately open a communication with the 3rd corps. The 4th corps d'armée was directed to move, at daybreak of the 1st of July, by the right of St. Denis, and to bombard this place during its march to Argenteuil, in which direction it was to effect a junction with the 1st and 3rd corps. The advanced posts of the 1st and 4th corps were to remain until relieved by the British troops, and then, in like manner, to follow the rest of the army.

These movements were punctually directed in the manner prescribed. As the 1st and 3rd corps d'armée moved off to the right, Count Bülow considered it necessary to strengthen the outposts of the 4th corps, so as to be prepared to meet the enemy should the latter debouch from St. Denis. He therefore ordered Colonel Hiller to take post in observation of this point, with six battalions, a regiment of cavalry, half of a 6-pounder battery, and two pieces of horse artillery.

About three o'clock in the afternoon, the Prussian outposts reported that French columns were advancing from St. Denis, and that the vedettes were already driven in. Colonel Hiller immediately pushed forward the sharpshooters of two battalions, as also two squadrons of cavalry, with two pieces of horse-artillery. At the same time, the troops at Stains got under arms, and were prepared to support. A very brisk tiraillade ensued, although there was no cover for the skirmishers on the plain, except the trees along the great road, and the high corn, which served to conceal their approach. The enemy had also sent detachments towards Epinay and Pierrefitte, but at these points, as also in advance of Stains, the French were compelled to give way and to retire, without having succeeded in their object of forcing back the Prussian outposts.

The main body of the 4th corps d'armée remained, during the 30th, in its position at le Bourget; its advanced guard, under General Sydow, was detached to the right, towards Argenteuil, to communicate with the 3rd corps d'armèe. As the former was to move off on the following morning, it became necessary to hold the outposts strictly on the defensive. Aubervilliers was the most open to attack. Two companies were posted at the outlets, towards the French side: and in rear of these, two other companies were formed in support. Still further to the rear was the main position, on which these troops, if overpowered, were to fall back. It lay along the villages of Chantourterelle, Courneuve, and Merville, connected together by a watercourse lined with bushes, and consisting of separate country-houses and châteaux, mostly within walls, which had been loopholed for tirailleurs. Six battalions, chiefly extended in skirmishing order, were considered sufficient to occupy the whole of this line, as far as the high road from le Bourget. Partial skirmishing, at a distance, was kept up; though, on the side of the Prussians, it was more for the purpose of diverting the attention of the enemy, and concealing from him the general movement to the right. Bivouac-fires were maintained during the night on the ground vacated by the different corps, in order to deceive the enemy by their apparent indication of the continued presence of the Prussian army in front of the lines of St. Denis.

On this day, the advanced guard of the Anglo-allied army (Vivian's hussar-brigade) reached Vauderlan. The British cavalry moved to Louvres.

Estorff's cavalry, attached to the 2nd corps, crossed the Oise at Creil, and proceeded by Chantilly to Luzarches. The infantry of this corps marched from Clermont to Chantilly.

The 1st corps moved from its camp near St. Martin Longeau, crossed the Oise at Pont St. Maxence, and advanced until the head of the column reached La Capelle, and its rear rested upon Senlis.

The reserve moved from its camp, near Gournay, by Pont St. Maxence, the head of the column reaching Fleurines, on the road to Senlis, and the rear resting upon Pont St. Maxence.

The following were the positions of the respective armies on the evening of the 30th:—

The 1st Prussian corps d'armée commenced its march, at half-past ten o'clock in the evening, from Blancmesnil and Aulnay towards St. Germain, passing, during the night, through Gonesse, Montmorency, and le Mesnil, to Carrière au Mont, near St. Germain—leaving its outposts in the position they had hitherto occupied.

The 3rd corps d'armée marched, during the night, from Dammartin to St. Germain, by Genosse and Argenteuil, at which latter place, however, its reserve-cavalry was halted.

The 4th corps d'armée remained in its position at le Bourget, to cover the march of the rest of the army. Its outposts continued at Stains, St. Denis, and Aubervilliers. Lieut. Colonel von Sohr, with the Brandenburg and Pomeranian hussars, crossed the Seine at St. Germain, and was advancing towards Versailles.

Major von Colomb, with the 8th hussars, occupied the bridge of St. Germain.

The head-quarters of Prince Blücher continued at Genosse.

The advanced guard of the Anglo-allied army was at Vauderlan.

The British cavalry was encamped on the plain about Louvres.

The Hanoverian cavalry was at Luzarches.

The 2nd and 4th divisions, and the Nassau troops, were upon the high road between La Capelle and Senlis.

The 5th and 6th divisions, the Brunswick troops, and the reserve-artillery, were upon the high road between Fleurines and Pont St. Maxence.

The pontoon-train and hawser-bridges were at Senlis.

The Duke of Wellington's head-quarters were at Louvres.

The French army remained within the lines of Paris.

Since the departure of Napoleon both the army and the citizens looked upon the parliament as the sole directing power; and, in full reliance upon its integrity, appeared willingly submissive to its dictates. Fouché, who had been in secret communication with the Allies, decided upon exercising, in accordance with their views, the great influence he had succeeded in acquiring over a very considerable portion of the deputies. It was mainly by means of this influence that he contrived to remove the principal obstacle in the way of all negotiation—the presence of Napoleon. His next step was to prepare the chamber for the return to power of the legitimate monarch, a measure which he could only hope to accomplish by holding it forth as the sole alternative to the destruction of Paris by the vast and overwhelming force of the Allied armies marching towards the capital from the north and east frontiers, and by combining with it the adoption of such modifications of the charter as should satisfy the desires of the constitutionalists and the moderately disposed of all parties. Aware that the army was animated with a spirit of determined resistance towards the Allies, he plainly saw that unless conciliated, the turbulent Buonapartists, with whom its ranks were filled, might speedily frustrate the accomplishment of his plans by which the peace of the capital was to be preserved, and ultimately prevent the attainment of that extended constitutional power for which the deputies were contending. He, therefore, with his usual adroitness, addressed himself to its chief, Marshal Davoust, Prince of Eckmühl; and by his skilful exposition of the political posture of affairs, he succeeded in gaining over the Marshal to his views. The latter wrote to him on the evening of the 29th that he had overcome his prejudices, and had arrived at the conclusion that the only safe course to be pursued, consisted in entering into an armistice, and proclaiming Louis XVIII. On the 30th, the Prince, as the head of the French army, addressed the following letter to both Wellington and Blücher:—

'Head-Quarters, La Villette, June 30, 1815.

'My Lord,

'Your hostile movements continue, although, according to the declarations of the Allied Sovereigns, the motives of the war which they make upon us no longer exist, since the Emperor Napoleon has abdicated.

'At the moment when blood is again on the point of flowing, I receive from Marshal the Duke of Albufera a telegraphic despatch, of which I transmit you a copy. My Lord, I guarantee this armistice on my honour. All the reasons you might have had to continue hostilities are destroyed, because you can have no other instruction from your government, than that which the Austrian generals had from theirs.

'I make the formal demand to your Excellency of ceasing all hostilities, and of our proceeding to agree to an armistice, according to the decision of congress. I cannot believe, my Lord, that my request will be ineffectual; you will take upon yourself a great responsibility in the eyes of your fellow-countrymen.

'No other motive but that of putting an end to the effusion of blood, and the interests of my country, has dictated this letter.

'If I present myself on the field of battle, with the idea of your talents, I shall carry the conviction of there combating for the most sacred of causes—that of the defence and independence of my country; and, whatever may be the result, I shall merit your esteem. 'Accept, &c.

'THE MARSHAL PRINCE OF ECKMUHL,
'Minister at War.'

To this the Duke of Wellington replied in the following terms:—

'Head-Quarters, July 1, 1815—10 A.M.

'MONSIEUR LE MARÉCHAL,

'I have just received your Excellency's letter of the 30th June, in which your Excellency communicates to me the intelligence you have received of an armistice having been concluded by General Frimont with Marshal the Duke of Albufera.

'I have already made known, in writing, to the French commissioners sent to the Allied powers, and verbally, to the commissioners sent to me, the reasons which have prevented me from suspending my operations; which reasons, I have cause to believe are fully adopted by the Allies of my Sovereign, and of those whose armies I have the honour of commanding.

'I have every wish to prevent the further effusion of the blood of the brave troops under my command; but it must be upon the conditions which shall secure the re-establishment and the stability of the general peace.

'I have the honour to be, &c.
'WELLINGTON."

Prince Blücher, who entertained a great contempt for diplomacy,* attributing as he did the cause of the renewal of

* On this point he always expressed himself openly and without reserve. A memorable instance occurred subsequently to the convention of Paris, at a large dinner party given by the Duke of Wellington, when, rising from his seat between the latter and the British minister, Viscount Castlereagh, he gave the following toast:—"May the diplomatists not again spoil with their pens, that which the armies have at so much cost won with their swords!" Not long after this, when the terms of the peace were under discussion, Blücher, conceiving that these would again be made too favourable to France, evinced the greatest mistrust, amounting almost to hatred of the diplomatists. Happening to meet the Prussian minister, Prince Hardenberg, he thus boldly addressed him—"I only wish I had you, gentlemen of the pen, exposed for once to a pretty smart skirmishing fire, that you might learn what it is when the soldier is obliged to repair with his life's blood the errors which you so thoughtlessly commit on paper." The following fact shows that no personal considerations restrained him from indulging in his splenetic humour against the great diplomatists of the day. It is well known that immediately after the convention of Paris, he was extremely desirous of destroying the bridge of Jena, and that he would undoubtedly have carried his intentions into effect had it not been for the urgent representations of the Duke of Wellington. On that occasion, Count von der Golz, formerly his aide-de-camp, and then Prussian ambassador in Paris, made a written application to him, in behalf, and in the name, of Prince Talleyrand; beseeching the preservation of the bridge. Blücher replied in his own hand-writing—"I have resolved upon blowing up the bridge; and I cannot conceal from your excellency how much pleasure it would afford me *if M. Talleyrand would previously station himself upon it;* and I beg you will make my wish known to him."

the war to the ill-concocted schemes to which that war had given birth, had hitherto refrained from either receiving in person, or noticing in writing, any communication addressed to him by the French authorities. He applied himself solely to the military solution of the great problem, on which depended the peace of Europe. Upon this occasion, however, tempted probably by the opportunity which was offered to him of sharply retorting upon the Marshal, under whose government of Hamburg the greatest excesses had been committed upon his countrymen, he was induced to pen the following reply, couched in his rough native German, as if to evince both his disdain of the usual diplomatic mode of communication, and his dislike of even the very language of the country he so thoroughly detested:—

'*To the French General Davoust.**

'Head-Quarters, July 1, 1815.

'Marshal,

'It is not conformable to truth that, because Napoleon has abdicated the throne, there exists no further motive for war between the Allied powers and France. His abdication is conditional; that is, in favour of his son: but a decree

---

* *Au den Franzöischen General Davoust.*

Mein Herr Marschall!

Es ist irrig dass zwischen den verbündeten Mächten und Frankreich alle Ursachen zum Kriege aufgehört haben, weil Napoleon dem Throne entsagt habe; dieser hat nur bedingungsweise entsagt, nämlich zu Günsten seines Sohnes, und der Beschluss der vereinigten Mächte schliesst nicht allein Napoleon, sondern alle Mitglieder seiner Familie vom Throne aus.

Wenn der General Frimont sich berechtigt geglaubt hat, einen Waffenstillstand mit dem ihm gegenüberstehenden feindlichen General zu schliessen, so ist dies kein Motiv für uns, ein Gleiches zu thun. Wir verfolgen unsern Sieg, und Gott hat uns Mittel und Willen dazu verliehen.

Sehen Sie zu, Herr Marschall, was Sie thun, und stürzen Sie nicht abermals eine Stadt ins Verderben; denn Sie wissen, was der erbitterte Soldat sich erlauben würde, wenn Ihre Hauptstadt mit Sturm genommen würde.

Wollen Sie die Verwünschungen von Paris eben so wie die von Hamburg auf sich laden?

Wir wollen in Paris einrücken, um die rechtlichen Leute in Schutz zu nehmen gegen die Plünderung, die ihnen von Seiten des Pöbels droht. Nur in Paris kann ein zuverlässiger Waffenstillstand Statt haben. Sie wollen, Herr Marschall, dieses unser Verhältniss zu Ihrer Nation nicht verkennen.

Ich mache Ihnen, Herr Marschall, übrigens bemerklich, das, wenn Sie mit uns unterhandeln wollen, es sonderbar ist, dass Sie unsere mit Briefen und Aufträgen gesendeten Offiziere gegen das Völkerrecht zurückhalten.

In den gewöhnlichen Formen conventioneller Höflichkeit habe ich die Ehre mich zu nennen,

Herr Marschall,
Ihren
dienstwilligen,

Blücher.

of the Allied powers excludes not only Napoleon, but every member of his family, from the throne.

'If General Frimont has considered himself authorised to conclude an armistice with your general opposed to him, that is no motive for us to do the same. We shall pursue our victory. God has given us strength and resolution to do so. Beware, Marshal, of what you do; and forbear devoting another city to destruction! for you know what liberties the exasperated soldiers would take, should your capital be carried by storm. Do you solicit the maledictions of Paris, in addition to those of Hamburgh?

'We shall enter Paris to protect the respectable inhabitants against the mob, by whom they are threatened with pillage. An armistice can be made with security nowhere but in Paris. This, our relative position towards your nation, be pleased, Marshal, not to mistake!

'Let me finally observe to you, Marshal, if you mean to negotiate with us, it is matter of surprise that, in defiance of the law of nations, you detain our officers dispatched with letters and orders.

'In the usual form of conventional civility, I have the honour to be,

'Marshal,

'Your obedient servant,

'BLÜCHER.'

Whilst thus endeavouring to draw the Allied generals into negotiation, Fouché and Davoust felt the necessity of carrying out their plans with the greatest caution, and in such a manner as to prevent any unfavourable construction being put upon their motives by the army. On the evening of the 30th of June there was an assemblage of general officers at the head-quarters in Villette, at which it was proposed to send up an address to the chamber of representatives, expressive of the determined spirit of resistance which animated the troops, and of their hostility to the Bourbons. It was adopted by the majority, and Davoust, though secretly working with Fouché for the restoration of Louis XVIII., did not hesitate to attach to it his signature. It was couched in the following terms:—

'Camp at Villette, 30th June.

'REPRESENTATIVES OF THE PEOPLE!

'We are in presence of our enemies. We swear before you and the world, to defend, to our last breath, the cause of our independence and the national honour.

'It is wished to impose the Bourbons upon us, but these princes are rejected by the immense majority of Frenchmen. If their return could be agreed to, recollect, representatives, that you would sign the annihilation of the army, which for twenty years has been the palladium of French honour. There are in war, especially when it has been long conducted, successes and reverses. In our successes, we have appeared great and generous. If it is wished to humble us in our reverses, we shall know how to die.

'The Bourbons present no guarantee to the nation. We received them with sentiments of the most generous confidence: we forgot all the calamities they had caused us in their rage to deprive us of our most sacred rights. Well! what return did they make for this confidence? They treated us as rebels and as vanquished. Representatives! these reflections are terrible, because they are true. History will one day relate what the Bourbons have done to replace themselves on the throne of France; it will also narrate the conduct of the army; of that army essentially national; and posterity will judge which best deserved the esteem of the world.

'The Marshal Prince of ECKMUHL, Minister at War,
'Count PAJOL, commanding the first corps of cavalry,
'Count D'ERLON, commanding the right wing,
'Count VANDAMME, General in chief.'
(And fifteen other generals.)

The chambers being thus appealed to, felt it incumbent on them to issue a proclamation explanatory of the political situation of France, and of their own intentions under all the critical circumstances in which it presented itself to their view. This document, cautiously drawn up by the constitutionalists, who formed the preponderating party in the state, and strongly marked by the policy which was pursued throughout by Fouché, was framed with great tact. Although it acknowledged the nomination of Napoleon's son to the empire, it manifested no hostility to the Bourbons; it expressed a desire to secure a monarchical and representative government, but, at the same time, declared that the head of the government, whoever he might be, must enter into a solemn compact and abide by the constitutional charter. In short, its general tone was sufficiently independent to secure for it, if not the approbation, at least the acquiescence, of both the liberals and the Buonapartists; whilst, on the other hand, it significantly indicated the terms upon which a Bourbon might re-ascend the throne, and rally round him the friends of constitutional order and civil rights. With but few exceptions it admitted of being reconciled with the proclamation published on the 28th of June by Louis XVIII.* It ran thus:—

'FRENCHMEN!

'The foreign powers proclaimed, in the face of Europe, that they were only armed against Napoleon, and that they wished to respect our independence, and the right which belongs to every nation to choose a government suitable to its habits and its interests.

'Napoleon is no longer the chief of the state. He has renounced the throne, and his abdication has been accepted by your representatives. He is removed from us. His son is called to the empire by the constitution of the state. The coalesced sovereigns are informed of this; and the war ought to be terminated, if the promises of kings have any foundation in truth.

'While plenipotentiaries have been sent to the Allied powers to treat for peace in the name of France, the generals of two of those powers have refused any suspension of arms. Their troops have accelerated their marches under favour of a moment of hesitation and trouble. They are now at the very gates of the capital, and no communication has stated for what object the war is continued. Our plenipotentiaries will soon declare whether we must renounce peace. In the mean time, resistance is not only legitimate, but necessary; and humanity, in requiring an account of the blood uselessly shed, will not accuse those brave men who only combat to repel from their houses the scourges of war, murder, and

* Appendix XLIX.

pillage, and to defend with their lives the cause of liberty, and of that independence the imprescriptible right of which has been guaranteed to them even by the manifestoes of their enemies.

'Amidst these circumstances, your representatives cannot forget that they were not chosen to stipulate for the interests of any individual party, but for the whole nation. Every act of weakness will dishonour them, and will only tend to endanger the future tranquillity of France. While the government is employing all the means in its power to obtain a solid peace, or, should that not be obtained without compromising our honour, to repel the battalions of foreigners, what more advantages to the nation can be done than to collect and establish the fundamental rules of a monarchical and representative government, destined to secure to all citizens the free enjoyment of those sacred rights, which sacrifices so numerous and so great have purchased; and to rally for ever, under the national colours, that great body of Frenchmen who have no other interest, and no other wish, than an honourable repose and a just independence.

'Meanwhile the chambers conceive that their duty and their dignity require them to declare that they will never acknowledge, as legitimate chief of the state, him who on ascending the throne, shall refuse to acknowledge the rights of the nation, and to consecrate them by a solemn compact. The constitutional charter is drawn up; and if the force of arms should succeed in temporarily imposing upon us a master—if the destinies of a great nation are again to be delivered up to the caprice and arbitrary will of a small number of privileged persons—then, in yielding to force, the national representation will protest in the face of the whole world against the oppression of the French people.

'Your representatives will appeal to the energy of the present and future generations to renew their claim both to national independence, and the rights of civil and religious liberty. For these rights they now appeal to the reason and the justice of all civilized nations.'

Notwithstanding the continued endeavours on the part of the French commissioners appointed by the chambers, to induce the Allied generals to enter upon an armistice, the military operations were not for a moment interrupted.

On the morning of the 1st of July, Bülow's corps d'armée (the 4th) moved off to its right, towards Argenteuil. During the movement, however, the enemy, as if at length aware, or desirous of ascertaining the nature, of Blücher's operation, attacked the village of Aubervilliers in front, from the canal of St. Denis, and penetrated as far as the church situated in the centre of the place. The French were here met by the Prussian support, and two battalions from the main position arriving immediately afterwards, they were prevented from making any further progress. Nevertheless a prolonged tiraillade, as well as a howitzer fire, on the part of the French, were maintained, during which the march of Bülow's corps continued in operation, the 14th brigade being left in support to the advanced posts until the arrival of the Anglo-allied troops.

In the afternoon, the Duke of Wellington's army reached le Bourget, and took up the position vacated by Prince Blücher, whose advanced posts it immediately relieved. Three companies of light infantry from Colville's division were thrown into Aubervilliers. The Prussians who had hitherto been stationed for the purpose of masking as much as possible the general movement of their army to the right, had kept up a desultory fire from that portion of the village which was in their possession, abstaining from making any direct attack, since this might have led to the advance of the French in great force at the moment the former were no longer supported by the main army, and before the Anglo-allied troops had arrived.

The British light companies, mentioned as having been thrown into Aubervilliers, were under no restraint of this kind, and Lieut. Colonel Sir Neil Campbell, who commanded them, determined to push forward, and possess himself, if possible, of the entire village. Having first gained two or three of the highest houses, he broke from the top of these into some that were lower, and thence forcing his way through the partition walls of others, without much firing, since the French did not appear disposed to make an obstinate resistance, (being by that time probably aware of the Prussian movement to the right, and of the arrival of the Anglo-allied army,) he succeeded in obtaining possession of one side of a whole street, and of the greater portion of the village. The French officer in command then proposed a truce, which was accepted, since the post he occupied lay between the British and a battery upon the canal. The remaining outposts were taken up from the Prussians without any molestation on the part of the enemy, and the main Anglo-allied army occupied a position, having its right upon the height of Richebourg, and its left upon the wood of Bondy.

It will be recollected that Lieut. Colonel Sohr, of the Prussian light cavalry, was directed to pass the bridge of St. Germain, on the morning of the 30th of June, and to show himself on the Orleans road upon the 1st of July. Starting at daybreak of the 30th, the brigade passed through Montmorency and Argenteuil, towards St. Germain, where it fell in with Major Colomb's detachment, consisting of the 8th hussars and two battalions of infantry. It then moved on about a league further, to Marly, upon the Versailles road, which it reached at nightfall, and where it bivouacked. On the morning of the 1st of July, Lieut. Colonel Sohr resumed his march, and took the direction of Versailles, which place, however, he did not reach until noon, much delay having occurred whilst passing through the intersected ground in that quarter, and in awaiting the reports from the detachments sent out in different directions to gain intelligence of the enemy.

This bold and hazardous movement of Lieut. Colonel Sohr's brigade, which was acting independently as a free corps for the time, did not escape the enemy's observation. General Excelmans, who commanded the French cavalry on the south side of Paris, on receiving information that two regiments of Prussian hussars were advancing by Marly upon Versailles, resolved to attack them. For this purpose he proceeded himself with the 5th, 15th, and 20th dragoons, and the 6th hussars, comprising a force of 3000 men, along the road from Montrouge towards Plessis-Piquet, against the front of the Prussian brigade. At the same time, the light cavalry-division of General Piré, together with the 33rd regiment of infantry, consisting of three battalions, were detached against the flank and rear of the Prussian brigade. The 5th and 6th lancers marched by the Sèvres road upon Viroflay; the 6th chasseurs proceeded to occupy the cross-roads connecting Sèvres with the northern portion of Versailles; the 1st chasseurs moved by Sèvres towards Rocquencourt, about three miles from Versailles, on the road to St. Germain; in which direction the 33rd infantry followed. Both the latter regiments were destined to cut off the retreat of the Prussian cavalry, should it be driven back by Excelmans. An exceedingly well planned ambush was now laid in and about Rocquencourt, and every precaution taken by the detaching of small parties on the look-out.

It was late in the afternoon when Lieut. Colonel Sohr received intelligence that the enemy's cavalry was approaching, and that his advanced guard was attacked. He immediately advanced with both his hussar-regiments, and drove back the enemy upon Villa-Coublai, in the defile of which village a sharp engagement ensued. In this attack the ranks of the Prussian hussars had become disordered, and, as the latter retired, they were fallen upon by the 5th and 6th French lancers, of Piré's light cavalry-brigade, before alluded to as having been posted in ambush. They then fell back upon Versailles, pursued by the French, who vainly endeavoured to force an entrance into the town, at the gate of which a gallant resistance was made by the Prussians. The short time that was gained by this resistance sufficed for collecting the main body of the brigade on the open space at the outlet leading to St. Germain, towards which point it might have retreated through the park, but, having received information of the advance of Thielemann's corps, and expecting every moment to derive from it a support, Lieut. Colonel Sohr retired by the more direct road through Rocquencourt. About seven o'clock in the evening, at which time the hussars had collected their scattered force together, and were on the point of commencing their further retreat upon St. Germain, Sohr received intelligence, upon which he could rely, that he had been turned by both cavalry and infantry, and that his line of retreat had been intercepted. His decision was instantly formed. He knew his men, their devotion, and their courage, and resolved upon cutting his way through the enemy with the sword.

On quitting Versailles the Prussian hussars were fired upon by the national guard from the barrier. They had not proceeded far when word was brought in, that Prussian and English cavalry were approaching from the side of St. Germain, but they were speedily undeceived. It was the 1st regiment of French chasseurs. In the next moment they were formed for attack, and advanced at a gallop. The chasseurs came on in the same style, but they were completely overthrown, and their commanding officer lay stretched upon the ground by a pistol-shot. As they were pursued by the hussars, a fire was unexpectedly opened upon the latter by two companies of the 3rd battalion of the 33rd French regiment, posted behind some hedges, near Lechesnay; whereupon Sohr, with the greater part of his hussars, struck into a field-road to the right, in order to turn this village which was occupied by the enemy. This, however, led them to a bridge, with adjacent houses, occupied by two more companies of the above battalion, from which they also received a sharp fire. Meeting with this new obstacle, and aware of the proximity of the great mass of cavalry under Excelmans, in their rear, the diminished and disordered remnant of the two Prussian regiments, about 150 hussars, rallying upon their chief, dashed across a meadow, with a determination to force a passage through the village of Lechesnay. Here the chasseurs again opposed them, but were once more overthrown, and the Prussians now followed a road which conducted them through the village, but which unfortunately led into a large court whence there was no other outlet. Not only was their further progress thus checked, but their whole body was suddenly assailed by a fire from infantry, already posted in this quarter, whilst the pursuing cavalry prevented every chance of escape. Their situation had become truly desperate, but their bravery, instead of succumbing, appeared incited to the highest pitch by the heroic example of Lieut. Colonel Sohr, who rejected the offer of quarter, and fell, severely wounded by a pistol-shot. Victory favoured the strongest; but it was a victory gained by immeasurably superior numbers over the dead and dying of a gallant band of warriors, who fought to the last, and did all that the most inflexible bravery could accomplish.

The losses incurred by this brigade during the short campaign had already reduced it, previously to this affair, to between 600 and 700 men: and on the present occasion it suffered a still further loss of 10 officers and from 400 to 500 men.

The detaching of these two regiments so much in advance of the Prussian general movement to the right, and the orders given to Lieut. Colonel Sohr, to cross the Seine on the morning of the 30th of June, appear a questionable measure. It is true that this officer was desired to consider himself as acting independently, and without reference to the troops that were to follow in the same direction; but then it must be recollected that he had to proceed along a very considerable portion of the circumference of a circle, from the centre of which the enemy could detach superior force along radii far shorter than the distance between the Prussian brigade and the main army: so that, with a vigilant look-out, the French possessed every facility of cutting off his retreat. His orders were, to interrupt the communication with Paris by the Orleans road, and to spread alarm and confusion on that side of the capital, but in issuing them the effect likely to be produced upon the *morale* of the citizens could have alone been contemplated; and, in all probability, it was at the same time conceived that, as no fortified works had been thrown up on the south side, the French troops intended to direct their attention mainly, if not wholly, towards the armies in front of the northern portion of the capital. The effect thus sought to be produced might have been obtained in the case of a weak garrison, but that of Paris, comprising as it did about 50,000 troops of the line, besides the national guards, was not to be so lightly treated. In carrying into execution the order to create alarm and confusion on the south side of Paris, these two regiments of hussars would naturally draw in that direction the attention of the French commanders, and thus lead, as the result proved, not only to the cutting off of so comparatively weak a force, but also to the posting of a respectable body of troops at the threatened point, in anticipation of the enemy's following up the attack in greater force. Even previously to obtaining the insight thus afforded into a part of the plan of the invaders, the movements of the latter had been more narrowly watched than was supposed, as may be readily inferred from the fact of Excelmans having been detached, on the 1st, towards Versailles, with a body of cavalry, and of the position at Montrouge having been occupied in considerable force. All circumstances considered, the preferable course would have been, to have employed Sohr's brigade as an advanced guard only, having immediate support from the main columns in its rear.

It so happened that the advanced guard of Thielemann's corps, consisting of the 9th infantry-brigade, under General Borcke, was on the march from St. Germain, (which it had left about seven o'clock in the evening) to take post at Marly, when it received intelligence of the two cavalry-regiments, under Lieut. Colonel Sohr, having been completely defeated. Borcke hastened forward, and it was not long before his advance became engaged with the French tirailleurs proceeding from Versailles. The enemy was immediately attacked, and driven back upon Rocquencourt. As darkness was setting in, Borcke drew up his force with caution. He pushed forward the fusilier-battalion of the 8th regiment, supported by the 1st battalion of the 30th regiment, and held the remainder in battalion-columns on the right and left of the road. The vigour of the attack made by the first named battalion was such, that the enemy retired in all haste upon the nearest suburb of Paris, whilst Borcke bivouacked at Rocquencourt.

Besides the cavalry under Excelmans, the remains of the 3rd and 4th French corps d'armée were detached to the south of Paris, on which side Vandamme, who commanded, took up a position, having his right upon the Seine, his left by Montrouge, and his centre in rear of Issy. He placed a portion of his troops in the villages of Vanves and Issy, the houses and walls of which appeared to offer great advantages for defence. His advanced guard occupied Chatillon, Clamord, Meudon, Sèvres, and St. Cloud. In the evening he was joined by the imperial guard, which he posted in support.

The following were the positions of the respective armies on the evening of the 1st of July:—

The 2nd corps of the Anglo-allied army, under Lord Hill, comprising the 2nd and 4th divisions, the Nassau troops, and Estorff's Hanoverian cavalry-brigade, was in the position previously occupied by the 4th Prussian corps; having its right upon the great road about Pierrefitte, its left upon the great road of Senlis, and its advanced posts at Aubervilliers and in front of St. Denis.

The 1st corps under Sir John Byng, comprising the 1st and 3rd divisions, and the Dutch-Belgian troops, were in the position previously occupied by the 1st

Prussian corps; having its right upon the great road behind le Bourget, its left upon the forest of Bondy, and its advanced posts along the Ourcq canal.

The reserve, under Sir James Kempt, was encamped between Louvres and Vauderlan.

The cavalry was encamped and cantoned about the villages of Groussainville, Vauderlan, and Roissy.

The pontoon-train and the hawser-bridges were at Sarcelles, on the Chantilly road to Paris.

The head-quarters of the Duke of Wellington were at Gonesse.

The 1st Prussian corps d'armée was encamped between the villages of le Mesnil and Carrière au Mont, on the left bank of the Seine, not far from St. Germain.

The 3rd corps was also on the left bank of the Seine, in the valley, and near St. Germain. Its advanced guard (the 9th brigade) was at Rocquencourt.

The 4th corps was upon the march to St. Germain.

Prince Blücher's head-quarters were at St. Germain.

The 3rd and 4th French corps d'armée and the imperial guard were on the south side of Paris, their right upon the Seine, their left by Montrouge; with the advanced guard at Chatillon, Clamord, Meudon, Sèvres, and St. Cloud.

The remainder of the French army continued within the capital.

The Prince of Eckmuhl's head-quarters were at Villette.

At daybreak of the 2nd of July, Blücher put the whole Prussian army in motion towards the south side of Paris, where he purposed taking possession of the advantageous position comprising the heights of Meudon and Chatillon, and their immediate vicinity. Thielemann's advanced guard (the 9th brigade) immediately proceeded to occupy Versailles. The corps itself halted two hours at Rocquencourt to wait for the arrival of Zieten's corps. As the latter corps advanced, it threw out a detachment to its left, consisting of the 1st battalion of the 1st West Prussian regiment, two pieces of horse-artillery, and a squadron of cavalry, under Captain Krensky, who was directed to proceed by Malmaison towards St. Cloud, communicating with Major Colomb, who had already been detached, with the force before mentioned as being under his command, towards the bridge of Neuilly, and to keep a look-out to the left of the direct road to Paris. On Zieten's advanced guard reaching Villedavray, whence it drove off a French picquet, information was obtained that the enemy was restoring the bridge of St. Cloud, which he had previously destroyed, and that he occupied the Bois de Boulogne in considerable force. The 3rd brigade was therefore ordered to proceed by its left towards St. Cloud, and to oppose any movement which might be attempted against that flank.

It was three o'clock in the afternoon when Zieten's 1st brigade, under Steinmetz, reached Sèvres. Here the French were strongly posted, occupying the place itself, the heights of Bellevue, and having their light troops well disposed amongst the adjacent gardens and vineyards. The 1st Prussian brigade was followed in support by the 2nd and 4th brigades; and, notwithstanding the very gallant defence that was made, these troops succeeded in forcing the French to abandon their stronghold, and fall back upon Moulineau. Here the French made another stand, but were again defeated by Steinmetz, who had closely pursued them. Whilst the 1st brigade was thus gaining ground, the 2nd, together with the reserve-artillery, advanced towards the heights of Meudon. The reserve-cavalry of the corps followed the 1st brigade, in support. The 4th brigade occupied Sèvres. Major General Jagow, who had been detached to the left, with the 3rd brigade, having ascertained that the enemy was not likely to undertake any movement from the Bois de Boulogne, and that Captain Krensky's detachment was on the look-out in that direction, proceeded to rejoin the corps, and on reaching Sèvres, towards evening, he was directed by Zieten to take up a position, with his brigade, to the right, on the heights of Meudon.

In the evening, the French, after having re-formed, and collected their defeated force at Issy, made an attempt to regain possession of Moulineau, but the attack failed, and they were driven back upon Issy. Here they were reinforced: 15 battalions were posted in and about Issy, supported by numerous guns and cavalry; their light infantry occupying the vineyards in front of the village. About half-past ten o'clock in the night, however, the Prussians, who kept a sharp look-out, heard these troops marching off, and perceived that their departure was conducted in rather a disorderly manner. Instant advantage was taken of this circumstance, and a part of the 1st and 2nd Prussian brigades attacked the French, who fled back upon the suburb of Vaugirard in such confusion, that Paris might have been entered at this moment, if more force had been at hand.

During the night, Zieten posted his corps in the following manner:—his right upon the height of Clamord, his centre upon that of Meudon, and his left in Molineau; Sèvres still occupied; the advanced-guard in Issy, in the rear of which village was the reserve-cavalry in support.

Whilst Zieten's corps had been thus successfully effecting its movement against the south side of the capital, Thielemann's, which formed the right column, proceeded towards Plessis-Piquet and pushed forward its advanced guard to the heights of Chatillon, which it reached late in the evening. Bülow's corps, acting as a reserve, occupied Versailles and its vicinity during the night.

During the whole of this day, the troops of the Anglo-allied army continued in position in front of the fortified lines on the north side of Paris. The Duke having established a bridge at Argenteuil, detachments were sent across the Seine: and these, having secured the villages of Anières, Courbevoie, and Suresnes, on the left bank of the Seine, opened a communication with the Prussians.

The Allied commanders had thus succeeded in shutting up the French forces within their lines. Wellington was perfectly prepared to attack the north side of Paris, if circumstances should render such a step necessary, or if a favourable opportunity should present itself; whilst Blücher, having secured a strong position in front of the south side, which was mostly open and defenceless, was equally ready to storm the capital with his collected force. The effect of this well-conceived and successfully-executed plan of operation was to divide the enemy's attention between two opposite points of the town. Should he attempt to assail the one army with his principal force, he would immediately find himself attacked by the other army, without possessing the means wherewith to carry on the contest with both simultaneously. On the other hand, should a general and formidable assault be made by those armies, on the opposite points, at the same time, the necessary division of his forces, in arranging his plan of defence, would render his situation still more desperate.

The provisional government, fully alive to this state of things, and duly aware of the approach of the Bavarian, Russian, and Austrian, armies, clearly saw the inutility of further resistance to the Allies, and instructed the commissioners to wait upon the Duke of Wellington, and report to his Grace the fact of Napoleon having quitted Paris on the 29th, to embark for the United States, and to press the point of a suspension of hostilities. To this representation the Duke replied that the great obstacle to the armistice having thus been removed, there remained only the question as to the terms, which he thought should be, the halting of the Anglo-allied and Prussian armies in their present positions, the withdrawal of the French army from Paris across the Loire, and the placing of the capital in the keeping of the national guards until the King should order otherwise. He offered, if they agreed to these terms, to endeavour to prevail on Prince Blücher to halt his troops and send an officer to settle the details; but, at the same time, he told them distinctly that he would not consent to suspend hostilities so long as a French soldier remained in Paris. Having received this explicit declaration on the part of his Grace the commissioners withdrew.

The following were the positions of the respective armies during the night of the 2nd of July: —

The troops of the Anglo-allied army continued in position in front of the lines of St. Denis. Detachments were at Anières, Courbevoie, and Suresnes, on the left bank of the Seine.

The 1st Prussian corps d'armée had its right on the height of Clamard, its centre on that of Meudon, its left at Moulineau, and its advanced guard at Issy: in rear of which point was the reserve-cavalry of the corps.

Of the 3rd corps, the 9th brigade was at Chatillon, the 10th and 11th brigades were in front of Velisy, the 12th brigade was at Chatenay and Sceaux. The reserve-cavalry of the corps bivouacked about Plessis-Picquet.

Of the 4th corps, the 16th brigade was at Montreuil, in advance of Versailles; the 13th brigade bivouacked near Viroflay; the 14th brigade bivouacked at Lechesnay bel Air, not far from Rocquencourt. The reserve-cavalry of the corps was partly in front of Versailles, and partly on the left of Montreuil.

The troops composing the right wing of the French army occupied the lines on the right bank of the Seine, whence they were watching the British. Some troops were posted in the Bois de Boulogne, and several posts were established along both banks of the river.

The left wing extended from the Seine as far as the Orleans road. It held Vaugirard strongly occupied, the main body was posted between the barrières de l'Ecole militaire and de l'Enfer.

At three o'clock on the morning of the 3rd of July, Vandamme advanced in two columns from Vaugirard to the attack of Issy. Between Vaugirard and the Seine, he had a considerable force of cavalry, the front of which was flanked by a battery, advantageously posted near Auteuil, on the right bank of the river. The action commenced with a brisk cannonade: the French having brought twenty pieces of cannon against the front of the village, which was then vigorously assailed by his infantry. The Prussians had constructed some barricades, and other defences, during the night, but these did not protect them from the sharp fire of case-shot which was poured upon them by the French batteries, the guns of which enfiladed the streets. The 12th and 24th Prussian regiments, and the 2nd Westphalian landwehr, supported by a half battery of 12-pounders, fought with great bravery. There was much loss on both sides. At length the French withdrew; but only to advance again, considerably reinforced.

The 2nd Prussian brigade was immediately ordered to join the 1st, and the whole of the troops of the 1st corps stood to their arms. Zieten sent a request to Prince Blücher for the support of two brigades of Bülow's corps; and, at the same time, begged Thielemann to advance (in conformity with instructions conveyed to him from head-quarters) from Chatillon, and threaten the enemy's left flank.

In the mean time, the French renewed their attack upon

Issy, which, however, again proved unsuccessful. This was followed by a heavy cannonade and by further assaults, without any decided advantage having been gained over the defenders. The French did not appear disposed to venture upon a more general attack, which would have offered them a much greater chance of forcing back the Prussian advanced guard, probably considering that, if unsuccessful, it might end in the suburbs of Paris being easily carried by storm; and hence, after four hours' continued, but fruitless, attempts upon Zieten's advanced position, they fell back upon Paris, the Prussian tirailleurs following them until they came within a very short distance of the barriers.

At a council of war, which had been held during the previous night in Paris, it was decided that the defence of the capital was not practicable against the Allied armies. Nevertheless, Davoust was desirous that another attempt should be made on the Prussian army; but now that this had failed in the manner described, that the two Allied armies were in full communication with each other, and that a British corps was likewise moving upon the left of the Seine, towards Neuilly, a capitulation was determined upon. Accordingly, at seven o'clock in the morning, the fire on the part of the French suddenly ceased; and General Revest was deputed to pass over to Zieten's corps, which of all the Allied troops was the nearest to the capital, for the purpose of offering a capitulation, and requesting an immediate armistice. Blücher, however, required from Marshal Davoust, the commander-in-chief of the French army, a negotiator possessing greater powers, before he would finally agree to a suspension of hostilities, and indicated the palace of St. Cloud, as the place where the negotiations should be carried on, to which point he then removed his head-quarters.

During the contest at Issy, the detachments on the left of the 1st Prussian corps, under Captain Krensky, were engaged rather sharply with the enemy between St. Cloud and Neuilly, which ended in the French being driven back upon the bridge at the latter place, towards which point also a body of British troops was advancing. Thus Zieten's corps, the same that had opened the campaign with the actions along the Sambre, had the honour of closing it with those at Issy and Neuilly on the Seine.

Officers furnished with full powers by their respective chiefs, soon met at St. Cloud, whither the Duke of Wellington had already repaired in person to join Prince Blücher; and the result of their deliberations was the following

Military Convention.

This day, the 3rd of July, 1815, the Commissioners named by the Commanders-in-chief of the respective armies; that is to say, the Baron Bignon, holding the portfolio of foreign affairs: the Count Guilleminot, chief of the general staff of the French army; the Count de Bondy, prefect of the department of the Seine; being furnished with the full powers of his Excellency the Marshal Prince of Eckmuhl, commander-in-chief of the French army, on one side: and Major General Baron Müffling, furnished with the full powers of his Highness the Field Marshal Prince Blücher, commander-in-chief of the Prussian army; and Colonel Hervey, furnished with the full powers of his Excellency the Duke of Wellington, commander-in-chief of the English army, on the other side, have agreed to the following articles.

Article I. There shall be a suspension of arms between the Allied armies commanded by his Highness the Prince Blücher and his Grace the Duke of Wellington, and the French army under the walls of Paris.

Art. II. The French army shall put itself in march to-morrow, to take up a position beyond the Loire. Paris shall be completely evacuated in three days; and the movement behind the Loire shall be effected within eight days.

Art. III. The French army shall take with it all its matériel, field-artillery, military-chest, horses, and property of regiments, without exception. All persons belonging to the depôts shall also be removed, as well as those belonging to the different branches of administration which appertain to the army.

Art. IV. The sick and wounded, and the medical officers whom it may be necessary to leave with them, are placed under the special protection of the Commanders-in-chief of the English and Prussian armies.

Art. V. The military, and those holding employments to whom the foregoing article relates, shall be at liberty, immediately after their recovery, to rejoin the corps to which they belong.

Art. VI. The wives and children of all individuals belonging to the French army shall be at liberty to remain in Paris. The wives shall be allowed to quit Paris for the purpose of rejoining the army, and to carry with them their property and that of their husbands.

Art. VII. The officers of the line employed with the *Fédérés*, or with the tirailleurs of the national guard, may either join the army, or return to their homes, or the places of their birth.

Art. VIII. To-morrow, the 4th of July, at mid-day, St. Denis, St. Ouen, Clichy, and Neuilly shall be given up. The day after to-morrow, the 5th, at the same hour, Montmartre shall be given up. The third day, the 6th, all the barriers shall be given up.

Art. IX. The duty of the city of Paris shall continue to be done by the national guard, and by the corps of the municipal gensd'armerie.

Art. X. The Commanders-in-chief of the English and Prussian armies engage to respect, and to make those under their command respect, the actual authorities, so long as they shall exist.

Art. XI. Public property, with the exception of that which relates to war, whether it belongs to the government, or depends upon the municipal authority, shall be respected, and the Allied powers will not interfere in any manner with its administration and management.

Art. XII. Private persons and property shall be equally respected. The inhabitants, and in general all individuals who shall be in the capital, shall continue to enjoy their rights and liberties, without being disturbed or called to account, either as to the situations which they hold, or may have held, or as to their conduct or political opinions.

Art. XIII. The foreign troops shall not interpose any obstacles to the provisioning of the capital, and will protect, on the contrary, the arrival and the free circulation of the articles which are destined for it.

Art. XIV. The present convention shall be observed, and shall serve to regulate the mutual relations until the conclusion of peace. In case of rupture it must be denounced in the usual forms at least ten days beforehand.

Art. XV. If any difficulties arise in the execution of any one of the articles of the present Convention, the interpretation of it shall be made in favour of the French army and of the city of Paris.

Art. XVI. The present Convention is declared common to all the Allied armies, provided it be ratified by the powers on which these armies are dependant.

Art. XVII. The ratifications shall be exchanged to-morrow, the 4th of July, at six o'clock in the morning, at the bridge of Neuilly.

Art. XVIII. Commissioners shall be named by the respective parties, in order to watch over the execution of the present Convention.

Done and signed at St. Cloud, in triplicate, by the Commissioners above named, the day and year before mentioned.

The Baron Bignon.
The Count Guilleminot.
The Count de Bondy.
The Baron de Müffling.
F. B. Hervey, Colonel.

Approved and ratified the present suspension of arms, at Paris, the 3rd of July, 1815.

The Marshal Prince of Eckmuhl.

Afterwards approved by Prince Blücher and the Duke of Wellington; and the ratifications exchanged on the 4th of July.

The terms of the Convention were literally fulfilled. On the 4th, the French army, commanded by Marshal Davoust, quitted Paris, and proceeded on its march to the Loire; and the Anglo-allied troops occupied St. Denis, St. Ouen, Clichy, and Neuilly. On the 5th, the latter took possession of Montmartre. On the 6th, they occupied the barriers of Paris, upon the right of the Seine, and the Prussians those upon the left bank. On the 7th, the two Allied armies entered Paris: the chamber of peers, having received from the provisional government a notification of the course of events, terminated its sittings; the chamber of deputies protested, but in vain. Their president (Lanjuinais) quitted his chair, and on the following day, the doors were closed, and the approaches guarded by foreign troops.

On the 8th, the French King, Louis XVIII. made his public entry into his capital, amidst the acclamations of the people, and again occupied the palace of his ancestors.

It was also on the 8th that Napoleon Buonaparte embarked, at Rochefort, on board the French frigate *La Saale*, and proceeded, accompanied by *La Méduse*, in which was his suite, to the roads of the Isle of Aix, with the intention of setting sail for America. On the 10th the wind became favourable, but a British fleet made its appearance, and Napoleon, seeing the difficulty of eluding the vigilance of its cruisers, resolved, after having previously communicated with Captain Maitland, upon placing himself under his protection on board the

Bellerophon, which vessel he accordingly reached on the 15th. On the following day, Captain Maitland sailed for England, and arrived at Torbay, with his illustrious charge, on the 24th. The Ex-Emperor was not permitted to land, and the British government having decided upon sending him to the island of St. Helena, he was removed to the Northumberland man-of-war, under Rear Admiral Sir George Cockburne, in which ship he sailed for that distant rock, the final abode on earth of the man whose extraordinary career marks the most stirring and eventful period in the history of Europe.

The Convention of Paris constituted a basis for the resumption of negotiations for the general peace which, a few months before, had been so unexpectedly interrupted. The celebrated statesmen of that remarkable period—Castlereagh, Nesselrode, Metternich, Hardenberg, and Talleyrand—aided by distinguished representatives of the minor European states, now perceived the importance of establishing a more closely cemented alliance; reconciling the clashing interests of emulative governments, securing the rights of the legitimate sovereign of France, and consolidating the re-established order of things in that country. The mere engagement of the French government to a treaty of peace and grateful amity, was not considered a sufficient guarantee for the long-desired repose of Europe. France, which dictated laws according to her own desires and interests, to the entire continent, was now, in her turn, to be subjected to the most severe conditions. In order to guarantee her compliance with the demands required of her by the wants and necessities of the nations panting for that peace which was to relieve their exhausted means, and to avert the dangers of internal dissensions, she was destined to witness the occupation of her frontier fortresses by a vast army, comprising contingent forces from the Allied powers, and requiring to be maintained upon a full war establishment, at her expense; whilst, at the same time, heavy contributions were laid upon her for the purpose of indemnifying the sovereigns who had been compelled again to take up arms against her.

But, notwithstanding these reverses and indemnities, France herself is, perhaps, the country that has most benefited by that general peace which was established on the ruins of her empire. The rational form of government which was secured to her by an enlarged constitutional charter, has gradually introduced among her people the most salutary reforms, and the most liberal institutions: the stimulus given to her industry by the cessation of harassing wars, of persecuting conscriptions, and of vexatious imposts, rapidly obtained for her a commercial prosperity to which she had long been a stranger; whilst an unusual period of tranquillity has so completely renovated and invigorated her resources, both moral and physical, as to place her again in the rank of the highest powers.

Now that the nation has completely recovered from the effects of the convulsive throes which attended its dissolution as an empire, and has assumed the calm and dignified attitude of repose, in its resuscitated strength it contemplates the past in a more rational and philosophic spirit, balancing the evil with the good. If the public mind of France dwell for a time upon the tyrannical exercise of Napoleon's power upon the people, the sadness of the reflection is palliated by his flattering, though personally ambitious, desire to render France the arbitress of Europe: if it perceive the rights of the citizens subverted for the furtherance of his designs, the impression thus produced vanishes at the contemplation of the *Code Napoléon:* if it appear shocked by the general perversion of labour from its natural sphere to purely military purposes, it is again soothed by the grandeur in design, and utility in effect, of mighty enterprises, conferring employment on myriads of artists and artisans: if it be disposed to disapprove of the spoliation authorized in foreign states, it is speedily flattered by the grand idea of rendering Paris the centre of civilization and of the arts: and finally, if it feel pained and subdued by a contemplation of the disasters of Moscow, Vittoria, Leipzic, and Waterloo, it revives and rejoices in recounting the glorious triumphs of Marengo, Austerlitz, Jena, and Wagram.

If one country more than any other required a lasting peace to enable her to recover from the effects of the immense sacrifices she had made, in life and treasure—sacrifices which proved, beyond doubt, the salvation of Europe—that country was Great Britain. Through the intelligence of her statesmen, the freedom of her constitution, the enterprise of her merchants, the industry of her artisans, and the bravery of her naval and military defenders, she continues to maintain her lofty position in the scale of nations; and even to extend her empire and her sway to the furthermost points of the earth. But to whom is she mainly indebted for this proud preeminence, this unparalleled grandeur? To such a question every Briton, no matter what may be the direction of his political feelings or party prejudices, will unhesitatingly reply —to the rare talent, the untiring zeal, and practised skill, of her Chief who led, as also to the inflexible courage, extraordinary endurance, and the perfect discipline, of her sons who fought, her last and ever-memorable struggle on the continent of Europe—the Battle of Waterloo. It was upon the solid foundation thus obtained that was raised that well-cemented superstructure, the solemn compact of sovereigns and states, constituting the General Peace of 1815; and although, as time rolls on, symptoms of decay may be traced in some portions of the edifice, still it stands, a monument of the downfall of an insatiable ambition, aiming at universal dominion, and continues to this day the surest guarantee of the preservation of that equitable balance of power which can alone secure the permanence of the tranquillity and prosperity of Europe.

SUPPLEMENT.

The Battle of Waterloo, followed as it was by the advance of the Anglo-allied and Prussian armies upon Paris, was so decisive in its effects, and so comprehensive in its results, that the great object of the war—the destruction of the power of Napoleon and the restoration of the legitimate sovereign—was attained while the armies of the Upper Rhine and of Italy were but commencing their invasion of the French territory. Had the successes attendant upon the exertions of Wellington and Blücher assumed a less decisive character, and, more especially, had reverses taken the place of those successes, the operations of the armies advancing from the Rhine and across the Alps would have acquired an immense importance in the history of the war; but the brilliant course of events in the north of France materially diminished the interest excited by the military transactions in other parts of the kingdom. Upon this ground it has been considered, that to enter into any very detailed account of the movements and dispositions of the Allies, on the eastern frontier, is unnecessary, and that the completion of the present work will be sufficiently accomplished by the addition of a simple outline of the daily progress and attendant circumstances of the advance of each army into the interior of the country.

Operations of the German Corps d'Armée.

This corps, which was composed of contingent forces supplied by the petty Princes of North Germany, was assembled, in the middle of April, in the vicinity of Coblentz. It amounted to 26,200 men, divided into 30 battalions, 12 squadrons, and 2½ batteries; and was placed under the command of General Count Kleist von Nollendorf. At a somewhat later period it crossed the Rhine at Coblentz and Neuwied, and took up a position on the Moselle and the Sarre, its right communicating with the 3rd Prussian corps d'armée, and its left with the Bavarian troops at Zweibrücken. Its advanced posts extended along the French frontier from Arlon to Mertzig. Its head-quarters were at Trier, on the Moselle.

In this position it remained until the 16th of June, when its commander, General von Engelhard (in the absence of Count Kleist, who was ill), advanced from Trier to Arlon, which it reached on the 19th. Here it continued until the 21st, when it received an order from Prince Blücher to move into France by Bastogne and Neufchâteau, and to gain possession of the fortresses of Sedan and Bouillon. On the 22nd, the corps commenced its march, in two columns; the one by Neufchâteau, upon Sedan, the other by

Recogne, upon Bouillon. Sedan, after a few days' bombardment, capitulated on the 25th of June. An attempt was made to take Bouillon by a *coup de main,* but its garrison was strong enough to frustrate this project. The place was not considered of sufficient importance to render a regular siege expedient, and it was therefore simply invested, from the 25th of June until the 21st of August, when it was blockaded at all points by troops of the Netherlands, under Prince Frederick of Orange.

On the 28th of June, Lieut. General von Hacke, who had been appointed to the command of the German corps, directed the advanced guard to move upon Charleville, which lies under the guns of the fortress of Mezières, and to carry the place by storm. The capture was successfully made by some Hessian battalions, and tended greatly to facilitate the siege of Mezières. Moveable columns were detached to observe the fortresses of Montmédy, Laon, and Rheims. The last named place was taken by capitulation on the 8th of July; and the garrison, amounting to 4,000 men, retired behind the Loire.

Lieut. General von Hacke, finding that notwithstanding his vigorous bombardment of Mezières, which he commenced on the 27th of June, his summons to surrender was unheeded by the commandant, General Lemoine, undertook a regular siege of the place, and opened trenches on the 2nd of August. On the 13th the French garrison gave up the town, and retired into the citadel, which surrendered on the 1st of September.

The efforts of the corps were now directed upon Montmédy, around which fortress it had succeeded in placing 12 batteries in position by the 13th of September. After an obstinate resistance, the garrison concluded a convention on the 20th of September, by which it was to retire, with arms and baggage, behind the Loire.

After the capture of Montmédy, the German corps d'armée went into cantonments in the department of the Ardennes, whence it returned home in the month of November.

Operations of the Army of the Upper Rhine, under the command of Field Marshal His Highness Prince Schwartzenberg.

This army consisted of four corps d'armée, and reserves, composed of troops of Austria, Bavaria, Wirtemberg, Saxony, of Hesse-Darmstadt, and of the petty Princes.

Its strength was as follows: —

			Battalions.	Squadrons.	Batteries.
1st corps de armée	24,400	men, in	26	16	8
2nd ...	34,350	...	36	26	11
3rd ...	43,814	...	44	32	9
4th ...	57,040	...	46	66	15
Austrian Reserve Corps	44,800	...	38	86	10
Blockade Corps	33,314	...	38	8	6
Saxon corps d'armée	16,774	...	18	10	6
Total	254,492	...	246	244	65

According to the general plan of operations projected by Prince Schwartzenberg, this army was to cross the Rhine in two columns. The right column, consisting of the 3rd corps, under Field Marshal the Crown-Prince of Wirtemberg, and of the 4th corps, or the Bavarian army, under Field Marshal Prince Wrède, was to cross the Rhine between Gemersheim and Manheim. The left column, consisting of the 1st corps, under the Master General of the Ordnance, Count Colloredo, and of the 2nd corps, under General Prince Hohenzollern Heckingen, together with the Austrian reserve corps, the whole being commanded by General the Archduke Ferdinand, was to cross the Rhine between Basle and Rheinfelden. The column formed by the right wing was to be supported by the Russian army, under Field Marshal Count Barclay de Tolly, which was expected to be collected at Kaiserslautern by the 1st of July. The object of the operations, in the first instance, was the concentration of the Army of the Upper Rhine and the Russian army at Nancy.

As soon as Prince Schwartzenberg was made acquainted with the commencement of hostilities in Belgium, he gave his orders for the advance of his army. The 4th, or Bavarian, corps d'armée was directed immediately to cross the Sarre, and, by turning the Vosgian Mountains, to cut off the French corps under General Rapp, collected in the environs of Strasburg, from its base of operations, and to intercept its communications with the interior of France.

A Russian corps, under General Count Lambert, forming the advance of the army of Count Barclay de Tolly, was united to the corps d'armée of Prince Wrède, who was to employ it principally in keeping up the communication with the North German corps d'armée, under Lieut. General von Hacke.

4th Corps d'armée, Prince Wrède.

On the 19th of June the Bavarian army crossed the Rhine at Manheim and Oppenheim, and advanced towards the Sarre. On the 20th, some trifling affairs of advanced posts occurred near Landau and Dahn. On the 23rd, the army having approached the Sarre, proceeded, in two columns, to take possession of the passages across the river at Saarbrück and Saargemünd.

The right column, under Lieut.-General Count Beckers, attacked Saarbrück, where it was opposed by the French General Meriage. The Bavarians carried the suburb and the bridge, and penetrated into the town along with the retiring French, of whom they made 4 officers and 70 men prisoners, and killed and wounded 100 men; suffering a loss, on their own part, of 3 officers and from 50 to 60 men killed and wounded. Count Beckers occupied the town, posted his division on the heights towards Forbach, and detached patroles along the road to Metz, as far as St. Avold, and to the right along the Sarre, as far as Saarlouis.

The left column, consisting of the 1st infantry division, under Lieut. General Baron von Ragliovich, and of the 1st cavalry-division, under his Royal Highness Prince Charles of Bavaria, advanced against Saargemünd, at which point the French had constructed a *tête de pont* on the right bank of the river. After some resistance, this was taken possession of by the Bavarians, whereupon Baron von Ragliovich marched through the town, and took up a position on the opposite heights, commanding the roads leading to Bouquenom and Lüneville.

The 4th infantry-division, under Lieut. General Baron Zollern, advanced towards the fortress of Bitsch, which, however, the French commandant, General Kreutzer, refused to surrender.

The Russian corps, under Count Lambert, attached to the right wing of Prince Wrède's army, advanced as far as Ottweiler and Ramstein.

On the 24th, Prince Wrède occupied Bouquenom, and detached the cavalry-division under Prince Charles towards Pfalzburg, to observe this place. His 2nd, 3rd, and 4th divisions, and the reserve, were collected at Saargemünd. The Russian troops under Count Lambert occupied Saarbrück, having previously detached the cavalry, under Lieut. General Czernitscheff, as far as St. Avold.

On the 26th, Prince Wrède's head-quarters were at Morhenge, and, on the 27th, his advanced posts penetrated as far as Nancy, where he established his head-quarters on the 28th. From St. Dieuze the Prince detached to the left, in order to discover the march of General Rapp; who, however, was still on the Rhine, and whose retreat had thus become cut off by the occupation of Nancy.

Prince Wrède halted at Nancy, to await the arrival of the Austrian and Russian corps d'armée. Upon his right, Lieut. General Czernitscheff crossed the Moselle, on the 29th, within sight of Metz, and carried by storm, on the 3rd of July, the town of Châlons sur Marne. The garrison of this place had promised to make no resistance, and yet fired upon the Russian advanced guard; whereupon the cavalry immediately dismounted, scaled the ramparts, broke open the gates, sabred a part of the garrison, made the remainder prisoners, including the French General Rigault, and pillaged the town.

After remaining four days in the vicinity of Nancy and Lüneville, Prince Wrède received an order from Prince Schwartzenberg to move at once upon Paris, with the 4th, or Bavarian corps, which was destined to become the advanced guard of the Army of the Upper Rhine. This order was given in consequence of the desire expressed by the Duke of Wellington and Prince Blücher, that the Army of the Upper Rhine should afford immediate support to their operations in front of Paris. On the 5th of July, the main body of the Bavarian army reached Châlons, in the vicinity of which it remained during the 6th. On this day its advanced posts communicated by Epernay, with the Prussian army. On the 7th, Prince Wrède received intelligence of the Convention of Paris, and, at the same time, directions to move towards the Loire. On the 8th, Lieut. General Czernitscheff fell in with the enemy between St. Prix and Montmirail, and drove him across the Morin, towards the Seine. Previously to the arrival of the corps at Château-Thierry, the French garrison had abandoned the place, leaving behind it several pieces of cannon, with ammunition. On the 10th of July, the Bavarian army took up a position between the Seine and the Marne, and Prince Wrède's head-quarters were at la Fertè sous Jouarre.

3d Corps d'armée, Crown Prince of Wirtemberg.

On the 22nd of June, a portion of the 3rd corps d'armée under the Crown Prince of Wirtemberg, took possession of the intrenchments of Germersheim, on the left bank of the Rhine. Lieut. Field Marshal Count Wallmoden was posted, with 10 battalions and 4 squadrons, in observation of the fortress of Landau, and the line of the Queich. The main body of the corps stood between Bruchsal and Philipsburg. On the 23d, the corps crossed the Rhine at Germersheim, and passed the line of the Queich without opposition.

The Crown Prince was directed to proceed by Weissenburg and Hagenau, with a view to complete, in conjunction with the 4th corps d'armée, the plan of intercepting the retreat of General Rapp.

On the 24th, the corps advanced to Bergzabern and Nieder-Ottersbach, at both of which points it fell in with the enemy, and drove him back. Count Wallmoden left a small detachment to observe Landau, and advanced, with the remainder of his force, as far as Rheinzabern. On the 25th, the Crown Prince ordered the advance towards the lines of Weissenburg, in two columns. The first column assembled at Bergzabern, and the second moved forward by Nieder-Ottersbach. Count Wallmoden was directed to advance upon Lauterburg. The Crown Prince advanced his corps still further along the Hagenau road. His advanced guard pushed on to Inglesheim, and the main body of the corps reached the lines of Weissenburg, which the French abandoned in the night, and fell back upon the forest of Hagenau, occupying the large village of Surburg. On the 26th, the Crown Prince attacked and defeated the enemy at the last mentioned place, with his right column, whilst the left column, under Count Wallmoden, was equally successful in an attack which it made upon the French General Rothenburg, posted, with 6,000 infantry and a regiment of cavalry, at Selz. On the following day, General Rapp fell back upon the defile of Brümath, but this he quitted in the night, and took up a favourable position in the rear of the Suffel, near Strasburg. His force comprised 24 battalions of infantry, 4 regiments of cavalry, and a numerous artillery, and amounted to nearly 24,000 men.

The Crown Prince of Wirtemberg, whose force amounted altogether to more than 40,000 men, succeeded, on the 28th, after a smart action, in forcing General Rapp to retire within the fortress of Strasburg. The loss of the 3rd corps on this occasion amounted to 75 officers, and 2,050 men, killed and wounded. That of the French was about 3,000 men.

Austrian Reserve-corps, Archduke Ferdinand.

The 3rd corps remained in front of Strasburg until the 4th of July, when it was relieved by the arrival of the 2nd Austrian corps, under Prince Hohenzollern, from the vicinity of Colmar. At this last point the advanced guard of the Austrian reserve-corps, under Lieut. Field Marshal Stutterheim, moved upon Remiremont, and the main body upon Ste Marie aux mines. The Austrian reserve-corps itself reached Raon l'Etape, whence it subsequently moved (on the 10th) to Neufchâteau. The 3rd corps, under the Crown Prince of Wirtemberg, marched into the vicinity of Molsheim.

On the 7th of July, the Crown Prince reached Lüneville, but instead of proceeding to Nancy, according to its original destination, the corps, on the 9th, took the road to Neufchâteau. The advance was in two columns; the one upon Bayon, and the other upon Rembervillers. These two columns moved respectively, the one, by Vaucouleurs, Joinville, Brienne le Château, Troyes, and Auxonne; and the other, by Neufchâteau, Chaumont, Bar sur Aube, Vendoeuvres, Bar sur Seine, and Chatillon; at which points (Auxonne and Chatillon) they halted on the 18th. On the 21st, the corps entered into cantonments between Montbard and Tonnerre.

1st and 2nd Corps—Count Colloredo and Prince von Hohenzollern.—Reserve-corps, Archduke Ferdinand.

The 1st and 2nd Austrian corps d'armée and the reserve-corps, forming the left wing of the army of the Upper Rhine, crossed this river at Rheinfelden and Basle in the night of the 25th of June. On the 26th, the 1st, under Count Colloredo, was directed upon Béfort and Montbelliard; and, on the same day, the Austrians invested the fortress of Huningen. The advanced guard of the 1st corps had an affair with a French detachment of 3000 men, belonging to the corps of General Lecourbe, and repulsed it as far as Donnemarie. On the 28th, the 1st corps fell in with the enemy near Chabannes, between Donnemarie and Befort, when the French force, amounting to 8000 infantry and 500 cavalry, was driven back upon Béfort. Major General von Scheither of the 1st corps was detached against Montbelliard, a town fortified and defended by a citadel. After having maintained a most destructive fire against the place, the Austrian troops carried it by storm; with a loss, however, of 25 officers and 1000 men, killed and wounded.

With the exception of a few sorties of little consequence, General Rapp remained very quiet in the fortress of Strasburg. The news of the capture of Paris by the British and Prussian troops led to a suspension of hostilities, which was concluded on the 24th of July, and extended to the fortress of Strasburg, Landau, Lutzelstein, Huningen, Schlettstadt, Lichtenberg, Pfalzburg, Neuf-Brisac, and Béfort.

The Russian Army.

The main body of the Russian army, commanded by Field Marshal Count Barclay de Tolly, and amounting to 167,950 men, crossed the Rhine at Manheim, on the 25th of June, and followed the army of the Upper Rhine. The greater portion of it reached Paris and its vicinity by the middle of July.

Operations of the Army of Italy.

The army of Italy, composed of Austrian and Sardinian troops, and amounting to 60,000 men, was under the command of General Baron Frimont. It was destined to act against the army of the Alps, under Marshal Suchet, posted in the vicinity of Chambery and Grenoble. It is uncertain what was the amount of force under Suchet, it having been estimated from 13,000 to 20,000 men; but the corps of observation on the Var, in the vicinity of Antibes and Toulon, under Marshal Brune, amounted to 10,000, and was not occupied with any enemy in its front.

Baron Frimont's army was divided into two corps; the one under Lieut. Field Marshal Radivojevich, was to advance by the Valais towards Lyons; and the other, which was in Piedmont, under Lieut. Field Marshal Count Bubna, was to penetrate into the south of France, through Savoy.

Marshal Suchet had received orders from Napoleon to commence operations on the 14th of June, and by rapid marches to secure the mountain passes in the Valais and in Savoy, and close them against the Austrians. On the 15th, his troops advanced at all points for the purpose of gaining the frontier from Montmeilian, as far as Geneva, which he invested. Thence he purposed to obtain possession of the important passes of Meillerie and St. Maurice, and in this way to check the advance of the Austrian columns from the Valais. At Meillerie the French were met and driven back by the advanced guard of the Austrian right column, on the 21st of June. By means of forced marches the whole of this column, which Baron Frimont himself accompanied, reached the Arve on the 27th of June.

The left column, under Count Bubna, crossed Mount Cenis on the 24th and 25th of June. On the 28th it was sharply opposed by the French at Conflans, of which place, however, the Austrians succeeded in gaining possession.

In order to secure the passage of the Arve the advanced guard of the right column detached, on the 27th, to Bonneville, on its left; but the French, who had already fortified this place, maintained a stout resistance. In the mean time, however, the Austrians gained possession of the passage at Carrouge, by which means the French were placed under the necessity of evacuating Bonneville, and abandoning the valley of the Arve. The column now passed Geneva, and drove the enemy from the heights of Grand Saconex and from St. Genix. On the 29th this part of the army moved towards the Jura; and, on the 1st July, it made its dispositions for attacking the redoubts and intrenchments which the French had thrown up to defend the passes. The most vigorous assault was made upon the pass of Les Rousses; but the Austrians were driven back. Reserves were then brought up, and the French having quitted their intrenchments to meet the latter, and a good opportunity having offered for a flank attack upon them with cavalry and artillery, the pass was captured by the Austrians; and the French were compelled to abandon both it and the other passes of the Jura. The Austrian advanced guard pursued the enemy, and reached, in the evening, St. Claude, on the road leading to the left from Gex, and St. Laurent, in the original direction of the attack, beyond Les Rousses.

In the mean time, the Austrian reserve-corps, under Lieut. Field Marshal Meerville, was directed to advance, and to throw back the French upon the Rhone. The latter, in retreating, destroyed the bridge of Seyselle; and, by holding the fort of l'Ecluse, closed the road from Geneva to Lyons. A redoubt had been constructed in front of the fort, and completely commanded the approach. It was gallantly stormed and carried by the regiment of Esterhazy. The fort itself was now turned by the reserve-corps along the left bank of the Rhone, with the design of forcing the passage at the Perte du Rhone. Here the French had constructed a *tête de pont*, which, however, they were forced to abandon in consequence of a movement made by the 1st corps under Lieut. Field Marshal Radivojevich. On retiring, they destroyed the very beautiful stone bridge then existing, and thus rendered it necessary for the Austrians to construct temporary bridges over the extremely narrow space between the rocks which confine the stream at this remarkable spot. The advanced guard of the reserve-corps, under General Count Hardegg, first crossed the Rhone, and found the enemy posted at Charix, in rear of Chatillon, on the road to Nantua. Count Hardegg immediately attacked him, and, after encountering an obstinate resistance, forced him to retire.

The troops of the 1st Austrian corps, which, in the mean time, were left in front of the fort l'Ecluse, had commenced a bombardment; and this, after twenty-six hours' duration, considerably damaged the fort. A powder-magazine exploded, which caused a general conflagration; to escape which the garrison rushed out, and surrendered at discretion to the Austrians: and thus, in three days, the high road from Geneva to Lyons was opened to the army of Italy.

On the 3rd July, General Bogdan, with the advanced guard of the 1st Austrian corps, having been reinforced by Lieut. Field Marshal Radivojevich, attacked the enemy with much impetuosity at Ojanax, beyond St. Claude, where the French General Maransin had taken up a favourable position, with 2,000 men. The Austrians turned his left flank, and forced him to retire. The corps reached Bourg en Bresse on the 9th July.

On the 10th July, a detachment, under Major General von Plüger, was pushed on to Maçon on the Saone, and gained possession of the *tête de pont* constructed there, and of the place itself.

On the 7th July, the 2nd corps, under Count Bubna, reached Echelles. A detachment, consisting principally of Sardinian troops, under Lieut. General Count Latour, had been directed to observe Grenoble, in front of which its advanced guard arrived on the 4th July. On the 6th, the suburbs were attacked, and the communication between this place and Lyons was cut off. The garrison, consisting of eight battalions of the national guard, offered to capitulate on the 9th, on the condition of being permitted to return to their homes. That a vigorous defence might have been maintained, was evident from the fact of the Austrians having found in the place 54 guns, and 8 mortars, and large quantities of provisions.

Count Bubna's corps and the reserve corps, by simultaneous movements, assembled together in front of Lyons on the 9th. An armistice was solicited by the garrison on the 11th July, and granted upon condition that Lyons and the intrenched camp should be evacuated, and that Marshal Suchet should retire with his corps behind the Loire, keeping his advanced posts within a stipulated line of demarcation.

Having secured possession of the line of the Rhone as far down as its junction with the Isère, as also of that part of the Saône between Maçon and Lyons, the army of Italy now proceeded towards the upper line of the latter river, leaving the 2nd corps, under Count Bubna, at Lyons, in front of Marshal Suchet. The 1st corps marched upon Chalons sur Saône, in order to gain the *tête de pont* at that point. At this time the 4th division of the army, under the French General Lecourbe, was at Salins, between Dôle and Pontarlier, and as Besançon had not yet been invested, Baron Frimont detached a part of the reserve-corps, under General Hecht, to Salins, whilst General Fölseis, detached from the 1st corps towards Dôle. The advanced guard of the 1st corps had arrived in front of the *tête de pont* at Chalons, and had completed its dispositions for attack, when the place surrendered. By the advance, at the same time, of Hecht upon Salins, and of Fölseis from Dôle upon Besançon, the retreat of the French General Laplane was completely cut off. This led to a convention which stipulated the dissolution of the national guards, the surrender of all the officers, and the abandonment of one of the forts of Salins to the Austrians.

On the 20th, the 1st corps d'armée advanced from Chalons sur Saône as far as Autun, and Besançon having in the mean time been occupied by the Austrian troops of the army of the Upper Rhine, a junction was effected with the latter by the army of Italy by Dijon.

The Sardinian General d'Osasca, who had been detached to Nice, concluded on the 9th of July an armistice with Marshal Brune, who commanded the army of the Var, in front of the Maritime Alps, and thus terminated all hostilities on that side of France.

The foregoing outline will suffice to show the nature, extent, and interconnection of the operations of the Allied armies which invaded France along her eastern and south-eastern frontier; and at the same time afford a clear proof that amongst the more immediate consequences of the decisive battle of Waterloo and speedy capture of

Paris must be ranked that of their having been the means of averting the more general and protracted warfare which would probably have taken place, had a different result in Belgium emboldened the French to act with vigour and effect in other parts of the country.

The reduction of the fortresses left in rear of the British and Prussian armies, adjoining their main line of operations, and which was confided to Prince Augustus of Prussia, with the 2nd Prussian corps d'armée, assisted by the British battering-train, was effected in the following manner:—

Maubeuge—siege commenced		8th July,	capitulated	12th July.
Landrecies	...	...	19th do.	...	21st do.
Marienberg	...	...	27th do.	...	28th do.
Philippeville	...	...	7th August,	...	8th August.
Rocroy	...	...	15th do.	...	16th do.

Prince Augustus had made every preparation for commencing the siege of Charlemont and its connecting forts, the two Givets and the Mont d'Hours, on the 8th of September, when the commandant, General Burcke, foreseeing that the occupation of the detached forts would divide his force too much, entered into negotiations, and surrendered those works on the 10th, withdrawing his troops into Charlemont; the bombardment of which was to have opened on the 23rd of September, but, on the 20th, Prince Augustus received information from Paris that hostilities were to cease throughout the whole of France.

APPENDIX.

I.

Declaration, on the 13*th of March*, 1815, *of the Allied Powers, upon the return of Napoleon Buonaparte to France.*

'à Vienne, ce 13 Mars, 1815.

'Les Puissances qui ont signé le Traité de Paris, réunies en Congrès à Vienne, informées de l'évasion de Napoléon Buonaparte, et de son entrée à main armée en France, doivent à leur propre dignité et à l'intérêt de l'ordre social une déclaration solemnelle des sentimens que cet événement leur a fait éprouver.

'En rompant ainsi la convention qui l'avait établi à l'isle d'Elbe, Buonaparte détruit le seul titre légal auquel son existence se trouvait attachée. En reparaissant en France, avec des projets de troubles et de bouleversemens, il s'est privé lui-même de la protection des lois, et a manifesté, à la face de l'univers, qu'il ne saurait y avoir ni paix ni trêve avec lui.

'Et quoiqu'intimement persuadés, que la France entière, se ralliant autour de son Souverain légitime, fera incessamment rentre dans le néant cette dernière tentative d'un délire criminel et impuissant, tous les Souverains de l'Europe, animés des mêmes sentimens et guidés par les mêmes principes, déclarent, que si, contre tout calcul, il pouvait résulter de cet événement un danger réel quelconque, ils seraient prêts à donner au Roi de France et à la nation Française ou à tout autre gouvernement attaqué dès que la demande en serait formée, les secours nécessaires pour rétablir la tranquillité publique, et à faire cause commune contre tous ceux qui entreprendraient de la compromettre.

'Les Puissances déclarent en conséquence que Napoléon Buonaparte s'est placé hors des relations civiles et sociales, et que, comme ennemi et perturbateur du repos du monde, il s'est livré à la vindicte publique.

'Elles déclarent en même tems que, fermement résolues de maintenir intact le Traité de Paris, du 30 Mai, 1814, et les dispositions sanctionnées par ce traité, et celles qu'elles ont arrêtées ou qu'elles arrêteront encore pour le completer et le consolider, elles emploieront tous leurs moyens et réuniront tous leurs efforts pour que la paix générale, objet des vœux de l'Europe et but constant de leurs travaux, ne soit pas troublée de nouveau, et pour la garantir de tout attentat qui ménacerait de replonger les peuples dans les désordres et les malheurs des révolutions.

'La présente Déclaration, insérée au Protocole du Congrès réuni à Vienne dans sa séance du 13 Mars, 1815, sera rendue publique.

'Fait et certifié véritable par les Plénipotentiaires des Huit Puissances signataires du Traité de Paris.

'Suivent les signatures dans l'ordre alphabétique les cours.

AUTRICHE	LE PRINCE DE METTERNICH, LE BARON DE WESSENBERG.
ESPAGNE	P. GOMEZ LABRADOR.
FRANCE	LE PRINCE TALLEYRAND, LE DUC DE DALBERG, LATOUR DU PIN, LE COMTE ALEXIS DE NOAILLES.
GRANDE BRETAGNE .	WELLINGTON, CATHCART, CLANCARTY, STEWART.
PORTUGAL	LE COMTE DE PALMELLA.
PRUSSE	LE PRINCE DE HARDENBERG, LE BARON DE HUMBOLDT.
RUSSIE	LE COMTE DE RASOUMOWSKY, LE COMTE DE STACKELBERG, LE COMTE DE NESSELRODE.
SUEDE	LÖWENHEIM.

II.

Treaty of Alliance of the 25th of March, 1815, *concluded between Austria, Russia, Prussia, and Great Britain.*

'Au nom de la Très Sainte et indivisible Trinité.

'Sa Majesté l'Empereur d'Autriche, Roi de Hongrie et de Bohème, et Sa Majesté le Roi du Royaume Uni de la Grande Bretagne et d'Irlande, ayant pris en considération les suites que l'invasion en France de Napoléon Buonaparte et la situation actuelle de ce royaume peuvent avoir pour la sûreté de l'Europe, out resolu d'un commun accord avec Sa Majesté l'Empereur de toutes les Russies, et Sa Majesté le Roi de Prusse, d'appliquer à cette circonstance importante les principes consacrés par le traité de Chaumont. En conséquence ils sont convenus de renouveller par un acte solemnel, signé séparément par chacune des quatre Puissances avec chacune des trois autres, l'engagement de préserver contre toute atteinte l'ordre des choses si heureusement rétabli en Europe, et de déterminer les moyens les plus efficaces de mettre cet engagement à exécution ainsi que de lui donner, dans les circonstances présentes, toute l'extention qu'elles reclament impérieusement.

'A cet effet Sa Majesté l'Empereur d'Autriche, Roi de Hongrie et de Bohème, a nommé pour discuter, conclure, et signer les conditions du présent traité avec Sa Majesté le Roi du Royaume Uni de la Grande Bretagne et d'Irlande le Sieur ; et Sa Majesté Britannique ayant de son côté nomme le Sieur , les dits Plenipotentiaires, après avoir échangé leurs pleinspouvoirs, trouvés en bonne et due forme, ont arrêté les articles suivants.

'ARTICLE 1.—Les Hautes Puissances Contractantes ci-dessus denommées s'engagent solemnellement à réunir les moyens de leurs états respectifs pour maintenir dans toute leur intégrité les conditions du traité de paix conclu à Paris le 30 Mai, 1814, ainsi que les stipulations arrêtées et signées au Congrès de Vienne, dans le but de completer les dispositions de ce traité, de les garantir contre toute atteinte, et particulièrement contre les desseins de Napoléon Buonaparte. A cet effet, elles s'engagent à diriger, si le cas l'exigeait, et dans le sens de la déclaration du 13 Mars dernier, de concert et de commun accord, tous leurs efforts contre lui et contre tous ceux qui se seraient déjà ralliés à sa faction, ou s'y réuniraient dans la suite, afin de le forcer à se desister de ses projets et de le mettre hors d'état de troubler à l'avenir la tranquillité et la paix générale, sous la protection de laquelle les droits, la liberté, et l'indépendence des nations venaient d'être placées et assurées.

'ARTICLE 2.—Quoiqu'un but aussi grand et aussi bienfaisant ne permette pas qu'on mesure les moyens destinés pour l'atteindre, et que les Hautes Parties Contractantes soient résolues d'y consacrer tous ceux dont, d'après leur situation respective, elles peuvent disposer, elles sont néanmoins convenues de tenir constamment en campagne, chacun 150,000 hommes au complet, y compris pour le moins la proportion d'un dixième de cavalerie et une juste proportion d'artillerie, sans compter les garnisons, et de les employer activement et de concert contre l'ennemi commun.

'ARTICLE 3.—Les Hautes Parties Contractantes s'engagent réciproquement à ne pas poser les armes que d'un commun accord, et avant que l'objet de la guerre désigné dans l'article 1 du présent traité n'ait été atteint, et tant que Buonaparte ne sera pas mis absolument hors de possibilité d'exciter des troubles et de renouveller ses tentatives pour s'emparer de pouvoir suprême en France.

'ARTICLE 4.—Le présent traité étant principalement applicable aux circonstances présentes, les stipulations du traité de Chaumont, et nommément celles contenues dans l'article 16, auront de nouveau toute leur force et vigueur, aussitôt que le but actuel aura été atteint.

'ARTICLE 5.—Tout ce qui est rélatif au commandement des armées combinées, aux subsistances, &c., sera réglé par une convention particulière.

'ARTICLE 6.—Les Hautes Parties Contractantes auront la faculté d'accréditer respectivement auprès des Généraux Commandants leurs armées des officiers qui auront la liberté de correspondre avec leurs gouvernemens, pour les informer des événemens militaires et de tout ce qui est rélatif aux opérations des armées.

'ARTICLE 7.—Les engagemens stipulés par le présent traité ayant pour but le maintien de la paix générale, les Hautes Parties Contractantes conviennent entr'elles d'inviter toutes les Puissance de l'Europe à y accéder.

'ARTICLE 8.—Le présent traité étant uniquement dirigé dans le but de soutenir la France, ou tout autre pays envahi, contre les entreprises de Buonaparte et de ses adhérens, Sa Majesté Trés Chrétienne sera spécialement invitée à donner son adhésion, et à faire connaître, dans le cas où elle devrait requérir les forces stipulées dans l'article 2, quels secours les circonstances lui permettront d'apporter à l'objêt du présent traité.

'ARTICLE 9.—Le présent traité sera ratifié, et les ratifications en seront échangées dans deux mois, ou plutôt, si faire se peut.

'En foi de quoi les Plénipotentiaires respectifs l'ont signé et y ont apposé le cachet de leurs armes.

'Fait à Vienne, le 25 Mars, de l'an de Grace, 1815.

(L.S.) LE PRINCE DE METTERNICH,
(L.S.) WELLINGTON,
(L.S.) LE BARON DE WESSENEBERG.

'Le même jour le même traité a été conclu entre la Russie et la Grand Bretagne ; ainsi qu'entre la Prusse et la Grande Bretagne.'

III.

Proclamation of the King of Prussia to his Army.

'When, in the hour of peril, I summoned my people to arms, to combat for the freedom and independence of their country, the whole mass of the youth, glowing with emulation, thronged around my standards, to bear with joyful self-denial unusual hardships, and heroically resolved to brave death itself. Then the best strength of the people intrepidly joined the ranks of my brave soldiers, and my generals led with me into battle a host of heroes, who have shown themselves worthy of the names of their ancestors, and heirs of their glory. Thus we and our allies, attended by victory, conquered the capital of our inveterate foe. Our banners waved in Paris. Napoleon abandoned his authority. Liberty was restored to Germany, security to thrones, and to the world the hope of a durable peace. This hope has now vanished, and we must again march to the combat. A perfidious conspiracy has brought back to France the man who, for ten successive years, inflicted on the world indescribable misery. The people, confounded by his unexpected appearance, have been unable to oppose his armed adherents. Though he, while still at the head of a considerable armed force, declared his abdication to be a voluntary sacrifice to the happiness and repose of France, he now disregards this, like every other convention. He commands a horde of perjured soldiers, who wish to render war eternal.

'Europe is again menaced. It cannot permit the man to remain on the throne of France, who loudly proclaimed universal empire to be the object of his continually renewed wars; who confounded all moral principles by his unceasing breach of faith, and who can therefore give the world no security for his peaceable intentions.

'Again, therefore, arise to the combat. France itself requires our aid, and all Europe is allied with us. United with your ancient companions in victory, and reinforced by the accession of new brethren in arms, you go, brave Prussians, to a just war with me, with the princes of my family, and with the generals who have always led you to conquest.

'The justice of the cause which we defend will insure our success. Arise, then, with God for your support, for the repose of the world, for morality, for your King and your country.'

IV.

Address of the Emperor Alexander to a numerous body of Russian troops which he reviewed on the 5th of April, 1815.

'Brave warriors!—the honour and the glory of the great empire with which Providence has intrusted me—your emperor comes once more to place himself at your head! He calls you a second time to the defence of humanity and the rights of Europe, which Napoleon, the vile and criminal artificer of fraud, has dared again to menace. Abusing our clemency, and violating those treaties which insured to him a secure asylum, he has succeeded in frustrating the hopes of those nations who had forgotten his atrocious cruelties and his insatiable ambition. Let us hasten to join the invincible phalanxes of our allies, and deliver France from the scourge of the human race, who once more governs it contrary to the wishes of every reasonable and peaceable inhabitant of that country.

'Soldiers! The sacred league which at present unites all the people of Europe, and which ought to guarantee them from all oppression, we know how to defend, and we will defend it, if necessary, to the last drop of our blood.

'Alexander is among you. You will always see him choose the path of true honour, that which leads to the happiness of mankind. This will entitle him to your confidence and affection.'

V.

The Convocation of the 'Champ de Mai.'

The convocation of the Champ de Mai took place on the 1st of June, and was remarkable for the solemnity with which the compact between the sovereign and the people was affirmed, the splendour with which the ceremony was surrounded, and the grandeur of a spectacle designed alike to appease the desires of the great political parties in the senate, and to resuscitate and keep alive in the minds of the people that thirst for military glory and national supremacy which was again to cement and uphold the power of the ambitious warrior-sovereign of France. It was held in the Champ de Mars, a large open piece of ground extending from the front of the military school nearly to the bank of the Seine, and in which the general assemblies of the nation were convoked together during the early periods of the French monarchy. These assemblies were instituted for the purpose of framing new laws, of adjusting differences among the barons, and of reviewing the national forces: and, as they met in the month of March, the place was called the *Champ de Mars*, until the middle of the eighth century, when Pepin altered the usual period to the month of May, whence arose the more modern appellation of the *Champ de Mai*.

The present convocation was summoned by Napoleon for the acceptance or rejection, by the nation, of a charter, which he had offered to the people, in the shape of "*An additional Act to the Constitutions of the Empire*," to be determined by the number of votes inscribed by all Frenchmen who had attained to years of maturity, in registries which were open for that purpose in every town and district. An altar was erected in the centre of the before mentioned arena. The throne was constructed in the front of the military school, the back of it adjoining the balcony of this building. Opposite the throne was a semicircular inclosure, affording accommodation to eighteen thousand persons. Along the entablature of the rotunda which encircled the altar were inscribed the names of the eighty-seven departments, intermingled with eagles and tri-coloured garlands. An immense multitude, besides fifty-thousand troops, filled the entire space of the Champ de Mars. Napoleon, habited in the imperial costume, took his seat on the throne, surrounded by his brothers, the great officers of his household, the ministers, and the marshals. A number of prelates, headed by M. de Baral, Archbishop of Tours, then advanced towards the steps of the altar and commenced the divine sacrifice. After the celebration of the mass, the grand-master of the ceremonies conducted to the foot of the throne a deputation of five hundred members of the electoral colleges, who were presented by the arch-chancellor. One of the members, M. Dubois d'Angers (representative of the department of the Maine and Loire) then pronounced the following address, in the name of the French people:—

'Sire! The French people had decreed the crown to you; you deposed it without their consent; its suffrages have just imposed upon you the duty of resuming it. A new contract is formed between the nation and your majesty. Collected from all points of the empire, around the tables of the law on which we are about to inscribe the wish of the people—this wish, which is the only legitimate source of power—it is impossible for us not to utter the voice of France, of which we are the immediate organs; not to say, in the presence of Europe, to the august chief of the nation, what it expects from him, and what he is to expect from it.

'What is the object of the league of the allied kings, in assuming that warlike preparation by which they alarm Europe, and afflict humanity? By what act, by what violation, have we provoked their vengeance, or given cause for their aggression? Have we since peace was concluded, endeavoured to give them laws? We merely wish to make and to follow those which are adapted to our habits. We will not have the chief whom our enemies would give us; and we will have him whom they wish us not to have. They dare to proscribe you personally; you, Sire, who, so often master of their capitals, generously consolidated their tottering thrones. This hatred of our enemies adds to our love for you. Were they to proscribe the most obscure of our citizens, it would be our duty to defend him with the same energy. He would be, like you, under the ægis of French law and French power.

'They menace us with invasion! And yet, contracted within frontiers which nature has not imposed upon us, and which, long before your reign, victory and even peace had extended, we have not, from respect to treaties which you had not signed, but which you had offered to observe, sought to pass that narrow boundary.

'Do they ask for guarantees? They have them all in our institutions, and in the will of the French people henceforth united to yours. Do they not dread to remind us of a state of things lately so different, but which may still be reproduced? It would not be the first time that we have conquered all Europe armed against us.

'They dare to dispute with the French nation, for the second time, in the nineteenth century, and in face of the civilized world, those sacred and imprescriptible rights, for which the most insignificant people have never pleaded in vain at the bar of justice and of history.

'Because France wishes to be France, must she be degraded, torn, dismembered; and must the fate of Poland be reserved for us? It is vain to conceal insidious designs under the sole pretence of separating you from us, in order to give us masters with whom we have nothing in common. Their pretence destroyed all the illusions attached to their name. They could not believe our oaths, neither could we rely on their promises. Tithes, feudal rights, privileges, every thing that was odious to us, were too evidently the fond objects of their thoughts, when one of them, to console the impatience of the present, assured his confidants, "that he would answer to them for the future." Every thing shall be attempted, every thing executed, to repel so ignominious a yoke. We declare it to nations: may their chiefs hear us! If they accept your offers of peace, the French people will look to your vigorous, liberal and paternal administration, for grounds of consolation for the sacrifices made to obtain peace; but if we are left no choice between war and disgrace, the whole country will rise for war. The nation is prepared to relieve you from the too moderate offers you have perhaps made in order to save Europe from a new convulsion. Every Frenchman is a soldier: victory will follow your eagles; and our enemies, who rely on our divisions, will soon regret having provoked us.'

At the conclusion of this address, the result of the votes, and the acceptance of the additional act, were proclaimed, amidst the loud and prolonged acclamations of the spectators.*

Napoleon, then addressing himself to the electors, spoke as follows:—

'Gentlemen, electors of the colleges of the departments and districts;—Gentlemen, deputies of the army and navy, to the Champ de Mai:—

'Emperor, consul, or soldier, I derive all from the people. In prosperity, in adversity, on the field of battle, in council, on the throne, and in exile, France has been the sole and constant object of my thoughts and actions.

'Like the king of Athens, I sacrifice myself for my people, in the hope of realizing the promise given to preserve to France her natural integrity, her honours, and her rights. Indignant at seeing those sacred rights, acquired by twenty years of victory, disavowed and lost for ever, and at hearing the cry of "French honour tarnished," the wishes of the nation have replaced me upon that throne which is dear to me because it is the palladium of the independence, the honour and the rights of the people.

'Frenchmen! in traversing, amidst the public joy, the different provinces of the empire to reach my capital, I had reason to rely on a lasting peace. Nations are bound by treaties concluded by their governments, whatever they may be. My thoughts were then all occupied with the means of establishing our liberty by a constitution conformable with the will and interests of the people. I convoked the Champ de Mai.

'I soon learned that the princes who have disregarded all principle, who have trampled on the sentiments and dearest interests of so many nations, wish to make war against us. They meditate the augmentation of the kingdom of the Netherlands, by giving it as barriers all our northern frontier-places, and the conciliation of the differences which still exist amongst them, by dividing Alsace and Lorraine.

'It was now necessary to provide for war. But, before personally encountering the hazard of battles, my first care has been to constitute the nation without delay. The people have accepted the act which I have presented to them.

'Frenchmen! when we shall have repelled these unjust aggres-

* The number of votes for the acceptance of the additional act amounted to 1,532,557; and, for its rejection, 4,802. Eleven departments had not sent in their registries. A great number of soldiers and sailors, unable to write their signatures, did not vote at all; and the registers of fourteen regiments did not arrive until after the scrutiny.

sions, and Europe shall be convinced of what is due to the rights and independence of twenty-eight millions of people, a solemn law, drawn up in the forms required by the constitutional act, shall combine together the different dispositions of our constitutions now dispersed.

'Frenchmen! you are about to return to your departments; inform the citizens that existing circumstances are of the highest importance; that with union, energy, and perseverance, we shall return victorious from this contest between a great people and their oppressors; that future generations will severely scrutinize our conduct; and that a nation has lost all, when she has lost her independence. Tell them that foreign kings, whom I have raised to the throne, or who owe to me the preservation of their crowns, who all, during my prosperity, sought my alliance and the protection of the French people now direct their blows against my person. Did I not perceive that it is the country they wish to injure, I would place at their mercy this existence, against which they show themselves so much incensed. But tell the citizens, that while the French people preserve towards me the sentiments of love, of which they have given me so many proofs, the rage of our enemies will be powerless.

'Frenchmen! my wish is that of the people; my rights are theirs; my honour, my glory, my happiness, can be no other than the honour, the glory, and the happiness of France.'

This harangue was received with the most enthusiastic plaudits, and with long continued shouts of "*Vive l'Empereur!*"

At length, when silence was restored, Napoleon swore, upon the New Testament, to observe and cause to be observed the constitutions of the empire, and, immediately, the arch-chancellor, Cambacérès, proclaimed the oath of obedience to the constitutions, and fidelity to the Emperor, on the part of the French people, represented by the electors. Then there arose from the latter, from the troops, and the great majority of the spectators, loud and reiterated cries of "We swear it!" The ministers of war and of marine, at the head of their respective deputations, now advanced and took the oath, as did also the minister of the interior, at the head of the electors, in the name of the national guards of France.

Te Deum having been sung, Napoleon laid aside the imperial mantle, and rising from the throne, addressed the military as follows:—

'Soldiers of the national guard of the empire! Soldiers of the land and sea forces! To your hands I confide the imperial eagle with the national colours. Swear to defend it at the sacrifice of your blood, against the enemies of France and of this throne. Swear that it shall always be your rallying signal.'

Loud and universal cries of "We swear it," immediately resounded among the troops. In the midst of these acclamations, Buonaparte proceeded to another throne in the middle of the Champ de Mars. The troops marched in battalions and squadrons, and surrounded the throne. He then, as colonel of the national and imperial guard, presented to each its eagle, and said :—

'Soldiers of the national guard of Paris ! Soldiers of the imperial guard! I confide to you the national eagles, and the national colours. You swear to perish, if necessary, in defending them against the enemies of the country and the throne.'

The whole army, drawn up in a close order around him, replied, with repeated exclamations of "We swear it !"

The drum rolled, and silence was restored. "You swear," continued Napoleon, "never to acknowledge any other rallying sign." Again the cries of "We swear it !" resounded on every side. "You, soldiers of the national guard of Paris, swear never to suffer foreigners again to pollute by their presence the capital of the great nation !" The most enthusiastic shouts of "We swear it !" burst from every rank, and were prolonged by the immense multitude who surrounded the inclosure.

The troops were now ordered to march past Napoleon, and, during two hours, which were occupied in the procession of the numerous battalions, the acclamations were continued with little or no intermission.

VI.

Effective Strength and Composition of the Anglo-allied Army, under the Command of Field Marshal the Duke of Wellington.

1st Corps.—His Royal Highness the Prince of Orange.

			Men
1st Division, M. General Cooke.	1st British Brigade, Major General Maitland.	2nd Batt. 1st Guards . . .	976
		3rd do. do. do. . . .	1,021
	2nd British Brigade, M. Gen. Sir John Byng.	2nd do. Coldstream Guards .	1,003
		2nd do. 3rd Guards . . .	1,061
			4,061
	Artillery, Lieut. Colonel Adye.	Capt. Sandham's British Foot-battery.	
		Major Kuhlmann's Horse-battery, K. G. Legion.	
3rd Division, L. Gen. Sir Charles Alten.	5th British Brigade, M. Gen. Sir Colin Halkett.	2nd Batt. 30th Regiment . .	615
		33rd Regiment	561
		2nd Batt. 69th Regiment . .	516
		2nd do. 73rd do. . . .	562
	2nd Brigade K. G. Legion, Colonel von Ompteda.	1st Light Battalion . . .	423
		2nd do. do.	337
		5th Line do.	379
		8th do. do.	388
	1st Hanoverian Brigade, M.G. Count Kielmansegge.	Field Batt. Bremen . . .	512
		Do. do. Verden . . .	533
		Do. do. York . . .	307
		Do. do. Lüneburg . . .	595
		Do. do. Grubenhagen . .	621
		Do. Jäger Corps	321
			6,970
	Artillery, L. Colonel Williamson.	Major Lloyd's British Foot-battery.	
		Captain Cleeves's Foot-battery, K.G. Legion.	
2nd Dutch-Belg. Division, L. General Baron de Perponcher.	1st Brigade, M. Gen. Count de Bylandt.	7th Regiment of the Line . .	701
		27th Jäger Battalion . . .	809
		5th Militia-Battalion . . .	482
		7th do. do. . . .	675
		8th do. do. . . .	566
	2nd Brigade, H.S.H. The Prince Bernhard of Saxe Weimar.	2nd Regiment of Nassau, 3 Battalions	2,709
		Regiment of Orange Nassau, 2 do.	1,591
			7,533
	Artillery, Major van Opstal.	Captain Byleveld's Horse-battery.	
		Captain Stievenaar's Foot-battery.	
3rd Dutch-Belg. Division, L. Gen. Baron Chassé	1st Brigade, M. General Ditmers.	2nd Regiment of the Line . .	471
		35th Jäger Battalion . . .	605
		4th Militia-Battalion . . .	519
		6th do. do. . . .	492
		17th do. do. . . .	534
		19th do. do. . . .	467
	2nd Brigade. M. General d'Aubremé.	3rd Regiment of the Line . .	629
		12th do. do. . . .	431
		13th do. do. . . .	664
		36th Jäger Battalion . . .	633
		3rd Militia-Battalion . . .	592
		10th do. do. . . .	632
			6,669
	Artillery, Major van der Smissen.	Captain Krahmer's Horse-battery.	
		Captain Lux's Foot-battery.	
		Total 1st corps . .	25,233 men, and 56 guns.

2nd Corps.—Lieut. General Lord Hill.

			Men.
2nd Division, L. Gen. Sir H. Clinton.	3rd British Brigade, Major General Adam.	1st Batt. 52nd Regiment. . .	1,038
		1st do. 71st do. . . .	810
		2nd do. 95th do. . . .	585
		3rd do. 95th do. . . .	188
	1st Brigade K. G. Legion, Colonel du Plat.	1st Line Battalion : . .	411
		2nd do. do.	437
		3rd do. do.	494
		4th do. do.	416
	3rd Hanoverian Brigade, Colonel Halkett.	Landwehr Batt. Bremervörde .	632
		Do. do. Osnabrück .	612
		Do. do. Quackenbrück .	588
		Do. do. Salzgitter . .	622
			6,833
	Artillery, Lieut. Colonel Gold.	Captain Bolton's British Foot battery. Major Sympher's Horse-battery, K.G. Legion.	
4th Division, L.Gen.Sir Charles Colville.	4th British Brigade, Colonel Mitchell.	3rd Batt. 14th Regiment . .	571
		1st do. 23rd do. . . .	647
		51st Regiment	549
	6th British Brigade, M. General Johnstone.	2nd Batt. 35th Regiment . .	570
		1st do. 54th do. . .	541
		2nd do. 59th do. . .	461
		1st do. 91st do. . .	824
	6th Hanoverian Brigade, M. Gen. Sir James Lyon.	Field Batt. Lauenburg . .	553
		Do. do. Calenberg . .	634
		Landwehr Batt. Nienburg . .	625
		Do. do. Hoya . . .	629
		Do. do. Bentheim . .	608
			7,212
	Artillery, L. Colonel Hawker.	Major Brome's British Foot-battery. Captain von Rettberg's Hanoverian Foot-battery.	
1st Dutch-Belg. Division, L. General Stedmann.	1st Brigade, M. General Hauw.	4th Regiment of the Line .	6,389
		6th do. do. .	
		16th Jäger Battalion . .	
		9th Militia do. . .	
		14th do. do. . .	
		15th do. do. . .	
	2nd Brigade, M. General Eerens.	1st Regiment of the Line .	
		18th Jäger Battalion . .	
		1st Militia do. . .	
		2nd do. do. . .	
		18th do. do. . .	
	Artillery . .	Captain Wynands's Foot-battery.	
Dutch-Belgian Indian Brigade, Lieut. General Anthing.		5th Regiment, 2 Battalions	3,583
		Flankers	
		10th Jäger Battalion . .	
		11th do. do. . .	
Artillery		Captain Riesz's Foot-battery.	
Detachments from 6th and 7th Line Battalions of the K. G. Legion, distributed among the other Battalions, and 2 Orderlies from Foreign Battalions			16
		Total 2nd corps .	24,033 men, and 40 guns.

Reserve.

			Men.
5th Division, L. Gen. Sir Thomas Picton.	8th British Brigade, M. Gen. Sir James Kempt.	1st Batt. 28th Regiment	557
		1st do. 32nd do.	662
		1st do. 79th do.	703
		1st do. 95th do.	549
	9th British Brigade. M. Gen. Sir Denis Pack.	3rd do. 1st do.	604
		1st do. 42nd do.	526
		2nd do. 44th do.	455
		1st do. 92nd do.	588
	5th Hanoverian Brigade, Colonel von Vincke.	Landwehr Battalion Hameln	669
		Do. do. Gifhorn	617
		Do. do. Hildesheim	617
		Do. do. Peine	611
			7,158
	Artillery, Major Heisse.	Major Rogers's British Foot-battery. Captain Braun's Hanoverian Foot-battery.	
6th Division, L. Gen. Hon. Sir L. Cole.	10th British Brigade, M. Gen. Sir John Lambert.	1st Batt. 4th Regiment	669
		1st do. 27th do.	698
		1st do. 40th do.	761
		2nd do. 81st do.	439
	4th Hanoverian Brigade, Colonel Best.	Landwehr Batt. Verden	621
		Do. do. Lüneburg	624
		Do. do. Osterode	677
		Do. do. Münden	660
			5,149
	Artillery, L. Colonel Brückmann.	Major Unett's British Foot-battery. Captain Sinclair's do. do.	
	British Reserve-Artillery, Major Drummond.	L. Col. Sir Hew Ross's Horse-battery. Major Beane's do. Major Morisson's Foot-battery. Captain Hutchesson's do. Captain Ilbert's do.	
7th Division . . .	7th British Brigade.	2nd Batt. 25th Regiment	388
		2nd do. 37th do.	491
		2nd do. 78th do.	337
	British Garrison Troops	13th Veteran Battalion	683
		1st Foreign do.	595
		2nd Garrison do.	739
			3,233
Brunswick Corps, H. S. H. The Duke of Brunswick.	Major von Rauschenplatt .	Advanced-Guard Battalion	672
	Light Brigade, L. Colonel von Buttlar.	Guard Battalion	672
		1st Light Battalion	672
		2nd do. do.	672
		3rd do. do.	672
	Line Brigade, L. Colonel von Specht.	1st Line do.	672
		2nd do. do.	672
		3rd do. do.	672
			5,376
	Artillery, Major Mahn.	Captain Heinemann's Horse-battery. Major Moll's Foot-battery.	
Hanoverian Reserve-Corps L. Gen. von der Decken.	1st Brigade, L. Colonel von Bennigsen.	Field Battalion Hoya	9,000
		Landwehr Battalion Mölln	
		Landwehr Battalion Bremerlehe	
	2nd Brigade, L. Colonel von Beaulieu.	Do. do. Nordheim	
		Do. do. Ahlefeldt	
		Do. do. Springe	
	3rd Brigade, L. Colonel Bodecker.	Landwehr Battalion Otterndorf	
		Do. do. Zelle	
		Do. do. Ratzeburg	
	4th Brigade, L. Colonel Wissel	Landwehr Battalion Hanover	
		Do. do. Uelzen	
		Do. do. Neustadt	
		Do. do. Diepholz	
Nassau Contingent, General von Kruse.	. . . . .	1st Regiment—3 Battalions	2,880
		Total Reserve	32,796 men, and 64 guns.

Cavalry.

			Men.
British, and King's German Legion.	1st Brigade, M. Gen. Lord E. Somerset.	1st Life Guards	228
		2nd do. do.	231
		Royal Horse Guards (Blue)	237
		1st Dragoon Guards	530
	2nd Brigade, M. Gen. Sir W. Ponsonby.	1st, or Royal, Dragoons	394
		2nd Dragoons (Scots Greys)	391
		6th (or Inniskilling) Dragoons	396
	3rd Brigade, M. Gen. Sir W. Dörnberg.	1st Light Dragoons, K.G. Legion	462
		2nd do. do. do.	419
		23rd Light Dragoons	387
	4th Brigade, M. Gen. Sir J. Vandeleur.	11th do. do.	390
		12th do. do.	388
		16th do. do.	393
	5th Brigade, M. Gen. Sir Colq. Grant.	2nd Hussars, K.G. Legion	564
		7th do.	380
		15th do.	392
	6th Brigade, M. Gen. Sir H. Vivian.	1st do. K.G. Legion	493
		10th do.	390
		18th do.	396
	7th Brigade, Col. Sir F. v. Arentsschildt.	3rd do. K.G. Legion	622
		13th Light Dragoons	390
	British Horse-batteries, attached to the Cavalry.	1. Major Bull's (Howitzers).	
		2. Lieut. Colonel Webber Smith's.	
		3. Lieut. Colonel Sir Robert Gardiner's.	
		4. Captain Whinyates's (with Rockets).	
		5. Captain Mercer's.	
		6. Captain Ramsay's.	
Hanoverian.	1st Brigade, Colonel von Estorff.	Prince Regent's Hussars	596
		Bremen and Verden Hussars	589
		Cumberland Hussars	497
	Brunswick Cavalry.	Regiment of Hussars	690
		Squadron of Uhlans	232
Dutch-Belgian.	1st Brigade, M. General Trip.	1st Dutch Carabiniers	446
		2nd Belgian do.	399
		3rd Dutch do.	392
	2nd Brigade, M. General de Ghigny.	4th Dutch Light Dragoons	647
		8th Belgian Hussars	439
	3rd Brigade, M. General van Merlen.	5th do. Light Dragoons	441
		6th Dutch Hussars	641
	Artillery	Captain Petter's half Horse-battery.	
		Captain Gey's half Horse-battery.	
			14,482 men. and 44 guns.

Artillery.

		Guns.	Men.
British	7 Foot-batteries of 6 guns each	42	3,630
	3 do. do. 4 do. (18-prs.)	12	
	8 Horse do. do. 6 do.	48	1,400
King's German Legion	1 Foot do. do. 6 do.	6	526
	2 Horse do. do. 6 do. each	12	
Hanoverian	2 Foot do. do. 6 do. do.	12	465
Brunswick	1 Foot do. do. 8 do. do.	8	510
	1 Horse do. do. 8 do. do.	8	
Dutch-Belgian	4 Foot do. do. 8 do. do.	32	968
	3 Horse do. do. 8 do. do.	24	667
		204	8,166

Engineers, Sappers and Miners, Waggon-Train, and Staff Corps . . . 1,240

Total Strength.

Infantry	82,062
Cavalry	14,482
Artillery	8,166
Engineers, Waggon-Train, &c.	1,240
Grand Total	105,950 men, and 204 guns.

VII.

Orders for the defence of the Towns of Antwerp, Ostend, Nieuport, Ypres, Tournai, Ath, Mons, and Ghent.

'1. Le moment que l'ennemi mettra le pied sur le territoire des Pays Bas les places ci-dessous nommées doivent étre déclarées en état de siége: c'est-a-dire, Anvers, Ostende, Nieuport, Ypres, Tournay, Ath, Mons, et Gand.

'2. Aussitôt qu'une place est déclarée en etat de siège, soit par l'effet de cet ordre, ou par un ordre particulièrement adressé au Gouverneur ou Commandant, toutes les précautions militaires doivent être adoptées; et le Gouverneur doit tout de suite rassembler le conseil de défense.

'3. Le conseil de défense doit consister du Gouverneur comme Président, du Commandant des troupes, du Chef de l'Artillerie, et du Chef de Génie.

'4. Il sera tenu un registre de leurs déliberations, qui sera signé par tous les membres du conseil.

'5. Le Gouverneur décidera seul sur toute question, ou de la défense ou de la police militaire ou autre, après avoir pris l'avis et entendu les discussions de son conseil, même contre leur avis; et chaque membre est autorisé de mettre sur le registre son opinion, signée par lui-même, avec tout le développement qu'il voudra.

'6. Les membres du conseil ne peuvent laisser transpirer aucun objet de déliberation, ou leur opinion personnelle sur la situation de la place qu'ils occupent, sans y être appellés par l'autorité supérieure.

'7. Le Gouverneur d'une des places ci-dessous nommées, c'est-à dire, Anvers, Ostende, Nieuport, Ypres, la citadelle de Tournay, Ath, la citadelle de Gand, qui, après avoir été en état de siège, aura consenti à la reddition de sa place avant que l'ennemi y ait fait brèche praticable, et que cette brèche ait été retranchée, et qu'elle ait soutenu un assaut, et sans avoir pris l'avis, ou contre l'aveu, de son conseil, sera coupable, non seulement d'une désobéissance militaire, mais de trahison.

'8. Il y aura ordre particulier pour la défense des villes de Mons, de Tournay, et de Gand, au lieu de l'Article 7.

'WELLINGTON.'

Orders for the defence of the Town of Tournay.

'La ville de Tournay doit être considérée comme un camp retranché, dont la citadelle est le réduit.

'La citadelle doit toujours contenir le tiers des troupes stationées à Tournay; et doit être défendue comme forteresse jusqu' à l'extrémité.

'Les flèches en avant des portes de la ville, les fossés, et les inondations de l'Escaut, qui pourraient se pratiquer, donneront la facilité aux troupes dans la ville de la défendre jusqu' à ce que l'ennemi en aurait détruit les défenses.

'Les troupes dans la ville doivent alors se retirer dans la citadelle jusqu'à la concurrence de ; et le surplus sur Bruxelles, ou le long de l'Escaut sur Audenarde, ou selon les ordres que le Gouverneur aura reçu.

'WELLINGTON.'

Orders for the defence of the Town of Mons.

'Le Gouverneur de Mons doit considérer la place comme un camp retranché, la défense de laquelle est facilitée par les ouvrages dernièrement construits, par les bons fossés de la ville, et par les inondations.

'Pour conserver ces dernières il faut occuper la redoute sur la route de St. Ghislain, avec 200 hommes; et celle sur Mont Palizel avec 400.

'Aussitôt que la place soit déclarée en état de siège il faut faire des coupures dans les chaussées qui l'approchent, et faire des abattis assez importans pour arrêter l'ennemi sous le feu des batteries.

'L'ennemi ne saurait faire une attaque sérieuse sur la place avant de saigner les inondations, après avoir pris les redoutes qui en gardent les écluses.

'Un Gouverneur Président observera ses mouvemens, et prendra les mesures pour assurer sa retraite, quand elle deviendrait nécessaire par les approches de l'ennemi, en faisant barricader les rues, &c.; et il se retirera soit sur Ath soit sur Bruxelles, selon les circonstances ou les ordres qu'il aura reçu, prenant garde de renforcer la garnison du Mont Palazel jusqu'à la concurrence de 600 hommes.

'WELLINGTON.'

Orders for the defence of the Town of Ghent.

'L'enceinte de Gand est énorme, et l'on ne peut considérer cette ville que comme un camp retranché, dont la citadelle est le réduit.

'Mais, malgré la grandeur de l'enceinte, quoique nuisible à une défense en règle avec une petite force; et comme les inondations aident beaucoup à la défense et rendent l'attaque sur tous les points très difficile, il y a lieu d'espérer que le Gouverneur pourrait même tenir la ville.

'1. Le tiers de la garnison doit toujours se trouver dans la citadelle.

'2. Ce tiers doit s'augmenter jusqu' a la concurrence de 1400 hommes, en cas que la citadelle soit la partie attaquée, ou que le Gouverneur se trouve dans le cas de se retirer de la ville.

'3. Si la ville est attaquée par la porte de Courtrai ou par la porte de Bruges, tous les efforts doivent être faits pour tenir les redoutes entre l'Escaut et le Lys en avant de la première, et les moulins et le village en avant de la seconde.

'4. Si le Gouverneur de la ville se trouve dans le cas de se retirer avec ses troupes après avoir laissé garnison suffisante dans la citadelle, il doit se retirer sur Anvers à moins d'avoir autres ordres de ses supérieurs.

'WELLINGTON.'

VIII.

Effective Strength and Composition of the Prussian Army under the command of Field Marshal Prince Blücher von Wahlstadt.

1st Corps d'armée—Lieut. General von Zieten.

		Batts.	Men.
1st Brigade, General von Steinmetz.	12th and 24th Regiments of the Line; 1st Westphalian Landwehr Regiment; 1st and 3rd Silesian Rifle Companies	9½	8,647
2nd Brigade, General von Pirch II.	6th and 28th Regiments of the Line; 2nd Westphalian Landwehr Regiment	9	7,666
3rd Brigade, General von Jagow.	7th and 29th Regiments of the Line; 3rd Westphalian Landwehr Regiment; 2nd and 4th Silesian Rifle Companies	9½	6,853
4th Brigade, General von Henkel.	19th Regiment of the Line; 4th Westphalian Landwehr Regiment	6	4,721
			27,887

Reserve-Cavalry of the 1st Corps—Lieut. General von Röder.

		Squad.	
Brigade of General von Treskow.	Brandenburg Dragoons (No. 5)	4	
	1st West Prussian Dragoons (No. 2)	4	
	Brandenburg Uhlans	4	
Brigade of L. Colonel von Lützow.	6th Uhlans	4	1,925
	1st and 2nd Kurmark Landwehr Regiments	8	
	1st Silesian Hussars	4	
	1st Westphalian Landwehr Regiment	4	

Reserve-Artillery of the 1st Corps—Colonel von Lehmann.

12-pounder foot-batteries Nos. 2, 6, and 9; 6- do. do. do. Nos. 1, 3, 7, 8, and 15; Howitzer-battery No. 1; Horse-batteries Nos. 2, 7, and 10	1,019
Total—34 Battalions, 32 Squadrons, 12 Batteries	30,831 men, and 96 guns.

2nd Corps d'armée—General von Pirch I.

		Batts.	Men.
5th Brigade, Gen. von Tippelskirchen.	2nd and 25th Regiments of the Line; 5th Westphalian Landwehr Regiment	9	6,851
6th Brigade, General von Krafft.	9th and 26th Regiments of the Line; 1st Elbe Landwehr Regiment	9	6,469
7th Brigade, General von Brause.	14th and 22nd Regiments of the Line; 2nd Elbe Landwehr Regiment	9	6,224
8th Brigade, Colonel von Langen.	21st and 23rd Regiments of the Line; 3rd Elbe Landwehr Regiment	9	6,292
			25,836

Reserve-Cavalry of the 2nd Corps—General von Jürgass.

		Squad.	
Brigade of Colonel von Thümen.	Silesian Uhlans	4	
	6th Neumark Dragoons	4	
	11th Hussars	4	
Brigade of Col. Count Schulenburg.	1st Queen's Dragoons	4	
	4th Kurmark Landwehr Regiment	4	4,468
Brigade of L. Colonel von Sohr.	3rd Brandenburg Hussars	4	
	5th Pomeranian Hussars	4	
	5th Kurmark Landwehr Regiment	4	
	Elbe Landwehr Regiment	4	

Reserve-Artillery of the 2nd Corps—Colonel von Röhl.

12-pounder Foot-batteries Nos. 4 and 8; 6-pounder do. do. Nos. 5, 10, 12, 34, & 37; Horse-batteries Nos. 5, 6, and 14	1,454
Total—36 Battalions, 36 Squadrons, 10 Batteries	31,758 men, and 80 guns.

3RD CORPS D'ARMÉE—LIEUT. GENERAL VON THIELEMANN.

		Batts.	Men.
9th Brigade, General von Borcke.	8th and 36th Regiments of the Line . . ; 1st Kurmark Landwehr Regiment . .	9 . .	6,752
10th Brigade, Colonel von Kämpfen.	27th Regiment of the Line . . ; 2nd Kurmark Landwehr Regiment . .	6 . .	4,045
11th Brigade, Colonel von Luck.	3rd and 4th Kurmark Landwehr Regiments	6 . .	3,634
12th Brigade. Colonel von Stülpnagel.	31st Regiment of the Line . . . ; 5th and 6th Kurmark Landwehr Regiments	9 . .	6,180
			20,611

Reserve-Cavalry of the 3rd Corps—General von Hobe.

		Squad.	
Brigade of Colonel von der Marwitz.	7th Uhlans	3	
	8th do.	4	
	9th Hussars	3	
Brigade of Colonel Count Lottum.	5th Uhlans	3	. . 2,405
	7th Dragoons	5	
	3rd Kurmark Landwehr Regiment . .	4	
	6th do. do. do. . .	4	

Reserve-Artillery of the 3rd Corps—Colonel von Mohnhaupt.

12-pounder Foot-battery No 7 . . . ; 6-pounder do. do. Nos. 18 and 35 . ; Horse-batteries Nos. 18, 19, and 20 .	 964
Total - 30 Battalions, 24 Squadrons, 6 Batteries	23,980 men and 48 guns.

4TH CORPS D'ARMÉE—GENERAL COUNT BÜLOW VON DENNEWITZ.

		Batts.	Men.
13th Brigade, L. General von Hacke.	10th Regiment of the Line . . . ; 2nd and 3rd Neumark Landwehr Regiments	9 . .	6,385
14th Brigade. General von Ryssel.	11th Regiment of the Line . ; 1st and 2nd Pomeranian Landwehr Regiments	9 . .	6,953
15th Brigade, General von Losthin.	18th Regiment of the Line . . . ; 3rd and 4th Silesian Landwehr Regiments .	9 . .	5,881
16th Brigade, Colonel von Hiller.	15th Regiment of the Line . . . ; 1st and 2nd Silesian Landwehr Regiments	9 . .	6,162
			25,381

Reserve-Cavalry of the 4th Corps—General, Prince William of Prussia.

		Squad.	
Brigade of General von Sydow.	1st West Prussian Uhlans . . .	4	
	2nd Silesian Hussars	4	
	8th Hussars	3	
Brigade of Colonel Count Schwerin.	10th do.	4	. . 3,081
	1st and 2nd Neumark Landwehr Regiments	8	
	1st and 2nd Pomeranian Landwehr Regiments	8	
Brigade of L. Colonel von Watzdorf.	1st, 2nd, & 3rd Silesian Landwehr Regiments	12	

Reserve-Artillery of the 4th Corps—Lieut. Colonel von Bardeleben.

12-pounder Foot-batteries Nos. 3, 5, and 13 ; 6 do do. do. Nos. 2, 11, 13, 14, & 21 ; Horse-batteries Nos. 1, 11, and 12	. . 1,866
Total—36 Battalions, 43 Squadrons, 11 Batteries	30,328 men, and 88 guns.

TOTAL STRENGTH.

	Infantry.	Cavalry.	Artillery.	Guns.
1st Corps d'armée .	27,817	1,925	1,019	96
2nd do. do. . .	25,836	4,468	1,454	80
3rd do. do. . .	20,611	2,405	964	48
4th do. do. . .	25,381	3,081	1,866	88
	99,715	11,879	5,303	312

Grand Total—116,897 men and 312 guns.

IX.

Effective Strength and Composition of the French Army, under the command of Napoleon Buonaparte.

Imperial Guard—Marshal Mortier, Duke of Treviso.

	(On the 16th June.)	Batt.	Men.
Lieut. General Count Friant.	1st and 2nd Regiments of Grenadiers	4	2,294
Lieut. General Count Roguet	3rd and 4th do. do.	3	1,623
Lieut. General Count Morand.	1st and 2nd do. Chasseurs	4	2,402
Lieut. General Count Michel.	3rd and 4th do. do.	4	2,069
Lieut. General Count Duhesme.	1st and 3rd do. Tirailleurs	4	2,043
Lieut. General Count Barrois.	1st and 3rd do. Voltigeurs	4	2,123
		Squad.	
Lieut. General Lef. Desnouettes.	Lancers and Chasseurs à Cheval	19	1,971
Lieut. General Count Guyot.	Dragoons and Grenadiers à Cheval	13	1,517
	Gendarmerie d'élite		102
Lieut. General Desvaux de St. Maurice.	9 Foot-batteries 4 Horse do. Marines (104)		
	Engineers		109
	Total—23 Battalions, 32 Squadrons, 13 Batteries		19,428 men, and 96 guns.

1st Corps d'Armée—Lieut. General Count d'Erlon.

	(On the 10th June.)	Batt.	
1st Division, Lieut. General Alix.	54th, 55th, 28th, and 105th Regiments of the Line	8	
2nd Division, Lieut. General Baron Donzelot	13th (Light), 17th, 19th, and 51st Regiments of the Line	9	16,200
3rd Division, Lieut. General Baron Marcognet.	21st, 46th, 25th, and 45th Regiments of the Line	8	
4th Division, Lieut. General Count Durutte.	8th, 29th, 85th, and 95th Regiments of the Line	8	
		Squad.	
1st Cavalry Division, Lieut. General Baron Jaquinot.	3rd and 7th Chasseurs 3rd and 4th Lancers	6 5	1,400
Artillery.	5 Foot-batteries 1 Horse-battery		1,066
	Engineers		330
	Total—33 Battalions, 11 Squadrons, 6 Batteries		18,996 men, and 46 guns.

2nd Corps d'Armée—Lieut. General Count Reille.

	(On the 10th June.)	Batt.	
5th Division, Lieut. General Baron Bachelu.	2nd (Light) 61st, 72nd, and 108th Regiments of the Line	11	
6th Division, Prince Jerome Napoleon.	1st (Light,) 1st, 2nd, and 3rd Regiments of the Line	11	
7th Division, Lieut. General Count Girard.	11th (Light), and 82nd Regiments of the Line, and 12th Light Infantry.	8	19,750
9th Division, Lieut. General Count Foy.	4th (Light), 92nd, 93rd, and 100th Regiments of the Line	10	
		Squad.	
2nd Cavalry Division, Lieut. General Baron Piré.	1st and 6th Chasseurs 5th and 6th Lancers	8 7	1,729
Artillery.	5 Foot-Batteries 1 Horse-battery		1,385
	Engineers		409
	Total—40 Battalions, 15 Squadrons, 6 Batteries		23,273 men, and 46 guns.

3rd Corps d'Armée—Lieut. General Count Vandamme.

	(On the 10th June.)	Batt.	
8th Division, Lieut. General Baron Lefol.	15th (Light), 23rd, 37th, and 64th Regiments of the Line	11	
10th Division, Lieut. General Baron Habert.	34th, 88th, 22nd, and 70th Regiments of the Line	12	14,508
11th Division, Lieut. General Berthezène.	12th, 56th, 33rd, and 86th Regiments of the Line	8	
		Squad.	
3rd Cavalry-Division, Lieut. General Baron Domon.	4th and 9th Chasseurs 12th Chasseurs	5 4	932
Artillery.	4 Foot-batteries 1 Horse-battery		936
	Engineers		146
	Total—31 Battalions, 9 Squadrons, 5 Batteries		16,522 men, and 38 guns.

4th Corps d'Armée—Lieut. General Count Gérard.

(On the 31st May.)		Batt.	Men.
12th Division, Lieut. General Baron Pecheux.	30th, 96th, and 63rd Regiments of the Line	10	
13th Division, Lieut. General Baron Vichery.	59th, 76th, 48th, and 69th Regiments of the Line	8	12,589
14th Division, Lieut. General Hulot.*	9th (Light), 111th, 44th, and 50th Regiments of the Line . . .	8	
		Squad.	
7th Cavalry-Division, Lieut. General Maurin,	6th Hussars	3	758
	8th Chasseurs	3	
Reserve Cavalry-Division, Lieut. General Baron Jaquinot.†	6th, 11th, 15th,‡ and 16th Dragoons .	16	1,608
Artillery.	4 Foot-batteries . . . . 1 Horse-battery		1,538
	Engineers		201
	Total—26 Battalions, 22 Squadrons, 5 Batteries . .		16,694 men, and 38 guns.

6th Corps d'Armée— Lieut. General Count Lobau.

(On the 10th June.)		Batt.	
19th Division, Lieut. General Baron Simmer.	5th, 11th, 27th, and 84th Regiments of the Line	9	
20th Division, Lieut. General Baron Jeannin.	5th (Light), 16th, 47th,§ and 107th Regiments of the Line . . .	6	8,152
21st Division, Lieut. General Baron Teste.	8th (Light), 40th,‖ 65th, and 75th Regiments of the Line . . .	5	
Artillery.	4 Foot-batteries . . . . 1 Horse-battery		743
	Engineers		189
	Total—20 Battalions, 5 Batteries		9,084 men, and 38 guns.

Reserve Cavalry—Marshal Grouchy.

1st Corps—Lieut. General Count Pajol.
(In June.)

		Squad.	
4th Cavalry-Division, Lieut. General Baron Soult.	1st, 4th, and 5th Hussars . . .	12	
5th Cavalry-Division, Lieut. General Baron Subervie.	1st and 2nd Lancers	8	2,324
	11th Chasseurs	4	
Artillery. .	2 Horse-batteries		317

2nd Corps—Lieut. General Count Excelmans.
(In June.)

		Squad.	
9th Cavalry-Division, Lieut. General Strolz.	5th, 13th, 15th, and 20th Dragoons .	16	2,817
10th Cavalry-Division, Lieut. General Baron Chastel.	4th, 12th, 14th, and 17th Dragoons .	15	
Artillery. .	2 Horse-batteries		246

3rd Corps—Lieut. General Kellermann (Count de Valmy).
(In June.)

		Squad.	
11th Cavalry-Division, Lieut. General Baron L'Heritier.	2nd and 7th Dragoons . .	7	
	8th and 11th Cuirassiers . . .	5	
12th Cavalry-Division, Lieut. General Roussel d'Hurbal.	1st and 2nd Carabiniers . . .	6	3,245
	2nd and 3rd Cuirassiers . . .	6	
Artillery.	2 Horse-batteries		309

4th Corps—Lieut. General Count Milhaud.
(On the 9th June.)

		Squad.	
13th Cavalry-Division. Lieut. General Wathier.	1st, 4th, 7th, and 12th Cuirassiers .	11	2,556
14th Cavalry-Division, Lieut. General Baron Delort.	5th, 6th, 9th, and 10th Cuirassiers .	13	
Artillery.	2 Horse-batteries		313
	Total—103 Squadrons, 8 Batteries		12,127 men, and 48 guns.

TOTAL STRENGTH.

	Infantry.	Cavalry.	Artillery.	Engineers, &c.	Guns.
Imperial Guard	12,554	3,590	3,175	109	96
1st Corps d'Armée	16,200	1,400	1,066	330	46
2nd do. do.	19,750	1,729	1,385	409	46
3rd do. do.	14,508	932	936	146	38
4th do. do.	12,589	2,366	1,538	201	38
6th do. do.	8,152	—	743	189	38
4 Corps of Reserve-Cavalry	—	10,942	1,185	—	48
	83,753	20,959	10,028	1,384	350

Grand Total—116,124 men, and 350 guns.

* This officer succeeded Lieut. General de Bourmont after the latter had deserted.
† Returned as commanding the light cavalry-division of the 1st corps on the 10th June.
‡ The 15th Dragoons formed part of the 9th cavalry-division of the 1st corps on the 10th June.
§ 47th detached to La Vendée (45 off—1003 men).
‖ 40th organizing its depôt at Senlis.

X.

Strength of the French Army, according to information received at the Prussian Head-quarters, shortly before the commencement of hostilities.

			Men.
1st Corps,	under	d'Erlon, at Lille . . .	22,000
2nd do.	do.	Reille, at Valenciennes . .	24,000
3rd do.	do.	Vandamme, at Mezières . .	18,000
4th do.	do.	Gérard, at Thionville . .	16,000
6th do.	do.	Lobau, at Laon . . .	14,000
Imperial Guard,	do.	Mortier, in Paris . . .	21,000
The 4 corps of reserve-cavalry		. . . .	15,000
			130,000 Men.

XI.

'ORDRE DU JOUR.

'Avesne, le 13 Juin, 1815.

'*Position de l'armée le* 14.

'Le grand quartier général á Beaumont. L'infanterie de la garde impériale sera bivaquée à un quart de lieue en avant de Beaumont, et formera trois lignes: la jeune garde, les chasseurs, et les grenadiers. M. le duc de Trévise reconnaîtra l'emplacement de ce camp: il aura soin que tout soit à sa place; artillerie, ambulance, équipage, etc.

'Le premier régiment de grenadiers à pied se rendra à Beaumont.

'La cavalerie de la garde impériale sera placée en arrière de Beaumont; mais les corps les plus éloignés n'en doivent pas être à une lieue.

'Le deuxième corps prendra position à Laire, c'est-à-dire, le plus près possible de la frontière, sans la dépasser. Les quatre divisions de ce corps d'armée seront réunies et bivaqueront sur deux ou quatre lignes; le quartier général au milieu; la cavalerie en avant, éclairant tous les débouchés, mais aussi sans dépasser la frontière, et la faisant respecter par les partisans ennemis qui voudraient la violer.

'Les bivouacs seront placés de manière que les feux ne puissent être aperçus de l'ennemi: les généraux empêcheront que personne ne s'écarte du camp: ils s'assureront que la troupe est pourvue de cinquante cartouches par homme, quatre jours de pain, et une demi-livre de riz; que l'artillerie et les ambulances sont en bon état, et les feront placer à leur ordre de bataille. Ainsi le deuxième corps sera disposé à se mettre en marche le 15 à trois heures du matin, si l'ordre en est donné, pour se porter sur Charleroi, et y arriver avant neuf heures.

'Le premier corps prendra position à Solre-sur-Sambre, et il bivaquera aussi sur plusieurs lignes, observant, ainsi que le deuxième corps, que ses feux ne puissent être aperçus de l'ennemi; que personne ne s'écarte du camp, et que les généraux s'assurent de l'état des munitions, des vivres de la troupe, et que l'artillerie et les ambulances soient placées à leur ordre de bataille.

'Le premier corps se tiendra également prêt à partir le 15, à trois heures du matin, pour suivre le mouvement du deuxième corps ; de manière que, dans la journée d'après-demain, ces deux corps manœuvrent dans la même direction, et se protégent.

'Le troisième corps prendra demain position à une lieue en avant de Beaumont, le plus près possible de la frontière, sans cependant la dépasser, ni souffrir qu'elle soit violée par aucun parti ennemi. Le général Vandamme tiendra tout le monde à son poste, recommandera que les feux soient cachés, et qu'ils ne puissent être aperçus de l'ennemi. Il se conformera d'ailleurs à ce qui presceit au deuxième corps pour les munitions, les vivres, l'artillerie, et les ambulances, et pour être prêt à se mettre en mouvement le 15 à trois heures du matin.

'Le sixième corps se portera en avant de Beaumont; et sera bivaqué sur deux lignes, à un quart de lieue du troisième corps. M. le comte de Lobau choisira l'emplacement, et il fera observer les dispositions générales qui sont prescrites par le présent ordre.

'M. le maréchal Grouchy portera les premier, deuxième, troisième, et quatrième corps de cavalerie, en avant de Beaumont, et les établira au bivouàc entre cette ville et Walcourt, faisant également respecter la frontière, empêchant que personne ne la dèpasse, et qu'on se laisse voir, ni que les feux puissent être aperçus de l'ennemi: et il se tiendra prêt à partir après demain, à trois heures du matin, s'il en reçoit l'ordre, pour se porter sur Charleroi, et faire l'avant-garde de l'armée.

'Il recommandera aux généraux de s'assurer si tous les cavaliers sont pourvus de cartouches, si leurs armes sont en bon état, et s'ils ont pour quatre jours de pain, et la demi-livre de riz qui ont eté ordonnés.

'L'équipage de ponts sera bivaqué derrière le sixième corps, et en avant de l'infanterie de la garde impériale.

'Le parc central d'artillerie sera en arrière de Beaumont.

'L'armée de la Moselle prendra demain position en avant de Philippeville. M. le comte Gérard la disposera de manière a pouvoir partir apès demain, le 15, à trois heures du matin, pour joindre le troisième corps, et appuyer son mouvement sur Charleroi, suivant le nouvel ordre qui lui sera donné ; mais le général Gérard aura soin de se bien garder sur son flanc droit, et en avant de lui, sur toutes les directions de Charleroi et de Namur. Si l'armée de la Moselle a des pontons à sa suite, le général Gérard les fera avancer le plus près possible, afin de pouvoir en disposer.

'Tous les corps d'armée feront marcher en tête les sapeurs, et les moyens de passage que les généraux auront réunis.

'Les sapeurs de la garde impériale, les ouvriers de la marine, et les sapeurs de la réserve, marcheront après le sixième corps, et en tête de la garde.

'Tous les corps marcheront dans le plus grand ordre et serrés. Dans le mouvement sur Charleroi, on sera disposé à profiter de tous les passages pour écraser les corps ennemis qui voudraient attaquer l'armée ou qui manœuvreraient contre elle.

'Il n'y aura à Beaumont que le grand quartier général. Aucun autre ne devra y être établi, et la ville sera dégagée de tout embarras. Les anciens règlemens sur le quartier général et les équipages, sur l'ordre de marche, et la police des voitures et bagages, et sur les blanchisseuses et vivandières, seront remis en vigueur. Il sera fait à ce sujet un ordre général; mais, en attendant, MM. les généraux commandant les corps d'armée, prendront des dispositions en conséquence; et M. le grand prévôt fera exécuter ces réglemens. L'empereur ordonne que toutes les dispositions contenues dans le présent ordre soient tenues secrètes par MM. les généraux.

'Par ordre de l'Empereur,
'Le marechal d'empire, major général,
'Duc de Dalmatie.'

XII.

Orders given by Lieut. General von Zieten, commanding the 1st Prussian Corps d'armée, on the 2nd May, 1815, *to be acted upon by his Brigadiers, in case of the enemy's attack.*

'Should the enemy advance by Binch or Maubeuge, and compel the advanced posts to retire, the brigades of the corps will assemble in the following manner:—

'The 1st brigade in rear of Fontaine l'Evêque,
2nd do. do. Charleroi,
3rd do. do. Fleurus,
4th do. do. Onoz,
Reserve-Cavalry, do. Gembloux, where it will receive further orders.
Reserve-artillery, do. Egheze.

'The 2nd brigade will leave a battalion at each of the points, Châtelet, Charleroi, and Marchienne, upon which the advanced posts can fall back, and the 1st brigade will leave 2 companies at Fontaine l'Evêque for a like purpose.

'As regards the outposts, the 2 rifle-companies of the 1st brigade will retire behind the defile of the Haine. The main body of the 1st Silesian hussars will collect in rear of Lerunes, towards which point its advanced posts will retire. The post at Lobbes will retire close along the left bank of the Sambre. The main body of the 6th uhlans will retire upon Charleroi, and unite with the 2nd brigade. The post of this regiment stationed at Thuin will await the arrival of the detachment from Lobbes with which it will then retire, by the left bank of the Sambre, to Marchienne. All the picquets between Thuin and Ham-sur-Heure will retire by Montigny de

Thigneu upon Marchienne: the posts between Ham-sur-Heure and Gerpinnes will fall back upon Charleroi.

'The 1st and 2nd squadrons of the Westphalian landwehr-cavalry at Près le Fort St. Eustache, will cross the Sambre at Châtelet, and join the 2nd brigade; the 3rd and 4th squadrons will cross the Sambre at Fallizole, their outposts falling back in the same direction, and the whole rejoining the 1st and 2nd squadrons on the left bank of the river.

'The passages across the Sambre, within the sphere of each respective brigade, will continue to be occupied until the brigades receive orders to retire from their points of assembly.

'The baggage and the train will be sent to the rear as far as Temploux.

'Should the enemy's dispositions render a further retrograde movement necessary—

'The 1st brigade after having sent on its artillery to Gosselies, will retire by Roux upon Jumet and Gosselies, and take post in rear of this town as advanced guard, and as a support to the posts on the Piéton.

'The 2nd brigade will take post in front of Fleurus.

'The 3rd and 4th brigades will take up a position in rear of Fleurus—the former on the right, the latter on the left, of the high road.

'Should the brigades receive orders to continue their retreat upon Fleurus, the 1st and 2nd will still hold the passages across the Piéton, the 2nd occupying that part of the river between Roux and its point of junction with the Sambre, and the 1st brigade that part between Roux and the Roman road. The 1st Silesian hussars and the 6th uhlans will remain as a support to the infantry posted on the Piéton. The reserve-cavalry will move upon Sombref; the reserve-artillery along the Roman road in the direction of the defile of Gembloux, in order to be at hand should an action take place in the position of Fleurus, or to strike into the high road to Namur, should a further retreat be ordered. In this latter case, the baggage of the brigades will proceed beyond Gembloux, accompanied by an officer, with the necessary escort from each brigade.

'Should the enemy advance from Beaumont or Philippeville, the foregoing disposition remains unaltered.

'In this case the 2nd brigade will continue to occupy the passages across the Sambre at Marchienne, Charleroi, and Châtelet, until the 1st brigade falls back upon the same line with it; the remainder of the 2nd brigade will form a support to these three posts, and then, taking up a position in rear of Gilly, upon the road from Charleroi to Fleurus, will become the advanced guard of the corps d'armée assembled at Fleurus.

'Should the enemy advance by Philippeville, and drive back the outposts of the 4th brigade, this brigade must defend the passages across the Sambre until the corps d'armée is assembled.

'Should individual French soldiers present themselves at the outposts, they must be warned to go back, unless they are deserters, but if they pay no attention to the warning, an endeavour must be made to capture them, and have them conveyed to head-quarters. In no case is a vedette to be allowed to retire in a peaceable manner.

'In the event of the 1st corps d' armée concentrating at Fleurus, the head-quarters will be in that town.

'von ZIETEN.'

'Charleroi,
the 2nd of May, 1815.'

'A correct copy,
'von REICHE,
'Chief of the Staff.'

XIII.

'ORDRE DU MOUVEMENT.

'Beaumont, 14 Juin, 1815.

'Demain, le 15, à deux heures et demie du matin, la division de cavalerie légère du genéral Vandamme montera à cheval, et se portera sur la route de Charleroi : elle enverra des partis dans toutes les directions, pour éclairer le pays, et enlever les postes ennemis ; mais chacun de ces partis sera au moins de cinquante hommes. Avant de mettre en marche la division, le général Vandamme s'assurera qu'elle est pourvue de cartouches.

'A la même heure, le lieutenant général Pajol réunira le premier corps de cavalerie, et suivra le mouvement de la division du général Domont, qui sera sous les ordres du général Pajol. Les divisions du premier corps de cavalerie ne fourniront point de detachemens ; ils seront pris dans la troisième division. Le général Domont laissera sa batterie d'artillerie, pour marcher après le premier battaillon du troisième corps d'infanterie. Le lieutenant général Vandamme lui donnera des ordres en conséquence.

'Le lieutenant général Vandamme fera battre la diane à deux heures et demie du matin ; à trois heures il mettra en marche son corps d'armée, et le dirigera sur Charleroi : la totalité de ses bagages et embarras seront parqués en arrière, et ne se mettront en marche qu'après que le sixième corps et la garde impériale auront passé ; ils seront sous les ordres du vaguemestre général, qui les réunira à ceux du sixième corps de la garde impériale et du grand quartier général, et leur donnera des ordres de mouvement.

'Chaque division du troisième corps d'armée aura avec elle sa batterie et ses ambulances ; toute autre voiture qui serait dans les rangs sera brûlée.

'M. le comte de Lobau fera battre la diane à trois heures et demie, et il mettra en marche le sixième corps d'armée à quatre heures, pour suivre le mouvement du général Vandamme, et l'appuyer ; il fera observer le même ordre de marche pour les troupes, l'artillerie, les ambulances, et les bagages, qui est prescrit au troisième corps.

'Les bagages du sixième corps seront réunis à ceux du troisième, sous les ordres du vaguemestre général, ainsi qu'il est dit.

'La jeune garde battra la diane à quatre heures et demie, et se mettra en marche à cinq heures; elle suivra le mouvement du sixième corps sur la route de Charleroi.

'Les chasseurs à pied de la garde battront la diane à cinq heures et se mettront en marche à cinq heures et demie, pour suivre le mouvement de la jeune garde.

'Les grenadiers à pied de la garde battront la diane à cinq heures et demie, et partiront à six heures, pour suivre le mouvement des chasseurs à pied. Le même ordre de marche, pour l'artillerie, les ambulances, et les bagages, prescrit pour le troisième corps d'infanterie, sera observé dans la garde impériale.

'Les bagages de la garde seront réunis à ceux de troisième et sixième corps d'armée, sous les ordres du vaguemestre général, qui les fera mettre en mouvement.

'M. le maréchal Grouchy fera monter à cheval, à cinq heures et demie du matin, celui des trois autres corps de cavalerie qui sera le plus près de la route, et lui fera suivre le mouvement sur Charleroi. Les deux autres corps partiront successivement à une heure d'intervalle l'un de l'autre; mais M. le maréchal Grouchy aura soin de faire marcher le cavalerie sur les chemins latéraux de la route principale que la colonne d'infanterie suivra, afin d'éviter l'encombrement; et aussi pour que sa cavalerie observe un mêilleur ordre. Il prescrira que la totalité des bagages restent en arrière, parqués et réunis jusqu'au moment où le vaguemestre général leur donnera l'ordre d'avancer.

'M. le comte Reille fera battre la diane à deux heures et demie du matin, et il mettra en marche le deuxième corps à trois heures; il le dirigera sur Marchiennes-au-Pont, où il fera en sorte d'être rendu avant neuf heures du matin; il fera garder tous les ponts de la Sambre, afin que personne ne passe. Les postes qu'il laissera seront successivement relevés par le premier corps; mais il doit tâcher de prévenir l'ennemi à ces ponts pour qu'ils ne soient pas detruits, surtout celui de Marchiennes, par lequel il sera probablement dans le cas de déboucher, et qu'il faudrait faire aussitôt réparer, s'il avait été endommagé.

'A Thuin et à Marchiennes, ainsi que dans tous les villages sur sa route, M. le comte Reille interrogera les habitans, afin d'avoir des nouvelles des positions et forces des armées ennemies; il fera aussi prendre les lettres dans les bureaux de poste, et les dépouillera, pour faire parvenir aussitôt à l'Empereur les renseignemens qu'il aura obtenus.

'M. le comte d'Erlon mettra en marche le premier corps à trois heures du matin, et il le dirigera aussi sur Charleroi, en suivant le mouvement du deuxième corps, duquel il gagnera la gauche le plutôt possible, pour le soutenir et l'appuyer au besoin. Il tiendra une brigade de cavalerie en arrière, pour se couvrir et pour maintenir par de petits détachemens, ses communications avec Maubeuge; il enverra des partis en avant de cette place, dans les directions de *Mons* et de *Binch*, jusqu'à la frontière, pour avoir des nouvelles des ennemis, et en rendre compte aussitôt. Ces partis auront soin de ne pas se compromettre et de ne point dépasser la frontière.

'M. le comte d'Erlon fera occuper Thuin par une division; et si le pont de cette ville était détruit, il le ferait aussitôt réparer, en même temps qu'il fera tracer et exécuter immédiatement une tête de pont sur la rive gauche. La division qui sera à Thuin gardera aussi le pont de l'abbaye d'*Alnes*, où M. le comte d'Erlon fera également construire une tête de pont, sur la rive gauche.

'Le même ordre de marche prescrit pour le troisième corps, pour l'artillerie, les ambulances et les bagages, sera observé aux deuxième et premier corps, qui feront réunir leurs bagages, et marcher à la gauche du premier corps, sous les ordres du vaguemestre le plus ancien.

'Le quatrième corps (armée de la Moselle) a reçu ordre de prendre aujourd'hui position en avant de Philippeville: si son mouvement est opéré, et si les divisions qui composent ce corps d'armée sont réunies, M. le lieutenant général Gérard les mettra en marche demain, à trois heures du matin, et les dirigera sur Charleroi;* il aura soin de se tenir à hauteur du troisième corps, avec lequel il communiquera, afin d'arriver à peu près en même temps devant Charleroi. Mais le général Gérard fera éclairer sa droite et tous les débouchés qui vont sur Namur; il marchera serré en ordre de bataille, fera laisser à Philippeville tous ses bagages et embarras, afin que son corps d'armée, se trouvant plus léger, soit plus à même de manœuvrer.

'Le général Gérard donnera ordre à la quatorizième division de cavalerie, qui a dû arriver aujourd'hui à Philippeville, de suivre le mouvement de son corps d'armée sur Charleroi, où cette division joindra le quatrième corps de cavalerie.

'Les lieutenans généraux Reille, Vandamme, Gérard, et Pajol, se mettront en communication par de fréquens partis, et ils régleront leur marche de manière à arriver en masse et ensemble devant Charleroi: ils mettront, autant que possible, à l'avant-garde, les officiers qui parlent flamand, pour interroger les habitans et en prendre des renseignemens; mais ces officiers s'annonceront comme commandans de partis, sans dire que l'armée est en arrière.

'Les lieutenans généraux Reille, Vandamme, et Gérard, feront marcher tous les sapeurs de leur corps d'armée, (ayant avec eux des moyens pour réparer les ponts,) après le premier régiment d'infanterie légère, et ils donneront ordre aux officiers du génie de faire réparer les mauvais passages, ouvrir des communications latérales,

* Le général Gérard reçut plus tard un nouvel ordre qui lui prescrivit de passer, avec son corps, la Sambre, au Châtelet.

et placer des ponts sur les courans d'eau où l'infanterie devrait se mouiller pour les franchir.

'Les marins, les sapeurs de la garde, et les sapeurs de la réserve, marcheront après le premier régiment du troisième corps ; les lieutenans généraux Rogniat et Haxo seront à leur tête : ils n'amèneront avec eux que deux ou trois voitures : le surplus du parc du génie marchera à la gauche du troisième corps. Si on rencontre l'ennemi, ces troupes ne seront point engagées, mais les généraux Rogniat et Haxo les emploieront aux travaux de passages de rivière, de têtes de pont, de réparations de chemin, et d'ouvertures de communication, etc. La cavalerie de la garde suivra le mouvement sur Charleroi, et partira à huit heures.

'L'Empereur sera à l'avant-garde sur la route de Charleroi. M.M. les lieutenans généraux auront soin d'envoyer à sa majesté de fréquens rapports sur leurs mouvemens et les renseignemens qu'ils auront recueillis ; ils sont prévenus que l'intention de sa majesté est d'avoir passé la Sambre avant midi, et de porter l'armée à la rive gauche de cette riviére.

'L'équipage des ponts sera divisé en deux sections : la première section se subdivisera en trois parties, chacune de cinq pontons et cinq bateaux d'avant-garde, pour jeter trois ponts sur la Sambre ; il y aura à chacune de ces subdivisions une compagnie de pontonniers ; la première section marchera à la suite du parc du génie, après le troisième corps.

'La deuxième section restera avec le parc de réserve d'artillerie, à la colonne des bagages ; elle aura avec elle la quatrième compagnie de pontonniers ; les équipages de l'Empereur, et les bagages du grand quartier général seront réunis, et se mettront en marche à dix heures. Aussitôt qu'ils seront passés, le vaguemestre général fera partir les équipages de la garde impériale, du troisième corps, et du sixième corps ; en même temps il enverra ordre à la colonne d'équipages de la réserve de la cavalerie, de se mettre en marche, et de suivre la direction que la cavalerie aura prise. Les ambulances de l'armée suivront le quartier général, et marcheront à la tête des bagages ; mais, dans aucun cas, ces bagages, ainsi que les parcs de réserve de l'artillerie, et la deuxième section de l'équipage de ponts, ne s'approcheront à plus de trois lieues de l'armée, à moins d'ordre du major général, et ils ne passeront la Sambre, aussi, que par ordre.

'Le vaguemestre général formera les divisions de ces bagages, et il y mettra des officiers pour les commander, afin de pouvoir en détacher ce qui sera ensuite appelé au quartier général, ou pour le service des officiers.

'L'intendant général fera réunir à cette colonne d'équipages la totalité des bagages et transports de l'administration, auxquels il sera assigné un rang dans la colonne. Les voitures qui seront en retard prendront la gauche, et ne pourront sortir du rang qui leur sera donné que par ordre du vaguemestre général.

'L'Empereur ordonne que toutes les voitures d'équipages qui

seront trouvées dans les colonnes d'infanterie, de cavalerie, ou d'artillerie, soient brûlées, ainsi que les voitures de la colonne des équipages qui quitteront leur rang, et intervertiront leur marche, sans la permission expresse du vaguemestre général.

'A cet effet, il sera mis un détachement de cinquante gendarmes à la disposition du vaguemestre général, qui est responsable, ainsi que tous les officiers de la gendarmerie et les gendarmes, de l'exécution de ces dispositions, desquelles le succès de la campagne peut dépendre.

'Par ordre de l'Empereur,
'Le maréchal d'empire, major général,
'LE DUC DE DALMATIE.'

XIV.

Memorandum for the Deputy Quarter Master General of the Anglo-allied Army, on the 15th of June, 1815.

'MOVEMENTS OF THE ARMY.

'Bruxelles, 15th of June, 1815.

'General Dörnberg's brigade of cavalry, and the Cumberland hussars, to march this night upon Vilvorde, and to bivouac on the high road, near to that town.

'The Earl of Uxbridge will be pleased to collect the cavalry this night at Ninhove, leaving the 2nd hussars looking-out between the Scheldt and the Lys.

'The 1st division of infantry to collect this night at Ath and adjacent, and to be in readiness to move at a moment's notice.

'The 3rd division to collect this night at Braine-le-Comte, and to be in readiness to move at the shortest notice.

'The 4th division to be collected this night at Grammont, with the exception of the troops beyond the Scheldt, which are to be moved to Audenarde.

'The 5th division, the 81st regiment, and the Hanoverian brigade of the 6th division, to be in readiness to march from Bruxelles at a moment's notice.

'The Duke of Brunswick's corps to collect this night on the road between Bruxelles and Vilvorde.

'The Nassau troops to collect at daylight to-morrow morning on the Louvain road, and to be in readiness to move at a moment's notice.

'The Hanoverian brigade of the 5th division to collect this night at Hal, and to be in readiness at daylight to-morrow morning to move towards Bruxelles, and to halt on the high road, between Alost and Assche, for further orders.

'The Prince of Orange is requested to collect, at Nivelles, the 2nd and 3rd divisions of the army of the Low Countries; and should that point have been attacked this day, to move the 3rd division of British infantry upon Nivelles, as soon as collected.

'This movement is not to take place until it is quite certain that the enemy's attack is upon the right of the Prussian army, and the left of the British army.

'Lord Hill will be so good as to order Prince Frederick of Orange to occupy Audenarde with 500 men, and to collect the 1st division of the army of the Low Countries, and the Indian brigade at Sotteghem, so as to be ready to march in the morning at daylight.

'The reserve artillery to be in readiness to move at daylight.

'WELLINGTON.'*

XV.

'MOVEMENT OF THE ARMY.

'*After orders*, 10 *o'clock*, p.m.

'Bruxelles, 15th of June, 1815.

'The 3rd division of infantry to continue its movement from Braine-le-Comte upon Nivelles.

'The 1st division to move from Enghien upon Braine-le-Comte.

'The 2nd and 4th divisions of infantry to move from Ath and Grammont, also from Audenarde, and to continue their movements upon Enghien.

'The cavalry to continue its movement from Ninhove upon Enghien.

'The above movements to take place with as little delay as possible.

WELLINGTON.'†

XVI.

Despatch from Napoleon to Marshal Ney.

A. M. LE MARÉCHAL,

PRINCE DE LA MOSKOWA.

'Charleroi, le 16 Juin, 1815.

'Monsieur le Maréchal, l'Empereur vient d'ordonner à M. le comte de Valmy, commandant le 3e corps de cavalerie, de le réunir et de le diriger sur Gosselies, où il sera à votre disposition.

'L'intention de Sa Majesté est que la cavalerie de la garde, qui

* "Despatches of Field Marshal the Duke of Wellington. Compiled by Colonel Gurwood, C. B."

† "Despatches of Field Marshal the Duke of Wellington. Compiled by Colonel Gurwood, C.B."

a été portée sur la route de Bruxelles, reste en arrière et rejoigne le restant de la garde impériale ; mais, pour qu'elle ne fasse pas de mouvement rétrograde, vous pourrez, aprés l'avoir fait remplacer sur la ligne, la laisser un peu en arrière où il lui sera envoyé des ordres dans le mouvement de la journée. M. le lieutenant général Lefebvre Desnouettes enverra, à cet effet, un officier pour prendre des ordres.

'Veuillez m'instruire si le l^er^ corps a opéré son mouvement, et quelle est, ce matin, la position exacte des 1er et 2e corps d'armée, et des deux divisions de cavalerie qui y sont attachées, en me faisant connaitre ce qu'il y a d'ennemis devant vous, et ce qu'on a appris.

'Le major général,

'DUC DE DALMATIE.'

XVII.

Order of Movement for Marshal Ney.

A. M. LE MARECHAL, PRINCE DE LA MOSKOWA.

'Charleroi, le 16 juin, 1815.

'Monsieur le Maréchal, l'empereur ordonne que vous mettiez en marche les 2e et 1er corps d'armée, ainsi que le 3e corps de cavalerie, qui a été mis à votre disposition, pour les diriger sur l'intersection des chemins dits les Trois-Bras (route de Bruxelles,) où vous leur ferez prendre position, et vous porterez en même temps des reconnaissances, aussi avant que possible, sur la route de Bruxelles et sur Nivelles, d'où probablement l'ennemi s'est retiré.

'S. M. désire que, s'il n'y pas d'inconvénient, vous établissiez une division avec de la cavalerie à Genappe, et elle ordonne que vous portiez une autre division du côté de Marbais, pour couvrir l'espace entre Sombref et les Trois-Bras. Vous placerez, près de ces divisions, la division de cavalerie de la garde impériale, commandée par le général Lefebvre Desnouettes, ainsi que le 1er régiment de hussards, qui a été détaché hier vers Gosselies.

'Le corps qui sera à Marbais aura aussi pour objet d'appuyer les mouvements de M. le maréchal Grouchy sur Sombref et de vous soutenir à la position des Trois-Bras, si cela devenait nécessaire. Vous recommanderez au général, qui sera à Marbais, de bien s'éclairer sur toutes les directions, particulièrement sur celles de Gembloux et de Wavre.

'Si cependant la division du général Lefebvre Desnouettes etait trop engagée sur la route de Bruxelles, vous la laisseriez et vous la remplaceriez au corps qui sera à Marbais par le 3e corps de cavalerie aux ordres de M. le comte de Valmy, et par le 1er régiment de hussards.

'J'ai l'honneur de vous prévenir que l'Empereur va se porter sur Sombref, où d'après les ordres de Sa Majesté, M. le maréchal Grouchy doit se diriger avec le 3e et 4e corps d'infanterie, et les

1er, 2e et 4e corps de cavalerie. M. le maréchal Grouchy fera occuper Gembloux.

'Je vous prie de me mettre de suite à même de rendre compte à l'Empereur de vos dispositions pour exécuter l'ordre que je vous envoie, ainsi que de tout ce que vous aurez appris sur l'ennemi.

'Sa Majesté me charge de vous recommander de prescrire aux généraux commandant les corps d'armée de fair réunir leur monde et rentrer les hommes isolés, de maintenir l'ordre le plus parfait dans la troupe, et de rallier toutes les voitures d'artillerie et les ambulances qu'ils auraient pu laisser en arrière.

'Le maréchal d'empire, major général,

'Duc de Dalmatie.'

XVIII.

Order of Movement for Count Reille.

A. M. LE COMTE REILLE,

Commandant le 2e corps d'armée.

'Frasnes, le 16 juin, 1815.

'ORDRE DE MOUVEMENT.

'Conformément aux instructions de l'Empereur, le 2e corps se mettra en marche de suite pour aller prendre position, la cinquième division en arrière de Genappes, sur les hauteurs qui dominent cette ville, la gauche appuyée à la grande route. Un bataillon on deux couvriront tous les débouchés en avant sur la route de Bruxelles. Le parc de rèserve et les équipages de cette division resteront avec la seconde ligne.

'La neuvième division suivra les mouvements de la cinquième, et viendra prendre position en seconde ligne sur les hauteurs à droite et à gauche du village de Bauterlet.

'Les sixième et septième divisions à l'embranchement des Quatre-Bras, où sera votre quartier général. Les trois premières divisions du comte d'Erlon viendrout prendre position à Frasnes ; la division de droite s'établira à Marbais avec la deuxième division de cavalerie légère du général Piré; la premiere couvrira votre marche, et vous éclairera sur Bruxelles et sur vos deux flancs. Mon quartier à Frasnes.

'Pour le Maréchal Prince de la Moskowa,

'Le Colonel, premier aide de camp,

'Heymes.'

'Deux divisions du comte de Valmy's s'établiront à Frasnes et à Liberchies.

'Les divisions* de la garde des généraux Lefebvre Desnouettes et Colbert resteront dans leur position actuelle de Frasnes.'

* This is evidently a mistake—it should be "régiments."

XIX.

Despatch from Count Reille to Marshal Ney.

A. M. LE MARECHAL, PRINCE DE LA MOSCOWA.

'Gosselies, le 16 juin, 1815, 10 heures et quart du matin.

'Monsieur le Maréchal,

'J'ai l'honneur d'informer Votre Excellence du rapport que me fait faire verbalement le général Girard par un de ses officiers.

'L'ennemi continue à occuper Fleurus par de la cavalerie légère qui a des vedettes en avant; l'on aperçoit deux masses ennemies venant par la route de Namur et dont la tête est à la hauteur de Saint-Amand; elles se sont formées peu à peu, et ont gagné quelque terrain à mesure qu'il leur arrivait du monde: on n'a pu guères juger de leur force à cause de l'éloignement; cependant ce général pense que chacun pouvait être de six bataillons en colonne par bataillon. On apercevait des mouvements de troupes derrière.

'M. le lieutenant-général Flahaut m'a fait part des ordres qu'il portait à Votre Excellence; j'en ai prévenu M. le comte d'Erlon, afin qu'il puisse suivre mon mouvement. J'aurais commencé le mien sur Frasnes aussitôt que les divisions auraient été sous les armes; mais d'après le rapport du général Girard, je tiendrai les troupes prêtes á marcher en attendant les ordres de Votre Excellence, et comme ils pourront me parvenir très vite, il n'y aura que très peu de temps de perdu.

'J'ai envoyé à l'Empereur l'officier qui m'a fait le rapport du général Girard.

'Je renouvelle à Votre Excellence les assurances de mon respectueux dévouement.

'Le général en chef du 2e corps,
'COMTE REILLE.'

XX.

Orders from Napoleon to Marshal Ney.

A. M. LE MARECHAL, PRINCE DE LA MOSKOWA.

'Charleroi, le 16 juin, 1815.

'Monsieur le Maréchal,

'Un officier de lanciers vient de dire à l'Empereur que l'ennemi présentait des masses du côté des Quatre-Bras. Réunissez les corps des comtes Reille et d'Erlon et celui du comte de Valmy, qui se met à l'instant en route pour vous rejoindre; avec ces forces, vous devrez battre et détruire tous les corps ennemis qui peuvent se présenter. Blücher était hier à Namur, et il n'est pas vraisemblable qu'il ait porté des troupes vers les Quatre-Bras; ainsi, vous n'avez affaire qu'à ce qui vient de Bruxelles.

'Le maréchal Grouchy va faire le mouvement sur Sombref, que

je vous ai annoncé et l'Empereur va se rendre à Fleurus; c'est là où vous adresserez vos nouveaux rapports à Sa Majesté.

'Le maréchal d'empire, major général,

'DUC DE DALMATIE.'

XXI.

Orders from Napoleon to Marshal Ney.

A. M. LE MARECHAL, PRINCE DE LA MOSKOWA.

'En avant de Fleurus, le 16 juin, à 2 heures.

'Monsieur le Maréchal, l'Empereur me charge de vous prévenir que l'ennemi a réuni un corps de troupes entre Sombref et Bry, et qu'à deux heures et demie M. le maréchal Grouchy, avec les troisième et quatrième corps, l'attaquera; l'intention de Sa Majesté est que vous attaquiez aussi ce qui est devant vous, et qu'après l'avoir vigoureusement poussé, vous rabattiez sur nous pour concourir à envelopper le corps dont je viens de vous parler.

'Si ce corps était enfoncé auparavant, alors Sa Majesté ferait manœuvrer dans votre direction pour hâter également vos opérations.

'Instruisez de suite l'Empereur de vos dispositions et de ce qui se passe sur votre front.

'Le maréchal d'empire, major général,

'DUC DE DALMATIE.'

XXII.

Orders from Napoleon to Marshal Ney.

A. M. LE MARECHAL, PRINCE DE LA MOSKOWA.

'Monsieur le Maréchal, je vous ai écrit, il y a une heure, que l'Empereur ferait attaquer l'ennemi à deux heures et demie dans la position qu'il a prise entre la village de Saint-Amand et de Bry; en ce moment l'engagement est très prononcé; Sa Majesté me charge de vous dire que vous devez manœuvrer sur-le-champ de maniére à envelopper la droite de l'ennemi et tomber à bras raccourcis sur ses derrières; cette armée est perdue si vous agissez vigoureusement; le sort de la France est entre vos mains. Ainsi n'hésitez pas un instant pour faire le mouvement que l'Empereur vous ordonne, et dirigez vous sur les hauteurs de Bry et de Saint-Amand, pour concourir à une victoire peutêtre décisive. L'ennemi est pris en flagrant délit au moment où il cherche à se réunir aux Anglais.

'Le major général,

'DUC DE DALMATIE.'

'En avant de Fleurus, le 16 juin, 1815, à 3 heures un quart.*

* Upon a duplicate of this order, despatched by another messenger, the time is stated to be half-past three o'clock.

~~5th B~~ QUATRE BRAS

2ND BOW -5TH MILITIA - GOOD

2ND LIGHT - BAD

3RD D/B CANNON - BAD

BRUNSWICK CORPS - BAD

2ND BRUNSWICK LIGHT - GOOD

KIELMANSEGG'S HANOVERIANS - GOOD

In column at quarter distance

XXIII.

Return of Killed, Wounded, and Missing, of the British Troops, at the Battle of Quatre-Bras.

Brigades.	Regiments.	Killed. Officers.	Killed. Serjeants.	Killed. Drummers.	Killed. Rank and File.	Killed. Horses.	Wounded. Officers.	Wounded. Serjeants.	Wounded. Drummers.	Wounded. Rank and File.	Wounded. Horses.	Missing. Officers.	Missing. Serjeants.	Missing. Drummers.	Missing. Rank and File.	Missing. Horses.	Total Rank and File, Killed, Wound and Missing.
	Royal Artillery	..	..	..	9	19	2	..	..	17	14	..	..	..	..	1	26
1st	1st Guards, 2nd Battn.	2	1	..	22	..	4	6	..	250	..	..	..	..	..	..	514
	1st Guards, 3rd Battn.	1	2	1	17	..	6	9	1	225	..	..	..	..	..	..	
2nd	2nd Guards, 2nd Battn.	..	..	..	..	..	..	..	..	..	..	..	..	..	..	..	7
	3rd Guards, 2nd Battn.	..	..	..	..	..	..	..	..	7	..	..	..	..	..	..	
5th	30th Regiment, 2nd do.	..	1	..	4	.	2	2	..	26	..	..	..	..	5	..	
	33rd do.	3	1	..	15	..	7	3	..	64	..	..	1	..	8	..	304
	69th do. do. do.	1	4	..	33	..	4	6	1	103	..	..	..	..	..	..	
	73rd do. do. do.	..	..	1	3	..	4	1	..	43	..	..	..	..	..	..	
8th	28th do. 1st do.	..	..	..	11	..	4	4	..	56	..	..	..	..	..	..	
	32nd do. do. do.	3	..	..	21	..	19	4	1	148	.	..	..	..	..	..	566
	79th do. do. do.	1	..	..	28	..	16	10	..	248	..	1	..	..	..	..	
	95th do. do. do.	1	2	..	6	..	4	3	..	48	..	..	..	..	..	..	
9th	1st do. 3rd do.	6	2	..	18	..	12	13	..	167	..	..	..	..	..	..	
	42nd do. 1st do.	3	2	..	40	..	15	14	1	213	..	..	..	..	..	..	788
	44th do. 2nd do.	2	..	1	9	..	15	12	..	82	..	..	1	2	14	..	
	92nd do. 1st do.	4	2	..	33	..	21	13	1	212	.	..	..	..	..	..	
	General Staff	2	..	..	..	..	5	..	..	..	..	..	..	..	..	..	
	Total ..	29	17	3	269	19	140	100	5	1909	14	1	2	2	27	1	2,205

XXIV.

Return of Killed, Wounded, and Missing, of the Brunswick Troops, at the Battle of Quatre-Bras.

Regiments.	Killed. Officers.	Killed. Non-commissioned Officers, and Privates.	Wounded. Officers.	Wounded. Non-commissioned Officers, and Privates.	Horses. Killed, and Wounded.	Missing. Rank and File.	Total Rank and File, Killed, Wounded, and Missing.
Regiment of Hussars ..	2	15	2	27	68		42
Squadron of Uhlans ..	..	4	..	10	8		14
Horse Battery	..	..	..	..	2		..
Foot Battery	..	..	..	..	..		..
Advanced-Guard Battalion	..	9	4	43	..		52
Guard Battalion	..	15	5	106	..		121
1st Light Battalion ..	..	..	..	3	..	210*	3
2nd do.	..	18	3	49	..		67
3rd do.	..	..	..	..	..		..
1st Line Battalion ..	1	16	2	86	..		102
2nd do.	2	23	4	162	..		185
3rd do.	..	4	1	19	..		23
General Staff	1	..	..	..	..		
							210*
Total ..	6	104	21	505	78	210	819

XXV.

Effective Strength of the French Army at the Battle of Ligny:
(including the 6th corps d'armée.)

	Infantry.	Cavalry.	Artillery and Engineers.	Guns.
Imperial Guard*	12,554	1,619	2,984	84
3rd Corps d'armée	14,508	932	1,082	38
4th do. do.	12,589	2,366	1,739	38
6th do. do.	8,152	.	932	38
7th Infantry-Division (Girard)	3,761	.	175	8
1st Cavalry-Corps	.	2,324	317	12
2nd do. do.	.	2,817	246	12
4th do. do.	.	2,556	313	12
	51,564	12,614	7,788	242

Grand Total 71,966 Men, and 242 Guns.

XXVI.

Effective Strength of the Prussian Army at the Battle of Ligny.

	Infantry.	Cavalry.	Artillery.	Guns.
1st Corps d'armée	27,887	1,925	1,019	96
2nd do. do.	†25,137	4,220	1,454	80
3rd do. do.	‡20,006	2,005	964	48
	73,030	8,150	3,437	224

Total, 84,617.

Deduct loss of 1st Corps on 15th of June 1,200.

Grand Total . 83,417 Men and 224 Guns.

* Deducting the light cavalry of the Guard, which was with Marshal Ney, in reserve.

† Deducting the 3rd batt. 21st regt. and 2 squadrons of the Neumark Dragoons, which had not rejoined from the vicinity of Philippeville.

‡ Deducting the 2nd batt. 3rd Kurmark landwehr, and 2 squadrons of the 6th Kurmark landwehr-cavalry, which had not rejoined from the vicinity of Dinant.

XXVII.

Orders from Napoleon to Marshal Ney.

A. M. LE MARECHAL, PRINCE DE LA MOSKOWA.

'Fleurus, le 17 juin, 1815.

'Monsieur le Maréchal, le général Flahaut, qui arrive à l'instant, fait connaître que vous êtes dans l'incertitude sur les résultats de la journée d'hier. Je crois cependant vous avoir prévenu de la victoire que l'Empereur a remportée. L'armée prussienne a été mise en déroute, le général Pajol est à sa poursuite sur les routes de Namur et de Liége. Nous avons déjà plusieurs milliers de prisonniers et 30 pièces de canon. Nos troupes se sont bien conduites: une charge de six bataillons de la garde, des escadrons de service et la division de cavalerie du général Delort a percé la ligne ennemie, porté le plus grand désordre dans ses rangs et enlevé la position.

'L'Empereur se rend au moulin de Bry où passe la grande route qui conduit de Namur aux Quatre-Bras; il n'est donc pas possible que l'armée anglaise puisse agir devant vous; si cela était, l'Empereur marcherait directement sur elle par la route des Quatre-Bras, tandis que vous l'attaqueriez de front avec vos divisions qui, à présent, doivent être rêunies, et cette armée serait dans un instant détruite. Ainsi, instruisez Sa Majesté de la position exacte des divisions, et de tout ce qui se passe devant vous.

'L'Empereur a vu avec peine que vous n'ayez pas réuni hier les divisions: elles ont agi isolément; ainsi, vous avez éprouvé des pertes.

'Si les corps des comtes d'Erlon et Reille avaient été ensemble, il ne réchappait pas un Anglais du corps qui venait vous attaquer. Si le comte d'Erlon avait exécuté le mouvement sur St. Amand que l'Empereur a ordonné, l'armée prussienne était totalement détruite, et nous aurions fait peut-être 30,000 prisonniers.

'Les corps des généraux Gérard, Vandamme, et la garde impériale ont toujours été réunis; l'on s'expose à des revers lorsque des détachements sont compromis.

'L'Empereur espère et désire que vos sept divisions d'infanterie et la cavalerie soient bien réunies et formées, et qu'ensemble elles n'occupent pas une lieue de terrain, pour les avoir bien dans votre main et les employer au besoin.

'L'intention de Sa Majesté est que vous preniez position aux Quatre-Bras, ainsi que l'ordre vous en a été donné; mais si, par impossible, cela ne peut avoir lieu, rendez-en compte sur-le-champ avec détail, et l'Empereur s'y portera ainsi que je vous l'ai dit;—si, au contraire, il n'y a qu'une arrière-garde, attaquez la, et prenez position.

'La journée d'aujourd'hui est necessaire pour terminer cette opération, et pour compléter les munitions, rallier les militaires isolés et fairé rentrer les détachements. Donnez des ordres en conséquence, et assurez-vous que tous les blessés sont pansés et transportés sur les derrières : l'on s'est plaint que les ambulances n'avaient pas fait leur devoir.

'Le fameux partisan Lutzow qui a été pris, disait que l'armée prussienne était perdue, et que Blücher avait exposé une seconde fois la monarchie prussienne.

'Le maréchal d'empire, major général,

'Duc de Dalmatie.'

XXVIII.

Orders from Napoleon to Marshal Ney.

A. M. LE MARECHAL, PRINCE DE LA MOSKOWA.

'4e corps d'armée, à Gosselies.

'En avant de Ligny, le 17 à midi.

'Monsieur le Maréchal, l'Empereur vient de faire prendre position, en avant de Marbais, à un corps d'infanterie et à la garde impériale; S.M. me charge de vous dire que son intention est que vous attaquiez les ennemis aux Quatre-Bras, pour les chasser de leur position, et que le corps qui est à Marbais secondera vos opérations ; S. M. va se rendre à Marbais, et elle attend vos rapports avec impatience.

'Le maréchal d'empire, major général,

'Duc de Dalmatie.'

XXIX.

Return of Killed, Wounded, and Missing, of the British Troops, and King's German Legion, on the Retreat from Quatre-Bras to Waterloo.

Regiments.	Killed.					Wounded.					Missing.					Total Rank and File, Killed, Wounded, and Missing.
	Officers.	Serjeants.	Drummers, or Trumpeters.	Rank and File.	Horses.	Officers.	Serjeants.	Drummers, or Trumpeters.	Rank and File.	Horses.	Officers.	Serjeants	Drummers, or Trumpeters.	Rank and File.	Horses.	
Infantry. 30th Regt. 2nd Battn.				1					2					8		11
33rd do.									3			1				3
69th do. 2nd Battn.							1		2							2
73rd do. do.	1			3												3
Cavalry. 1st Life Guards				8	9	1	2		7							15
Royal Horse Guards				3	8				5							8
1st or Royal Dragoons				1	2											1
7th Hussars	1			6	17	1	5		16	20	2		1	14	22	36
11th Light Dragoons					4	1								2		2
13th Light Dragoons														1		1
18th Hussars				1					1							2
23rd Light Dragoons		1			5				3					2	8	5
2nd Light Dragoons, K G.L.				1					2					1		4
1st Hussars, K.G.L.												1		2	3	2
General Staff											1					..
Total	2	1	..	24	45	3	8	..	41	20	3	2	1	30	33	95

XXX.

Effective Strength of the Anglo-allied Army at the Battle of Waterloo.

Infantry.

Divisions.	Brigades.	British.	K. G. Legion.	Hanoverian.	Brunswickers.	Nassauers.	Dutch-Belgians.
1st . .	1st British .	1,997					
	2nd do. . .	2,064					
2nd . .	3rd do. . .	2,621					
	1st K. G. Legion	..	1,758				
	3rd Hanoverian	..	..	2,454			
3rd . .	5th British .	2,254					
	2nd K. G. Legion	..	1,527				
	1st Hanoverian	..	..	3,189			
4th . .	4th British .	1,767					
5th . .	8th do. . .	2.471					
	9th do. . .	2,173					
	5th Hanoverian	..	..	2,514			
6th . .	10th British .	2,128					
	4th Hanoverian	..	..	2,582			
Brunswick .	Light Infantry .	..	..	..	3,360		
	Line . . .	..	..	..	2,016		
Nassau . .	1st Regiment .	..	..	..	..	2,880	
2nd Dutch-Belgian	1st Brigade .	..	..	..	..	..	3,233
	2nd do. . .	..	..	..	..	..	4,300
3rd Dutch-Belgian	1st do. . .	..	..	..	..	..	3,088
	2nd do. . .	..	..	..	..	..	3,581
Detachment of the King's German Legion		..	16				
		17,475	3,301	10,739	5,376	2,880	14,202
Deduct losses on the 16th and 17th of June.		2,294	..	481	790	..	about 800
	Total . . .	15,181	3,301	10,258	4,586	2,880	13,402

Grand Total, 49,608 Infantry.

Cavalry.

Brigades.	British.	K. G. Legion.	Hanoverians.	Brunswickers.	Dutch-Belgians.
1st	1,226				
2nd	1,181				
3rd	387	881			
4th	1,171				
5th	772	6*			
6th	786	493			
7th	390	622			
1st Hanoverian	..	..	497		
Brunswick	..	..	..	922	
1st Dutch-Belgian	..	..	..	..	1,237
2nd do.	..	..	..	..	1,086
3rd do.	..	..	..	..	1,082
	5,913	2,002	497	922	3,405
Deduct losses on the 16th and 17th of June	70	5	..	56	about 200
Total	5,843	1,997	497	866	3,205

Grand Total, 12,408 Cavalry.

* These 6 men of the 2nd Hussars, K. G. Legion, were employed as orderlies to different General Officers; the regiment itself was still on the frontier near Ypres.

Artillery.

	British.		K. G. Legion.		Hanoverians.		Brunswickers.		Dutch-Belgians.	
	Men.	Guns.	Men.	Guns.	Men.	Guns.	Men.	Guns.	Men.	Guns.
Foot-Artillery .	1,781	30	526 {	6	465	12	510 {	8	510	16
Horse-Artillery .	1,212	48		12	..	..		8	667	16
Deduct losses on 16th and 17th of June }	2,993	78	526	18	465	12	510	16	1,177	32
	26	..	..*	..	..*	..	..	..	..	..
Total . .	2,967	78	526	18	465	12	510	16	1,177	32

Grand Total, 5,645 Artillery, and 156 Guns.

Total Strength.

Infantry	49,608
Cavalry	12,408
Artillery	5,645

Grand Total, 67,661 Men, and 156 Guns.

XXXI.

Effective Strength of the French Army at the Battle of Waterloo.

	Infantry.	Cavalry.	Artillery, and Engineers.	
			Men.	Guns.
Imperial Guard .	12,554	3,590	3,284	96
1st Corps d'armée .	16,200	1,400	1,396	46
2nd do.† .	15,989	1,729	1,619	38
6th do.‡ . .	5,836	..	771	30
3rd Cavalry Corps .	..	3,245	309	12
4th do. do. .	..	2,556	313	12
3rd Cavalry Division	..	932	174	6
5th do. do. .	..	1,090	163	6
	50,579	14,542	8,029	246
Deduct previous losses	§ 3,000	§ 750	§ 500	
Total . .	47,579	13,792	7,529	246

Grand Total, 68,900 Men, and 246 Guns.

* Returns of the casualties that occurred in the King's German Legion, in the Hanoverian subsidiary corps, and among the Dutch-Belgian troops, during the 16th, 17th, and 18th, will be found in Appendix.

† Deducting the 7th Division which was at Ligny,

‡ Deducting the 21st Division, which was with Marshal Grouchy.

§ According to the "Mémoires de Napoléon," livre ix.

XXXII.

List of Officers of the King's German Legion, who were present at the Defence of La Haye Sainte.

2nd Light Battalion. Majors—G. Baring; A. Bösewiel, *killed.* Captains—E. Holtzermann, *taken prisoner;* W. Schaumann, killed. Lieutenants—F. Kessler, *wounded,* C. Meyer; O. Lindam, *wounded;* B. Riefkugel, *wounded;* A. Tobin, *taken prisoner;* T. Carey, *wounded;* E. Biedermann; D. Græme, *wounded;* S. Earl. Ensigns—F. von Robertson, *killed;* G. Frank, *wounded;* W. Smith; L. Baring. Lieut. and Adjutant—W. Timmann, *wounded.* Surgeon—G. Heise.

1st *Light battalion.* Captains—von Gilsa, *wounded;* von Marschalck, *killed.* Lieutenant—Kuntze. Ensign—Baumgarten.

Skirmishers of 5th Line Battalion. Captain—von Wurmb, *killed.* Lieutenants—Witte, *wounded;* Schläger. Ensign—Walther, *wounded.*

XXXIII.

Effective Strength of the Prussian Troops on the Field of Waterloo.

			Infantry.	Cavalry.	Artillery.	Guns.
At half-past 4 o clock	Part of 4th corps	15th Brigade	5,881	..	1,143	64
		16th Brigade	6,162	..		
		Reserve Cavalry	.	2,720		
At 6 o'clock .	Remainder of 4th corps .	13th Brigade	6,385			
		14th Brigade	6,953			
At 7 o'clock .	Part of 1st corps	Part of 1st Brig.	2,582	1,670	274	16
	Part of 2nd corps	5th Brigade	6,851	4,468	380	24
		6th Brigade	6,460			
		Total,	41,283	8,858	1,803	104
			Grand Total 51,944 Men, and 104 Guns.			

XXXIV.

Lines descriptive of the part taken in the Battle of Waterloo by the 6th brigade of British cavalry, upon the repulse of the last attack by the French; with the death of Major the Hon. Frederick Howard.

BY AN OFFICER OF THE 10TH HUSSARS, WHO WAS PRESENT.

Back rolls the tide of war; its refluent wave
E'en Ney arrests not, *bravest of the brave.**
For ever turn'd, in wild confusion throng
Horse, cannon, infantry, the slope along;
And while with parting glare the sun illumes
Helm, cuirass, sabre, lance, pennons, plumes,
Such splendid pageantry of glorious war
Alone must swell the soul; but higher far
The feelings rose, to see the pride of France
Thus routed, mingled, while our bands advance,
Each serried column formed in order due,
Each eye elate this glorious end to view.
Hark! on the right exulting shouts arise,
And the huzza of Britons rends the skies;
From the left flank, in column, winding far,
Speeds with a whirlwind's force the swift hussar,
Tho' to their thund'ring hoofs the plain resounds.
Still cautious discipline their ardour bounds.
Who, with a hero's port and lofty form,
With waving sabre onward guides the storm?
While through the tangled corn and yielding clay
His spurs incessant urge his panting grey—
'Tis Vivian, pride of old Cornubia's hills,
His veins th' untainted blood of Britons fills.
  Him follows close a Manners,† glorious name,
In him a Granby's soul aspires to fame,
Or such as erst, when Rodney gained the day,
Ebb'd from his kinsman's wound with life away.

* *"Brave des braves."*

† *Lieut. Colonel Lord Robert Manners,* 10*th Hussars.*

"Front form the line!" cries Vivian, still its course
The head maintain'd, the rear with headlong force
Speeds at the word, till troops to troops combine,
And each firm squadron forms the serried line.
Now to their head as eager Uxbridge rush'd,
Fate check'd his wish to lead, as sudden gush'd
A purple torrent from his ebbing wound,
And from his charger hurl'd, he press'd the ground;
No groan he utter'd, breath'd no fainting sigh,
But on our squadrons bent his anxious eye.
Th' heroic eye spoke firm contempt of pain,
But disappointment not to lead again.
Then pierc'd the fatal ball young Gunning's heart,
Headlong he fell, nor felt one instant's smart:
Calm, pale as marble forms on tombs, he lay
As days had sped since pass'd his soul away.
His charger onward on the squadron's flank
To battle rush'd, and kept its master's rank.
Vain! (tho' still worthy of their former fame,
And from a gen'rous foe respect to claim,)
Vain the attempt! some gallant bands appear
Arrang'd to check the fierce hussars' career,
Awhile protection for their rear to form
And shield it from the desolating storm—
The helm'd dragoon upon our right bears down,
Couch'd are the lances of a band that crown
The hill's low brow, and down at speed they burst,
Sabre meets lance, and blow encounters thrust.
They turn, they fly—Vain hope to rally! vain!
To stem our onward course; o'er all the plain
Amid their bands confusion reigns supreme,
While o'er their heads our threat'ning sabres gleam.
At length a pause—A band of vet'rans true,
Whom no dire terrors of pursuit subdue,
Form the close square, and on a swelling brow
Unmov'd they stand, undaunted; onwards flow
The streaming fugitives, yet still they stand
Resolv'd to perish for their *beauteous land.**
Resolv'd, indignant, ere the field they leave,
The stains on Gallic honour to retrieve.
Here, should they rest, by their example warm'd
Others may join, and conflict fierce be form'd—
Charge, Howard, charge! and sweep them from the field,
To British swords their bayonets must yield—
To high emprize upon the battle's plain
When was the name of Howard call'd in vain?
Worthy his great progenitors he heard
The call, exulting, and with ready word,

* "*La Belle France.*"

"Charge, brave hussars!" he cried, and wav'd on high
His gleaming sword—forward at once they fly—
No tighten'd rein, no high curvetting airs,
(As their cuirassiers hover'd round our squares,
In hopes, perchance, some trembling files to spy,
Vain hopes, in bands where all were prompt to die.)
Now to each panting steed the spurs were press'd,
His mane wav'd o'er the rider's forward breast—
Thus rush'd the gallant squadron on the foe,
Yet firm they stood, their arms in levell'd row
Their volleying thunders pour'd our ranks among,
Where foremost blade on foremost musket rung.
Three gallant youths the van exulting led,
Three by the deadly volley instant bled—
Arnold and Bacon fall, again to rise,
From three fell wounds brave Howard's spirit flies:
Full many a warrior on that dreadful day,
Brave, generous, gentle, breath'd his soul away,
But one more gentle, generous, or brave,
Never in battle found a soldier's grave—
Alas! what tears shall dim the lovely eyes
Of her who now for absence only sighs—
Her whom to leave gives death its keenest smart,
Its deepest anguish to his bursting heart.
  Short were your pangs, but ere the spirit fled,
Heaven grant you saw that not in vain you bled;
That your brave followers on the broken foe
With vengeance wing'd dealt many a deadly blow,
Till mercy check'd each hand, and bade them spare
The suppliant remnants of the vanquish'd square.

XXXV.

List of British Officers who were present at the defence of Hougomont.

2nd Battalion of Coldstream, or 2nd Regiment of Foot Guards. MAJOR—A. G. Woodford, Colonel. CAPTAINS and LIEUT. COLONELS—J. Macdonell, *wounded;* D. Mackinnon, *wounded;* Hon. J. Walpole; H. Dawkins; Hon. E. Acheson; H. Wyndham, *wounded.* LIEUTENANTS and CAPTAINS—G. Bowles; T. Sowerby; W. L. Walton; W. G. Baynes; C. A. F. Bentinck, Adj.; J. S. Cowell; E. Sumner, *wounded;* J. L. Blackman, *killed;* B. Lord Hotham; Hon. R. Moore, *wounded;* T. Chaplin. ENSIGNS—Hon. J. Forbes; H. Gooch; A. Cuyler; M. Beaufoy; H. F. Griffiths, *wounded;* J. Montague, *wounded;* G. R. Buckley; J. Hervey; H. Vane; F. J. Douglass; R. Bowen; A. Gordon; Hon. W. Forbes; C. Short. ADJUTANT—C. A. F. Bentinck. QUARTER MASTER—B. Selway. SURGEON—W. Whymper. ASST. SURGEONS—G. Smith; W. Hunter.

2nd Battalion of the 3rd Regiment of Foot Guards. MAJOR—F. Hepburn, Lieut. Col. CAPTAINS and LIEUT. COLONELS—H. W. Rooke; W. C. Master; D. Mercer; C. Dashwood, *wounded;* F. Home; E. Bowater, *wounded;* C. West. *wounded.* LIEUTENANTS and CAPTAINS—W. Stothert, Adj. W. Drummond; R. B. Hesketh, *wounded;* H. Hawkins; R. H. Wigston; Hon. J. B. Rodney; C. J. Barnet; J. W. Moorhouse; E. B. Fairfield; G. Evelyn, *wounded;* Hon. H. Forbes, *killed;* J. Elrington; H. B. Montgomerie, *wounded;* T. Crawford, *killed;* J. Ashton, *killed.* ENSIGNS—C. Lake, *wounded;* Hon. E. Stopford; B. Drummond; G. D. Standen; D. Baird, *wounded;* W. James; W. F. Hamilton; Hon. G. Anson; T. Wedgewood; W. Butler; A. C. Cochrane: J. Prendergast; C. Simpson, *wounded;* H. S. Blane; H. Montague. ADJUTANT—W. Stothert, Capt., *wounded.* QUARTER MASTER—J. Skuce. SURGEON—S. Good. ASST. SURGEONS—J. R. Warde; F. G. Hanrott.

1st Regiment of Foot Guards. CAPTAINS and LIEUT. COLONELS—Lord Saltoun; C. P. Ellis, *wounded.**

* I know not the names of the remaining officers of the light companies of the 1st Brigade of Guards detached to Hougomont.—W. S.

XXXVI.

Return of Killed, Wounded, and Missing, of the British Troops at the Battle of Waterloo.

	Brigades.	Regiments.	Killed. Officers.	Killed. Troop Quarter-Masters, and Serjeants.	Killed. Trumpeters or Drummers.	Killed. Rank and File.	Killed. Horses.	Wounded. Officers.	Wounded. Troop Quarter-Masters, and Serjeants.	Wounded. Trumpeters or Drummers.	Wounded. Rank and File.	Wounded. Horses.	Missing. Officers.	Missing. Troop Quarter-Masters, and Serjeants.	Missing. Trumpeters, or Drummers.	Missing. Rank and File.	Missing. Horses.	Total Rank and File Killed, Wounded, and Missing.
		Royal Artillery .	5	2	..	51	337	24	13	..	198	123	..	..	..	10	35	259
		Royal Engineers .	..	..	..	..	..	1	..	..	..	..	..	..	..	..	..	..
		Royal Staff Corps .	..	..	..	..	..	2	..	..	..	..	..	..	..	..	..	..
Cavalry.	1st	1st Life Guards .	2	4	..	12	39	3	4	..	36	21	..	..	..	4	25	525
		2nd do. . .	1	2	..	14	100	1	5	1	34	20	..	3	..	94	53	
		Rl. H. Guards (Blues)	1	2	..	14	54	4	5	..	51	15	1	..	..	20	34	
		1st Dragoon Guards	3	3	..	37	55	4	4	2	94	13	4	9	..	115	243	
	2nd	1st Dragoons . .	4	6	..	79	161	9	6	1	81	35	1	..	..	9	..	533
		2nd do. (Scots Greys)	6	3	1	92	179	8	9	..	80	47	..	..	..	..	2	
		6th do. (Inniskillings)	1	5	1	66	105	5	10	2	99	49	1	..	..	27	53	
	3rd	*1st Light Drag. K. G. L.*	..	..	..	..	..	..	..	..	..	..	..	..	..	..	..	64
		2nd do. . .	..	..	..	..	..	..	..	..	..	..	..	..	..	..	..	
		23rd Light Dragoons	1	3	..	10	20	5	..	..	23	26	1	..	..	31	33	
	4th	11th do. . .	1	1	..	10	17	4	4	..	20	38	..	1	2	20	18	167
		12th do. . .	2	6	..	39	28	3	4	1	56	22	..	..	..	..	60	
		16th do. . .	2	2	..	6	35	4	2	..	16	20	..	..	..	..	..	
	5th	*2nd Hussars, K. G. L.*	..	..	..	..	..	..	..	..	..	..	..	..	..	..	..	207
		7th Hussars . .	..	1	..	55	84	6	9	1	83	116	..	..	..	..	..	
		15th do. . .	2	2	..	19	31	3	3	..	45	52	..	..	..	5	22	
	6th	*1st Hussars, K. G. L.*	..	..	..	..	..	..	..	..	..	..	..	..	..	..	..	174
		10th Hussars . .	2	..	..	20	40	6	1	1	38	35	..	..	1	25	41	
		18th do. . .	..	..	..	12	19	2	9	..	62	41	..	..	..	17	37	
	7th	*3rd Hussars, K. G. L.*	..	..	..	..	..	..	..	..	..	..	..	..	..	..	..	86
		13th Light Dragoons	1	..	..	11	15	9	10	2	57	46	..	..	..	18	52	
Infantry.	1st	1st Guards, 2nd Battn.	1	..	..	50	..	5	7	..	89	..	..	..	..	..	..	456
		1st Guards, 3rd Battn.	3	2	..	79	..	6	7	..	238	..	..	..	..	..	..	
	2nd	2nd Guards, 2nd Battn.	1	1	..	53	..	7	13	..	229	..	..	..	1	3	..	500
		3rd Guards, 2nd Battn.	3	2	..	37	..	9	10	..	178	..	..	..	..	..	..	
	3rd	52nd Regiment, 1st do.	1	..	..	16	..	8	8	..	166	..	..	..	..	..	..	624
		71st do. do.	1	1	..	23	..	14	7	3	150	..	..	..	..	3	..	
		95th do. 2nd do.	..	2	1	31	..	14	6	2	171	..	..	..	..	20	..	
		95th do. 3rd do.	..	..	..	3	..	4	1	1	34	..	..	..	..	7	..	
	4th	14th do. 3rd do.	..	..	..	7	..	1	5	..	16	..	..	..	..	..	..	131
		23rd do. 1st do.	4	2	..	9	..	6	7	..	71	..	..	..	..	..	..	
		51st do. do.	..	..	1	8	..	2	..	..	20	..	..	..	..	..	..	
	5th	30th do. 2nd do.	6	3	1	41	..	14	6	..	145	..	..	..	2	12	..	679
		33rd do. do.	2	1	1	31	..	10	8	..	84	..	..	..	3	45	..	
		69th do. 2nd do.	4	..	..	14	..	3	..	..	50	..	..	..	2	13	..	
		73rd do. 2nd do.	5	3	1	43	..	12	13	2	160	..	..	..	..	41	..	
	8th	28th do. 1st do.	1	1	..	17	..	15	6	1	136	..	..	..	..	..	..	588
		32nd do. 1st do.	..	..	..	28	..	9	11	..	126	..	..	..	..	..	..	
		79th do. 1st do.	2	2	..	27	..	11	7	4	121	..	..	..	..	1	..	
		95th do. 1st do.	1	4	..	16	..	11	7	1	116	..	..	..	..	..	..	
	9th	1st do. 3rd do.	2	1	..	12	..	14	4	..	111	..	..	..	..	..	..	325
		42nd do. 1st do.	..	..	..	5	..	6	6	..	33	..	..	..	..	..	..	
		44th do. 2nd do.	..	..	..	4	..	3	3	..	54	..	..	..	..	..	..	
		92nd do. 1st do.	..	1	..	13	..	6	3	..	93	..	..	..	..	..	..	
	10th	4th do. do.	..	2	..	10	..	9	6	..	107	..	..	..	..	..	..	746
		27th do. do.	2	7	..	96	..	13	10	2	348	..	..	..	..	..	..	
		40th do. do.	2	5	..	25	..	10	16	1	142	..	..	..	..	18	..	
		General Staff . .	10	..	..	..	..	40	..	..	..	..	2	..	..	..	..	
		Total . .	85	82	7	1245	1319	365	7 1	28	4261	719	10	13	11	558	708	6064

XXXVII.

Return of Killed, Wounded, and Missing, of the King's German Legion at the Battle of Waterloo.

	Brigades.	Regiments.	Killed.					Wounded.					Missing.					Total Rank and File, Killed, Wounded, and Missing.
			Officers.	Non-commissioned Officers.	Trumpeters or Drummers.	Rank and File.	Horses.	Officers.	Non-commissioned Officers.	Trumpeters or Drummers.	Rank and File.	Horses.	Officers.	Non-commissioned Officers.	Trumpeters or Drummers.	Rank and File.	Horses.	
		Artillery	1	3	..	16	51	6	1	..	50	..	..	..	..	4	..	70
Cavalry.	3rd	1st Light Dragoons	3	3	1	26	42	11	7	1	91	93	..	..	..	10	14	127
	3rd	2nd do.	2	..	1	17	29	4	5	..	47	14	..	..	..	2	25	66
	3rd	*23rd British do.*	..	..	..	..	..	..	..	..	..	..	..	..	..	..	..	..
	6th	1st Hussars	..	..	..	1	9	1	..	..	5	13	..	..	..	..	..	6
	6th	*10th British do*	..	..	..	..	..	..	..	..	..	..	..	..	..	..	..	..
	6th	*18th do. do.*	..	..	..	..	..	..	..	..	..	..	..	..	..	..	..	..
	7th	3rd Hussars	4	2	1	37	63	8	7	..	71	24	..	..	..	..	15	108
	7th	*13th British Light Dragoons*	..	..	..	..	..	..	..	..	..	..	..	..	..	..	..	..
Infantry.	1st	1st Line Battalion	1	2	1	19	..	6	6	..	63	..	..	..	1	16	..	98
	1st	2nd do.	1	1	1	16	..	2	4	..	75	..	..	1	..	6	..	97
	1st	3rd do.	1	1	..	16	..	5	2	1	90	..	..	..	..	31	..	137
	1st	4th do.	1	1	..	12	..	7	3	..	74	..	..	..	1	13	..	99
	2nd	1st Light Battalion	4	1	..	36	..	9	6	3	73	..	..	..	..	13	..	122
	2nd	2nd do.	3	6	..	34	..	9	8	1	111	..	1	2	..	27	..	172
	2nd	5th Line Battalion	2	1	..	35	..	3	6	1	40	..	..	..	..	74	..	149
	2nd	8th do.	3	2	1	41	..	4	4	..	76	..	..	1	2	13	..	130
		General Staff	1	..	..	..	..	2	..	..	..	..	..	..	..	..	..	..
		Total	27	23	6	306	194	77	59	7	866	144	1	4	4	209	54	1381

XXXVIII.

Return of Killed, Wounded, and Missing, of the Hanoverian Troops on the 16th, 17th, and 18th of June, 1815.

	Brigades.	Regiments.	Killed.					Wounded.					Missing.					Total Privates Killed, Wounded, and Missing.
			Officers.	Non-commissioned Officers.	Buglers and Drummers.	Privates.	Horses.	Officers.	Non-commissioned Officers.	Buglers and Drummers.	Privates.	Horses.	Officers.	Non-commissioned Officers.	Buglers and Drummers.	Privates.	Horses.	
		1st Battery of Foot Artillery	..	1	..	7	..	..	1	..	26	..	..	..	..	..	..	33
		2nd Battery of Foot Artillery	..	..	..	..	..	..	..	..	..	..	..	..	..	..	..	..
Cavalry.	1st	Prince Regent's Hussars	..	..	..	..	..	..	..	..	..	..	..	..	..	..	..	..
	1st	Bremen and Verden Hussars	..	..	..	..	..	..	..	..	..	..	..	..	..	..	..	..
	1st	Duke of Cumberland's do.	1	2	..	15	..	..	3	..	30	..	..	..	..	2	..	47
Infantry.	1st	Rifle Corps	..	..	..	12	..	3	..	1	37	..	..	..	..	19	..	68
	1st	Field Batt. Bremen	1	1	..	10	..	8	8	1	104	..	..	..	1	34	..	148
	1st	Field Batt. Verden	..	3	..	60	..	7	6	1	87	..	..	..	2	51	..	198
	1st	Field Batt. Duke of York's	2	..	1	21	..	4	2	..	66	..	..	..	1	44	..	131
	1st	Field Batt. Lüneburg	3	1	1	27	..	5	4	1	132	..	1	..	1	46	..	205
	1st	Field Batt. Grubenhagen	1	1	..	14	..	6	4	1	67	..	..	..	1	47	..	128
	3rd	Landwehr Batt. Bremervörde	2	..	..	16	..	4	1	1	15	..	2	2	..	5	..	36
	3rd	Do. Osnabrück	3	1	..	16	..	6	..	1	61	..	..	..	..	6	..	83
	3rd	Do. Quackenbrück	1	..	..	1	..	..	1	..	9	..	..	..	..	2	..	12
	3rd	Do. Salzgitter	..	1	..	19	..	2	3	..	57	..	..	..	..	1	..	77
	4th	Do. Verden	2	..	..	10	..	4	1	..	96	..	3	1	..	42	..	148
	4th	Do. Lüneburg	..	..	..	10	..	5	1	..	36	..	..	..	..	..	..	46
	4th	Do. Osterode	2	..	..	12	..	5	2	..	91	..	..	..	..	14	..	117
	4th	Do. Münden	..	1	..	11	..	6	4	1	92	..	..	..	1	16	..	119
	5th	Do. Hameln	..	..	..	9	..	4	3	..	57	..	..	..	..	7	..	73
	5th	Do. Gifhorn	2	..	..	13	..	3	4	..	65	..	..	..	..	..	..	78
	5th	Do. Hildesheim	..	..	..	3	..	1	1	2	17	..	..	..	..	..	..	20
	5th	Do. Peine		..	..	8	..	2	1	1	38	..	..	..	1	5	..	51
		General Staff	..	..	..	..	..	2	..	..	..	..	..	..	..	..	..	..
		Total	20	12	2	294	..	77	50	11	1183	..	6	3	8	341	..	1818

XXXIX.

Return of Killed, Wounded, and Missing, of the Brunswick Troops, at the Battle of Waterloo.

Regiments.	Killed.		Wounded.		Horses.	Missing.	Total Rank and File, Killed, Wounded, and Missing.
	Officers.	Non-commissioned Officers, and Privates.	Officers.	Non-commissioned Officers, and Privates.	Killed, and Wounded.	Rank and File.	
Regiment of Hussars ..	1	27	5	45	40		72
Squadron of Uhlans ..	..	..	2	13	15		13
Horse Battery	1	2	..	6	16		8
Foot Battery	..	..	..	18	6		18
Advanced-Guard Battalion	..	7	1	20	..		27
Guard Battalion	..	14	1	36	..		50
1st Light Battalion ..	..	4	3	41	..	50*	45
2nd do.	2	37	2	73	..		110
3rd do.	1	35	5	75	..		110
1st Line Battalion ..	..	9	..	46	..		55
2nd do.	1	2	1	6	..		8
3rd do.	..	10	2	51	..		61
General Staff	1	..	4	..	..		..
							50*
Total ..	7	147	26	430	77	50	627

XL.

Return of Killed, Wounded, and Missing of the Troops of the Nassau Contingent (1st Regiment) at the Battle of Waterloo.

Killed : .	5 Officers,	249 Under-officers and Privates.	
Wounded . .	19 .	370	.. ..
Total Killed and Wounded	24 .	619	.. ..

XLI.

*List of Officers of the British Army who were present in the Actions on the 16th, 17th, and 18th of June, 1815, including those posted near Hal on the 18th, and distinguishing such as were Killed, Wounded, or Missing.**

Staff.

Commander-in-Chief—Field Marshal His Grace the Duke of Wellington, K.G., G.C.B., &c. *Military Secretary*—Lieut. Colonel Lord FitzRoy Somerset, 1st F. Gds. *w. Aides-de-Camp*—Lieut. Colonels, J. Fremantle, 2nd F. Gds., C. F. Canning, 3rd F. Gds. *k.*, Hon. Sir Alex. Gordon, 3rd F. Gds. *k.*, Lieut. Lord George Lennox, 9th Lt. Drns., Hered. Prince of Nassau Usingen. *Extra A.D.C.'s*—Lieut. Colonel Hon. Henry Percy, 14th Lt. Drns., Captain Lord Arthur Hill, h.p., Lieutenant Hon. George Cathcart, 6th Drn. Gds.

General H.R.H. The Prince of Orange, *w. Aides-de-Camp*—Lieut. Colonel Tripp, 60th Foot, Captains, Lord John Somerset, h.p., Hon. Francis Russell, h.p., *Extra A.D.C.'s*—Captain Earl of March, 52nd Foot, Lieutenant H. Webster, 9th Lt. Drns.

Lieut. General the Earl of Uxbridge, G.C.B. *w. Aides-de-Camp*—Major W. Thornhill, 7th Huss. *w.*, Captain H. Seymour, 60th Foot, *w. Extra A.D.C.'s*—Captains T. Wildman, 7th Huss. *w.*, J. Fraser, 7th Huss. *w.*

* The names of those killed, wounded, or missing, are marked *k*, *w*, and *m*, respectively.

Lieut. General Lord Hill, G.C.B. *Aides-de-Camp*—Major R. Egerton, 34th Foot, Lieut. Colonel C. Hill, R. H. Gds. *w.*, Major C. H. Churchill, 1st F. Gds., Captain D. Mackworth, 7th Foot. *Extra A.D.C.*—Captain Hon. O. Bridgeman, 1st F. Gds. *w.*

Lieut. General Sir Thomas Picton, G.C.B. *k.* *Aides de-Camp*—Captains, J. Tyler, 93rd Foot. *w.*, N. Chambers, 1st F. Gds. *k.* *Extra A.D.C.*—Captain B. Price, h.p.

Lieut. General Sir Henry Clinton, G.C.B. *Aide-de-Camp*—Captain F. Dawkins, 1st F. Gds.

Lieut. General C. Count Alten, K.C.B. *Aide-de-Camp*—Lieutenant W. Havelock, 43rd Foot, *w.*, Major Ch. Heise, 2nd Batt. K.G.L.

Lieut. General Sir Charles Colville, G.C.B. *Aides-de-Camp*—Captain J. Jackson, 37th Foot, Lieut. F. W. Frankland, 2nd Foot. *Extra A.D.C.*—Captain Lord James Hay, 1st F. Gds.

M. General V. Count Alten. *Aide-deCamp*—Lieutenant Baron Estorff, 2nd Drns. K.GL.

M. General Sir John Vandeleur, K.C.B. *Aide-de-Camp*—Captain W. Armstrong, 19th Lt. Drns. *Major of Brigade*—Major M. Childers, 11th Lt. Drns.

M. General Cooke, *w.* *Aide de-Camp*—Captain G. Desbrowe, 1st F. Gds. *Extra A.D.C.*—Ensign A. Cuyler, 2nd F. Gds.

M. General Sir James Kempt, K.C.B. *w.* *Aide-de-Camp*—Captain Hon. Charles Gore, h.p. *Major of Brigade*—Captain C. Eeles, 95th Foot.

M. General Hon. Sir W Ponsonby, K.C.B. *k.* *Aide-de Camp*—Lieutenant B. Christie, 5th Drn. Gds. *Extra A.D.C.*—Major D. Evans, 5th W. I. Regt. *Major of Brigade*—Major Reignolds, 2nd Drns. *k.*

M. General Sir John Byng, K.C.B. *Aide de-Camp*—Captain H. Dumaresq, 9th Foot, *w.* *Major of Brigade*—Captain W. Stothert, 3rd F. Gds. *k.*

M. General Sir Denis Pack, K.C.B. *w.* *Aide de Camp*—Major E. L'Estrange, 71st Foot, *k.* *Major of Brigade*—Captain C. Smith, 93rd Foot, *k.*

M. General Lord E. Somerset, K.C.B. *Aide-de-Camp*—Lieutenant H. Somerset, 18th Huss. *Major of Brigade*—Major H. G. Smith, 25th Foot, *k.*

M. General Sir Colquhoun Grant, K.C.B. *w.* *Aide-de-Camp*—Lieutenant R. Mansfield, 15th Huss. *w.* *Extra A.D.C.*—Captain W. Moray, 17th Lt. Drns. *w.* *Major of Brigade*—Captain Jones, h.p.

M. General Sir James Lyon, K.C.B. *Aide-de-Camp*—Lieutenant J. M'Glashan, 2nd Lt. Bn. K.G.L. *Major of Brigade*—Captain Richter, 1st Ceylon Regt.

M. General P. Maitland. *Aide-de-Camp*—Ensign Lord Hay, 1st F. Gds. *k.* *Extra A.D.C.*—Cornet Lord William P. Lennox, R.H. Gds. *Major of Brigade*—Captain J. Gunthorpe, 1st F. Gds.

M. General G. Johnstone. *Aide-de-Camp*--Capt. C. G. Gray, 25th Foot. *Major of Brigade*—Captain S. Holmes, 78th Toot.

M. General F. Adam, *w.* *Aide-de-Camp*—Lieutenant R. P. Campbell, 7th Foot. *Extra A.D.C.*—Captain C. Yorke, 52nd Foot. *Major of Brigade*—Major Hunter Blair, 91st Foot, *w.*

M. General Sir Colin Halkett, K.C.B. *w.* *Aides-de-Camp*—Captains, H. Marschalk, 1st Lt. Bn. K.G.L. *k.*, A. Holme, 2nd Lt. Bn. K.G.L. *Major of Brigade*—Captain W. Crofton, 54th Foot, *k.*

M. General Sir Hussey Vivian, K.C.B. *Aide-de-Camp*—Captain E. Keane, 7th Huss. *Extra A.D.C.*—Lieutenant C. A. Fitzroy, R. H. Gds. *Major of Brigade*—Captain T. N. Harris, h.p. *w.*

Adjutant General.—M. General Sir Edward Barnes, K.C.B. *w.* *Aide-de-Camp*—Major A. Hamilton, 4th W.I. Regt. *w.* *Dep. Adj. General*—Colonel Sir John Elley, K.C.B. R. H. Gds. *w.* *Assist. Adj. General*—Lieut. Colonels, S. Waters, Unatt. *w.*, Sir George H. Berkeley, K.C.B. 35th Foot, *w.*, Sir Guy Campbell, Bt. 6th Foot, Sir Noel Hill, K.C.B., 1st F. Gds., D. Barclay, 1st F. Gds., H. Rooke, 3rd F. Gds., E. Currie, 90th Foot, *k.*; Majors, A. Wylly, 7th Foot, G. Evatt, 55th Foot, W. Darling, h.p., F. Breymann, 2nd Lt. Bn. K.G.L. *Dep. Assist. Adj. Gen.*—Captains, Hon. E. S. Erskine, 60th Foot, *w.*, Lord Charles Fitzroy, 1st F. Gds., C. Bentinck, 2nd F. Gds., L. Grant, 78th Foot, H. Blanckley, 23rd Foot, Hon. W. Curzon, 69th Foot, *k.*; Lieutenants, J. Hamilton, 46th Foot, *w.*, J. Harford, 7th R. V. Bn., E. Gerstlacher, 3rd Huss. K.G.L., J. Rooke, h.p. *Dep. Judge Advocate*—Lieut. Colonel S. Goodman. h.p.

Dep. Quarter Master General.—Col. Sir William Delancey, K.C.B. *k.* *Assist. Quar. Mas. Gen.*—Colonels, Hon. A. Abercromby, 2nd F. Gds., *w.*, F. B. Hervey, 14th Lt. Drns., Lieut. Colonels, R. Torrens, 1st W. I. Regt., Sir Charles Broke, K.C.B. Perm., Sir Jeremiah Dickson, K.C.B. Perm., Lord Greenock, Perm., J. Woodford, 1st F. Gds., C. Grant, 11th Foot, Sir William Gomm, K.C.B. 2nd F. Gds., Sir Henry Bradford, K.C.B. 1st F. Gds. *w*, Sir George Scovell, K.C.B., h.p., D. Kelly, 73rd Foot; Majors, W. Campbell, 23rd Foot, Hon. George L. Dawson, 1st Drn. Gds. *w.*, E. Beckwith, 95th Foot, *w.*, J. Shaw, 43rd Foot, J. Jessop, 43th Foot, *w.* *Dep. Assist. Quar. Mas. Gen.*—Captains, E. Fitzgerald, 25th Foot, *w.*, T. Wright, R. Staff Corps, *w.*, H. McLeod, 35th Foot, *w.*, J. Mitchell, 25th Foot, *w.*, W. Moore, 1st F. Gds., G. Hillier, 74th Foot, J. Fraser, 90th Foot, W. Cameron, 1st F. Gds., F. Read, R. Staff Corps; Lieutenants, P. Barrailler, 33rd Foot, B. Jackson, R. Staff Corps, A. Brauns, R. Staff Corps.

Commandant at Head-Quarters—Colonel Sir Colin Campbell, K.C.B. 2nd F. Gds.

Cavalry.

1st *Life Guards.* Major—S. Ferrier, Lieut. Col. *k.* Captains—J. Whale, *w.*; M. Lind, *k.*; E. Kelly, *w.*; J. Berger, Maj. Lieutenants—G. Randall; W. Mayne; H. Wyatt. Sub. Lieutenants—W. S. Richardson, *w.*; S. Cox, *w.*; W. Wombwell; G. Storey. Surgeon—R. Gough. Asst. Surgeon—J. H. James. Vet. Surgeon—F. Dalton.

2nd Life Guards. MAJOR—Hon. E. P. Lygon, Lieut. Col. CAPTAINS—W. Boyce, Maj.; R. Fitzgerald, Lt. Col. *k.*; Hon. H. E. Irby; J. P. M. Kenyon. LIEUTENANTS—R. Meares; W. Elliott; S. Waymouth, *w.* and *m.*; C. Barton. SUB LIEUTENANTS—A. Kenyon; T. Martin; A. M'Innes; J. Clues, Adj. SURGEON—S. Broughton. ASST. SURGEON—T. Drinkwater. VET. SURGEON—J. Field.

Royal Horse Guards, Blue. LIEUT. COLONELS—Sir John Elley, Col. *w.*; Sir R. C. Hill, *w.* MAJOR—R. C. Packe, *k.* CAPTAINS—J. Thoyts; W. R. Clayton; C. Hill, Lt. Col. *w.*; W. T. Drake. LIEUTENANTS—J. B. Riddlesden; W. C. Shawe, *w.*; E. W. Bouverie, *w.*; H. E. Boates; T. B. Tathwell; G. Smith; Hon. G. J. Watson. CORNETS—J. K. Picard; J. Arnold. SURGEON—D. Slow. VET. SURGEON—J. Seddall. TROOP QUARTER MASTERS—T. Varley, *w.*; P. Watmough; T. Hardy; J. Varley, *w.*; T. Troy.

1st (or King's) Dragoon Guards. LIEUT. COLONEL—W. Fuller, Col. *k.* CAPTAINS—H. Graham, Maj. *k.*; M. Turner, *w.*; J. F. Naylor, *w.*; W. Elton; J. D. Brughurst, Maj. *k.*; J. P. Sweeny, *w.*; R. Wallace; T. N. Quicke; G. E. Battersby, *k.* LIEUTENANTS—J. Leatham; W. Sterling; R. Babington; F. Brooke, *k.*; R. T. Hamley; T. C. Brander; T. Shelver, Adj. *k.*; E. Hamill; W. D. A. Irvine, *w.*; J. E. Greaves; J. N. Hibbert. CORNETS—G. Quicke; J. F. Middleton; Hon. H. B. Bernard, *k.*; W. W. Huntley, PAYMASTER—J. Webster. SURGEON—J. Going. ASST. SURGEONS—W. M'Auley; Robert Pearson.

1st Royal Dragoons. LIEUT. COLONEL—A. B. Clifton. MAJOR—P. Dorville, Lieut. Col. CAPTAINS—C. E. Radclyffe, Maj. *w.*; A. K. Clark, *w.*; P. Phipps; R. Heathcote; E. C. Windsor, *k.*; C. L. Methuin; C. Foster, *k.* LIEUTENANTS—H. R. Carden; G. Gunning, *w.*; T. R. Keily, *w.*; S. Trafford, *w.*; S. Windawe, *w.*; C. Bridges; C. Ommaney, *w.*; C. Blois, *w.*; S. Goodenough, *w.*; R. Magniac, *k.* CORNETS—W. Sturges; J. C. Sykes, *k.* ADJUTANT-CORNET—T. Shipley, *k.* QUARTER MASTER—W. Waddel. SURGEON—G. Steed. ASST. SURGEON—T. Prosser.

2nd, or Royal North British, Dragoons, (Scots Greys). LIEUT. COLONEL—J. J. Hamilton, Col. *k.* MAJOR—J. B. Clarke, Lieut. Col. *w.*; T. P. Hankin, Lieut. Col. *w.*—CAPTAINS—E. Cheney, Maj.; J. Poole, *w.*; R. Vernon, Maj. *w.*; T. Reignolds. *k.*; C. L. Barnard, *k.*; E. Payne. LIEUTENANTS—John Mills, *w.*; F. Stupart, *w.*; G. H. Falconer; J. Wemyss; J. Carruthers, *w.*; A. Hamilton; T. Truther, *k.*; J. Gape; C. Wyndham, *w.*; J. R. T. Graham; H. M'Millan. CORNETS—E. Westby, *k.*; F. C Kinchant, *k.*; L. Shuldam, *k.*; W. Crawford. PAYMASTER—W. Dawson. QUARTER MASTER—J. Lennox. SURGEON—R. Dunn. ASST. SURGEON—J. Alexander. VET. SURGEON—J. Trigg.

6th, or Inniskilling, Dragoons. LIEUT. COLONEL—J. Muter, Col. *w.* MAJORS—F. S. Miller, Lieut. Col. *w.*; H. Madox. CAPTAINS—W. F. Browne, *w.*; W. F. Hadden; Hon. S. Douglass, *w.*; E. Holbech; T. Mackay. LIEUTENANTS—T. Biddulph; A. S. Willett; J. Linton; H. W. Petre; A. Hassard, *w.*; F. Johnson; R. Down; B. Barry; P. Ruffo, *m.*; M. Dames. CORNET—J. D. Allingham. ADJUTANT—M. M'Cluskey, *k.* REGIMENTAL QUARTER MASTER—J. Kerr. SURGEON—J. Bolton. ASST. SURGEONS—W. H. Rickatts; W. Campbell. VET. SURGEON—R. Vincent. PAYMASTER—W. Armstrong.

7th Light Dragoons. COLONEL—Earl of Uxbridge, Lt. Gen. *w.* LIEUT. COLONEL—Sir Edward Kerrison, Col. MAJORS—Edward Hodge, *k.*; W. Thornhill, *w.* CAPTAINS—W. Verner, *w.*; T. W. Robbins, *w.*; E. Keane; P. A. Heyliger, *w.*; T. Wildman; J. J. Frazer, *w.*; J. D. Elphinstone, *w*; E. Wildman, *w.* LIEUTENANTS—S. O'Grady; W. Shirley; W. Grenfell; R. Douglass, *w.*; R. Uniacke; J. R. Gordon, *w.*; Henry Lord Paget; J. Daniel; E. J. Peters, *w.*; J. Wildman; F. Beatty, *w.*; S. Rice; F. Towers. PAYMASTER—T. Feltom. LIEUT. ADJ.—A. Meyers, *w.* QUARTER MASTER—J. Greenwood. SURGEON—D. Irwin. ASST. SURGEONS—R. A. Chermside; J. Moffit. VET. SURGEON—R. Dorville.

10th Hussars. LIEUT. COLONEL—George Quentin, Col. *w.*; Lord Robert Manners. MAJOR—Hon. F. Howard, *k.* CAPTAINS—T. W. Taylor, Maj.; H. C. Stapleton; J. Grey, *w.*; J. Gurwood, *w.*; C. Wood, *w.*; H. Floyd; A. Shakespeare. LIEUTENANTS—J. W. Parsons; C. Gunning, *k.*; W. S. Smith; H. J. Burn; R. Arnold, *w.*; W. Cartwright; J. C. Wallington; E. Hodgson; W. C. Hamilton; A. Bacon, *w.*; W. H. B. Lindsey. PAYMASTER—J. Tallon. LIEUTENANT and ADJUTANT—J. Hardman. ASST. SURGEON—G. S. Jenks. VET. SURGEON—H. C. Sannerman.

11th Light Dragoons. LIEUT. COLONEL—J. W. Sleigh. MAJOR—A. Money, Lt. Col. CAPTAINS—J. Bouchier; B. Lutyens, Maj.; M. Childers, Maj.; J. A. Schreiber; J. Jenkins; T. Binney; J. Duberley. LIEUTENANTS—G. Sicker; F. Wood, *w.*: W. Smith; R. Coles, *w.*; B. Lye; E. Phelips, *k.*; J. R. Rotton; J. S. Moore, *w.*; B. Des Voeux; R. Millingan, *w.* CORNETS—B. P. Browne; H. Orme; G. Schreiber, *w.*; H. R. Bullock; P. H. James. PAYMASTER—D. Lutyens. ADJUTANT—G. Sicker. QUARTER MASTER—J. Hall. SURGEON—J. O'Meally. ASST. SURGEON—H. Steel.

12th, or Prince of Wales's Light Dragoons. LIEUT. COLONEL—Hon. F. C. Ponsonby, Col. *w.* MAJOR—J. P. Bridger. CAPTAINS—S. Stawell; G. F. Erskine; E. W. T. Sandys, *w.*; H. Wallace; A. Barton; H. Andrews. LIEUTENANTS—W. Heydon; J. Chatterton; J. Vandeleur; W. Hay; W. H. Dowbiggen, *w.*; A. Goldsmid; J. D. Calderwood; L. J. Bertie, *k.*; T. Reed. CORNETS—J. E. Lockhart, *k.*; J. H. Slade. ADJUTANT—J. Griffiths.

13th *Light Dragoons.* LIEUT. COLONEL—P. Doherty, Col. MAJOR—S. Boyse, Lt. Col. *w.* CAPTAINS—B. Lawrence, Maj.; J. Doherty, *w.*; J. Macalister, Maj.; M. Bowers; J. Gubbins, *k.*; C. Gregorie; F. Goulbourn; J. Moss; G. Doherty, *w.*; J. H. Drought; C. R. Bowers, *w.*; A. T. Maclean; J. Geale, *w.*; R. Nesbitt; G. Pym, *w.*; W. Turner; J. Mill, *w.*; G. H. Pack, *w.*; H. Acton; J. Wallace; J. E. Irving, *w.*; J. Wakefield. PAYMASTER—A. Strange. QUARTER MASTER—W. Minchin. SURGEON—T. G. Logan. ASST. SURGEON—A. Armstrong. VET. SURGEON—J. Constant.

15th Hussars. LIEUT. COLONEL—L. C. Dalrymple, *w.* MAJOR—E. Griffith, *k.*; CAPTAINS—J. Thackwell, *w.*; S. Hancox; J. Whiteford, *w.*; P. Wodehouse; F. C. Philips; W. Booth; J. Buckley, *w.*; J. Carr. LIEUTENANTS—E. Barrett, J. Sherwood, *k.*; W. Bellairs; H. Lane; W. Byam, *w.*; E. Byam, *w.*; G. A. F. Dawkins, *w.*; H. Dixon; J. J. Douglass; W. Stewart. PAYMASTER—J. C. Cocksedge. LIEUTENANT and ADJUTANT—J.

Griffith. Surgeon—T. Cartan. Asst. Surgeons—S. Jeyes; W. Gibney. Vet. Surgeon—C. Dalwig.

16th Light Dragoons. Lieut. Colonel—James Hay, *w.* Majors—Hon. H. B. Lygon; G. H. Murray. Captains—J. H. Belli, Maj.; C. Swetenham; R. Weyland, *w.*; W. Persse; J. P. Buchanan, *k.*; W. Tomkinson; C. King. Lieutenants—J. Barra. W. Osten, *w.*; T. Wheeler; G. Baker; R. Beauchamp; N. D. Crichton, *w.*; E. B. Lloyd; W. Nepean; J. A. Richardson; J. Luard; W. Harris; Hon. C. T. Monckton. Cornets—W. Beckwith; W. Polhill; G. Nugent. Paymaster—G. Neyland. Lieutenant and Adjutant—J. Barra. Quarter Master—J. Harrison. Surgeon—J. Robinson. Asst. Surgeon—J. M. Mallock. Vet. Surgeon—J. Jones.

18th Light Dragoons. Lieut. Colonel—Hon. H. Murray. Captains—A. Kennedy; R. Croker; R. Ellis; J. Grant, Maj.; G. Luard; J. R. L. Lloyd. Lieutenants—C. Heste, *w.*; T. Dunkin; J. Waldie; G. Woodberry; Hon. L. C. Dawson; M. French; T. Prior; R. Coote; J. T. Machell; D. M'Duffie; H. Somerset; W. H. Rowlls; J. R. Gordon; C. C. Moller; W. Monins. Paymaster—W. Deane. Lieutenant and Adjutant—H. Duperier, *w.* Surgeon—W. Chambers. Asst. Surgeons—L. Pulsford; J. Quincey. Vet. Surgeon—D. Pilcher.

23rd Light Dragoons. Lieut. Colonel—Earl of Portarlington, Col. Majors—J. M. Sutcliffe, *w.*; P. A. Latour. Captains—C. W. Dance, *w.*; P. Z. Cox; J. Martin; T. Gerrard, Maj. *w.*; R. M'Neil; H. Grove, Maj.; J. M. Wallace. Lieutenants—G. Dodwell; A. Bolton; S. Coxen, *k.*; C. Tudor; J. Banner; J. Lewis; C. Bacon; B. Disney, *w.*; R. Johnson; T. B. Wall, *w.*; G. W. Blathwayte. Cornet—W. Hemmings. Paymaster—T. Dillow. Lieutenant and Adjutant—H. Hill. Quarter Master—J. Grouchley. Surgeon—S. Steele. Asst. Surgeon—H. Cowen. Vet. Surgeon—J. Ship.

Infantry.

1st Regt. Foot Guards (2nd and 3rd Batts.) Majors—H. Askew, Col. *w.*; Hon. W. Stuart, *w.* Captains and Lieut. Colonels—Hon. H. Townsend, *w.*; R. H. Cooke, *w.*; E. Stables, *k.*; Sir F. D'Oyly, K.C.B. *k.*; L. G. Jones; H. D'Oyly, *w.*; G. Fead, *w.*; C. Thomas, *k.*; Lord Saltoun; J. Reeve; W. Miller, *w.*; Hon. J. Stanhope; J. G. Woodford; C. Colquett; W. H. Milnes, *w.*; Sir H. W. Bradford, K.C.B. *w.*; Sir T. N. Hill, K.C.B.; D. Barclay, K.C.B.; Sir U. Burgh, K.C.B.; Lord F. Somerset, K.C.B. Lieutenants and Captains—R. Adair, *w.*; T. Streatfield, *w.*; J. H. Davis; Lord James Hay, *k.*; E. Grose, *k.*; J. Gunthorpe, Adj.; Hon. R. Clements, *w.*; Lord C. Fitzroy; J. H. Hutchinson; R. Ellison; H. W. Powell; George Desbrowe; W. G. Cameron; Lonsdale Boldero; R. W. Phillimore; C. P. Ellis, *w.*; J. Simpson, *w.*; A. F. Viscount Bury; E. Clive; W. F. Johnstone; E. F. Luttrell, *w.*; T. Brown, *k.*; E. P. Buckley; F. Dawkins; J. Nixon; C. F. R. Lascelles, *w.*; W. G. Moore; S. W. Burgess, *w.* Ensigns—R. Batty, *w*; R. Master; W. Barton, *w.*; Hon. H. S. V. Vernon; E. Pardoe, *k.*; J. Butler; T. R. Swinburne; C. J. Vyner; F. D. Swan: J. P. Dirom, Lt.; J. F. M. Erskine; R. Bruce, *w.*; Hon. T. S. Bathurst; Hon. E. A. Edgcumbe; G. Fludyer, *w.*; W. F. Tinling; A. Greville; G. T. Jacob; D. Cameron; L. Hurd; F. Norton; H. Lascelles; G. Mure; G. Allen; T. E. Croft, *w.*; Hon. S. S. P. Barrington, *k.*; J. St. John; D. Tighe; J. Talbot. Adjutant—C. Allix, Capt. Quarter Master—R. Colquhoun. Surgeons—W. Curtis; W. Watson. Asst. Surgeons—J. Harrison; A. Armstrong; J. Gardner; F. Gilder.

Coldstream, or 2nd Regt. Foot Guards (2nd Batt.) Major—A. G. Woodford, Col. Captains and Lieut. Colonels—J. Macdonell, Lt. Col. *w.*; D. MacKinnon, Lt. Col. *w.*; Hon. J. Walpole; H. Dawkins; H. A. Abercromby, *k.*; Sir C. Campbell, K.C.B.; Hon. E. Acheson; Sir W. Gomm, K.C.B.; H. Wyndham, *w.* Lieutenants and Captains—G. Bowles; T. Sowerby; J. Fremantle, Lt. Col.; W. L. Walton; W. G. Baynes; C. A. F. Bentinck, Adj.; J. S. Cowell; E. Sumner, *w.*; J. L. Blackman, *k.*; Lord Hotham; Hon. R. Moore, *w.*; T. Chaplin. Ensigns—Hon. J. Forbes; H. Gooch; A. Cuyler; M. Beaufoy; H. F. Griffiths, *w.*; John Montagu, *w.*; G. R. Buckley; J. Hervey; H. Vane; F. J. Douglas; R. Bowen; A. Gordon; Hon. W. Forbes; C. Short. Adjutant—C. A. F. Bentinck, Capt. Quarter Master—B. Selway. Surgeon—W. Whymper. Asst. Surgeons—G. Smith; W. Hunter.

3rd Foot Guards (2nd Batt.) Major—F. Hepburn, Col. Captains and Lieut. Colonels—H. W. Rooke; D. Mercer; Hon. Sir A. Gordon, *k.*; C. Dashwood, *w.*; F. Home; C. F. Canning, *k.*; E. Bowater, *w.*; C. West, *w.* Lieutenants and Captains—W. Stothert, Adj.; W. Drummond; R. B. Hesketh, *w.*; H. Hawkins; R. H. Wigston; C. J. Barnet; J. W. Moorhouse; E. B. Fairfield; G. Evelyn, *w.*; Hon. H. Forbes, *k.*; J. Elrington; H. B. Montgomerie, *w.*; T. Crawford, *k.*; J. Ashton, *k.* Ensigns—C. Lake, *w.*; Hon. E. Stopford; B. Drummond; G. D. Standen; D. Baird, *w.*; W. F. Hamilton; W. James; Hon. G. Anson; T. Wedgewood; W. Butler; A. C. Cochrane; J. Prendergast; C. Simpson, *w.*; H. S. Blane; H. Montagne. Adjutant—W. Stothert, Capt. *w.* Quarter Master—J. Skuce. Surgeon—S. Good. Asst. Surgeons—J. R. Warde; F. G. Hanrott.

1st Regt. Foot, or Royal Scots, (3rd Batt.) Major—Colin Campbell, Lt. Col. *w.* Captains—L. Arquimbau, Maj. *w.*; R. Macdonald, Maj. *w.*; H. Massy, Maj. *w.*; W. Buckley, *k.*; W. Gordon; R. Dudgeon, *w.* Lieutenants—A. Morrison, *w.*; J. Armstrong, *k.*; J. E. O. Neil, *k.*; W. J. Rea, *w.*; J. Ingram, *w.*; W. Clarke, *w.*; G. C. Johnstone; T. Gordon; A. Cameron, Adj. *w.*; J. Stoyte, *w.*; R. H. Scott, *w.*; G. Lane, w.; J. Symes, *w.*; J. Alstone, *w.*; W. G. Young, *k.*; J. Mann, *w.*; W. Dobbs, *w.*; J. F. W. Millar, *w.*; G. Stewart, *w.*; J. L. Black, *w.* Ensigns—A. Glen; C. Mudie; J. G. Kennedy, *k.*; C. Lewis; C. Graham, *w.*; T. Stephens, *w.*; J. MacKay, *w.*; A. Robertson, *k.*; W. Anderson, *k.*; L. M. Cooper, *w.*; W. Thomas. Paymaster—J. C. Thompson. Adjutant—A. Cameron, *w.* Quarter Master—T. Griffith, *w.* Surgeon—W. Galliers. Asst. Surgeons—W. Finnie; T. Bolton.

4th Regt. Foot (King's Own.) LIEUT. COLONEL—F. Brooke. CAPTAINS—G. D. Wilson, Maj. *w.*; C. J. Edgell, *w*; W. L. Wood; J. W. Fletcher; H. T. Shaw; R. Erskine; D. S. Craig; E. S. Kirwan; J. Browne, *w.* LIEUTENANTS—G. Vincent; B. Martin; G. Richardson, *w.*; P. Boulby; H. Boyd, *w.*; G. H. Hearne; B. Collins, *w.*; W. Squire, *w.*; J. Bushel; R. Mulholland; W. Lonsdale; E. Boulby; W. Clarke; W. Richardson, Adj.; F. Field; W. Reddock; A. Gerard, *w.*; J. L. Fernandez; W. Blagrave; C. Levinge. ENSIGNS—W. Taylor; E. Newton; W. M. Matthews, *w.*; J. E. H. Holland; I. Beer. PAYMASTER—J. Lansdale. QUARTER MASTER—T. Richards. SURGEON—F. Burton. ASST. SURGEONS—W. Morrah; J. French.

14th Regt. Foot (3rd Batt.) MAJORS—F. S. Tidy, Lt. Col.; J. Keightley. CAPTAINS—G. Marley, Maj.; T. Ramsay; W. Turnor; W. Ross; R. Adams; C. Wilson; J. L. White; W. Hewett. LIEUTENANTS—W. Akenside; C. M. Brannan; L. Beachcroft; W. Buckle, Adj.; G. Baldwin; J. Nickson; L. Westwood; D. Slocock; J. C. Hartley; H. Boldero. ENSIGNS—W. Reed; J. Mackenzie; F. R. Fane; R. B. Newenham; C. Frazer; A. T. E. Adamson; W. Keowen; J. M. Wood; A. Ormsby, *w.* (24th); J. R. Smith; A. Cooper, *w.*; J. Bowlby; J. P. Matthews; R. J. Stackpoole; R. B. Holmes; Hon. G. T. Keppel. PAYMASTER—R. Mitton. QUARTER MASTER—A. Ross. ASST. SURGEONS—A. Shannon; Henry Terry.

23rd Regt. Foot (Royal Welsh Fusiliers.) LIEUT. COLONEL—Sir H. W. Ellis, K.C.B, Col. *w.* MAJORS—T. Dalmer, Lt. Col.; J. H. E. Hill, Lt. Col. *w.* CAPTAINS—J. Hawtyn, Maj. *k.*; P. Brown, Maj.; F. Dalmer, Maj.; H. Wynne; T. Strangeway; W. Campbell, Maj.; C. Jolliffe, *k.*; T. Farmer, *k.*; H. Johnson, *w.*; H. S. Blanckley. 1st LIEUTENANTS—F. O'Flaherty; J. Milne; W. Walley; E. M. Brown; F. L. G. Cowel; G. Hensham, *k.*; R. Smith; H. Palmer; J. W. Harris; J. Enoch, Adj.; G. Philips; J. Macdonald; G. Fielding; R. P. Holmes; C. Fryer; W. A. Griffiths, *w.*; J. Clyde, *w.*; A. A. Brice; A. D. Sidley, *w.*; A. Clayhills; E. Methold. 2nd LIEUTENANTS—T. Lilly; G Dunn; G. Stainforth; G. FitzGibbon; W. Leebody, *k.* (24th); T. Towers; T. Allan. PAYMASTER—R. Julian. LIEUT. and ADJUTANT—J. Enoch. QUARTER MASTER—G. Sidley. SURGEON—J. Dunn. ASST. SURGEONS T. Smith, J. Williams.

27th (Inniskilling) Regt. Foot. CAPTAINS—J. Hare, Maj. *w.*; J. Tucker, *w.*; G. Holmes, *k.* LIEUTENANTS—G. Macdonald, *w.*; W. Henderson, *w.*; R. Handcock, *w.*; E. W. Drewe, *w.*; J. Betty; W. F. Fortescue, *w.*; W. Talbot; J. Millar, *w.*; C. Manley, *w.*; T. Craddock, *w.* ENSIGNS—W. Kater; T. Handcock, *w.*; T. Smith, *w.*; S. Ireland, *k.*; J. Ditmas, *w.* QUARTER MASTER—T. Taylor. ASST. SURGEONS—T. Mostyn: G. FitzGerald.

28th Regt. Foot. LIEUT. COLONELS—Sir Charles Philip Belson, K.C.B., Col.; R. Nixon, *w.* MAJORS—W. P. Meacham, *k.*; W. Irving, *w.*; R. Llewellyn, *w.* CAPTAINS—C. Cadell; R. Kelly, *w.*; J. Bowles, *w.*; T. English, *w.*; C. Teulon, *w.* LIEUTENANTS—J. H. Crummer; J. F. Wilkinson. *w.*; M. Semple; R. P. Gilbert, *w.*; R. P. Eason, *w.*; W. Irwin, *w.*; H. Hilliard, *w.*; S. Moore; J. Coen, *w.*; C. B. Carruthers, *w.*; J. T. Clarke, *w.*; J. W. Shelton, *w.*; J. Deares, *w.*; E. E. Hill; G. Ingram, *w.*; T. W. Colleton; J. Parry. ENSIGNS—R. T. Stewart; W. Serjeantson; R. Martin; J. Simpkin; W. Mountsteven, *w.*; W. Lynam. LIEUTENANT and ADJUTANT—T. Bridgeland, *w.* PAYMASTER—J. Dewes. QUARTER MASTER R. Reynolds. ASST. SURGEON P. H. Lavens.

30th Regt. Foot (2nd Batt.) LIEUT. COLONEL—A. Hamilton, *w.* MAJORS—N. W. Bailey, *w.*; C. A. Vigoureux, *w*; T. W. Chambers, *k.* CAPTAINS—A. M'Nab, *k.*; R. Howard; A. Gore, *w.*; M. Ryan; D. Sinclair-Finneane. LIEUTENANTS—B. W. Nicholson; J. Gowan; R. Mayne; M. Andrews; R. Heaviside; R. C. Elliot, *w.*; A. W. Freear; J. Rumley, *w.*; R. Daniells, *w.*; P. Neville;* J. Roe, *w.*; T. O. Halloran; R. Hughes, *w.*; P. Lockwood, *w.*; J. Pratt, *w.*; H. Beere, *k.*; E. Prendergast, *k.*; W. O. Warren, *w.*; T. Moneypenny, *w.*; R. Harrison; J. Roe; F. Tincombe. ENSIGNS—R. N. Rogers; J. James, *k.*; E. Macready; J. Bullen, *k.* PAYMASTER—H. B. Wray. LIEUTENANT and ADJUTANT—M. Andrews, *w.* QUARTER MASTER—Williamson. SURGEON—J. G. Elkington. ASST. SURGEONS—J. Evans; P. Clarke.

32nd Regt. Foot. MAJORS—J. Hicks, Lt Col.; F. Calvert. CAPTAINS—C. Hames, Maj.; H. R. Lewen; W. H. Toole, Maj. *w.*; J. Crowe, *w*; J. Boyce, *k.*; T. Cassan, *k.*; E. Whitty, *k.*; H. Harrison, *w.*; C. Wallett, *w.*; S. Cane. LIEUTENANTS—H. W. Brookes, *w.*; G. Barr, *w.*; M. W. Meighan, *w.*; S. H. Lawrence, *w.*; T. Butler; J. Boase, *w.*; T. Ross Lewin, *w.*; H. Butterworth, *w.*; J. S. M'Culloch; J. R. Colthurst, *w.*; B. Hill; J. Harvey; J. Robinson, *w.*; G. Brock; R. T. Belcher; J. Fitzgerald, *w.*; T. J. Horan, *w.*; E. Stephens, *w.*; H. Quill, *w.*; J. Jagoe, *w.*; G. Small; B. R. O'Connor; H. Newton; J. Peyton. ENSIGNS—J. Lucas; J. M'Conchy; H. Metcalf, *w.*; J. Birtwhistle, *w.*; A. Stuart, *w.*; G. Brown, W. Bennet, *w.*, C. Dallas, *w.* LIEUTENANT and ADJUTANT—D. Davis, *w.* PAYMASTER—T. Hart. QUARTER MASTER—W. Stevens. SURGEON—W. Buchanan. ASST. SURGEONS—R. Lawder; H. M'Clintock.

33rd Regt. Foot (2nd Batt.) LIEUT. COLONEL—W. K. Elphinstone. MAJORS—G. Colclough; E. Parkinson, *w.*; CAPTAINS—W. M'Intyre, *w.*; C. Knight, *w.*; J. Haigh, *k.*; J. M. Harty, *w.*; R. Gore; J. Longden. LIEUTENANTS—T. Reid, *w.*; G. Barrs; H. R. Buck, *k.*; A. H. Trevor; J. Boyce, *k.*; A. Gore, *k.*; J. Hart; J. Markland, *w.*; T. H. Patterson; R. Westmore, *w.*; T. D. Haigh, *w.*; G. Whannel; J. G. Ogle, *w.*; S. A. Pagan, *w.*; E. Clabon; J. Lynam; J. Archibald; J. Forlong, *w.*; J. Cameron, *w.* ENSIGNS—H. Bain, *w.*; J. Alderson, *w.*; J. A. Howard, *w.*: A. Watson; C. Smith; W. Hodson; G. Blackall; G. Drury, *w.*; W. H. Grote. PAYMASTER—E. Stoddart. ADJUTANT—W. Thain, *w.*; QUARTER MASTER—J. Fazakerly. SURGEON—R. Learer. ASST. SURGEONS—W. Fry; D. Finlayson.

35th Regt. Foot (2nd Batt.) MAJORS—C. Macalister; J. Slessor, Lt. Col. CAPTAINS—C. W. Wall; W. Rawson; H. Rutherford; T. M'Niell; R. Cameron; N. Dromgoole. LIEUTENANTS—S. S. Scarfe; J. W. Amos; J. Osbourne; T. M'Donough; R. Thobourne; W.

* This officer was employed in the Engineer Department, reconnoitring on the frontiers, and retired to join his regiment on the advance of the French army.

Farrant; A. Barnwell: J. Hildebrant; P. Murdock; J. Wilder; N. R. Tompkins; E. Shewell; W. Rainsford; G. Wilkins; J. Middleton. ENSIGNS—J. M. Bliss; W. L. Hedding; J. Hewetson; W. Macalister; J. B. Wyatt; Lord S. Ker; N. M'Donnell; R. Pottenger; A. D. Hamilton; J. Thomas. PAYMASTER—W. Bury. ADJUTANT—C. S. Brearey. QUARTER MASTER—R. Foot. SURGEON—C. S. Doyle. ASST. SURGEONS—W. Keoghoe; J. Purcell.

40th Regt. Foot. MAJORS—A. R. Heyland, *k.*; F. Browne. CAPTAINS—S. Stretton, Maj.; R. Turton; C. Ellis, *w.*; J. H. Barnet, *w.*; R. Philips; W. Fisher, *k*; E. C. Bowen; P. Bishop; J. D. Franklyn; W. Kelly. LIEUTENANTS—J. Thoreau; M. Chadwick; R. Moore, *w.*; W. O. Sandwith; J. Butler; H. Millar; J. Richardson; J. Anthony, *w.*; C. Gorman; J. Mill, *w.*; — Glynne; W. Neilly; R. Hudson; H. Wilkinson; J. Foulkes; T. Campbell, *w.*; H. B. Wray; R Jones; Hon. M. Browne, *w.*; D. M'Donald: F. Fort; G. Hibbert: R. Rudd. ENSIGNS—H. Helmsley; J. L. Wall; W. Clerke: G. Atkinson; R. Thornhill; J. Murphy; W. J. M'Carthy. PAYMASTER—F. H. Durand. ADJUTANT—W. Manning, Lieut. SURGEON—W. James. ASST. SURGEONS—W. Barry; G. Scott.

42nd Regt. Foot (Royal Highlanders.) LIEUT COLONELS—Sir Robert Macara, *k.*; R. H. Dick, *w.*; MAJOR—A. Menzies, *w.* CAPTAINS—J. Campbell, Lt. Col.; G. Davidson, Maj. *w.*; M. Macpherson, *w.*; D. M'Donald, *w.*; D. M'Intosh, *w.*; R. Boyle, *w.* LIEUTENANTS—D. Chisholm, *w.*; D. Stewart, *w.*; D. M'Kenzie, *w.*; H. A. Frazer, *w.*; J. Malcolm, *w.*; A. Dunbar, *w.*; J. Brander, *w.*; R. Gordon, *k.*; R. Stewart; J. Robertson; K M'Dougall; D. M'Kay; A. Innes; J. Grant; J. Orr, *w.*; G. G. Munro, *w.* ENSIGNS—G. Gerard, *k.*; W. Fraser, *w.*; A. L Fraser, *w.*; A. Brown; A. Cumming. ADJUTANT—J. Young, *w.* QUARTER MASTER—D. M'Intosh, *w.* SURGEON—S. M'Leod. ASST. SURGEONS—D. M'Pherson; J. Stewart.

44th Regt. Foot (2nd Batt.) LIEUT. COLONEL—J. M. Hamerton, *w.* MAJOR—G. O'Malley, Lt. Col. CAPTAINS—A. Brugh, *w.*; D. Power, *w.*; W. Burney, *w.*; M. Fane, *w.* LIEUTENANTS—R. Russell, *w.*; R. J. Twinberrow; R. Grier, *w.*; W. Tomkins, *k.*; W. B. Strong, *w.*; J. Campbell, *w.*; N. T. Kingsley; J. Burke, *w.*; H. Martin; W. M. Hern, *w.*; A. Reddock. ENSIGNS—Christie, *w.*; B. Whitney, *w.*; G. Dunlevie; P. Cooke, *k.*; T. M'Cann, *w.*; J. C. Webster, *w.*; A. Wilson, *w.* PAYMASTER—J. Williams. ENSIGN and ADJUTANT—T. M'Cann, *w.* QUARTER MASTER—H. Jones. SURGEON—O. Halpin. ASST. SURGEONS—J. Collins; W. Newton.

51st Foot LIEUT. COLONEL—H. H. Mitchell, Col. MAJOR—S. Rice, Lt. Col. CAPTAINS.—J. T. Keyt, Maj.; J. Campbell; W. Thwaits, Maj.; R. Storer; J. H. Phelps; James Ross; J. Ross; S. Beardsley, *w.*; E. Frederick. LIEUTENANTS—T. Brook; B. B. Hawley; F. Minchin; W. Mahon; W H. Hare; O. Ainsworth; H. Read; F. Kennedy; J. Dyas; J. J. Flaman, *k.*; W. H. Elliott; W. D. Simpson; F. Mainwaring; C. W. Tyndall, *w.*; H. Martin; H. H. Roberts; E. Isaacson; E. J. Taylor; T. Troward; J. Lintott. ENSIGNS—G. F. B. St. John; F. Percy; W. K. Krause; R. B. Walton; W. Johnstone; A. Fraser; J. Blair; H. Lock. PAYMASTER—J. Gibbs. LIEUT. and ADJUTANT—W. Jones. QUARTER MASTER—T. Askey. SURGEON—R. Webster. ASST. SURGEONS—J. F. Clarke; P. Fitzpatrick.

52nd Foot. LIEUT. COLONEL—Sir John Colborne, K.C.B., Col. MAJOR—C. Rowan, Lt. Col. *w.* CAPTAINS—P. Campbell, Maj.; W. Chalmers, Maj.; W. Rowan Maj. *w.*; J. F. Love, Maj. *w.*; C. Earl of March, Maj.; C. Diggle, Maj. *w.*; J. Shedden; G. Young; J. M'Nair; E. Langton; J. Cross; C. Yorke. LIEUTENANTS—C. Dawson, *w.*; M. Anderson, *w.*; C. Kenny; G. H. Love; W. Ripley; J. C. Barrett; W. H. Clerke; G. Hall; W. R. Nixon; G. Gawler; G. Whichcote; W. Ogilvy; E. R. Northey; Hon. W. Browne; E. Scoones; G. Campbell, *w.*; W. Austin; J. Snodgrass; J. S. Cargill; W. Hunter; W. C. Yonge; T. Cottingham, *w.*; C. Holman; G. Moore; E. Mitchell; C. Shawe; J. Hart; G. E. Scott; H. T. Oakes; J. R. Griffith; J. Burnett; R. Steward; G. Robson; F. W. Love. ENSIGNS—J. Jackson; T. Massie; W. Nettles, *k.*; J. Macnab; J. Montagu; J. F. May; E. Monins; W. Leeke. PAYMASTER—J. Clarke. LIEUT. and ADJUTANT—J. Winterbottom, *w.* QUARTER MASTER—B. Sweeten. SURGEON—J. B. Gibson. ASST. SURGEONS—P. Jones; W. Macartney.

54th Regt. Foot. LIEUT. COLONEL—J. Earl Waldegrave. MAJORS—Sir Neil Campbell, Col.; A. Kelly. CAPTAINS—T. C. Kirby; R. Blakeman; W. Crofton. Brig. Maj. *k.*; J. Leslie; G. J. Tappenden; G. Black, Brig. Maj.; T. Chartres. LIEUTENANTS—G. Fraser; G. Bromhead; E. A. Evanson; J. Pillon; R. Woodgate; W. Claus; R. Kelly; J. Grey; P. Mandilhon; J. H. Potts; R. Seacroft; F. Taylor; E. Marcon; J. Reid; R. Stacpoole; F. Burgess; W. Pilkington; W. Persse; D. Denham; F. Hutchinson; M. S. H. Lloyd. ENSIGNS—E. Nugent; T. Fraser; C. Hill; J. Clark; C. W. Thomas; A. Mathewson; P. Clarke. PAYMASTER—H. Irwin. ADJUTANT—J. Dowdell. QUARTER MASTER—W. Coates. SURGEON—G. Redmond. ASST. SURGEONS—M. F. Finan; G. Leech.

59th Regt. Foot (2nd Batt.) LIEUT. COLONEL—H. Austen. MAJORS—F. W. Hoysted, Lt. Col.; C. Douglas. CAPTAINS—F. Fuller; J. Cockburn; A. Pilkington; J. A. Crawford; J. M'Gregor; J. Fawson. LIEUTENANTS—R. Preedy; W. F. Mayne; A. Dent; J. Cowper; H. Brown; A. Macpherson; E. Duncan; N. Chadwick; L. Carmichael; H. Hartford; P. O'Hara; W. Veall; W. Pittman; W. H. Hill; G. Robinson; R Scott. ENSIGNS—A. C. Ross; H. K. Bloomfield; R. F. Hill; C. Makepeace. PAYMASTER—C. Marr. ADJUTANT—A. Campbell, Lt. QUARTER MASTER—W. Baird. SURGEON—J. Hagan. ASST. SURGEONS—P. K. Lambe; A. Calvin.

69th Regt. Foot (2nd Batt.) COLONEL—C. Morice, *k.* MAJOR—G. Muttlebury, Lt. Col. CAPTAINS—J. L. Watson, Maj. *w.*; H. Lindsay, Maj. *w.*; G. S. Cotter; C. Cuyler; B. Hobhouse, *k.*; H. W. Curzon, *k.*; R. Blackwood, *k.*; G. W. Barlow. LIEUTENANTS—W. Harrison; R. Franklyn; S. Parke; B. Pigot, *w.*; C. Busteed, *w.*; N. Ray; C. W. Ingle; J. Hill; H. Oldershaw, Adj.; C. L. Dickson; E. M. Wrightwick, *k.*; H. Anderson, *w*; J. Stewart, *w.* ENSIGNS—E. Hodder, *w.*; W. Bartlett; C. Seward; H. D. Keith; G S. H. Ainslie; Volunteer Clarke, *w.* PAYMASTER—P. Vyvyan. QUARTER MASTER—M. Stevens. SURGEON—C. Bancks, M.D. ASST. SURGEON—J. Bartlet.

71st Light Infantry (Glasgow Highlanders.) LIEUT. COLONEL—T. Reynell, Col. *w.*

MAJORS—A. Jones, Lt. Col. *w.*; L. Walker. CAPTAINS—S. Reed; J. T. Pidgeon; A. Armstrong; D. Campbell, *w.*; E. L'Estrange, Maj. *k.*; W. A. Grant, *w.*; J. Henderson, *w.*; A. J. M'Intyre; C. Johnstone, Maj. *w.*; A. Grant. LIEUTENANTS—J. Baraillier, *w.*; L. Richards; J. R. Elwes, *k.*; C. Stewart; R. Baldwin; W. C. Hanson, *w.*; R. Lind, *w.*; J. Roberts, *w.*; J. Coates, J. Fraser; E. Gilborne; J. Whitney; W. Long; R. Lawe, *w.*; C. T. Cox; C. Lewin, *w.*; W. Woolcombe; W. Torriano; G. W. Horton; J. Coote, *w.*; C. Moorhead; D. Soutar; H. Mamro; N. Campbell. ENSIGNS—A. Moffit; W. Smith; H. W. Thompson; J. Todd, *k.*; J. Barnett; A. M. Henderson; J. Spalding; J. Impett; A. L'Estrange. PAYMASTER—H. Mackenzie. ADJUTANT—W. Anderson, Lieut. *w.* QUARTER MASTER—W. Gavin. SURGEON—A. Stewart. ASST. SURGEONS—J. Winterscale; L. Hill.

73rd Regt. Foot (2nd Batt.) COLONEL—G. Harris, *w.* MAJOR—A. J. Maclean, *w.* CAPTAINS—H. Coane, *w.*; A. Robertson, *k.*; W. Wharton, *w.*; J. M. Kennedy, *k.*; J. Garland, *w.* LIEUTENANTS—R. Leyne; J. W. H. Strachan, *k.*; J. R. M'Connell, *w.*; M. Hollis, *k.*; J. Acres, *w.*; J. Dowling; T. Reynolds, *w.*; D. Browne, *w.*; J. Y. Lloyd, *w.*; R. Stewart. ENSIGNS—R. G. Hesilrige, *w.*; W. MacBean, *w.*; T. Deacon, *w.*; C. B. Eastwood, *w.*; G. D. Bridge, *w.*; G. Hughes; W. S. Lowe, *k.*; A. Blennerhasset; C. Page, *k.* ADJUTANT—J. Hay, *w.* PAYMASTER—J. Williams. SURGEON—D. M'Dearmid. ASST. SURGEONS—J. Riach; F. B. White.

79th Regt. Foot (Cameron Highlanders,) LIEUT. COLONEL—Neil Douglas, *w.* MAJORS—A. Brown, Lt. Col. *w.*; D. Cameron, Lt. Col. *w.* CAPTAINS—T. Mylne, Maj. *w.*; P. Innes; R. Mackay, *k.*; J. Campbell, *w.*; N. Campbell, *w.*; W. Marshall, *w.*; M. Fraser, *w.*; — M'Kay, *k.*; W. Bruce, *w.*; J. Sinclair, *w.* LIEUTENANTS—A. Cameron, *w.*; D. Cameron, *w.*; T. Brown, *w.*; W. Maddocks, *w.*; W. Leaper, *w.*; J. Fraser, *w.*; D. M'Pherson, *k.*; D. M'Phee, *w.*; F. Robertson; E. Cameron, *w.*; A. Forbes, *w.*; C. M'Arthur, *w.*; K. J. Leslie; J. Powling, *w.*; J. Cameron; E. Kennedy, *k.*; W. A. Riach, *w.*; J. Thompson; G. Harrison. ENSIGNS—J. Mackenzie; C. J. Maclean; J. Nash, *w.*; J. Robertson, *w.*; A. Cameron; A. S. Crawford, *w.*; J. Campbell; Volunteer Cameron, *w.* ADJUTANT—J. Kynock, Lt. *k.* PAYMASTER—J. M'Arthur. QUARTER MASTER—A. Cameron. SURGEON—G. Ridesdale. ASST. SURGEONS—W. G. Burrell; D. Perston.

91st Regt. Foot. LIEUT. COLONEL—Sir W. Douglas, K.C.B., Col. CAPTAINS—J. Walsh, Maj.; T. H. Blair, Maj.; W. Steuart; A. Campbell; D. Campbell; J. C. Murdoch; A. J. Collender, Maj.; A. Campbell; R. Anderson. LIEUTENANTS—J. Campbell; J. Russell; A. Campbell; R. Stewart; A. M'Lochlan; C. Egan; A. Cathcart, *w.* (24th); J. M'Dougall; J. Hood; A. Smith; T. L. Hemmick; T. Murray; R. S. Knox; C. Stuart; J. M'Donald; E. Brown; A. Campbell; G. Scott, Adj.; W. Smith; J. Black, *w.* (24th); A. Sword. ENSIGNS—N. Lamont; W. Trimmer; J. Paton; D. Ducat; A. Smith; L. Lind. PAYMASTER—D. Campbell. ADJUTANT—G. Scott, Lt. QUARTER MASTER—J. Stewart. SURGEON—R. Douglass. ASST. SURGEONS—G. M'Lachlan; W. H. Young.

92nd Regt. Foot (Highlanders). LIEUT. COLONEL—J. Cameron, *k.* MAJORS—J. Mitchell, Lt. Col. *w.*; D. Macdonald. CAPTAINS—G. W. Holmes, *w.*; D. Campbell, *w.*; P. Wilkie, *w.*; W. C. Grant, *k.*; W. Little, *k*; A. Ferrier, *w.* LIEUTENANTS—C. Alexander, Adj.; J. J. Chisholm, *k.*; R. Winchester, *w.*; T. Hobbs, *w.*; T. Macintosh, *w.*; D. Macdonald, *w.*; A. Will; J. K. Ross, *w.*; R. Macdonald, *w.*; T. Gordon; H. Innes, *w.*; G. Logan, *w.*; E. Campbell; R. M'Donald; J. Mackinlay, *w.*; R. Peat; G. Mackie, *k.*; A. M'Pherson, *w.*; E. Ross, *w.*; J. Hope, *w.* ENSIGNS—J. Branwell, *w.*; R. Logan, *w.*; J. Clarke; A. M'Donald, *w*; A. Becher, *k.*; R. Hewit; R. M'Pherson, *k.*; J. M. M'Pherson. PAYMASTER—J. Gordon. ADJUTANT—C. Alexander, Lt. SURGEON—G. Hicks. ASST. SURGEON—J. Stewart, *w.*

95th Regt. (Rifle Corps,—1st and 2nd Batt. and 2 Companies 3rd Batt.) LIEUT. COLONEL Sir A. F. Barnard, K.C.B. Col. *w.* MAJORS—A. G. Norcott, Lt. Col. *w.*; G. Wilkins, Lt. Col. *w.*; J. Ross, Lt. Col. *w.*; A. Cameron, Lt. Col. *w.* CAPTAINS—J. Leach, Maj.; F. Glasse; G. Miller, Maj. *w.*; C. Beckwith, Maj.; J. Logan; C. G. Gray; J. Fullerton, Maj.; H. Lee; H. G. Smith, Maj.; E. Chawner, *w.*; W. Johnston, *w.*; T. M'Namara; J. G. M'Collock, *w.*; W. Eeles, Maj.; C. Eaton; C. Eeles, *k.*; F. Le Blanc; J. R. Budgen. 1ST LIEUTENANTS—W. Humbley, *w.*; J. C. Hope; T. Cochrane; J. Layton; J. Molloy, *w.*; T. Smith, Adj.; J. Cox; F. Bennett; A. Stewart; F. Dixon; W. Chapman; C. Coxon, *w.*; R. B. Freer; J. Gardiner, *w.*; D. Cameron, *w.*; J. Kincaid, Adj.; G. Simmons, *w.*; J. Stilwell; R. Cochran, *w.*; J. A. Ridgeway, *w.*; J. Fry, *w.*; J. P. Gardner, *w.*; W. Haggup; G. Vickers; T. T. Worsley, Adj.; J. G. Fitzmaurice, *w.*; G. Drummond; E. Madden; V. Webb, *w.*; G. H. Shenley; C. C. Urquhart; J. Lynam, *w.*; O. Felix, *w.*; G. Drummond. 2ND LIEUTENANTS—D. Macfarlane; A. Stewart; C. Rochfort; W. Wright; J. Church; R. Fowler; A. Milligan; T. B. Sheean; C. Probart; W. Shenley; R. C. Eyre, *w.*; J. P. Walsh, *w.* PAYMASTERS—J. Mackenzie; A. M'Donald. ADJUTANTS—T. Smith; J. Kincaid. QUARTER MASTERS—D. Ross; J. Bagshaw. SURGEONS—J. Burke; F. Scott. ASST. SURGEONS—J. Robson; R. H. Hett; J. Armstrong; T. P. M'Cabe; R. Scott.

ARTILLERY.

Staff. COLONEL Sir George A. Wood, Kt., Com. LIEUT. COLONEL Sir Augustus Frazer, K.C.B. com. British Horse Artillery. LIEUT. COLONEL A. Macdonald, com. under Sir Augustus Frazer. LIEUT. COLONEL Sir John May, K.C.B., Asst. Adj. Gen. CAPTAIN H. Baynes, *w.*, Brigade Major. LIEUTENANTS, J. Bloomfield, G. Coles, F. Wells, Staff Adjuts. to Sir George Wood. LIEUTENANT W. Bell, Staff Adjut. to Sir Augustus Frazer. FIELD OFFICERS com. two batteries of Foot Artillery attached to each division of the Army—LIEUT. COLONELS S. G. Adye, C. Gold, J. S. Williamson, J. Hawker. FIELD OFFICER com. Reserve-Artillery—MAJOR P. Drummond. Com. Battering Train—LIEUT. COLONEL Sir Alexander Dickson, K.C.B.

Troops of British Horse Artillery. 1. MAJOR R. Bull, *w.*; CAPTAINS, R. M. Cairnes,

Maj. *k.*, M. Louis; LIEUTENANTS, W. Smith, *w.*, J. Townsend. (Heavy 5½ in. Howitzers.) 2. LIEUT. COLONEL Webber Smith; CAPTAINS, E. Y. Walcott, D. Crawford, *w.*; LIEUTENANTS, D. J. Edwards, H. Foster, *w.* (Light 6-pounders.) 3. LIEUT. COLONEL Sir Robert Gardiner, K.C.B.; CAPTAINS, T. Dyneley, Maj., R. Harding; LIEUTENANTS, W. Swabey, W. B. Ingleby. (Light 6-pounders.) 4. CAPTAIN E. C. Whinyates, Maj. *w.*; CAPTAINS, C. C. Dansey, *w.*, A. Wright; LIEUTENANTS, T. Strangways, *w.*, A. Ward, R. H. Ord. (Light 6-pounders and Rockets.) 5. CAPTAIN A. C. Mercer; CAPTAIN R. Newland; LIEUTENANTS, H. M. Leathers, J. Hincks, J. Breton (9-pounders.) 6. CAPTAIN W. N. Ramsay, Maj. *k.*; CAPTAINS, A. Macdonald, Maj., W. Brereton, *w.*; LIEUTENANTS, P. Sandilands, W. Robe, *k.* (9-pounders.)

Troops in Reserve. LIEUT. COLONEL Sir Hew D. Ross, K.C.B.; CAPTAINS, J. B. Parker, Maj. *w.*, R. Hardinge; LIEUTENANTS, J. Day, *w.*, F. Warde, P. V. Onslow. (9-pounders.) CAPTAIN G. Beane, Maj. *k.*; CAPTAINS, W. Webber, *w.*, J. E. Maunsell; LIEUTENANTS, J. R. Bruce, M. T. Cromie, *k.* (Light 6-pounders).

Batteries of British Foot Artillery. CAPTAIN C. F. Sandham; CAPTAIN W. H. Stopford; LIEUTENANTS, G. Foot, G. M. Baynes, D. Jago. (9-pounders.) CAPTAIN S. Bolton, *k.*; CAPTAIN C. Napier, *w.*; LIEUTENANTS, G. Pringle, W. Anderson, C. Spearman, *k.*, W. Sharpin, B. Cuppage. (9-pounders.) CAPTAIN W. I. Lloyd, Maj. *k.*; CAPTAIN S. Rudyerd; LIEUTENANTS, S. Phelps, W. Harvey, *w.* (9-pounders.) CAPTAIN J. Brome, Maj.; CAPTAIN J. J. G. Parker; LIEUTENANTS, R. J. Saunders, T. O. Cater, A. O. Molesworth. (9-pounders.) CAPTAIN G. W. Unett; CAPTAIN G. Browne; LIEUTENANTS, D. Lawson, W. Montagu, C. G. Kett.

Battery in Reserve. CAPTAIN J. Sinclair; CAPTAIN F. Macbean; LIEUTENANTS, J. A. Wilson, W. H. Poole, *w.*, R. B. Burnaby.

Subaltern Officers present but unattached. LIEUTENANTS, W. Lemoine, E. Trevor, E. W. Wood, G. S. Maule, T. Watkis, G. T. Hume.

Attached to Captain Cleeves's Foot Battery, K. G. L. LIEUTENANT R. Manners, *k.*

ROYAL ENGINEERS.

Staff. LIEUT. COLONEL J. Carmichael Smyth, commanding Engineer. MAJOR Sir George Hoste, Bart., K.F.M., commanding Engineer to 1st Corps. MAJOR J. Oldfield, Major of Brigade. LIEUTENANT J. Sperling, Adjutant. CAPTAINS—F. Stanway, A. Thomson, *w.* (26th). LIEUTENANTS—J. W. Pringle, *w.*, M. A. Waters, F. B. Head, F. Y. Gilbert, A. D. White.

ROYAL STAFF CORPS.

LIEUT. COLONEL W. Nicolay, Col. CAPTAINS, T. Wright, *w.*, W. Staveley, F. Read. LIEUTENANTS, G. D. Hall, *w.*, B. Jackson, A. C. G. Brauns. ENSIGNS, T. W. Colleton, J. S. Sedley, J. Milliken.

ROYAL WAGGON TRAIN.

LIEUT. COLONEL T. Aird. CAPTAINS, T. Pardoe, B. Jackson. LIEUTENANTS, W. Aitkin, W. Smith, J. M'Dowall, H. O'Neill, W. Dean, R. Parkinson, C. Bott, R. Kerr. CORNETS, T. Glendening, J. Fenn. SURGEON, T. Wynne. VET. SURGEON, F. Cherry.

MEDICAL STAFF.

INSPECTOR, J. R. Grant, M.D. DEPUTY INSPECTORS, W. Taylor, J. Gunning, (*Surgeon in Chief*), S. Woolriche, J. R. Hume, M.D. PHYSICIAN, G. Denecke, M.D. SURGEONS, H. G. Emery, M.D., M. A. Burmeister, R. Grant, J. Maling, J. G. Van Millingen, S. B. Bruce. ASST. SURGEONS, J. Dease, W. Twining. APOTHECARY, W. Lyons.

XLII.

List of the Officers of the King's German Legion, Killed, Wounded, and Missing, in the Actions on the 16th, 17th, and 18th of June, 1815.*

KILLED.

Staff. Captain C. von Bobers, Brigade Major. (Attached to 7th brigade of cavalry.)

Artillery. 1st Lieutenant C. von Schultzen. (Attached to 1st battery of Hanoverian Artillery.)

1st Dragoons. Captain F. Peters. Lieutenants, F. C. von Levetzow, O. Kuhlmann.

* From a Return compiled by Major L. Benne, K.H. of the Hanoverian Staff.

2nd Dragoons. Captain F. von Bülow. Cornet H. Drangmeister.

3rd Hussars. Lieut. Colonel F. L. Meyer. Captains, A. von Kerssenbruch, G. Janssen. Lieutenant H. Brüggemann. Cornet W. Deichmann.

1st Light Battalion. Captains, P. Holtzermann, H. von Marschalk, A. A. von Goeben. Lieutenant A. Albert.

2nd Light Battalion. Major A. Bösewiel. Captains, F. M. W. Schaumann, H. Wiegmann, (acting Brigade Major to 1st Infantry Brigade, K.G.L.) Ensign F. von Robertson.

1st Line Battalion. Captains, C. von Holle, A von Saffe. Ensign H. von Lücken.

2nd Line Battalion. Lieut. Colonel J. C. von Schröder. Captain G. Tilee.

3rd Line Battalion. Captain F. Didd. Lieutenants, F. von Jeinsen, F. Leschen.

4th Line Battalion. Colonel G. C. A. du Plat, (commanding 1st infantry-brigade, K.G.L.) Majors, G. Chüden, G. Lewis Leue. Captain G. Heise. Ensign E. T. von Cronhelm.

5th Line Battalion. Colonel C. von Ompteda, (commanding 2nd infantry brigade, K.G.L.) Captain E. C. C. von Wurmb. Lieutenant J. L. Schuck.

8th Line Battalion. Captains, A. W. von Voigt, T. von Westernhagen. Lieutenant W. von Marenholtz.

Wounded.

Staff. Brigade Majors, Captain G. von Einem, (attached to 2nd infantry-brigade, K.G.L.) Captain M. von Cloudt, (attached to 3rd cavalry-brigade.)

Artillery. Major A. Sympher. 2nd Captains, W. Braun, F. Erythropel. 1st Lieutenants, W. von Goeben, H. Hartmann. 2nd Lieutenant L. Heise.

1st Dragoons. M. General Sir William von Dörnberg. Lieut. Colonel J. von Bülow. Major A. von Reizenstein. Captains, P. von Sichart, G. von Hattorf, B. von Bothmer. Lieutenants, W. Mackenzie, W. Fricke, O. von Hammerstein, H. Bosse. Cornets, S. H. Nanne, E. Trittau.

2nd Dragoons. Lieut. Colonels, C. de Jonquières, C. von Maydell. Captains, C. T. von Harling, L. Lüderitz. Lieutenant H. H. Rittor. Cornet F. Lorentz.

1st Hussars. Lieutenant G. Baring.

3rd Hussars. Captains, Q. von Goeben, W. von Schnehen. Lieutenants, H. True, C. Oehlkers. Cornets, F. Hoyer, C. von Dassel, H. von Hodenberg.

1st Light Battalion. Major Hans von dem Bussche. Captains, F. von Gilsa, C. Wynecken. Lieutenants, A. Wahrendorff, C. Heise, H. Wollrabe, E. F. Koester, H. Leonhart, N. de Miniussir, E. Gibson. Ensigns, G. Best, A. A. von Gentzkow, C. Behne, A. Heise.

2nd Light Battalion. Captain E. A. Holtzermann. Lieutenants, G. Meyer, F. G. T. Kessler, O. Lindham, B. Riefkugel, M. T. H. Tobin, G. D. Græme, W. Timmann, T. Carey. Ensigns, G. Frank, A. Knop.

1st Line Battalion. Major W. von Robertson. Captain G. von Schlütter. Lieutenants, F. Schnath, A. Müller, D. von Einem, H. Wilding, jun. Ensign C. A. von der Hellen.

2nd Line Battalion. Captain F. Purgold. Lieutenants, C. von der Decken, C. Fischer, F. la Roche, A. F. Ziel.

3rd Line Battalion. Major A. Boden. Lieutenants, A. Kuckuck, H. E. Kuckuck.

4th Line Battalion. Captain W. Heydenreich. Lieutenants, C. von Both, A. von Hartwig, W. L. de la Farque, A. von Langwerth. Ensign A. Appuhn.

5th Line Battalion. Captain F. Sander. Lieutenants, C. Berger, G. Klingsöhr.

7th Line Battalion. Lieutenant G. Klingsöhr.

8th Line Battalion. Captain C. E. W. Rougemont. Lieutenants, F. Brinckmann, C. Sattler. Ensign W. von Moreau.

Missing.

2nd Light Battalion. Captain E. A. Holtzermann. Lieutenant M. T. H. Tobin.

XLIII.

List of the Officers of the Hanoverian troops, Killed, Wounded and Missing, in the Actions of the 16*th,* 17*th, and* 18*th of June,* 1815.*

Killed.

Cumberland Hussars. Captain F. S. von Winterstedt.

Field Battalion Bremen. Lieut. Colonel W. L. von Langrehr.

Field Batt. Duke of York. Captain R. von. Pawel; Ensign A. C. Müller.

Field Batt. Lüneburg. Captains, F. Bobart, C. T. Korfes; Ensign C. B. von Plato.

Field Bat. Grubenhagen. Lieut. Colonel F. L. A. von Wurmb.

Landwehr Batt. Bremervörde. Lieutenant C. C. Löper; Ensign T. von Holt.

Landwehr Batt. Osnabrück. Captain C. H. Quentin; Lieutenant G. F. Uffel; Ensign H. Bergtroff.

Landwehr Batt. Quackenbrück. Major C. W. von dem Bussche Hünefeldt.

Landwehr Batt. Verden. Lieutenants, C. E. Wegener, C. E. von Hinüber.

Landwehr Batt. Osterode. Lieutenant T. Fenisch; Ensign C. A. Schanz.

Landwehr Batt. Gifhorn. Major G. von Hammerstein; Lieutenant H. C. Schmidt.

* From a Return compiled by Major L. Benne, K.H., of the Hanoverian Staff.

Wounded.

Staff. Colonel von Berger. Lieutenant and Aide-de-Camp Hanbury.

Rifle Corps. Captain von Reden; Lieutenants, Grote, Schutze.

Field Battalion Bremen. Major Müller; Captains, Bazoldo, von Lepel; Lieutenants, von Quistorp I., von Quistorp II., Welmer; Ensigns, Brüel, Meyer.

Field Batt. Verden. Major von Schkopp; Captain Jacoby; Lieutenants, Gehrhard, Brandis I., Brandis II., Selig, Suffenplan.

Field Batt. Duke of York. Major von Bülow; Lieutenants, Moll, von Mahrenholz; Ensign Rabins.

Field Batt. Lüneburg. Lieut. Colonel von Klencke; Lieutenants, Völger, von Plato; Ensigns, Sachse, von Weyhe.

Field Batt. Grubenhagen. Captain Bauer; Lieutenants, Westphal, Marwedel; Ensigns, von Bülow, Ernst, Stieppel.

Landwehr Batt. Bremervörde. Lieutenants, Warnecke, Meyer; Ensigns, Hotthusen, Wilken.

Landwehr Batt. Osnabrück. Major Count Münster; Captain Gotthard; Lieutenants, Winkler, Richers; Ensigns, Nichenke, Meyer.

Landwehr Batt. Salzgitter. Captain von Hammerstein; Lieutenant von Spangenberg.

Landwehr Batt. Verden. Captain von Witzendorf; Lieutenants, H. Wynecken, Hurtzig; Ensign Siegener.

Landwehr Batt. Lüneburg. Captains, von Reiche, von Kemps; Lieutenant von Dassel; Ensigns, Dormauer, Meyer.

Landwehr Batt. Osterode. Major von Reden; Captains, von Ingersleben, Papet; Lieutenants, Greve, Laubrecht.

Landwehr Batt. Münden. Captain von Hanstein; Lieutenants, Wrisberg, Brenning, Schwenke II.; Ensigns, Murray, Oppermann.

Landwehr Batt. Hameln. Major von Strube; Captain Blankhard; Lieutenants, Krahle, Kistner.

Landwehr Batt. Gifhorn. Captain Wiedenfeld; Lieutenant and Adj. Schwake; Ensign Brüggemann.

Landwehr Batt. Hildesheim. Major von Rheden.

Landwehr Batt. Peine. Captain von Bertrap; Ensign Köhler.

Missing.

Field Batt. Lüneburg. Major von Dachenhausen.

Landwehr Batt. Bremervörde. Lieutenant Ehlers; Ensign Ress.

Landwehr Batt. Verden. Lieutenant von der Horst; Ensigns, Plati, Kotzebue.

XLIV.

*List of Officers of the Brunswick Troops, Killed in the Action of the 16th, and 18th of June, 1815.**

16th of June. His Serene Highness the Reigning Duke FREDERICK WILLIAM: Major von Cramm, commanding the regiment of hussars; Captain von Pawel, of the hussars: Ensign Hercher, of the first line-battalion: Major von Strombeck, commanding 2nd line battalion: Captain von Bülow, of the 2nd line battalion.

18th of June. Lieut. Colonel von Heinemann, of the Staff: Lieutenant Lambrecht, of the hussars: Lieutenant Diedrich, of the horse-artillery: Ensigns, Bruns and Sensemann, of the 2nd line battalion: Captain von Praun, of the 3rd light battalion: Ensign von Vechelde, of the 2nd line battalion.

* From a return furnished by Lieut. General Aug. von Herzberg, of the Brunswick service, but which does not comprise the names of the *wounded* officers.

XLV.

Return of Killed, Wounded, and Missing, of the Dutch-Belgian Troops, on the 16th, 17th, and 18th of June, 1815.

Divisions.	Brigades.	Regiments.	Killed. Officers.	Killed. Under-Officers, and Privates.	Killed. Horses.	Wounded. Officers.	Wounded. Under-Officers, and Privates.	Wounded. Horses.	Missing. Officers.	Missing. Under-Officers, and Privates.	Missing. Horses.	Total Under-Officers and Privates, Killed, Wounded, & Missing.
2nd	1st	27th Chasseurs . .	1	14	..	6	172	..	2	156	..	342
		7th Regiment of the Line	2	18	..	4	134	..	1	82	..	234
		5th Militia . . .	3	70	..	7	132	..	7	102	..	304
		7th do. . . .	..	20	..	7	57	..	..	201	..	278
		8th do. . . .	..	17	..	4	103	..	..	70	..	190
	2nd	1st Battn.	1	26	..	5	92	..	..	59	..	177
		2nd do.	1	20	..	9	86	..	..	38	..	144
		3rd do.	..	18	..	8	105	..	..	3	..	126
		Orange Nassau 1st Battn.	1	4	..	3	33	..	..	20	..	57
		Orange Nassau 3rd do.	..	6	..	4	42	..	..	52	..	100
3rd		Artillery Train . .	1	14	114	6	83	..	..	14	..	111
	1st	35th Chasseurs . .	..	8	..	3	60	..	..	..	..	68
		2nd Regt. of the Line	..	6	..	4	24	..	..	57	..	87
		4th Militia . . .	..	6	..	..	26	..	..	38	..	70
		6th do. . . .	1	4	..	..	15	..	..	22	..	41
		17th do. . . .	..	1	..	3	24	..	..	30	..	55
		19th do. . . .	..	1	..	3	25	..	..	50	..	76
	2nd	36th Chasseurs . .	..	3	..	..	10	..	..	41	..	54
		3rd Regiment of the Line	..	1	..	1	23	..	..	56	..	80
		12th do.	..	2	..	..	13	..	1	8	..	23
		13th do. . .	..	6	..	..	20	..	..	34	..	60
		3rd Militia . . .	..	5	..	..	26	..	..	2	..	33
		10th do. . . .	..	7	..	1	14	..	..	3	..	24
		Horse-Artillery . .	..	2	13	..	16	6	..	..	..	18
		Foot do. . .	..	..	..	..	3	..	..	10	..	13
		Train	..	3	17	..	2	..	...	12	11	17
Cavalry.	Heavy	1st Regt. Carabiniers .	..	12	101	9	66	..	2	13	49	91
		2nd do. . .	1	57	86	4	64	..	..	30	76	151
		3rd do. . .	..	6	39	2	29	..	..	26	43	61
	Light	4th Light Dragoons .	4	50	71	8	135	..	1	51	233	236
		5th do. . .	..	10	24	2	74	..	..	71	99	155
		6th Hussars . .	2	10	122	6	64	..	1	131	180	205
		8th do. . . .	1	10	79	6	145	..	..	122	189	277
		Horse-Artillery . .	..	8	31	..	9	..	..	4	4	21
		Train	..	1	27	..	10	..	..	4	12	15
		General Staff . .	1	..	4	3	..	..	..	..	..	..
		Total . .	20	446	728	118	1936	6	15	1612	896	3904

XLVI.

Return of Killed, Wounded, and Missing, of the Prussian Troops, at the Battle of Waterloo.

Corps.	Brigades.	Regiments.	Killed.					Wounded.					Missing.					Total Privates Killed, Wounded, and Missing.
			Officers.	Under-Officers.	Drummers or Trumpeters.	Privates.	Horses.	Officers.	Under-Officers.	Drummers or Trumpeters.	Privates.	Horses.	Officers.	Under-Officers.	Drummers or Trumpeters.	Privates.	Horses.	
1st	1st Brigade.	. . . .	..	1	2	28	5	7	10	1	139	2	..	2	..	109	2	276
	Reserve Cavalry	. . . .	..	..	..	2	9	1	..	..	10	17	..	..	..	..	..	12
	Reserve Artillery	. . . .	..	..	..	1	4	..	1	..	3	2	..	..	..	..	..	4
2nd	5th Brigade	1st Pomeranian Regiment	1	2	..	2	..	1	4	1	40	..	..	..	1	17	..	59
		25th Regiment	..	..	..	..	..	..	..	..	8	..	..	..	..	..	..	8
		5th Westphalian Landwehr	..	..	..	2	..	..	..	..	8	..	..	..	..	..	..	10
		Volunteer Light Company	..	..	..	..	..	..	..	..	..	..	..	..	..	7	..	7
	7th Brigade	2nd Elbe Landwehr	..	..	..	1	..	..	..	..	4	..	..	..	..	..	..	5
	8th Brigade	21st Regiment	..	..	..	..	..	..	1	..	14	..	..	..	..	4	..	18
		23rd do.	..	..	..	7	..	..	5	..	31	..	..	..	1	8	..	46
		3rd Elbe Landwehr	..	1	..	20	..	2	1	..	65	..	4	1	..	45	..	130
	Reserve-Cavalry	Brandenburg Hussars	..	..	..	..	3	..	..	1	..	3	..	1	..	7	7	7
		Pomeranian do.	..	..	..	1	6	..	1	..	2	1	..	..	..	1	2	4
	Reserve-Artillery	6.pr. Foot-Battery No. 10	..	..	..	..	..	..	1	..	2	1	..	..	..	..	..	2
		Horse-Battery No. 6	..	..	..	..	4	..	1	..	2	2	..	..	..	..	..	2
4th	13th Brig.	1st Silesian Regiment	..	3	..	41	..	10	16	..	195	..	1	2	..	6	..	242
		2nd Neumark Landwehr	1	2	..	7	..	2	6	..	97	..	..	8	1	100	..	204
		3rd do. do.	1	3	..	23	1	7	7	3	116	..	..	3	..	131	..	270
	14th Brig.	2nd Silesian Regiment	2	4	..	35	..	13	18	4	285	..	2	1	2	86	8	406
		1st Pomeranian Landwehr	2	10	..	103	3	11	17	4	226	..	..	..	..	..	..	329
		2nd do. do.	..	10	1	276	..	15	17	3	143	..	..	2	..	104	..	523
	15th Brig.	18th Regiment	2	6	..	124	2	19	43	5	528	..	..	..	..	88	..	740
		3rd Silesian Landwehr	3	5	..	135	3	13	43	..	369	..	..	3	..	54	..	558
		4th do. do.	..	5	..	33	..	5	10	2	200	..	..	1	..	100	..	333
	16th Brig.	15th Regiment	2	6	1	59	4	18	40	2	509	5	..	..	..	25	..	593
		1st Silesian Landwehr	5	9	1	141	2	10	17	9	381	..	4	1	..	50	..	572
		2nd do. do.	1	4	..	32	1	7	11	4	170	3	27	3	..	278	..	480
	Cavalry	2nd Silesian Hussars	..	1	..	6	18	1	6	1	66	72	1	4	..	40	49	112
		West Prussian Uhlans	..	..	..	1	2	1	4	..	15	16	..	..	..	..	..	16
		10th Hussars	..	..	..	1	7	..	1	..	4	10	..	2	..	13	15	18
		8th do.	..	1	..	7	19	8	6	1	43	25	..	..	..	2	..	52
		1st Neumark Landwehr Cav.	..	..	..	1	5	..	..	..	..	13	..	..	..	..	..	1
		2nd do. do. do.	..	1	..	6	39	5	7	..	93	102	..	1	..	9	..	108
		1st Pomeranian do. do.	..	..	..	..	4	..	..	..	3	9	..	..	..	..	..	3
		1st Silesian do. do.	..	..	..	1	26	..	..	..	1	1	..	..	..	3	..	5
		2nd. do. do. do.	..	..	..	1	26	1	..	..	14	6	..	1	1	2	3	17
		3rd do. do. do.	..	1	1	10	35	2	6	..	34	22	..	..	..	6	14	50
	Artillery	12-pr. Batteries Nos. 3, 5, & 13	..	..	..	5	17	..	6	..	22	14	..	..	..	3	..	30
		6-pr. do. Nos. 2, 11, 13, 14, & 21	..	..	..	5	20	..	3	..	14	12	..	..	..	7	..	26
		Horse-Batteries, Nos. 1, 11, & 12	..	..	..	5	21	2	6	..	13	18	..	..	..	..	..	18
		General Staff	2	..	..	..	..	1	..	..	..	..	..	..	..	..	..	..
		Total	22	75	6	1122	286	162	315	41	3869	356	39	36	6	1305	100	6296

XLVII.

List of the Officers of the Prussian Army, Killed, Wounded, and Missing, at the Battle of Waterloo.

Killed.

II. Corps. *2nd Regt. of Infantry*—1st Lieutenant von Mirbach.

IV. Corps. 13th Brigade—*2nd Neumark Landwehr*—1st Lieutenant von Stoberts.—*3rd Neumark Landwehr*—2nd Lieutenant von Norrmann.

14th Brigade—*11th Regt. of Infantry*—Major von Aulok. 2nd Lieutenant von Dewette. *1st Pomeranian Landwehr*—2nd Lieutenants, von Lindner, von Kuhfass.

15th Brigade—*18th Regt. of Infantry*—2nd Lieutenants, von Schlemmer, von Wehlermann. *3rd Silesian Landwehr*—1st Lieutenants, von Treutter, von Teiminger, von Becker.

16th Brigade. *15th Regt. of Infantry*—Captain von Seidlitz. 2nd Lieutenant von Quanstedt. *1st Silesian Landwehr*—Major von Seidlitz. Captains, von Wittich, von Geisler. 2nd Lieutenants, von Hildebrandt, von Briesen, von Gregor. *2nd Silesian Landwehr*—2nd Lieutenant von Zimmermann.

Reserve-Cavalry—Colonel and Brigadier Count von Schwerin. Lieut. Colonel and Brigadier von Watzdorf.

Wounded.

I. Corps. *Brandenburg Dragoons*—Captain von Puttkammer. *Silesian Rifle Battalion*—Lieutenant von Hotten. *12th Regt. of Infantry*—Captain von Wenkstern. *24th Regt. of Infantry*—Major von Lowenklau. Captain von Blankenstein. Lieutenants von Maller, von der Golz, Lampresch.

II. Corps. *2nd Regt. of Infantry*—2nd Lieutenant von Stempel. *3rd Elbe Landwehr*—Captain von Bülzingslöwen. 2nd Lieutenant von Scholmer.

IV. Corps.—13th Brigade. Colonel and Brigadier von Lettow. *10th Regt. of Infantry* Major von Marsigli. 1st Lieutenants, von Doringkowski, von Torzilowsky, von Nordhausen. 2nd Lieutenants, von Barth, von Kretschmer, von Marguardt, von Witzleben, von Bartke. *2nd Neumark Landwehr*—Captain von Solta. 2nd Lieutenant von Liebich. *3rd Neümark Landwehr*—Major von Osten. Captain von Zamori. 2nd Lieutenants, von Münchow, von Szandabelly, von Moritz, von Alter, von Achterberg.

14th Brigade. *11th Regt. of Infantry*—Captains, von Niesemauschel, von Kuensberg, von Morgenstern. 1st Lieutenant von Aulock. 2nd Lieutenants, von Biederstein, von Ciriacy, von Rahden, von Podewil, von Bentivigni, von Egloffstein, von Koepke, von Bender, von Walter. *1st Pomeranian Landwehr*—Lieut. Colonel von Brandenstein. Majors, von. Nettelhorst, von Toll. Captains, von Andrees, von Spalding, von Loeper, von Wolter. 2nd Lieutenants, von Zirkel, von Nehring, von Hoepfner, von Doebke. *2nd Pomeranian Landwehr*—Majors, von Katt, von Stojenthin. Captains, von Steinwehr, von Pauly, von Wedell. 2nd Lieutenants, von Stricker, von Preussendorf, von Barth, von Ewald, von Dolist, von Hagemann, von Schmidt, von Ludwig, von Heinze.

15th Brigade. *18th Regt. of Infantry*—Captains, von Pogursch, von Gluschinsky. 1st Lieutenants, von Wedelstädt, von Bursche, von Elsner, von Kurstein, von Wallenroth, von Taubenheim. 2nd Lieutenants, von Arnim, von Bath, von Lutermann, von Alberti, von Koeppen, von Bindemann, von Wiedermauth, von Broene, le Blanc, von Schömfeldt, von Kerzieg. *3rd Silesian Landwehr*—Major von Zischwitz. Captains, von Osten, von Loepell. 1st Lieutenant von Krause. 2nd Lieutenants, von Pari, von Lützow, von Büttseher, von Pietsch, von Schreiber, von Wende, von Platius. *4th Silesian Landwehr*—Captain von Schirche. 1st Lieutenant, von Stemler. 2nd Lieutenants, von Wagner, von Liebich, von Schedelbach.

16th Brigade. *15th Regt. of Infantry*—Major von Boek, com. Captains, von Jutrzenka, von Bionstierna, von Cawizinsky. 1st Lieutenant von Redeker. 2nd Lieutenants, von Preuss (and Adjutant), von Nadler, von Mousers, von Hering, von Frohreich, von Hassenstein, von Luck, von Hülsen, von Sinel, von Lindenhöfer, von Wittke, von Fittscherini, von Helm. *1st Silesian Landwehr*—Captains, von Maistre, von Salisen, von Schrötter. 1st Lieutenants, von Herzberg, von Vogt, von Laubak. 2nd Lieutenants, von Louve, von Bemda, von Stürmer. *2nd Silesian Landwehr*—Major von Schwemmler. 2nd Lieutenants, von Richter, von Brandt, von Krickmuth, von Arnim, von Beyer, von Sack.

Reserve-Cavalry. *Staff*—Major von Drigalsky. *2nd Silesian Hussars*—Captain von Wander. *West Prussian Uhlans*—Lieutenant von Knobelsdorf. *8th Regt. of Hussars*—Captain von Erichson. 2nd Lieutenants, von Bauhöfen, von Möllendorf, von Plieth, von Dieringsfeldt, von Winterfeldt, von Genny. *2nd Neumark Landwehr Cavalry*—Lieut. Colonel von Hiller. Captains, von Goerz, von Preussendorf. Lieutenants, von Braun, von Oestreich. *2nd Silesian Landwehr Cavalry*—Lieutenant von Schweinitz. *3rd Silesian Landwehr Cavalry*—Captain von Altenstein. *Horse Artillery*—Captains, von Zinken, von Pfeil.

Missing.

IV. Corps. *1st Silesian Landwehr*—2nd Lieutenant von Siegberg. *11th Regt. of Infantry*—Captain von Riesemenschel. 2nd Lieutenant von Bieberstein. *2nd Silesian Landwehr*—2nd Lieutenant von Koeszegy. *2nd Silesian Hussars*—N— R.

XLVIII.

Despatch from the Duke of Wellington to Earl Bathurst.

Waterloo, June 19, 1815.

My Lord,—Bonaparte having collected the 1st, 2nd, 3rd, 4th, and 6th corps of the French army and the imperial guards, and nearly all the cavalry, on the Sambre, and between that river and the Meuse, between the 10th and 14th of the month, advanced on the 15th, and attacked the Prussian posts at Thuin and Lobez, on the Sambre, at daylight in the morning.

I did not hear of these events till the evening of the 15th, and I immediately ordered the troops to prepare to march; and afterwards to march to their left, as soon as I had intelligence from other quarters, to prove that the enemy's movement upon Charleroi was the real attack.

The enemy drove the Prussian posts from the Sambre on that day; and General Zieten, who commanded the corps which had been at Charleroi, retired upon Fleurus; and Marshal Prince Blücher concentrated the Prussian army upon Sombref, holding the villages, in front of his position, of St. Amand and Ligny.

The enemy continued his march along the road from Charleroi towards Bruxelles, and on the same evening, the 15th, attacked a brigade of the army of the Netherlands, under the Prince de Weimar, posted at Frasne, and forced it back to the farm-house on the same road, called Les Quatre Bras.

The Prince of Orange immediately reinforced this brigade with another of the same division, under General Perponcher, and in the morning early regained part of the ground which had been lost, so as to have command of the communication leading from Nivelles and Bruxelles, with Marshal Blücher's position.

In the mean time I had directed the whole army to march upon Les Quatre Bras; and the 5th division, under Lieut. General Sir Thomas Picton, arrived about half-past two in the day, followed by the corps of troops under the Duke of Brunswick, and afterwards by the contingent of Nassau.

At this time the enemy commenced an attack upon Prince Blücher with his whole force, excepting the 1st and 2nd corps, and a corps of cavalry under General Kellermann, with which he attacked our posts at Les Quatre Bras.

The Prussian army maintained their position with their usual gallantry and perseverance, against a great disparity of numbers, as the 4th corps of their army, under General Bülow, had not yet joined, and I was not able to assist them as I wished, as I was attacked myself, and the troops, the cavalry in particular, which had a long distance to march, had not arrived.

We maintained our position also, and completely defeated and repulsed all the enemy's attempts to get possession of it. The enemy repeatedly attacked us with a large body of infantry and cavalry, supported by a numerous and powerful artillery; he made several charges with the cavalry upon our infantry, but all were repulsed in the steadiest manner. In this affair His Royal Highness, the Prince of Orange, the Duke of Brunswick, and Lieut. General Sir Thomas Picton, and Major General Sir Jas. Kempt, and Sir Denis Pack, who were engaged from the commencement of the enemy's attack, highly distinguished themselves, as well as Lieut. General Charles Baron Alten, Major General Sir C. Halkett, Lieut. General Cooke, and Major Generals Maitland and Byng, as they successively arrived. The troops of the 5th division, and those of the Brunswick corps were long and severely engaged, and conducted themselves with the utmost gallantry. I must particularly mention the 28th, 42nd, 79th, and 92nd regiments, and the battalions of Hanoverians.

Our loss was great, as your Lordship will perceive by the enclosed return, and I have particularly to regret His Serene Highness the Duke of Brunswick, who fell fighting gallantly at the head of his troops.

Although Marshal Blücher had maintained his position at Sombref, he still found himself much weakened by the severity of the contest in which he had been engaged, and as the 4th corps had not arrived, he determined to fall back, and concentrate his army upon Wavre; and he marched in the night after the action was over.

This movement of the Marshal's rendered necessary a corresponding one on my part, and I retired from the farm of Quatre Bras upon Genappe, and thence upon Waterloo the next morning, the 17th, at ten o'clock.

The enemy made no effort to pursue Marshal Blucher. On the contrary, a patrole which I sent to Sombref in the morning, found all quiet, and the enemy's videttes fell back as the patrole advanced. Neither did he attempt to molest our march to the rear, although made in the middle of the day, excepting by following with a large body of cavalry, brought from his right, the cavalry under the Earl of Uxbridge.

This gave Lord Uxbridge an opportunity of charging them with the 1st Life Guards, upon their debouch from the village of Genappe, upon which occasion his Lordship has declared himself to be well satisfied with that regiment.

The position which I took up in the front of Waterloo, crossed the high roads from Charleroi and Nivelle, and had its right thrown back to a ravine near Merke Braine, which was occupied; and its left extended to a height above the hamlet Ter la Haye, which was likewise occupied.—In front of the right centre, and near the Nivelle road, we occupied the house and garden of Hougomont, which covered the return of that flank; and in front of the left centre we occupied the farm of La Haye Sainte. By our left we communicated with Marshal Prince Blücher at Wavre through Ohaim; and the Marshal had promised me, that in case we should be attacked he would support me with one or more corps, as might be necessary.

The enemy collected his army, with the exception of the third corps, which had been sent to observe Marshal Blücher, on a range of heights in our front, in the course of the night of the 17th and yesterday morning: and at about ten o'clock he commenced a furious attack upon our post at Hougomont. I had occupied that post with a detachment from General Byng's brigade of guards, which was in position in its rear; and it was for some time under the command of Lieut. Colonel Macdonel, and afterwards of Colonel Home; and I am happy to add, that it was maintained throughout the day with the utmost gallantry by these brave troops, notwithstanding the repeated efforts of large bodies of the enemy to obtain possession of it.

This attack upon the right of our centre was accompanied by a very heavy cannonade upon our whole line, which was destined to support the repeated attacks of cavalry and infantry occasionally mixed, but sometimes separate, which were made upon it. In one of these the enemy carried the farm-house of La Haye Sainte, as the detachment of the light battalion of the Legion which occupied it, had expended all its ammunition, and the enemy occupied the only communication there was with them.

The enemy repeatedly charged our infantry with his cavalry, but these attacks were uniformly unsuccessful, and they afforded opportunities to our cavalry to charge, in one of which, Lord E. Somerset's brigade, consisting of the Life Guards Royal Horse Guards, and 1st Dragoon Guards, highly distinguished themselves, as did that of Major General Sir W. Ponsonby, having taken many prisoners and an eagle.

These attacks were repeated till about seven in the evening, when the enemy made a desperate effort with the cavalry and infantry, supported by the fire of the artillery, to force our left centre near the farm of La Haye Sainte, which after a severe contest was defeated; and having observed that the troops retired from this attack in great confusion, and that the march of General Bülow's corps by Euschermont upon Planchenoit and La Belle Alliance had begun to take effect, and as I could perceive the fire of his cannon, and as Marshal Prince Blücher had joined in person, with a corps of his army to the left of our line by Ohaim, I determined to attack the enemy, and immediately advanced the whole line of infantry, supported by the cavalry and artillery.

The attack succeeded in every point; the enemy was forced from his position on the heights, and fled in the utmost confusion, leaving behind him, as far as I could judge, one hundred and fifty pieces of cannon, with their ammunition, which fell into our hands. I continued the pursuit till long after dark, and then discontinued it only on account of the fatigue of our troops, who had been engaged during twelve hours, and because I found myself on the same road with Marshal Blücher, who assured me of his intention to follow the enemy throughout the night; he has sent me word this morning that he has taken sixty pieces of cannon belonging to the Imperial guard, and several carriages, baggage, &c. belonging to Bonaparte, in Genappe.

I propose to move, this morning, upon Nivelles, and not to discontinue my operations.

Your Lordship will observe, that such a desperate action could not be fought, and such advantages could not be gained, without great loss; and I am sorry to add that ours has been immense. In Lieut. General Sir Thomas Picton, His Majesty has sustained the loss of an officer who has frequently distinguished himself in his service, and he fell gloriously leading his division to a charge with bayonets, by which one of the most serious attacks made by the enemy on our position was defeated. The Earl of Uxbridge, after having successfully got through this arduous day, received a wound by almost the last shot fired, which will, I am afraid, deprive His Majesty for some time of his services.

His Royal Highness the Prince of Orange distinguished himself by his gallantry and conduct till he received a wound from a musket-ball through the shoulder, which obliged him to quit the field.

It gives me the greatest satisfaction to assure your Lordship, that the army never, upon any occasion, conducted itself better. The division of Guards, under Lieut. General Cooke (who is severely wounded), Major General Maitland, and Major General Byng, set an example which was followed by all; and there is no officer nor description of troops, that did not behave well.

I must, however, particularly mention, for His Royal Highness's approbation, Lieut. General Sir H. Clinton, Major General Adam, Lieut. General Charles Baron Alten, severely wounded; Major General Sir Colin Halkett, severely wounded; Colonel Ompteda, Colonel Mitchell, commanding a brigade of the 4th division; Major General Sir James Kempt and Sir Denis Pack, Major General Lambert, Major General Lord E. Somerset, Major General Sir W. Ponsonby, Major General Sir C. Grant, and Major General Sir H. Vivian; Major General Sir O. Vandeleur; Major General Count Dörnberg. I am particularly indebted to General Lord Hill for his assistance and conduct upon this as upon all former occasions.

The artillery and engineer departments were conducted much to my satisfaction by Col. Sir G. Wood and Col. Smyth; and I had every reason to be satisfied with the conduct of the Adjutant General Major General Barnes, who was wounded; and of the Quarter-master-general Colonel Delancy, who was killed by a cannon-shot in the middle of the action. This officer is a serious loss to His Majesty's service and to me at this moment. I was likewise much indebted to the assistance of Lieut. Colonel Lord Fitzroy Somerset, who was severely wounded, and of the officers composing my personal staff, who have suffered severely in this action. Lieut. Colonel the Hon.

Sir Alexander Gordon, who has died of his wounds, was a most promising officer, and is a serious loss to His Majesty's service.

General Kruse of the Nassau service, likewise conducted himself much to my satisfaction, as did General Trip, commanding the heavy brigade of cavalry, and General Vanhope, commanding a brigade of infantry of the King of the Netherlands.

General Pozzo di Borgo, General Baron Vincent, General Müffling, and General Alava, were in the field during the action, and rendered me every assistance in their power. Baron Vincent is wounded, but I hope not severely; and General Pozzo di Borgo received a contusion.

I should not do justice to my feelings, or to Marshal Blücher and the Prussian army, if I did not attribute the successful result of this arduous day to the cordial and timely assistance I received from them.

The operation of General Bülow upon the enemy's flank was a most decisive one; and even if I had not found myself in a situation to make the attack which produced the final result, it would have forced the enemy to retire, if his attacks should have failed; and would have prevented him from taking advantage of them, if they should unfortunately have succeeded.

I send, with this despatch, two eagles, taken by the troops in this action, which Major Percy will have the honour of laying at the feet of His Royal Highness.

I have the honour, &c.

WELLINGTON.

XLIX.

Proclamation of Louis XVIII. to the French People.

'The gates of my kingdom at last open before me. I hasten to bring back my misguided subjects to their duty, to mitigate the calamities which I had wished to prevent, and to place myself a second time between the Allies and the French armies, in the hope that the feelings of consideration of which I may be the object, may tend to their preservation.

'This is the only way in which I have wished to take part in the war. I have not suffered any prince of my family to appear in foreign ranks, and have restrained the courage of those of my servants who had been able to range themselves around me.

'Returned to my native country, I feel a peculiar pleasure in speaking confidence to my people. When I first re-appeared among you, I found men's minds heated and agitated by conflicting passions. My views encountered difficulties and obstacles on every side. My government was liable to commmit errors: perhaps it did commit them. There are times when the purest intentions are insufficient to direct, and sometimes they even mislead. Experience alone can teach; it shall not be lost. All that can save France is my wish.

'My subjects have learned by cruel experience, that the principle of the legitimacy of sovereigns is one of the fundamental bases of social order;—the only one upon which, amidst a great nation, a wise and rational liberty can be established. This doctrine has just been proclaimed as that of all Europe. I had previously consecrated it by my charter, and I will add to that charter all the guarantees which can secure the benefits of it.

'The unity of the ministry is the strongest that I can offer. I design that it should exist, and that the frank and firm march of my council should guarantee all interests and calm all troubles.

'Some persons have spoken of the restoration of tithes and feudal rights. This fable, invented by the common enemy, does not require refutation. It will not be expected that the King should stoop to refute calumnies and lies. The success of the treason has too clearly indicated their source. If the purchasers of national property have felt alarm, the charter should suffice to re-assure them. Did I not myself propose to the chambers, and cause to be executed sales of such property? This proof of my sincerity is incontrovertible.

'In these latter times, my subjects of all classes have given me unequivocal proofs of their love and fidelity. I wish them to know how sensibly I feel them, and that it is from among all Frenchmen I shall delight to choose those who are to approach my person and my family. I wish to exclude from my presence none but those whose celebrity is matter of grief to France, and of horror to Europe.

'In the plot which they contrived, I perceive many of my subjects to have been misled, and some guilty. I promise—I who never promised in vain (as all Europe can witness)—to pardon to misled Frenchmen all that has transpired since the day when I quitted Lille, amidst so many tears, up to the day when I re-entered Cambray, amidst so many acclamations.

'But the blood of my people has flowed in consequence of a treason unprecedented in the annals of the world. That treason has summoned foreigners into the heart of France. Every day reveals to me a new disaster. I owe it, therefore, to the dignity of my crown, to the interest of my people, and to the repose of Europe, to except from pardon the instigators and authors of this horrible plot. They shall be delivered over to the vindication of the laws by the two chambers, which I propose forthwith to assemble.

'Frenchmen! such are the sentiments which he brings among you, whom time has not been able to change, nor calamities, fatigues, nor injustice, made to stoop. The King, whose fathers reigned for eight centuries over yours, returns to consecrate the remainder of his days in defending and consoling you.

'Given at Cambray, the 28th of June, 1815, and of our reign the twenty-first.

'LOUIS.'

THE END.